Computer Organization

PRINCIPLES OF COMPUTER SCIENCE SERIES

Series Editors
ALFRED V. AHO, *Bell Telephone Laboratories, Murray Hill, New Jersey*
JEFFREY D. ULLMAN, *Stanford University, Stanford, California*

Narain Gehani
Advanced C: Food for the Educated Palate

Narain Gehani
C: An Advanced Introduction

Narain Gehani
C for Personal Computers: IBM PC, AT&T PC 6300, and Compatibles

David Maier
The Theory of Relational Databases

Leonard R. Marino
Principles of Computer Design

Christos Papadimitriou
The Theory of Database Concurrency Control

Theo Pavlidis
Algorithms for Graphics and Image Processing

Jeffrey D. Ullman
Computational Aspects of VLSI

ISSN 0888-2096

Computer Organization

MICHAEL ANDREWS

Colorado State University and Space Tech Corporation

COMPUTER SCIENCE PRESS

Computer Science Press, Inc.
1803 Research Boulevard
Rockville, Maryland 20850

    1   2   3   4   5   6   91   90   89   88   87

    The figures on pages 231, 233, 236, and 237; the tables on pages 242, 243, and 245; and the examples on pages 245 and 246 are reprinted by permission from *VAX Architecture Handbook*, Copyright, Digital Equipment Corporation, 1981. All rights reserved.
    The figures on pages 227 and 247 and the tables on pages 239 and 240 are reprinted by permission from *VAX Technical Summary*, Copyright, Digital Equipment Corporation, 1982. All rights reserved.

Library of Congress Cataloging-in-Publication Data

Andrews, Michael, 1940-
   Computer organization.

   Bibliography: p.
   Includes index.
   1. Computer architecture.   I. Title.
QA76.9.A73A53   1987   001.64   85-9654
ISBN 0-88175-114-6

CONTENTS

PREFACE

This text is useful for a second course in Computer Science/Engineering following a course employing a procedural language such as Pascal. As such, second course subject matter can address hardware, software, or both. *Computer Organization* focuses on the middle ground, admittedly a difficult task. Its objectives are (1) to impart an understanding of elementary computer structures, (2) to provide a working knowledge of assembly language (to a limited extent only), and (3) to impart an elementary comprehension of different yet cohesive abstractions of computational systems. The difficulty lies in the bridging of software to hardware. As an engineering text, the outline may be followed consecutively. In a computer science course, Chapter 2 may be dealt with toward the end of the course, possibly just before Chapter 8. In any case, extensive use of the accompanying lab manual is recommended, especially for objective 2.

A computer organization may be hierarchically viewed from hardware levels or software levels. Each view is useful. The hardware levels (solid state phenomena, logic gates, MSI/LSI/VLSI circuits, CPU/MU/IOU,...) help a circuit designer understand how individual logic functions are employed. Yet, without programs, a computer is a static system. The software levels (microprograms, machine programs, assembly programs, operating system programs, and virtual machine programs) capture the dynamism of a computer system. In a hierarchical fashion, each level whether hardware or software is implemented with components from a lower level. It is worthwhile to consider a computer system as levels of virtual machines, especially from the software view. Each chapter builds upon previous chapters attempting to portray the various software and hardware levels.

Chapter 1 overviews organization, architectures, programs, instructions, and the stored program machine. From these general perspectives, the functions of the four basic building blocks (central processor unit, control unit, memory unit, and input/output unit) are identified. Although the control unit is not often portrayed separately but rather embedded in the central processor unit, future machines appear to be gravitating toward microprogrammed control units. Hence, separate treatment of the control unit is appropriate. All topics in Chapter 1 are treated briefly, relying on subsequent chapters to more fully explain the intimate organizational details within each building block.

Chapter 2 describes the register transfer level (RTL), which represents our lowest level considered. The RTL is useful for functionally analyzing machine instructions. Typical circuit components found in the central processing unit, memory unit, input/output unit, and control unit are studied. RTL coupled with physical descriptions then illustrate machine instructions. From this coupling, the reader should understand how each component of Sections 2.1 and 2.2 supports the computer organization. Because digital logic design is often covered separately in an earlier computer science course, this chapter could serve as a review. It does not so much demonstrate "how" a circuit works, but rather "where" and "why" a circuit can be found in a computer system. A study of computer organization necessarily begins at this lowest level, especially if a deep understanding of a microprogram or assembly language program is desired.

Chapter 3 builds upon the RTL descriptions to portray the conventional machine level. Here, a brief introduction to instruction sets and addressing modes lays a foundation for assembly language programming. The input to an assembler is source code generated by a user at the conventional machine level. The assembler output or object code is machine language instructions that manipulate hardware (mainly registers and ALU resources) and soft-ware (microprograms) at the RTL level. A study of Chapter 3 identifies the system resources that an assembly language programmer can directly manip-ulate (programming model registers, ALU operations, memory and input/output registers). Because assembly language programs inherently can be very fast and use fewer machine resources, this chapter is important for determining just how much optimization can be achieved.

Chapters 4 and 7 deal mainly with the PDP-11 and VAX. Here, many examples and exercises are intended to illustrate organizational issues and assembly language programming. These families of computers are represen-tative of a wide class of stored program or Von Neumann architectures. Except for the use of octal notation, nearly all other features exist in various machines. Nevertheless, the reader should not succumb to the "not-designed-here" syndrome. The DEC machines are not utopian architectures. Many good systems are now available and machine organizations are as diverse as humans.

Chapter 5 focuses on implementing structure in assembly programs. Pro-grammers should generate modular and structured programs. There can be calling routine procedures, called routines, subroutines, and high or low level modules. In this chapter can be found the fundamental elements of program-ming (modularity, linkage, stacks, and data parameter passage). Later sec-tions introduce coroutines, recursion, and reentrant code. Such topics, optional for the subject of computer organization, can be expected to be found in a later course on operating systems.

Chapter 6, which is similar to Chapter 5, expands even further on program organization now invoking other introduction sets such as the 370, VAX, and 68000. However, programming within the context of a cohesive computer system should be emphasized. For instance, the reader should be able to determine how I/O suports throughput, how data is transformed and processed internal to the I/O unit, and how I/O programs buffer, translate, and transmit packed and unpacked data. Chapter 8, focusing on input/output, first covers simple I/O registers. Device handler programs and buffering follow. Finally, the chapter ends with the important topic of interrupts.

Chapter 8 deals with computer organization at the operating system level. Here, the reader is introduced to the important concepts of a virtual machine and virtual machine levels. As soon as any program can be loaded into a computer, that provision allows the program not only to process data in the traditional sense, but also to simulate or emulate other computers. To some "users" this simulation/emulation capability makes the host machine transparent and the emulated machine virtual. Most machines contain an operating system of some sort. An operating system has a dual purpose as a "supervisor" of the system and as a "servant" to the user. Simply stated, the supervisor manages system resources to best serve all users. Maximum system throughput is highly desired and a good operating system does just that. From this chapter, the reader should begin to grasp the "big picture" of a computer system that is comprised of diverse software and hardware components. Previous chapters should now clearly come into focus in terms of computer organization.

Enough assembly language details are covered to produce exercises so that the reader can gain experience in programming a specific computer. However, concepts and techniques applicable to a broad range of computers are and should be emphasized. Neither is this a text solely devoted to assembly language programming. Some understanding at this level of programming is important; however, organizational mechanisms of computer systems attendant to this level are crucial.

No hypothetical machines are emphasized, because the author believes that learning details about a specific machine better illustrates basic concepts. Of course, the only hazard in such a presentation is the "not-designed-here" syndrome. Students studying one machine in such intimate detail tend to believe that their machine is the ideal model. A course instructor should appropriately convey the more global view that the current machine is only one of a variety of machines.

An instructor's manual and a laboratory manual are available. Solutions to selected exercises, sample test questions, and additional computer organization topics are found in the instructor's manual. Laboratory exercises on an LSI-11 contained in the lab manual introduce the student to increasingly complex programs coupled to new computer organization issues illustrated in subsequent chapters. The first exercise assembles and executes a simple predefined program while exposing some of the system software aids. Intermediate exercises track topical coverage of Chapters 4 through 8 of this text. The last exercise requires the student to employ complex array manipulating instructions to perform data conversion for BCD numbers.

The text has been used in a second-year course entitled "Computer Organization" at Colorado State University and follows a general programming course on high level languages. Many students have actively contributed to the clarity and accuracy of the material. The author especially recognizes the efforts of the following courageous students:

Ken Baab	Dean Glover
Chan Benson	Carol Huang
Robert Edward Boring	Paul Nosker
Cindy Brodhead	Julie Raiss
Robert Fenerty	R.L. Ritter
Kathryn Francavilla	Philip Sweaney

Many months of typing and editing with patience and love by my wife, Sandra, and my daughter, Jennifer, have made the task of generating another textbook a pleasurable experience. Carrie Meyers helped revise the manuscript along with countless students. During much of the writing, constant support, guidance, and encouragement by Jimmie R. Suttle, Army Research Office, was received. The vision of quality computer science research is evident there under Dr. Suttle's direction. For these overwhelmingly supportive people, I am very grateful.

Michael Andrews

This text is dedicated to

Jennifer

Christopher

Ginger

Rebecca

and all their children

"children are fun"

Chapter 1

COMPUTER STRUCTURE

La science sans conscience, ce n'est rien que la mort de l'ame.

—François Rabelais

Every object rightly seen unlocks a quality of the soul.

—Ralph Waldo Emerson

And he who is versed in the science of numbers can tell of the regions of weight and measure, but he cannot conduct you thither.

—Kahlil Gibran

The Analytical Engine weaves algebraical patterns just as the Jacquard loom weaves flowers and leaves.

—Ada Augusta, Countess of Lovelace

1.1 CHAPTER OBJECTIVES

In this chapter, foundations of computer organization are introduced. Computers are a tool of society; hence, they are useful only if they provide the capacity to enhance our understanding of the world around us. Computers, then, are data processing machinery. Data manipulation, or data processing, depends very much upon the computer's organization. A poor organization can destroy inherent system efficiency. Any system organization is based upon building blocks. Ours are the control unit, the central processing unit, the memory unit, and the input/output unit (see Figure 1.1). Because each unit can be found in every computer, the study of computer organization focusing on these building blocks is widely applicable to any computer. Finally, computers operate on data manipulated by machine instructions in a program. We only introduce the notion of machine instructions in this chapter, leaving the important details to a later chapter (Chapter 4) after a further understanding of organizational features has been developed.

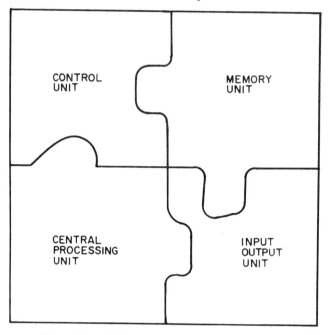

Figure 1.1   Building Blocks of a Computer System

This text is organized as follows. Only the most general issues are presented in this first chapter, which should then serve as a road map to further study in the text. Each section presents a topical coverage of material otherwise illustrated in greater detail in remaining chapters. As with any top-down methodology, a lower level (early chapters) in the study increases understanding by adding more information, judiciously "letting in" only sufficient data to enable you to grasp the next level. Recognize that as you study each "part" in Chapter 1, you will also subsequently return to the same topics, but with greater appreciation for the "sum of the parts." Efficient, powerful, and reliable computers are similarly designed, manufactured, and used in this top-down fashion.

From this chapter, a general understanding of the four basic building blocks should be obtained. Within this framework, the concepts of a stored-program computer, of program control, of programming languages, and of computer storage in all of its various forms can be interpreted. Such interpretations are necessary because a computer is only a static device until a program is translated to a form that is directly executable. Once execution begins, the computer is in a dynamic environment. Data is being processed, information is being manipulated, and our understanding of the world is increasing. All of this can only begin when we grasp the "first" principles of computer organization.

1.2 HISTORY

Images of modern computing can be found in the design of the Analytical Engine proposed by Charles Babbage about 1825. This remarkable machine, although never built, along with Babbage's almost-working prototype of another "computer," the Difference Engine, hinted at much of what we know about computers today. Babbage and others, notably Ada Augusta, Countess of Lovelace, identified many important attributes of machines and programs —a parallel addition algorithm with carry lookahead, multiple-precision operations, error detection, rounding, overflow detection, languages for expressing programs, loop control, index variables, to name just a few. Babbage realized early that a computer could be very beneficial to society, but he also recognized the complexity of the machine. He wrote, in *The Life of a Philosopher* (1864):

> If, unwarned by my example, any man shall undertake and shall succeed in really constructing an engine embodying in itself the whole of the executive department of mathematical analysis upon different principles or by simpler mechanical means, I have no fear of leaving my reputation in his charge, for he alone will be fully able to appreciate the nature of my efforts and the value of their results.

A computer is a myriad of electronic circuits organized to process information for human use. It has an *input* or source for the information and an *output* or destination for the results or processed information. Information may come from people or other sources, machines, mechanical, electrical, or otherwise. Information may even come from or go to another computer. Regardless of the source of information, all computers can perform useful tasks when they process the information. Processing information, then, is the ultimate goal of a computer.

As electronic technology advanced from electromechanical switches to vacuum tubes and now transistors, the understanding of computers as a discipline or science also experienced concomitant change. Many of the machines even helped advance our knowledge by using the computer itself to solve design problems and thereby gather additional insight. The 1930s saw rapid hardware developments. By 1939, John V. Atanasoff built a breadboard model of a special-purpose digital computer. By the 1940s, Howard H. Aiken of Harvard

University, Atanasoff of Iowa State University, George R. Stibitz of Bell Telephone Laboratories, and Konrad Zuse of the Technische Hochschule in Stuttgart formulated many of the concepts that allowed Aiken, Stibitz, and Zuse (working independently) to build general-purpose programmable digital computers. In 1946, J.P. Eckert and J.W. Mauchly of the Moore School of Electrical Engineering at the University of Pennsylvania produced the ENIAC (Electronic Numerical Integrator and Calculator), the first operational electronic digital computer. The ENIAC was organized not with electro-mechanical relays, but instead with high-speed electronic vacuum tubes arranged in logical groups. Each tube represented a binary digit, 0 or 1. By using electrical voltages across each vacuum tube, the ENIAC design eliminated many moving parts, and only a few switches were used to command the initial state of the machine and load programs.

Later, von Neumann, Goldstine, and Burks from The Institute for Advanced Studies (IAS) in Princeton proposed a key ingredient to cause the machine to execute the steps repeatedly with a very high rate of speed. These computer pioneers saw the benefits of a *stored-program digital computer* in which both data and instructions could be stored in the computer itself (an important topic to be discussed later in this chapter). This machine was unlike the ENIAC, which saved only data in resident storage, acquiring instructions sequentially and externally. Von Neumann also recognized that manually rewiring connections as with the ENIAC could be eliminated by allowing the computer to modify instructions as needed. If the instructions were stored as numbers, the computer could process them just as if they were data. The first stored-program digital computer began executing instructions in May 1949 upon the completion of the Electronic Delay Storage Automatic Calculator (EDSAC), built at Cambridge University.

In time, the ILLIAC at the University of Illinois, the MANIAC at Los Alamos, the WHIRLWIND (operational in 1951) at the Massachusetts Institute of Technology, and the JOHNNIAC at Rand Corporation were built. By the 1950s, the new computer industry had emerged. The twentieth century became the age of both the microprocessor and megaprocessor fueled by technological breakthroughs from the vacuum tube, the transistor, integrated circuits, and microminiaturization.

This scaling down of technology paralleled the scaling up of computer system sophistication and availability. The ENIAC consumed a room full of hardware, while the UNIVAC, developed at Sperry Corp., reduced the physical size of a computer to a few racks of electronic gear. Companies like Digital Equipment Corporation and Hewlett Packard helped spawn the minicomputer, a single cabinet of electronics (and even less). Large scale integration (LSI) encouraged greater miniaturization. The first microprocessor chip appeared in the early 1970s with the Intel 4004, a 16-pin, 117 mil by 159 mil integrated circuit device (1 mil = 1/1000 of an inch), which heralded the age of microcomputers. Today's computers are far more powerful than the ENIAC, yet are packaged in small desk-top units. Prices have plummeted and popularity has widened to every facet of our lives. Apple Computer, Inc., was selling machines at a rate of 6,000 per month by mid 1985. Shortly thereafter, the first 32-bit microcomputer devices were produced commercially by Hewlett Packard, National Semiconductor, and others.

1.3 WHAT IS A COMPUTER?

Definition 1.1: A *computer* is a machine that reckons with basic units of information called *data* to process, store, and/or retrieve such information from the outside world or from memory.

Humans direct computers through computer programs that cause sequencing of internal machine action upon physical devices such as gates, registers, an arithmetic logic unit, and memory cells.

Definition 1.2: A *program* is a unified and ordered collection of instructions that directs the necessary operations specified by an algorithm.

A program is written in a computer *language*. And, as would be expected from what is known about our native verbal language, a computer language has an alphabet, a set of rules or *syntax* for forming acceptable strings of symbols in the alphabet, and rules or *semantics* for forming a meaning from those acceptable strings.

A running program or a program in execution is called a *process*. The notion of a process is fundamental to understanding computer organization. Unlike a program, which is static, a process is dynamic. A computer may be handling several processes at a time, each of which is in a certain evolutionary state ranging from just initiating execution to just terminating execution. A process state should constitute the program, its current control flow (which instruction is to be executed next), the status of supporting hardware (input/output), and the values of program variables and data. The totality of these four factors is a state vector, which undergoes change with time. However, since a program that changes itself or modifies its code is considered undesirable, a process has a static part, i.e., the program, and a changing or dynamic part. A process runs on a *processor*, the main arithmetic and/or data processing element of a computer. The notion of a process is very important at the operating system level, to be discussed in Chapter 8.

Any program before execution is in one of various stages of evolution. When first written by a programmer, the program is likely to be written in a high-level language (HLL) such as Pascal or Ada, or in an intermediate-level language called an assembly language. Before actual execution, the program must be compiled or translated into machine-executable code or machine language. An HLL program is in *source* code and a program in intermediate-level language is in machine-executable code or *object* code.

Definition 1.3: An *algorithm* is a logical set of clear and concise steps required to produce meaningful results.

Any program is the embodiment of the algorithm and, as such, is a static statement of actions to be performed. Organizing these static statements requires a "guide," or algorithm, toward specific goals. Hence, no program generation should be started without an algorithm to guide the programmer. A sorting algorithm is now described in order to illustrate the differences between a program and an algorithm.

Example 1.1   Sorting Algorithm. Ten random characters are to be listed in alphabetical order starting with the letter "A." An algorithm to accomplish this must first find or determine if the character "A" exists in the list. If so, that character is saved on a new list, and the character is also removed from the old list. Next, the character "B" is searched for. If successfully found, that character is saved below the previous character on the new list and removed from the old list. This sorting process continues until all ten characters have been successfully sorted.

The description of the solution can be written in the following algorithm.

0. Use "A" as the first letter to be searched.

1. Search the old character list for the current letter.

2. If it is found, save the character on the new list and delete the character from the old list.

3. If it is not found, use the next letter.

4. If all letters are tested, stop.

5. Otherwise, return to Step 1.

This algorithm is not directly executable by a computer, but it does help a programmer to eventually write one. Most programs are not written in a form that is directly executable by the computer. The computer executes a machine language program.

The internal machine sequences of the computer are specified by machine language instructions.

Definition 1.4: A *machine instruction* is a command to the executing elements of a computer to perform primitive tasks.

An instruction, in reality, is a specification of an operation. Computer operations are organized around this concise, ordered collection of instructions called a *machine language program*. This program or software, coupled with the computer's functional hardware, processes information. That is, to produce useful results without taxing human endurance, the computer processing must terminate in a finite number of steps. Furthermore, the computer must operate only upon an unambiguous and definite set of steps which depends on algorithm development and which we translate (as programmers) into correct programs.

The *basic units* of information in a computer are bits, digits, bytes, and words (see Figure 1.2). A bit (*BInary digiT*) is the basic unit of information in a computer. A *bit,* common to nearly all computers, takes on the values "0" or "1." Hence, the computer's alphabet corresponds to a finite set of symbols, which at the machine level is a binary alphabet (0, 1). A bit actually represents one of two voltage levels. Computer designers in the past proposed ternary bits (a three-valued bit), but the economics of electronic technology better support binary-valued symbols. Hence, binary machines dominate the field. A *digit* is a contiguous collection of 4 bits. A *byte* is a collection of digits and contains 8 bits. A *word* is a collection of bytes. A word is not necessarily 16 bits, as shown in Figure 1.2. Some computers have a 16-, 18-, 24-, 32-, 60-, or 64-bit word. Both the byte and the word can represent numeric or nonnumeric information.

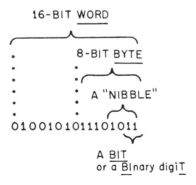

Figure 1.2 Common Units of Information

Data internal to the computer, regardless of its representation, is manipulated by several logical elements. Momentary or temporary storage between primitive processing steps occurs in *registers* which hold words. More permanent storage is built up of memory units such as disks, magnetic tapes, and solid state devices. Data processing on bits, bytes, or words occurs in a central facility, appropriately called the *central processing unit* (CPU), primarily with an *arithmetic logic unit* (ALU), as shown in Figure 1.3. The ALU can add, subtract, multiply, and divide numeric information. The ALU can also perform logical operations on numeric as well as non-numeric data. *Gates* are switches, opening or closing signal paths between primitive elements. It is important to realize that data as well as machine instructions may flow through these paths. In fact, machine instructions are data and constitute a data type.

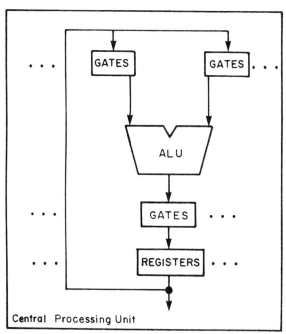

Figure 1.3   Primitive Elements Within a Central Processing Unit

Figure 1.3 represents only part of a machine that contains numerous gates, registers, and logic elements (several million). Such digital logic views are not a main focus of computer organization, but they are important to computer architecture. In fact, completely ignoring the level at which binary information is physically manipulated or processed portrays a distorted overall picture of computer machinery. Data processing is not instantaneous simply because electronic circuits are involved. Instructions command data (ultimately electrical signals) to flow among registers, gates, the ALU, etc. All of this traffic physically moves through typical circuits as seen in Figure 1.3, each one of which will propagate the data in finite intervals (typically nanoseconds). Computers that are designed and organized satisfactorily tend to minimize propagation delays, and this greatly contributes to higher performance.

A more comprehensive or global view of computer organization is illustrated by the four functional building blocks of Figure 1.4. Interconnecting paths among the blocks permit either data flow or control flow. Every computer organization can be studied via these four functions. The functional building blocks are now briefly defined and subsequent sections of this chapter will analyze each block in more detail.

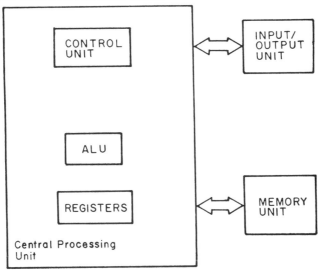

Figure 1.4 One CPU Computer Organization

Definition 1.5: The *central processing unit* (CPU) functions as the primary data and instruction manipulation facility of a computer. It performs numeric and non-numeric data transformations and consists of registers (temporary storage) and an arithmetic logic unit (computational element).

Definition 1.6: The *memory unit* retains temporary as well as permanent information used in programs. It consists of cells or words that store information (information is the *contents* of the cell), each cell possessing a unique pointer to the cell called an *address*.

Definition 1.7:   The *input/output (I/O) unit* serves as the primary connection, called the *interface,* to external devices or peripherals such as CRTs, printers, and keyboards.

Definition 1.8:   The *control unit (CU)* serves as the mastermind of the computer system, performing precise timing on machine operations such as instruction execution and synchronization among the other building blocks.

The two interconnecting paths in Figure 1.4 between the CPU, input/output, and memory are called buses. A *bus* is a collection of wires designated for transporting information. Early computer designers made great distinctions between data paths and instruction paths among the four building blocks. Some computer systems actually isolated this flow using separate wires for each function. Data would flow only on data wires; instructions or, more appropriately, programs would flow only on program wires. Today, however, computer systems carry or transport data information as well as instruction information on the same paths or wires. Since the control unit does not process data, data paths do not normally exist between the control unit and other units. The three remaining units primarily facilitate data processing; hence, control paths do not exist between them.

Impact of Word Size and Bus Width

At first glance, a computer user might contend that a large word length is always better than a short word length, but other factors must be considered. For example, the IBM PC has a 16-bit word length, but data paths between the CPU and the memory unit are 8 bits. This constriction often causes programs to execute much more slowly than if 16-bit data paths existed everywhere. Hence, the net offset of word length must be considered along with the width of the buses. □

1.4   A COMPUTER'S DESCRIPTION

The inherent structure or "personality" of a CPU is depicted in its block diagram and/or programming model. An assembly language programmer will find that the net effect of a CPU structure is best described by its block diagram and/or programming model. At this programming level, efficient programming builds on the knowledge of the number and types of registers. Such programs make extensive use of registers for temporary storage of intermediate results, for passing data to/from different programs, and for maintaining/monitoring the status of the machine and programs. Obviously, the more registers the more opportunities and greater flexibility for assembly language programmers, but this flexibility does not come free. Switching new programs into the CPU may generate frequent register maintenance tasks.

Such opportunities and subsequent tradeoffs are of slight concern to a Pascal programmer, but they are of vital concern to the assembly language programmer.

The *block diagram* depicts the available resources commonly found in the CPU, and is primarily useful to someone designing computer hardware. For example, an electronics engineer might use the block diagram as a guide in the circuit design process. The *programming model* contains essential information about the CPU important to an assembly language programmer. The address space or *memory map* categorizes, by location in memory, the functions of certain regions in memory. For example, some of the memory space is available only to the operating system, and other space, called user space, is available to users. Like the programming model, the memory map is also vital to programming at the assembly language level.

1.4.1 BLOCK DIAGRAMS

Most block diagrams available from computer manufacturers depict available data paths and their widths (1-bit, 4-bit, 8-bit, 16-bit,...) internal to the CPU. Interconnections from the CPU to other devices in the computer machinery may also be identified. The block diagram is of great use to a hardware system designer, expecially when working with microprocessors. For small computers, users ofter "package" their own systems by purchasing boards, accessories, and low-cost circuits in kit form. In fact, manufacturers provide a number of hardware devices or chips to aid this process. Block diagrams, then, not only inform the system designers how information can flow among the registers and resources internally but also indicate what connections to the block diagram exist externally.

The block diagram of the computer is merely a "snapshot" of the physical resources found primarily in the CPU, but it implies something about the machine's instruction set by identifying the legal data and instruction paths among the internal CPU resources. With such information, a block diagram can tell a user whether data is transferable between one specific register and another. If the diagram shows a line between two elements, information flow between the two elements is possible. Also, the width of the data path may be indicated. For example, in the block diagram shown in Figure 1.5, the address bus is 16 bits wide and is connected to all registers. The data bus, however, is 8 bits wide and is connected to the same registers.

Microprocessor Units

The MPU is basically the data processing engine of the CPU. The term MPU primarily refers to a single physical device or chip. Many computers do not use a single chip but rather several discrete devices for the CPU. This is because lightning-fast speed is required in the CPU. Current technology employing a single MPU does not yet provide this speed. However, aggressive research at IBM, Bell Labs, and universities with various novel technologies (Josephson junctions, gallium arsenide, etc.) is altering this picture drastically. □

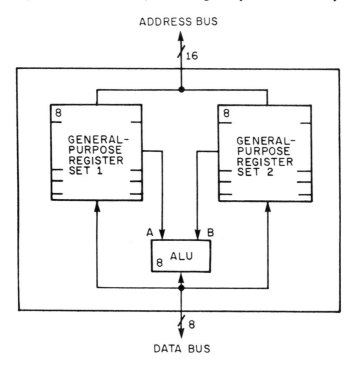

Figure 1.5   Generic Block Diagram

1.4.2   PROGRAMMING MODEL

Unlike the case of the block diagram (of interest mainly for its hardware information), nearly all users like to know what physical resources are available for programming. The *programming model* commonly depicts those resources (primarily registers) available to a programmer and is essential to the assembly language programmer. Computer manufacturers actually condense very detailed documentation into a form easily recognizable by the programmer. The programming model of the PDP-11 is depicted in Figure 1.6.

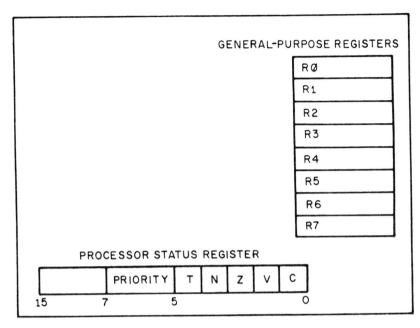

Figure 1.6 PDP-11 Programming Model

It is common to include the number, lengths, and types of registers found in the CPU along with general information about their function. However, in contrast to the block diagram, the programming model of a computer seldom depicts the data and instruction paths among the registers. Typically, a programming model depicts the general-purpose registers and their widths (4-bit, 8-bit, 16-bit,...), accumulator(s), or other special-purpose registers, and/or memory locations of interest to a programmer.

The PDP-11 family programming model contains eight general-purpose registers labeled R0, R1,..., R7. R0 through R5 are truly general purpose and serve a variety of functions including temporary storage or accumulation of results (commonly called *accumulators*). R6 and R7 serve as special registers called the *stack pointer* and the *program counter*, to be described later. In the status register, we can find flags that indicate the status of results of a current computation. For example, the N flag in the PDP-11 processor status register indicates the sign of the current arithmetic result that was just generated in the CPU. The Z flag indicates whether the result is zero or nonzero. We will not be concerned about the actual functions of each register for now. Later chapters will clearly describe their usage.

1.4.3 MEMORY MAP

A computer's address space or *memory map* suggests how the manufacturer allows a user to view the primary or main memory of the computer. Important information that a typical memory map indicates to a programmer, as depicted in Figure 1.7, includes the reserved system locations, the blocks of memory reserved for system software such as a monitor or an operating system, and the blocks of memory available to users or programmers of a computer. User space is primarily RAM storage. System software space often utilizes both RAM and ROM storage.

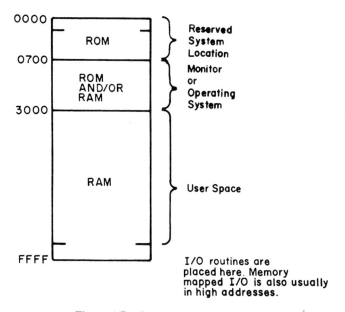

Figure 1.7 Computer Memory Map

It is not realistic to portray large computer personalities solely by a block diagram, programming model, or memory map. Large computers, called *mainframes*, like the IBM 370, 30XX, and 43XX[1] series, VAX-11, CYBER

---

[1]"30XX" means replace the last two digits with specific model numbers. The IBM 370 computer series is a family of models including the 115, 168, 3031, 3032, 3033, 4331, 4341, and 3081. The organization of each 370 model is quite similar. Hence, this text, when referring to a 370, implies the organization of most features of all models. Model features differ mostly in capacity and speed. Later models employ smaller and faster semiconductor technology and often include additional instructions.

172, and Burroughs B77, are a class of systems that must be characterized with additional information. For example, the personality of large systems will convey information about the size and availability of the I/O and memory units. These issues can be resolved more effectively by studying system attributes, better described by the organizational aspects of a computer via a *system block diagram*. Consequently, a clearer picture of the totality of computer systems, large and small, is obtained by studying how the basic functional building blocks (CPU, I/O, CU, and MU) are related. A system block diagram is still a snapshot of a computer system, but the view is distant from intimate machine details. The next section examines the organization of computers via system block diagrams.

1.5   ORGANIZATION VERSUS ARCHITECTURE

The organization and the architecture of any system are two different perspectives that help us to understand the system. *Webster's Dictionary* defines organization and architecture as follows:

> **or-gan-i-za-tion**—...4. any unified, consolidated group of elements; systematized whole;...

> **ar-chi-tec-ture**—...3. a style of construction... 4. design and construction. 5. any framework, system,...

Computers possess both an architecture, which is a stylized framework of hardware, and an organization, which is a unified collection of functional elements. Each is viewed as important according to the information provided to each audience. Electronics engineers, software engineers, programmers, and systems analysts want to know about different aspects of a computer. This section examines what information is important to each group and why.

Computers are *implemented* (manufactured) with electronic circuits on printed circuit boards that contain integrated circuits. Although informative to a hardware engineer, this view lacks information pertinent to a software engineer. A computer implementation is a specific architecture possessing an instruction set, registers, ALU(s) in the CPU, and an address space or map. This architectural level is of some interest to software engineers who develop the system software. Assembly language programmers work at this level. A higher level, representing a comprehensive view of a computer system, is the organization level that a computer system designer uses to assemble a complete system. Most programmers will write high-level code, and thus need to understand the organization level. All of these levels are nested in the hierarchical fashion of Figure 1.8. This text focuses primarily on computer organization.

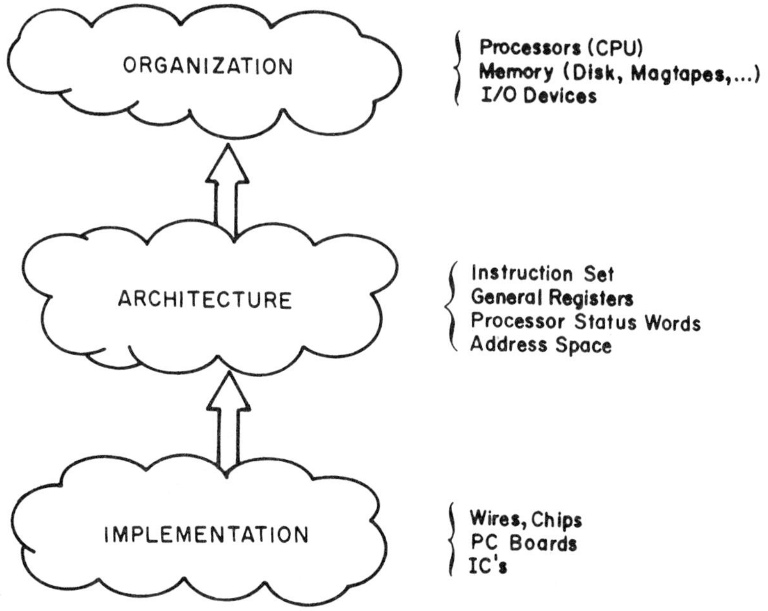

Figure 1.8.   Computer Hierarchy of Views

1.5.1   ORGANIZATION

Computer system designers have a great interest in the *organization* of the separate system elements (disk, drums, RAM, ROM, CPU, printers, CRTs, etc.). Systems are organized according to a plan based on economics and utility. A system designer organizes a computer system to maximize throughput while simultaneously minimizing costs. *Throughput* is a measure of the speed at which data processing tasks are completed. Much study has been applied to organizing efficient systems. As a result, device utilization formulas (how often a device is used) play an important role in "sizing" a system. The capacity of memory, CPU activity, and input/output flexibility constitute basic sizing parameters. Organization, then, is concerned with a systematized development of a computer system from a set of functional devices, such as memory, input/output, control, and central processing unit, as shown previously in Figure 1.4.

A designer of computer systems translates user requirements into an organization of computer devices. The designer's building blocks are the central processing units (CPU), video data terminals (VDT), printers, disks, magnetic tapes, input/output controllers (IOC), ROM, and RAM. The system designer organizes the interconnections among these basic units via system buses to build a cohesive structure in which a software manager, such as an operating system, can direct traffic. The organization is established to exploit the speed or response time of each device. For example, most frequently required tasks will reside "close" to the CPU, perhaps in the fast RAM. Seldom-accessed tasks or jobs might reside in a magnetic disk unit. As such, devices with slow responses are reserved for less frequent operations, while fast devices like RAMs are commonly utilized for frequent tasks.

The *system block diagram* portrays how a computer system is organized about its bus(es). The single-bus organization depicted in Figure 1.9 requires all units to pass information through one bus, often precluding parallel operation. A single-bus system tends to become a traffic bottleneck. However, its simplicity supports economical add-on of other devices. The computer system depicted in Figure 1.4 is a multibus organization. This bus organization forces the I/O data to pass through the CPU before reaching memory. In principle, I/O transfers are directly controlled or programmed by the CPU. However, unlike the multibus configuration of Figure 1.4 (often found in small computers), the bus organization of Figure 1.10 allows direct I/O transfers to memory. These I/O configurations enhance parallel or simultaneous activity among the active channels. Once the CPU initiates a data transfer, it can release the control to I/O and return to some other task. IBM 370 machines are multibus oriented.

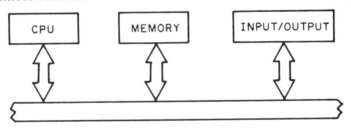

Figure 1.9   Single Bus Organization

Figure 1.10   Multibus Organization

1.5.2   ARCHITECTURE

Architecture, unlike organization, reflects the style or personality of a particular hardware or software architect in assembling basic building blocks into a cohesive functioning entity. At this level, a CPU processor architect, in contrast, views these blocks or elements as flip-flops, registers, switches, lamps,

LEDs, transistors, gates, and counters. Choosing one semiconductor technology over another reflects the cost, speed, style, and framework to which the hardware architect is largely accustomed. The software architect is more concerned with the available programming resources, such as the type of instruction set or the logical power in the CPU. This designer may want a computer architecture with a fast ALU and a large memory space. The software architect working with an instruction set translates the capabilities of the computer into languages immediately useful to programmers. The tools of program development are assemblers, compilers, editors, debuggers, and diagnostic software.

Software Architecture

A software architect may work in the discipline of software engineering. The basic building blocks include an operating system, executive, monitor, utilities, handlers, support software such as assemblers, compilers, interpreters, and applications software such as procedure-oriented language (PL/1, Pascal, Ada) and/or problem-oriented language (ECAP, STRESS,...). The software engineer translates user requirements into an economically organized set of basic programs in order to maximize system throughput. Software engineering and "software architecture" are emerging disciplines.

Boehm[2] defines software engineering as "the application of science and mathematics by which the capabilities of computer equipment are made useful to man via computer programs, procedures, and associated documentation."

Software engineering is becoming increasingly important because software itself is becoming large and increasingly costly and makes a large impact on human welfare. Dijkstra[3] advises programmers to employ the "separation of concerns" principle: complex jobs are easily handled when the problem is well-defined and separated into manageable parts. Good software engineers not only generate computer programs, but also produce documentation, along with the operational procedures needed to use the programs. □

Although much can be said about the organization of a computer by examining its architecture, bus structure, and how I/O or memory devices are connected to the bus, this remains a static view of a computer system. How does the system actually work? The block diagram, system block diagram,

---

[2]Barry W. Boehm, *Software Engineering Economics*, Englewood Cliffs, N.J.: Prentice-Hall, 1981, p. 16.

[3]Edsger W. Dijkstra, *A Discipline of Programming*, Englewood Cliffs, N.J.: Prentice-Hall, 1976.

and programming model are only *static* pictures. For example, the programming model in Figure 1.6 has eight general-purpose registers. The model does not tell us how to get data into a register. For such answers we need to know how the instruction set is organized. What constitutes a program? What kinds of programs are there? Where does a program reside, and in what state or level? We will now look at a dynamic picture of a computer.

1.6   COMPUTER SOFTWARE

Although the focus of this book is on computer organization, that is best understood at the conventional machine level where assembly language programming occurs. All software may be classified into three general groups: system, support, or applications. Assembly language programs are found in each group. The amount of programs is sensitive to the intended tasks of the specific computer system. In the past, operating systems and compilers were generated with assembly languages. Today, however, such software is often written with high-level languages. Nevertheless, segments of operating systems may be coded in assembly language because machine-specific resources, such as I/O devices, are best programmed at this level.

Machine Independent Software

"Machine-independent software, which operates the same way regardless of the particular computer system that is executing it, has been a traditional way of easing the transition from one machine to another. AT&T Laboratories' UNIX operating system, for example, has been transported to any number of minicomputers, and microcomputer versions are on the way; for 8-bit microcomputers, Digital Research Inc.'s CP/M operating system has also become a standard. These "portable" operating systems and other similar pieces of portable software rely on defining a standard set of operations that the operating system can perform for input and output, isolating the hardware-dependent sections of the input/output routines (so only those sections must be recoded for a new piece of hardware) and then insisting that all input and output be done by calls to these operating-system routines."[4] □

1.6.1   CLASSIFICATION

Computer software is a collection of programs, some of which may be generated by a user and some of which are provided by the computer system to aid the user. From a computer's perspective, one program is no different from any

---

[4]*IEEE Spectrum*, December 1983, page 24.

other. To the computer, every program is a collection of machine language instructions. Of course, some programs must reside in the computer all the time (resident software), while others may be called in as needed (nonresident or transient software). From a user's perspective, computer software can be meaningfully classified according to its functionality rather than according to its degree of residency in the computer. At any given moment, a typical computer may be executing one of the instructions from system software, support software, or applications software listed in Table 1.1. The characteristics of each group depend upon the functional goals of the software.

Table 1.1   Classification of Computer Software

System Software

Operating Systems including monitor, executive, or supervisor
Loaders
Utility Programs
Libraries
DOS 3.1, SOS, MP/M, CP/M, Unix, Venix

Support Software

Assemblers
Interpreters for BASIC, APL, LISP, SNOBOL, etc.
Compilers for FORTRAN, Pascal, Ada, etc.
Editors

Application Software

STRuctural Equation System Solver (STRESS)
Electronic Circuit Analysis Program (ECAP)
A company payroll or inventory program
Word processing programs (WordStar, APPLEWRITER, . . .)
Video game arcade programs (PAC-MAN)

System software is a collection of programs generally resident in the computer to provide for the translation, loading, and/or monitoring of user programs. The inclusion of system software in a computer environment is a remarkable improvement over the first computers. In such vintage machines, programs were loaded by setting switches on the machine's operator panel, later observing panel lamps to determine program activity. Back then, a typical computer system did not consist of a complex array of terminals, printers, and memory systems. Today, this manual activity is unheard of, because it would be virtually impossible to orchestrate the large collection of peripherals in a computer system solely by human interaction. System software, such as an operating system, can help us to program, monitor, and even fine tune a computer system to maximize throughput (the number of programs or processes completed per unit of time).

The *operating system* or a derivative of it is the workhorse of system software. An operating system may be very complex, as in large multiuser systems, or simple, as in small, dedicated computers that perform the same task day after day. Simple machines are seldom used to create new programs. Furthermore, only a single user is likely to be operating such a machine, using a monitor, which is quite satisfactory to oversee the single task. A monitor helps the user load his or her program, execute it, and terminate it.

An executive or *supervisor* is a more elaborate monitor program. A supervisor has some I/O programs to assist a user's program development on the computer itself. These I/O programs along with other supervisor capabilities help to manage the stages through which a user's program proceeds. As we have seen, when first coded, the program may be in a high-level form called *source code*. By execution time, the same program has been translated into a machine-compatible form called *object code*. The supervisor calls up the translator (compiler or assembler) to convert the source code to object code, and later a loader to transfer the user's program from auxiliary storage to main memory for execution. Loaders may also ensure that no information has been lost or corrupted during the transfer.

System software can include utility programs (utilities). Utilities perform general support functions that are auxiliary to program execution. A program to convert codes in one representation to another (such as from binary to hexadecimal) is often part of the system software utilities. Sorting, merging, and copying processes or tasks are also common utility functions.

Support software such as editors, debuggers, compilers, and interpreters help us create and modify programs. They can be excellent tools for program generation, maintenance, and diagnosis. Creation of applications software is greatly aided by these software tools. *Text editors* help a programmer to modify his or her source program. Some text editors have the capability to detect and analyze coding errors (only if such errors are in syntax or semantics). Editors invoke commands to allow the programmer to manipulate whole programs (such as print out the source code), a line of code (e.g., delete or insert a line), and even a single character in a line (e.g., add a "period" here). Program, line, and character editing are always found in powerful editors. A good editor makes a programmer's life enjoyable, especially if programmer-convenient attributes are available.

An assembler or *compiler* is a program that translates "source" code into object code. The level of source code language and the type of translation process distinguish translators. Programs written in a high-level language (HLL) like Pascal use a compiler to translate this code into object code. An *interpreter* also translates HLL into object code; however, each HLL line is being translated and immediately executed, unlike a compiler whose translated code is executable only after being completely translated. An HLL BASIC program uses an interpreter (although some BASIC compilers can now be found). An assembler translates "intermediate" or assembly-level languages into object code. An assembly language programmer uses symbols and mnemonics (a shorthand form of a synonym) instead of a natural language such as English in high-level languages. An assembler makes one or more entire passes through the source program to generate a machine language program, which is then directly executable on the computer.

A machine language uses sequences of microinstructions to control the actual machine steps at the most primitive level of operation. This primitive level activates gates, registers, counters, and memory cells. Machine language programs involve very long and detailed statements of the problem. To reduce programming at the machine level to a reasonable effort, assemblers are used, and assembly language programs are written instead of machine language programs. Programmers resort to assembly language (rather than high-level languages) when fast program execution is desired and/or memory is limited. Assembly language programming involves a tradeoff between the CPU register usage and the memory cycle time. In Example 1.2, two assembly language programs are compared. Such analytical comparisons are important to an assembly language programmer for the reasons just noted.

Example 1.2   Choosing Assembly Language Instructions. Suppose you have a task that requires the following mix of instructions. Only two types of instructions are being used: instructions that operate directly in the CPU and instructions that reference memory locations. CPU instructions operate twice as fast as memory reference instructions. You have generated two programming solutions to the task at hand.

Solution 1: Program A utilizes ten CPU instructions for every memory reference instruction. The program takes a total of 66 instructions.

Solution 2: Program B utilizes eight CPU instructions for every memory reference instruction. A total of 63 instructions are needed.

Question: If minimum execution time is sought, which solution is best?

Answer: The first solution takes

$$60x + (6 * 2x) = 72x \text{ units of time}$$

where x is the time one CPU instruction takes to execute. The second solution takes

$$56x + (7 * 2x) = 70x \text{ units of time}$$

It is clear that the first solution is slower than the second solution. But this is only one criterion. Which was clearer (easier to maintain)? Which was faster to program? (Hardware is cheap; programmers are expensive.)

Applications software are programs written for specific purposes required by their users. Business inventory, accounts receivable, or payroll programs are examples of applications software. Applications software may be as lengthy and complicated as the programs to manage the United States Social Security payments or as simple and concise as the program that totals cash register transactions at the supermarket. Applications software may be written in an intermediate assembly language or in a high-level language. However, most applications software is written in either procedure-oriented languages or problem-oriented languages (POLs). Pascal and Ada are common procedure-oriented languages. Such high-level languages were invented because machine languages are oriented toward a specific machine and not toward the application of the user. This situation was much like telling a construction worker to dig a hole by talking about a shovel rather than about moving dirt.

Why Problem/Procedure-Oriented Language?

Programmers recognized long ago that routines frequently called upon should not be generated over and over again by the programmer. Such routines could become modules that perform single-purpose tasks to become physically inserted in other program modules. As a result, modularity was encouraged and supported by POLs (and still is!). A computer programmer should always practice and encourage quality programming. Modularity is one such attribute. Program segments can be made short and concise. This helps us to better maintain code. Also, shorter code segments are easier to create, understand, and correct. □

Problem-oriented languages such as STRESS (STRuctural Equation System Solver) and ECAP (Electronic Circuit Analysis Program) are high-level software packages geared directly to specific applications. A civil engineer regularly calls upon STRESS to compute beam loading and concrete foundation designs, all in a familiar language. The electronics engineer uses ECAP to design electronic circuits such as transistors and amplifiers, again using the familiar "talk of the trade."

1.6.2   A PROGRAM LANGUAGE HIERARCHY

Computer languages possess a hierarchy of abstraction levels. At a low level are microprograms (programs residing in the control unit), while at the most "real" or readily understandable level are high-level languages. Microprograms can be written in a type of register transfer language. At this level, farthest from most users, microprograms reside in the control unit of a computer. For many large-scale machines, microprograms are written by the original equipment designers. However, small machines, which are often dedicated to specific tasks (such as instrumentation or process control), may be user-microprogrammed. Most users, however, will never write or see a microprogram. Surrounding microprograms are a number of software support tools such as assemblers, editors, and debuggers. The language of the support tool class is an assembly language.

Surrounding these levels of software are the software support tools, such as translators, interpreters, and compilers, which assist programmers who work with high-level languages, the least abstract level of programming activity. The language of the translators, interpreters, and compilers may also be an assembly language. Thus, computer languages can possess a hierarchy related somewhat to the level of language understanding and popularity. The most real language level is readily understandable, uses natural grammar, and dominates programming activity today. The most abstract level is least understandable, very symbolic, and is invoked by only a few computer users (such as designers).

1.7   THE STORED PROGRAM AND COMPUTER STORAGE

As we have seen, all programs must be stored somewhere in the computer in one form or another before execution can even begin. It is important to realize that a program can be in various stages of evolution before actual execution. A Pascal program when first written is not directly executable on a computer. It must be compiled by a compiler. The as yet uncompiled Pascal program is called a source program. An untested source program may need to be edited and revised before it runs correctly. Source programs during testing are in the development stage. After compilation, the program is an object program in a machine-executable stage. After further transformations to ensure that the object code is ready for execution, execution of the program begins. These further transformations may require additional code from the computer's library to perform the input/output operations. At each of these stages, the program and its transformations may reside in different memory areas. These are discussed next.

As a consultant to the Moore School of Engineering at the University of Pennsylvania observing the construction of the ENIAC, John von Neumann, from the Princeton Institute for Advanced Study, sensed the power of "storing" programs in a computer's memory. The ENIAC was not programmable as we know it today. Sequences of machine steps were laboriously entered, hardwired, and fixed. Specific computational tasks were firmly embedded in hardware, mostly to compute ballistic trajectories. Hence, the ENIAC in many ways was a dedicated, special-purpose computer.

Apparently influenced by the ENIAC, von Neumann conceived a machine organization that has dominated the computer field from then on. This organization consisted of four basic units: the memory unit, the arithmetic logic unit (in the CPU), the input/output unit, and the control unit, much like those depicted in Figure 1.11. Von Neumann and his colleagues recognized that the computer's processing activity could be programmed with steps similar to those in the figure (for an addition operation). However, the program (only steps 11, 12, and 13 of a typical program are depicted in Figure 1.11) should reside in a memory that can be easily reprogrammed for another task when desired instead of in a bank of switches.

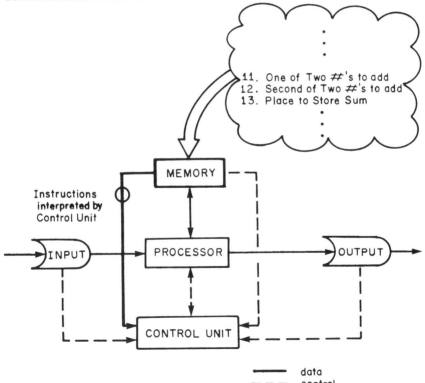

Figure 1.11   Stored-Program Computer

At the same time, Maurice Wilkes of Cambridge University, also visiting the ENIAC project, perceived that control should consist of memory similar to the stored program memory of the system, but whose function is devoted primarily to controlling machine sequences at a primitive level. Subsequently, a memory system was perceived as a storage medium for more than just tables of numbers or data.

Technological limitations prevented satisfactory implementation. However, the von Neumann organization with its stored program and its other innovative contributions (including an ALU operating in parallel instead of in serial fashion) stands as a significant engineering feat. Wilkes' control memory scheme advanced computer developments even further as it sought to make the computer and its designing process simpler by "centralizing internal control statements" within memory. Wilkes influence can be found in today's microprogrammable machines.

1.7.1 CONTROL MEMORY VERSUS PRIMARY MEMORY

With increased understanding of computers, designers realized that a microprogram for CPU control could effectively reside in a memory unit (instead of switch settings as in the ENIAC). As a result, computer organizations were proposed where the memory, even if only a single entity, could be partitioned into control memory and program memory. Hence, this dual function of memory, conceived by Wilkes, carried the original stored program concept one step further, that is, to store a "microprogram" as well as a "program" in memory. To this day, the contents of each storage area have distinctly different types of instructions.

1. *Control memory*—contains instructions governing the actions of the computer at a low level seldom seen by or accessible to the typical computer programmer, but essential to perform the user tasks requested in his or her program. Such instructions are called *microinstructions*.

2. *Primary memory*—contains instructions and data of a higher level than the control memory instructions, provided by and accessible to the computer programmer. Such instructions are called *machine language instructions*.

1.7.2 HIERARCHICAL MEMORY SYSTEMS

Just as computer languages possess a hierarchy, a similar hierarchical scheme carries over to a memory system organization, as shown in Figure 1.12. However, the memory hierarchy depends on the relative speed and capacity of the medium, rather than on some level of understanding. Memory in the smallest area of the figure possesses the fastest response or retrieval time and is used for *control memory* (CM) to contain microprograms that can respond within nanoseconds. The CM is usually read only memory (ROM) and is provided with the necessary microprograms already installed when the computer is acquired. Today, *random access memory* (RAM) is also used in the CM. *Primary memory* containing machine language programs and data need not operate as fast. The assumption is that several microinstructions must be executed for every machine language instruction anyway. Hence, this less frequent access of machine language instructions is traded off against relatively slower response. Primary memory often has greater storage capacity than control memory, and it must be read/write memory so programs can be stored here during execution.

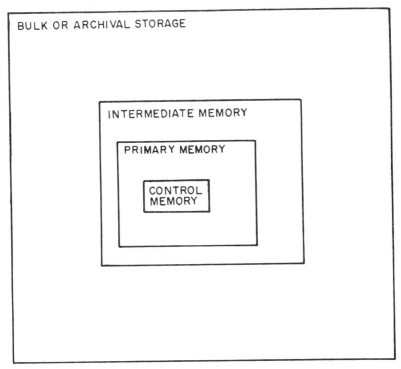

Figure 1.12 A Hierarchy of Memory

Programs about to be processed in some fashion (processing may even include compiling, interpreting, etc.) reside in *intermediate storage*, also called secondary storage. Access to intermediate storage is expected to be even less frequent than that of primary memory because such access generally transfers an entire program over to primary memory and vice versa. Programs in source languages such as Pascal, Ada, and other high-level language programs would commonly reside in intermediate memory (although the language type does not necessarily govern whether they will exist in intermediate storage or not). Since computers often execute many tasks or programs simultaneously, the capacity of intermediate storage is much larger than that of primary memory. Even though it might seem desirable to be able to run a program when it is first loaded into primary memory, in practice the program may be temporarily returned or offloaded to intermediate storage. This may occur when data for the program is not available or when another program has a greater priority.

Bulk or *archival storage* is used for off-line, often manual retrieval of information that itself seldom changes. However, such storage can be characterized primarily by its manual retrieval operations. For instance, the magnetic tape libraries of a university center are archival storage. Tape recordings of a central bank's daily activity used as a backup copy could be considered archival storage. In these situations, information to be retrieved first requires a human operator to find the magnetic tape on the shelves and then mount the tape on a tape drive. Actual information retrieval may take only minutes.

1.8   CENTRAL PROCESSOR UNIT ORGANIZATION

1.8.1   PROGRAM CONTROL

In the preceding section, we studied where programs may be stored. In this and in the remaining sections of the chapter, we want to understand how a program directs or controls machine activity to process data. In a stored-program computer, the program (once ready for execution) must somehow be accessed one instruction at a time. The primitive yet essential machine resources that assist in program control are the *program counter* and *instruction register*. These two resources are actually embedded in a very large and complex sequential circuit. A sequential circuit can be analyzed by partitioning the circuit into a memory part and a nonmemory part or combinational logic part, much like that depicted in Figure 1.13.

Although a modern computer can be considered as a sequential state machine (hence, a sequential circuit), once a program is loaded, that same program becomes, in fact, a carefully selected set of bit settings in certain memory locations and CPU registers. Executed line by line as machine instructions, the program transforms a large and very complex sequential circuit into a dynamic machine capable of processing airline reservations, controlling missile flights, monitoring weather information, and supporting countless other societal tasks all under program control.

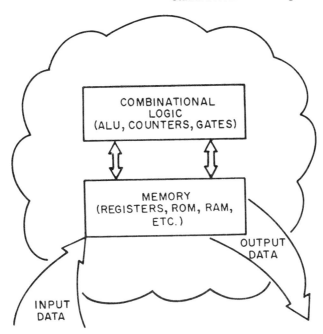

Figure 1.13   Computer as a Sequential State Machine

Programs we write or data we need are loaded into memory. To a computer memory, the type of stored information is immaterial. During execution, processed data is output.

To execute a stored program, the computer memory must be accessed and program information must be converted to control signals for use by the CPU and other machine resources. Every computer has distinct *control paths* and *information paths*. A control path is a "street" or a connection between the control unit and the remaining machine resources. A control path allows information to flow through an information "street" or path. Information may be data or instructions, both of which may flow on a typical information path. Control and data paths for the program counter and instruction register for typical lines of code are depicted in the diagram of Figure 1.14. The sequence of control steps generated by the control unit to execute lines 1, 2, and 3 of the illustrated program are:

•
•
•

1. The PC contents select location 2 of main memory.

2. Location 2 contents are transferred to the IR.

3. The IR is decoded, causing the "ADD" control line to the ALU to be asserted or activated.

4. Data is input to L and R of the ALU.

5. The ALU output is generated.

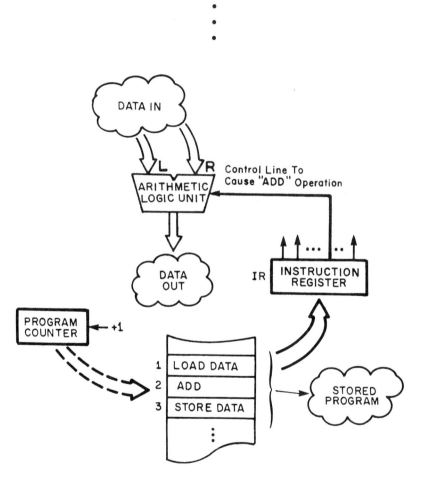

Figure 1.14   Execution of a Stored Program

Note that the program is automatically updated or incremented by 1 in this illustration to point to the next line of code. The "output" of the program counter is an adressable location. The PC simply tells memory where to look for the next instruction. The "output" of memory is information. As illustrated, program instructions are being deposited one by one into an IR for decoding purposes. The "output" of the IR is a set of control signals. Each control signal flows on a control path. For the five steps of the program listed above, all of the necessary decoded control signals were derived from the program instructions. Program control is directly asserted in this manner using the PC and the IR.

The following are the key elements of a stored-program computer for implementing program control:

1. The memory circuits that retain the program, the individual instructions to be accessed in the sequence desired via a program counter (PC).

2. An instruction register (IR) and circuitry, which decodes the instructions to determine which machine sequences should occur and which operands must be accessed.

3. The actual data processing elements of the CPU.

When a program is properly generated and translated into directly executable machine language instructions by a translator (the compiler), the static sequential machine potentially becomes a dynamic data processing entity. A machine instruction energizes information paths via control signals that have been indirectly generated by the program. In this book, computer organization at this level is primarily concerned with how instructions perform such activity. To a large extent, instructions undergo the following basic cyclic phases.

1.8.2   FETCH/EXECUTE CYCLE

Computers, as we know them today, operate on data with programs we have generated. Such programs are a collection of instructions to be used by the computer. For every instruction in our program, the computer has a precisely defined sequence of steps found in the control unit that it follows. The specific sequence for each instruction depends upon the particular instruction being executed. For example, some instructions cause activity in the ALU, such as arithmetic operations. Others may request the memory reference. Some instructions cause data input/output transfer. However, every instruction in our program must undergo the same two steps, repetitively: the acquiring or fetching of the instruction from memory and the execution of the actual instruction (see Figure 1.15).

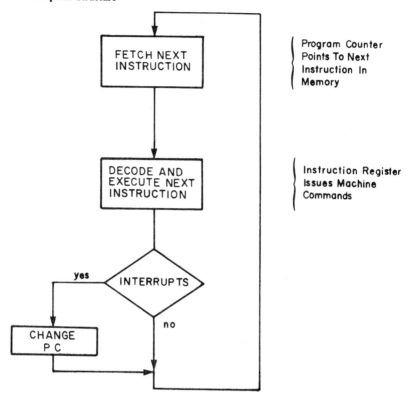

Figure 1.15 Simple Fetch/Execute Cycle

The instruction fetch phase is nearly identical from instruction to instruction. That is, the same sequence of internal machine actions takes place. Common to most computers during the fetch phase, an instruction from a program stored in memory is retrieved and placed into an instruction register (IR). However, the execute phase is not identical from instruction to instruction. A different sequence of internal machine actions takes place for each individual instruction. In the last section, a sequence to add data was illustrated. This sequence and all other machine sequences depend heavily on the specific instruction and the internal architecture of the computer.

The control unit plays an essential role in fetching/executing instructions. It contains a special program (namely, a control program or *microprogram*) to accomplish the fetch/execute cycle that has been generated by the manufacturer of the computer or by a microprogrammer. This control program has been stored in the control unit of the computer at machine fabrication time. When we power up or "initialize" a computer, this program is ready to begin fetching our instructions. As it is executed, the program directs the CPU in the correct steps to accomplish fetching and executing instructions from main memory.

In almost every computer, the fetch/execute cycle is more elaborate. For example, a computer can be interrupted by external circumstances (such as a line printer running out of paper). Interruptions modify the fetch/execute cycle to allow the computer to "jump" to an instruction sequence not normally a part of the currently executing program. Another even more important modification to the fetch/execute cycle is the "branch" to an instruction (leave the current sequential execution). A branch is achieved by replacing the contents of the program counter with an operand in the instruction register.

1.9   INPUT/OUTPUT UNIT ORGANIZATION

Computers indeed process information, at least once it is inside the computer. But where does this information come from? And how does it get into the data processing elements of a computer? Information or data initially comes from the external world, from people, other machines, instruments, and even other computers. We already know that unfortunately our information or data is not suitable for direct data processing by a computer. It may be pictures, sounds, numbers, or characters. But it is seldom strings of bits, and it is almost never transferred at rates identical to the computer's machine cycle. How is this information transformed and synchronized with the computer?

The functions of the input/output unit of a computer are to manipulate the representation of data into a form suitable for the computer, when acquiring the information from the external world, and to synchronize the transfer rate. When transmitting the processed data back to us, the reverse procedure is also necessary. I/O devices or peripheral devices, such as CRTs, keyboards, etc., connect to the I/O unit. The connection point is called the *interface*.

The I/O unit plays a vital role in a general-purpose computer destined for a multitude of diverse tasks. Computer applications are numerous and diverse, all of which directly affect the I/O communications required of the machine. We can now find computers in the home, at the office, behind the dashboard of a car, at the supermarket checkout, in a ball point pen, and even on the human wrist. How the computer communicates in each environment is very dependent on the speed, timing, and coding of the information in that particular application and the external devices connected or interfaced to the computer.

Therefore, speed, timing, and coding capabilities are three principal factors in the design of the I/O units in a computer. Since the majority of computer activity involves the CPU and memory unit, the relative speeds of these units compared with those of the peripheral devices (such as a CRT or printer) must be carefully balanced within the software or hardware design process. That same design process must recognize that the internal or master clock timing of a computer may be entirely different from the timing of peripheral devices. Furthermore, real-world information is generally in the form of strings of alphanumeric characters. This alphanumeric code must be converted eventually to a binary code for internal data processing within the computer. Computer information must necessarily be machine-oriented and not human-oriented (to allow processing). Within the I/O units, we can find *transducer devices*, called *encoders* or *decoders*, which perform the code translation process necessary between the computer and peripherals. Input/output units may also contain temporary storage or *buffers* to hold batches or blocks of data to be transferred between the CPU, the memory unit, and peripheral devices. Buffers facilitate data transfer by allowing the CPU activity to commence while data transfer to an I/O device takes place.

1.10 SUMMARY

This chapter has introduced the concept of computer organization. The organization of a computer is formulated around four basic units: the central processing unit, the memory unit, the input/output unit, and the control unit. Each unit has a very clear and distinct function. Functions within and among these basic building blocks are implemented with machine language instructions, probably the lowest level of programming effort for most of us. These machine instructions comprise a program, and in most computers the program is stored in main memory just prior to and during execution. There are multiple levels of programming effort, starting from the low level or machine language level and terminating at high-level language software. This text focuses more on assembly language programming, which is found at the conventional machine level.

The programming model, block diagram (primarily found in small computers), and system block diagram provide a capsule view of a computer's personality. Such information helps us make quick comparisons among machines. However, the personality of a computer depends very much on its instruction set. Instruction sets can be classified in many ways. However, a classification scheme that focuses on the ability to manipulate data and programs results in a clearer understanding of the power of a digital computer. Instructions that guide the sequences of internal machine steps within a computer are controlled by a basic fetch/execute machine cycle, which first retrieves an instruction from a stored program and subsequently decodes and executes that instruction.

The important properties of any digital computer are its capacity to

1. Retrieve and store information
2. Process data according to desired sequences of program steps
3. Process information with Boolean operations and arithmetic
4. Transmit intermediate and processed data
5. Support interruptions to current tasks and conditional branches

This chapter only briefly introduces us to these properties at the top level. How a computer does all of this is precisely the subject matter for the remainder of this text.

1.11 KEY WORDS

alphabet	machine instruction
architecture	memory unit
arithmetic logic unit	organization
binary	process
bit	program
block diagram	programming model
bus	register
central processing unit	semantics
control unit	stored-program computer
fetch/execute cycle	syntax
high-level language	system block diagram
input/output unit	word

1.12 SUGGESTED READING

Andrews, Michael, *Programming Microprocessor Interfaces for Control and Instrumentation,* Englewood Cliffs, N.J., Prentice-Hall, 1982.
   Additional information on programming classes can be found on pages 23-29. This book focuses primarily on the 6809 microprocessor and has limited applicability to general computer organizations. Hence, only one small, maybe even myopic, view of the world of computers can be obtained from later chapters.

Boehm, B. W., *Software Engineering Economics*, Englewood Cliffs, N.J., Prentice-Hall, 1981.
   Chapter One sets the theme for the new discipline of software engineering. This in-depth, authoritative reference is complete with principles and real-life applications.

Capron, H.L., and Williams, Brian K., *Computers and Data Processing*, Menlo Park, Calif., Benjamin/Cummings, 1982.

A general coverage of computer issues is nicely presented in a top-down fashion. No single computer dominates the coverage other than that of the "stored-program" variety. Applications abound in the colorfully descriptive narrative. The text can serve as an introduction to the topic of computer organization.

Gear, C. William, *Computer Organization and Programming*, 3rd ed. New York, McGraw-Hill, 1980.

Intended for a second course in programming, this textbook focuses on the IBM 370, PDP-11, CYBER 170, and an 8080 at the machine language level. This third edition provides a sound introduction to machine-level programming, emphasizing skills applicable to many types of computers.

IBM System/370 Principles of Operation, Poughkeepsie, N.Y., International Business Machines Organization, 1981.

This manual is part of the IBM library of authoritative reference materials for system analysts, programmers, and operators of IBM systems, but it is of main use to System/370 assembly language programmers. Chapter Two describes the "logical organization" of 370s which consists of main storage, one or more CPUs, operator facilities, channel sets, channels, and input/output devices. IBM calls the physical identity of each unit a "model" to help distinguish the various 370 implementations.

Kuck, David J., *The Structure of Computers and Computations,* Vol. 1, New York, John Wiley & Sons, 1978.

An excellent historical coverage of computer developments from Babbage to Watson (IBM) is presented on pages 52-72. Insight into the very heated race during the 1940s and 1950s to build "the" computer is helpful for understanding today's computer organization centered on a single CPU machine. Later chapters may serve nicely as in-depth references for the remaining chapters of your current text.

Stone, Harold S., *Introduction to Computer Organization and Data Structure*, New York, McGraw-Hill, 1972.

Some simple Turing machine examples are discussed on pages 8-13. The book focuses on the IBM 360/370 and the HP 2116 minicomputer.

1.13 EXERCISES

1.1   Explain how the computer can be a useful tool of society. When does this fail to be true?

1.2   What is a computer program? How does it differ from a TV program or a concert program?

1.3   Both are a set of rules, but what is the difference between syntax and semantics?

1.4   Why must an algorithm precede a program? What could happen if an algorithm is not "used"?

1.5   Generate an algorithm to sort 10 characters found in the English alphabet. Do not use the algorithm of Example 1.2. Why? Does Example 1.2 need an inner loop?

1.6   A program is a static statement of machine action to be performed. What does it mean if a program is a "dynamic" statement of actions?

1.7   Convert the algorithm in Example 1.2 to a computer program. Use a language you are familiar with such as Pascal, FORTRAN, or BASIC.

1.8   Why must a computer's alphabet correspond to a finite set of symbols? Is it also correct to say "...a finite set of variables"?

1.9   Distinguish the differences between a bit, digit, byte, and word.

1.10   Describe the four functional building blocks of a computer organization.

1.11   What are some implications to a computer user if a direct path between the input/output unit and the memory unit exists in Figure 1.4?

1.12   Devise various methods by which buses can be characterized. Which of your characterizations best helps a computer system purchaser to make an intelligent selection?

1.13   What is one significant drawback to a single-bus computer system? What obvious improvement can be made? At what expense?

1.14   Describe the advantages and disadvantages of single-bus and multibus organizations.

1.15   What are the distinguishing features of the block diagram and the programming model of a computer?

1.16   Match the computer "user" who is most likely to need the following information.

Information	"User"
block diagram	assembly language programmer
programming model	computer architect

1.17   In two different computers of your choice, identify the general-purpose registers. How wide are they? What functions do they perform?

1.18   Why is it reasonable to also call the programming model of a computer the register model?

1.19   Briefly describe the possible functions of each register found in the following programming model. (This programming model is not complete.) What could you add to this model to at least make what it is more meaningful?

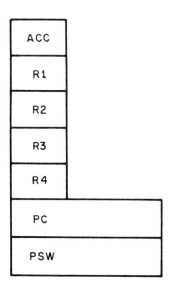

1.20   What is an operating system?

1.21   Although both are "operating systems," how does a monitor differ from a supervisor?

1.22   While high-level languages are more readily understood, why do programmers still program at the assembly language level?

1.23   What is source code? Object code?

1.24   Name three languages that require a compiler to produce machine-executable code.

1.25   Even though both are "translators," how does a compiler differ from an interpreter?

1.26   What significant advantage did von Neumann see in a stored-program computer organization?

1.27   If a Wilkes machine can store a microprogram that essentially tells the computer how to step through its primitive tasks, is it not possible to "redesign" such a machine by simply storing a new microprogram in the control memory? What are the implications of this feature?

1.28 Briefly list the characteristics and storage roles of control memory, primary memory, and secondary memory.

1.29 Suppose a computer is organized as in the figure below. What important implications must be made about this scheme? What if the CPU block is replaced by an ALU?

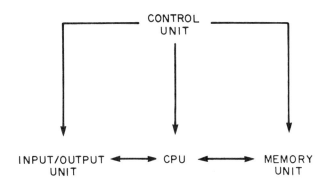

1.30 Match the "programs" likely to be found in the memory units listed below.

Memory	Program
control memory	uncompiled Pascal program
primary memory	machine language program
secondary memory	microprograms

1.31 Describe the typical storage life of a program entered on a desk-top microcomputer. Assume that a file cabinet filled with floppy disks serves as bulk storage, a floppy disk drive is available, and the microcomputer has 256K of main primary memory. Would your answer be affected if only 4K of primary memory existed?

1.32 In Figure 1.14, where does the stored program reside: in primary or main memory, in intermediate storage, or in bulk storage? Explain your choice.

1.33 What modification to Figure 1.14 would be required if lines of code were found in every other address instead of as shown?

1.34 In Figure 1.14, only one control signal is identified. Identify other control signals that these lines of code might generate. Remember that the instruction register output can control more than just the ALU.

1.35 Suppose a program occasionally requires the fetching of more than one "instruction" before instruction execution and decoding is initiated. How should Figure 1.15 be altered to reflect this new fetch/execute cycle?

1.36 The control unit in a microprogrammable computer not only contains a microprogram to control the fetch/execute cycle, but also has many other microprograms. What are some others? (Hint: How is the computer initialized at power-on time? Suppose the machine begins to malfunction. What can help repair it? ...)

1.37 Consider this analogy. A computer is like a city with traffic, traffic lights, intersections, parking lots, high-speed avenues, and low-speed school zones. A city has a city council, city planner, police force, and refuse collectors. Identify analogous computer resources for each of these city attributes. Explain.

1.38 What principal factors guide I/O unit design in a computer?

1.39 What resources are likely to be found in an I/O unit?

1.40 Why does machine language programming seldom occur? Why study machine language instructions?

1.41 What aids are employed to convert high-level language and assembly-level languages into machine language?

1.42 A number of computer definitions can be found in the *Encyclopedia of Computer Science,* 2nd ed. Ralston, Anthony, and Meck, Chester L., eds. (New York: Van Nostrand Reinhold, 1981). Review the list of key words found in this chapter. Do any of them disagree?

Chapter 2

THE REGISTER TRANSFER LEVEL

Don't sweat it—it's only ones and zeros.

—P. Skelly

2.1 CHAPTER OBJECTIVES

A computer is a very large digital system. Even though all digital systems are sequential, the logic state machines constructed with flip-flops, gates, state tables, and diagrams completely describing a computer would be enormous. Hence, computer hardware is described in more compact notation using a *register transfer language* (RTL) at a register transfer logic level. Information flow and execution of elementary tasks are more meaningfully explained at this logic level. RTL provides the computer scientist with a notation for specifying:

1. Sets of registers in a computer.

2. Sets of interconnections among modules (registers, ALU,...).

3. Gating or transfer behavior (serial, parallel) between digital logic elements in the computer.

4. Operational functions of the individual digital logic elements (add, subtract, shift,...).

This chapter demonstrates how some basic logical elements formulated by Boolean algebra can be employed in computer hardware. The chapter focuses on the actual hardware elements typically assigned to the arithmetic logic unit, input/output unit, memory unit, and control unit. One objective is to show how the complicated details of machine behavior can be described in the powerfully efficient notation called register transfer language (RTL). This language, like any language, contains a notation, symbols, and a set of rules to be followed. Because the language generates simple yet compact statements, RTL can describe very complicated hardware operations. In fact, the main purpose of RTL is to describe computer behavior at the hardware level.

Computer architects use RTL to document, analyze, and develop new machines. Those interested only in computer organization can use the RTL of

41

a specific machine to more fully describe the behavior of individual machine or assembly language instructions. For example, with RTL the intimate and primitive interaction of gates, flip-flops, memory cells, and operations within the ALU can be described. However, for the most part, a machine's RTL serves as an aid to the architect in the design of control units. Therefore, it should be understood that much of this chapter deals with issues about control units even though ALUs, memory, and other modules are described. Hence, the sections on micro-operations delineate events at the register transfer logic level that are controlled by hardware and software. In this case, the software, more appropriately called firmware, is microprograms residing within a control unit.

Is it enough to portray a machine by its register transfer language? No, not at all. A register transfer language only partially helps us to understand machine behavior and its relation to the control unit. A complete description of a computer should consider the various levels of representation as depicted in Figure 2.1. The most primitive building blocks (gates and flip-flops) represent one level. In this chapter can be found the next level, register transfer logic, where the descriptions of functional units and I/O interface belong. The next higher level of representation is the global system structure (system diagrams in Sections 1.4 and 1.5). All levels of representation are useful.

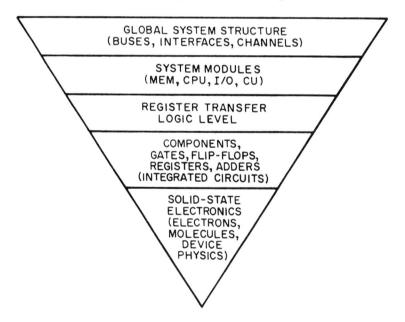

Figure 2.1   Levels of Representation

However, higher levels such as the system level can be better understood in the light of lower levels such as the RTL level considered here.

2.2 BASIC COMPONENTS

2.2.1 REGISTERS

When transferring information internally among the various logical units of a computer, the information is generally stored as a word in a register. A register is a logic circuit comprised of n discrete memory devices, commonly flip-flops with associated gating circuitry. However, registers do not need to be configured solely by flip-flops. Information in a register is generally considered temporary, in contrast to information on a magnetic tape or disk which may last forever. Recall from our discussions about the programming model that machines have general-purpose registers as well as special-purpose registers (program counter, index, program status, . . .). These registers would be considered as a form of scratchpad where information is temporarily held. This temporary "storing" action is called *latching*. Registers that have no clock input have sometimes been called latches for this reason.

A register may be hidden or visible to an assembly language programmer. A visible register is generally accessible to the programmer through a machine instruction. A hidden register may be used by a programmer, but only indirectly and, most likely, without his or her knowledge. The registers in the programming models seen in Chapter 1 are obviously visible. Some registers in the input/output unit may also be visible. Registers internal to the ALU are seldom visible to a programmer, although they are necessary for data processing.

There are four ways to transfer information into and out of a register. They are serial in and out, serial in/parallel out, parallel in/serial out, and parallel in/parallel out. Transfer can be synchronized with a clock input. It is a simple matter to clear the entire register with the single clear input signal. Some registers allow us another input signal to set all of the flip-flops as well.

Registers are either operational or storage. An *operational* register "stores" as well as performs some data manipulation task. A shift register, which we will soon see, is an operational register. A *storage* register merely holds binary information. Any associated gating circuitry merely aids in the input or output of data with that register. The program counter (PC) is an operational register because it can hold information as well as increment it. Incrementing its contents by one or more than one is necessary to keep the PC current. A current PC points to the next instruction in the program presently under execution. The general-purpose registers are storage registers since they can only retain information. A shift register inside the ALU is an operational register.

Figure 2.2 indicates a register capable of loading or latching n input lines. This is indicated by the small n with the slash mark across the input arrow. This register is capable of a parallel transfer, so we should expect to see n output lines as shown. The least significant bit in this register occupies the rightmost position of this register indicated by the small 0. The leftmost bit or most significant bit occupies the n-1 position in the register. (Not all computer manufacturers assign bit designations this way. Some designate the rightmost bit as bit n and the leftmost bit as bit 0.) This register can also be cleared. For brevity, we omit the clock pulse input, which, of course, is assumed for most registers.

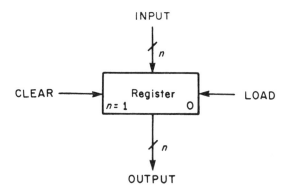

Figure 2.2 Register Symbol

2.2.2 SHIFT REGISTERS

Registers that permit us to enter data serially into the registers or output the data serially are called *shift registers*. An n-bit shift register contains n flip-flops with associated circuitry which permit the contents of the register to move or shift across the register itself. Some shift registers permit us to shift from left to right as well as from right to left. A shift register, as seen in Figure 2.3, capable of shifting from left to right will transfer a bit in flip-flop position n-k to flip-flop position n-k-1, assuming the rightmost bit or least significant bit occupies flip-flop position 0 and the leftmost bit or the most significant bit occupies flip-flop position n-1. A register capable of shifting from right to left transfers a bit of information from flip-flop position n-k-1 to flip-flop position n-k. A control signal to the shift register must indicate which direction the shifting will occur. The shifting occurs across the entire word itself. For instance, if we had an 8-bit shift register capable of shifting to the right upon activation of the shift right signal, and if the contents of the shift register were 01110110, after one shift the register would contain 00111011.

BEFORE SHIFT

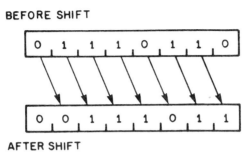

AFTER SHIFT

Figure 2.3 Right Shift Micro-Operation

Some shift registers are capable of not only shifting to the right and to the left, but also of parallel loading into the register. Likewise, shift registers are very important in serial-to-parallel as well as parallel-to-serial transmission of information. Much activity between a computer and a user depends on signals that are transmitted or received serially. A teletype is a serial device. It transmits information sequentially one bit at a time to and from the computer. Information that travels over telephone lines via logic circuits called modems also carries serial data. Shift registers are found in a variety of locations in the computer from the arithmetic logic unit to special input/output units.

2.2.3 COUNTERS

Computers can count with an adder. To do so, we could simply load a register with a predetermined value and begin adding "1" to that register using the adder in the arithmetic logic unit if we want to count up. If we want to count down, we could subtract "1" using the adder with this register. There are many occasions, inside the computer, where it would be too slow to use the adder for counting or the adder itself is being used for other purposes. Recall that in our control unit, a special register called the program counter is necessary to keep track of the current instruction being executed in our program. The program counter in the control unit is not implemented with an adder at all, but has its own digital logic circuitry to make it a counter.

An *n*-bit counter is a collection of *n* flip-flops and associated gating circuitry that forces this sequential circuit to go through a predetermined sequence of states when input pulses occur. These counting pulses can occur at random intervals or at very precise instances in time. A counter with *n* flip-flops can count up to 2^n-1. Hence, a counter with three flip-flops can count up to seven, and a counter with four flip-flops can count up to fifteen and so on. Since a counter is a sequential circuit, counters may behave synchronously or asynchronously. Synchronous counters cause all flip-flops to make the state transitions simultaneously in synchronization with the input pulses. Asynchronous counters make flip-flop transitions dependent on the output transitions of other flip-flops. Asynchronous counters are also called ripple counters. Besides their function as the program counter in the control unit, counters in general can perform many useful functions where it is necessary to control the number of occurrences of an event or to measure the interval of a sequence of events.

2.2.4 DECODERS

The input/output unit in a digital computer serves as the gateway for external devices such as a CRT or keyboard. To select a device from several available, the I/O unit internally could employ a digital logic circuit called a *decoder*. Suppose, as in Figure 2.4, that our I/O unit must select one of four devices at any given moment for the computer with a 1-of-4 decoder as shown. A decoder is a combinational logic circuit with n input lines and 2^n output lines. Only one device-enable line is activated or selected for any given set of inputs. The inputs may be control signals generated by a computer instruction to select a unique device. Decoders help gate, route, or direct data within the computer as well as devices into and out of the computer itself. In our I/O unit, we employ a 1-of-4 decoder to select one of the four devices shown in Figure 2.4.

2.2.5 MULTIPLEXERS

The decoder of Figure 2.4 in our I/O unit can only select a device for the computer. The decoder as shown cannot simultaneously enable the device and transmit or receive data from the computer. A logic circuit that both selects the device and permits data transfer is called a *multiplexer*. A multiplexer receives binary information from 2^n lines and transmits it out on one single line. Only one input line is connected to the output line at any one given time. Example 2.1 illustrates one possible use of a multiplexer in a computer.

Example 2.1 An Input Port. A computer system has only one input port but storage requirements must be satisfied by four disk drive units. An I/O program is to be generated to "select" one of the four disk units when input is desired. In Figure 2.5, a multiplexer is employed in this input port. The I/O program must activate appropriate disk drive selector signals to the multi-plexer. The IBM 370, among many other computers, uses multiplexers to enable and transfer data between I/O devices and the computer.

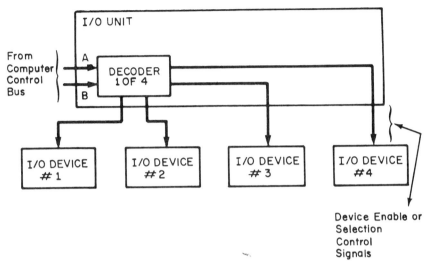

Figure 2.4   Decoder in an I/O Unit

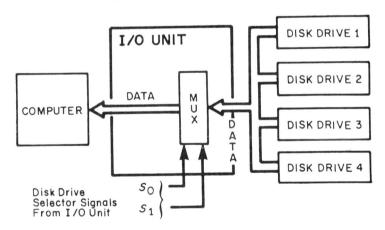

Figure 2.5   4-by-1 MUX in a Data Input Port

This 4-by-1 multiplexer in an I/O unit could select and transmit data from one of four external devices into the computer itself. Thus, if we wanted to "read" a particular device, we could employ this kind of circuit by connecting the data lines of the device to A, B, C, or D and enable one of the four lines in

Figure 2.5 with S_0 and S_1. Data would then transfer from one device through the multiplexer to the computer. Of course, multiplexers can be used in a variety of applications besides reading data from a device. Also, the read operation is possible by means other than a multiplexer.

2.2.6 DEMULTIPLEXERS

Suppose a computer is to output information from one of many possible sources internal to the computer. A demultiplexer can perform this logic function. The 4-by-1 demultiplexer in Figure 2.6 is identical to the 1-of-4 decoder in Figure 2.4. The only difference now is that we have interpreted the enable line of Figure 2.4 as a data input line. Input lines A and B in the demultiplexer perform the selection operation on the four AND gates. In fact, any decoder with an enable line can be used as a demultiplexer by just assigning the data input to the enable line and performing the selection with the remaining input lines. The demultiplexer can now perform a "storing" operation from the computer out to an external device. Just like a multiplexer, a demultiplexer can also be a data routing device.

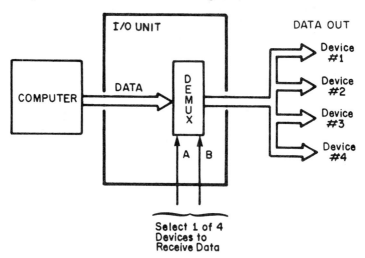

Figure 2.6   4-by-1 Demultiplexer

2.3 MAJOR COMPONENTS

2.3.1 ARITHMETIC LOGIC UNIT

The primary data processing unit in a digital computer is the arithmetic logic unit. The ALU is found in the CPU section of a computer. Data transfer to the *adder* may be derived from several sources including a register in the CPU, the adder output itself, memory, or the data bus as shown in Figure 2.7. Since arithmetic operations occur in the adder, the status of the current result is always kept in the *processor status word* (PSW). In this depiction, negative (N), zero (Z), overflow (V), and carry (C) status are maintained. Inputs to the PSW partially come from the adder, but all of the N, Z, V, and C status are generated within the ALU. Some or all of the status may be monitored by circuits within the CU. The CU can monitor the PSW to alter program execution depending on conditions found in the ALU. In fact, conditional branch instructions described in the next chapter utilize this status generated in the CPU for just such a purpose.

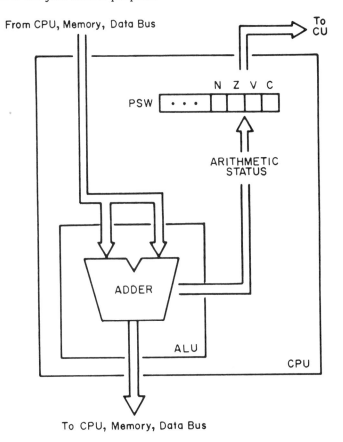

Figure 2.7 CPU Data Flow for the ADDER

2.3.2 INPUT/OUTPUT UNIT

The primary function of an I/O unit is to support communications between the computer and peripherals. The design of an I/O unit must then allow for a variety of interfaces. However, there is no universal I/O unit available. The myriad of peripheral devices along with their varied characteristics make the concept of a universally applicable I/O unit almost impossible. Large-scale mainframe computers typically employ channel selector or auxiliary processors as found in the IBM 360/370 series. (A channel selector decides which pathway from CPU to I/O device is being involved.) At the other extreme, microprocessor manufacturers provide several sophisticated support chips called *programmable peripheral interface chips* (or simply, peripheral chips), which permit a microcomputer designer to interface very specialized devices. The peripheral chips mimic the behavior of auxiliary processors only to a very limited extent. Both I/O units, however, must be capable of matching disparate I/O transfer rates with CPU clocks, temporarily holding data, and performing coding as needed.

Large computer systems utilize buses, channel selectors, or multiplexers when many I/O devices are connected to the same channel. Such subsystems in an I/O unit direct the flow of information between the I/O devices and main storage, provide a means for connecting various types of I/O devices to the CPU and main storage, and contain facilities for the control of I/O operations. During a typical I/O operation, a channel unit may assemble or disassemble data and synchronize data byte transfer with other computer cycles (such as a main storage access cycle). Within a channel unit as part of the I/O operation, addresses for data and a count of the data may be maintained and updated. Some I/O unit configurations permit an I/O operation to be overlapped or function concurrently with other CPU activity (appropriately called I/O overlapped operation). When available, I/O overlapped operation does not interfere with the currently executing CPU program (unless both the CPU and I/O device refer to the same storage area). Of course, it may slow down the program execution.

The IBM 370 employs three types of channels for I/O operation: selector, byte multiplexer, and block multiplexer. Any IBM 370 I/O operation must occur either in a burst or a byte-multiplex mode. In the burst mode, the channel is monopolized by the I/O device. Hence, such transfer causes the device to remain logically connected to the channel for the entire duration of the "burst" of information, and no other device may communicate on that channel. A burst may be a few bytes, many bytes, a group of blocks with associated control and status information, a whole block of data, or other status information which causes channel monopolization. In the byte-multiplex mode, an I/O device stays connected for shorter durations. The duration commonly occupies time for only one operation to transfer a segment of information, which may be a single byte of data, a few data bytes, a device status report, or control information to initiate a new operation.

Computer systems can support I/O operations between two storage media without interfering with CPU activity. IBM channels and I/O overlapped operations are one such technique. *Direct memory access* (DMA) is another I/O transfer scheme. In a DMA transfer, the I/O operation must maintain the source and destination addresses of the data as well as a current count of the data. Hardware within an I/O processor, as part of the I/O unit facilities, automatically updates the address and count. In a DMA transfer, transfer between two devices occurs without the need to pass data through any accumulator or registers in the CPU. This "bypass" operation effectively increases computer performance and is highly desirable for concurrent operation of the CPU and I/O.

2.3.3   MEMORY DEVICES

The system cost of a computer is still very sensitive to the cost of the memory unit and its separate memory devices. The memory or storage elements of a computer utilize a variety of media from magnetic tape, plated wire, and disk to bubble memory and solid state RAM semiconductor. A memory system is a hierarchy of these media. An ideal memory would have a very large capacity, operate extremely fast, and have very low power requirements. Above all, such memory ought to be very inexpensive. Since this ideal memory does not exist, our selection remains a tradeoff between the speed of the device and its cost. Device cost is directly related to the cost per bit of information stored and access speed.

Main memory generally does not contain huge amounts of information, but it must be relatively fast. Main memory should exist electronically and physically close to the CPU. If we want to maximize the throughput[1] of the machine, one way is to ensure that any action we take with the main memory should be nearly as fast as the action or the data processing steps that occur in the CPU itself. Because fast memory is relatively expensive, main memory does not contain nearly the amount of information that secondary memory does.

Today main memory is generally built from semiconductor devices. In the past, it was built with core memory as illustrated in Figure 2.8. Core storage consists of planes of ferrite toroids (small "doughnuts" of magnetic material). A toroid or core exists at each intersection of wires which reads ("senses") the

---

[1]Throughput is a measure of the performance of a computer system and is the amount of processing per unit time.

direction of magnetic flux and wires that write into each core. The direction of flux can be reversed by the direction of electrical current flowing around each toroid. One flux direction signals a binary "1" while the opposite direction signals a binary "0." Cores are very small with an approximately 1/4" outside diameter. The major expense in core storage is the auxiliary circuitry needed to amplify, sense, read, and write the data in each individual core.

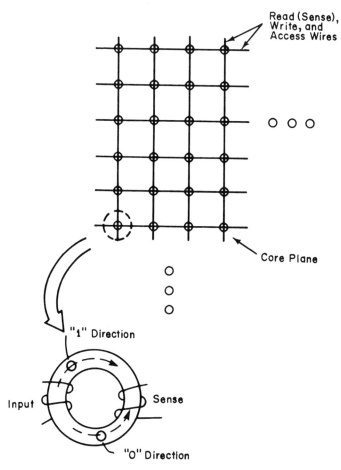

Figure 2.8 Core Memory

Magnetic core is an obsolete technology, but it had one advantage. It was nonvolatile. Core holds information even when the circuits are unpowered, in contrast to some semiconductor memory which must have power at all times.

Engineers spend a great deal of time developing devices that will retain information with very little power. Magnetic bubble memory is a natural successor to magnetic core memory because it too is nonvolatile.

Magnetic bubble memory is a high-density, solid state storage device used for memory. A magnetic bubble memory stores data in the form of cylindrical magnetic domains in a thin film of magnetic material. The presence of a domain (a bubble) is interpreted as a binary 1, and the absence of a domain is interpreted as a binary 0. Bubbles are created from electrical signals by a bubble generator within the memory and reconverted to electrical signals by an internal detector. An external rotating magnetic field propels these cylindrical domains through the film. Metallic patterns or chevrons deposited on the film steer the domains in the desired directions. Transfer rates, once started, are in the tens of thousands of bits per second, but because the data circulates past a pickup point at which it becomes available to the outside world, there is a delay, averaging tens of milliseconds, before data transfer can begin.

Magnetic Field in Bubbles

In these respects, magnetic bubble memories are serial high-density storage devices like electromechanical disk memories. However, in a disk, the stored bits are stationary on a moving medium. In the magnetic bubble memory, the medium is stationary and the bits move. Small metallic patterns deposited on the thin film control the movement of the bubbles for data storage. Asynchronous chevrons encourage the bubbles to move in only one direction as in Figure 2.9.

When an electric current passes through a wire laid across a magnetic bubble film, the bubbles are attracted to it and follow it as if they are moved. In particular, if the wire is physically rotated, the bubbles move in circles. They do so because a magnetic field is associated with the current in the wire. If the current in the wire is directed from top to bottom across the film, the magnetic field under the wire is directed to the right and pulls the magnetic bubbles in that direction. (The magnetic field above the wire is directed to the left, but since it is farther from the film, it has less effect on the bubbles, which react more strongly to the nearby part of the field.) □

The principal advantage of magnetic bubble memories is their nonvolatility; that is, if power fails, the stored data is retained. Products incorporating bubble memories therefore do not require battery backups. Magnetic bubble memories share this feature with read only memories (ROMs), erasable programmable PROMs (EPROMS), and electrically erasable PROMs (E²PROMs). However, unlike any of these technologies, magnetic bubble memories can have data written into them at any time, at speeds comparable to those at which data is read. Furthermore, unlike disk memories, bubble memories are quiet and very reliable, because they have no moving parts. With a million or more bits per device, a bubble can store 16 to 64 times the amount of data as alternative semiconductor memories, providing very high storage capability in a compact space.

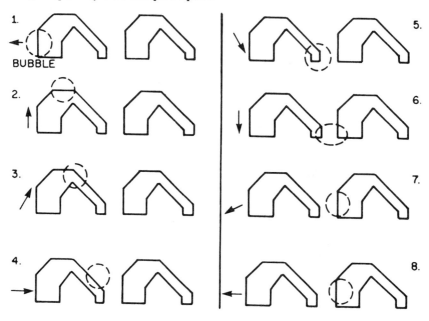

Figure 2.9 Bubble Movement

Regardless of whether it is semiconductor, core, bubble, or otherwise, a memory device must have a set of address selection lines that select a specific location in memory. A device that employs k lines permits selection among 2^k locations. A memory device must also allow a control to distinguish a read operation from a write operation. By convention, we read from memory and I/O into the CPU and we write into memory and I/O from the CPU.

Example 2.2 A Semiconductor Memory Device. Semiconductor devices require a set of lines called the chip enable lines since the devices are only 14- to 16-pin chips. Sometimes the p chip enable lines are used in conjunction with the k address selection lines to select an address among several chips. For instance, if each chip had three chip enable lines, a semiconductor memory system could be organized with eight chips and could assign locations to each chip. Now the k address lines and the p chip enable lines could serve as a $k+p$ set of address lines in the computer. Each memory chip would be capable of receiving or transmitting n bits of information. Thus, n data input/output wires would be required.

The storage capacity of a memory device can be measured in terms of the total number of bits of information dimensioned by the number of words (W) and the number of bits (B) per word. The memory width is the width of a word, and its length is the total number of words. The *address* of a word is its unique location in memory. The *content* is the actual information stored in the addressed location in memory. A memory chip with 256 words by 1-bit is commonly called a 256-bit chip. Chips are also available in a 1024-by-1 bit, 4096-by-4 bit, and larger. A 1024-word by 1-bit chip is called a 1K device while the 4096-by-1 bit is a 4K device or chip. Designers are expending considerable energy to develop very compact memory devices with great bit densities. The *density* of a device is a measure of the number of bits per unit area of the device.

Computers seldom address an individual bit in a memory device; hence, memory devices are rarely designed to be bit addressable. *Words*, commonly, are addressable in a memory system. Again, a word consists of n bits of information, and is generally the nominal amount of information communicated. A word is not the only addressable data size in memory. The 68000, PDP-11, and IBM 360/370 series allow us to address a byte (eight bits) in memory. We should not say that the word size in a machine is necessarily the same as the width of memory. The IBM 370 is a 32-bit word machine, yet we can address 8, 32, and even 64-bit quantities. The CYBER 170 is a 60-bit machine with memory that is not organized about a 60-bit word.

Since the cost of a memory device is sensitive to the speed, main memory is primarily reserved for storage of programs and data that are currently, or are about to be, processed. The *access time* of memory is the interval of time between a request for information, either to or from memory, and the moment that the information is available. For example, in a read operation, the memory access time is the interval from memory address selection to the moment that the data appears at the requesting device. The write access time is not always identical to the read access time, although it is very close. The write access time is the interval of time required from the moment of address selection to the moment that data has been stored in the memory device. Some memory devices lose their contents upon reading the actual location. This destructive readout requires a restoring or a writing back into the location. The time to read plus restore the information in destructive memory devices is called the memory *cycle time*. A core memory is a destructive readout device.

The memory devices discussed so far are commonly used for control memory or main memory. Memory devices not suited to the fast access required of control or main memory, but found in secondary memory, are storage media based on rotating machinery. Disks and drums are such devices. Data storage is accomplished by writing bits of information onto circular tracks. Writing is accomplished by setting the direction of magnetic fields in minute spots called magnetic domains on the medium, which has been precoated with an oxide material capable of magnetizing.

Magnetic Domains

Magnetic domains can be established in many types of magnetic materials including iron bars, the coating on magnetic tape, and ferrite toroids (the most common form of computer memory in the 1960s). Each domain is a group of atoms with parallel magnetic orientations. When the material in bulk is unmagnetized, the domains have a random orientation. Magnetization to a level less than saturation orients some of the domains to a common direction, but leaves many of them randomly oriented. When a domain orientation changes, usually by the imposition of an external magnetic field, the domain itself does not physically move, but boundaries between domains that formerly had different orientations become indistinct or disappear altogether.

There are a variety of recording techniques. Some are listed in Table 2.1. Newer techniques include perpendicular and laser (for optical storage devices) recording. Unlike conventional or longitudinal recording, the magnetization of the disk surface material occurs at angles *perpendicular* to the surface, as shown in Figure 2.10. Conventional longitudinal recording creates magnetized zones *along* the surface. Much higher storage densities are available in perpendicular recording with typically 100,000 flux reversals per inch possible. □

Table 2.1   Magnetic Recording Techniques

Technology	Versatility	Lineal Density	Areal Density
longitudinal recording	read and write	15,000 flux reversals per inch	165×10^8 flux reversals per square inch
perpendicular recording	read and write	100,000 flux reversals per inch	100×10^8 flux reversals per square inch
laser (optical) recording	read/write	25,000 impressions per inch	6.25×10^8 impressions per square inch

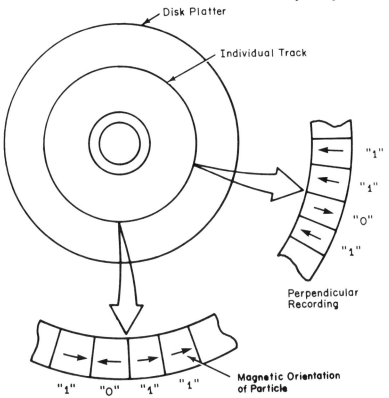

Figure 2.10 Disk Platter with Magnetic Domains

A disk system is comprised of a disk drive mechanism with disk platters as in Figure 2.11. The disk drive system includes a motor to spin the disk platters and servomotors to position a movable arm that contains the head above and/or below the disk platter. The head reads and writes onto tracks. A track is a concentric circle of data on a disk. The recording area, regardless of whether it is in a fixed or a moving head disk system, is always organized into tracks consisting of these circular rings of recorded data. When a disk system contains multiple heads, the removable disk package that holds multiple disks is called a disk pack.

Tracks on a disk can be organized in sectors. Data is synchronized on a disk with a timing track to help recognize the sectors. Since a track in a given sector near the outer edge of the disk platter is longer than a track at the center of a disk, bits are recorded with unequal density. Those tracks near the center have a much higher density than those tracks at the outer edge. One design objective is to equalize the number of bits on all tracks. In Figure 2.11, a sequential sector organization with eight sectors is depicted. A sequentially organized disk has ordered sectors. Organization may also be nonsequential.

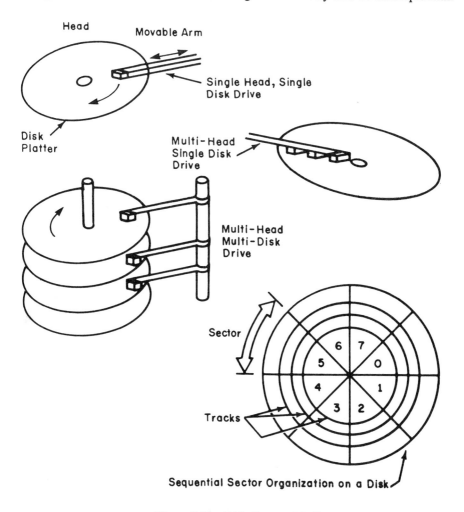

Figure 2.11   Disk Storage Media

To assist in data location on a disk, index marks are placed on the tracks. They are actually special sectors that indicate the beginning of a track. Some multi-head disk drive systems can move heads over the platters in unison. The radial position of all the heads as measured from the spindle forms a set of addresses within a cylinder, hence, a radial position in such configurations is called a *cylinder address*.

The rotation time it takes for positioning the datum under the head while on the desired track is called *latency*. The time to place the head over a specific track is the *seek time*. However, more time may be needed to eventually access a datum on the disk because the datum, although in the current track, may not yet be under the head. The average duration of this interval is one-half of the time to move the head from the innermost to the outermost track. An unused disk must first be formatted. Formatting involves placing specific "header" information on a disk to specify details about its size and physical location.

Disks can be either floppy or hard. A floppy disk is a flexible circular sheet of mylar, again coated with some magnetizable material. Its extremely low cost is attractive to a microcomputer user, generally one-tenth to one-twentieth of the cost of a hard disk platter. Information storage capacity is much less on a small floppy such as depicted in Figure 2.12. Floppies are sold in a 3½", 5¼", or 8" diameter. Data organization on a floppy is similar to that of a hard disk. Because they can be handled and therefore damaged more easily, floppies are less reliable and less durable than hard disks.

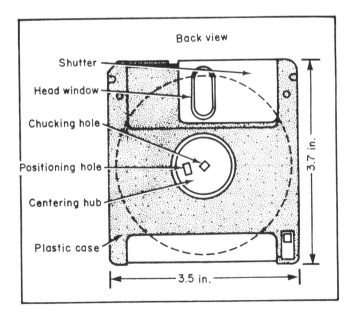

Figure 2.12 Floppy Disk

Recording on a disk is accomplished with heads housed in disk drive units. Head technology today uses either the Winchester or Whitney configurations as shown in Figure 2.13. Whitney heads, first used in the IBM 3380, require less space between platters than Winchester heads and can get closer to inner and outer edges, thus allowing additional tracks. The heads are smaller, also. Typical disk drive characteristics are listed in Table 2.2 for Winchester hard disk systems and typical soft or floppy disk systems.

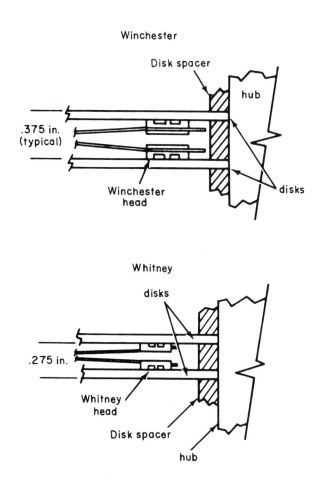

Figure 2.13 Disk Head Technology

Table 2.2 Typical Winchester Disk Drive Characteristics

Performance	Winchester (Hard)
Formatted Capacity:	
Per Drive	5 Mbytes
Per Surface	1.25 Mbytes
Per Track	8,192 bytes
Per Sector	512 bytes
Sectors per Track	16
Transfer Rate:	5 M b/s
Average Access Time:	17.0 msec
Functional Specifications:	
Rotational Speed	3600 RPM
Densities	254 tracks per inch

Performance	5¼″ Disk System (Floppy)
Formatted Capacity:	
Per Drive	819 Kbytes
Diskettes per Drive	1
Number of Recorded Surfaces	2
Per Track	5,120 bytes
Per Sector	512 bytes
Sectors per Track	10
Transfer Rate:	250 K b/s
Random Access Time:	264 msec
Functional Specifications:	
Rotational Speed	300 RPM
Densities	96 tracks per inch

2.3.4 MAGNETIC TAPE

Magnetic tape, the major medium for archival storage, is a serially accessed device. Data is stored on tracks on a flexible nylon plastic tape medium with a magnetized coating to store information as in Figure 2.14. Magnetic tapes come in various widths from ½″ to 1″. The ½″ tape in the figure indicates nine tracks that run parallel to the edge of the tape. Data, then, can be stored across the tape in 9-bit characters. Generally, one track is reserved for parity. *Parity* is an error detection scheme that essentially performs an exclusive-OR operation on the bits in the character. A 9-track tape would store an 8-bit character plus parity. Using an exclusive-OR operation on the eight bits would then indicate whether a single error had occurred in the reading or writing of a character. For example, suppose that we were writing a word onto the tape with even parity. We could then exclusive-OR the eight bits of the character, and if the outcome of the exclusive-OR of these eight bits was zero, our parity would be assigned a "0" to force even parity. If, however, the exclusive-OR of these bits was a one, we would assign a "1" to the parity bit to ensure that the parity of all eight bits is indeed a zero. Odd-parity is also used.

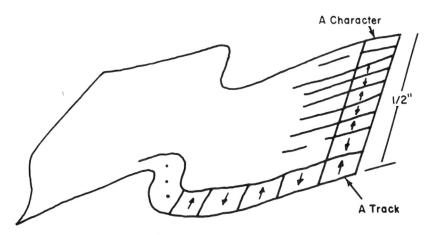

Figure 2.14   Segment of a 9-Track Magnetic Tape Medium

Parity detection is implemented both in hardware and software. Two types of parity checks can be employed. Transverse parity checks a character in each row across the tape as mentioned above. A longitudinal parity detects an error along a track for several bits along this single track. Not all tape drives or systems provide for both of these techniques. Some of the low-cost magnetic tape systems such as cassette tapes found commonly in microcomputers may have no parity checks at all.

Magnetic tapes are wound on reels, generally about 2400, 1200, or 600 feet long. Tapes are mounted on a tape drive device with both a tape supply reel and a takeup reel. As the tape moves across a read and a write head, data is transferred accordingly. Tapes move about 120 inches a second with bit densities of 200, 556, 800, 1600, and 6250 or more bits per inch. With such densities and speeds, obviously we could not start or stop a tape between characters. Data on a tape is organized as records with the boundary between records called inter-record gaps.

A *character* is the basic unit of information on a tape. These characters are then grouped into fields which may represent names or addresses or even some numerical data. The groups or fields are now combined into a record. A *record* is a logical group of information of interest to a user. Sometimes the word *block* has been used synonymously with record, but recently a block has been interpreted to mean a physically recorded group of information. Records can also be combined if they have something in common. Such a group of records is a *file* or *data set*. Files then are delineated on the magnetic tape by an end-of-file mark. (A file is a named collection of related information.)

Tapes may be formatted or unformatted. A *formatted* tape has an additional timing track by which data is located character by character on the tape. *Unformatted* tapes contain no timing track. Since the magnetic tape medium is sequential access, it is not convenient to access records randomly or directly. Rather, the tape must wind or unwind toward the desired record, passing through the intermediate records and proceeding through all blocks one at a time. Some tape handling machines allow you to read and write while traveling in either direction.

Small computers and microcomputers employ a poor man's version of magnetic tape storage or cassettes. These cassette tapes and drives behave much like the larger tape mediums we have just discussed, although they are very low-cost devices. Reliability is not as good as with larger tape drives. Cassette tapes can be unformatted with only one track. Two-track cassette tapes are available.

Smaller computers such as microcomputers predominantly employ a cassette tape recoruer. Large main frame computers tend to employ either IBM-compatible transports or nonstandard tape transports. Minicomputers may employ a combination, although cartridge recorders are very popular. A *transport* is simply the tape drive mechanism. It includes the motors to turn the tape plus its takeup reel if necessary. The performance of cartridge recorders generally exceeds that of the cassette recorder, but, of course, cartridge recorders are a bit more expensive. Some tape systems can handle more than one transport. The low-cost cassette recorders generally have a single track which records strings of ones and zeroes in one single track. Cartridge records may have a single track or multiple tracks. Usually, a timing track is included in a cartridge recorder system.

2.3.5 CONTROL UNIT

It is not an assembly language program that causes the hardware to execute the basic fetch/execute cycle, but a microprogram already residing in the control unit. However, not all control units are microprogrammable. Some are designed to handle control functions by other means, one of which is by directly "hardwiring" or fixing the control sequences into digital logic instead of into a control memory. No matter what implementation scheme is used, the same basic fetch/execute cycle can be found in all computational machines.

A two-step procedure portrays a very general view of the actual procedures used within a computer to execute programs. Details that might alter this basic cycle have not yet been considered. For example, a computer might be "interrupted" during the normal processing (fetch, execute, fetch, execute,...). Circuits and special control programs are then activated to service interrupts. Furthermore, such programs alter the fetch/execute cycle slightly to allow the computer to fetch an instruction from sources external to the currently executing program. (More accurately, they replace the contents of the PC after saving the previous contents for a return. The instruction cycle stays fixed.) Interrupt service programs initiate sequences of steps (different machine instructions) to process the algorithms related to the interrupts. When interrupt processing is completed, the computer automatically returns to the interrupted program (where it was interrupted) and continues normal processing. This is a very simplified explanation of only one modification to the fetch/execute cycle. There will be other examples later in the text. Among those are instructions that require multiple fetches before the instruction execution phase begins. Regardless of whether a basic or altered fetch/execute occurs, supporting this cyclic nature of a computer is an internal clock that essentially "times" events in a precise manner.

The structure of a control unit falls into one of two classes: decentralized (random logic) or centralized (microprogrammable). A *decentralized control unit* distributes the control hardware about the machine in hardware that comprises a myriad of different devices. In contrast, a *centralized control unit* contains a control memory and memory access devices all together and centrally located. The control memory contains microprograms that issue microinstructions to the remaining computer hardware. A *microinstruction* is an ordered collection of micro–operations. A microinstruction is fetched and executed when a machine language instruction from main memory is decoded from the instruction register. Some machine language instructions cause several microinstructions to be executed. However, it is the micro-operations specified by a microinstruction that directly assert control signals throughout the computer.

The basic function of the control unit is to translate machine language instructions into a sequence of timing pulses and control signals. These synchronized control signals implement the register transfer language micro-operations in a digital computer. A master clock generator within the control unit synchronizes the flow of these timing signals throughout the computer. The basic hardware of a control unit is shown schematically in Figure 2.15.

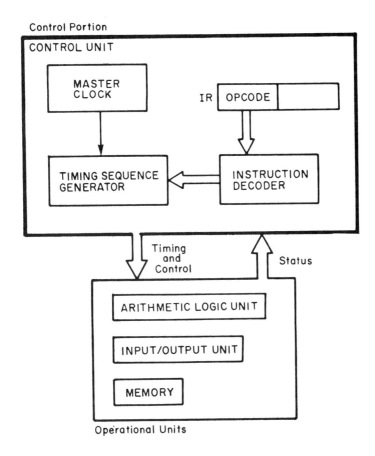

Control Portion

CONTROL UNIT

MASTER
CLOCK

IR | OPCODE

TIMING SEQUENCE
GENERATOR

INSTRUCTION
DECODER

Timing
and
Control

Status

ARITHMETIC LOGIC UNIT

INPUT/OUTPUT UNIT

MEMORY

Operational Units

Figure 2.15 Control Unit Block Diagram

This control unit contains a master clock, timing sequence generator, instruction register, and instruction decoder. The output from the control unit is a set of pulses from the timing sequence generator, as in Figure 2.16. These pulses synchronize micro-operation activity in the operational units. During instruction execution, operational units may generate status signals which are then fed back to the control unit. A typical status signal might be the occurrence of an arithmetic overflow from an ALU operation. Along with the timing signals from the control unit are actual control signals that emanate from the instruction decoder.

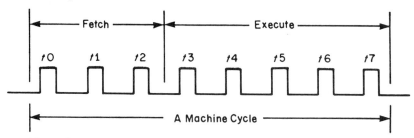

Figure 2.16   Example of a Control Unit Timing Circuit Pulse Sequence

To portray the control unit's timing influence upon the assertion of a micro-operation, a control statement precedes the micro-operation as follows:

Control Statement		Micro-operation(s)
$tk \wedge N$	:	R3 ← (R2)
This is the Boolean control statement. If true, the primitive step is performed. If false, the primitive step is ignored.		This is the primitive step to be performed.

A *control statement* is a Boolean function of binary variables. There may be one or more variables in each statement. In the control statement above, the Boolean variables, tk and N, must both be true for the primitive steps to be executed. These variables belong to the Boolean function of the control statement for a specific micro-operation in the sequence. In this example syntax, control statements are separated from micro-operations by a colon. The micro-operation(s) is performed only if the control statement is true. In the above micro-operations, the contents of R2 (Register 2) will be transferred to R3 when tk is true *and* N is true. (Note that N could be the negative flag in the program status register. If so, this micro-operation will be performed at time tk only if N has been set.)

For most of the examples in this section, a control statement will contain a variable representing an instant of time in a machine cycle (such as tk above). Since a timing sequence generator in the control unit generates these clock pulses and since the micro-operations must be synchronized to specific clock pulses, that same clock pulse will be indicated along with the micro-operations. If there are any machine status signals that become part of the control statement, they will also be indicated in that control statement. Later examples describe a simple set of control statements that include a machine status of the arithmetic conditions in the ALU.

In Chapter 1, a general instruction fetch/execute cycle was described. This cycle is controlled by the control unit with a special microprogram as found in Example 2.3.

Example 2.3 Instruction Fetch Micro-Operations. The micro-operations required during the fetch phase of every machine cycle are listed below:

Fetch Control Statements	Micro-Operations
t0:	MAR ← (PC)
t1:	IR ← (MDR), PC ← (PC+1)
t2:	Decoder ← (IR)

IR refers to the instruction register, PC refers to the program counter, MAR refers to the memory address register, MDR refers to the memory data register.

Two micro-operations are necessary. The first is a register transfer of the contents of the program counter to the memory address register, which causes the memory to be accessed at the location pointed to by the memory address register. At clock pulse t1, the contents of memory are transferred to the instruction register via the memory data register. Also, the program counter is incremented. At clock pulse t2, the instruction register is decoded. Corresponding gates and fetch micro-operations are shown in Figure 2.17.

Notice that an AND gate connects the timing pulse t0 and the decoder output to cause the memory address register transfer. This AND gate then feeds a set of control gates between the program counter and memory address register. When these control gates are closed, the data in the program counter is capable of being transferred to the memory address register. This transfer occurs when a load signal is activated in the memory address register itself. The load signal must not be activated at the same time that these control gates are enabled between the two registers. There is a slight time delay involved in the enabling of these control gates, and this delay must be inserted in the load signal line as shown. This delay will cause the contents of the memory address register to be loaded properly. There are alternative mechanisms to perform a parallel load.

Example 2.4 A Parallel Register Transfer. Suppose that we want to make a transfer of the contents of register R1 into register R2. A scheme similar to the previous example is now possible. Realize, however, that these micro-operations occur during an execute phase of the basic fetch/execute cycle. This is a simple micro-operation which can occur early in the execute phase. Pulse t3 is sufficiently early to assert the register transfer command as shown in Figure 2.18. The AND gate that couples t3 with the register transfer command is fed to the control gates between R1 and R2. To compensate for propagation, a delay is required at the load signal input to R2 to prevent ambiguous data from being loaded into R2.

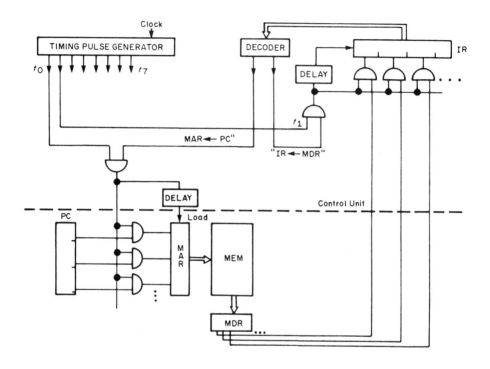

Figure 2.17   Micro-Operations in the Fetch Phase of a Machine Cycle

Example 2.5 Register Addition.   Suppose that we want to add the contents of register R1 to R2. The sequence of micro-operations for this process is indicated in Table 2.3. In the table, we see the set of micro-operations that causes the gating of the data between R1 and the ALU and R2 and the ALU. The gating or control signals come from the control unit. A timing circuit capable of generating eight pulses from t0 to t7 is used to synchronize activities between the registers and the ALU. The timing circuit generates a sequence of pulses as seen earlier in Figure 2.16. Let's assume that the first three pulses are assigned to the fetch phase of the machine cycle. The remaining five pulses are assigned to the execute phase of the machine cycle.

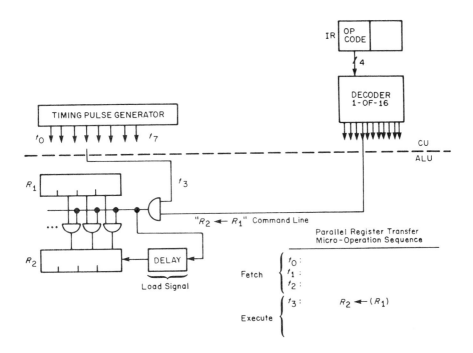

Figure 2.18 Register-to-Register Transfer Micro-Operations

Table 2.3 Sequence of Micro-Operations for
Register-to-Register Addition of the Form R1 ← R1+R2

	Control Statement	Micro-Operation
	t0 :	MAR ← (PC)
Fetch	t1 :	IR ← (MDR), PC ← (PC+1)
Phase	t2 :	Decoder ← (IR)
	t3 :	ABUS ← (R1), BBUS ← (R2)
	t4 :	ALU ← (R1+R2)
Execute	t5 :	CBUS ← (ALU)
Phase	t6 :	R1 ← CBUS
	t7 :	No Operation

The sequence of micro-operations listed in Table 2.3 indicates the set of control signals that must be generated by the control unit. These entries are the necessary control statements for the respective micro-operations. The micro-operation is performed only when the control statement is true. This register transfer language notation is helpful to describe the activity within the control unit itself. The register addition requires seven clock pulses, t0 through t6. However, this control unit assumes that a machine cycle will consist of eight clock pulses. Any machine instructions, such as this register addition, which do not utilize all clock pulses, will cause the machine to "coast‛ through the extra clock pulses. In this case, t7 indicates a "no operation."

The first three steps in the sequence are assigned to the fetch phase of the instruction for the register addition. Every machine instruction requires a fetch phase. The remaining four clock pulses are used in the execute phase. At pulse time t0, an instruction in program memory is pointed to by the memory address register. This is a read operation on the memory unit. At pulse t1 the actual contents of the location are passed via the memory data register into the instruction register of the control unit. At the same time, the program counter is incremented by one. At time t2 in the timing sequence, the opcode field of the instruction is decoded to determine which signals are output from the decoder. Next, the decoding determines that a register addition sequence is required. At time t3, the register addition cycle begins. Registers R1 and R2 are connected to the A and B buses. At time t4, the arithmetic logic unit receives a control signal on its function select lines to cause an addition of the two inputs on the A and B buses connected to the ALU. This control signal is activated at the ALU at time t4, and this synchronization is established with an AND gate that ANDs the timing pulse t4 with the "add‛ signal from the decoder. Figure 2.19 depicts this AND gate outside of the control unit. In practice, these control gates reside in the control unit itself. At time t5 and t6, the sum is returned to R1. Since t7 is not needed, an NOP occurs. Control statements t3 through t6 need additional inputs, not shown. For example, t3 should be replaced by "ADD"$\land$+3.

At the onset of the next t0 clock pulse, the fetch phase of the machine cycle is repeated and a new instruction is retrieved from program memory. Figure 2.19 does not depict all of the control gates necessary to execute the sequence of micro-operations. Realize that there will be a set of control gates (possibly a very large set) for each of these clock pulses from t0 through t7. For instance, to transfer the contents of the program counter to the memory address register, this parallel register transfer requires a load signal into the memory address register. This load signal would be generated by the decoder in the control unit.

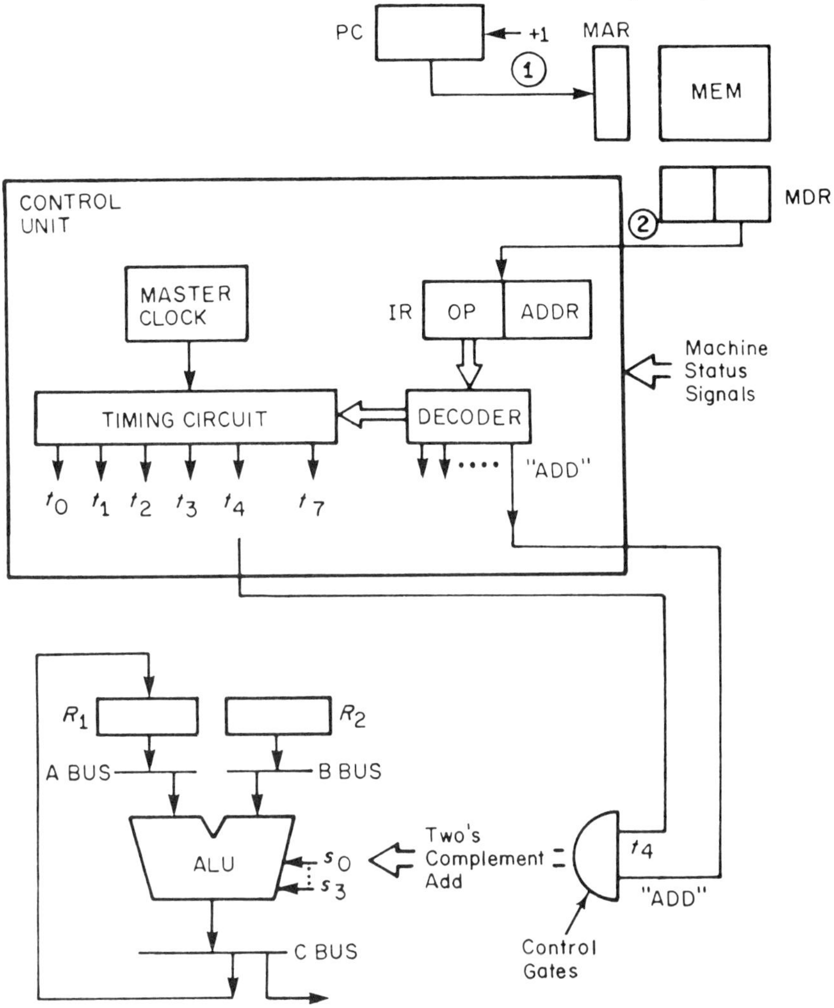

Figure 2.19 Control Unit Decoding the Register Add Micro-Operation

The sequence of micro-operations and control statements in Table 2.3 does not indicate any signals returning to the control unit from the operational units such as status. If the sequence of micro-operations is modified to consider arithmetic overflow, a signal from the arithmetic logic unit or elsewhere would so indicate the overflow and must be included. This status signal would then be used in the control unit to alter the sequence of steps. Also, a control statement, possibly at clock pulse t4 or t5, would be changed to alter the sequence of actual micro-operations. This modification would include a condition on a control statement to cease execution of this instruction and cause a new fetch phase. None of this capability is indicated in either Table 2.3 or Figure 2.19. The program status register now is introduced, which does have the capability to latch conditions for the control unit (seen later in Example 2.6).

Suppose that capability now exists in hardware to determine whether an arithmetic overflow occurs or not after an addition micro-operation. The machine hardware that monitors the arithmetic status and stores the current machine status is called the *machine status register* or status register. It may also be called the *program status register*. The function of the status register is to retain the current conditions of the machine in one register. The register contains flags as in Figure 2.20. A *flag* is a 1-bit storage cell whose sole purpose is to provide vital information about current activity within the machine. These bits are flags because they are intended to "capture" an executing program's interest. A flag can be used in a program to alter the current sequence of steps if an abnormal condition in the machine occurs. To alter the normal sequence, the contents of the program counter must be changed. Normally, the program counter is incremented to fetch the next sequentially located instruction. If, however, a flag is raised, the machine is being alerted to a possible non-sequential instruction fetch.

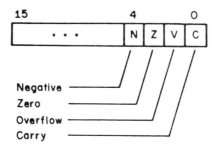

Figure 2.20   Machine Status Register

In Example 2.6, the status register contains four flags: negative, zero, overflow, and carry. The *negative flag* is set to a one when the result of an arithmetic operation is negative or less than zero. The *zero flag* is set to a one when the result is zero. A zero result occurs when all of the bits in the result are zero. The *overflow flag* is set to a one when the machine, after performing some arithmetic operation, was asked to generate a result which is larger than that representable in the machine. The overflow flag is monitoring an output from the ALU. Likewise, the *carry flag*, or C flag, also monitors the results of the current arithmetic operation. The C flag latches or holds the carryout of the most significant bit or the sign bit. The C flag is useful for multi-bit arithmetic when it is necessary to add the carry from the least significant byte or word into the next significant byte or word.

Example 2.6 Control Statements with Machine Status. Suppose that the machine in Example 2.5 contains a status register. It is monitoring the results in the arithmetic logic unit shown in Figure 2.19. Now it is desired to alter the machine's normal sequence if an overflow occurs. To do so, the fetch phase micro-operations must be modified. This modification is shown in Table 2.4. The overflow flag is ANDed with clock pulse t0. If the overflow flag has been set, the machine fetches an instruction from a special location. Location 001C is chosen in this example. In this location of memory, provisions have been made to handle overflow. (In a very simple machine, the control unit could illuminate a red lamp on the front panel that would indicate overflow and stop the machine. An operator would then have to come and fix the problem.)

Table 2.4   Fetch Phase Modified by Machine Status

$$V' \wedge t0 : \quad MAR \leftarrow (PC),$$
$$V \wedge t0 : \quad MAR \leftarrow 001C$$
$$t1 : \quad IR \leftarrow (MDR), PC \leftarrow (PC+1)$$
$$t2 : \quad Decoder \leftarrow (IR)$$

If the overflow flag is not set, then this micro-operation is not executed. In fact, the normal micro-operation seen in an earlier fetch phase is executed. In Table 2.4, notice that the control statements are now modified to include the status signal (V) from the status register. The circuit necessary to do this is a simple two-input AND gate with an extra inverter as shown in Figure 2.21. In most machines, the program status register retains the overflow condition and the computer continues program execution. In this event, the assembly language program should have additional statements to test and handle the overflow. (It is very easy to generalize Table 2.4 for traps and interrupts by changing the PC after saving it. Can you do it?)

It is certainly possible to modify the control statements to include the status from the other arithmetic status indicators in the status register. For instance, one could alter the micro-operations in the fetch phase when a zero result has indeed occurred. Furthermore, it is just as easy to alter the fetch phase micro-operations when the negative flag is set. The hardware in Example 2.6 is representative of possible circuitry available in a control unit to perform the fetch phase portion of the cycle when the machine status signals are input to the control unit. There are many other machine status signals that could enter the control unit. They may include a status indication that electrical power is failing, that the computer itself is heating up, or that a human operator wishes to alter the sequence of events manually. (For example, an operator might want to halt the machine by depressing a HALT pushbutton on the front panel.)

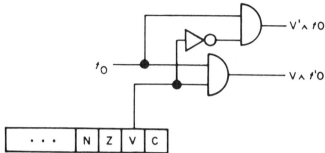

Figure 2.21   Modified Control Unit Circuits for Overflow Conditions

2.3.6   TIMING

Programs to a computer are like music to an orchestra. Both follow a "score" which governs activity. Just as an orchestra needs a conductor to keep the pace and tempo, a computer needs a timer serving as a master clock. A computer is essentially a large synchronous sequential state machine. Although we (as computer users) may never see it, the master clock (timer) by which the computer stays in step exists in every computer. The master clock generator produces a regular sequence of pulses called a *machine cycle* that flows through the internal machine to cause information to arrive at registers, counters, and ALUs (e.g., neither early nor late). These sequences of pulses are the control signals to gate information at the proper time.

Why is timing so important? Consider this analogy. Suppose there were no traffic lights whatsoever on the streets in your city. What method would be possible to maximize traffic flow and minimize accidents? Computers are like cities. The data and information paths are city streets. Data (cars) must arrive at specific computer elements without colliding: neither too early nor too late. Traffic lights (instructions) guide movement through the city (computer). Someone (computer architect) must lay out the streets (hardware). Someone else (software engineer) must devise a master plan to control the traffic lights.

Consider our basic two-step machine cycle with fetch and execute phases. We have just seen how these steps can be integrated as internal commands (from the control unit) to the computer elements to acquire an instruction from program memory and load it into the instruction register (fetch phase). The execute phase then follows. A timing circuit for such activity usable within a control unit could be the sequencer, as depicted in Figure 2.22, which is capable of generating pulses t_0 and t_2, reserved for the fetch and execute phases, respectively. Pulses t_1 and t_3 are not assigned as yet, but are available when modifications to this cycle are needed. The t_0 pulse could be used as a signal to the program counter to point to and access program memory. The t_2 pulse could be used to decode and execute the instruction just placed into the IR. The "X" input signal initiates or starts up the fetch/execute cycle. If "X" were cleared to zero, the fetch/execute cycle would cease. CP is a clock pulse signal derived from the master clock. Example 2.7 illustrates a preliminary design exercise for a control unit likely to use the sequencer.

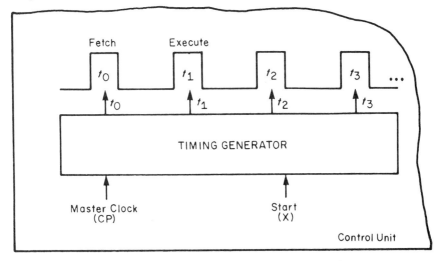

Figure 2.22   Timing Pulses from the Control Unit

Example 2.7 Master Clock Timing.   Suppose that a sequencer built with the circuitry of Figure 2.22 is used to generate the fetch/execute phases of a control unit. Suppose also that the particular computer utilizes two clock pulses each for fetch and execute phases. If the computer requires a fetch phase equal to 100 nanoseconds, what should the clock pulse width equal? The answer is obtained by counting the number of clock pulses required for a fetch phase interval and dividing the fetch phase by this number. This intermediate result produces the width of a clock cycle. But a clock cycle consists of the "one" state as well as the "zero" state. If the clock is symmetrical, then the "one" state interval equals the "zero" state interval. Assuming a symmetrical clock, the clock pulse width that is normally the "one" state interval is found by halving the intermediate result. From Figure 2.22, we see that two clock cycles are needed for every fetch phase. The intermediate result of 50 nanoseconds, now obtained, must be halved to 25 nanoseconds. Hence, the clock pulse width for this control unit is 25 nanoseconds.

2.4   REGISTER TRANSFER LEVEL ORGANIZATION

A computer can be described in terms of the programs that reside in it, from its high-level language programs down to its microprograms in the control store, or a computer can be described by its hardware organization. The basic organization just observed in earlier sections comprises a structural description of a computer (predominantly at the basic component level), including the ALU, the I/O, and the memory, but the behavior of a computer is best described in terms of functions that each of the separate basic elements performs. Design tools such as Boolean algebra, sequential state machines, truth tables, and state tables are indeed useful to explain the behavior of a single flip-flop or set of flip-flops.

However, computers can be organized about hardware modules, each of which may contain one or more registers, counters, or other primitive elements or components. Describing the behavior of a computer would be hopelessly confusing if each individual state of a flip-flop was noted in some documentation. Recognizing, then, that modules, not gates and flip-flops, comprise the basic hardware elements at this level, a new language is necessary to efficiently describe computer behavior. This language is called "register transfer language" or RTL. Like other languages, it contains symbols and rules with notation to be understood by its users. RTL attempts to make the description of register transfer logic clear and concise. In fact, a computer architect can describe most computers of considerable complexity with only a few pages of register transfer documentation.

Hardware modules may be simple (containing only a single register) or complex (possessing data processing capabilities). In any case, operations internal to a module are described by a micro-operation being performed. A *micro-operation* is an elementary step performed on data internal to the module. Micro-operations may be executed in one clock pulse or less. A micro-operation represents a very basic operation of the digital computer. A set of micro-operations comprises a microinstruction. A microinstruction, then, describes the activity of the modules at the register transfer logic level. Microinstructions reside in the control store or control memory of a computer. The collection of microinstructions to perform a specific task is a microprogram.

2.4.1   RTL NOTATION

Many register transfer languages are currently in vogue. One purpose of any register transfer language could be to design a digital computer. More important, RTL helps us comprehend the primitive operations within a computer by coupling these operations on primitive elements to micro-operations. Micro-operations form the basis of assembly language instructions. Subsequent sections describe some pseudo-programs with RTL. Here, it will be seen that as a programming language, the register transfer language is inadequate.

The notation and symbols to be used are found in Table 2.5. Since the descriptions explain the operations between special registers and processing

Table 2.5 Symbols in Register Transfer Language

Symbol	Meaning	Examples
capital letters with or without numerals	a register	B, R4, MAR, MDR, PC, IR, PSR, PSW, ACC
subscripts	one or more bits of a register	$R4_3$, B_{1-6}
( )	parentheses enclose a logical group or field of a register and indicate "contents of"[2]	IR(4-7)
M( )	a location in memory pointed to by register in parentheses	M(MAR)
← MDR	a memory read operation	R4 ← (MDR)
MDR ←	a memory write operation	MDR ← (R4)
←	transfer information from right-hand side to left-hand side	R4 ← (R7)
,	comma to separate one or more micro-operations taking place simultaneously or within subclock cycles	B ← C, D ← E
+	add	R0 ← R1+R7
−	subtract	R2 ← R1-R7
V	inclusive-OR	B ← AVR3
∧	and	B ← A∧R3
'	complement	R0 ← R1'
shr	logical shift right, vacated bit positions are zero	R1 ← shr R1
shl	logical shift left, vacated bit positions are zero	R6 ← shl R2
cil	circular logical shift left, vacated bit position receives shifted out bit (also called "rotate")	R6 ← cil R6
cir	circular logical shift right, vacated bit position receives shifted out bit	R6 ← cir R6
asl	arithmetic shift left, vacated bit is zero	R2 ← asl R2
asr	arithmetic shift right, sign bit copied back into vacated bit position	R2 ← asr R2

---

[2]Where it is obvious, the parentheses may be omitted.

capabilities, certain capital letters are reserved for such use. M always refers to memory and when used with parentheses indicates a location in memory pointed to by the register in parentheses. Again, IR refers to the instruction register, PC refers to the program counter, MAR refers to the memory address register, and MDR refers to the memory data register. PSW is the program status word while PSR is the program status register. Some of the symbols are self-explanatory and have been seen earlier.

Some micro-operations may be performed simultaneously. When hardware exists to support such opportunities, RTL statements may denote this "concurrency of operation" by concatenating micro-operations in a single statement. As shown below, micro-operation 1 (MO_1) and micro-operation 2 (MO_2) can be executed concurrently and are so indicated by a comma between them.

$$MO_1 , MO_2$$

If the duration of a clock pulse is long enough, some micro-operations can be performed early and others late in the same pulse duration. In these cases, the leftmost micro-operation in a concurrent statement is assumed to be executed first and the rightmost micro-operation is assumed to be executed last.

2.4.2   MICRO-OPERATIONS

Transfer between two registers can be parallel, as shown in Figure 2.23, in which case all bits of one register are transferred to the identical bit positions in the destination register as depicted in the following transfer between R2 (the source register) and R1 (the destination register). The horizontal arrow implies that information is passed from R2 to R1. Information in R2 has not been lost and is still retained. Since it is obvious that the contents of R2 and not R2 itself are transferred to R1, the parentheses could be omitted.

$$R1 \leftarrow (R2)$$

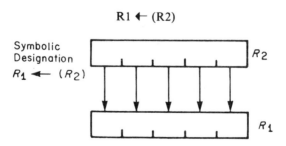

Figure 2.23   Parallel Transfer

Transfer can also take place between a register and a memory location. In this case, a special symbol is used for the memory, namely M. The pointer into the memory is the memory address register, MAR. The symbols to indicate a *read* operation (for instance, from memory into R4) are indicated in the following notations.

$$R4 \leftarrow M(MAR) \text{ or } R4 \leftarrow (MDR)$$

In this read operation, the contents of a memory location pointed to by MAR will be transferred to register R4. As a source register, MDR sends out data from a memory location pointed to by MAR. This is also equivalent to "reading" a memory location.

It is also possible to denote a *write* operation in register transfer language in one of two ways.

$$M(MAR) \leftarrow (R4) \text{ or } MDR \leftarrow (R4)$$

Here, R4 is again used, but now the contents of R4 will be transferred to a memory location pointed to by MAR. MDR is a special register. When specified, as above for a write operation, it implies more than just a single register transfer. As a destination register, MDR receives data *and* places the same data into a memory location pointed to by the MAR. This is the corresponding "write" operation.

2.4.3 ALU MICRO-OPERATIONS

Unlike the previous micro-operations between registers which do not modify the contents of the source register, arithmetic micro-operations are capable of modifying both the source and the destination registers. Arithmetic micro-operations represent the bulk of the data processing tasks in a computer for scientific applications. A simple addition micro-operation between registers R3 and R1 is indicated in Figure 2.24. R1 and R3 are source registers. The "+" sign now indicates the add micro-operation instead of the Boolean ORing operation. The single destination register, R3, will obviously be modified to contain the result of the addition micro-operation. A control signal to the ALU will command the ALU to perform the add micro-operation. This control signal emanates from the control store of the machine.

The symbolic designation for the subtraction operation involving the ALU is shown in Figure 2.25. Here, R1 is subtracted from R3 with the result placed in R3. Just as in the addition micro-operation, this subtraction operation results in modifying one register, the destination register. No specific symbols will be assigned to the addition and subtraction operations to indicate whether a one's complement, two's complement, or even sign/magnitude is taking place. The actual number representation will be assumed, and the computer hardware is then capable of performing that specific arithmetic operation with the assumed number representation.

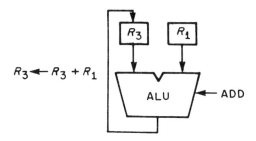

Figure 2.24   Add Micro-Operation

Many program segments rely on a counter with the ability to repeatedly count up (increment) or count down (decrement) in a particular register. Such a counter is necessary for controlling the number of iterations through a loop in a program. This is especially evident for incrementing a PC. The symbolic representation for increment and decrement can be implemented by using the addition and subtraction micro-operations of the ALU as in Figure 2.26. To increment, you add one to the counter. To decrement, you subtract one from the counter. The counter in this figure is R2. There may be hardware in a computer to perform the counting operation with registers instead of relying on the ALU, and, in that case, the register capable of incrementing and decrementing will perform the counting operation directly. Any registers capable of counting directly are identified during the machine specification phase of design. Complementation in a binary machine can take the form of one's complement or two's complement.

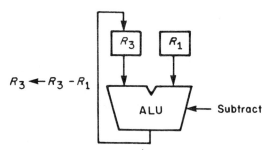

Figure 2.25   Subtract Micro-Operation

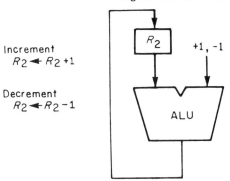

Figure 2.26   Increment and Decrement Micro-Operations

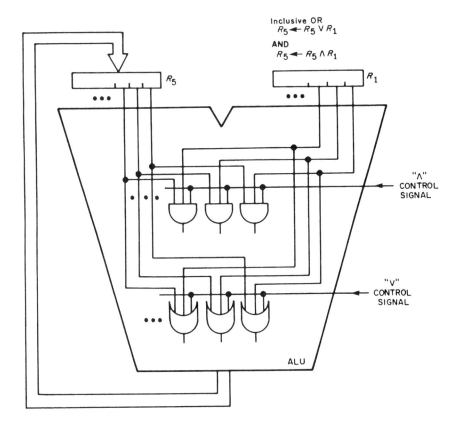

Figure 2.27   "OR" and "AND" Micro-Operations in the ALU

Let's return to Table 2.5 and look more closely at the Boolean micro-operations (AND, OR, NOT) possible in an arithmetic logic unit. The inclusive-OR and the Boolean AND operation are indicated in Figure 2.27. R5 with R1 are source registers with the Boolean micro-operations performed in the ALU with sets of AND gates for the ANDing operation and sets of OR gates for the ORing operation. Only the first three bits of R1 and R5 are shown. If these registers were n-bit registers, there would be two rows of n-bit gates for these functions in the ALU. A control signal from the control store would activate the AND gates for the ANDing operation. A control signal from the control store would also activate the OR gates for the inclusive-OR operation. Complementation in the ALU is performed as in Figure 2.28.

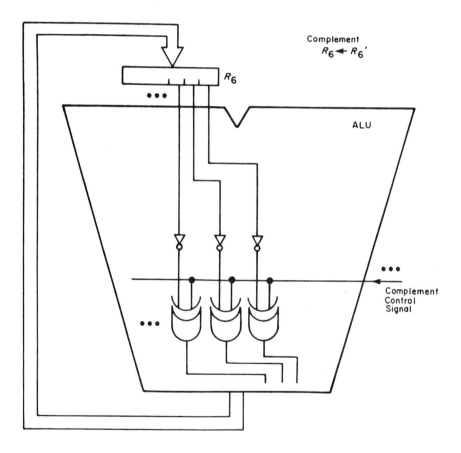

Figure 2.28   Complementing in the ALU

(Is it one's or two's complement?) Here, a set of XOR gates enables the Boolean micro-operation for complementation of R6. Again, a "complement" control signal would be issued to the ALU to request this micro-operation. Complementation can be performed outside the ALU if circuitry exists inside the computer at the register or the source itself.

Most arithmetic logic units can perform several Boolean micro-operations other than the logical AND and OR. Sixteen Boolean micro-operations of two variables are listed in Table 2.6.

Table 2.6   Micro-Operation Opcodes for an Arithmetic Logic Unit

Selection Code S3 S2 S1 S0	RTL Designation	Name	Function
0 0 0 0	...00000	Null	Binary constant 0
0 0 0 1	...11111	Identity	Binary constant 1
0 0 1 0	A'	Complement A	Not A
0 0 1 1	B'	Complement B	Not B
0 1 0 0	← A	Transfer	A
0 1 0 1	A∧B	AND	A and B
0 1 1 0	A/B	Inhibition	A but not B
0 1 1 1	B/A	Inhibition	B but not A
1 0 0 0	← B	Transfer	B
1 0 0 1	A⊕B	Exclusive-OR	A or B but not both
1 0 1 0	A V B	Inclusive-OR	A or B
1 0 1 1	(AVB)'	NOR	Not-OR
1 1 0 0	A⊙B	Equivalence	A equals B
1 1 0 1	A ⊂ B	Implication	If B then A
1 1 1 0	A ⊃ B	Implication	If A then B
1 1 1 1	(A∧B)'	NAND	Not-AND

An ALU that can perform the 16 micro-operations listed in Table 2.6 is shown in Figure 2.29. Except for flip-flops in the adder sections, an ALU has no memory in it. Circuits are mainly combinational, although some of the combinational circuits can be rather complicated. This is an n-bit parallel ALU, which is capable of executing the 16 functions on each of the n bits on the A side and B side of the ALU.

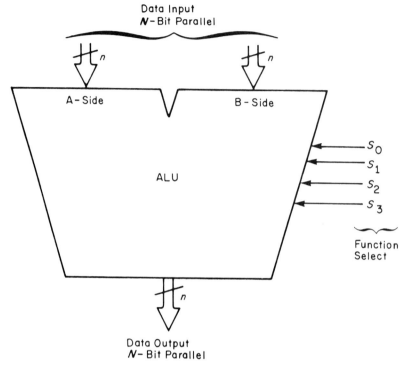

Data Input
N-Bit Parallel

A-Side

B-Side

ALU

S_0
S_1
S_2
S_3

Function
Select

Data Output
N-Bit Parallel

Figure 2.29   N-Bit Parallel Arithmetic Logic Unit

Selection of one of the 16 micro-operations is accomplished with four function select lines labeled S0, S1, S2, and S3. The corresponding micro-operation selected is indicated in Table 2.6. Only one micro-operation can be executed at a time. To execute a selected micro-operation, the inputs must be available during selection time. After a time interval required for the data to pass through the combinational circuits (be processed), the output is available on the data output lines. This ALU is also capable of performing micro-operations on a single input, either A or B. Such micro-operations are then called *unary* micro-operations, in which case only one variable is affected. Micro-operations on two variables are called *binary* micro-operations. There are ten binary micro-operations in Table 2.6.

Shift micro-operations involve the transfer of bits across a single register or between two registers. Three types of shifts are possible: logical, circular, and arithmetic shifts. Arithmetic shift micro-operations are reserved for signed binary numbers. Logical shift and circular shift may be used for signed binary numbers, but they can also be used for any character or datum in a register.

A shift within a register displaces all bits to the left or to the right simultaneously. The symbolic designation for a serial transfer from one register to another can be described by our register transfer language. Suppose that, as in Figure 2.30, a serial transfer is desired with register R2 as a source and register R1 as the destination register. By performing a right shift the least significant bit of R2 will enter the most significant bit of R1. Bits vacated in R2 will become zero. This is the rule for the shift regardless of its direction. Thus, with one clock pulse then, two micro-operations are executed. A shift right on R2 occurs, and bit 0 of R2 enters bit n-1 of R1. Bit 0 is the rightmost bit and bit n-1 is the leftmost bit in both registers.

$$shr \quad R_2 , R_{1_n} \leftarrow R_{2_0}$$

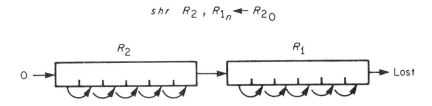

Figure 2.30 Serial Transfer with a Shift Right Micro-Operation

A shift right micro-operation obeys the procedure with the symbolic notation indicated in Figure 2.31. In both the shift left and the shift right micro-operations, the source register will be cleared to zero if we perform each operation n times. Such serial transfer of information is useful in the input/output interface between a computer and peripheral devices. Some peripheral devices transmit or receive serial data. However, an n-bit computer is basically organized with n-bit parallel paths. The I/O unit performs the necessary serial-to-parallel micro-operations for inputting data and the necessary parallel-to-serial operations for outputting data.

$$shl \quad R_2 , R_{1_0} \leftarrow R_{2_n}$$

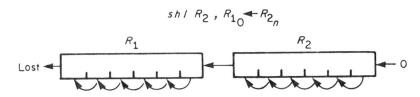

Figure 2.31 Serial Transfer with a Shift Left Micro-Operation

2.4.4 BUS MICRO-OPERATIONS

The preceding sections have illustrated transfers between registers or registers and memory always with one single source and one single destination. Suppose, however, that a selection must occur between one of many inputs to a particular device, as in Figure 2.32. Here, four registers, R1–R4, are capable of interconnection to an input side of an arithmetic logic unit. The input or output junction of the four registers is called a *bus*. A bus is essentially like a street with data intersections and traffic lights. An input bus can be made of multiplexers. The traffic lights are the selection codes on each multiplexer. Since only four registers are available, a 4-by-1 multiplexer will suffice. The micro-operation for bus transfer is also shown in Figure 2.32. The specific micro-operations connect R1 to the ALU through the bus.

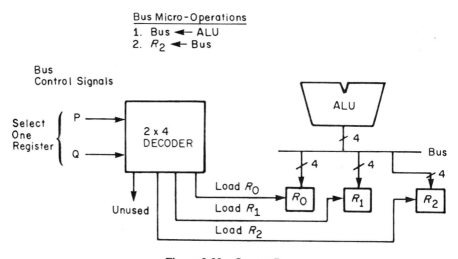

Bus Micro-Operations
1. Bus ← ALU
2. R_2 ← Bus

Figure 2.32 Output Bus

Similarly, it is possible to connect the output of an ALU to one of several destinations. In that case, the circuitry again employs a bus, but now the bus that controls information flow is implemented with a decoder. The output of the ALU in Figure 2.33 has the capacity to connect to one of three registers, R0, R1, or R2. The selection process is made possible with a decoder, and an output bus transfer occurs when the proper control signals are applied to the decoder. Two control signals are necessary for this 2-by-4 decoder to select one of three registers. Since a 2-by-4 decoder generates a possibility of four one of four selections, and since the bus needs only three selections, one of the output lines of the decoder is unused. (Remember that it may be necessary to have a no-op for this bus.) The number of lines from the ALU to each register is four, as indicated by the number "4" near the slash mark on each data path. The bus micro-operation to transfer the ALU to register R2 is also depicted in Figure 2.33.

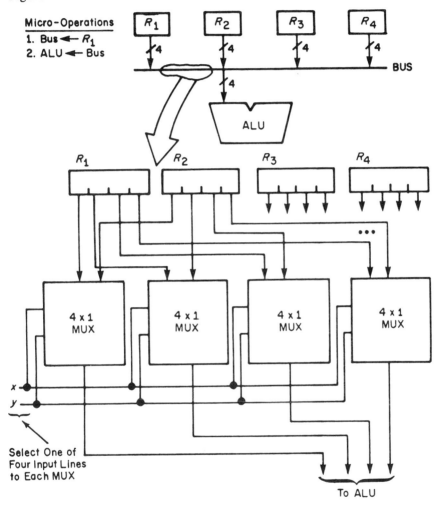

Figure 2.33 Input Bus

When it is clear, listing the bus transfer micro-operation may be eliminated. One should understand that there is an intermediate step requiring the data to pass through the bus. The implication applies also to an input bus transfer, as in the case of Figure 2.33. If R1 were to be connected to the ALU via the bus, the abbreviated micro-operation step might be "R1 being transferred directly to the ALU."

$$\text{ALU} \leftarrow (\text{R1})$$

Bus micro-operations are extremely useful not only for an ALU, but also between the computer and the outside world via an input/output unit. A bus may be unidirectional or bidirectional. In many small computers, there are three primary buses in a computing system: the address bus, the data bus, and the control bus. Where data or information must flow from several sources to one destination or from one source to several destinations, a bus could be employed. Similar hardware is then required for the address, data, and control bus.

2.5 SUMMARY

This chapter demonstrates how basic logical elements are physically employed in computer hardware. It is, however, only a brief introduction to possible implementations for the building blocks themselves. For the most part, such topics belong to the study of computer architecture.

A computer architect requires very extensive documentation to describe his or her machine, especially during the design phase. Documentation such as schematics and signal timing diagrams are only part of the total machine description, and they are necessary for the machine builder. But there are other forms of documentation more appropriate for those who want to understand and use machines, such as RTL. RTL is effective because it condenses the myriad of hardware details into short descriptive statements called micro-operations.

There are many computer languages besides microprogramming languages, RTL, and assembly languages. Each has a specific function. Some are programming languages, and others are descriptive or "design" languages. As a descriptive language, RTL is powerful. It is introduced specifically to facilitate understanding of both how primitive hardware building blocks are employed and how assembly language instructions can be described.

Conceivably, the micro-operations listed in the various examples could be embedded as microinstructions in a microprogramming language. Microprogramming is the lowest level of programming possible in a machine. Most readers may never microprogram. Some at one point may program at the assembly language level. An assembly language is more compact than a register transfer language, and thus portrays machine behavior with even more conciseness. In fact, a typical assembly language instruction implies more than one micro-operation (generally several micro-operations). Assembly language is a programming language. Hence, it is not used to describe a machine, but to write programs.

2.6 KEY WORDS

access time	negative flag
adders	operational register
address	overflow
arithmetic shift	overflow flag
binary counter	parallel load
borrow	parity
buffer register	RAM
carry	read operation
carry flag	register
circular shift	ROM
content	RTL
cycle time	seek time
cylinder address	sector
data selector	shift register
decoder	status register
demultiplexer	storage register
destructive read out	track
latency	volatile
logical shift	write operation
main memory	zero flag
micro-operation	
multiplexer	

2.7 SUGGESTED READING

Andrews, Michael. *Principles of Firmware Engineering in Microprogram Control.* Rockville, Md.: Computer Science Press, 1980.
    This advanced textbook covers the design of control units of digital machines. Building micro-operations into microinstructions is described in early chapters.

Optimizing microprograms (making them shorter and faster) is the topic of later chapters.

Gschwind, Hans W., and McCluskey, Edward J. *Design of Digital Computers.* New York: Springer-Verlag, 1975.
Content-addressable or associative memory systems are briefly described on pages 413-416. A 4 × 4, CAM similar to the Intel 3104, is depicted on page 415. Solid state semiconductor memory cells of the bipolar and MOS varieties are covered on pages 401-406.

Kline, Raymond M. *Digital Computer Design.* Englewood Cliffs, N.J.: Prentice-Hall, 1977.
A lucid presentation of memory cells and units can be found on pages 303-340. Diagrams of 2-D and 2½ D memory registers are depicted. Much detailed information about semiconductor memory systems helps one to understand RAM and ROM organization.

Myers, Glenford J. *Digital System Design with LSI, Bit-Slice Logic.* New York: John Wiley & Sons, 1980.
Using the AMD 2900, 3000, and MC10800 logic families, many principles of control unit designs are covered. Though primarily hardware-oriented, the text offers some insight into general microprogramming languages. Emphasis is placed on designing with LSI in the control unit.

Peatman, John B. *Microcomputer-Based Design.* New York: McGraw-Hill, 1977.
In this text dealing with the 6800 microprocessor, considerable detail at the hardware level is provided. The material focuses on using microprocessors in dedicated small computer applications primarily for instrumentation tasks. Earlier chapters are primarily motivational. Chapter 3 is a useful adjunct to this text and portrays general microcomputer hardware principles.

Sloan, M. E. *Computer Hardware and Organization.* Chicago: Science Research Associates, 1976.
A brief but clear explanation of magnetic recording techniques such as return-to-zero (RZ), return-to-bias (RB), and nonreturn-to-zero (NRZ) can be found on pages 364-368. Discussion of core memory follows much of Kline but is more brief.

Weitzman, Cay. *Minicomputer Systems.* Englewood Cliffs, N.J.: Prentice-Hall, 1974.
A thorough discussion of the storage mediums and the motivation for frequently employing disks and magnetic tapes is covered on pages 118-137. Cassette cartridge systems are described on pages 101-107.

2.8   EXERCISES

2.1   What are the basic building blocks at the register transfer level?

2.2   Which discipline in computer science is likely to employ a register transfer language?

2.3   What machine resources commonly exist in the CPU?

2.4   The status of arithmetic operations is kept in which register? Does a path exist from the CPU to the CU for this same purpose?

2.5   The ALUs in this book use *n*-bit parallel adders. That is, two operands, each *n*-bits wide, are processed in parallel *n*-bit fashion. Suppose an ALU is designed with a 1-bit adder section. What effect does the 1-bit adder have on machine instruction execution time?

2.6   What logic circuit in this chapter can be used to select 1 of 4 destinations for an ALU output?

2.7   What are the primary functions of the I/O unit?

2.8   What is the primary difference between a storage register and an operational register?

2.9   Of the two types of registers, which is general purpose?

2.10   What type of register is the program counter? Where is the PC found?

2.11   In Chapter 1, we found that the memory unit can be organized in hierarchical fashion. Match the devices below to the most likely level.

Device	Level
magnetic tape	Control Memory
solid state memory	Primary Memory
bubble memory	Secondary Memory
hard disk media	Bulk/Archival Memory
floppy disk media	

2.12   Why are magnetic tape media often called sequential access media?

2.13   Define the following terms:
    a. Character   d. Inter-record gap
    b. Record   e. Block
    c. File   f. Sector

2.14   RTL is not a programming language. Why?

2.15   Why is RTL important to the computer scientist? To the computer architect?

2.16   What is a micro-operation?

2.17   What two broad classes of control units exist?

2.18   What is a microinstruction?

2.19 In the control unit, timing is critical to the assertion or activation of micro-operations. Why?

2.20 Obtain a set of micro-operations from Table 2.5 which performs the following between register A and register B:

    a. Interchanges registers B and A.

    b. Interchanges the contents of registers A and B using circular shift micro-operations.

2.21 Obtain a sequence of micro-operations from Table 2.5 which multiplies register R1 by five. (Hint: Use the arithmetic shift left micro-operation.)

2.22 Obtain a sequence of micro-operations from Table 2.5 which divides register R1 by seven. (Hint: Use a spare register to help you.)

2.23 Of the following languages, which ones are primarily descriptive? Which ones are primarily programming languages?

    a. microprogramming languages

    b. register transfer languages

    c. assembly languages

2.24 For a computer you are already familiar with, using the programming model, instruction set, and RTL, describe one instruction from each of the data movement, data manipulation, program movement, and program manipulation classes.

2.25 What are the implications of a control unit architecture in which the PC has no incrementing capability?

2.26 In Section 2.3, the control statements and examples illustrate how micro-operations may be skipped over or ignored. Suppose that actual branching from one statement to another is desired. What hardware do you expect to find in the control unit to handle this feature? (Hint: See Figure 2.21.)

2.27 What two capabilities must exist in a DMA I/O unit?

Chapter 3

THE CONVENTIONAL MACHINE LEVEL

You can now buy more gates with less pages of specifications than at any other time in history.

—Kenneth Parker

There are two laws discrete,
Not reconciled,—
Law for Man, and law for thing;
The last builds town and fleet,
But it runs wild,
And doth the man unking.

—Ralph Waldo Emerson

3.1 CHAPTER OBJECTIVES

In this chapter, we briefly introduce the next level in the hierarchy of programming languages, which is in the conventional machine level (see Figure 3.1). This is the machine language level. Machine language programming is impractical by human standards and hence is seldom practiced. Rather, a machine program is generated by an assembler that has translated source code into directly executable machine code or object code. In point of fact, a machine language program is "programmed" by another program (the assembler). Machine languages use, appropriately, machine instructions which are merely strings of bits. Machine instructions are best understood by examining the micro-operations they perform described in register transfer language (RTL).

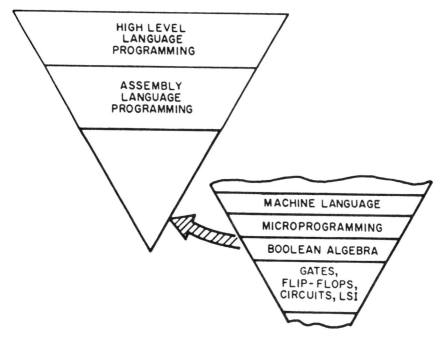

Figure 3.1 Programming Levels

Machine instructions are primarily obtained indirectly from programs. Rarely are machine instructions directly used by humans. If the programs are in FORTRAN or Pascal, the respective machine instructions are obtained via the compiler (from a compilation process). If the programs are written in an assembly language, machine instructions are obtained via an assembly process. If the programs are written in a machine language, the machine instructions come directly from these programs.

We need to study machine language instructions in order to determine the power of a computer. The power of a digital computer as a general-purpose digital system lies in its ability to execute many different tasks. This is often easier when a rich instruction set or repertoire is available. We need to study machine language instructions in order to understand how assembly language and high-level language instructions direct circuits within internal machine resources. In this chapter, we briefly introduce the notion of an instruction, its format, and general classes of instructions. Chapter 4 is devoted to the detailed operations of machine language instructions.

Prior to introducing the PDP-11, three popular addressing modes (direct, indirect, and immediate) are illustrated for a generic machine. This machine is a generic stored-program computer. Register-deferred addressing of the PDP-11 is identical to indirect addressing, does exist, and will be discussed in the next chapter. The PDP-11 computer of this chapter is simplified purposely to keep hardware details to a reasonably understandable level. (Computer architecture is not the main focus of this text.) We want only to identify machine resources and micro-operations that make up common machine instructions. You can extend these concepts to other instructions you may encounter. The brief introduction to micro-operations in the last chapter will be used in this chapter as a basis for describing machine instructions.

The actual programming language at the conventional machine level is assembly language. Why should we want to program at the assembly language level? Primarily because such code can be very fast and efficient. Fast code is executed in the least amount of time. Efficient code tends to take the least amount of program memory. But to generate such fast and efficient code, we must peer into the behavior of the machine at the micro level. This behavior will tell us the number of machine cycles required for each instruction as well as the number of bytes or words required in memory. Because we have closest and direct access to the computer at this level, we can choose instructions that are short and fast. However, programming with an assembly language does not automatically guarantee speedy programs. Any programmer at any language level must understand the power of the language and practice with it.

Assemblers are translators that generally follow the same set of rules from one assembler to the next. Of course, adherence to the particular syntax and semantics for a specific assembler must be maintained. Most of the characteristics of the MACRO-11 assembler (for the PDP-11 family) are commonplace. Developing a programming style at this level is achieved by a clear understanding of the symbol set, reserved symbols, labels, and opcodes.

Any assembly language has an inherent structure composed of lines of code called *statements*, each of which has one or more fields assigned to distinct functions. An assembly language programmer can not only invoke machine instructions, called *imperative statements*, but also issue assembler commands. Such commands, found in declarative and control statements, direct the assembler to perform useful environmental tasks.

In fact, each line of assembly code is a statement of one of three possible types: declarative, imperative, and control. Just as in a high-level language, a declarative statement in assembly code "declares" or defines data and storage attributes. For example, in Pascal, TYPE and VAR statements are called declarations. In PL/1, the key word for all data definitions is *DCL*, short for *DECLARE*. These same constructs can be found in an assembly language.

Imperative statements in an assembly language contain code that eventually will be executable in the computer at run time. They are similar to assignment statements in Pascal. Control statements in assembly language command the assembler to modify the assembly process. They alter the environment (do not print, skip next page, etc.). An equivalent Pascal control statement is *INCLUDE*, which brings other modules into the process.

3.2 MACHINE LANGUAGE

As shown in Figure 3.1, machine language is at a level just above microprogramming languages. The inverted pyramid also implies (and rightly so) that the increasing programming activity occurs with high-level languages. Why? Few users of a typical computer will have prior knowledge of internal computer hardware of sufficient depth to enable them to microprogram. Besides, microprogramming is not intended for the average user. Furthermore, machines are much easier to program with high-level languages. At this level, the rules, the notation, and the body of programming knowledge required depend primarily on concepts already familiar to the average computer user. High-level languages tend to reflect the application terminology.

The lower the level in the inverted pyramid of Figure 3.1 the greater amount of knowledge required of the hardware details of any computing system. Machine languages appropriately occupy a very low level. A machine language is not used as a human programming language because it is strings of binary patterns. This language is used by the computer to execute our programs. Humans, however, program at the assembly language level and use an assembler to translate their source code into machine language or object code.

We program a machine primarily at the assembly language level when we need to execute the fastest code possible using the least amount of program memory. However, these desirable goals do not necessarily exclude programming at higher levels. Sometimes it is most important to complete the software project quickly (no matter what language or level is used). Oftentimes, access to the machine's assembly language is not even available. But when fast code is desired, there are few substitutes for programming at this level. An assembly language programmer has direct and immediate access to the working registers in the central processing unit. He or she has direct access to the many data flow paths from the CPU to the memory and I/O units. Furthermore, an assembly language programmer is not necessarily at the mercy of a compiler (which may choose slower code if it is not an optimizing compiler). Hence, object code generated by the assembler is not subject to modification by some other software.

The price paid for this flexibility in generating fast code (measured in program size and speed) often is a greater investment in actual programming time. Furthermore, an assembly language programmer may also have to learn a great deal more about the particular computer system. This cost, however, may be unavoidable. Suppose that a new compiler is needed for a computer. Although it is unnecessary and indeed uncommon today to use an assembly language, the new compiler can be written in some assembly language. Suppose that on some new system no assembler exists, which means that an assembler must be created. Finally, there are many computer applications that primarily utilize assembly language programs. Dedicated computers, which must have extremely fast response time in such applications as process control for the chemical industry, are one example. Many computer applications may also be sensitive to the maximum size of main memory. In such limited space, high-level language programs may not even fit in memory.

3.2.1 A MACHINE INSTRUCTION

The machine language that computers directly execute is in *binary*, and, of course, to be executable, machine instructions must be encoded properly (be recognizable by the computer). Unfortunately, a machine language for one computer does not work on another computer, unless, of course, the computer hardware is identical. Machine languages are different from high-level languages, which are highly portable, are able to run on many different machines, and are very understandable. A machine instruction has a format specific to the machine. For example, the following is an instruction to load register R6 with the constant 624 (base 8) in the PDP-11 in binary:

	Machine Instruction		RTL Description
Binary Representation	Octal Representation		
0001010111000110	012706		R6 ← 0624
0000000110010100	000624		

This machine instruction causes the octal number 000624, found in memory directly below the opcode, to be placed into R6 as shown in Figure 3.2. In the fetch phase (not shown), the address (2074) of the current machine instruction (012706) has been transferred to R7, which serves as a program counter. The instruction has also been placed into the instruction register. Once this is completed, the execution phase of this instruction causes 000624 to be transferred from primary memory in the memory unit across the data bus of the computer and into register R6 of the CPU.

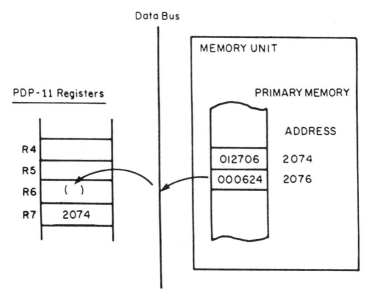

Figure 3.2 Machine Instruction Execution Step

It is important to realize that if, somehow, the binary strings

0001010111000110   and   0000000110010100

were placed into the primary memory of another computer (such as the IBM 370), the resultant action would not be the same. In fact, this object code would be completely unrecognizable to the new machine. Machine code is not portable (usable) across different computers, and this is a nontrivial disadvantage to machine language programming. (And as we will see shortly, the same disadvantage exists with assembly language programming.)

3.2.2 INSTRUCTION CLASSES

Computers have many machine instructions, anywhere from tens to hundreds. In this chapter, we only want to sort them into meaningful groups or classes of instructions, leaving detailed discussion to follow. In the past, computer designers avidly sought to classify instructions according to the physical hardware resources upon which the instructions executed. This portrayal resulted in several classes and explained much about machine resources. For instance, those instructions that manipulated the arithmetic logic unit were called arithmetic instructions. Those that invoked Boolean operations were called Boolean instructions. Instructions that worked with the memory unit were called memory reference instructions. Instructions that passed data to and from the I/O unit were called I/O instructions. This classification was used with many popular machines, from the small PDP-8 minicomputer to the large IBM 360/370.

Although instructions so classified are useful for understanding the relationship of an instruction to its specific hardware, we could just as easily make a classification scheme that directly relates the power of an instruction to the data and program activity (instead of the hardware). We could then directly assess the capacity of a specific machine to store, retrieve, process, and otherwise move or manipulate data and programs. Only four major classes need to be identified.

The four classes of instructions are data movement, data manipulation, program movement, and program manipulation. A listing of typical machine language mnemonics assigned to each class is indicated in Table 3.1. The list is not exhaustive, but is merely representative of common machine language instructions and their mnemonics. When we classify instructions in this manner, we can quickly grasp the power of a specific instruction repertoire. Powerful computers possess rich instruction sets.

Table 3.1   Machine Instruction Classes

Data Movement	Data Manipulation
Load (LDA)	Add (ADD)
Store (STA)	Subtract (SUB)
Stack (POP, PUSH)	Logical (LSR, LSL,...)
Transfer (TFR)	Rotate (ROR, ROL)
Move (MOV)	

Program Movement	Program Manipulation
Program Jump (JMP)	Status Testing (CHK)
Call Subroutines (CALL)	Interrupt Enable/Disable (EN, DIS)
Jump to Subroutines (JSR)	Set Masks
Program Branch (BRA)	PSW Commands

Assume that we have a computer with a physical organization and resources as shown in Figure 3.3. Not all data and control paths are indicated. Our memory unit contains 4,096 locations in memory, an input register that points to the current location accessed, called the *memory address register* (MAR), and a register that holds the data before transfer, called the *memory data register* (MDR). Our CPU contains 16 general-purpose registers (GPR), an arithmetic logic unit, and a single program status word register (PSW). The control unit contains an instruction register (IR) with two fields:

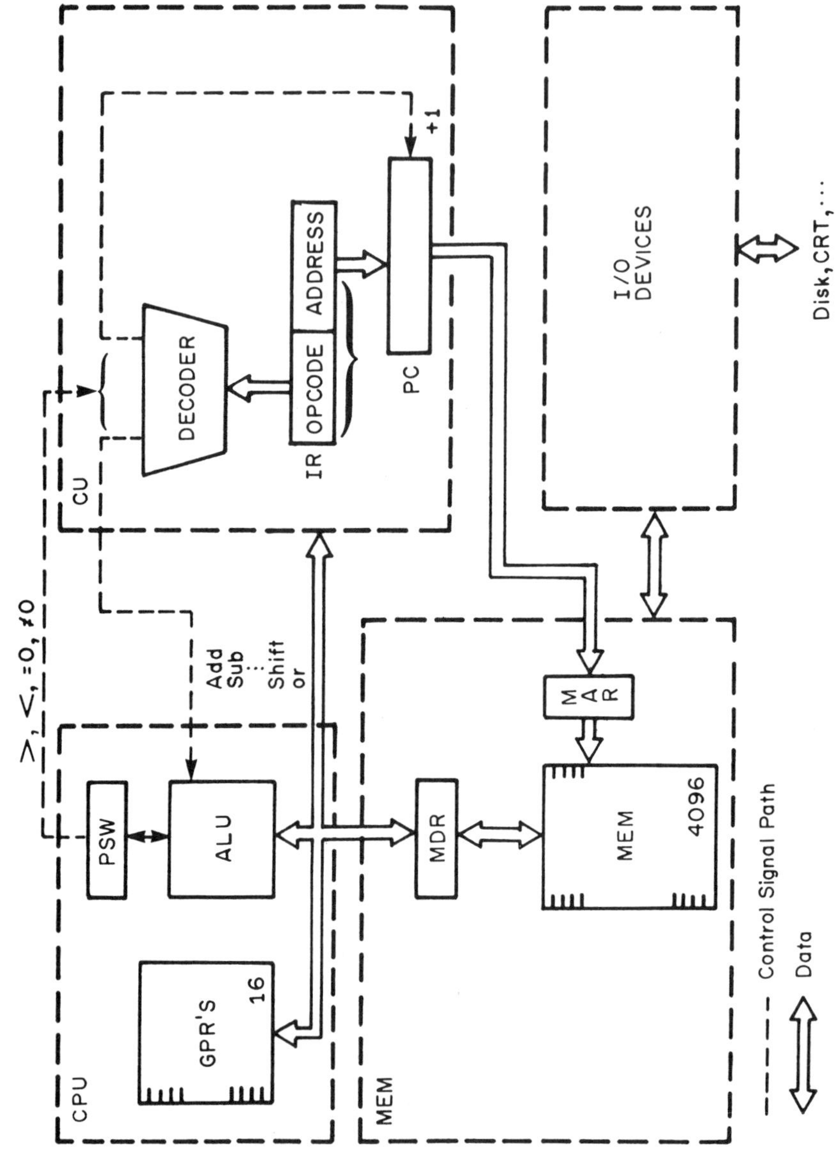

Figure 3.3 Physical Organization of Internal Computer Resources

an opcode field and an address field. The address field can feed into a program counter (PC) whose contents is the address of the current instruction in the program and into the MAR directly (path not shown). Since most programs will involve instructions that are sequentially accessed, our program counter has a control signal, "+1," to increment the program counter. The IR, PC, and a control decoder, which deciphers the instruction register opcode field and transmits command signals to the machine, comprise our control unit. Let's now use this simplified organization to briefly study machine instruction classes.

3.2.3   DATA MOVEMENT INSTRUCTIONS

Data movement instructions imply that we are going to move or transfer data from one physical unit in the machine to another, as well as internally within a single unit. The first instruction, load, with its mnemonic, LDA, could transfer information from the memory unit to the CPU. The store instruction, with its mnemonic, STA, could transfer or move information from the CPU to memory. Both STA and LDA must have a destination and a source designated in the address field of the instruction, respectively. A general rule among computer manufacturers assumes that instructions such as load and store make reference to an information transfer which is relative to the CPU. That is, we *load* data "into" the CPU and we *store* data "out of" the CPU.

3.2.4   DATA MANIPULATION INSTRUCTIONS

Often a computer processes data using the ALU. The arithmetic operations, such as add (ADD) and subtract (SUB), perform arithmetic operations on numeric data. Since computers must also manipulate data that is not necessarily numeric, other instructions exist for the ALU operations. For example, logical data manipulation instructions, such as logical shift right (LSR) and logical shift left (LSL), might be used to place the lower four bits of a word into the upper four bits of a data word.

3.2.5   PROGRAM MOVEMENT INSTRUCTIONS

A corresponding classification exists for the program-oriented instructions. Program movement instructions do not affect the CPU like the data movement or manipulation instructions, but primarily affect the program counter (PC). In fact, the first instruction listed as a program jump (JMP) would force a specific address into the PC. This causes our program to jump to this new address. The last instruction, program branch (BRA), also modifies the PC, but, here, this modification is made relative to the existing contents of the PC. The former JMP instruction makes no reference to the current PC contents. Program movement instructions operate mainly upon the program counter in the control unit.

3.2.6   PROGRAM MANIPULATION INSTRUCTIONS

Program manipulation instructions utilize (among other resources) the contents of the program status word, which monitors the machine state. Our program status word in Figure 3.3 tells us that the program status word can send back to the control unit the indication of a $>$, $<$, $=0$, and 0 resulting from comparing a datum to zero or to another datum. Program manipulation instructions use this information to make decisions about taking different paths through program memory. Program manipulation instructions do more than just monitor the PSW. Some instructions change program status when interrupts occur, either internally or externally. Other instructions change the PSW and thus enable or disable interrupts.

3.3   MACHINE INSTRUCTION SETS

3.3.1   HOW MACHINE INSTRUCTION SETS ARE CHOSEN

Instruction sets are partly determined by the marketplace, because companies make computers to sell them to the largest possible market. To do so, instruction sets are chosen by market survey demands or by selecting a set based upon past experience (but still heavily influenced by previous successful sets). In some cases, candidate instruction sets are analyzed by correlating results among statistical studies about various instruction mixes. For instance, scientific applications make extensive use of ALU operations (add, subtract, multiply, and divide). Business applications predominately require file manipulation instructions. Word processing applications need instructions that manipulate characters and strings of characters easily. Fine tuning the instruction selection process is possible by testing candidate sets in benchmark programs tailored for specific applications.

"Gibson Mix"

Instruction sets seem to be selected on the basis of tradition rather than the application of scientific methods. The selection is very critical to microprocessor architectures, which must contend with restrictions on chip area, power dissipation, speed, and complexity. However, some intelligent selection schemes are possible. For example, one scheme, based on frequency of instruction usage and which uses the "Gibson Mix,"[1] may gauge the worth of a

---

[1] J. C. Gibson, "The Gibson Mix," IBM Technical Report TR-00.2043, 1970.

computer to a user and thus help plan data processing systems. This mix groups instructions by common characteristics according to their respective functions, but the complexity of instruction sets seems to defy identifying the optimal set. Different mixes to test the utility of candidate instruction sets have appeared.

Computer machinery falls into two broad categories, special-purpose computers and general-purpose computers, each of which may dictate entirely different instruction sets. The instruction set of a special-purpose computer along with its hardware is narrowly defined and fitted to a specific application. For example, a microcontroller is a special-purpose dedicated computer used to perform precise operations day after day in a specific industry. A microcontroller would generate control signals, for instance, for an automatic welding machine that tacks automobile chassis together. A general-purpose computer aims at a much broader class of applications. Selecting an instruction set for this environment is much more challenging. General-purpose computers or mainframes are to be found in the industrial, scientific, and military communities. They could perform word processing, business data processing, and scientific computations. Obviously, the appropriate instruction set must support a wide variety of applications.

Selection of an instruction set is often considered within a hierarchy or family of computers. Computer manufacturers often develop a set or a family of computers that range from physically small, low-cost individual machines to large and high-cost systems. To be attractive to the largest customer base, the machine instruction set ought to be compatible across this entire range. Although a reduced version of the instruction set may operate on the low-cost machines, that same kernel set or subset of instructions must be executable on even the largest systems. Economics and software longevity also provide key motivation for instruction set compatibility. In addition, manufacturers hope that customers who, in time, upgrade their systems can reduce later programming costs and capitalize on familiarity and the compatibility of the current instruction set with that of their previous machines.

So far, all of the reasons cited for selecting an instruction set are actually determined by *external* factors. That is, such factors are found outside the computer itself and are primarily derived from market surveys, economic costs, or computer family longevity issues (extending a product life time). Selection of instruction sets can also be determined by factors or considerations internally related to the computer architecture (such as memory width versus ALU width, etc.). To understand this, further explanation of the machine instruction itself is necessary.

3.3.2 INSTRUCTION ENCODING

Machine instructions possess a format. The *format* is the specification of the assignment of the bits in an instruction word to particular operations. A format may specify bit groups as *fields*. A field within a format categorizes classes of activity. A format may be as simple as an opcode field, an address field, or both as in Figure 3.4. The opcode field specifies certain primitive machine operations, whereas the address field identifies the source or destination of operands used by the opcode. The width of one field does not necessarily equal that of the other field. However, the sum of the two widths is often governed by memory width, the internal width of data paths, and the number of opcodes and addressing modes.

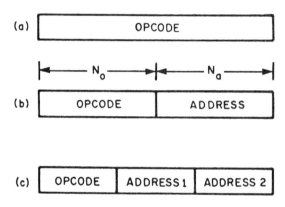

Figure 3.4 Three Typical Instruction Formats

There are many possible formats, but each machine instruction must somehow specify:

1. The operation or that field in the instruction which determines the actual machine operation. This is called the opcode or operation code field and is in the opcode field of the instruction.

2. The source of the data which is found in the address field of an instruction word where multiple data are required, such as in two-operand instructions, and all source addresses must be provided.

3. The destination of the result of the operations and/or the source of the next instruction. Any or all addresses may be explicit or implicit.

A bit assignment that maps machine operations and addresses onto bits in each field is called *encoding*. Encoding is an architectural tool often governed by the number of instructions and the addressability of operands. For example, the MIT TX-0, the forerunner of the PDP family of computers, used an instruction format with 18 bits, 2 bits assigned to the instruction or opcode field and 16 bits assigned to the address field. The TX-0 designers obviously saw a greater need to access memory and less need to have many instructions (two opcode bits implies four instructions).

The TX-O's successor, the PDP-1, employed five bits to encode an instruction and the remaining thirteen for addressing tasks. Initially, the PDP-1 was designed primarily for control applications (lab control, message switching, and time sharing) at a low cost. Only three different data types were available: the word, integer, and a Boolean vector or logical. By today's standards, the PDP-1 was a simple machine containing only one accumulator (a sort of general-purpose register) and few control instructions. In its production version, 28 instructions were eventually employed. In contrast to the narrow role of the PDP-1, the PDP-8, an immensely popular 12-bit successor, was a very general-purpose machine. Its instruction set included far more instructions than those found in the PDP-1. Even so, the PDP-8 still did not have a large instruction set.

The PDP-11, VAX, and IBM 370 are designed as truly general-purpose machines. The instruction set of the VAX is encoded to handle a very flexible addressable space. Although fewer modes are available in the VAX than in the PDP-11, the chosen set facilitates memory accesses across 2^{32} locations. The PDP-11 can access only 2^{18} locations. In addition, the VAX has 16 general-purpose registers while the PDP-11 has 8. The IBM 370 is a 32-bit machine, has 16 general-purpose registers,[2] and can access 2^{24} locations. As with the PDP-11 and VAX, the smallest addressable unit in the 370 is the *byte*, consisting of eight bits. In the PDP-11, a word is two bytes as in the VAX, while with in the 370, a word is four bytes.

The most common datum size handled by a computer also impacts on the size of the instruction word. It is sometimes desirable to make the width of an instruction comparable if not equivalent to the word length of a datum. Suppose, for instance, that in some rare cases, a half-byte and byte are considered to be four and eight bits, respectively. Hence, a natural "word" size could be 4, 8, 16, 24 bits, etc. Choosing an instruction word length equivalent to 4, 8, 16, or 24 bits, etc., potentially allows more efficient use of main memory. Furthermore, if chosen accordingly, a complete instruction fetch may often require fetching only one word from main memory, thus reducing memory accesses (which can be relatively slow). Accessing a byte, a

[2]Actually, 20 registers are available in the 370 at this conventional machine level. Four are used for floating-point arithmetic.

character, or a word from memory is also made easier, partly because fewer memory accesses are involved. This is illustrated in Example 3.1.

Example 3.1 Datum Size Versus Instruction Size.   Ignoring other factors, a computer architect is given the option to select one of three primary memory access widths as shown in Figure 3.5. In the intended applications, this computer will predominantly encounter half-word and word size datum equally. An important factor for the architect to consider is the typical number of memory fetches per instruction and per datum. From Table 3.2, the architect can see that if a "typical" program has an equal number of instructions, half-words, and word data, a memory width of 24 bits is best. If, however, the number of instructions approximately equals the sum of half-words and words, a 16-bit memory width is better.

Memory

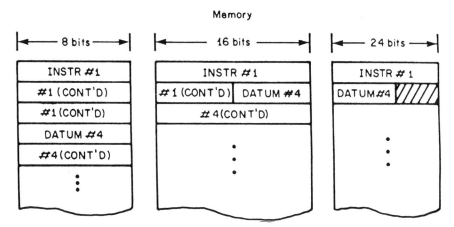

Figure 3.5   Memory Widths

Table 3.2   Memory Widths

Memory Width	Number of Fetches/Instructions	Number of Fetches/Half-Words	Number of Fetches/Word
8	3	1	2
16	2	1	1
24	1	1	1

When a machine has few instructions and a very wide memory word, it is even possible to pack more than one instruction into a word. *Packing* is the inclusion of more than one instruction in the same word, as shown in Figure 3.6.

The ratio of instruction width to memory width is a significant design factor in a computer because several related factors such as the average number of fetches per instruction are affected. Variable instruction widths pose similar challenges. When the difference between a short instruction word and a long instruction word is large, a variable length instruction word must be employed. Variable instruction widths are now common. In the IBM 370, there are at least five instruction formats, as we shall soon see. In the PDP-11 minicomputer family and even most microprocessors today, several formats exist.

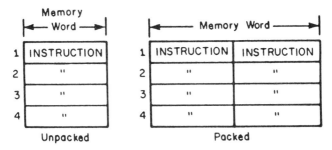

Figure 3.6 Memory Word Versus Instruction Length

The *opcode* field in an instruction word determines which machine operation is to be performed, and the width of the opcode field indicates the maximum number of machine operations permissible. A field with four bits could specify one of 16 different operations. Hence, a field of 8 bits could specify one of 256 operations. Obviously, a machine with many operations must have a very large opcode field. If an instruction consisted entirely of the opcode field, and the machine data word was 16 bits wide, many instructions could theoretically be possible (65,536), but that is not realistic. An instruction must not only specify the operations to be performed, but must also specify *where to find the operands*. The opcode field width is influenced by this need.

3.3.3 EXPANDING OPCODES

Figure 3.4 illustrates three formats, each of which depicts a constant instruction width, namely, $N_o + N_a$. However, it is possible to design instruction formats such that the total width is neither constant nor are N_o or N_a individually fixed. When the total width is constant but N_o/N_a is not, an expanded code concept may be used. In simplest terms, certain opcodes in the expanded set are used strictly to specify the meaning of other fields. Hence, fields can take on different meanings dependent upon specific opcodes. Example 3.2 illustrates the PDP-11 expanded opcode set.

Example 3.2 PDP-11 Formats.   The family of PDP-11 computers also employs variable instruction formats as depicted in Figure 3.7 (only three of thirteen formats are shown). An instruction with only one operand assigns bits 0 through 5 to the address field. Bits 6 through 15 are assigned to the opcode field. A machine instruction with two operands specifies the operand's locations in bits 0 through 11. Bits 0 through 5 specify the destination and bits 6 through 11 specify the source. (Note that the bits are numbered from right to left.)

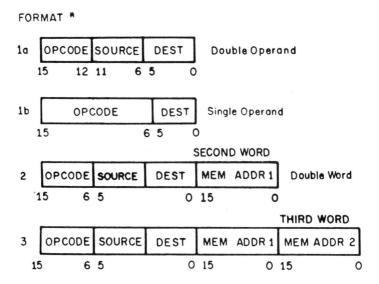

* Note that DEC Literature assigns the leftmost bit position as bit position 15. IBM 370 Literatures uses the opposite bit assignment.

Figure 3.7   Some PDP-11 Instruction Formats

Formats 1, 2, and 3 specify 16-bit, 32-bit, and 48-bit instructions, respectively. Note, however, that the opcode is always found in the first memory word. It is standard to have the opcode in the first word because, at the very minimum, an opcode may determine the remaining number of fetches for the current instruction. The remaining words are data words, which will be described shortly. As an expanded opcode scheme, the PDP-11 uses bits 12 to

14 to specify length in the following manner. A double operand instruction is indicated by the numbers 1 to 6 in bits 12 through 14. Otherwise, the opcode is found in the leftmost 7, 8, or 10 bits.

3.3.4   VARIABLE LENGTH INSTRUCTIONS

Example 3.3 IBM 370 Principal Formats.   The IBM 370 has five instruction formats, as depicted in Figure 3.8. (Note that the bits are numbered from left to right.) Some of these are multi-word instructions. The RR instruction format assigns bits 0 through 7 to the opcode, and bits 8 through 15 to the register specifications. The RR format is a register to register transfer. The IBM 370 also allows register to storage or memory transfer operations. The RX format requires 32 bits for an instruction, as shown in Table 3.3. Notice that bits 8 through 31 specify the necessary addressing tasks between the register and memory. The RR format occupies two bytes in the program memory. A byte in the 370 is eight bits. The RX format occupies four bytes. RS, SI (I stands for immediate addressing mode), and SS formats are similarly specified.

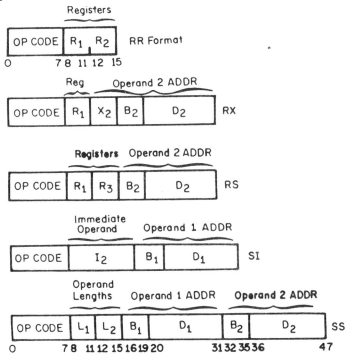

Figure 3.8   IBM 370 Instruction Formats

The length of the actual machine instruction is specified by the two leftmost bits,[3] as shown in Table 3.3. In essence, these two bits in the opcode field specify the meaning of other fields.

Table 3.3 IBM 370 Instruction Length (IL) Bits

Operand Type	IL Bits 0,1	Instruction Length
RR	00	16-Bit Instruction
RX	01	32-Bit Instruction
RS or SI	10	32-Bit Instruction
SS	11	48-Bit Instruction

In general, the length of an instruction depends upon the number of memory addresses used by the instruction. For the 370, an SS formatted instruction uses two memory addresses, which also means that two memory fetches are required before an SS formatted instruction can be completely executed (assuming main memory is 16 bits wide, as it was for the 138 and 148).

The source or destination field of an instruction may contain not only the address(es) of the operand(s), but also the mode of addressing. The addressing *mode* specifies the method of generating the actual or physical address or location of the operand, called the *effective address*. In the next section, popular addressing modes are examined.

3.3.5   ADDRESS ENCODING

We could conceive of an address field for a very simple machine, such as a computer with only 16 general-purpose registers and no memory, which needs only four bits in the address field. This is simplistic since such an address field could not even access a memory location (directly) even if memory did exist in the machine. Therefore, to access both general-purpose registers and memory locations, the address field and modes are likely to be extended (to include more bits). We can either extend the bits in the instruction word itself, or we can add a second word to the total instruction (as is common).

Machines could then be conceived that are strictly zero-address, one-address, two-address, etc., instructions, but each format has its own advantages and disadvantages. A zero-address machine can take advantage of the entire N instruction bits for operations. For a 16-bit machine, 2^{16} or 65,536

---

[3]IBM calls these bits the "instruction length code." Manufacturer's documentation then refers to variable length codes rather than expanded codes.

different operations can be specified. However, the underlying architecture is markedly different from a machine that employs address fields. The essential difference is the degree to which the operand sources are explicitly identified. In a zero-address machine, addressing is very implicit and obviously inflexible. Because of this, no real machines strictly employ a zero-address mode.

Conceptually, a zero-address machine assumes that the source and destination of operands are found in one implied area. This implied area could be a stack in which current operands can be retrieved or stored from one end. The stack depicted in Figure 3.9 has an associated stack pointer that updates itself during transactions with the stack. Briefly, an instruction that adds A to B in a zero-address machine could find A and B on the stack, perform the addition operation, and place the result on top of the stack. The computer is designed to include the assumption that A can be found on the stack, that B is next to it (shown above A in Figure 3.8), and that the result will be placed above B. The opcode itself does not specify the location of A, B, or C.

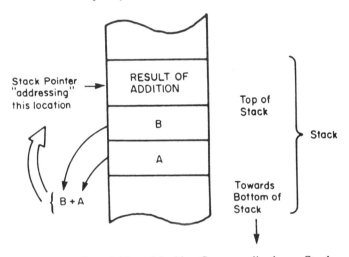

Figure 3.9 Zero-Address Machine Conceptualized as a Stack

A one-address machine may explicitly specify the source or the destination of a single operand, but not both simultaneously. The implicit or "implied" address for a second operand must be defined by other means (such as a rule or assumption). One candidate rule for a one-address machine could be that the implicit address of one-source all-destination operands is an accumulator (one of the registers in the ALU). Machines in the past have been designed with a single accumulator (and no general-purpose registers, but that is rare today). A two-address machine offers more flexibility. Both the source and destination addresses of two-operand operations can be explicitly specified simultaneously. A three-address machine allows the programmer even greater flexibility. Here, the addresses of two source operands and the destination can be explicitly defined. However, multiple-address machines require more instruction words.

The width of an address field depends on the maximum addressable space. An n-register machine requires at most $\log_2 n$ bits in the register field. A K-word main memory in a computer with a word as the smallest addressable unit requires at most $\log_n K$ bits in the address field. The width of an instruction word, not including the opcode, must be large enough to specify the individual address fields as well as their modes. Four popular modes are now described.

3.4   DIRECT, INDIRECT, IMMEDIATE, AND REGISTER ADDRESSING MODES

Memory in a computer consists not only of primary or main memory and secondary memory, but also of registers in the CPU. Whether storage is regarded as temporary (as in registers or primary memory) or permanent (as in secondary memory), access to any memory device can be made possible through different modes. Briefly, operations with registers occur in a register addressing mode while operations with memory (primary or secondary) can occur in one of several modes (direct, indirect, immediate, etc.). There are many more addressing modes (to be described in Chapter 4), but these four modes are sufficient to describe many computers.

A candidate machine instruction format is shown in Figure 3.10. The addressing modes are encoded in fields as follows. When the address mode field contains all zeroes, the instruction decoder recognizes a direct mode of addressing. *In the direct mode of addressing, the instruction itself in program memory (in the following sequential locations) contains the actual or effective address of the operand.* The contents of this addressed location is the operand required by the current machine instruction. When the addressing mode field contains 1000, the machine instruction is employing the indirect mode of addressing. *In the indirect addressing mode, the instruction contains the address (or pointer) of an address of an operand.* If an indirect addressing mode instruction is contained in two words in memory with the second word reserved for addressing, the second word contains a pointer to a location that contains another pointer to the actual operand. The effective address is not contained in the next sequential location below the current instruction in program memory, but, in fact, the effective address is contained in the location pointed to by this second word in this two-word instruction.

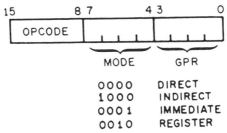

Figure 3.10 One-Address Machine Instruction with Addressing Modes

The *immediate* mode of addressing, indicated by 0001 in the addressing mode field of the machine instruction, informs the instruction decoder that this instruction contains the actual operand value itself. For example, if the second word of a two-word machine instruction, operating with the immediate mode of addressing, is 02E4 in hexadecimal, the program code would contain this actual hexadecimal number. Any subsequent operations on this second word would interpret that word as a datum whose value is 02E4. Thus, we could take its literal meaning. We do not have to go anywhere else in memory to find the value of the datum as in the direct or indirect mode of addressing. Furthermore, the effective address is the location immediately following the first word of the current machine instruction.

For the *register* mode of addressing, bits 4 through 7 of the mode field must contain "0010" or "2." When so specified, the machine operation will involve a register in the CPU. In the register mode, a register may serve as a source, destination, or both. To specify how a register is to be used requires some additional encoding in the mode field (not shown). Register addressing modes will be revisited when the PDP-11 is examined shortly.

Example 3.4 Simple Addressing Modes.   Suppose our program counter contained the address 200. During instruction decode, one of three addressing modes has been detected: direct, indirect, or immediate. Bits 4 through 7 of the instruction register determine the addressing mode. These three cases are depicted in Figure 3.11, assuming the addressing mode assignment of Figure 3.10. In the direct mode of addressing, the effective address of the operand is 02E4H and is found in the next sequential location of program memory (201H). The actual operand is found in location 02E4H and its datum is 24FFH. A direct mode of addressing instruction would operate on 24FFH. The indirect mode of addressing requires a second memory fetch. Location 201H contains an address just as before. However, the computer will retrieve the information from location 02E4H and interpret it as another address. This second address or pointer, 24FFH, is our effective address. In location 24FFH, the actual operand, 8CE3H, is found. This operand will be employed in this indirect addressing mode machine instruction. The situation is much simpler in the immediate mode of addressing. When the instruction register decodes the immediate mode of addressing, location 201H contains the actual datum. The effective address in this mode is 201H. The operand is 02E4H.

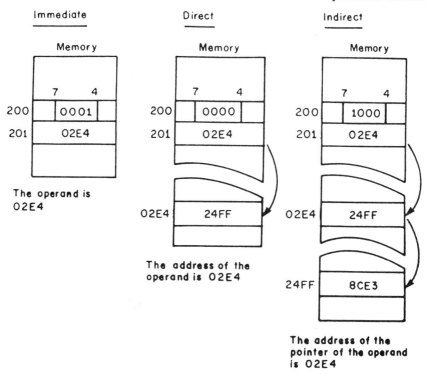

Figure 3.11   Simple Addressing Modes

Observe from the previous example that some additional micro-operations are required to execute the direct, indirect, and immediate addressing modes. In essence, the micro-operations cause additional memory fetches. Instructions operating with these modes are also called *memory reference instructions*. In the direct addressing mode, not only must the CPU fetch the original instruction, but it must return to memory one more time to obtain the address of the operand. In the indirect addressing mode, an additional memory access micro-operation is necessary. In Examples 3.5, 3.6, and 3.7, possible sequences of micro-operations that could perform an operand fetch with direct, indirect, and immediate addressing modes are illustrated. At this conventional machine level, a programmer often wants to know how many machine cycles are needed to execute an instruction. Note carefully how much longer the fetch phase of the indirect addressing mode takes compared with the immediate mode.

Example 3.5 Micro-Operations for Direct Addressing.   Suppose that it is necessary to access the contents of location 02E4H as shown in Figure 3.11. The actual micro-operations that could be performed to do this are depicted in Table 3.4. Suppose that a simple sequencer much like that described in Section 2.2 is used. Only now, additional clock pulses must be made available. At clock pulse t3, if instruction register bits 4 through 7 are cleared, an additional memory access will be performed. Here, the memory data register contains the address of the operand (not an operand!). This address is transferred into the memory address register at time t5. Between pulse t5 and the initiation of pulse t6, the memory is being read at a location pointed to by the memory address register. This new data will reside in the memory data register before t6. At clock pulse t5, this new data, which is our actual operand, is transferred to some destination that is symbolically represented by *DEST*.

A read operation in the direct addressing mode is executed at clock pulse times t3 and t4 (OPCODE bits are not shown for the *READ*). Carefully observe how the control statements are modified to include the addressing mode indicator bits. The direct addressing occurs if IR(4-7) are cleared.

Table 3.4   Direct Addressing Mode Micro-Operations (Fetch Phase)

Read from Memory

IR(4-7)′ ∧ t3:	MAR ← PC+1
IR(4-7)′ ∧ t4:	PC ← (MDR)
IR(4-7)′ ∧ t5:	MAR ← PC
IR(4-7)′ ∧ t6:	DEST ← (MDR)

End of Fetch Phase

Example 3.6 Micro-Operations for Indirect Addressing (Fetch Phase).   In Figure 3.11, the indirect addressing mode causes, first, the address of an operand to be fetched, second, another address or "pointer" to be fetched, and finally, the actual operand itself to be fetched. The micro-operations necessary require additional clock pulses, and a sequence depicted in Table 3.5 is possible.

Table 3.5   Indirect Addressing Mode Micro-Operations (Fetch Phase)

Read from Memory

IR(7) ∧ IR(4-6)′ ∧ t3:	MAR ← PC+1
IR(7) ∧ IR(4-6)′ ∧ t4:	PC ← (MDR)
IR(7) ∧ IR(4-6)′ ∧ t5:	MAR ← PC
IR(7) ∧ IR(4-6)′ ∧ t6:	PC ← (MDR)
IR(7) ∧ IR(4-6)′ ∧ t7:	MAR ← PC
IR(7) ∧ IR(4-6)′ ∧ t8:	DEST ← (MDR)

End of Fetch Phase

Example 3.7 Micro-Operations for Immediate Addressing (Fetch Phase). The immediate mode of addressing uses fewer micro-operations than either the indirect or direct mode. This is important to remember because when time is critical and there is a high probability that a constant will not need changing in the future, the immediate mode should be chosen. An assembly language programmer knows this and takes advantage of the immediate mode whenever possible. However, the immediate address mode accesses a *constant* (and not a variable). Manipulating a *variable* requires another addressing mode. From Figure 3.11, the actual operand is to be fetched from location 201. Note that only two micro-operations are needed to perform the fetch phase for the immediate addressing mode as indicated in Table 3.6.

Table 3.6   Immediate Addressing Mode Micro-Operations (Fetch Phase)

Read from Memory

IR(5-7)' ∧ IR(4) ∧ t3:	MAR ← PC+1
IR(5-7)' ∧ IR(4) ∧ t4:	DEST ← (MDR)

End of Fetch Phase

The machine described in Examples 3.4 through 3.7 does not exactly portray the PDP-11. First, the instruction format in Figure 3.10 does not exist in the PDP-11. (It could, however, exist in other machines.) Second, the PDP-11 has eight registers instead of sixteen, so the GPR field need only be three bits wide instead of four as shown. Finally, the PDP-11 has many more addressing modes, some of which manipulate single operands while others manipulate double operands. Examples 3.4 through 3.7 only discuss single-operand instructions. In spite of these differences, the PDP-11 and most other computers functionally behave somewhat like this machine with its micro-operations and addressing modes portrayed in this section. The important point is to recognize that *certain addressing modes are slower because additional memory fetches are necessary.*

3.5 ASSEMBLY LANGUAGE, BRIEFLY

Strictly speaking, no complete or extensive machine language programs have been demonstrated as yet. Had a user really programmed in machine language, he or she would have resorted to manipulating strings of binary ones and zeroes much like the actual machine language program shown in Example 3.8 which adds up some variables in an array.

Example 3.8 A Machine Language Program.

Binary	Octal
0000101000011111	005037
0000000000011010	000032
0001010111000000	012700
0000001000000000	001000
0001010111011111	012737
0000000010010010	001022
0000000000011100	000034
0110010000011111	062037
0000000000011010	000032
0010011111000000	023700
0000000000011100	000034
0000001011111011	001373
0000000000000000	000000

Computers directly execute tasks specified by machine instructions that consist of binary strings. Most humans, however, become hopelessly lost after just a few instructions, behaving quite erratically (or irrationally) during such an endeavor. Imagine trying to recall the meaning of each machine instruction in Example 3.8. One would have to carry a very long table around in one's head. That's not the most efficient behavior for humans, but it is simple to accomplish using computers. The program listed in Example 3.8 is a machine language or object program. If this program were loaded directly into the primary memory of a PDP-11, the computer would execute this program with no translation required. However, without a mental translation into mnemonic symbols, one is lost as to its intended purpose.

Shortly, we will discard the octal notation (common to the PDP-11 and other older designs) in favor of the mnemonics offered by the manufacturer for each specific instruction. *A mnemonic is a memory aid to help us recall the function of a specific machine instruction.* Although mnemonics for machine instructions (some were seen in Chapter 1) are popular, we are not forced to use those specific mnemonics. A programmer could even invent a new set. For example, the *MOV* instruction could be changed to a *LOAD* (when transferring from memory to the CPU). One could replace *MOV* with *STORE* (when transferring from CPU to a resource outside). In any case, programming life is made much easier if one employs mnemonics not only for machine instructions, but if we also utilize *symbolic representations* for addresses, variables, constants, etc.

At the conventional machine level, the micro-operations of Chapter 2 are not visible. Micro-operations are only viewed at a lower level. Any computer is functionally described in terms of the instruction set it realizes, and the machine language level is only a useful starting point. Hence, understanding the current level requires information about the computer described at the next lower level (therefore, micro-operations). The previous sections have portrayed some aspects (but not all) of the conventional machine level, primarily building upon micro-operations within machine instructions. It is neither desirable nor even necessary to continue describing instructions this way. From now on, this text will use assembly language notation rather than machine instruction notation (binary or octal strings).

Assembly language programming, then, allows us to do just that. In this chapter, we'll perform only the hand assembly of programs. From this, we will appreciate the utility of the automatic translation process of an assembler. An assembler translates symbolic code (mnemonics and symbolic addresses, variables, and constants) into an object code (binary strings) directly executable by the machine hardware.

3.5.1   WHY ASSEMBLERS?

As we have seen, binary programs are beset with a number of human difficulties. Such programs are tedious to write. One would become bored after the first binary string instruction in Example 3.8. The list of binary strings in the example gives no indication of the actual machine task, and, therefore, does not help a user to understand the current program behavior. Such programs are almost impossible to verify and debug. Finally, programmers are prone to make mistakes with so many clerical tasks.

An assembly language program consists of mnemonics and symbols which overcome many of the penalties of binary programming. *The assembly process, then, is the procedure of translating a user source program written with mnemonics into the machine language program called the "object" program.* The object program is the actual binary program executable by the computer.[4] The assembly task can be performed manually by the programmer or by the computer. It makes better sense to let the computer perform the assembly task because the assembly itself can be done in an error-free fashion. A computer will obey the set of rules of assembly to provide the correct code. It will do it correctly for every statement and every time; that is, a computer is a deterministic machine.

---

[4]An assembler by itself does not produce directly executable code. Often, a linker and loader, which further process the code (to relocate it, acquire needed variables not in the code), may also copy it elsewhere.

3.5.2   WHAT ASSEMBLERS DO

Assemblers can do more than just convert source language into binary numbers. Assemblers keep track of where instructions reside in memory, what symbols are used, and what current values they possess. In doing so, assemblers remove much of the drudgery from machine language programming. In fact, as illustrated in the remainder of this text, assemblers, coupled with other software support tools such as linkers and loaders, can:

1. Generate addresses
2. Assign symbols to information
3. Build tables that equate the symbols with designated values when requested
4. Generate error diagnostics to help debug programs
5. Determine where to actually put binary coded programs in program memory
6. Keep track of general-purpose registers, locations in memory, data, instructions, and flags
7. Produce a consistent form of documentation

3.5.3   WHAT LINKERS DO

A source program undergoes several processing stages before execution. The assembler generates object code which may not be directly executable as an object module. One reason is that the object code may access data, variables, information, or another program outside of the code. For example, an existing system library program may be needed to convert input data from ASCII to binary. As another example, suppose that separately generated source programs, possibly by different programmers, are to be combined. A *linker* is a system program that performs the task of connecting, for instance, separately assembled or compiled system library program routines to the object module, combining different programs, and otherwise causing object modules to be combined into a complete machine language program.

3.5.4   WHAT LOADERS DO

A *loader* places the object module in main memory for the execution phase of the code. This would be a simple task for the loader if the programmer knew beforehand precisely where the program was to be stored all of the time. However, that is seldom possible because more than one program may reside in main memory, and the operating system moves programs to different locations, sometimes to make room for other programs by removing seldomly used programs. Since available main memory space is commonly in short supply, the operating system manages memory dynamically to keep it filled with active programs. Some loaders will even modify a user's object code in order to relocate it.

Such a relocating loader will take the object code which starts at location P and adds or subtracts the necessary offsets to the starting location and any other modifiable addresses in the code to relocate it. If a relocating loader is not available, the programmer may have to take special precautions with the several addressing modes at his or her disposal. One precaution may be to initially generate code that can be relocated without the need for a relocatable loader in the first place. Such code is called *position-independent code*. In practice, using addressing modes that are relative to the contents of some register (to the PC, as in the PDP-11) is helpful. Other position-independent coding techniques are described in Chapters 7 and 8.

3.6   AN ASSEMBLY LANGUAGE PROGRAM

An assembly language program employs the mnemonics and permissible symbols provided by the computer manufacturer, along with a set of rules and syntax belonging to the specific assembler. The brief programs already observed are only pieces of assembly source code. True assembly language programs would contain not only the mnemonics, but also symbols, expressions, and comments to direct or control the assembly process. The next example is provided only to contrast assembly language with machine language. In Example 3.9, we have substituted the object code of Example 3.8 with the mnemonics of the PDP-11 instruction set and the symbols *SUM*, *COUNT*, and *LOOP*. Even this program, although replaced by symbols, still could be made more understandable. The program actually accumulates the sum of ten numbers, placing the final result in *SUM*. Of the two programs (Example 3.8 and Example 3.9), which one is more comprehensible? Clearly, the program in Example 3.9 provides us with greater understanding. One could not determine instantly what this program is doing without studying it carefully, line by line. Soon, skills will be acquired that will make assembly language programming more meaningful.

Examine this assembly language program more closely in order to contrast an assembly language program and a machine language program. First, we don't have to memorize long octal strings (for the machine language instructions). Instead, the mnemonics, CLR, MOV, ADD, etc., are used. In so doing, we at least begin to discern a general understanding of the program behavior.

Example 3.9 Some Assembly Language Code.

Line #	Location Count	Object Code	Label	Opcode	Operands
1				.TITLE	SUM OF NUMBERS
2				.ENABL	AMA
3		000000'		LC=.	
4	000000	005037 000032'	START:	CLR	SUM
5	000004	012700 001000		MOV	#1000,R0
6	000010	012737 001022 000034'		MOV	#1022,COUNT
7	000016	062037 000032'	LOOP:	ADD	(R0)+,SUM
8	000022	023700 000034'		CMP	COUNT,R0
9	000026	001373		BNE	LOOP
10	000030	000000		HALT	
11	000032		SUM:	.BLKW	1
12	000034		COUNT:	.BLKW	1
				.END	START

SYMBOL TABLE

COUNT	000034R	LC =	000000R	LOOP	000016R
START	000000R	SUM	000032R		

(Surely, the first line of code, CLR SUM, is more understandable than 005067!) Also, we don't have to compute address values. The assembler will assign a location value to LOOP. Is this helpful? Yes, often a programmer does not know where his or her program will reside in memory space. The assembler allows the programmer to use symbols instead of absolute binary strings. Later, the assembler will assign the value.

Documentation Is Important

Example 3.9 illustrates an incomplete assembly language program. Notably missing is information describing this program found in comment fields. Even though the label, opcode, and operand fields contain much information about the function of the program, no assembly language program (or any program, for that matter) is complete without a full disclosure of its purposes, author, use of data, input and output requirements, control, etc. Undocumented code at any programming level is, at best, poor programming.

Obviously, the purpose of a program is made partially clearer with assembly language statements. Why? Mnemonics instead of octal opcode or binary opcode indicate line-by-line activity. Symbols as operands for the opcodes amplify the machine instruction. Symbols called labels to the left of the opcode of the mnemonic give some indication of program flow. These features (and more) contribute to the clarity of employing assembly language programs.

To continue examining a machine at the conventional level, an actual computer should be studied. In later sections of this chapter, the instruction set and organization of the PDP-11 are used. During this study, the reader is encouraged to refer to earlier chapters as needed. For instance, the actual micro-operations implementing the instructions in Examples 3.10 to 3.23 can be determined from material found in the preceeding sections. Hardware to implement these micro-operations is described in Chapter 2 and is organized much like that found in Chapter 1. Studying the micro-operations will not only enable you to understand computers functionally, but also to estimate the relative execution times of the various machine instructions. Indeed, if a programmer is to take advantage of the execution speed and parsimonious use of memory at the assembly language level, familiarity with primitive steps (micro-operations) is essential.

3.7   THE PDP-11 ARCHITECTURE, BRIEFLY

The reader now has enough understanding about computers to look at the PDP-11 in greater detail. This computer has, at least, the following characteristics.

1. 16-bit parallel ALU

2. 2's complement arithmetic logic unit

3. Eight general-purpose registers

4. Four addressing modes

5. General-purpose applications

6. Memory expandable to 65,536 locations (each of which contains a byte that can be accessed directly)

7. WORDs consisting of 16 bits

8. BYTEs consisting of 8 bits

The programming model of this machine contains eight general-purpose registers, R0 through R7, and a special 16-bit register called the *processor status word* (PSW) as in Figure 3.12. Because it is understood that electrical connections between the various hardware resources are made with control gates and control paths, the remaining machine instruction examples will no longer specify timing generator requirements (which are implemented in the control unit).

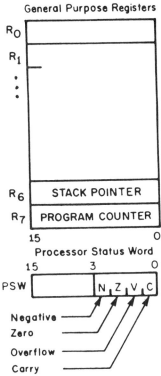

Figure 3.12 PDP-11 Computer Programming Model

Tables 3.7 through 3.10 depict the available machine instructions for the PDP-11 computer. The remaining sections of this chapter describe the mnemonics of each instruction listed under the machine language column. The first column contains the octal notation for each machine instruction. In the first row of Table 3.8, the machine instruction CLR d is encoded with the octal notation 0050DD. We should understand that the "DD" is replaced by an addressing mode and an actual register number. Since this is a single-operand instruction, that number is found in bits 5 through 0 of the machine instruction. Our DD specifies a destination operand. Our destination operands are described by registers R0 through R7. If we desired register R0 as our destination, the instruction DD would be replaced by all zeroes. If we desired register R3, DD would be replaced by 03.

Note that the flag settings in the examples happen at the end of the operation and depend on the result operand. Some operations do not affect some flags and it is important to know which instructions they are.

Table 3.7   Data Movement Machine Instructions for the PDP-11

Octal Code	Instruction	Processor Status Word Effects NZVC	Action
01SSDD	MOV s,d	**0-[a]	Move (equivalent to load or store).
0003DD	SWAB d	**00[b]	Swap upper and lower bytes in same word.

[a] * affected,

   - not affected

   1,0 set or cleared as depicted

[b] PSW effects apply to LSI-11 and 11/03.

Table 3.8   Data Manipulation Machine Instructions for the PDP-11

Octal Code	Instruction	Processor Status Word Effects NZVC	Action
		Logical	
0050DD	CLR d	0100	Clear contents to zero.
0051DD	COM d	**01	Form 1's complement.
0060DD	ROR d	****	Circular shift right.
0061DD	ROL d	****	Circular shift left.
02SSDD	CMP s,d	****	Compare and set condition codes accordingly (s-d).
0057DD	TST d	**00	Zero, positive, or negative?
03SSDD	BIT s,d	**0-	Bit-wise Boolean AND.
04SSDD	BIC s,d	**0-	Bit-wise clear.
05SSDD	BIS s,d	**0-	Bit-wise set.
		Arithmetic	
0052DD	INC d	***-	Increment contents.
0053DD	DEC d	***-	Decrement contents.
0054DD	NEG d	****	Form 2's complement.
0062DD	ASR d	****	Arithmetic shift right, copy sign bit.
0063DD	ASL d	****	Arithmetic shift left, C flag receives sign bit.
06SSDD	ADD s,d	****	2's complement addition.
0055DD	ADC d	****	Add carry bit.
16SSDD	SUB s,d	****	2's complement subtraction (d ← d−s).
0056DD	SBC d	****	Subtract carry bit.

Table 3.9 Some Program Movement Machine Instructions for the PDP-11

Octal Code	Instruction	Processor Status Word Effects NZVC	Action
0001DD	JMP d	—	Jump to another program memory location.
0004**ᵃ	BR	—	Branch always.
0010**	BNE	—	Branch if not equal to zero (if Z=0).
0024**	BLT	—	Branch if less than (if N XOR V=1).
1034**	BLO	—	Branch if lower (if C=1).

ᵃ Rightmost digits determined by the offset.

Table 3.10 Program Manipulation Machine Instructions for the PDP-11

Octal Code	Instruction	Processor Status Word Effects NZVC	Action
000000	HALT	—	Stop machine.
000005	RESET	—	Return machine to special state called RESET.
000241	CLC	—0	Clear C flag.
000261	SEC	—1	Set C flag.
000240	NOP	—	No operation.

Single-operand addressing modes will be specified by the format of Figure 3.13. Three bits are assigned to the address mode field and three bits are assigned to the register field. Our machine contains eight registers, hence, the register subfield only requires three bits. Obviously, eight operand address modes could be made available in this computer. Tables 3.11 and 3.12 list some PDP-11 register and memory addressing modes, respectively.

Table 3.11 PDP-11 Register Addressing Modes (R0-R7)

Mode (Octal)	Name	RTL	Operand's Location	Explanation
0	Register	Rn	Rn	Operand is in Rn.
1	Register-Deferred	(Rn)	memory	Address of operand is in Rn.

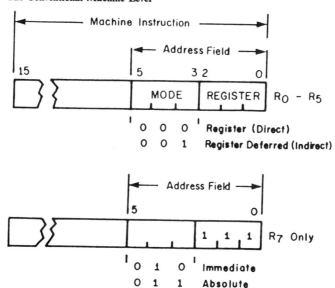

Figure 3.13 Computer Address Field (Single-Operand)

Table 3.12 PDP-11 Memory Addressing Modes with Register R7 Only

Mode (Octal)	Name	RTL	Operand's Location	Explanation
2	Immediate	#n	memory	Operand n follows instruction.
3	Absolute	@#A	memory	Address A follows instruction.

Only four addressing modes are shown: register, register-deferred, immediate, and absolute. The absolute and the immediate mode of addressing are identical to the direct and immediate mode of addressing illustrated in Example 3.4. Table 3.12 applies only to register R7, which is the PC. An indirect mode of addressing is encoded as mode 1 in the register mode field and is called the *register-deferred mode*. It is similar to the indirect mode of addressing, but not identical. In the register-deferred addressing mode, the address of the pointer of an operand is obtained from a register. In the indirect addressing mode of Example 3.4, the address of the pointer of the operand is found in the second location of an instruction in program memory. Remaining modes possible with our machine will be described in Chapter 5. For now, sufficient capability will be introduced to describe the various machine language instructions.

Indirect Versus Deferred Addressing

Historically, the indirect mode of addressing has often employed a memory location (rather than a register) in the intermediate stages of computing the effective address. Interestingly, two mainframes, the IBM 370 and CYBER 170, do not have indirect addressing, per se. The 370 does have register indirect branches. In some microprocessors, such as the 68000, nine registers in the programming model are distinctly called address registers to perform the register and register-deferred addressing modes. The remaining registers in the 68000 programming model are called data registers to clearly distinguish between the functions of these two sets of registers. □

In subsequent examples, actual machine code is shown to help you understand address modes and instruction lengths. The first column, labeled the address column, indicates the location in the program memory of the actual instruction. The machine instruction contained at that address is found in the second column. Our mnemonic which describes the machine instruction is found in the third column. The symbols # and @# in this column are used to indicate the memory addressing mode (immediate and absolute, respectively). These same symbols also belong to the symbol set in assembly language programming which we will see later. The last column describes the micro-operations which represent the register transfer activity in our basic computer using register transfer language.

In our examples, SS and DD in the coded instructions have been replaced with the actual source and destination, respectively. Although many simple one or two-line programs start at location 0 in program memory, there is no requirement to do so. These programs could exist anywhere in memory. How many lines of code each instruction requires should be studied. Some instructions require a second and/or third word to indicate addresses of operands. Programmers who must fit code into very little memory need to employ one- or only two-word instructions. All addresses and numeric data are in octal representation for each example.

Note carefully that the PC has been incremented a sufficient number of times always to point to the next instruction (and not the next word in the current instruction). Since the PDP-11 PC always points to an even word, incrementing by two or by four will take place automatically. This automatic updating of the PC is important to remember because certain instructions which use the PC take this into account (namely, the branch relative instructions). Nearly all computer PC's behave similarly.

3.8   DATA MOVEMENT INSTRUCTIONS

Two instructions in the computer belong to the data movement set. They are the move instruction, MOV, and the swap byte instruction, SWAB. Has a fundamental weakness of our machine just been encountered given only two data movement instructions? No. As will be seen, the many addressing modes available permit the move operation to actually make data transfer anywhere in the computer. The move instruction can perform both the load and store operations among registers, register to memory, and memory to memory operations. Later, you will even see how the move operation transfers data into and out of a computer.

Example 3.10 Register to Memory Transfer

Address	Contents	Machine Instruction	Micro-Operations
000000	010337	MOV R3,@#42	M(42) ← (R3)
000002	000042		Address of operand

This instruction and its addressing modes require two lines of code. The first word is the instruction, 010337. The second word contains the address of the operand. This move instruction transfers the contents of register R3 into program memory at location 42. The symbols "@#" denote the absolute addressing mode using register R7. Register R7 is a general-purpose register but has a unique function. It is also the program counter in the PDP-11. This means that internal machine hardware exists which automatically modifies the contents of R7 with each instruction fetch. Registers R0 through R5 are limited to the addressing modes shown in Table 3.10. This MOV instruction transfers 16 bits from R3 into location 42. The word, 002766, is transferred to memory location 000042 (see Figure 3.14).

3.9   DATA MANIPULATION INSTRUCTIONS

Most data manipulation instructions belong either to the arithmetic machine instructions or to the logical machine instructions. This classification is made only to recognize that signed numbers are typically manipulated by arithmetic instructions. Characters, then, are manipulated by logical instructions (although this is not mandatory).

This one-line instruction performs the circular right shift on register R3 with the following modification. In the PDP-11, the processor status register is actually location 177776 and contains the processor status word. Four flags are in the PSW. One of these is the carry (C) flag, which represents the carry

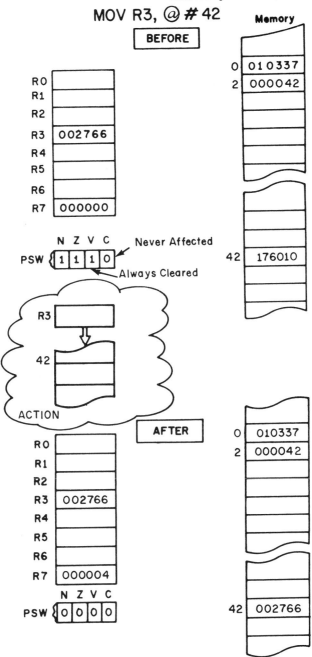

Figure 3.14   Register to Memory Transfer

Example 3.11 Rotate Register R3

Address	Contents	Machine Instruction	Micro-Operations
000000	006003	ROR R3	R3(15) ← C,
			R3(14) ← R3(15),
			R3(13) ← R3(14),
			•
			•
			•
			R3(0) ← R3(1),
			C ← R3(0)

bit out of the most significant bit out of a word in data manipulation machine instructions. In this instruction, the carry flag enters the vacated bit, 15, of R3. The C flag is then replaced by the exiting bit (bit 0 of R3). The remaining bits are individually shifted to the right one position. The right rotate and left rotate instructions each employ the carry flag. Only the direction of shifting changes. Our address mode is the register mode, as indicated by the 0 in the mode field, with address R3 specified by the octal 3 in the register field. Note how the V flag is affected to reflect that the sign of the result is different from the sign of the operand. V is set if N XOR C is one. In Figure 3.15, the V flag is set. Example 3.12 illustrates a simple multiplication routine using ROR.

Example 3.12 Multiplication Using ROR. Multiplication can be done through a combination of rotates and additions or through repetitive additions. R0 will contain the 8-bit product. R1 and R2 contain the multiplicand and multiplier, respectively. The algorithm tests the MSB of R2. If the shifted out bit is one, add the multiplicand and shift the partial product. Otherwise, simply shift the partial product. The algorithm terminates after eight shifts with the final product in R0. Assume the following code uses an 8-bit word.

```
              CLC                ;INITIALIZE CARRY
              CLR R0             ;CLEAR PRODUCT
              MOV #7,CNT         ;SET UP COUNTER FOR 8-BITS
    AGAIN:    ROR R2             ;GET MSB OF MULTIPLIER INTO C FLAG
              BCC NOADD          ;ADD MULTIPLICAND?
              ADD R1,R0          ;IF MSB IS "1", ADD
                                 ;MULTIPLICAND
    NOADD:    ROL R0             ;UPDATE PARTIAL PRODUCT
              ROR R1             ;ALIGN MULTIPLICAND WITH
                                 ;PARTIAL PRODUCT
              DEC CNT            ;8 BITS USED?
              BNE AGAIN          ;NO, TEST NEXT SIGNIFICANT BIT
```

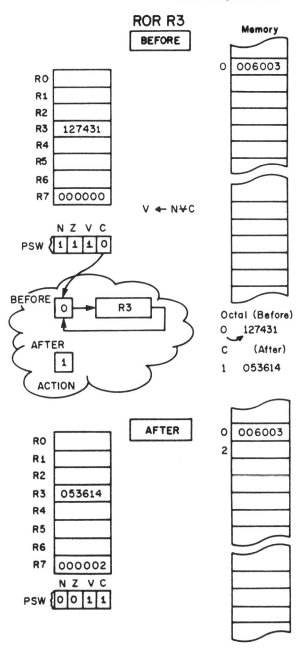

Figure 3.15   Rotating Register R3

Example 3.13 Comparing Two Registers

Address	Contents	Machine Instruction	Micro-Operations
000000	020405	CMP R4,R5	R4 − R5

This one-word instruction compares a source with a destination. Our example shows the contents of register R4 compared with the contents of register R5 (see Figure 3.16). The octal code for this instruction, 020405, indicates the compare instruction, CMP, with the 02 in the opcode field, 04 for the register mode of addressing with register R4, and 05 for the register addressing mode with R5 in the address mode fields. The micro-operation performed is the subtraction of R5 from R4. The result of this subtraction goes nowhere. This instruction causes changes in the processor status word. All four flags (N, Z, V, C) are affected. It is important to note that the C and V flags are set according to the *same* rules as those found in subtraction. For this 2's complement subtraction, if R5 is equal to R4 upon execution of this instruction, the Z flag is set. If R5 is greater than R4, the result is negative, and the N flag is set to indicate a negative result. If R5 is less than R4, the result is positive.

This instruction could be used to test the end of a loop. Suppose we want to loop through some code ten times. We could place 10 in R4 and use R5 as a counter. Each time we iterate through the loop, 1 could be added to R5 (assuming R5 was set to a 0). When R5 equals R4, the loop would be exited by monitoring the flags in the processor status word. A later instruction does this. The subtraction in the CMP machine instruction is a 2's complement subtraction. All flags are affected according to the rules of subtraction. The C flag is set if there is a borrow (no carry out of MSB), and the overflow flag, V, is set if N XOR C = 1.

Example 3.14 ANDing Bits

Address	Contents	Machine Instruction	Micro-Operations
000014	032713	BIT #000017,(R3)	M(R3)∧17 operand
000016	000017		Modify PSW flags

In this example, two different addressing modes are used. Our source mode of addressing is the immediate mode, indicated by the octal 27 in the machine instruction. The digit 2 corresponds to the immediate addressing mode. Our operand is found in program memory following this instruction. Register R7 is currently pointing to this location; hence, 27 is the desired address field code for the source. The destination addressing mode is the register-deferred mode. In our destination field of the instruction, we find 13. The 1 specifies the register-deferred addressing mode, while the 3 specifies the register involved.

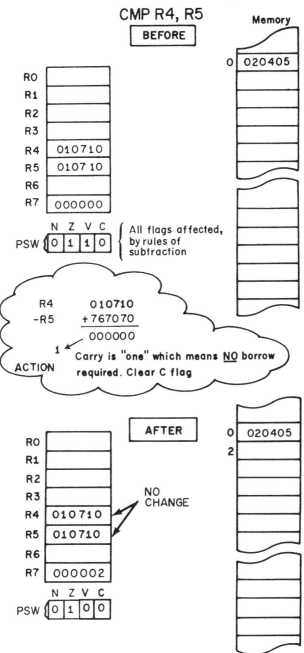

Figure 3.16 Comparing Two Registers

The other operand in this Boolean *AND*ing operation is found in program memory at a location pointed to by register R3. In Figure 3.17, we find R3 containing 24. This is a pointer to memory for this machine instruction. Memory location 24 contains 32. Hence, 32 is *AND*ed to 17 to produce the octal digits 000012. Our processor status word had both the negative and zero flags set, prior to this instruction. After execution of this instruction, although all four flags can be affected, only the negative and zero flags have changed. They are now both cleared. Our result is neither negative nor zero. Note carefully that this instruction alters no operands! It affects only the PSW.

Example 3.15 Halving a Number

Address	Contents	Machine Instruction	Micro-Operations
000004	006237	ASR @# 6	M(16) ← asr M(16),
			C ← exiting bit
000006	000016		operand address

In this two-word instruction starting at location 4 in program memory, we find the octal opcode 006237, which designates the arithmetic shift right operations in the absolute addressing mode. The absolute address is found in program location 6. It is 000016. Suppose location 16 contains the numbers 000041. Upon execution of this instruction, the contents of location 16 are arithmetically shifted right. The final contents of location 16 are 000020. What happened to the least significant digit 1? The exiting bit in this instruction enters the carry flag. All flags are affected by this instruction. The remaining three flags are cleared to zero, since the result is neither negative nor zero, nor have we overflowed the machine. If our original operand were an even number, this instruction would accurately halve the number. If, however, the operand is an odd number, we do not exactly divide the number by two. Arithmetic instructions preserve the sign bit of a number. We assume that the arithmetic instructions operate on signed numbers. Hence, arithmetic shift right, which we'll see next, must maintain that sign in the sign bit position. If our number had been negative, the most significant bit would have been 1 to indicate the negative sign. Upon shifting right in an arithmetic sense, this 1 from bit 15 enters bit 14 of the operand (see Figure 3.18).

3.9.1 MULTIPLE-PRECISION SHIFTING

In Examples 3.16 and 3.17, we want to perform an arithmetic right shift and an arithmetic left shift between two 16-bit numbers. In order to perform each task properly, we must ensure that the vacating bit of one register enters the vacated bit position of the other register. This must occur on both ends of both registers.

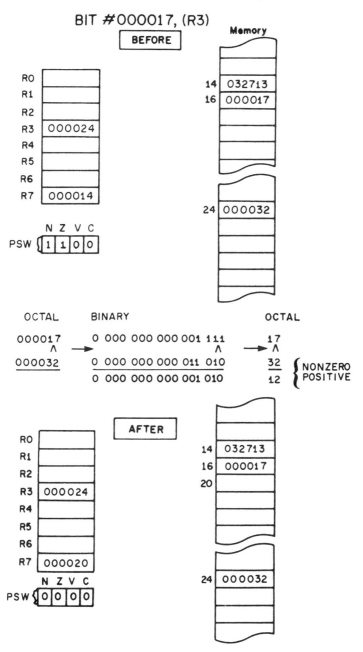

Figure 3.17   ANDing Bits

ASR @ #16

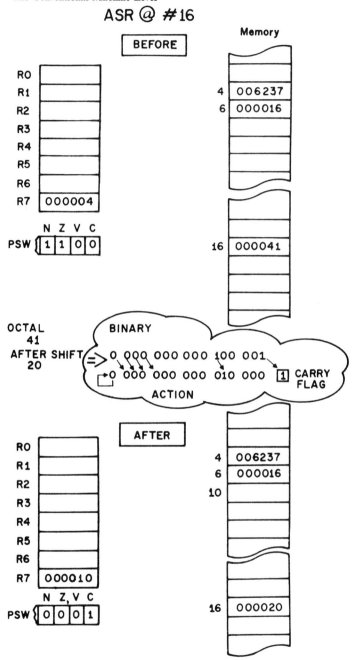

Figure 3.18   Halving a Number

Example 3.16 Double Arithmetic Right Shift

R0 = Most Significant Bits

R1 = Least Significant Bits

Multiple Right Shift

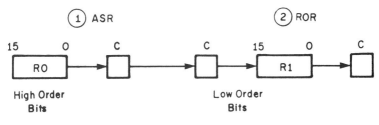

Machine Code   ASR R0 /High Order Bits
               ROR R1 /Low Order Bits

Figure 3.19   Multiple Right Shift

In Example 3.16, we want to perform a right shift between R0 and R1. The most significant digits of our data are in R0 and the least significant digits of our data are in R1. Multiple-precision right shifting is accomplished in the following manner. The first step is to perform an arithmetic shift right (ASR) on the high-order bits. The next step is to perform a rotate right (ROR) on the low-order bits. The machine code consists of two instructions as shown in Figure 3.19. Notice carefully how the carry bit is filled with the vacating bit position 0 of the high-order bits in the first step. In the second step, the right rotate instruction forces the carry flag into the vacated bit (bit 15) of the low-order bits. A right rotate also causes the vacating bit (bit 0) to enter the carry flag. If our arithmetic right shifting operation was required over three or more registers, we would need simply to perform a right rotate for each additional register. The same operations apply not only to registers, but also to memory locations. The only difference in our machine code would be the addressing mode utilized in each instruction.

Example 3.17 Double Arithmetic Left Shift

R0 = Most Significant Bits

R1 = Least Significant Bits

In Example 3.17, we want to perform a multiple left shift on registers R1 and R0 (see Figure 3.20). Assume that R0 contains the most significant digits and R1 contains the least significant digits. The first step is to perform an arithmetic shift left (ASL) on the low-order bits. This causes the sign bit of

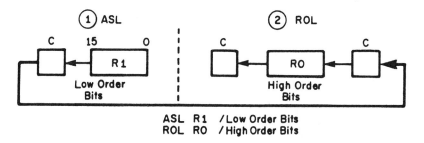

Figure 3.20   Multiple Left Shift

R1 to enter the carry flag. The next step requires a rotate left (ROL) on the high-order bits. This causes the carry flag to enter bit 0 of R0. The result of this multiple left shift causes the entire 32 bits of our data word to be shifted to the left by one position. Notice that multiple left shifts are initiated on the *low-order bits* first with an ASL instruction. In contrast to this, multiple right shifts are performed initially with an ASR operation on the *high-order bits*.

Example 3.18 Subtraction with Two Memory Locations

Address	Contents	Machine Instruction	Micro-Operations
000006	161513	SUB (R5),(R3)	M(R3) ← M(R3)−M(R5)

In this example, a memory location, pointed to by R5, is to be subtracted from a memory location pointed to by R3 (see Figure 3.21). This instruction uses the register-deferred mode of addressing both for the source and for the destination. This 2's complement arithmetic operation causes the location pointed to by R3, which is 104710, to be reduced by the contents of the location pointed to by register R5, which is 104712. When we perform the subtraction of 16 from 14 leaving a result of a negative 2, our negative flag is set to a 1. The Z and V flags are cleared by this result. Since this is a 2's complement subtraction operation, the carry flag is now interpreted as a borrow flag. For a 2's complement number in a subtraction operation, a carry from the MSB causes the C flag to be cleared. *No* carry causes the C flag to be set (as in this example).

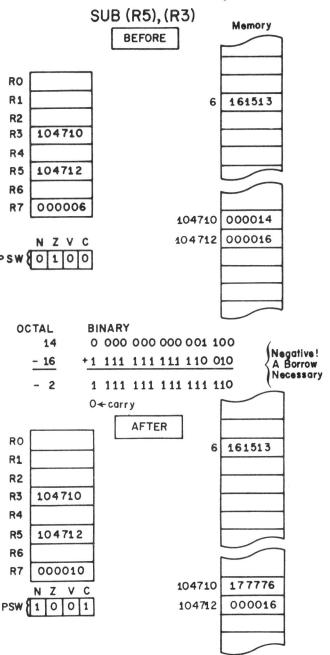

Figure 3.21 Subtraction with Two Memory Locations

Example 3.19 Double-Precision Subtraction (Base 10)

$$
\begin{array}{r}
232\ 769 \\
-182\ 841 \\
\hline
49\ 928 \\
\end{array}
$$

1 Borrow

Before			After		
R0	769		R0	928	
R1	841		R1	841	
R2	232		R2	49	
R3	182		R3	182	

An Assembly Language Program

.
.
.

```
SUB R1,R0      ;SUBTRACT LOWER HALF
SBC R2         ;BORROW FROM HIGH-ORDER BITS
SUB R3,R2      ;SUBTRACT UPPER HALF
      .        ;NOTE! OVERFLOW NOT MONITORED HERE
      .
      .
```

Suppose that we have a 3-digit word length and we want to perform a double-precision subtraction. We would subtract the least significant digits first. The least significant digits are in R0 and R1. The first subtraction operation, SUB R1,R0, subtracts R1 from R0 with the result returned to R0. The second subtraction operation, SBC R2, subtracts the carry (which should be considered a borrow flag here) if it has occurred for this least significant digit operation. The final subtraction, SUB R3,R2, subtracts R3 from R2 leaving the result in R2. The final result can be found in R0 (LSDs) and R2 (MSDs). Notice that our two numbers did require a borrow from the upper half, as shown in the example. Hence, we must subtract one from the upper digits with the second subtraction instruction (SBC R2).

3.10   PROGRAM MOVEMENT INSTRUCTIONS

Program movement instructions directly affect the program counter of a computer. Since the PDP-11 computer employs register R7 as the program counter, program movement instructions employ or modify the contents of R7. The first instruction in our set of program movement instructions of Example 3.20 is the jump instruction. The JMP instruction is equivalent to the FORTRAN GO TO instruction. Both instructions cause a change in the flow of program sequences.

FORTRAN	Assembly	Comments
GO TO 4024	JMP (R1)	;R1 POINTS TO PROGRAM ;LOCATION 4024

Example 3.20 Jump To Program Memory Location 4024

Address	Contents	Machine Instruction	Micro-Operations
000000	000111	JMP (R1)	PC ← M(R1)
			or
			PC ← 004024

The octal code for this jump instruction is found in program location 0 using R1 with the register-deferred mode of addressing (see Figure 3.22). This register points to a location in memory which contains the octal code, 004024. This address is loaded into register R7. When R7 is loaded, program flow automatically jumps to location 004024 in program memory. Here, another instruction, not data, should be found. Why? The machine will return to a fetch phase at which point the contents of location 004024 will be loaded into the instruction register for an instruction execute phase. We mention this because a frequent programming error is to cause a jump to a line of code containing data instead of an instruction. Similarly, JMP R1 is not allowed because R1 is a register, not an address.

Example 3.21 Branching Forward

Address	Contents	Machine Instruction	Micro-Operations
000010	000402	BR NEXT	PC ← (PC)+2+2(offset)

The 6-digit opcode consists of eight bits (upper half) for the opcode and eight bits (lower half) for the offset.

Short jumps are best accomplished using branch instructions instead of jump instructions (see Figure 3.23). Only one memory fetch is required (rather than two). Here in Example 3.21, the octal code for a branch instruction is in location 10. This instruction causes us to branch to location 16. The offset is used with the current value in the program counter to cause the program jump. The offset is a function of the distance from the current instruction. However, the offset is not the effective address.

Calculation of the effective address is accomplished in the following manner. The PDP-11 computer assumes that the memory is divided into even and odd locations (like any other machine). However, instructions must be found only in even addresses. This means that the program counter is automatically incremented by two (not one). Also, the two least significant octal digits of the opcode are assumed to be one-half the actual distance, because the PDP-11 computer automatically multiplies this number by two to calculate the effective address. More precisely, the computer uses the following formula:

$$\text{NEW PC} = \text{CURRENT PC} + 2(\text{OFFSET})$$

Note that the current PC value is the value of the address of our current instruction *plus* two. The "NEW PC" is the effective address. Our instruction in Example 3.21 starts at location 000010, so our "CURRENT PC" is 000012. In our example, we will branch six locations from the current location. To obtain the lower eight bits of the branch opcode, simply subtract the

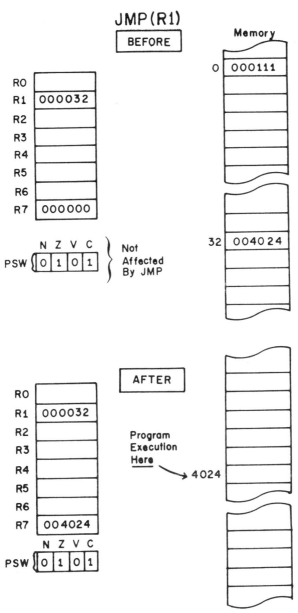

Figure 3.22 Jump to Program Memory Location 4024

current PC from the new PC and divide this result by two. Then, truncate the result to eight binary bits to obtain the numerical value to be found in the low-order eight bits of the opcode. This offset must be a signed binary number in the range from +127 (decimal) to −128 (decimal). The truncated offset required in our example is 02. Hence, the opcode 000402 is found in location 000010. It is possible to branch backward as well as forward. Tables 3.13 and 3.14 are useful for calculating the offset necessary for the branch instructions.

Table 3.13   Branch Forward Offsets in the PDP-11

*Distance From Current Instruction (Decimal)	Truncated Offset (Octal)
0	−1
2	0
4	1
6	2
8	3
10	4
12	5
14	6

*Assumes the PC points to first word of current instruction

Table 3.14   Branch Backward Offsets in the PDP-11

*Distance From Current Instruction (Decimal)	Truncated Offset (Octal)
0	377
− 2	376
− 4	375
− 6	374
− 8	373
−10	372
−12	371
−14	370
−16	367
−18	366
−20	365

*Assumes the PC points to first word of current instruction

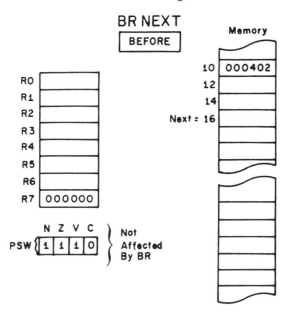

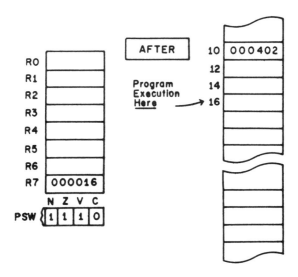

Figure 3.23   Branching Forward

3.10.1 LOOPING

Just as we have seen the need for looping through FORTRAN and other high-level code, the same task is required of assembly language programs. Generating code to perform a program loop requires us to do the following:

1. Initialize the loop parameters.

2. Update those parameters with each loop iteration.

3. Test for the end of the loop sequence.

Let's examine the following simple example which performs the sum of the integers, $1 + 2 + 3 + 4 + ... + 8$. Our FORTRAN code in Example 3.22 assumes that the loop parameters consist of K, a counter set initially to 8, and a variable, L, representing the running sum. The equivalent machine language code is also depicted. We initialize the loop by setting the running sum to 0, and the counter to the number of iterations desired through this loop (eight are desired). The running sum is generated in program location 20, with the machine instruction *ADD K,L*. The loop counter, K, is decremented in the next machine instruction and tested for zero with the *TST K* instruction. Finally, the program returns to location 20 if K is not equal to zero. Otherwise, we have executed the loop eight times. The program then proceeds out of the loop. *This test for loop end is very dangerous and should never be used.* Test for less than or equal to zero because the loop would go forever if zero was "missed" for some strange reason (e.g., DO $>$ I=1,7,2).

Example 3.22 Computing the Sum of 8 Numbers

	FORTRAN	Program Location	Machine Language Instruction
	L = 0		CLR L
	K = 8		MOV #8,K
20	L = L+K	000020	ADD K,L ←
	K = K-1		DEC K
			TST K
	IF(K.NE.0) GO TO 20		BNE ──┘
60	•		•
	•		•
	•		•

Example 3.23 Branch If Less Than

Address	Contents	Machine Instruction	Micro-Operations
000160	002412	BLT NEXT	N ⊻ V: PC ← (PC)+2+2(offset) (N ⊻ V): PC ← (PC)+2

The BLT instruction, or branch if less than, is a conditional branch instruction that monitors the negative flag and the overflow flag. The particular test on these flags is an exclusive-OR of the negative flag with the overflow flag, as shown in Example 3.23. If either the negative flag or the overflow flag is set, but not both, a branch will occur. In Example 3.23, we want to branch to a location 10_{10} locations from the current location. The calculated offset, from Table 3.13, requires an offset of 4, which is found as part of the octal opcode for BLT NEXT. Our current instruction is at location 000160. Upon testing the processor status word flags, we find that the condition is satisfied, and our program branches to location 000172. A machine instruction should be found here, not a data word. No flags in the processor status word are modified (see Figure 3.24).

3.11 PROGRAM MANIPULATION INSTRUCTIONS

Program manipulation instructions, in contrast to program movement instructions, do not necessarily cause the program counter to be modified. Program manipulation instructions tend to change the state of the machine. One possible way, obviously, is to stop or start programs. The *HALT* and *RESET* instructions, respectively, do just that. Recall that the state of a machine is indicated in the processor status word. Hence, machine instructions that modify or alter the contents of these flags belong to the program manipulation instruction set. Modifying any of the flags with an instruction does not always directly alter the behavior of a program. Processor status word modifying instructions must be accompanied by instructions that test these altered flags to directly change subsequent program behavior.

The set of program manipulation machine instructions found in Table 3.9 is not complete, but only representative. For instance, we indicate the capability to modify the carry flag, which is certainly necessary for arithmetic operations, but we already know that an overflow flag, when set by current activity that has caused overflow, should be capable of being restored to zero. The full set of PDP-11 program manipulation instructions will be found in the next chapter. Let's look at one example which can manipulate a program.

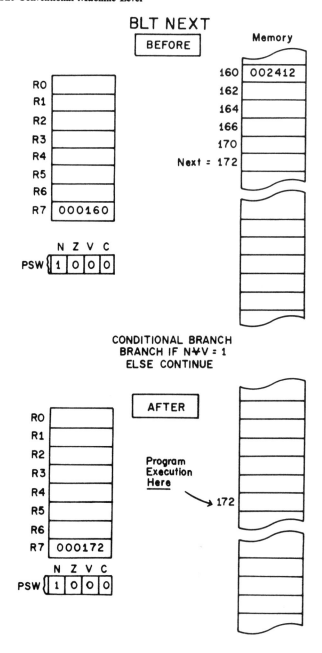

Figure 3.24 Branch If Less Than

Example 3.24 Clear Carry Flag

Address	Contents	Machine Instruction	Micro-Operations
001160	000241	CLC	C ← 0

The CLC, or clear carry flag, in the machine instruction is a simple one-line instruction that resets the C flag in the processor status word to a zero. Its octal opcode is 000241. In Example 3.24, it is found in location 001160. When this instruction is executed, the C flag will have been reset to zero. This is an important instruction in many arithmetic operations. The CLC instruction is often found at the beginning of code to initialize the carry. A programmer may monitor the carry flag not only to perform multiple-precision arithmetic, but also to properly shift across two or more words. CLC is also useful when the C flag has been set by instructions other than arithmetic instructions, and subsequent program activity requires the C flag to be cleared or reinitialized.

3.12   SYNTAX OF ASSEMBLER LANGUAGES

An assembly language program consists of source statements. In general, an assembly source statement of an assembly language program corresponds to and is translated into one machine language instruction of a computer. A source statement consists of one or more fields specifying a machine language instruction or another task (required of the assembler). The four common fields are: *label, opcode, operand,* and *comment.* Each field is variable in length and is set apart by a delimiter. The delimiter may consist of special characters from the ASCII character set and can be a space, colon, or other special character. Converting a program into a correct assembly language program requires that the programmer abide by the *rules of syntax* required by the assembly language program of the specific computer.

   Assemblers employ three types of source statements: declarative, imperative, and control. Each of these is used as follows:

1. *Declarative statements* allocate space for symbols or values and assign contents to addressable locations. Declarative statements *are not executable at run time*, but rather cause activity of the assembler during assemble time.

2. *Imperative statements* define the actual machine language instructions in symbolic or mnemonic form. Imperative statements *are executable at run time*.

3. *Control statements* are commands to the assembler by the programmer to modify or alter the assembly process itself. Control statements command such activities as start a new page, do not print contents of location counter, skip next page, etc. Control statements generate housekeeping tasks.

3.12.1 LOCATION COUNTER

To keep track of the program location, assemblers use a *location counter*, often designated by the assembly programmer as LC. The location counter, much like a program counter, can then specify the current location of an instruction in the source code. In many respects, the location counter is similar to the line number in a BASIC or FORTRAN program. During assembly, the location counter is updated as each new symbolic statement is translated. For many assemblers, the value of the location counter is printed alongside the machine opcode for every imperative statement. Declarative statements are not converted to object code since they are not used during execution time of the program anyway.

The partial assembly language program of Example 3.9 is shown with the additional symbols and notation required for completeness in Example 3.25. In the leftmost field or label field of source statements can be found the symbolic addresses, *START, LOOP, SUM,* and *COUNT,* needed in this program. These symbolic addresses are used to represent either a program location (such as *START* and *LOOP*) or the addresses of operands (such as *SUM* and *COUNT*). The second field contains the operation codes of our program. They include more than the machine language mnemonics. For example, *.TITLE, .ENABL, .BLKW,* and *.END* are special commands to the assembler to request specific activity of the assembler itself. The third field consists of the operands required by the instructions. The fourth field consists of the comments that help programmers to understand the program behavior.

The structure of the program in Example 3.25 includes, first, a declarative part consisting of information about the program useful to the programmer, second, the body of code or instructions (imperative statements), and third, statements about the data area. In this data area are the values (addressable locations) for the symbols. For instance, during execution the program finds "COUNT" in location 000034. The statements containing .TITLE, .ENABL, and LC=. are control statements. The statements beginning with the label START and ending with the opcode HALT are imperative statements. The reserved storage statements SUM: and COUNT: are declarative statements.

The rules of syntax for each field described are those of MACRO-11, but they are common to most assemblers. For the most part, the rules apply across all fields. Those rules that apply only to a specific field are identified.

Example 3.25 Fields of an Assembly Language Program

Label	Opcode	Operands	Comments

;"SUM OF NUMBERS" OBTAINS THE SUM OF 10 FIXED-POINT NUMBERS FROM A TABLE
;STARTING AT LOCATION 1000, USING REGISTER R0 AS A COUNTER AND AS AN
;INDIRECT POINTER TO THE TABLE OF VALUES. THE RESULT IS FOUND IN SUM.
;COUNT IS USED WITH R0 TO TEST FOR LAST POINTER LOCATION. PRE-SCALE
;VALUES. OVERFLOW NOT MONITORED. CHRIS ANDREWS - JUN 1986 - REV 1.

	.TITLE	SUM OF NUMBERS	
	.ENABL	AMA	;RECOGNIZE ;ABSOLUTE ADDRESSING
	LC=.		;SET SYMBOL LC TO VALUE ;OF ;LOCATION COUNTER WHICH ;IS ZERO

;BODY OF CODE TO FORM THE SUM NOW FOLLOWS

START:	CLR	SUM	;INIT SUM TO ZERO
	MOV	@#1000,R0	;SET UP POINTER
	MOV	@#1022,COUNT	;INIT COUNT TO LAST ENTRY
LOOP:	ADD	(R0)+,SUM	;SUM=DATA+SUM
	CMP	COUNT,R0	
	BNE	LOOP	;DONE? NO, ADD AGAIN
	HALT		;YES, STOP COMPLETELY!
SUM:	.BLKW	1	;STORAGE FOR SUM
COUNT:	.BLKW	1	;STORAGE FOR COUNT
	.END	START	;DONE NOW

;DATA AREA USED IN "SUM OF NUMBERS" NOW FOLLOWS
SYMBOL TABLE

START	000000	LOOP	000016
COUNT	000034	SUM	000032

;END OF PROGRAM

3.12.2 LABEL FIELD

A label is the symbolic name of a memory location or cell. The label field of an assembly language program contains names or symbolic addresses. In Example 3.25, the executable program actually begins at the statement named or labeled START. The first line clears the location called SUM. The remaining fields of this line labeled START specify the contents of the memory cell. Labels are composed of one to six alphanumeric characters (letters and numbers). Valid and invalid labels are depicted in Table 3.15. Valid labels may consist of a single character, although these are not very descriptive, and such brevity is discouraged. Invalid labels contain characters other than letters and numbers. A?XZ contains "?". The ? is not allowed in a label. *A label should not exceed six alphanumeric characters.* Assemblers generally do not recognize more than six characters; hence, the label TERMINAL is indistinguishable from the label TERMINATE to an assembler. Periods and dollar signs can be used in names or labels as if they were letters. But such usage in a label field is discouraged because these symbols have special meanings to many assemblers.

The delimiter for the label field in the PDP-11 is a colon (:), which must immediately follow a label. This terminating rule is specific to the label field. Labels may begin anywhere on a statement line; however, by convention, labels start in column one. No other fields may precede a label field on any given statement.

Table 3.15   Valid and Invalid Labels/Symbols

Valid	Invalid	Reason Invalid
START	A?XZ	CONTAINS "?"
LOOP	TERMINAL	8 CHARACTERS (assembler ignores "AL")
BEGIN	A/C	CONTAINS "/"
AGAIN	%TEN	CONTAINS "%"
ABAD	A+BAD	CONTAINS "+"
AGOOD	A-GOOD	CONTAINS "-"
COMMA	COM,MA	CONTAINS ","
BLANK	BL ANK	CONTAINS " "

In Example 3.25, the symbolic addresses START and LOOP are names or labels found in the label field. However, symbolic names may exist outside the label field. In this same example, SUM and COUNT are symbolic names which represent symbolic addresses. These symbolic addresses are analogous to variable names in FORTRAN and BASIC. Just as in those high-level languages, these variable names are names of memory locations that contain "numbers." Such numbers can be manipulated by the program just as if they were data. The symbolic addresses START and LOOP are analogous to such statement labels in a FORTRAN or BASIC program (if allowed). They are names of memory locations which contain machine language instructions. In high-level languages, every attempt is made to distinguish between variable names and statement labels. This is not so in assembly language programs.

This distinction actually does not exist. In fact, a symbolic address is the name of a memory location or cell, and it does not matter whether the contents of that memory cell is a number or an instruction. The rules for labels apply to symbolic names found in the operand field. The notation of symbolic names is very crucial; we will return to its usage in Chapter 6.

3.12.3   OPERATION CODE FIELD

The operation code field may contain not only the mnemonics of machine language instructions, but also assembler instructions called *assembly directives, pseudo-operations,* or *pseudo-instructions.* Most assemblers distinguish between operation codes and assembly directives with a special symbol. In MACRO-11, assembly directives always begin with a period (.). The legal operation codes and assembler directives consist only of those available from the manufacturer's table of mnemonics and directives that an assembler recognizes. Example 3.25 contains the legal mnemonics CLR, MOV, ADD, CMP, BNE, and HALT. MOV is a valid mnemonic and will be recognized by the assembler, but MOVE is not.

An assembler will generate an error diagnostic message calling attention to an illegal mnemonic. The assembly directives in the program include .TITLE, .ENABL, .BLKW, and .END. These are special instructions to the assembler to perform numerous housekeeping tasks which make assembly language programming life less burdensome. The four assembly directives are definitely *not* operation codes. An assembler directive commands activity during the assembly process. No object code is generated for a directive. Consequently, directives are *not* executed during program execution time.

Besides liberally documenting a program with the comment fields, an assembly language programmer should always title his or her program. The assembly directive .TITLE allows a programmer to assign a name to the program. SUM OF NUMBERS is the desired title for Example 3.25. The .TITLE assembly directive will place this name on the first and every succeeding page of a printout of the program (should the program require more than one page of printout). The .ENABL AMA assembly directive informs the assembler that absolute addressing is being requested. Recall that the PDP-11 has two general memory addressing modes: relative and absolute. In the absolute mode, the actual numerical address is used in the instruction. Example 3.25 uses the absolute addresses, @#1000 and @#1011. However, invoking .ENABL AMA forces the assembler to assemble relative addresses (mode 6) using mode 3. In Example 3.25, the symbols SUM, COUNT, and LOOP are assembled in the relative addressing mode. This directive is useful during the debugging phase of program development.

Every label or symbol resides at or is assigned to some memory location by the assembler. The operands of the current machine instructions, SUM and COUNT, indicate names of memory locations. In this example, the programmer wants to reserve one word location for each of these symbols. The .BLKW 1 assembly directive assigns one 16-bit word to each symbol. The number following the .BLKW directive is called the argument and indicates the number of words desired in the block. For example, if a symbol table requires six words, the statement

TABLE: .BLKW   6

directs the assembler to reserve six consecutive locations in memory at starting address TABLE. The first entry in "TABLE" is not necessarily "6". The argument of .BLKW specifies length not content. The last assembly directive in the program simply denotes the physical end of the program. The .END directive contains one operand, which generally is the label of the first line of code in our program.

3.12.4 OPERAND FIELD

Machine language instructions may require no operands (as in HALT), one operand (as in CLR SUM), or more than one operand (as in MOV @#1000,R0). An assembler obeying the rules of syntax will monitor each opcode and watch for the correct number of operands. When two or more operands are required as in MOV @#1000,R0, the assembler will make provisions for both operands. It updates the location counter by four and makes symbol table assignments when necessary. It is instructive to determine how much the location counter will be updated after MOV @#1022,COUNT. From Example 3.9, we find that the PC is incremented by 6. Extra or leading zeroes of a number may be deleted. In the statement MOV @#1000,R0, it is unnecessary to enter the statement MOV @#001000,R0.

3.12.5 COMMENT FIELD

A program is more than just computer software. It should represent diligent effort and careful thought. Programs are seldom cast into concrete. They are more likely to be altered, changed, and modified months after the original creation. Often, such changes are done by someone else. Documenting a program for posterity is definitely advised.

The comment field option is provided by the manufacturer not as an afterthought, but to intentionally help us to understand programs. Comment fields begin anywhere on a line, but they are assumed to be the last field of that line. No other fields can follow a comment field (i.e., an operand field cannot follow a comment field). This is so because comment fields are not assembled into object code. Hence, any symbols or expressions that follow a semicolon are ignored at object code generation time. A program that is well documented will contain much information about program behavior, the name of the programmer, the latest revision number, and other pertinent information. The comments preceding a program make up the *header*.

Comments should not just mimic the current opcode and operands. *Comments should be up-to-date, accurate, complete, and understandable.* They should tell a user of your program what the intent is of the program itself. Misleading or absent comments represent a waste of time and money. Comments help everyone to maintain and adapt programs. An astute programmer always acknowledges that some day his or her code may be modified to fit into another machine or may even be attached to another program. The eventual user, then, should be able to know exactly what every program does and what it needs, without resorting to further consultation with its author. A well-documented program should stand alone. Remember that programs will last long after their author. In the source code of Table 3.16, good and bad comments are illustrated. These are only representative of many possible alternatives.

Table 3.16 Good and Bad Comments

Source Code	Bad Comments	Good Comments
ADD (R0)+,SUM	;SUM=SUM+(R0)	;SUM=SUM+DATA AND UPDATE POINTER
BNE LOOP	;BRANCH TO LOOP	;LAST DATA ADDED? NO, THEN DO IT AGAIN
MOVB R5,(R3)+	;(R3)+ ← R5	;STORE CHAR IN ARRAY, UPDATE INDEX
MOV PC,SP	;SP ← PC	;INITIALIZE STACK POINTER TO START

In the first line of code, "R0" as a comment repeats the source code listing, but "DATA" does not. It tells the programmer something about R0. The good comments in the second line of code indicate something about internal loop behavior. The remaining code and comments are self-explanatory.

3.13 THE MACRO-11 ASSEMBLER

The assembler developed for a PDP-11 programmer is MACRO-11, a machine-dependent programming language which runs only on a PDP-11 computer. The MACRO-11 language provides the programmer with additional capabilities to access all of the features of the operating system of the PDP-11 (i.e., RT-11). The MACRO-11 assembly language employs the PDP-11 instruction set. The language also assumes that only the mnemonic instructions that correspond to various PDP-11 computer operations are invoked. As such, a MACRO-11 program is a sequence of lines or, more appropriately, source language statements. An assembly language statement has the following format:

label: operator   operand(s)   ;comments

A MACRO-11 assembly language program is not very different from those generated in other assembly languages. The operator and/or operand may be: (1) an instruction selected from the PDP-11 instruction set, (2) data needed by the instructions (for example, absolute addresses), and (3) assembler directives of the MACRO-11 assembler directive set. The statement label is optional, but is useful to identify significant statement lines so that the programmer can refer to the instructions or data on that line from other parts of the program. Comments are optional, but are strongly encouraged. Sequences of language statements constitute a routine (hopefully to perform a useful specific function). Groups of routines with the respective data compose an entire executable program. A "complete" program also includes effective documentation.

The MACRO-11 language processor is the PDP-11 assembler that accepts information in one format (a source program containing source statements) and translates it into another format (binary opcodes of a machine language program). The assembler interprets and processes assembly language statements, one at a time, to generate one or more computer instructions or data items. Source statements will be composed of characters in ASCII format. The MACRO-11 program translates this code into a machine format that the computer can directly execute. The output of the MACRO-11 assembly process is a new version of the program in object format, called an object module. Should one desire and request it, the assembler will also produce a listing of the source program at the same time. During assembly processing, the MACRO-11 assembler does the following:

1. Recognizes all instructions used within the source program to determine their relative position in computer memory (using the location counter)

2. Keeps track of all user-defined symbols (such as macros) and their respective values in a symbol table

3. Converts assembly language mnemonics, user-defined symbols, and data values into their respective machine language equivalents (binary object code).

The MACRO-11 assembler provides the *automatic assembly process*, converting source code into object code. This translation process allows users to employ meaningful symbols rather than a numerical code which has no mnemonic value. These symbols employed are then assembled into absolute binary code capable of being executed by the PDP-11. The MACRO-11 assembler will accept addresses of the form:

$$symbol + constant$$

Unless explicitly directed otherwise, addresses are assembled in the relative addressing mode. The addresses in Example 3.26 are valid. Every symbolic address must be somehow defined. The address may be defined as a label by means of an assignment directive (symbol = expression) or by the .GLOBL directive.

Example 3.26 Symbols and Expressions

```
MOV R1+4,R0    ;R1+4 MEANS R5, NOT ADD 4 TO R1!
               ;R1+4 IS AN ADDRESS CONTAINING A
               ;SYMBOL AND A CONSTANT
CLR BUFFER     ;BUFFER IS A VALID SYMBOLIC ADDRESS
               ;WITH NO CONSTANT
```

MACRO-11 is a two-pass assembler. In the first pass, addresses for the symbols are determined and a symbol table is generated. In the second pass, the assembler, which now has the addresses defined, will generate the machine language code for each and every assembly language instruction. Briefly, a symbol table is constructed by scanning the assembly language program during *pass one* of the assembly process. This symbol table is then used to construct the actual machine language program. This construction process is accomplished during *pass two*. Construction of a machine language program requires two tables: the operation code table and the symbol table. The operation code table used in pass two is identical to the tables of opcodes found in Chapter 2, while the symbol table generated during pass one is made up of user-defined symbols. The assembler actually substitutes numbers for the symbolic names (both symbols and machine mnemonics). The output of an assembler is an absolute binary code or the relocatable object code and is of type .OBJ. This code, when generated by a MACRO-11 assembler and loaded into a PDP-11 assisted by a linker and loader, can then be executed.

3.13.1 RESERVED CHARACTERS

Special characters in an assembler's character set are reserved for specific action or meaning for that assembler. Such special characters help the programmer to recognize labels, constants, pseudo-operations, decimal values, comments, and so on. These characters consist of the printable ASCII character set listed here. Other special characters will be described later.

$$. \$: = \% \# @ ( ) ; ' " + - \& !$$

We have already noted the use of the colon to designate the end of the label symbol. The semicolon is used to indicate the initiation of a comment field. The nonprinting space character also has a special meaning, although it does not affect the assembly process.

3.13.2 THE PERIOD

In MACRO-11, the period symbol, ".", has several meanings. We have seen how an assembler directive or pseudo-operand requires a period before the actual directive, such as .END and .WORD. The period symbol is more commonly used as the symbol for the assembler location counter (LC). The location counter in an assembler performs the same function as the program counter of the program. The location counter contains the address of the current line of code of the assembly language program. When the period symbol is used in the operand field of an instruction, it represents the address of the first word of the current instruction. In Example 3.27, a period in the operand field informs the assembler to place the contents of the location counter in the assembled code for the program.

Example 3.27 A Poor Use of "."

Location Counter	Program Contents	Label	Opcode	Operands	Comments
000200	005027	STOP:	CLR	#.	;HALT MACHINE
000202	000200				;THIS IS POOR
					;PROGRAMMING

In this example, the period in the operand field informs the assembler to use location 200. The assembler generates code, which is then assembled in the column labeled program contents, placing the value 000200 in the second line of this two-word instruction. Recall that the # sign represents the immediate addressing mode. It is instructive to examine what this simple program does. When executed, this code will place all zeroes in location 200. Hence, the next time this same code is executed, the machine will halt, which illustrates the worst form of self-modifying code! Notice that the machine will *not* halt during the first execution of the program. Example 3.27, at best, involves tricky coding of the type that should be avoided at all costs!

3.13.3   RESERVING STORAGE SPACE

The period can represent the decimal point in an assembler. For example, if you want to assign the decimal number 8 to a location in memory, the following code informs the assembler to accomplish just such a task.

EIGHT: .WORD 8.

MACRO-11 assumes that all numbers are in octal, unless otherwise specified. Hence, should you desire that a number be interpreted as a decimal number, the period must be used. One could allow both octal and decimal numbers in a program. The following valid table stores the octal numbers 1 through 7 and the decimal numbers 8, 9, and 10, starting at location TABLE.

TABLE: .WORD   1,2,3,4,5,6,7,8.,9.,10.

or

TABLE: 1,2,3,4,5,6,7,8.,9.,10.

If a table as shown above is desired, it is not necessary to include the .WORD assembler directive, but it is encouraged. Without it, another programmer may not recognize the intended data size. This assembler directive may have one, two, or more operands. If more than one operand is used, these will be stored in successive words in the object program. Such operands must be legally formed expressions. Numbers have been chosen above. Should the operator field be left blank, the assembler will assume the .WORD directive is being invoked if the operand field contains one or more expressions. Hence, the second line of code above is valid. If .WORD is omitted and no operands follow, be prepared for some surprising problems. Some assemblers will not indicate any error! Worse yet, in some assemblers the location counter will not be updated.

3.13.4   DIRECT ASSIGNMENT

Oftentimes, a programmer will need to assign a specific value to a symbol. *The direct assignment defines the value of a symbol.* That statement must occur the first time the symbol is entered in the program. The symbol will be entered into the assembler's symbol table with the specified value associated with it. It is possible to subsequently redefine a symbol. The symbol value retains the most current assigned value. The general expression for direct assignment statements is

symbol = expression

This direct assignment statement is equivalent to the *EQUATE* (*EQU*) in other assemblers. Direct assignment statements are helpful for amplifying the information content of a program and enhancing the clarity. Commonly used values or expressions for symbol names should then be given in the direct assignment.

In MACRO-11, a user can assign to the location counter an initial value. The direct assignment statement then becomes

$$LC=.$$
$$. = 4000 + LC$$

In the preceding, the programmer is adding the value of 4000 to the current contents of the location counter. This direct assignment statement is equivalent to the common assembler directive ORG, found in other assemblers; ".=4000", by itself, is an illegal assignment to the LC. The direct assignment statement is an assembly directive. Just as with *.TITLE*, *.ENABL*, etc., assembly directives are "executed" at assembly time, not at program execution time. For instance, $A=A+1$ causes the value of A in the symbol table to be incremented. This occurs at assembly time. It does not cause location A in program memory to be incremented.

To specify a general-purpose register in the PDP-11 programming model, a programmer could use the % sign (see Example 3.28).

Example 3.28 The Meaning of %

```
          MOV    #4,%2
   LOOP:  ADD    %3,%4
          DEC    %2
          BNE    LOOP
```

"%" is not the best way to indicate R, is it? "%" does not resemble "R". However, with a direct assignment statement, a programmer can force the otherwise ordinary symbol strings R0, R1, R2, ..., R7 to take on the very specific meaning of a general-purpose register in the PDP-11. In Example 3.28, a wise programmer will precede the program code with

$$R1 = \%1 \qquad R3 = \%3$$
$$R2 = \%2 \qquad R4 = \%4$$

Each symbol, "%n", is replaced by Rn to make the program clearer. If we return to Example 3.25, we see that it is still not complete because direct register assignment statements, as above, should precede the imperative statements.

3.13.5   THE PERIOD AND BRANCHING

The "." symbol can be used for calculating branch or jump addresses as follows. In the instruction, BR .-6 of Example 3.29, the computer will execute an instruction three words preceding this instruction. In Example 3.29, the opcode, BR .-6, causes program execution to resume at location 000012. The "." in the operand field informs the assembler to compute the new PC using the current value of the location counter, which is 000020 (and *not* the current value of the PC!). The operand, -6, causes a backward branch three words preceding this instruction. Using the "." for branch addresses is not recommended. A frequent mistake a careless programmer is prone to make is to want to jump back six locations and write BR .-6 when, in fact, a backward branch to three words will occur. The reason for this error is that the PDP-11 instructions can occupy one, two, or even three words, but the PDP-11 is both half-word and word addressable. It is strongly advised that you make branch addresses explicitly defined. Example 3.30 employs the recommended procedure: *use a label instead of the period.*

Example 3.29 Implicit Branching from Current LC (Undesirable)

Location Counter	Program Contents	Label	Opcode/Operand	Comments
000012		HERE:		
000014				
000016				
000020	000774	GOBACK:	BR .-6	;UNDESIRABLE CODING
000022				

Example 3.30 Explicit Branching from Current LC (Desirable)

Location Counter	Program Contents	Label	Opcode/Operand	Comments
000012		HERE:		
000014				
000016				
000020	000774	GOBACK:	BR HERE	;DESIRABLE CODING;
000022				;TELLS PRECISELY ;WHERE BRANCHING ;OCCURS

3.14   MORE ASSEMBLER DIRECTIVES

In MACRO-11, it is possible to conveniently command the assembler to store data as consecutive bytes. Such 8-bit binary data is then stored by the assembler with the .BYTE directive in the following directive:

.BYTE 101,041,130,033

This directive will then store the following octal numbers in two consecutive words of memory:

041101
033130

Data arriving from a teletype or another serial peripheral device frequently will be represented in ASCII code. The assembler can be informed to store the ASCII code of a string of consecutive bytes with the following directive:

.ASCII "delimiter" ASCII string "delimiter"

All ASCII codes are printed characters. To utilize a nonprinting character with an ASCII code, n, we employ $<n>$. The following statements store "IT IS TIME FOR A COFFEE BREAK" in consecutive memory locations.

.ASCII /IT IS TIME /
.ASCII /FOR A COFFEE /
.ASCII /BREAK/<7>

Note that the above code will store the character strings in memory. Don't forget the nonprinting space after TIME and COFFEE. The nonprinting ASCII character, whose octal representation is 7, will cause the bell to ring on a teletype when this code is transmitted to the peripheral device (maybe to wake up a computer operator!). A user could replace the slash, "/", with any character not in the string except $<$ and $=$. The slash marks are simply *delimiters* to indicate to the assembler the beginning and the ending of the character string.

The MACRO-11 assembler can reserve a storage block of n words or bytes with the directives, .BLKW and .BLKB, respectively. The operand field must contain a number, called the *argument*, to indicate the desired length of the block. In the example below, 20 words and 8 bytes are desired or a total of 24 words. Don't confuse .BLKW with .WORD. The numbers 20 and 8 are not stored in any table.

$$\begin{array}{l} \text{.BLKW 20} \\ \text{.BLKB 8.} \end{array}$$

Example 3.31 Storing ASCII Characters

Directives	Memory
.WORD 16.,20,"A6	000020
.BYTE ^B1101,'L	000020
	033101
	046015

The preceding directives will store in consecutive memory locations the words and bytes as shown. In memory can be found four consecutive words containing the octal numbers. The first three octal words stored represent the decimal number, 16, the octal number, 20, and the ASCII character pair, A6. The ASCII pair is stored with 6 as the most significant binary bit of the 16-bit word. The ASCII character, A, is found in the lower eight binary bits of the ASCII word. The fourth word stored comprises the ASCII character, L, in the upper eight bits (the "'" designates ASCII) and the binary number, 1101, in the lower bits of the same 16-bit word. Packing and unpacking of ASCII characters will be covered in Chapter 4 in Section 4.3. In Example 3.31, we assumed that the most significant bit of an ASCII character is zero, thus ignoring parity.

Sometimes, certain areas of a program must regard all subsequent numbers as base-R numbers, where R represents the radix 2, 4, 8, or 10. The assembly directive .RADIX R will cause the interpretation of all subsequent numbers as decimal if R is replaced by 10. Numbers will then be interpreted as decimal unless individually designated otherwise, such as with the prefix ^B, ^O, or ^C. These symbols denote a binary, octal, or the complement of the number, respectively. One radix directive can be canceled by another radix directive. Using a radix directive eliminates the need for the suffix "." as well as the prefix ^D for decimal numbers. The MACRO-11 assembler when not otherwise directed will assume that all numbers are octal.

3.14.1   EVEN AND ODD ADDRESSES

Sometimes coding will cause the next line of code to be at an odd address when an even address is wanted, and vice versa. With the MACRO-11 assembler, the programmer can force the next address to be either even or odd. *The .EVEN directive will cause the location counter to become the next even address, if it is odd. The .ODD directive will cause the location counter to become the next odd address, if it is even.*

Directives Are Not Executable Code

Remember that directives are a means to control assembly behavior. They can be interspersed among the assembly language instructions anywhere, and they need not reside at the beginning of a program or at the end of a program. Directives are instructions to the assembler to be obeyed during assembly time. Such instructions are ignored (in fact, they no longer exist in the executable code) during run time when the program is actually executed. Can you recall any other fields in an assembler that are ignored during run time? How about the comment field?

3.15   VAX-11 MACRO FACILITIES

The VAX-11 MACRO assembler is the input source module translator to take a user's machine language program into relocatable object code for eventual execution. Do not confuse macro with MACRO, which is the name for the DEC VAX assembler. The VAX-11 MACRO is similar to the PDP-11 MACRO, but its instruction mnemonics correspond to the VAX native instructions. A native instruction is one that the assembler built for the VAX recognizes. A cross assembler is not needed to translate native instructions. VAX-11 MACRO or MACRO, from now on, has the following characteristics:

1. Relocatable object modules
2. Global symbols for linking separately assembled object programs
3. Global arithmetic, global assignment operator, global label operator, and global default declarations
4. User-defined macros
5. Program sectioning directives
6. Conditional assembly directives
7. Assembly and listing directives span (environmental)

Three types of symbols can be defined for use within the MACRO source programs:

1. Permanent symbols
2. User-defined symbols
3. Macro symbols

The permanent symbols are the VAX instruction mnemonics and MACRO directives. A user doesn't need to define these symbols. User-defined symbols are labels or symbols defined in a direct assignment directive. Macro symbols are found in macro names. MACRO maintains a symbol table for each type. The value of the symbol depends on its use in the source program. MACRO determines the value of a symbol in the operator field by first searching the macro symbol table, then the user symbol table, and finally the permanent symbol table in that order. User-defined symbols are either internal to a source program module or global (externally available). As a rule, internal symbol definitions are limited to the module in which they appear. Internal symbols, in effect, are local definitions resolved by the assembler. A global symbol can be defined in one module and referenced in another module. Unless explicitly defined as global, a user-defined symbol is internal.

3.16 SUMMARY

In this chapter, a generic machine was briefly introduced to set the stage for three popular addressing modes: direct, indirect, and immediate. The PDP-11 computer was introduced later partly because the PDP-11 does not have true indirect addressing. In the PDP-11, a register-deferred mode of addressing is offered as an alternative to the indirect mode, but, obviously, we cannot use a memory location to address the pointer of the operand. The IBM 370 also does not have an indirect addressing mode. Machines like the PDP-11 and IBM 370 may have enough compensating general-purpose registers. It is worthwhile to contrast the addressing modes of the PDP-11 with those of the generic machine, especially in the one-address instruction format. A tradeoff among the number of address modes, the number of general-purpose registers, and the number of opcodes must always be made if only a fixed and finite number of bits are to be allocated to an instruction.

Only a representative few in each of the four classes of instructions (data movement, data manipulation, program movement, and program manipulation) are described in this chapter. Those included were chosen basically to illustrate the more commonly found instructions across several machines, how they function, and what flags are affected. For many of these instructions, programmers haphazardly tend to ignore the program status word (erroneously considering its influence as a harmless side effect). This should not be done. Assembly language programmers must diligently implement code, fully aware of the state of the program status word at all times.

One additional point, which may not be obvious, is the need for an assembler. To illustrate this, examples stepping through offset calculations (for the branch address) were offered. In practice, seldom are offsets hand assembled.

Rather, an assembler is or should be provided because no one seriously programs at the machine language level.

In this chapter, you should have learned the following:

1. How machine instructions can be identified with their respective micro-operations.

2. How instructions within the four classes listed below behave.
   a. Data movement
   b. Data manipulation
   c. Program movement
   d. Program manipulation

3. How some addressing modes function in the programming model.
   a. Register (direct)
   b. Register-deferred (indirect)
   c. Absolute
   d. Immediate

4. How offsets are used with a program counter to branch to locations displaced from the current PC.

5. How signed and unsigned conditional branches operate.

The PDP-11 computer is introduced briefly. Its characteristics are representative of stored-program computers in general. The next chapter presents the remaining properties of the PDP-11 family.

3.17   KEY WORDS

absolute address

address mode field

direct address

effective address

encoding

flags (N, Z, V, C)

immediate address

indirect address

instruction format

instruction mnemonics

label

machine language programming

offset

overflow

pointer

processor status word

register address mode

register-deferred mode

undefined label

3.18   SUGGESTED READING

Eckhouse, Richard H., Jr., and Morris, L. Robert. *Minicomputer Systems*, 2nd Ed. Englewood Cliffs, N.J.: Prentice-Hall, 1979.
> Intimate details of the PDP-11 family of computers are covered along with advanced programming concepts (in later chapters). Although not an introductory text for machine language programming, the depth of coverage provides us with a clear understanding of machine instruction principles. The entire book is devoted to the PDP-11 family of computers. Useful examples on programming techniques and structure are found in many chapters.

Flores, Ivan. *Computer Organization.* Englewood Cliffs, N.J.: Prentice-Hall, 1969.
> Details of the IBM 360 machine organization and instructions are covered in Chapter Nine. This is an advanced text with much obscure notation. More recent texts cover the IBM 360, 370, and 3300/4300 series with more clarity (e.g., see Struble).

Gear,C. William. *Computer Organization and Programming*, 3rd ed. New York: McGraw-Hill, 1980.
> Much coverage of the hardware organization of the IBM 370, PDP-11, Cyber 170, and Intel 8080 can be found in Chapters Two and Three. The instruction formats of each machine are briefly covered on pages 30-40, 41-42, 43-44, and 45-46, respectively. More detailed explanations are found on later pages of Chapter Two. Chapter Four on programming techniques is especially strong.

Gill, Arthur. *Machine and Assembly Language Programming of the PDP-11*. Englewood Cliffs, N.J.: Prentice-Hall, 1978.
> Further coverage of signed and unsigned conditional branch tests can be found on pages 91-97. Useful addressing mode examples abound in the first forty pages. The first five chapters provide the reader with foundational material to write simple programs. Later chapters proceed through greater operational details of the PDP-11.

Kapps, Charles, and Stafford, Robert L. *Assembly Language for the PDP-11*. Boston: Prindle, Weber & Schmidt, 1981.
> This book focuses entirely on assembly language programming for the PDP-11 and is intended as a self-study guide. It provides readers with the fundamental principles of assembly language programming on a minicomputer. Looping, conditional branching, and multiple-precision arithmetic examples are found on pages 88, 89-94, 98-101, 125-127, and 137-142.

Katzan, Harry, Jr. *Computer Organization and the System/370.* New York: Van Nostrand Reinhold, 1971.
> The entire text is devoted to the IBM 370 hardware and instruction set. Coverage is conceptually comprehensive, although advanced. No machine language programming examples are offered.

Mano, M. Morris. *Computer System Architecture*, 2nd ed. Englewood Cliffs, N.J.: Prentice-Hall, 1982.

> The basics of computer organization, developed by supporting examples of micro-operations in Chapter Five, help us to understand machine language instructions. This chapter makes heavy use of control statements to enable us to more fully understand the hardware in the control unit. Instruction formats with examples for the IBM 370 and PDP-11 are found in Chapter Seven.

Soucek, Branko. *Minicomputers in Data Processing and Simulation*. New York: Wiley-Interscience, 1972.

> Chapter Three covers basic computer instructions of the PDP-8 minicomputer. The PDP-8 architecture is discussed in Chapter Six, along with the Varian 620, HP 2100 minicomputer, and the PDP-11. Coverage is basic and easily readable. The general intent of this book is to provide a basic working knowledge of minicomputers for the design and use of laboratory digital systems.

Struble, George W. *Assembler Language Programming: The IBM System/360 and 370*. Reading, Mass.: Addison-Wesley, 1975.

> This text has a considerable number of examples to help us program the IBM 360 and 370 at the machine language level. As a companion text to Katzan, *Computer Organization and the System/370*, this book has programming coverage that balances the extensive hardware organization of Katzan.

3.19   EXERCISES

3.1   What is the main purpose of all machine languages?

3.2   How is a machine language program generated?

3.3   What is the input and output of an assembler called?

3.4   What features of machine language programming are unattractive to humans?

3.5   What features of assembly language programming are attractive to humans?

3.6   What features of assembly language programming are unattractive to humans?

3.7   What external factors govern the selection of an instruction set? What internal factors?

3.8   Characterize the kinds of instructions most likely to be used in the following:

   a. Scientific applications

b. Word processing

c. Personal computers

d. University computer center

e. Chemical processing plant

f. Automobile assembly line

3.9 Define the following terms:

a. Field

b. Format

c. Machine instruction

d. Encoding

e. Packing

3.10 What two basic tasks must every machine instruction perform?

3.11 What criteria are used to select instruction sets?

3.12 A computer has been designed to accommodate all instructions in one memory word. The memory width is 16 bits, and N_o and N_a represent the number of opcode and address bits, respectively. Using the following table, determine the maximum allowable number of opcodes and operand addresses for each case:

N_o	N_a
16	0
8	8
4	12
2	14
0	16

3.13 A computer primary memory organization is needed with a constant bit capacity. If two design teams exist, one team promoting an 8-bit byte as the memory width and another team a 32-bit word as the memory width, what is the bit capacity of this memory? Assume that the primary memory utilizes $1K \times 8$-bit RAMs and no more than 64 RAMs are allowed.

3.14 For Exercise 3.13, explain the advantages and disadvantages of each choice. (For example, if a character is 8 bits long, the basic machine operation of comparing two characters is made easier by an 8-bit wide memory.)

3.15   Describe the advantages and disadvantages of zero-address, one-address, two-address, and three-address machines.

3.16   A 370 memory is 16 bits wide. Eight IBM instructions are found within a certain segment of memory: two SS, one RS, one SI, and four RR formatted instructions, in that order. How much memory space is required for this segment?

3.17   There are 13 different instruction formats in the PDP-11. Describe them. (Three are already depicted in Figure 3.6.)

3.18   Why would unused opcodes be useful to a manufacturer?

3.19   Computer manufacturer XYZ has taken numerous samplings of programs found in his marketplace. On the average, a "typical" program contains operations involving registers and memory locations on an equal basis when a machine with 16 registers is used. However, a machine with only four registers causes the mix of register and memory operations to change drastically. Here, only 10% of the activity is register related. In order to maintain throughput, an architect has the option to select a zero-address, one-address, or two-address machine. Choose a machine that best meets the throughput criterion. Explain your choice carefully.

3.20   Explain why the immediate addressing mode cannot specify a destination in a computer.

3.21   For the general computer described in this chapter, generate a sequence of micro-operations to perform the following. Show only clock pulses in the control statements.

   a. Indirect read from memory into R2

   b. Indirect write into memory from R2

   c. Immediate mode of addressing with a memory location into R2

3.22   True/False: In a subtraction operation with 2's complement numbers, the C flag in the computer of this chapter is cleared when no carry from the MSB occurs.

3.23   True/False: In a subtraction operation with 2's complement numbers, when overflow occurs, the V flag in the computer described in this chapter will be set to one if the operands are of opposite signs and the sign of the result is the same as that of the number subtracted.

3.24 How are the N, Z, V, and C flags affected in the PDP-11 computer for the following arithmetic operations? Identify the number system you have chosen in each case.

a.	14	b.	14	c.	0	d.	+1
	$\underline{-2}$		$\underline{-16}$		$\underline{-1}$		$\underline{-1}$

e.	32,768	f.	16,384	g.	+1
	$\underline{-65,536}$		$\underline{+32,768}$		$\underline{-(-1)}$

3.25 Show by example that the V flag is set by the expression N (XOR) C in the ASL instruction.

3.26 Identify a corresponding assembly language instruction(s) for the following FORTRAN statements:

FORTRAN	Assembly
K = 4	MOV #4,R1 for example.

a.	K = K+1
b.	K = K−1
c.	J = J−K
d.	GO TO 6
e.	STOP
f.	J = J/2
g.	J = 2(J)
h.	IF(M.NE.0) GO TO 20

3.27 What are the machine language instructions (octal) for the following?

	Program Location	Mnemonic
a.	600	MOV #177562,R5
b.	400	MOV @#177562,R5
c.	000	NEG R1
d.	010	SEC
e.	670	ROR R0
f.	020	MOV (R2),(R2)
g.	300	MOV @#130,R0
h.	200	CMP R0,#132

3.28 What is the PDP-11 assembly language instruction for the following?

	Program Location	Opcode
a.	602	012712
	604	177777
b.	040	012701
	042	176000
c.	077	042700
	100	177700
d.	000	005013
e.	002	010302
f.	002	062716
	004	000005
g.	034	005537
	036	000014
h.	477	161513
i.	500	020407
j.	000	005727
	002	000042
k.	004	006227
	006	000016
l.	404	006237
	406	000016
m.	000	005600
n.	000	000000

3.29 Find the octal opcode for each instruction in Example 3.22 in the subsection on Looping. Note that each line of code is sequentially listed in program memory. Let R1 contain L and let R2 contain K.

3.30 Write a program to swap two registers without using a third register.

3.31 Write a program to swap the contents of two memory locations.

3.32 Assemblers commonly employ reserved symbols such as "., $, :, =, %, #," etc. Suppose that these symbols are not reserved. What does this imply?

3.33 Storage space can be reserved by several means. Identify and explain the purpose of each method. Which methods lead to clear programming? Are there any that should be discouraged?

3.34 Describe the meaning of the period in each example below.

    a. .TITLE   d. CMP R6,#.

    b. MOV #.,R1   e. TABLE: .WORD   4.,6,18.,0

    c. .=300+LC

3.35 For Example 3.31, generate the octal numbers stored in memory if even parity is assumed.

Chapter 4

THE PDP-11 AND VAX

Counting in octal is just like counting in decimal if you don't use your thumbs.

—Tom Lehrer

Counting in binary is just like counting in decimal if you are all thumbs.

—Glaser and Way

4.1 CHAPTER OBJECTIVES

In this chapter, the architecture of the PDP-11 family of computers is presented. Among the myriad choices ranging from the large Cyber 205 and CRAY mainframes to the smallest microcomputer, why should the study of this DEC computer family be made? First, its instruction set and organization are typical of most members of this family and of many computers today, although the octal notation is awkward in the light of the more common hexadecimal notation. (However, not all of the instructions in this chapter are available on every PDP-11, partly because the size of the instruction set depends very much on the available hardware.) Second, the instruction sets of many microprocessors bear a strong resemblance to that of the PDP-11 machines. Third, detailed study of one member of a computer family often facilitates the understanding of all members of that family. This is so partly because computer manufacturers would rather capture new technology with the same instruction set than make an entirely new machine for compatibility (a marketing play). Many computer manufacturers tend to produce a family of machines, from large-scale mainframes to single chip microprocessors for just this reason.

One objective of this chapter is to further increase one's understanding of assembly language instructions and addressing modes. These two concepts linked together directly expose the programming power and flexibility of a computer, regardless of whether assembly language programming or high-level language programming is executed.

175

By now, an appreciation of the hierarchical nature of a computer system should be realized. This chapter builds upon the concepts of previous chapters. For instance, a machine language instruction is implemented by one or more microinstructions. Microinstructions are implemented by internal digital hardware. Digital hardware obeys the rules of Boolean algebra, and Boolean algebra constitutes an underlying language of our computer processing tasks. Programming in the assembly language is best accomplished with full knowledge of the hierarchical nature of a computing system.

The complete set of addressing modes in the PDP-11 architecture is examined in this chapter. You will learn how each mode is efficiently applied to the several and varied data processing tasks. Simple addressing modes (e.g., direct or register) are important in short programs where speed is critical and memory space is precious. More complex addressing modes (such as the autoincrement/decrement and deferred) are vital to manipulating tables and arrays of data which are multi-dimensional. A common task is to compute the physical location of a double subscripted variable found in a two-dimensional matrix.

Floating-point number representation for the PDP-11 is introduced. Here you should comprehend the difference between integers and real numbers, and how each is handled in a computer. The PDP-11, as well as many other computers, employs a type of excess notation for the exponent and a normalization rule for the mantissa or fraction. In general, the principles applied to this notation are similar on many machines and should be mastered for at least one real machine. Because floating-point standards are now accepted, it is worthwhile to identify the capabilities of the PDP-11 (and other machines) which support such standards.

4.2   PDP-11 ARCHITECTURE

4.2.1   PROGRAMMING MODEL

The architecture of a computer is ultimately the set of resources seen by a programmer. Such resources for the assembly language programmer include the machine instruction set, general-purpose registers, and certain status words found in the programming model. In the programming model shown in Figure 4.1 can be found eight general-purpose registers labeled R0 through R7 organized as 16-bit words in the PDP-11. Registers R6 and R7 are not only general-purpose registers, but R6 also serves as a stack pointer (SP) and R7 serves as the machine's program counter (PC). In this capacity, these two registers have additional addressing modes. The complete set of addressing modes for R0 through R7, with the additional addressing modes for R6 and

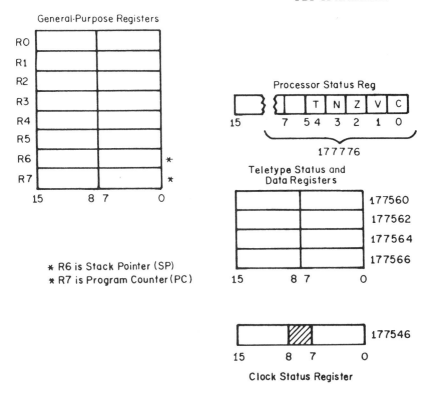

Figure 4.1   PDP-11 Programming Model

R7, will be shown later. Recall that the addressing modes of the previous chapter are available in the PDP-11.

The programming model depicts reserved memory locations for a clock and teletype. A minimal PDP-11 configuration would include such peripherals with the locations in memory as indicated reserved for these devices. Notice also that the processor status register is a memory location (177776). To examine the processor status register, a programmer addresses this location to observe the contents of that register. There are processor status register instructions to manipulate those flags, two of which have already been seen in the previous chapter.

4.2.2   PROGRAM STATUS REGISTER (PSR)

The programming model also depicts a processor status register. The PDP-11 status register is 16 bits with bits 0 through 4 assigned to the carry (C), overflow (V), zero (Z), negative (N), and trap (T) flag functions, respectively. The contents of the status register is called the program status word (PSW). For convenience, their functions are indicated in Table 4.1 and an explanation of addition and subtraction effects on these bits follows.

Table 4.1   Processor Status Register (PSR) Flags

	Addition	Subtraction
C =	1 if carry from MSB. 0 otherwise.	1 if no carry from MSB. 0 otherwise.

V =	1 if operands of same
	   sign and sum is of
	   opposite sign.
	0 otherwise.
		1 if operands are of
		   opposite signs and
		   difference is of
		   same sign as number
		   subtracted.
		0 otherwise.

Z =	1 if result is 0 (000000 octal). 0 otherwise.	same.

N =	1 if result is negative
	   (sign bit or bit 15
	   is 1).
	0 if result is positive
	   or zero.
		1 if result is negative
		   (sign bit or bit 15
		   is 1).
		0 if result is positive
		   or zero.

T =	1 if trap. 0 if no trap.	not a function of arithmetic operations.

C, V, N, Z, and T describe bits 0 through 4 of the program status register. Bit 4 is used in traps (special program flow situations to be described later). Bits 5 through 7 are used for masks for interrupt priority scheduling, a concept we will study later. Bits 8 through 15 are very useful for very high rate data transfer operations that might occur with an interrupt service routine. For this chapter, the reader need only be concerned with the five status flags.

4.2.3   ADDITION/SUBTRACTION EFFECTS ON THE PSW

In some computers, including the PDP-11, the effects of certain instructions on the PSR flags are not always obvious. For example, in the PDP-11, the subtraction instruction (SUB) and its counterpart, the compare instruction (CMP), reverse the source and destination operands for the subtrahend as follows. The number subtracted is the *source* operand in the SUB instruction, while the number subtracted is the *destination* operand in the CMP instruction. This reversal policy has significant effects on the machine's rule for setting the V flag in subtraction, and it is instructive to point out that the following apply to the flags in the processor status register.

1. In addition operations, if both operands are positive, C is always cleared, and the sum is incorrect only if the sign of the sum is negative (N=1).

2. In addition operations, when both operands are negative, C is set, and the sum is incorrect only if the sum is positive (V=1).

3. In addition operations, if the operands are of opposite signs, overflow is not possible (V is cleared), but C can be either 0 or 1.

Some Programming Hints

The PSR flags are helpful to quickly determine the status of the CPU results. To use the flags of the processor status register correctly, the programmer must observe certain rules. Violation of these rules tends to cause considerable programming grief. *First, numbers should be treated consistently.* Do not assume a number is signed in one area of a program and unsigned elsewhere. This inconsistency confuses a later user of the code. *Second, addresses should be treated as unsigned numbers, never as signed numbers.* Manipulating addresses for programming's sake assumes that any processor status flags set or cleared by address instructions which compute addresses observe unsigned numbers. *Third, conditional branch instructions, which monitor or test the processor status flags, depend very much on whether signed or unsigned conditional branches are being executed.* (Conditional branch instructions will be revisited with much greater detail shortly.) Since the PDP-11 addresses are unsigned 16-bit binary numbers, address comparison and branching (if desired) are possible using CMP and unsigned branches. □

The following examples in Table 4.2 illustrate how the flags in a PSR are affected. Two's complement arithmetic is assumed and the flags are affected as in Table 4.1. In case one, a small negative number (−2 in base 10) is added to or subtracted from a small positive number (+1 in base 10). The result from addition is −1. From subtraction, it is +1. Only the negative flag is set by the addition operation. In cases two and three, the same operands are used. However, the subtrahend becomes the minuend and vice versa in case three. 100001 is a very large negative number. 077776 is a very large positive number. Carefully observe that the overflow flag is not set in any addition operation of Table 4.2. *Adding unlike signed numbers will never cause an overflow.*

Table 4.2   Arithmetic Effects on the PSR

Case	Operands	(Octal)	Addition (A+B)				Subtraction (A−B)			
	A	B	N	Z	V	C	N	Z	V	C
1	000001	177776	1	0	0	0	0	0	0	1
2	100001	077777	0	1	0	1	0	0	1	0
3	077777	100001	0	1	0	1	1	0	1	1

In Example 4.1, we will determine the interval or distance between two addresses. Such information is often needed by a loader to determine where in memory enough space is available to load a program.

Example 4.1 Using Addresses as Operands.   A program in disk space is about to be moved into main memory. Prior to doing so, the system software must determine whether sufficient memory is available. Writing into certain memory spaces may create havoc. For reasons to be discussed later, addresses can and should be considered as unsigned numbers only. For instance, a machine with 65,536 memory locations using a 16-bit address could assign location 000000 (octal) to the top of memory space and 177777 (octal) to the bottom.

Suppose that available memory space is determined by operands A and B in Table 4.2. That is, operands A and B are two addresses which bound the top and bottom of some available space. If the program to be moved requires 40 locations, only the space bounded by the addresses in case one is large enough (in fact, it is very large). Only two free locations are available in cases two and three!

4.3   MEMORY MAP

Just as certain memory locations are reserved for the clock and teletype in a minimal PDP-11 system, other memory locations are reserved for additional peripheral devices, as well as the system software. The memory map of the PDP-11 family in Figure 4.2 assumes that the memory space spans the 16-bit address space (65,536 base 10 bytes). Not all machines have 65,536 base 10

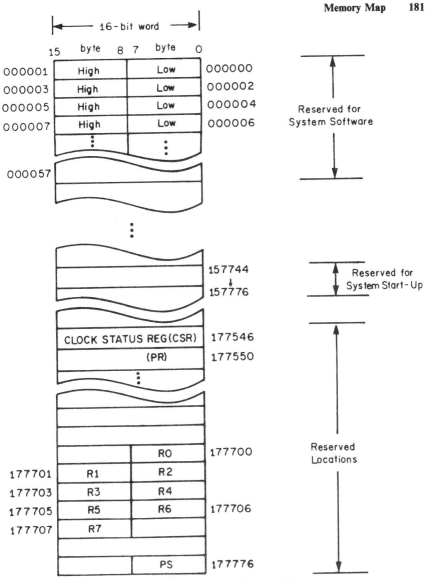

Figure 4.2   PDP-11 Memory Map

bytes of storage. In those installations, a reduced memory map is used. Such details need not concern the reader for now. Regardless of the size of memory, the length of a byte and a word are standard across the family. Words are sixteen bits with bits 0 through 7 assigned to the low-order 8-bit byte, and bits 8 through 15 assigned to the high-order byte, if bytes are being used. The low byte of a 2-byte word will always be found in even addresses, and the high byte or most significant byte will be found in the odd addresses of the same word. *All words are addressed only on even address boundaries.* Since instructions are at least one word, instructions must be found in even addresses.

An address is an unsigned (assumed positive) 16-bit binary number. For brevity, an address can be indicated by its octal equivalent, which is then a six-digit quantity. The most significant digit can only take on the value 0 or 1. Not all addresses are available to an end-user. Reserved locations are needed by the operating system or system software. Locations reserved for system software at least include locations 000000 through 000057. These locations are reserved for trap vectors. A *trap vector* is a location in memory to which a program will jump to acquire information to handle special situations. For example, if power failed in the computer, it would be helpful to save the contents of the general-purpose registers and machine status. Reserved locations 000024 through 000027 are used for the power fail trap vector. Reserved locations are used for more than just trap vectors. Further discussion on trap vectors is deferred to a later chapter.

Locations 000040 through 000057 also are used for the system software. In a full memory system, locations 157744 through 157776 are reserved for the system start-up. Here a bootstrap loader has been stored by the manufacturer. This program initializes the active registers and sets the proper status of the machine when power is first applied (the machine is "booted up"). Most of the remaining memory space is available to the end-user. However, if one is operating with system software, such as a disk operating system (DOS) or executive package, additional memory space is utilized by this software. Never assume that all of the memory locations not assigned in the memory map are available to the general user. Available memory is determined by both the memory map and the current system software package in a computer. Further details may be found in the documentation of the installed computer system.

If the specific PDP-11 computer does not contain the full 65,536 memory locations, the memory map is modified to incorporate reserved space at different locations. Such details belong to the study of system design. The PDP-11 memory always consists of an address space in multiples of 4K words. A PDP-11 memory of 8K words has 8192 locations or 16,384 bytes. Larger memories are possible; however, the exact size varies from one installation to another. Word addresses are always even. Byte addresses can be even or odd. The upper 4K words in any PDP-11 memory system are reserved for special input/output operations. Devices which transmit or receive information from a PDP-11 use these memory locations, some of which have already been seen for a teletype in our programming model of the previous section.

4.4 DATA REPRESENTATION

In the binary computer, data can be represented as fixed-point numbers (integers), floating-point numbers, and alphanumeric characters, as in Figure 4.3. Each of these data representations has supporting instructions to handle addition, subtraction, multiplication, division (if special hardware is available), complementing, and shifting; but all of the arithmetic instructions treat

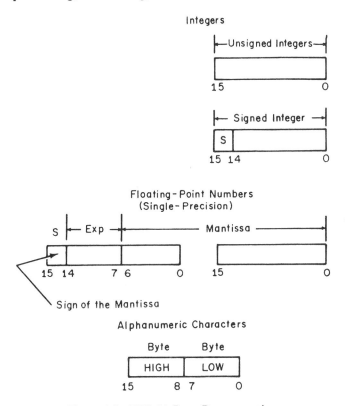

Figure 4.3 PDP-11 Data Representations

words (sixteen bits) as 2's complement (signed) numbers. Note that because the most significant bit of a 2's complement number always indicates the sign, this bit can be conveniently used for conditional branch tests. Recall that the N flag in the PSR copies the MSB for many (but not all) instructions.

Instructions and conditional branch tests also exist to treat integers as unsigned quantities.

One of the most important unsigned operands is an address. Address manipulation instructions, then, assume an unsigned number representation. The reader should realize that the PDP-11 is basically a 2's complement machine. Hence, performing 1's complement arithmetic is not as simple as 2's complement arithmetic. Also, 1's complement notation introduces a second representation for zero. This undesirable aspect motivates many computer (including those of the PDP family) designers to implement a 2's complement hardware. The sign/magnitude form, although available as a representation, is rejected in favor of the complement notation. Sign/magnitude adders are much more complex logic circuits and are seldom implemented directly in hardware.

4.4.1   FIXED-POINT NUMBERS (INTEGERS)

In the PDP-11 family, integers can be represented as *bytes*, *words*, or *longwords*. The size, type, and range are indicated in Table 4.3. Bytes are organized in the memory as two bytes per word. The lower byte or least significant byte is always found on an even address. The most significant byte is always found on an odd address. Bytes range, in decimal, from −128 to +127 as signed numbers. As unsigned numbers, bytes range from 0 to 255. The range of words and longwords is indicated in the table. Note that the largest positive number represented as a longword is $2^{31}-1$ (approximately ten decimal digits). Longwords may be generated from the product of word multiplication and from the dividend in division. Not every PDP-11 has hardware to execute multiplication and division as machine instructions. When hardware is not available, multiplication and division must be done with software algorithms, such as repeated additions or successive subtractions, respectively.

Table 4.3   Integer Representation in the PDP-11

Type	Size	Decimal Range	
		Signed	Unsigned
Byte	8 bits	−128 to +127	0 to 255
Word	16 bits	−32768 to +32767	0 to 65535
Longword	32 bits	-2^{31} to $2^{31}-1$	0 to $2^{32}-1$

Fixed-point numbers assume that the machine point is found in the same bit position for every number represented as a fixed-point number. When considered as an integer, the machine point is to the right of the least significant bit

(bit 0). Fixed-point numbers are frequently found in business applications. Consider the following example. Although money is dollars and cents (hundredths of a dollar), it is convenient, in such programming languages like COBOL, to consider $42.57 as the integer 4257. Thousandths of a dollar are not necessary. As with any fixed-point number system, the underlying assumption is that a least number exists. In the American dollar monetary system of representation, it is the penny. All numbers are then scaled to become integers (hence, eliminating any needs for a fraction). For example, a dollar is 100 pennies.

For many numbers in this text, an octal representation is assumed, only for the sake of brevity. This will always occur when our unsigned integers are representing addresses. The range of integers, for signed as well as unsigned numbers as words in the PDP-11, was not chosen casually. Registers in the PDP-11 family are sixteen bits long. Unfortunately, integers of finite size (sixteen bits) have a fixed upper bound on the size of the numbers to be represented. For many applications, sixteen bits used in a fixed-point representation does not provide a sufficient *range*. In those cases, a floating-point data representation is employed.

4.4.2 FLOATING-POINT NUMBERS

Although quite convenient to program with, integers represented in a computer lack the dynamic range necessary for many scientific applications. The *dynamic range* of the numbers used in a computational process is a measure of the distance from the lowest possible number expected in a machine to the greatest possible number. Mathematical computations in astronomy and physics require numbers within extreme ranges of the real number system. 16-bit integers fail miserably to reach either end. Such integers lack the range of magnitudes necessary in these computations, even though the data may be occasionally represented with sufficient precision. To overcome these difficulties, a floating-point number representation is used. The PDP-11 floating-point number representation, shown in Figure 4.3, employs two 16-bit words. These two words are partitioned into a *sign* bit field (bit 15 of the upper word), an *exponent* field (bit 14 through bit 7 of the upper word), and a *mantissa* field consisting of the concatenation of bits 6 through 0 (of the upper word) and bits 15 through 0 (of the lower word). The software designers in the PDP family assumed that the mantissa represents a fraction; hence, some literature calls these bits the fractional part of a floating-point number. The floating-point representation of Figure 4.3 is a single-precision floating-point representation. The numbers are actually stored in two contiguous 16-bit words in memory.

Adding and subtracting floating-point numbers necessarily requires the computer to "align" the exponents, just as a person might do manually. Example 4.2 illustrates why this is necessary. Addition and subtraction can then be performed correctly. First, the exponents must be adjusted to be equal. Either the smallest exponent can be increased to equal the largest exponent or the largest exponent can be reduced to equal the smallest exponent. In both cases, the mantissa of the adjusted exponent must also be adjusted. Increasing the exponent value necessarily decreases the mantissa value (moves the decimal point to the left) in order to maintain a constant magnitude for the floating-point data. Otherwise, if exponents are not aligned, the mantissa operations would be incorrect. Obviously, in Example 4.2, 55.85 is not equal to 192.83*10.

Example 4.2   Floating-Point Number Addition

$$15.22*10**2 = 152.20*10$$
$$+40.63*10**1 = +40.63*10$$
$$\overline{}$$
$$55.85* \ ? = 192.83*10$$
$$\text{WRONG!} \qquad \text{RIGHT!}$$

Exponent scaling is performed because the actual addition and subtraction operations in the computer are performed in fixed-point arithmetic. Floating-point numbers in many computers are also assumed to be *normalized*. The normalized form of a floating-point number assumes that the first bit of the fraction is a one. Unnormalized numbers contain a zero in this first bit. Normalized numbers are desired for two reasons. First, they allow the largest possible number of bits to be used to represent the actual fraction (that is, they maintain maximum precision). Second, the normalized form of representation greatly simplifies the process of performing floating-point operations.

As with most binary computers, the PDP-11 expresses floating-point numbers internally in binary rather than in decimal numbers. Because of this, the decimal number in a binary computer is expressed with a fraction as a binary number (23 bits) and an exponent which is a power of 2 instead of a power of 10. Within the PDP-11, the exponent stored in the first word is in *excess* 128_{10} notation. Excess notation efficiently represents signed numbers without explicitly using a sign bit. The PDP-11 floating-point representation assigns the sign bit of the 32-bit word to the fraction (and *not* to the exponent). The sign bit of the exponent is not explicit, but rather is interpreted within the excess 128 notation. The power of the exponent range in the PDP-11 ranges from −128 to +127, and is approximately equivalent to 10 raised to the power

−38 to +38, respectively. As shown in Table 4.4, the smallest positive number in the exponent (+1) is represented in binary by 10000001.

Table 4.4 Range of Stored Exponents in the PDP-11 with Single-Precision

Relative Value of True Number	True Decimal Exponent	Stored Binary in Excess Notation	Stored Octal Representation
largest positive	+127	11111111	377
	+2	10000010	202
smallest positive	+1	10000001	201
	0	10000000	200
least negative	−1	01111111	177
	−2	01111110	176
smallest (zero)	−128	00000000	000

To determine the true exponent, subtract the excess, which is worth 128, from the exponent field. When 10000000 is subtracted from 10000001, 00000001 is obtained which represents 2**1. Notice that the exponent field in this representation always contains integers. Any stored exponent less than 10000000 represents a negative exponent.

Mathematically, a floating-point number, X, has the form
$$X = (2**K)*F$$
where K is an integer and F is a fraction. For any nonvanishing number, K and F will be uniquely determined if we enforce the rule that
$$1/2 < F < 1$$
If F adheres to these limits, we say that the fraction is normalized. Again, in a mathematical sense, if $X=0$, then F must be assigned the value zero, but K may be indeterminate. Within the PDP-11 computer representation, the *stored exponent* is
$$K + 200_8$$
In order to squeeze even more precision out of the floating-point representation, the PDP-11 designers indirectly provide users with 24 bits for the fraction part, even though the stored fraction field has 23 bits. This is possible because in normalized floating-point representation, the leading digit of the fraction is always a "one." Consequently, there is no need to store this "one" in the fraction field. This most significant bit, called the *hidden bit*, is ignored and left out. However, one slight problem occurs when we assume that this bit is always one, yet is "hidden" from the machine. Computer hardware is incapable of recognizing such assumptions. The major effect of the hidden "one" assumption eliminates the precise representation of the floating-point number, zero. A zero cannot be represented precisely in a computer with this

notation. Hence, the computer architects purposely assign -128 to the exponent in order to represent the zero. No matter what number exists in the fraction field, if the exponent contains 00000000, this is taken to mean the number zero. In practice, this is called a "dirty zero" in contrast to a "clean zero" which has all zeroes in the stored fraction *and* stored exponent. Some numbers for the floating-point representation in the PDP-11 are found in Example 4.3.

Example 4.3   Some Stored Floating-Point Numbers

True Decimal Number	32-Bit Binary Stored Number		
	Sign	Exponent	Fraction
$1/2 * 2**127$	0	11111111	00000000000000000000000
$35/64*2**7$	0	10000111	00011000000000000000000
$15/32*2**1$	0	10000000	11100000000000000000000
$+1 = 2**0$	0	10000001	00000000000000000000000
$35/64*2**0$	0	10000000	00011000000000000000000
$+1/2 = 2**-1$	0	10000000	00000000000000000000000
0	0	00000000	00000000000000000000000
$-1/8 = -(2**-3)$	1	01111110	00000000000000000000000
$-1/4 = -(2**-2)$	1	01111111	00000000000000000000000
$-1/2 = -(2**-1)$	1	10000000	00000000000000000000000
$-(35/64*2**0)$	1	10000000	00011000000000000000000
$-1 = -(2**0)$	1	10000001	00000000000000000000000
$-(35/64*2**7)$	1	10000111	00011000000000000000000
$-32 = -(2**5)$	1	10000110	00000000000000000000000

Unless a multiple word is used, floating-point number representations suffer from one severe penalty. They lose precision. If in a 16-bit machine, one bit is assigned to the sign of the number, E bits are assigned to the exponent, and M bits are assigned to the fraction. If $E+M+1=6$, unless E is very small, M will not have sufficient precision for most scientific applications. For example, if $E=6$, then $M=9$. A common solution is to assign two or more words to the floating-point representation.

The procedure for obtaining the octal representation of PDP floating-point numbers in order to obtain the two words of storage is called *packing*. In Example 4.4, the number 70 (decimal) is packed into two contiguous memory locations. The first octal number is 041614 and the second octal number is all zeroes. To do so, consider the full 32-bit binary number as follows. First, adjust the exponent of the number so that a fraction less than one-half is obtained. Next, convert the lower 16 bits to their octal equivalent. This representation is then stored in the least significant digits location in memory.

Example 4.4 Packing a Floating-Point Number in the PDP-11 with Single-Precision Representation.   Consider the number
$$35/64*2**7$$
In decimal notation, this number equals
$$35/64*128 = 0.546875*128 = 70 \text{ in decimal}$$
The octal number stored in two contiguous memory locations for this floating-point number is

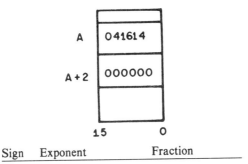

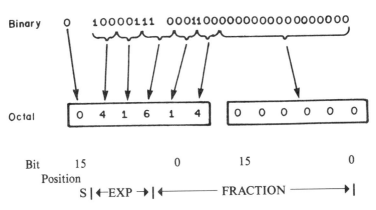

In Example 4.4, the data is all zeroes in the word found in addressed location $A+2$. The most significant digits are obtained with a combination of the remaining upper seven bits of the binary fraction and the stored exponent with the sign. The upper seven bits of the fraction generate the octal digits 14. The most significant bit of the fraction is combined with the two least significant bits of the exponent to generate the least significant octal digit of the exponent. This is 6. The remaining octal digits (041) are derived from the remaining exponent bits and the algebraic sign bit of the original number. Notice that it is almost impossible to determine the exponent and fraction from the octal representation.

To summarize, in the PDP-11 family, 32-bit single-precision floating-point numbers possess the following properties.

1. The mantissa is expressed as a normalized 24-bit positive fraction (frac) where $0.5 \leq$ frac < 1. The binary point is positioned to the left of the most significant bit. Since this bit is always a 1, it is not stored in the fraction field. This enables the remaining bits of the fraction to be stored in 23 bits. Fractions are stored in a sign magnitude representation.

2. The exponent is stored as a biased 8-bit positive integer E. That is, when 128 (10000000 in binary) is subtracted from E, this result is the power of 2 by which the mantissa is multiplied to obtain the true value of the floating-point number. The stored exponent is not the true exponent. This is called "excess -128" notation.

3. The sign of the number is positive when s (the sign bit or bit 15 of the first word) is 0, and negative when $s=1$.

Twenty-three bits assigned to the fraction allow approximately seven decimal digits of precision. If this is not sufficient, a second 32-bit word (one longword) can be appended to this fraction to yield almost sixteen decimal digits of accuracy. In that case, the user is employing a double-floating-point number representation. Not all members of the PDP family support this extended arithmetic base. Such representations depend very much on the available hardware of the installed computer system.

4.4.3   FPP ARCHITECTURE

It is important to recognize that the basic PDP-11 is not equipped to directly handle "real" numbers without optional hardware. The IBM PC without the 8087 and the TRS 80 are also examples. To employ real numbers in the floating-point representation without the optional hardware requires additional software. That software must consist of programs to independently manipulate the mantissa and the exponents. Exponent alignment is generally the first step. Normalization is commonly the last step. Addition and subtraction in software become more difficult than multiplication and division. When available, the optional hardware found in the PDP-11 extended instruction set option (EIS) and the floating-instruction set (FIS) make one's programming life much more comfortable. The FIS is optional on the PDP-11/35, 11/40, and LSI-11. A floating-point processor (FPP) is available on the PDP-11/60 and other mid-range computers. The floating-point processor is configured in Figure 4.4.

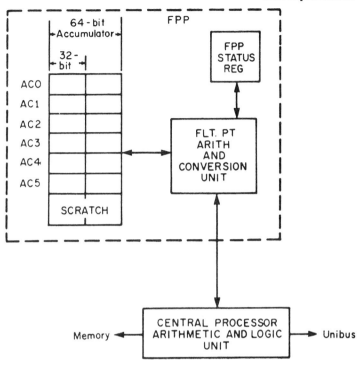

Figure 4.4 Floating-Point Processor (FPP)

The FIS consists of four instructions (FADD, FSUB, FMUL, and FDIV) which operate on single-precision floating-point formats. A second set of floating-point instructions (FP11) is available as microcode or as a hardware option to specific members of the PDP-11 family. Either set is an attempt to speed up the data processing and facilitate programming with this data representation. The FPP is a hardware or microcode implementation of the FP11 set.

The FPP contains scratch registers, a floating exception address pointer (FEA), status/error registers, six general-purpose accumulators (AC0-AC5), and a program counter. These resources are intended to perform floating-point arithmetic operations and integer to floating-point format conversion. AC0-AC3 are available to perform data transfer between general registers/memory and the FPP. All six accumulators can function as 32 bits or 64 bits.

An FPP attached to a CPU can execute an instruction in parallel with a CPU instruction. This concurrency increases throughput. Any interaction is automatic, delaying the CPU only when necessary to fetch an FPP instruction (hence, the need for a program counter in the FPP). In the following sequence, an FPP executes the first three instructions. The CPU will execute an SOB after the ADDD is fetched into the FPP. The CPU also calculates the effective address of the STCDI instruction. All instructions assume double-precision (64 bits). STCDI is a store and convert from double to integer format. It is instructive to compare this code to the code required to perform double-precision multiplication without an FPP.

```
              •
              •
              •
         LDD     (R1)+,AC2    ;ACQUIRE MULTIPLIER
ADDFP    LDD     (R1)+,AC1    ;ACQUIRE MULTIPLICAND
         MULD    AC2,AC1      ;PRODUCT NOW IN AC1
                              ;CPU EXECUTES NEXT SOB AND
                              ;CALCULATES EFFECTIVE ADDRESS
         ADDD    AC1,AC0      ;ACCUMULATE RUNNING TOTAL IN AC0
         SOB     R3,ADDFP     ;LAST PRODUCT FORMED?
         STCDI   AC0,(R4)     ;YES, CONVERT TO INTEGER AND STORE
              •
              •
              •
```

4.4.4   ALPHANUMERIC CHARACTERS

In the PDP-11, an *alphanumeric* character is represented by an 8-bit binary number which occupies one byte. Since memory is both word addressable and byte addressable, low-order bytes in memory should be found in even addresses, and high-order bytes of a 2-byte word should be found in odd addresses. A byte is eight bits; hence, the low byte would occupy bit positions 7 through 0. The character code of any computer is generally determined by the type of input/output device used for reading or printing the characters. In the PDP-11, a frequently used code is the ASCII (American Standard Code for Information Interchange) and is standard for teletypewriters (TTY). Other codes seldom used but nevertheless available for the PDP-11 include the Hollerith (punched card code) and Radix-50 or RAD50. The 7-bit ASCII and Radix-50 codes are found in the appendices.

A full 7-bit ASCII system uses 128 codes; 33 are used for control functions such as linefeed and carriage return. The remaining 95 are used for printing characters. Those 95 printable characters consist of the following:

26 Uppercase Letters

26 Lowercase Letters

10 Numerals

1 Blank Space (really,
non-printing character)

32 Punctuation Marks

The full set of 32 punctuation marks includes:

! " # $ % & ' + , - . / < > : ; = ? @ [\ ] - ^ ` { | } ~ ( ) *

Less expensive teletypes and printers use less than the 128 possible codes, and printing of 64 characters which includes the following are common.

26 Uppercase Letters

10 Numerals

1 Blank Space

27 Punctuation Marks

(the marks ` { | } ~ are not included)

The most common control characters of the full set of 33 are the following.

BEL—Rings the bell on the typewriter

BS—Backspaces the typewriter

HT—Horizontal tab

LF—Line feed, advances the paper one line

VT—Vertical tab

FF—Form feed, advances the paper to a new page

CR—Carriage return, moves the print mechanism back to the beginning of the line

ASCII is a 7-bit code in which each character is representable within a 7-bit number. However, a character in the PDP-11 is found in an 8-bit string or byte. The "free" leftmost bit of a byte in a computer representing an ASCII character can be used for a parity bit. The parity bit is used for error detection. One of two error detection schemes is frequently employed when transmitting a character from some peripheral device to the computer where noise is often encountered. An *even parity* scheme ensures that the parity bit value is designated to make the total number of bits in the byte even. For example, the capital letter "H" with even parity (ASCII code 110 in octal) is stored as 110 (octal) with even parity assumed since the number of ones in its ASCII code is already even. However, the small letter "h" has the octal code 150. When represented in the computer with even parity, the letter "h" is stored as 350 to force the number of ones to be even.

A similar procedure applies to an odd parity scheme. Error detection with an even/odd parity scheme is a simple process. If the number of ones transmitted for a character is odd (but was supposed to be even!), an erroneous transmission of some bit in that byte has occurred. The parity scheme for error detection will detect an error of one erroneous bit. It will not detect an erroneous error occurring with two bits. However, the likelihood of 2-bit errors is extremely small compared with 1-bit errors. Obviously, when ASCII characters are manipulated in the PDP-11 which have been received from peripheral devices like a teletype, a programmer must insure that the nonzero parity bit is ignored. In the other direction, transmitting an ASCII character with a parity bit to a printer has no effect on the printer. The printer will simply ignore this parity bit if it is so designed. In the PDP-11, two ASCII characters stored in memory occupy the upper and lower bytes as shown in Example 4.5 for the character string BD. Try to represent BD in a 16-bit word assuming even parity.

Example 4.5 Alphanumeric Character Packing

"_" is the 8th bit or parity bit if it exists.

4.5   SYMBOLIC INSTRUCTION FORMATS

Although instructions exist to manipulate 8-bit bytes, the PDP-11 family belongs to the class of 16-bit *general-purpose stored-program computers*. As such, the PDP-11 family contains hardware with an instruction set which deals mainly with 16-bit words. Integers are signed 16-bit numbers, and addresses are unsigned 16-bit integers. Since the address space and the primary data type are both sixteen bits, the basic design decision to utilize truly general-purpose registers in the programming model, in contrast with a single accumulator, found in many earlier computers (e.g., PDP-8), helps facilitate assembly language programming in the PDP-11. Any of the eight registers in the programming model can be used to manipulate both addresses and data.[1] This flexibility and consistency contribute to the power of any computer architecture. This flexibility is carried across to the instruction formats in the PDP-11. There are at least five instruction formats: operate, single-operand, double-operand, branch, and status register instructions.

The notation used in Tables 4.6, 4.7, and 4.8 employs the symbols whose meanings are explained in Table 4.5. Most of the instructions operate on bytes as well as words. For byte instructions, a (B) is appended to the mnemonic to indicate that byte manipulation is possible. Then, the octal code for byte manipulation instructions in the table replaces the "." with a "1" to indicate byte manipulation. When a word is manipulated, the (B) is deleted from the mnemonic and the "." is replaced with a "0" in the octal designation. The notation is very similar to RTL (but not equivalent).

Table 4.5   PDP-11 Symbolic Notation

	For Address Codes
•	Word/Byte Bit; set for byte instruction, cleared for word instruction
SS	Source Field (Mode, Register)
DD	Destination Field (Mode, Register)
XX	Offset (8-bit)
Rn	General-Purpose Register n
PSR	Processor Status Register
SP	Stack Pointer

---

[1]However, R6 and R7 are recognized by the hardware as the stack pointer and program counter, respectively. System software uses these registers often when it is least expected.

For Operations	
( )	Contents Of
'	Not
∧	And
∀	Or
∀	Exclusive-OR
−(SP) ←	"Is pushed onto the processor stack"
← (SP)+	"The contents of the top of the processor stack is popped and becomes"

For Condition Codes	
*	Set Conditionally
-	Not Affected
0	Cleared
1	Set

4.5.1   OPERATE INSTRUCTIONS

The operate instruction format, seen in Figure 4.5, consists entirely of an opcode utilizing bits 0 through 15. All instructions in the operate group are one word long (no longer). No field of the opcode is designated for a source or a destination. As is typical of the other computer operation formats, none is needed. Operate instructions belong to the class of program manipulation instructions. Program manipulation instructions can stop the computer, place it in a wait state, or return it to a reset state. Other functions of the operate instructions, such as RTI, RTT, IOT, and BPT, control program flow, a topic to be studied in a later chapter. As such, the operate instructions do not directly affect data, but rather alter the state of the machine which is directly influenced by a program under execution.

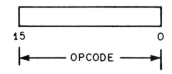

Figure 4.5   Operate Instruction Format

Table 4.6   Operate Instructions

Mnemonic	Instruction Operation	Opcode	Condition Codes NZVC
HALT	HALT Processor stops; (R0) and the HALT address in lights on operator panel	000000	no effect
WAIT	WAIT Processor releases bus, waits for interrupt	000001	no effect
RTI	ReTurn from Interrupt (PC) ← (SP)+ (PSR) ← (SP)+, T-bit trap enabled	000002	loaded from (SP)
RTT	ReTurn from Trap (PC) ← (SP)+ (PSR) ← (SP)+, T-bit trap disabled for one instruction	000006	loaded from (SP)
IOT	Input/Output Trap −(SP) ← (PSR) −(SP) ← (PC) (PC) ← (20) (PSR) ← (22)	000004	loaded from (22)
RESET	RESET An INIT pulse is issued by the CPU	000005	no effect
EMT	EMulator Trap −(SP) ← (PSR) −(SP) ← (PC) (PC) ← (30) (PSR) ← (32)	104000-104377	loaded from (32)
TRAP	TRAP −(SP) ← (PSR) −(SP) ← (PC) (PC) ← (34) (PSR) ← (36)	104400-104777	loaded from (36)
BPT	Break Point Trap −(SP) ← (PSR) −(SP) ← (PC) (PC) ← (14) (PSR) ← (16)	000003	loaded from (16)

Mnemonic	Instruction Operation	Opcode	Condition Codes NZVC
NOP	No OPeration Used to delete unwanted instructions during debugging	000260	no effect

4.5.2 SINGLE-OPERAND INSTRUCTIONS

Many data processing tasks in a computer require the programmer to manipulate only a single operand. The instruction format for the first word of all single-operand instructions is found in Figure 4.6. Single-operand instructions may occupy more than one word in program memory. Bits 15 through 6 specify the opcode of these instructions. Bits 5 through 3 specify the addressing mode with bit 3 assigned to the direct (if 0) mode of addressing or deferred (if equivalent to the indirect mode) mode of addressing. Bits 2 through 0 specify one of eight general-purpose registers in the programming model. If register R0 is desired, bits 2 through 0 become 000. Bits 0 through 5 form the 6-bit field called the *destination address field*. Single-operand instructions only specify the destination address. When a second word is required by a single-operand instruction, it may contain a 16-bit address or a data constant. A data constant follows the first word of a single-operand instruction, if we are

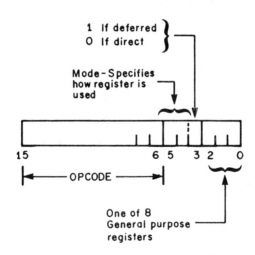

Figure 4.6 Single-Operand Instructions

executing the immediate addressing mode. In that case, bits 5 through 3 contain the octal digit 2. If a 16-bit address is to be found in the second word of a single-operand instruction, the absolute addressing mode is assumed, and bits 5 through 0 now contain the octal digit 3. Other addressing modes of the PDP-11 are described in the next section.

Table 4.7   Single-Operand Instructions

Mnemonic	Instruction Operation	Opcode	Condition Codes NZVC
CLR(B)	CLeaR (Byte) DD ← 0	.050DD^2	0100
COM(B)	COMplement (Byte) DD ← DD'	.051DD	**01
INC(B)	INCrement (Byte) DD ← DD+1	.052DD	***−
DEC(B)	DECrement (Byte) DD ← DD-1	.053DD	***−
NEG(B)	NEGate (Byte) DD ← -DD	.054DD	****
ADC(B)	ADd Carry (Byte) DD ← DD+(C)	.055DD	****
SBC(B)	SuBtract Carry (Byte) DD ← DD-(C)	.056DD	****
TST(B)	TeST (Byte) DD ← DD-0	.057DD	**00
ROR(B)	ROtate Right (Byte) Rotate right 1 place with C	.060DD	****
ROL(B)	ROtate Left (Byte) Rotate left 1 place with C	.061DD	****
ASR(B)	Arithmetic Shift Right (Byte) DD ← DD/2, result truncated (shift right with sign extension)	.062DD	****
ASL(B)	Arithmetic Shift Left (Byte) DD ← 2*DD (shift left with low-order bit zeroed)	.063DD	****
SWAB	SWAp Bytes Bytes of a word are exchanged	0003DD	**00
SXT	Sign eXTend DD ← -1*(N)	0067DD	−*0−

---

^{2}Replace "." with a zero if the operand is a WORD. Otherwise, use a one for byte length operands.

4.5.3   DOUBLE-OPERAND INSTRUCTIONS

Double-operand instructions can be found in the data manipulation class, as well as the data movement class of machine instructions. The opcode field of double-operand instructions occupies bits 15 through 12. The source address field occupies bits 11 through 6 and is subdivided into the source address mode field and the register subfield, bits 11 through 9, and 8 through 6, respectively. The destination address field occupies bits 5 through 0. Both fields are coded identically as shown for the source address field in Figure 4.7. The upper two bits (11 and 10) specify how a register is to be used. Bit 9 specifies the direct or the deferred mode. The destination field designates the location of the second operand which is also the result. For example, the instruction "SUB R0,R1" subtracts the contents of the source operand (R0) from the destination operand (R1), and places the result in R1. The contents of the source (R0) will be unchanged. Not all of the instructions in the double-operand group are found in every member of the PDP-11 family. Instructions in the double-operand group can be one, two, or three words long, because the flexible addressing of both the source and destination could require two words following the double-operand instruction. Table 4.8 lists the double-operand instructions in the PDP-11.

Table 4.8   Double-Operand Instructions

General Double-Operand Group

Mnemonic	Instruction Operation	Opcode	Condition Codes NZVC
MOV(B)	MOVe (Byte) DD ← SS	.1SSDD	**0–
CMP(B)	CoMPare (Byte) compute SS-DD, set condition codes	.2SSDD	****
BIT(B)	BIt Test (Byte) compute SS "ANDed with" DD on a bit-wise basis, set condition codes	.3SSDD	**0–
BIC(B)	BIt Clear (Byte) DD ← SS'∧DD	.4SSDD	**0–
BIS(B)	BIt Set (Byte) DD ← SSVDD	.5SSDD	**0–
ADD	ADD DD ← SS+DD	06SSDD	****
SUB	SUBtract DD ← DD-SS	16SSDD	****

Register Double-Operand Group[3]

MUL	MULtiply (R,R+1) ← (R)∗SS (R) ← high-order word of product (R+1) ← low-order word of product	070RSS	∗∗0∗
DIV	DIVide (R) ← quotient of (R,R+1)/SS (R+1) ← remainder of (R,R+1)/SS, R even Dividend high-order 16 bits in R Dividend low-order 16 bits in R+1	071RSS	∗∗∗∗
ASH	Arithmetic SHift (R) ← (R)∗2∗∗SS	072RSS	∗∗∗∗
ASHC	Arithmetic SHift Combined (R,R+1) ← (R,R+1) ∗2∗∗SS, R even	073RSS	∗∗∗∗
XOR	eXclusive-OR DD ← (R) ∀ DD	074RDD	∗∗0–

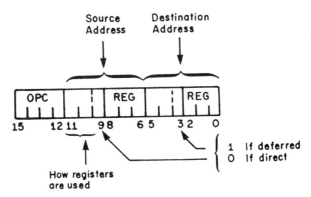

Figure 4.7 Double-Operand Instructions

---

[3]Not found in all members of PDP-11 family.

4.5.4 UNCONDITIONAL BRANCH INSTRUCTIONS

Two unconditional branch instructions exist in the PDP-11 family. They are branch (BR) and jump (JMP). Table 4.9 lists these instructions including their opcode. Both instructions belong to the program movement set of instructions. The behavior of these instructions is identical to those found in Chapter 3. BR is used for control of program movement within the range −128 to +127 program locations of the current PC. JMP is an absolute branch instruction capable of causing program movement anywhere in program memory (up to the full 16-bit address space).

Table 4.9 Unconditional Branch Instructions

Mnemonic	Instruction Operation	Opcode	Condition Codes NZVC
BR	BRanch (unconditionally) (PC) ← loc, XX means "plus 8-bit offset"	0004XX	———
JMP	JuMP (PC) ← DD	0001DD	———

4.5.5 CONDITIONAL BRANCH INSTRUCTIONS

Conditional branch instructions are one-word instructions belonging to the program manipulation class, with the format shown in Figure 4.8. The format of these instructions consists of two fields: the opcode field in bits 15 through 8, and the offset field in bits 7 through 0. Hence, the offset in the low byte contains an 8-bit signed word offset (seven bits plus sign). This offset is used to specify the branch target address or effective address, relative to the PC. Branch instructions can cause the program execution to branch backward up to 128 words. Branch instructions can cause forward branches up to 127 words (towards memory location 1777...). Manual calculation of the correct value to place in the offset is rather awkward; however, this task is aided greatly by the use of an assembler. By execution time, the CPU recognizes the effective address as follows:

1. Extend the sign of the offset (bit 7) through bits 8 through 15.
2. Perform an arithmetic shift left operation (effectively multiplying the signed offset by 2).
3. Add this result to the current value of the PC to form the final branch address.

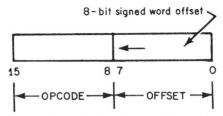

Figure 4.8 Conditional Branch Instructions

Since the CPU performs these steps to calculate the effective address during program execution, we must perform the reverse sequence of steps to obtain the correct offset. Don't forget that the PC is pointing to the word following the branch instruction. We compute the offset with the following formula.

OFFSET = (EA - PC - 2)/2 (truncated to 8 bits)

where EA is the effective address (of the branch instruction in program memory). Example 4.6 illustrates the procedure.

Example 4.6 Computing the Offset for the Branch Instructions

Program Location	Opcode		Instruction
000120	010001	BACK	MOV R0,R1
000176	000750		BR BACK

We calculate the offset as follows:

effective address	000120
current address	000176
difference (120-200)	177722
less 2 locations	177720
divide by 2	177750
truncate to 8 bits	350

The branch instruction BR BACK becomes

000400 + 350 = 000750

where 000400 is the opcode for BR before the offset is included (see Table 4.9). Notice that when 177750 is truncated to eight bits, the result is 350 and not 750! Truncating a six octal digit word to eight bits is not simply a matter of deleting the upper three octal digits. Furthermore, the difference step uses 200 and not 176. Recall that the PC is pointing to the location following the BR instruction.

Table 4.10   Conditional Branch Instructions

Mnemonic	Instruction Operation	Opcode	Condition Codes NZVC
BNE	Branch if Not Equal (Zero) (PC) ← loc if Z = 0	0010XX	——
BEQ	Branch if EQual (Zero) (PC) ← loc if Z = 1	0014XX	——
BGE	Branch if Greater or Equal (Zero) (PC) ← loc if N ⊻ V = 0	0020XX	——
BLT	Branch if Less Than (Zero) (PC) ← loc if N ⊻ V = 1	0024XX	——
BGT	Branch if Greater Than (Zero) (PC) ← loc if Z V (N ⊻ V) = 0	0030XX	——
BLE	Branch if Less than or Equal (Zero) (PC) ← loc if Z V (N ⊻ V) = 1	0034XX	——
BPL	Branch if PLus (PC) ← loc if N = 0	1000XX	——
BMI	Branch if MInus (PC) ← loc if N = 1	1004XX	——
BHI	Branch if HIgher (PC) ← loc if C = 0 and Z = 0	1010XX	——
BHIS	Branch if HIgher or Same (PC) ← loc if C = 0	1030XX	——
BLO	Branch if LOwer (PC) ← loc if C = 1	1034XX	——
BLOS	Branch if LOwer or Same (PC) ← loc if C V Z = 1	1014XX	——
BVC	Branch if oVerflow Clear (PC) ← loc if V = 0	1020XX	——
BVS	Branch if oVerflow Set (PC) ← loc if V = 1	1024XX	——
BCC (or BHIS)	Branch if Carry Clear (PC) ← loc if C = 0	1030XX	——
BCS	Branch if Carry Set (PC) ← loc if C = 1	0014XX	——
SOB[4]	Subtract One from register, Branch if not zero (R) ← (R)-1 (PC) ← loc if (R) ≠ 0	077RXX	——

[4]Not available in all members of PDP-11 family.

4.5.6 STATUS REGISTER INSTRUCTIONS

The processor status word can be modified by a set of instructions which individually or collectively sets or clears the four flags. The format for this instruction is found in Figure 4.9. Bits 3 through 0 specify the negative flag (N), zero flag (Z), overflow flag (V), and the carry flag (C), respectively. These four flags, also called the condition code, can be modified by each instruction in Table 4.11. For example, if one desires to set the overflow flag, SEV would set bit 1 in the processor status register to 1. All remaining flags are unchanged. The PDP-11 family allows us to actually "AND" the operations together to form a combination (e.g., CLN!CLC where "!" is taken to mean "AND" by the assembler in this case). The opcode for this selectable combination of clearing two flags is 000254. Because bit 4 in this instruction selects either a set or a clearing operation in the flag field, it is impossible to "AND" the set with a clear operation. Notice that if our machine opcode is 000240, no flags are affected. The same is true for the opcode 000260. These two opcodes are equivalent to the NOP or no operation instruction in the PDP-11 family. If it is 277, all flags are set.

Table 4.11 Processor Status Register Instructions

Mnemonic	Instruction Operation	Opcode	Condition Codes NZVC
CLC	CLear Carry flag C ← 0	000241	———0
CLV	CLear oVerflow flag V ← 0	000242	——0—
CLZ	CLear Zero flag Z ← 0	000244	—0——
CLN	CLear Negative flag N ← 0	000250	0———
SEC	SEt Carry flag C ← 1	000261	———1
SEV	SEt oVerflow flag V ← 1	000262	——1—
SEZ	SEt Zero flag Z ← 1	000264	—1——
SEN	SEt Negative flag N ← 1	000270	1———

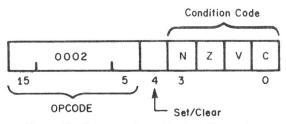

Figure 4.9 Processor Status Register Instructions

4.6 ADDRESSING MODES

There are three general classes of addressing modes in the PDP-11 family: *direct*, *deferred* (PDP-11 version of indirect), and *relative* addressing. Table 4.12 lists both direct and deferred addressing modes for the general-purpose

Table 4.12 General Register Addressing Modes (R0-R7)

Mode	Name of Mode	Symbolic	Operand's Location
0	Register	Rn	Operand is in Rn.
1	Register-Deferred	(Rn) or @(Rn)	Address of operand is in Rn.
2	Autoincrement	(Rn)+	Address of operand is in Rn; Rn←(Rn)+2 after operand is fetched. But Rn←(Rn)+1 if instruction is byte instruction and n<6.
3	Autoincrement-Deferred	@(Rn)+	Address of address of operand is in Rn; Rn←(Rn)+2 after operand is fetched.
4	Autodecrement	−(Rn)	Rn←(Rn)−2 before address is computed; address of operand is in Rn. But Rn←(Rn)−1 if instruction is byte instruction and n<6.
5	Autodecrement-Deferred	@−(Rn)	Rn←(Rn)−2 before address is computed; address of address of operand is in Rn.
6	Index	X(Rn)	Address of operand is X + (Rn). Address of X is in PC and is the second word of the instruction; PC←(PC)+2 after X is fetched.
7	Index-Deferred	@X(Rn)	Address of address of operand is X + (Rn). Address of X is in PC; PC←(PC)+2 after X is fetched.

registers. Table 4.13, restricted to R7, lists the relative addressing modes. According to the instruction formats from the previous section, the direct mode of addressing is identified with a zero in the direct/indirect bit of the mode field. Hence, all even modes (0, 2, 4, and 6) designate the direct addressing mode. These direct addressing modes are register, autoincrement, autodecrement, and index. The indirect addressing modes, also called deferred modes, are register-deferred, autoincrement-deferred, autodecrement-deferred, and index-deferred. All eight registers in the PDP-11 programming model (R0-R7) can employ these eight modes.

However, registers R6 and R7 have some additional features provided by facilities in the assembler. R6 is also a special register called the stack pointer

(SP). R7 is the program counter (PC) in the PDP-11 family. Its additional addressing modes are found in Table 4.13. These addressing modes for R7 include immediate, absolute, relative, and relative-deferred. In essence, modes 2 and 3 are non-relative while modes 6 and 7 are relative. A relative addressing mode determines the effective address using an offset or displacement from the current PC value. This mode is quite useful when programs must be written which can be loaded in program memory, independent of the area used in program memory. This important attribute of programming is called *position-independent coding* (PIC). Program counter relative addressing modes assist us in generating position-independent code. This important concept will be considered in more detail in a later chapter. Addressing modes with the general registers permit a programmer to use the registers in any of the following ways:

1. *Accumulators*—manipulated data resides within the register.

2. *Pointers*—the register contents is an address of the data, rather than the data itself.

3. *Stack pointers*—self-modifying pointers which, when used in a program, automatically point to the location and update themselves to the next location. When stepping forward (toward location 177...), this automatic pointer update is called autoincrement addressing. When stepping backward (toward location 00000), this automatic update is called autodecrement addressing. Stacks can be used for nesting programs and creating temporary storage.

4. *Index registers*—the contents of an index register and a word immediately following the instruction are summed together to produce the effective address of the operand or data. The index register contents remain unchanged.

Table 4.13 Register R7 Addressing Modes

Mode	Name of Mode	Symbolic	Operand's Location
2	Immediate	#n	Operand follows instruction.
3	Absolute	@#A	Absolute address of operand follows the instruction.
6	Relative	A	Address of operand relative to the instruction follows the instruction.
7	Relative-Deferred	@A	Address of location containing a pointer to operand relative to the instruction follows the instruction.

All eight registers can individually behave as accumulators, pointers, stack pointers, and index registers. However, R6, called the *stack pointer* (SP), has some additional capabilities that enhance using R6 as *the* stack pointer. Not only does R6 behave as a stack pointer under program control, but certain instructions, which facilitate subroutine programming and program interruption, automatically use R6. Behaving as a "hardware stack pointer," R6 functions best if it is used primarily for that purpose only. Hence, mode 3 in Table 4.12 is predominantly used for R6. As a hardware stack pointer, the special attribute of R6 is that autodecrements and autoincrements are always executed in steps of two (because words are found on even boundaries and the stack is often thought of as an address holder).

In a later chapter, the concept of a stack is developed. For now, assume that a stack is a contiguous set of addressable locations which a programmer may use as a sort of temporary scratch pad for a data area or other purposes. A stack not only conveniently allows for temporary holding of information, but also is manipulated with special stack instructions, each of which updates the stack pointer and accesses the stack in one short opcode.

R7, like R6, has special addressing modes because of the unique function R7 possesses as a program counter. These addressing modes are sometimes called the PC addressing modes. Whenever the CPU uses R7 as a program counter to acquire a word from memory, the program counter is automatically incremented by two to contain the address of the next word of the instruction to be executed, *or* the address of the next instruction, itself. *Just as with R6, even when the program uses the PC to locate byte data, the PC is still incremented by two.*

Note! There are real dangers using R6 and R7 as "just registers." System software uses R6 and R7 and returns the program execution to an unknown place or causes a branch.

4.7   DIRECT ADDRESSING

4.7.1   REGISTER MODE (0)

As shown in Table 4.12, the four basic addressing modes used in direct addressing are: register, autoincrement, autodecrement, and index. The register mode of addressing has already been examined in a previous chapter. As a review, the following example demonstrates the register addressing mode with the ADD instruction. The symbolic notation for the register addressing mode is

OPR Rn

OPR represents the operation (e.g., ADD, SUB, etc.) and Rn is a general register (R0...R7). If two operands are involved, the symbolic notation becomes "OPR Rn,Rm," where Rn is the source and Rm is the destination.

Example 4.7   Register Direct Addressing Mode

Symbolic	Octal Code	Instruction Name
ADD R0,R5	060005	2's complement word addition

Operation: Add the contents of R0 to the contents of R5. Place result in R5.

Before				After			
Program Memory		Register		Program Memory		Register	
1676	060005	R0	000432	1676	060005	R0	000432
1700		R5	000410	1700		R5	001042

Data Memory	Data Memory
(not used)	(not used)

4.7.2   AUTOINCREMENT MODE (2)

Suppose that a programmer must access sequential elements in a table of data which is found in data memory as a set of contiguous locations. The address at the top of the table is found in a general register. If it is necessary to automatically step through the data, acquiring one piece of data after another for some repeated operation (such as a running sum), the autoincrement mode of addressing can be used to perform the automatic stepping through the program with one single instruction. That instruction not only retrieves the data, but also updates the pointer. The symbolic notation for the autoincrement mode is

OPR (Rn)+

Rn represents a general register and OPR represents the general instruction mnemonic. The + sign designates the autoincrement mode of addressing and appears to the right of the parentheses deliberately to indicate that the pointer is incremented by "one" for bytes, and by "two" for words *after* the access is made. If R6 and R7 are used, they are always incremented by two. Placing the + sign in this position helps us to remember that the effective address is used first, then the pointer is updated. This autoincrement mode is extremely helpful in *processing arrays of data*, whether they are one-dimensional, two-dimensional, or n-dimensional. The autoincrement mode is useful in accessing an element of a table and stepping the pointer to address the next datum in that same table.

Example 4.8   Autoincrement Mode on a Word

Symbolic	Octal Code	Instruction Name
CLR (R4)+	005024	Clear

Operation: Contents of R4 contain an address of the operand. First, clear selected operand pointed to by contents of R4. Second, increment contents of R4 by 2.

Before				After			
Program Memory		Register		Program Memory		Register	
200	005024	R4	001700	200	005024	R4	001702

Data Memory		Data Memory	
1700	003714	1700	000000

Suppose that a table stored in memory is to be cleared. Using the autoincrement mode makes this table access trivial. In the following loop of Example 4.9, a CLR instruction in the autoincrement mode executes the task on a 16_8 element linear array.

Example 4.9   Incrementing Through an Array of Data

```
       MOV   #TOP,R0    ;INITIALIZE R0 TO POINT TO TOP OF
                        ;TABLE
       MOV   #16,R1     ;INITIALIZE R1 TO LENGTH OF ARRAY
LOOP:  CLR   (R0)+      ;PROCESS NEXT ARRAY ELEMENT AND
                        ;UPDATE POINTER
       DEC   R1         ;R1 CONTAINS LENGTH OF ARRAY
       BNE   LOOP       ;GO BACK IF NOT DONE
```

Array Picture

4.7.3 AUTODECREMENT MODE (4)

Like the autoincrement mode, the autodecrement mode is very useful for processing data in an array or a list. However, the processing occurs in the reverse direction from that of the increment mode. The autodecrement mode first causes the effective address to be decremented (by 2 for word instructions, and by 1 for byte instructions). This step is the pointer update step. Second, this effective address is then used as the address of the operand for data. The symbolic notation for the autodecrement mode is

OPR -(Rn)

Keep in mind that the register is decremented *before* using the register as a pointer. The "-" sign before the (Rn) is placed ahead of the register to help us remember which occurs first. This is contrasted with autoincrementing where the pointer update is performed *after* the pointer is used and the "+" sign follows.

4.7.4 INDEX MODE (6)

Suppose a computer is to be organized so that memory space looks somewhat like a box of 3 × 5 file cards or index cards. Between each index card in our card file is information which belongs to each index. For example, this could be the names of people living in one political precinct, with each index representing the precinct number. To efficiently search this database, we could first examine each index. Upon selecting the desired index, we could move through its subfile to find the actual data. This two-step process is equivalent to using the index addressing mode in the PDP-11. In the index mode, the contents (also called the base address) of the selected register and the index word following your instruction word are summed together to form the effective address of the operand. The index word must be a 2's complement signed 16-bit number. We assume that the contents of the selected register are used as an index for calculating a series of addresses. The symbolic notation for the index addressing mode is of the form

OPR X(Rn)

where X is the base address and is located in the memory location immediately following the instruction word, and Rn is the selected general register containing the index word. Note that two words are necessary to specify the index mode of direct addressing. The first word contains the opcode and the second word contains the base address.

Example 4.10   Direct Addressing Index Mode

Symbolic	Octal Code	Instruction Name
ADD 20(R4),10(R5)	066465	Add with index mode
	000020	direct addressing
	000010	

Operation: The contents of a location pointed to by an effective address, computed by adding 20 to the contents of R4, are added to the contents of a location pointed to by the effective address, computed by adding 10 to the contents of R5. The latter location is also the destination.

Before

Program Memory		Register	
40	066465	R4	001016
42	000020	R5	002032
44	000010		

Data Memory

1036	000042
2042	001770

After

Program Memory		Register	
40	066465	R4	001016
42	000020	R5	002032
44	000010		

Data Memory

1036	000042
2042	002032

The index addressing mode is especially suited to table accesses which require entering every nth location in the table. Assume that a 4 × 3 array is stored in memory, as shown in Table 4.14. The code in Example 4.11 accesses

Table 4.14   Memory Map of 4 × 3 Matrix

Location	Matrix Element	Location	Matrix Element	Location	Martix Element
600	A_{11}	610	A_{12}	620	A_{13}
602	A_{21}	612	A_{22}	622	A_{23}
604	A_{31}	614	A_{32}	624	A_{33}
606	A_{41}	616	A_{42}	626	A_{43}

each element in the first row using an index addressing mode. The index is 12_8. The base address is 600_8, the top of the array in memory. Only three elements need to be processed so R1 is initialized to -3 and tested in the loop. ASR 600(R0) does not modify the contents of R0 which is the index word.

Example 4.11 Accessing the First Row of a Matrix

```
        CLR   R0        ;INITIALIZE POINTER TO ARRAY
        MOV   #-3,R1    ;INITIALIZE LENGTH OF ROW ACCESS
LOOP:   ASR   600(R0)   ;DIVIDE A ROW ELEMENT BY TWO
        ADD   #12,R0    ;ADJUST POINTER TO NEXT ELEMENT IN ROW
        INC   R1·       ;UPDATE COUNTER
        BNE   LOOP      ;EVERY ROW ELEMENT MODIFIED?
                        ;YES
```

4.8 DEFERRED ADDRESSING

Processing of arrays, tables, and lists are so important that a general-purpose computer can make effective use of many more addressing modes than those already shown. The deferred addressing mode is invaluable for these address manipulation intensive tasks. Deferred addressing uses an intermediate operand as an address to another, or final, operand. In the deferred addressing mode, two addresses can be found: the intermediate address (or pointer to an address) and the effective address (the actual address of the operand). The simplest of the deferred addressing modes in the PDP-11 is the register-deferred addressing mode. All deferred modes are indicated with the parentheses around the register for the register-deferred mode. Modes 3, 5, and 7, the autoincrement-, autodecrement-, and index-deferred modes, employ the "at" sign, @, in addition to the parentheses.

4.8.1 REGISTER-DEFERRED MODE (1)

In the register-deferred mode, the address of the operand is found in a general-purpose register (and not the operand). This address directs the computer to the actual operand which can be located outside the CPU, in memory, or in an I/O register. *This mode is quite useful for sequential lists, indirect pointers and data structures, top of stack manipulations, and jump tables.* Jump tables are arrays of addresses which a program uses to jump to other tables. The symbolic notation for the register-deferred mode is

OPR (Rn)

where Rn represents the general register name, and OPR represents the general instruction mnemonic. The parentheses designate the register-deferred mode of addressing. When it is clear to the particular machine and its assembler, the register-deferred mode may be indicated simply with parentheses around the general register.

The register-deferred mode of addressing is quite similar to the index mode of addressing, although there are some subtle differences. In the register-deferred mode, the effective address is found directly as the contents of a general–purpose register. However, in the index register addressing mode, an effective address is obtained by computing the sum of a base address (found as the second word of the instruction) and the contents of a general–purpose register. Notice that in the register-deferred mode, the machine performs no address computations.

How could a programmer simulate the register-deferred addressing mode with the index addressing mode? One simple solution would be to place all zeroes in the second word of the instruction, which is also the base address. When added to the index register, the effective address is, then, simply the contents of the index register itself. Why is the register-deferred mode of addressing useful? The answer is that the index register mode of addressing is a two-word instruction while the register-deferred mode is only a one-word instruction. If program memory space is precious, a register-deferred addressing mode may help, since one less line of code is necessary, thus saving memory space.

4.8.2   AUTOINCREMENT-DEFERRED MODE (3)

The autoincrement-deferred and autodecrement-deferred modes are very effectively employed with tables of addresses. In the autoincrement-deferred mode, the specified register in the register field contains an address. This address is used to point to another address, which is the address of the actual operand. After the operand has been accessed, the register containing the address is automatically incremented. These two steps in the addressing process are performed with one single instruction. The symbolic notation for the autoincrement-deferred mode is

OPR @(Rn)+

Whereas the autoincrement mode (mode 2) is used to access operands that are stored in consecutive locations, the autoincrement-deferred mode (mode 3) can be used to access lists of operands stored anywhere in the computer. The operands do not have to reside in adjoining locations. It is useful to employ mode 2 for tasks which step through a table of *operands*, while mode 3 is useful to *step through a table of addresses*. The indirect mode 3 always increments the register by 2, regardless of whether these addresses point to word or byte operands.

Recognize that whenever an instruction invokes mode 2 or 3, the address is incremented each time the instruction is executed. If a byte is accessed in mode 2, the address is incremented by one. If a word is accessed in mode 2, the address is incremented by two. But, since R6 and R7 are special registers, they are always incremented by two, regardless of whether one uses a byte or a word instruction.

4.8.3   AUTODECREMENT-DEFERRED MODE (5)

The autoincrement-deferred mode allows a programmer to access locations in memory in a sequential fashion, sequentially moving toward address 177777. The autodecrement-deferred mode allows us to step through a table of addresses in the reverse order; that is, toward location 000000. The effective address is calculated by first decrementing a pointer in the register specified in the instruction. This decrementing by 2 is accomplished for both word and byte operations. Next, this updated pointer is used to retrieve an *address* word stored outside the CPU. The symbolic notation for this addressing mode is

OPR @-(Rn)

As with autoincrement-deferred, the autodecrement-deferred does not require the operands to reside in consecutive locations. The autodecrement-deferred mode is an indirect addressing mode and is primarily used for *manipulating tables of addresses*. Since addresses are always found on even boundaries in the PDP-11, the autodecrement step decrements the register by 2. Notice that decrementing occurs before the address is used in the autodecrement mode.

Example 4.12   Autodecrement-Deferred Mode

Symbolic	Octal Code	Instruction Name
XOR R2,@-(R1)	074251	eXclusive-OR

Operation: The contents of register R2 are exclusive-ORed with the destination operand specified by R1 in the addressing mode indicated. The result is stored in the destination address. The contents of register R2 are unaffected.

Before				After			
Program	Memory	Register		Program	Memory	Register	
64	074251	R1	001772	64	074251	R1	001770
		R2	000243			R2	000243

Data Memory		Data Memory	
1760	003377	1760	003134
1770	001760	1770	001760
1772	004237	1772	004237

4.8.4   INDEX-DEFERRED MODE (7)

The index-deferred mode is much like the index mode of addressing; however, the index-deferred mode is an indirect addressing mode. Here, a base address is added to an index word. The result of this sum is a pointer to an address, rather than the effective address, itself. Mode 7 is similar to mode 6, except that the address computation step produces a pointer to an address, instead of a pointer to an operand. The index-deferred mode provides us with the capability to randomly access operands, using a table of operand addresses. The symbolic notation for the index-deferred mode is

OPR @X(Rn)

This two-word machine instruction contains the operation code in the first word along with the designated addressing modes. The second word contains the index. The base address is found in a general–purpose register. Notice that the index-deferred mode does not necessarily increment or decrement a pointer by one or two. Rather, the address computation step uses a base address (found in the register) and an index word. Either the base address or the index word could contain the values $+1$, $+2$, -1, and -2. However, autoincrement and autodecrement using the index-deferred mode is not recommended for this mode. Neither the base address nor the index word are modified by this addressing mode.

Example 4.13   Index Register Deferred Mode

Symbolic	Octal Code	Instruction Name
ASRB @1000(R3)	106273	Arithmetic shift
	001000	right of a byte.

Operation: An effective address points to a location in which all bits are shifted to the right one place in the lower byte. The high-order bit is replicated. The carry bit is loaded from the low-order bit of the destination. In effect, ASRB performs signed division of the destination by two, rounded to minus infinity.

Before				After			
Program	Memory	Register		Program	Memory	Register	
22	106273	R3	000100	22	106273	R3	000100
24	001000			24	001000		

Data Memory		Data Memory	
400	000200	400	000300
1100	000400	1100	000400

Note that location 400 contains 200. After executing this instruction, 300 is found in location 400. Since 400 is a negative byte, signed division by two must retain the sign. Hence, the most significant bit (which is a one) in the byte will be copied leaving a negative number in the result.

4.9   RELATIVE ADDRESSING

Relative addressing assumes that two elements are needed to generate an effective address. One element is the "base" address from which the second, a "displacement," is made. The *sum* of the displacement plus this base generates the effective address. In the relative addressing mode, some computer systems may assume that the base is the program counter. Hence, relative addressing is sometimes called *PC relative addressing*. Computation of the displacement in the PDP-11 is done in 2's complement arithmetic using the PC. The displacement must be a signed 2's complement number. Since all addresses are in sixteen bits, the displacement must be a 16-bit word.

There is some similarity between the use of register 7 in the index mode and register 7 in the relative addressing mode. Recall that in the index mode, the effective address is computed by adding a base address, X, to the contents of the designated register. If R7 is chosen, then this effective address in the index mode is equivalent to this effective address in relative addressing.

The two relative addressing modes of the PC are modes 6 and 7, relative and relative-deferred, respectively, found in Table 4.13. Both facilitate the handling of unstructured data. For our purposes, unstructured data is data that might reside anywhere in memory and not necessarily in contiguous locations. For instance, an isolated datum found in a random location is easily addressed in the PC absolute mode. If a single datum were desired as a constant, then the PC immediate mode of addressing would be used. However, the PC relative mode of addressing greatly enhances the ability to write programs which can be relocated in program memory, without major programming revisions. This concept of position-independent coding assumes that we can invoke the PC relative addressing modes. If an instruction and its objects or datum are moved in such a way that the relative distance between them is not altered, the same offset relative to the PC can be used in all positions in memory. Thus, position-independent coding usually references locations relative to the current location.

4.9.1   PC RELATIVE MODE (6)

In the PC relative mode, the operand's address is calculated by adding the word that follows the instruction, called a displacement or offset, to the updated contents of the PC. PC + 2 directs the CPU, not to the next instruction, but to the offset that always follows the instruction. Hence, PC + 4, not PC + 2, is added to the displacement to produce the effective address of the operand. In the relative addressing mode, the address of an operand is always determined with respect to the updated PC. The distance between the updated PC (PC + 4) and the operand is called the *displacement* or *offset*. Whether the program is assembled by hand or by an assembler, this offset appears in the next word following the instruction. The symbolic notation for this mode is

OPR A

Example 4.14   PC Relative Mode

Symbolic	Octal Code	Instruction Name
ASH R4,A	072467	16-bit arithmetic shift

Operation: This instruction (072RSS) performs a shift by a certain number of bits specified in a count field (bits 5 through 0 of the source operand) on a single 16-bit operand (R4). The effective address is computed by summing PC + 4 with the contents of PC + 2. The shift count is contained in the low-order six bits of this address location. This number ranges from −32 to +31. A negative number is a right shift. A positive number is a left shift.

Before				After			
Program	Memory		Register	Program	Memory		Register
16	072467	R4	007070	16	072467	R4	000707
20	001700			20	001700		

Data Memory		Data Memory	
1716		1716	
1720		1720	
1722	000075	1722	000075

4.9.2 RELATIVE-DEFERRED MODE (7)

In the PDP-11, the relative-deferred addressing mode is provided only with register R7, just as with the relative mode previously examined. The relative-deferred mode is equivalent to the index-deferred mode, except now we use the PC. A pointer to an operand's address is calculated by adding an offset to the updated PC. The offset is the second word of this two-word instruction. Realize that all deferred modes are equivalent to indirect addressing modes. Hence, the sum of the offset or displacement and updated PC (PC +4) serves as a pointer to an address, and not as a pointer to an operand. Only after the address is retrieved, could it then be used to locate that operand. The symbolic notation for this mode is

OPR @A

4.10   MORE ON CONDITIONAL BRANCHES

When handling data, a continuing source of major confusion is the testing of the relative magnitude of pairs of numbers. Since numbers may be considered as signed or unsigned, the tests which compare relative magnitudes depend greatly on this single issue. Obviously, comparing a signed number to an unsigned number quickly leads to trouble. Not so obvious is the fact that comparing numbers with the same representation must also be carefully done. One can see that, in Table 4.15 for positive numbers from 0 to 32767 in decimal (077777 in octal), the signed and unsigned interpretations are identical. However, once a binary one is encountered in the most significant digit, all similarity ceases. The number 100000 (octal) represents the unsigned number 32768. The same octal code represents the signed number −32768. Incrementing the octal number to 100001 and so on causes the unsigned number to increase. Finally, the 16-bit word, 177777, represents the unsigned number, 65535, but its signed interpretation is −1. Because of this, comparing and testing such numbers depends on more than just examining the most significant bit (normally the sign bit for signed numbers, that is).

Table 4.15   Signed and Unsigned Numbers in a 16-Bit Machine

Signed Interpretation	Unsigned Interpretation	Octal Contents
0	0	000000
1	1	000001
•	•	•
•	•	•
•	•	•
7	7	000007
8	8	000010
9	9	000011
10	10	000012
11	11	000013
•	•	•
•	•	•
•	•	•
32766	32766	077776
32767	32767	077777
−32768	32768	100000
−32767	32769	100001
−32766	32770	100002
•	•	•
•	•	•
•	•	•
−4	65532	177774
−3	65533	177775
−2	65534	177776
−1	65535	177777

Computers have instructions to test signed and unsigned numbers. In the PDP-11, two instructions, CMP and TST, are invaluable for these purposes. Both instructions, used in conjunction with signed conditional branches and unsigned conditional branch instructions, can process every expected result encountered in a digital computer, including overflow. To do so, consider the processor status register flags as condition codes or condition bits. Then the conditional branch instructions, upon monitoring these codes (N, Z, V, and C), can make a branch determination on one or more of these codes. Let's look at how the codes are affected by the TST and CMP instructions.

TST merely examines the operand and sets or clears bits accordingly. If the operand is 0, the Z bit is set to 1. If the operand is negative, the N bit is set to 1, and so on. The operand itself is not modified, nor are any other registers in the machine. CMP is similar to TST, except that CMP is a double-operand instruction. It tests the result of a 2's complement subtraction process between a source (SS) and a destination (DD). However, "destination" is a misnomer here, because the result of the CMP instruction only modifies the condition codes. The result is "destined" for nowhere.

Table 4.10 lists seventeen conditional branch instructions. This set consists of two types: those which test signed numbers, and those which test unsigned numbers. Signed conditional branches regard operands as 16-bit 2's complement numbers. Any operations performed on this representation and subsequently compared obey the rules for signed numbers. The add and subtract arithmetic instructions assume that we are operating with signed numbers. CMP makes the same assumption. The CMP instruction performs a 2's complement subtraction and sets the condition code bits, C and V, according to the definition for a subtraction operation.

How CMP Affects the PSW

1. The carry flag is defined to be a borrow into the most significant bit position of the word. Similarly, a carry from the most significant bit causes the C flag to be cleared. No carry from the most significant bit causes the C flag to be set.

2. Overflow is defined to have occurred whenever the operands were of the opposite sign and the result generated is of the same sign as the subtrahend. For the CMP instruction, the *destination* operand is the subtrahend.

Consider Example 4.15 and notice how the condition bits are affected.

Example 4.15   Comparing Two Numbers

Case One	Case Two
•	•
•	•
•	•
CMP R0,R1	CMP R0,R1
BMI SMALLER	BLT SMALLER
•	•
•	•
•	•

These two programs cause the PSW flags to be affected by the result of the operation

$$R0 - R1$$

Suppose R0 and R1 become (octal)

$$R0 = 100001$$
$$R1 = 077777$$

Then,

$$R0 - R1 = 100001 - 077777 = 2$$

and the PSR becomes

N	Z	V	C
0	0	1	0

Suppose that a program is needed which would branch to program location SMALLER if R0 is less than R1. Which program above will branch? BMI tests only the N flag, so the first program will not branch. BLT tests the relation N XOR V (which is one). The second program branches. How should a user interpret each program? The answer in each case is to examine the conditional branch test. BMI is a signed conditional branch instruction. If R0 is less positive than R1, the program should branch, but it didn't! In the second program, a branch occurred as desired. Why? The BLT is designed to handle overflow and sign tests, and BMI is designed to handle a simple sign test (N). In fact, when overflow occurs with signed numbers, the true sign of the result is reversed. From this example, obviously BLT is the correct instruction to use when it is necessary to test the relative magnitude of two signed numbers.

Suppose that a program is needed to branch if R0 is lower than R1. Now one desires to test two unsigned numbers (since "lower than" and "higher than" are unsigned relative magnitude tests). BMI SMALLER fails to branch, even though R0 is lower than R1 (see Table 4.15). Obviously, BMI is not an adequate unsigned conditional branch instruction. How about BLT?

Does it adequately test unsigned numbers? In this case, yes, because R0 is lower than R1. But what if

$$R0 = 077777$$
$$R1 = 100001$$

Well, the difference between R0 and R1 becomes

$$R0 - R1 = 077777 - 100001 = 177776$$

and the PSW becomes

$$\underline{N\ Z\ V\ C}$$
$$1\ 0\ 1\ 1$$

So BLT does not cause a branch (N XOR V = 0) here, and it shouldn't. R0 is no longer lower than R1. Let's try one more case, namely

$$R0 = 000001$$
$$R1 = 177776$$

By now, the reader should be able to quickly detect that R0 is lower than R1, so this conditional branch test should cause a branch. Does BLT work properly here? No, since N XOR V = 0. The correct instruction to use is BLO. Table 4.16 lists the correct application of all conditional branch instructions.

Table 4.16   Conditional Branch Instructions

Unsigned		Signed		
BEQ	BNE	BEQ	BNE	Equality or zero test
none		BPL	BMI	Sign test
BCS	BCC	BVS	BVC	Overflow test
BLO	BLOS	BLT	BLE	Relative magnitude
BHIS	BHI	BGE	BGT	Relative magnitude

A programmer should always use *unsigned* conditional branch instructions and nothing else for address tests. Why? Addresses are considered best as unsigned (assumed positive) numbers. For example, suppose that one desires to move a table of data from one area of program memory to another area. The first location of the table is 2000. The location of the last table entry is 6000. The first location of the new area is 17660. (The reader should perform the octal addition to obtain the last location.) The following examples illustrate the errors which could occur if one uses a signed conditional branch instruction.

Example 4.16 Comparing Addresses

```
              MOV    #17660,R5
              MOV    #2000,R3
              MOV    #6000,R4
       LOOP:  MOV    (R5)+,(R3)+
              CMP    R4,R3
              BGE    LOOP
                      •
                      •
                      •
```

BGE treats the operands (R4 and R3) as signed 2's complement numbers. The entire table is moved correctly, because the loop will terminate when R3 contains 6002. Everything appears reasonable, but consider Example 4.17 where the table is found between locations 057776 and 170000.

Example 4.17 Moving a Table Incorrectly

```
              MOV    #17660,R5
              MOV    #057776,R3
              MOV    #170000,R4
       LOOP:  MOV    (R5)+,(R3)+
              CMP    R4,R3
              BGE    LOOP
                      •
                      •
                      •
```

This program fails to move the entire table. In fact, it makes only one data movement and exits because the N flag has been set, causing the program to exit the loop (BGE branches if N XOR V = 0).

```
     170000      N Z V C
    -060000
     110000      1 0 0 1
```

The correct solution to effect the movement of the entire table requires BGE to be replaced with BHIS as follows:

```
              MOV    #17660,R5
              MOV    #057776,R3
              MOV    #170000,R4
       LOOP:  MOV    (R5)+,(R3)+
              CMP    R4,R3
              BHIS   LOOP
                      •
                      •
                      •
```

In the above code, the BHIS branch instruction asks the question,

"Is R4 higher or the same as R3?"

With BHIS, only the C flag is tested (a simple conditional test). As long as the C flag is 0, the loop is executed. The C flag is set only when R3 is identical to R4. BHIS is an unsigned conditional branch test and will work regardless of the values of the addresses (even if unsigned overflow occurs).

Many computer instructions (besides arithmetic instructions) affect the condition codes. Such capabilities exist to test address manipulation for end-of-loop comparisons, end-of-table transfers, etc. INC, DEC, NEG, MOV, and TST all affect the PSW, but in a variety of ways. Because such instructions modify the PSW, usage of CMP and TST may be unnecessary as indicated in the following examples. In Example 4.18, CMP is superfluous because DEC already sets or clears the N, Z, and V flags as necessary. In Example 4.19, TST is redundant because the preceding SUB instruction modifies all four flags accordingly.

Example 4.18   An Extra CMP

```
            •
            •
            •
    DEC    R3
    CMP    R3,#0    ←Redundant
    BNE    AGAIN
            •
            •
            •
```

Example 4.19   An Extra TST

```
            •
            •
            •
    SUB    R0,R1
    TST    R1       ←Redundant
    BEQ    AGAIN
            •
            •
            •
```

Programming at the machine level demands careful attention to PSW modifying instructions. In the previous examples, memory space is wasted (as well as program execution time) because superfluous instructions are invoked. In Example 4.20, execution time could also be reduced because the testing of two conditions simultaneously can be accomplished with one instruction.

Example 4.20   Testing Two Conditions

Slow Program		Fast Program	
	•		•
	•		•
	•		•
CMP	R3,#3	CMP	R3,#3
BGT	AGAIN	BHI	AGAIN
TST	R3		•
BLT	AGAIN		•
	•		•
	•		
	•		

BHI performs the same task as BGT and BLT, because negative numbers are always higher than any positive numbers (when treated as unsigned numbers).

Sometimes program behavior can be obscured by using instructions for something other than their intended purposes. In the following example, TST and CMP are used solely to increment or decrement registers. A programmer might possibly detect this misuse when no conditional branch instruction follows each instance of usage. Such programming practices are discouraged. They only trap the unwary programmer who has been asked to modify or maintain obscure code.

Example 4.21   Increment/Decrement with CMP and TST

CMP	(R2)+,(R2)+	R2	← R2+4
TST	(R3)+	R3	← R3+2
TST	−(R6)	R6	← R6−2

Recommended usage of instructions and conditional branch tests are listed as guidelines.

Some Programming Guidelines

1. *Always* treat addresses as unsigned (assumed positive) numbers. Use unsigned conditional branches only.

2. Treat any number in your program *consistently*. Don't allow a given operand to be considered as an unsigned number in one section of code and as a signed number in another section.

3. Do *not* use the following conditional branches with signed numbers.

BCS	BCC
BHIS	BHI
BLO	BLOS

4. The four unsigned conditional branch instructions (BLO, BHIS, BLOS, BHI) should only be used after CMP.

5. Do *not* use the following conditional branch instructions with unsigned numbers. They examine the N or V bits.

BLT	BLE
BGE	BGT
BPL	BMI
BVS	BVC

6. The four signed conditional branch instructions (BLE, BGT, BLT, BGE) should be used after CMP *only* for signed number tests.

7. Because BEQ and BNE test only the Z bit, they can be used with *both* signed and unsigned numbers.

8. Signed and unsigned overflow need to be treated *separately*. The instructions, ADD, INC, SUB, DEC, and NEG, each modify the V bit. INC and DEC can be used with signed and unsigned numbers, but remember that these instructions do not affect the C bit. Hence, INC and DEC cannot reliably cause unsigned overflow, but note that the result is zero when unsigned overflow occurs with INC. MOV and TST cause neither signed nor unsigned overflow. Both always clear the V bit.

4.11 PDP-11 INTERFACE

4.11.1 UNIBUS

A typical PDP-11 system consists of the elements shown in Figure 4.10. In a PDP-11 system, data transfer is accomplished between the central processor and peripheral devices through a communications bus called the UNIBUS. The UNIBUS is a collection of wires among the various units within the system that carries information signals which consist of address, data, and control signals. The actual bus is capable of simultaneous signal transfer including the ability to transfer sixteen bits of a memory word. The actual number of lines in a PDP-11 UNIBUS consists of 56 signal lines which are connected to all devices, including the processor, in parallel.

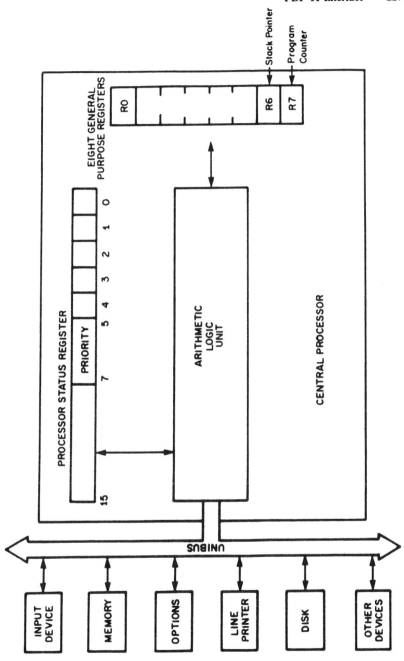

Figure 4.10   PDP-11 System Block Diagram

4.11.2   MASTER/SLAVE COMMUNICATIONS

Communication between any two devices on the UNIBUS is in a master/slave relationship. During a bus operation, one device (namely, the bus master) controls the bus on communicating with another device. The CPU is not necessarily always the master. The other device is called the slave. For example, to fetch an instruction from memory, the processor, as a master, would access the data bus and seek data transfer from a slave, such as the memory unit. As another example, a disk, serving as the master unit, could transfer data directly to the memory as a slave unit. Communication among the devices then obeys a dynamic master/slave relationship. Any peripheral device may be a master at any given time.

Although only one device gains control of a bus at any point in time, remaining devices can access the bus with a priority circuit which arbitrates between the units. Such device communications are interlocked. That is, for each command issued by a master device, a slave must transmit a response signal to complete the data transfer. Unlike some bus configurations, device communication is completely asynchronous. The device communication does not depend on the actual physical length of the bus or response times between master and slave devices. The data transfer is bidirectional and asynchronous. The overriding design concept of the PDP-11 family assumes that each device communicates in identical fashion. Hence, I/O units have the same power and flexibility as the processor and memory units to access the bus. This commonality of communication develops a very flexible interface medium which permits peripherals to migrate from one computer system to another. This is highly attractive to the end-user who expects to upgrade his system to a more powerful PDP-11 family member, without having to buy new peripherals.

The PDP-11 UNIBUS at first failed to anticipate future expansion of a computer system. The increasing disparity between processor and memory speeds caused the UNIBUS to slow down data transfer. Even the later expansion of the 18-bit memory address became an eventual limitation. Most of the shortcomings of the UNIBUS have been overcome by clever interfacing and memory management concepts. In that sense, the PDP-11/70 and VAX machines represent major breakthroughs over the original UNIBUS concepts.

4.11.3   TTY REGISTERS

In a basic system, the PDP-11 communicates to the outside world with a teletype via a keyboard and printer. A teletype data transfer is accomplished with the four registers indicated in the programming model. They include the keyboard status register (address 177560), keyboard data register (address

177562), printer status register (address 177564), and printer data register (address 177566). The fields of each register serve specific functions, as shown in Figure 4.11. Both data registers hold the encoded form of the character in bits 0 through 7. The keyboard data register, obviously, is a *read only* register, while the printer data register is a *write only* register. Both status registers indicate the ready status of the device by placing a one in bit 7 of each register. When bit 7 is cleared to zero in the keyboard status register, an instruction has been executed which refers to the keyboard data register. A MOV instruction, transferring data from the keyboard data register to CPU or elsewhere, causes bit 7 to be cleared. Similarly, bit 7 of the printer status register is cleared when a character has been loaded into the printer data register. A simple way to determine if a data transfer has been accomplished is to monitor bit 7, which can be considered a sign bit. For example, to determine whether the keyboard has a character for the CPU, a simple test on a byte, located in 177560, to determine whether a negative number exists would indicate the desired status.

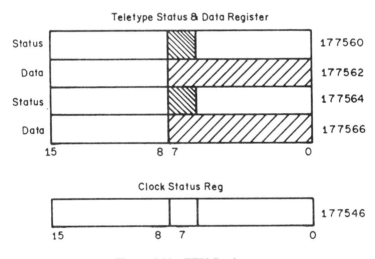

Figure 4.11   TTY Registers

The conversion of ASCII characters to the internal representation of a number as well as the conversion of an internal number to ASCII in I/O operations presents a challenge. Example 4.22 takes the 16-bit word in R1 and stores the corresponding six ASCII characters in the buffer addressed by R2. R3 is a temporary location for intermediate results. Suppose that the symbol, TKBUF, points to location 177562, which is the data register of a TTY input device. Example 4.22 converts a six octal datum to ASCII to output to a printer. This routine does not check the status of the printer (as it should). A complete program to access an I/O device is found in Chapter 8.

Example 4.22   ASCII Conversion

```
        MOV    #177566,R2    ;SET UP PRINTER BUFFER POINTER
OUT:    MOV    #5,R0         ;LOOP COUNT FOR 6 CHARACTERS
LOOP:   MOV    R1,R3         ;COPY WORD INTO R3
        BIC    #177770,R3    ;ONE OCTAL VALUE
        ADD    #'0,R3        ;CONVERT TO ASCII
        MOVB   R3,-(R2)      ;STORE IN BUFFER
        ASR    R1            ;SHIFT
        ASR    R1            ;RIGHT
        ASR    R1            ;THREE POSITIONS
        DEC    R0            ;TEST IF DONE
        BNE    LOOP          ;NO, DO IT AGAIN
        BIC    #177776,R1    ;GET LAST BIT
        ADD    #'0,R1        ;CONVERT TO ASCII
        MOVB   R1,-(R2)      ;STORE IN BUFFER OF PRINTER
        RTS    PC            ;DONE, RETURN
        .END   OUT
        .EXIT
```

4.11.4   CLOCK REGISTER

A simple PDP-11 contains a line clock which counts 60 times per second. The clock status register (address 177546) designates bit 7 as the 1/60 of a second bit. Bit 7 is a one every 1/60 of a second. Provisions are provided by other bits in the clock status register to cause bit 7 to return to zero shortly after each tick. As with the other status registers, we can detect the clock pulses by recognizing a negative number in byte 177546.

4.11.5   MASSBUS

Between the PDP-11/70 and the VAX family of machines is a high speed communications interface called the MASSBUS. The main functions of this interface are the following:

1. Maps addresses from virtual or program memory to actual or physical memory. (Virtual memory is discussed in Chapter 8.)

2. Provides a method to buffer data for transfers between main memory and the MASSBUS.

3. Transfers interrupts from MASSBUS devices to the system.

A VAX machine, such as the VAX-11/750, can support up to three MASS-BUS adapters (MBA), with each adapter supporting up to eight device controllers. A MASSBUS subsystem is depicted in Figure 4.12. A device controller links peripheral devices such as disk and other storage media, and performs the necessary control signal transmission and data capture for each device. In the VAX system architecture, only one controller transfers data at any one given time with a data transfer rate dependent on the particular device being accessed. Just as with the UNIBUS, a MASSBUS has an interface, internal registers, control paths, and data paths to support a communication's highway among the system elements. An MBA accepts and executes appropriate commands from the CPU and returns necessary status changes and fault conditions.

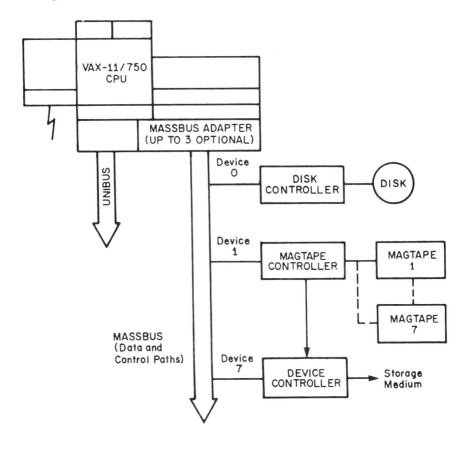

Figure 4.12   MASSBUS Subsystem

4.12   VAX ARCHITECTURE

The successor to the PDP-11 family of DEC computers is the VAX series, which the manufacturer has called their Virtual Address Extension machines. The designers of the VAX series sought to make this family an extension of the popular 11 series. Hence, instructions running on the 11 series are able to run on the VAX series in a particular mode. Likewise, this compatibility between the two families exists in the interconnection or interface bus of the VAX. There are some anomalies between the software and hardware compatibilities but they are not significant.

A typical VAX system is composed of a processor, peripherals, operating system, languages, utilities and program development tools, information management facilities, and data communication facilities. For each specific implementation (e.g., VAX 11/782, VAX 11/780, VAX 11/750, and VAX 11/730), the processor serves as the basic central processing unit. Except for minor variations in technology and performance levels such as speed and power, the same VAX instruction set and programming model exist for the user. Typical VAX architectures are shown in Figure 4.13

4.12.1   PROGRAMMING MODEL

To the typical user of a VAX machine, the VAX processor provides 32-bit addressing, sixteen 32-bit general registers and 32 interrupt priority levels. The programming model is shown in Figure 4.14. The 32-bit address space allows a user to reach across four billion locations, hence the name "virtual." To do so, an elaborate memory management scheme is invoked in the VAX system; this is described in detail in Chapter 8. The outcome of this scheme is a perception to the programmer that nearly all of the four billion addresses are available.

The sixteen general registers provide temporary address and data storage. They are designated R0 through R15. These registers do not have memory addresses, but are explicitly accessed by including the register name, Rx, in an operand specifier, or implicitly by machine operations which make reference to specific registers. A VAX programmer should realize that certain registers have specific uses and special names recognized by the system software and hardware. Because these registers serve the system, a user should never assume that the registers are vacant. Similarly, when writing into these registers, a user might consider preserving prior register contents. The specific uses and names are listed below in Table 4.17.

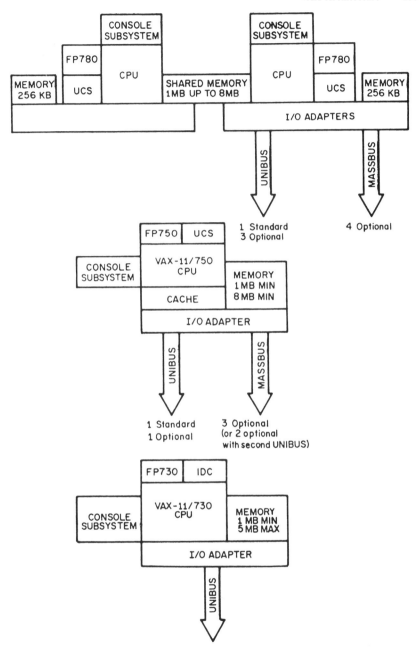

Figure 4.13 VAX Architectures

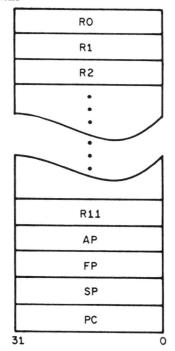

Figure 4.l4   VAX Programming Model

DEC designers have sought to assign more global significance to the high-numbered registers, while allowing the low-numbered registers to be "used for" temporary, local purposes. This is strictly a matter of convention. A programmer may use any register in any fashion. However, this arbitrary usage may hinder later program development and use, especially if a different person must handle the code and documentation is poor. It is recommended that users be consistent with the designer scheme. High-numbered registers are used for pointers needed by all software and hardware, while low-numbered registers can be used for working storage of string-type instructions.

4.12.2   PROGRAM STATUS REGISTER

The VAX system does not have a program status register as simple as the PDP-11 series because the VAX is a sophisticated system. In many ways the VAX supports multiple user activity far exceeding the capabilities of a PDP-11. Because a VAX may be handling several users or processes, several processor state variables associated with each process are then grouped together into a 32-bit Processor Status Longword, PSL, as depicted in Figure 4.15. (Assume for now that a process is a single stream of machine instructions executed in sequence.) The low order bits, bits 15:0 are designated the proces-

Table 4.17   Special VAX Register Uses and Names

Registers	Hardward Use	Conventional Software Use
PC (R15)	Program counter	Program counter
SP (R14)	Stack pointer	Stack pointer
FP (R13)	Frame pointer saved & loaded by CALL, used & restored by RET	Frame pointer; condition signalling
AP (R12)	Argument pointer saved & loaded by CALL, restored by RET	Argument pointer (base address of argument list)
R6:R11	None	Any
R3,R5	Address counter in character & decimal instructions	Any
R2,R4	Length counter in character & decimal instructions	Any
R1	Result of POLYD; address counter in character & decimal instructions	Result of functions (not saved or restored on procedure call)
R0	Results of POLY, CRC; length counter in character & decimal instructions	Results of functions, status of services (not saved or restored on procedure call)

sor status word, PSW. These bits contain unprivileged information. Simply stated, such unprivileged bits define status freely controllable by any program. Any user can access these bits and deliberately modify them if so desired. Bits 31:16 have an altogether different meaning. They are privileged status bits and are not available to anyone at any time.

The four least significant bits are defined as the condition code bits. A programmer could normally consider these bit values reflecting the status of the most recent instruction which affects them. It is the burden of the user to know which instructions affect which bits. Although processor designers try to invoke logical meaning to the cause and effect relationship between each bit and instruction, the programmer must not make assumptions about bit changes. The conditional branch instructions test the bits and use them to decide whether to branch or not.

The C bit designates bit 0. It is the carry condition flag and is usually set after arithmetic operations in which a carry out of, or borrow into, the most significant bit occurred. C is cleared after arithmetic operations which generated no carries or borrows. Other instructions either clear or have no affect on C. One other important function of C is its use as an input variable to the ADWC (add with carry) and SBWC (subtract with carry) instructions. These two instructions are important to multiple-precision arithmetic operations.

The V bit is bit 1 and flags an overflow condition in which the magnitude of the algebraically correct result is too large to be represented in the available space. The V bit is cleared after an arithmetic operation, in which case the result fits. If appropriately used, the V bit can also cause a program to trap to some code which could cause the condition to be exposed to a user. To do so, special trap enable bits must be set.

A result of an arithmetic operation which generates a zero sets the Z bit which is bit 2. The Z bit is cleared if the result is not zero. Most important, this reflects the actual result, even if overflow occurs. A negative result of an arithmetic operation causes the N bit, bit 3, to be set. An instruction which generates a positive or zero result clears this bit. Some instructions affect the N bit according to a stored result. In such cases, N reflects the actual result, even if the sign of the result is algebraically incorrect as a consequence of overflow.

The special conditions under which a program should cease execution and flag or correct an arithmetic operation are facilitated by the trap-enable bits or bits 7:4 of the PSL. When set these bits cause traps to occur under the special conditions. DV bit, bit 7, is the decimal overflow trap enable. FU bit, bit 6, is the floating underflow trap enable. A result which cannot be represented in floating point notation, because it is too small in magnitude, sets the trap to occur. A floating point underflowed result is always stored as zero. The integer overflow trap enable bit is bit 5, IV bit. The V condition bit, bit 5, is set independently of this bit. Should a trap occur, it would be useful to trace instructions. Bit 4, T bit, is used to debug programs and help single stepping through instructions. If any instruction is traced and causes an arithmetic trap, the trace trap occurs after the arithmetic trap.

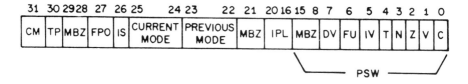

Figure 4.15   Processor Status Longword

The remaining bits in the PSL are explained later. In general, these bits facilitate system-wide operations. Bits 20:16 designate the processor's interrupt priority level. Other bits flag the mode (unprivileged or privileged, etc.).

4.13   VAX MEMORY MAP

Essential to any assembly language programmer's understanding is the space of addresses which are available and which are designated for other functions prescribed by the system software. This information is provided by the memory map of the machine. The VAX memory depicted in Figure 4.16 indicates that from the programmer's point of view, the bottom two billion bytes of virtual address space can be used for programs without the need to be concerned about special memory handling requirements. When the most significant address bit is set, that half of memory is addressing system space. System space comprises the operating system software and system-wide data. Processes can use this space to share the system-wide data and facilitate interrupt handling.

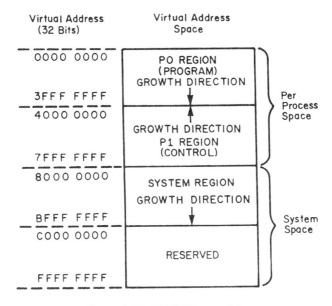

Figure 4.16   VAX Memory Map

The lower half of memory space is termed the process space. Each space is separately defined for each process. Process space is further defined or partitioned into P0 space and P1 space. P0 space contains program images and most of their data. P1 space contains the stacks and other process-specific data. As is explained later in this text, a stack can shrink or grow dynamically. Proper memory management requires that P1 and P0 space be appropriately allocated in the "working" space of a process. Because P1 space can grow towards lower addresses, it is unique in that it is allocated from the high address downward.

4.14 VAX DATA REPRESENTATION

There are seven categories of data types used in the VAX, each grouped below according to the groups of instructions that operate on them.

Integer and Floating data types
Character String data types
Numeric String data types
Packed Decimal data types
Queue data types
Variable Length data types
Special Table data types

These data types can be characterized by both size and format flexibility. Their usefulness is self-evident; however, their representation is not. In a 32-bit machine, an integer is not represented the same way as it is in a 16-bit machine. The VAX supports five different integer data representations. This means that machine language instructions exist which can manipulate 8-, 16-, 32-, 64-, and 128-bit sizes, termed byte, word, longword, quadword, and octaword integers, respectively. All integers are stored in memory in binary format (because the VAX is a binary computer) and can be treated as signed or unsigned. Unsigned integers extend upward from the value zero. Signed integers are represented in 2's complement notation. The MSB is zero for positive and zero quantities. The MSB is 1 otherwise.

A byte is eight contiguous bits numbered from the right 0 through 7. Each byte starts on an addressable byte boundary or in a register such as Rn<7:0>. A signed quantity as a byte is a 2's complement integer with bits increasing in significance from bit 0 through bit 6 with bit 7 designating the sign. A word is two contiguous bytes and starts on an arbitrary byte boundary. When in a register, the word is represented as Rn<15:0>. The bits are then numbered in increasing weight from bit 0 to bit 15. If an integer is being represented by the word, the MSB is zero (bit 15) for positive numbers and zero. A negative number contains a one in the MSB (bit 15). Other data types are listed in Table 4.18. Their representations are listed in Table 4.19.

Table 4.18   VAX Data Types

DATA TYPE	SIZE	RANGE (decimal)	
Integer		Signed	Unsigned
Byte	8 bits	-128 to $+127$	0 to 255
Word	16 bits	-32768 to $+32767$	0 to 65535
Longword	32 bits	-2^{31} to $+2^{31}-1$	0 to $2^{32}-1$
Quadword	64 bits	-2^{63} to $+2^{63}-1$	0 to $2^{64}-1$
Octaword	128 bits	-2^{127} to $+2^{127}-1$	0 to $2^{128}-1$
F –and D –floating point		$\pm 2.9 \times 10^{-37}$ to 1.7×10^{38}	
F –floating point	32 bits	approximately seven decimal digits precision	
D –floating	64 bits	approximately sixteen decimal digits precision	
G –floating point		$\pm 0.56 \times 10^{-306}$ to 0.9×10^{306}	
G –floating	64 bits	approximately fifteen decimal digits precision	
H –floating point		$\pm 0.84 \times 10^{-4932}$ to $\pm 0.59 \times 10^{4932}$	
H –floating	128 bits	approximately thirty-three decimal digits precision	
Packed Decimal String	0 to 16 bytes (31 digits)	numeric, two digits per byte sign in low half of last byte	
Character String	0 to 65535 bytes	one character per byte	
Variable-length Bit Field	0 to 32 bits	dependent on interpretation	
Numeric String	0 to 31 bytes (DIGITS)	$-10^{31}-1$ to $+10^{31}-1$	
Queue	$\geq$ 2 longwords/ queue entry	Queue entries at arbitrary displacement in memory	

Briefly, the data type of an instruction operand designates how the number of bits are to be treated as a unit and what meaning each unit possesses. A VAX processor's native instruction set recognizes four primary data types: integer, floating point, packed decimal, and character string. The several variations on these data types are listed in the previous tables.

Floating point values are stored as a signed exponent and a binary normalized fraction. Just as in the PDP-11, the normalization bit is not represented.

Table 4.19 VAX Data Type Representations

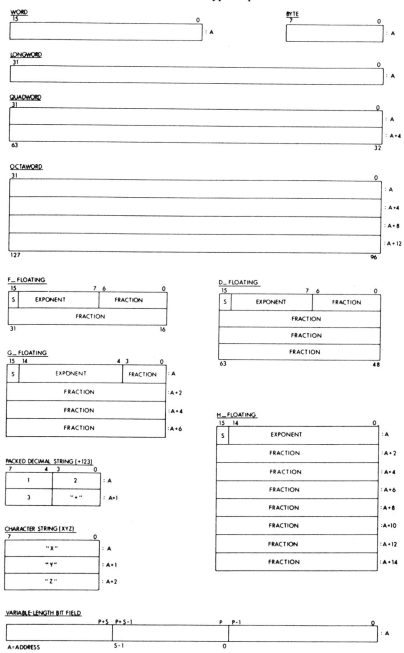

Also compatible with the PDP-11, two floating point formats (F-floating) and (D-floating) are standard on all VAX machine families. However, to make effective use of the true 32-bit capability of the VAX family, two additional floating point formats are available. They are extended range formats (G-floating and H-floating). Notice from the tables how the range increases with these two additional formats. A range of 33 decimal digits is possible with the H-float representation.

Packed-decimal data are stored as a string of bytes, again each byte is divided into two four-bit nibbles. One decimal digit is stored in each nibble with the highest order digit stored in the first byte as depicted in Figure 4.19. The sign of the packed-decimal quantity is found in the low order nibble of the last byte in the string. It is important to remember that there are two forms of decimal digits represented in a VAX; the decimal string data type in which each decimal digit occupies one byte, and the previously described packed-decimal data type which makes more efficient use of memory. The former is termed a numeric string and has several forms, two of which are the "leading separate numeric string" and the "trailing numeric string."

The leading numeric string has two attributes in a contiguous sequence of bytes in memory. The first attribute is the address A of the first byte (containing the sign character), and the length of the string in digits (not the length in the string of bytes). Digits of decreasing significance are assigned to bytes of increasing addresses. The trailing numeric string is a contiguous string of bytes in memory again described with two attributes. The first attribute is the address A of the first byte (most significant digit) of the string. The second attribute is the length of the string in bytes (not digits). Digits of decreasing significance are assigned to the increasing addresses.

Except for the least significant digit byte, all bytes of a trailing numeric string must contain ASCII decimal digit characters (0–9). The representation of the "non-least significant" digits must be:

digit	decimal	hex	ASCII character#
0	48	30	0
1	49	31	1
2	50	32	2
•	•	•	•
•	•	•	•
•	•	•	•
9	57	39	9

The highest addressed byte will contain an encoding of the least significant digit and the sign of the numeric string. DEC system software supports three encodings. They are briefly:

1. Unsigned numeric in which there is no sign and the least significant digit contains an ASCII decimal digit character.

2. Zoned numeric.

3. Overpunched numeric.

The reader is referred to manufacturer's literature for details of these later two formats. Table 4.20 lists the representation of LSD and sign.

Table 4.20   Representation of the Least Significant Digit and Sign

	Zoned Numeric Format			Overpunch Format			
digit	deci-mal	hex	ASCII char.	deci-mal	hex	ASCII char. norm	alt.
0	48	30	0	123	7B	{	0 [?
1	49	31	1	65	41	A	1
2	50	32	2	66	42	B	2
3	51	33	3	67	43	C	3
4	52	34	4	68	44	D	4
5	53	35	5	69	45	E	5
6	54	36	6	70	46	F	6
7	55	37	7	71	47	G	7
8	56	38	8	72	48	H	8
9	57	39	9	73	49	I	9
−0	112	70	p	125	7D	}	] : !
−1	113	71	q	74	4A	J	
−2	114	72	r	75	4B	K	
−3	115	73	s	76	4C	L	
−4	116	74	t	77	4D	M	
−5	117	75	u	78	4E	N	
−6	118	76	v	79	4F	O	
−7	119	77	w	80	50	P	
−8	120	78	x	81	51	Q	
−9	121	79	y	82	52	R	

4.15   VAX ADDRESSING MODES

Just as with the PDP-11, it is important to recognize the addressing capabilities of the VAX with registers as well as with memory locations. Instruction operands are often temporarily stored in registers or accessed through them.

In fact, registers can be used for temporary storage, accumulators, base registers, and index registers. As a base register, addressing of a software data structure such as a table is convenient and fast. When a register is used as an index register, the same expedient processing occurs for a logical offset into a data structure. Normally, a register used to contain data holds the data in the same format as it would appear in memory. A quad-word or double-floating datum would be stored in two adjacent registers. For example, a user who stores a double floating point number in register R5 loads both R5 and R6. As noted earlier, some registers have special meaning to certain software. These registers also have special addressing capabilities, most notably among them are the program counter and stack pointer.

The addressing modes and assembler syntax for the VAX are listed in Table 4.21. They are very similar to the PDP-11 addressing modes already discussed in this chapter.

Table 4.21 VAX Addressing Modes

Mode	Symbol	
Literal (immediate)	$\left\{ \begin{matrix} S\uparrow \\ I\uparrow \end{matrix} \right\}$ # constant	
Register	Rn	
Register Deferred	(Rn)	Indexed [Rx]
Autodecrement	−(Rn)	
Autoincrement	(Rn) +	
Autoincrement Deferred (Absolute)	@ (Rn) + @ # address	
Displacement	$\left\{ \begin{matrix} B\uparrow \\ W\uparrow \\ L\uparrow \end{matrix} \right\}$ displacement (Rn) address	
Displacement Deferred	@ $\left\{ \begin{matrix} B\uparrow \\ W\uparrow \\ L\uparrow \end{matrix} \right\}$ displacement (Rn) address	

n = 0 through 15
x = 0 through 14

The autodecrement-deferred mode is not listed. Can the reader see why? Six modes can be modified to allow indexed addressing. The register mode does not allow it. The other modes when so modified simply append the "index" name to them when in the indexed mode. For example, autoincrement modes with indexing would be "autoincrement indexed." A VAX processor recognizes six indexed addressing modes. In any indexed addressing mode, two registers are involved. One register is used to compute the base address of a data structure while the other register is used to compute an index offset into the data structure. Computation of the operand's effective address is accomplished as follows in the indexed mode:

1. The processor computes the base operand address provided by one of the basic addressing modes (except for the register mode).

2. Obtains the value in the index register and multiplies it by the given operand size.

3. Adds the resultant product to the operand address.

Note that the index register is not affected by these computations so that it could be used again and again. As in autoincrement and autodecrement addressing, the index is calculated in the context of the operand data type. Double-indexing is also possible and is left as an exercise to the reader. In short, the base address can be selected from a table of base addresses, using the displacement-deferred mode and then an index register can be used to provide the offset into the particular data table selected. Table 4.22 lists the index addressing modes. Rn specifies a general register and Rx specifies an index register.

Table 4.22   Index Addressing Modes

MODE	ASSEMBLER NOTATION
Register deferred index	(Rn) [Rx]
Autoincrement indexed	(Rn) + [Rx]
Immediate indexed	I# constant [Rx] which is recognized by assembler but is not generally useful. Operand address is independent of value of constant.
Autoincrement deferred indexed	@(Rn) + [Rx]
Absolute indexed	@#address [Rx]
Autodecrement indexed	−(Rn) [Rx]
Byte, word or longword displacement indexed	@B↑D(Rn)[Rx] @W↑D(Rn)[Rx] @L↑D(Rn)[Rx]
Byte, word or longword displacement deferred indexed	@B↑D(Rn)[Rx] @W↑D(Rn)[Rx] @L↑D(Rn)[Rx]

In Example 4.23 below, the index addressing mode is used in a Clear instruction. The full addressing mode is autoincrement deferred indexing. R2 contains the address of the operand address. The index value a is obtained as was described earlier. First, multiply the contents (5) of the index register which is R3 by the contents of the data type, which is 2. The W in CLRW specifies this data type as a word. Notice that the calculated word address is cleared as was desired by this CLRW @(R2)+[R3] instruction.

Example 4.23   Autoincrement Deferred Index Mode—CLRW @(R2)+[R3]. This example shows a Clear Word instruction using the autoincrement deferred indexing mode. R4 contains the address of the operand address. The index value A is obtained by multiplying the contents (5) of the Index register by the context of the data type, which is 2. The calculated word address is cleared.

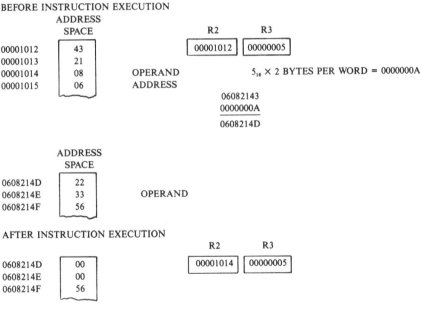

The displacement and displacement-deferred modes operate as follows. In the displacement mode a value is stored as a base address in a register. A byte, word, or longword unsigned constant is added to this base address. The resulting sum becomes the effective address of the operand. In the displacement-deferred mode, the only difference is that the resulting sum is the address of a location that contains the actual address of the operand. This is a form of indirect addressing. Does the PDP-11 have an equivalent displacement mode?

Example 4.24 illustrates a displacement deferred addressing mode in the MOVE LONG instruction, MOVL @↑X14 (R3)[R5],R7. The displacement of 14 is added to the contents of R3. The sum 0001026 is considered an address and the contents of this location produces an operand address, 44332211. This is now added to the index to obtain an indexed operand address of 44332211. The MOVL instruction now causes the contents of this address to be moved into R7 as shown.

Example 4.24 Displacement Deferred Index Mode - MOVL@↑X14 (R3)[R5],R7. This example shows a Move Long instruction using displacement deferred indexed addressing. The displacement of 14 is added to the contents of R1 yielding 00001026. The contents of this location yield the operand address (44332211). This quantity is added to the index yielding the indexed operand address of 44332221. The contents of this address are then moved into R5 as shown.

BEFORE INSTRUCTION EXECUTION

ADDRESS SPACE

Address	Space
00001012	12
00001013	34
00001014	56
00001015	78
00001026	11
00001027	22
00001028	33
00001029	44
44332221	01
44332222	23
44332223	45
44332224	67
44332225	89

R3
00001012

R5
00000004

R7
00000000

$4_{16} \times 4$ BYTES PER LONGWORD
$= 10_{16}$ (INDEX)

00001012	CONTENTS OF R3
00000014	DISPLACEMENT
	ADDRESS OF OPERAND
00001026	ADDRESS
44332211	OPERAND ADDRESS
00000010	INDEX
44332221	INDEXED OPERAND ADDRESS

AFTER INSTRUCTION EXECUTION

R3
00001012

R5
00000004

R7
67452301

4.16   VAX INPUT/OUTPUT STRUCTURE

As with any computer system the input/output structure is complex. The VAX is no different. However, much of the I/O programming requirements for data transfer into and out of the processor is made transparent to the typical user. I/O is a process of communicating between the processor and the peripheral devices. In some systems, I/O controllers do most of the work once the user has set up the interface correctly. Because I/O is complex and can cause real problems when someone else's CRT screen view is destroyed (for instance), a user seldom has the option to program I/O directly. System programs do most of the work for the user. A user is responsible for specifying the logical structure of some data but not responsible for the myriad attending details of setting a printer head to move and print along a line. These functions are served by the system software. The VAX uses a utility called Record Management Services (RMS) to handle files, their organization, and I/O operations. Chapter 8 covers these details.

Perhaps a good overview of a typical VAX I/O structure is possible by examining the VAX 11/780 system. The 11/780 is designed as a multi-user system for both program development and application system execution. It is intended as a priority-scheduled, event-driven system. As such an assigned priority determines the level of services given to a user. Time critical jobs receive service as needed while the system manages allocation of CPU time and memory residency for normal executing processes. A VAX 11/780 computer system consists of the central processor unit, the console subsystem, the

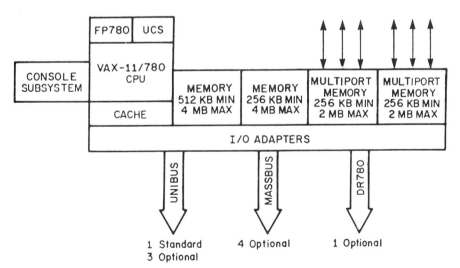

Figure 4.17   VAX 11/780 Hardware Configuration

main memory subsystem, and the I/O subsystem. A Synchronous Backplane Interconnect (SBI), UNIBUS, and MASSBUS subsystems comprise the I/O subsystem as depicted in Figure 4.17. PDP-11 computers and peripherals would conceivably connect to the UNIBUS, which is the basic bus of the PDP-11 family.

4.17 SUMMARY

Although this chapter focuses on the PDP-11, the organization of this family of computers is typical of many computer organizations from the small micro-computer to the larger mainframes. The important concepts to be learned apply across the spectrum of computers. They are:

1. How some numbers and characters can be formatted in a typical computer, including their representation in a finite number of bits.

2. How instruction formats depend on the number of operands and respective addresses.

3. How several addressing modes behave, including direct addressing, indirect addressing, and relative addressing.

4. How offsets and displacements are generated in the relative addressing mode both automatically and manually.

5. How the use of conditional branch instructions critically depends on the type of arguments (signed versus unsigned numbers).

The instructions presented in this chapter may be found in large general-purpose computers as well as in small microcomputers! However, different instructions and mnemonics are possible and certainly available. But those mnemonics not yet seen can be easily understood from those presented so far. For example, the MOV instruction of the PDP-11 is similar to the LDA (load) and STA (store) instructions of the Motorola 6809. Often the computer designer sought to use abbreviated forms for the actual instruction. BR for "branch," LA for "load address," and CLR for "clear" are a few examples. The reader is encouraged to examine other machines' assembly language instructions. Whether the PDP-11 or some other machine's language is studied, none of these issues is as important as good programming practices. Later sections of this chapter illustrated only a few such practices.

4.18 KEY WORDS

ASCII	autoincrement
autodecrement	biased exponent

byte	packing
computer family	parity
excess notation	PSR
exponent	register-deferred
fraction	signed conditional branches
hidden bit	stored exponent
index register	trap vector
longword	true exponent
machine compatibility	unsigned conditional branches
memory map	virtual address space
multi-user environment	word
normalization	

4.19 SUGGESTED READING

Andrews, Michael. *Microprocessor Interfaces for Control and Instrumentation.* Englewood Cliffs, N.J.: Prentice-Hall, 1982.

Chapter 4 includes a brief discussion of the instruction set of the Motorola 6809 8-bit microprocessor with sixteen examples. Later chapters provide some additional programming illustrations. The 6809's instruction set and addressing modes mimic many of the PDP-11's instructions and addressing modes. An interesting exercise would be to contrast the autoincrement and autodecrement modes in the 6809 with the PDP-11. They are very similar.

Bell, C. Gordon, Mudge, J. Craig, and McNamara, John E. *Computer Engineering, A DEC View of Hardware Systems Design.* Bedford, Mass.: Digital Press, 1978.

A good description of the PDP-11 family organization and the UNIBUS can be found on pages 269–276. A number of bus parameters, such as the maximum number of connections and delay in connecting, are discussed. The concepts presented are very detailed and tend to be advanced. A good description of the history of the DEC LSI-11 can be found on pages 301–326. The PDP-11 has been emulated with LSI bit-slice circuits. This implementation is recorded on pages 449–462. The implementation (CMU-11) actually falls between the PDP-11/10 and the PDP-11/40. Interestingly, the CMU-11 performs at twice the speed of the LSI-11. Intel 3000 microcomputer circuits were employed. The CMU-11 instructions emulating this overflow detection were costly because the 3000 bit-slice architecture has no overflow output.

Eckhouse, Richard H., Jr., and Morris, L. Robert. *Minicomputer Systems.* Englewood Cliffs, N.J.: Prentice-Hall, 1979.

The authors of this text, who are employed at Digital Equipment Corporation and have access to numerous facts, describe the PDP-11 operation in meticulous detail. The instructions are well-defined on pages 59–83. The reader can never understand enough about conditional branch instructions. Pages 143–145 contain some additional examples. How the PDP-11 handles floating-pointing numbers is discussed on pages 55–58. The focus is less upon concepts and more upon concrete examples. The explanations, however, tend to be brief.

Gear, C. William. *Computer Organization and Programming*. New York: McGraw-Hill, 1980.

Chapter 2 has a comparative study of the hardware organizations of the PDP-11, IBM 370, CYBER 170, and Intel 8080. The several tables list the machine instructions of each machine (pages 39, 53, 56–58, 73, 84). A number of contrasting machine language programs are also offered in this chapter to illustrate the computing power of each machine.

Gill, Arthur. *Machine and Assembly Language Programming of the PDP-11*. Englewood Cliffs, N.J.: Prentice-Hall, 1978.

This book moves along at a rapid pace. A useful coverage of branch instructions is found on pages 35–38 and 93–97. Page 95 contains several branch examples with a 4-bit machine, clearly illustrating the resultant condition codes and their effects on signed and unsigned conditional branch instructions. It is easy to read.

Greenfield, S.E. *The Architecture of Microcomputers*. Cambridge, Mass.: Winthrop Publishers, 1980.

General coverage of instructions and addressing modes is clearly described in Chapters 8 and 9. Unlike most books, the instructions are grouped according to the number of operands, as in Chapter 4. Overflow indicators are discussed on pages 270–274.

Kapps, Charles, and Stafford, Robert L. *Assembly Language for the PDP-11*. Boston, Mass.: Prindle, Weber & Schmidt, 1981.

Signed and unsigned numbers, including conditional branch instruction guidelines, can be found on pages 119–127. This is a very clear textbook on assembly language programming for the PDP-11. Topics are presented in an orderly fashion, beginning with elementary concepts and progressing toward complex issues.

Leventhal, Lance. *Introduction to Microprocessor Software, Hardware and Programming*. Englewood Cliffs, N.J.: Prentice-Hall, 1978.

The microprocessor instruction sets for the Intel 8080 and Motorola 6800 microprocessors are thoroughly covered in Chapter 3. Later chapters present numerous useful examples from numeric and nonnumeric data processing. This is a good book to obtain a comprehensive coverage of two popular 8-bit microprocessor chips.

Osborne, Adam, and Kane, Gerry. *Osborne 16-Bit Microprocessor Handbook*. Berkeley, Calif.: OSBORNE/McGraw-Hill, 1981.

Summaries of instruction sets for several 16-bit microprocessors are presented. They include the National Semiconductor PACE, General Instrument CP 1600, Texas Instruments TMS 9900, 9980, NOVA 9440, Intel 8086, Zilog Z8000, and

Motorola 68000. This handbook assumes considerable prior knowledge of micro-processors; however, detailed coverage is sometimes provided. Much of the discussion centers around instruction timing.

PDP-11 Processor Handbook. Maynard, Mass.: Digital Equipment Corporation, 1981.
Precise details of machine language instructions and the architecture of these members of the PDP-11 family can be found in Chapter 4 (instruction set) and Chapters 7 through 10. Advanced topics discussed are the floating-point instruction set in Chapter 11 and the commercial instruction set in Chapter 12. Chapter 3 includes additional examples on addressing modes. Manufacturer's data such as this processor handbook remains the most authoritative source on machine operation (except for the machine execution itself).

4.20 EXERCISES

4.1 What are the chief advantages to the manufacturer of a hierarchy of computers? To the user?

4.2 What two features of floating-point data representation in most computers help facilitate manipulation of the numbers internal to the computer?

4.3 Not all numbers in the PDP-11 floating-point representation contain a "hidden" one. Identify one number which is an exception to this normalization rule.

4.4 Suppose two floating-point numbers are expressed as
$$N_1 = S_1 * f_1 * 2 ** e_1$$
and
$$N_2 = S_2 * f_2 * 2 ** e_2$$
where S_i, f_i, and e_i are the sign, fraction, and exponent of the ith number.

  a. Express the product of N_1 and N_2
  b. Express the result of dividing N_1 by N_2.
  c. If fractions are normalized in a binary machine, how many bit shifts may be required to normalize the product?
  d. If fractions are normalized in a binary machine, how many bit shifts may be required to normalize the quotient?

4.5 Obtain the octal representation for the following PDP-11 floating-point numbers. The numbers are currently in decimal. (Hint: First obtain a fraction between ½ and 1.)

a. $41/64*2**7$

b. $-1.7*2**0$

c. 82

d. -82

e. $-1.2195122*10**-2$

f. -832

g. 0.0390625

4.6 What decimal numbers have the following single-precision PDP-11 floating-point representation?

a. 041377   b. 137000
   010001   100111

4.7 A 16-bit machine has the following floating-point representations:

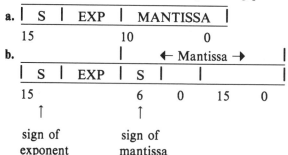

What is the range of numbers possible in single-precision and no hidden bit?

4.8 Compare the PDP-11 floating-point conventions with the IEEE #754 floating-point standard. What differences exist? How can the PDP-11 format be made compatible with the #754?

4.9 Generate the octal equivalent representation as stored in PDP-11 memory for each character string below assuming no parity.

a. AB   c. Lm

b. CE   d. #@

4.10 Repeat Problem 4.9, except assume even parity.

4.11 Repeat Problem 4.9, except assume odd parity.

4.12 The following condition code operators perform what functions?

a. 000252   c. 000277

b. 000257   d. 000263

4.13 Write an assembly language program to form a double-precision 2's complement. Assume that R0 contains the LSD's and R1 contains the MSD's.

4.14 Write an assembly language program to perform a double-precision addition. Assume the following:

R0—least significant digits of the first word
R1—most significant digits of the first word
R2—least significant digits of the second word
R3—most significant digits of the second word

4.15 What do the following PDP-11 machine instructions do?

a. 062204   e. 105161
                       000200

b. 105025   f. 005150

c. 105240   g. 005077
                       000020

d. 005064   h. 063703
   000200   002000

4.16 Why are the autoincrement and autodecrement addressing modes efficient?

4.17 In the PDP-11 autodecrement mode, $Rn \leftarrow Rn-1$ if $n < 6$. Why?

4.18 Obtain the octal representations for the following PDP-11 instructions.

a. ADD R2,R4   g. COM 200(R2)

b. COMB R4   h. ADD 40(R3),40(R2)

c. CLR (R7)+   i. COM @−(R1)

d. ADD (R1)+,R3   j. SUB @2000(R1),R3

e. ADD −(R1),R3   k. COM +(R1)

f. ADDB −(R1),R3   l. ADD 41(R6),R0

4.19 Devise code that does the same operations as these instructions. Ignore the PSR effects for all except f and g.

a. INC R1   e. INC @(R3)
                         INC R3
                         INC R3

b. DEC R5   f. CLC!SEV

c. MOV #1100,R0   g. CLC!CLV!CLZ!CLN

d. DEC R4
   DEC R4
   COM @(R4)

4.20 What do the following instructions do?

a. 072327   b. 073427
   000000   000000

4.21 Show by example that comparing unsigned numbers can be accomplished with tests on only a single condition. Show by example that single condition tests fail for comparing signed numbers.

4.22 Show that

                        •
                        •
                        •
              BIT   #177774,R3
              BNE   AGAIN
                        •
                        •
                        •

is equivalent to the code in Example 4.22.

4.23 What does the following one-word instruction do?
                     000400

4.24 Why do the following assembly language instructions represent poor programming practices?

  a. CMP   (R0)+,(R0)+   **b.** CMPB   (R0)+,(R0)+

4.25 What is the machine instruction (octal) for the following?
                     MOV (I)+,R0

4.26 Recode Example 4.12 to use register R4 as a stack pointer. Clearly specify the top of the stack.

4.27 Why are direct addressing modes preferred over indirect addressing modes?

4.28 Suppose a computer's addressing modes included a post-decrement and a pre-increment option. How would the "−" and "+" symbols be appropriately used in a typical assembly instruction?

4.29 Explain why certain addressing modes are preferred for manipulating tables of addresses while others are preferred for manipulating tables of data.

4.30 The PDP-11 uses parentheses to enclose an operand to indicate "indirection" or the deferred addressing mode. Examine two other computers and find other symbols to represent indirection.

4.31 The PDP-11 uses a form of relative addressing using the PC. Is it possible to build an addressing mode which is not relative to the PC in the PDP-11? In another machine?

4.32 Generate a routine to do the same task as the MACRO-11 .FLT 2 instruction in the PDP-11 assembly.

4.33 Flowchart a procedure to process single-precision floating-point numbers in the PDP-11 to perform the following:

    a. addition   **b.** multiplication

    b. subtraction   **c.** division

4.34 In the PDP-11, is it possible to implement indirect addressing using only memory locations and not a register? For example, will MOV (@#1000),R3 work?

4.35 Arithmetic operations on floating-point numbers consist of addition, subtraction, multiplication, and division. Using the following steps as a guide, generate an assembly language program to perform the requested operation. Assume that the numbers are single-precision, are found in 2's complement notation, and all outputs are to be normalized. Recall that the PDP-11 stored exponent is represented in excess 128 and the fraction is stored in sign magnitude notation.

    a. Add/Subtraction

        i. Shift the mantissa of the number with the smaller exponent to the right where the number of steps required is equal to the difference in the exponents.

        ii. Now adjust the exponent of this number to equal the other exponent.

        iii. Perform the desired arithmetic operation (add/subtract) on the mantissas.

        iv. Adjust the sign of the result.

        v. Normalize the result.

        vi. Check for overflow/underflow. Overflow occurs when the exponent is not in the allowable range.

    b. Multiplication

        i. Add the exponents and subtract 128.

        ii. Multiply the mantissas.

        iii. Normalize the result.

        iv. Check for overflow/underflow.

4.36 Repeat Problem 4.35 for double-precision numbers. Do you recall how to handle multi-byte arithmetic operations using the carry/borrow flag?

4.37 Using the most efficient addressing modes within a loop, generate a PDP-11 assembly language program which clears an array with the following.

a. one dimension

b. two dimensions

c. four dimensions

4.38 What two VAX instructions are useful in multiple-precision arithmetic operations?

4.39 What bits are designated the PSW bits in the PSL?

4.40 What is unique about P1 space in the VAX process space?

4.41 What two spaces constitute the "working" space of a process?

4.42 Which VAX addressing modes are not found in the PDP-11?

4.43 How is the effective operand address computed in an indexed mode?

4.44 Explain how to perform double-indexing in the VAX?

4.45 What are the three trailing numeric string encodings supported by VAX system software?

4.46 In the VAX, is the index register modified by an indexed addressing mode instruction? How about in the PDP-11?

Chapter 5

ELEMENTS OF PROGRAM ORGANIZATION

To iterate is human; to recurse, divine.

—L. Peter Deutsch

Inside every large program, there is a small program struggling to get out.

—C.A.R. Hoare

5.1 CHAPTER OBJECTIVES

This chapter is a distinct departure from earlier chapters, in which we looked at short segments of code completing primitive tasks. Now we examine code which is organized into a unitized, cohesive, structured program consisting of one or more modules. The concepts in this chapter will provide a means to do so.

In this chapter, we will see why and how sequences of instructions should be organized into self-contained procedures, subprograms, subroutines, and to a lesser extent, coroutines. Much of this chapter deals ostensibly with subroutines. However, subprograms in general (of which functions and subroutines are examples), and procedures utilize the same computer resource support mechanisms. These modular concepts are so fundamental to programming that nearly every imaginable program uses some of them. We initially examine why modules such as these are important and how to use them in computer programming. You could consider a subroutine as the assembly language counterpart of a procedure in an HLL. In reality, there is no difference in behavior or purpose. Often, our discussion will make no distinction between the two "modules."

Subroutines may be serially reusable, reentrant, recursive, or none of these. It is important to know when and how to employ such properties. Reentrant code is vital to system programs. Serially reusable subroutines, less stringently defined than reentrant code, are expected to be completely executed before reentry. Reentrant subroutines may be reentered any time under any circumstance or regardless of past history of usage. Recursive subroutines generate elegant mathematical routines but at the expense of complicated programming. All subroutines, however, are slower than equivalent code embedded in the main routine. The expense is the time to execute the call and the return.

The abstraction of a subroutine is quite similar to that of a procedure. Both are sets of statements commonly called or invoked. Both have definitive initiating and terminating statements. (Subroutines use the notion of a "starting address" in the JSR and return address in RTS, while procedures are often nested within BEGIN and END statements.) Both require a linkage mechanism to name the invoked code, pass values or parameters into the code, and provide output to the caller. Although subroutines have been used to illustrate program segmentation and linkage, the underlying hardware architecture supports the same requirements for procedures and procedure invocations.

A stack can play a major role in software that contains calling and called routines. The stack is useful to pass variables (by reference or otherwise), allocate local and/or global storage space, and maintain nested entry/exit linkages to called routines. A variety of parameter passage techniques is possible. Advantages and disadvantages need to be understood in relation to the properties or the intended behavior of the code. The key to effective stack usage among the many uses of software is consistency. One consistent stack picture is presented in this chapter. There are others.

In this chapter, the computer resources (primarily the program counter and stack pointer) which support modular program execution are described. Here, you should comprehend the associations among program control flow, program counter, and stack pointer. The point is to illustrate the processor mechanisms used to implement transfers, parameter passing, and return address manipulation. Terminating or temporarily suspending code execution in one module to begin execution elsewhere (a type of context switching) may require the intermediate results and status of the machine to be preserved before switching to the new module. Likewise, upon return to the previous module, the intermediate results, which may be found in registers and/or memory, may need to be restored. This preservation/restoration task should be consistently applied to the many procedures and users of assembly language code (or, in fact, of any language).

5.2 THE CONCEPT OF PROGRAM STRUCTURE

In the previous chapters, we have said very little about the relationship between individual steps in a program which comprise an algorithm. Most of our programs were actually straight-line structures or segments. That is, each source statement execution is followed by one and only one choice of statement execution. Conditional branches do not exist in straight-line structures. Conditional branches allow a program to select one of several paths to take, depending on the conditions at the current branch point. In these programs, not all of the instructions will be executed. Some lines have code which may be skipped over, at least temporarily. These segments are obviously not straight-line structures. Another common program structure is the loop. Here, the computer makes use of program control to reuse statements, which therefore specifies much more processing with fewer instructions. Earlier, we studied macros in another attempt to define structure in a source program. Macros make use of an assembler's ability to copy code elsewhere in the program, and thus relieve programming effort. All possible programming structures have not been exhausted here. We also need to study the general concept of a module.

5.2.1 MODULES

Recall from our higher level language experience that functions and subroutines (both also called subprograms), all of which are predefined modules, can add some structure to a program. A *module* is simply a self-contained segment of code; and for our purposes, assume that it is a section of a program which will be treated as a unit of assembly code. The term "module" delineates an assignment of programming responsibility within a team effort. But more importantly, a module is a unit in the subdivision of a program's functional specification. Such "modules" can be usefully employed as basic building blocks for constructing algorithms. In this chapter, we will examine these concepts further in order to illustrate what computer architecture resources support structured programs.

5.2.2 CONTROL CONSTRUCTS

Of course, there is more to program structure than just macros, procedures, functions, subprograms, and subroutines. For some time, the computer science community has recognized the need to encourage a few standard methods (constructs) in programming. By now, you should have been introduced to the Pascal control constructs (IF/THEN/ELSE, WHILE/DO, REPEAT/UNTIL, FOR, and CASE) which are built into the Pascal language. Pascal inherently encourages structure. A Pascal program organization is very specific:

1. You write the program name.

2. You make statements defining data and the particular kind or type of data.

3. You identify functions and procedures.

4. You develop the main part of the program.

The popularity of some of these same control constructs can be seen in BASIC which now includes IF-THEN and GOTO, as well as FOR/NEXT. We are not concerned with control constructs in this text, since they belong to the study of programming styles and practices. Nevertheless, we mention them here to remind us of the many aspects of program structure.

Modules in a program obey a hierarchy similar to that of programs and subprograms we commonly find developed with a high-level language. Modules could be called high-level modules or low-level modules, corresponding to programs and subprograms, respectively. Low-level modules, of course, can provide the same actions that high-level modules do. These include the ability to:

1. Accept data.

2. List out the computation or data processing task.

3. Return the results.

However, low-level modules should be considered as programs designed for a unique and specific purpose. Low-level modules should be able to receive data from high-level modules and return the desired results to the high-level modules. The high-level module could be considered the manager or boss who issues commands or directions to a subordinate. A low-level module, then, behaving as a subordinate, would return the results when available to the manager. The high-level module *calls* or *invokes* the low-level module. When the call occurs, the low-level module is expected to perform the specific task and *return* the control back to the high-level module. Do not expect that the low-level module will be called from the same place in the high-level module every time. There is no reason why the low-level module could not be called from different places. This is shown in Figure 5.1.

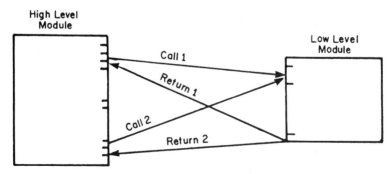

Figure 5.1 Module Invocation

One important aspect of a module call is the assumption that the low-level module returns control to the program at the point the call was made. In Figure 5.1, strange program behavior could be expected if call 1 to the low-level module would generate a return 2. Also, modules are well-written if a single entry and a single exit point exist in each module. Generally, the entry of a low-level module occurs at the beginning or at the first source statement of the module, and the exit occurs at the end or at the last source statement of the module. Obviously, it is much easier for us to understand modules when there is only one way to get into and out of each module in the total program.

5.3 SUBROUTINES

Subroutines are segments of code which are inherently modular. Although we normally do not consider a subroutine as a module, we could. The term, module, has typically been reserved for structures in programs written in a high-level language, such as FORTRAN, Ada, or Pascal. In a high-level language, a module can actually be a subroutine itself, but a subroutine is seldom called a module. Nevertheless, the point is that, except for minor differences, a subroutine provides the same capacity as a module to develop highly structured code. Of course, subroutines can be found in high-level code, just as modules can be found in low-level code, such as assembly language programs.

5.3.1 SUBROUTINES VERSUS MACROS

Subroutines are not macros, although they appear quite similar. A subroutine possesses a definition just as a macro does. However, no assembler directive is required (such as .XXXXX) to define a subroutine. You generate the subroutine code outside of the main program execution area. Make sure that if the subroutine follows a main program, the last executable statement in the main program does not permit the subroutine to be executed. A subroutine should be executed only when "called." In contrast to a macro, a subroutine's code is generated only once at assembly time. Whereas, a macro, when called, informs the assembler to expand the macro definition at the position of the macro call at assembly time, not execution time. A macro produces a copy of the code. A subroutine call or, more appropriately, a subroutine JUMP does not cause a copy to be inserted at the calling line of code. Rather, a subroutine call causes the program control flow to exit the calling program, execute the subroutine, and then return to the calling program at the point of the subroutine call. Subroutines are highly desirable when program memory space is precious.

5.3.2   SUBROUTINE CALLS AND RETURNS

Subroutines are advantageous when we desire to execute a particular sequence of code from several different positions in the main program.[1] For example, we may desire a message to be printed out on a terminal at several instances in a program. If the messages are identical, the subroutine can conveniently perform this task at each instance. In Example 5.1, the

Example 5.1   Subroutine Calls in the PDP-11

```
;MAIN PROGRAM
                        •
                        •
                        •
            JSR  PC,ADDP        ;CALL DOUBLE-PRECISION
                                ;SUBROUTINE
            MOV R0,RESULT       ;NEXT INSTRUCTION IN MAIN
            CLR TEN             ;PROGRAM
                        •
                        •
                        •
            JSR  PC,ADDP        ;CALL DOUBLE-PRECISION
                                ;SUBROUTINE
MORE:       COM NINE            ;NEXT MAIN PROGRAM
            BR   OUT            ;INSTRUCTION
                        •
                        •
                        •
;SUBROUTINE
ADDP:       MOV R0,-(SP)        ;PRESERVE ACTIVE REGISTERS
            MOV R1,-(SP)
            MOV R2,-(SP)
            MOV ARG1,R0         ;BODY OF SUBROUTINE
            MOV ARG2,R1
            ADD R1,R0           ;ADD LOW 16 BITS
            MOV ARG3,R1
            MOV ARG4,R2
            ADC R1
            ADD R2,R1           ;ADD HIGH 16 BITS
            BVS  ERROR          ;OVERFLOW?
            MOV R1,HIGHSUM      ;SAVE HIGH WORD RESULT
            MOV R0,LOWSUM       ;SAVE LOW WORD RESULT
            MOV (SP)+,R2        ;RESTORE ACTIVE REGISTERS;
            MOV (SP)+,R1        ;NOTE; THE ORDER OF
            MOV (SP)+,R0        ;RESTORATION
RETURN:     RTS PC             ;RETURN TO MAIN PROGRAM AT
                                ;LOCATION "MORE"
```

---

[1]The discussion, in reality, describes the general class of subprograms which includes functions and subroutines. A procedure is an HLL synonym for a subprogram. The reader should realize that calls and returns to a subprogram, function, subroutine, and procedure are similar in many respects.

subroutine, ADDP, is called twice from the main program. This subroutine performs double-precision addition.

This PDP-11 assembly language program uses a JSR instruction (jump to subroutine) with the address of the starting location of the subroutine following the first operand (PC in this case). The first operand in the JSR instruction determines where the program counter will be saved when the program jumps to the subroutine. Saving the PC is necessary so that upon returning from the subroutine to the main program, the PC will find the proper address. Various jump-to-subroutine instructions and their corresponding machine operations for the PDP-11, HP 2100, and IBM 360/370 are shown in Examples 5.2 to 5.4.

Example 5.2   PDP-11

Assembly Language	Machine Operation	Comments
JSR REG,ADDP	-(SP) ← PC	;PC STORED IN A REGISTER
	REG ← PC	;AS WELL AS ON A STACK
	PC ← ADDP	;POINTED TO BY R6; FINALLY,
		;PC POINTS TO SUBROUTINE

Example 5.3   HP 2100

Assembly Language	Machine Operation	Comments
JSB ADDP	MEM[ADDP] ← PC	;PC STORED IN FIRST LINE
	PC ← ADDP	;OF SUBROUTINE; NOTE
		;SELF-MODIFYING CODE
		;OCCURS IN FIRST LINE OF
		;SUBROUTINE

Example 5.4   IBM 360/370

Assembly Language	Machine Operation	Comments
BAL RETURN,ADDP	REG ← PC	;BRANCH AND LINK (BAL)
	PC ← ADDP	;CAUSES PC TO BE STORED
		;IN A REGISTER
		;DETERMINED BY "RETURN"
		;(RETURN AND REG MUST
		;BE SAME REGISTER)

The return from subroutine action must place the return address of the calling point in the PC. This operation for each of the above computers occurs as follows:

PDP-11 (Example 5.2)

Assembly Language	Machine Operation	Comments
RTS REG	PC ← REG	;REG CONTAINS RETURN
	REG ← (SP)+	;ADDRESS, OLD VALUE OF
		;REG NOW RESTORED

HP 2100 (Example 5.3)

Assembly Language	Machine Operation	Comments
JMP ADDP,I	PC ← ADDP	;INDIRECT ADDRESSING TO
		;FIRST LINE OF SUBROUTINE
		;WHERE RETURN ADDRESS WAS
		;SAVED

IBM 360/370 (Example 5.4)

Assembly Language	Machine Operation	Comments
BR RETURN	PC ← REG	;A GENERAL PURPOSE
		;REGISTER, REG, HAS
		;THE RETURN ADDRESS

A subroutine call behaves much like the module invocation in Figure 5.1. Here, a high-level module makes a call to a low-level module, at which point the low-level module executes the task and returns to the high-level module at the calling point. Both subroutines and modules have a single entry point and a single exit point.

5.3.3   SUBROUTINE STRUCTURE

Figure 5.2 illustrates the structure of a subroutine. The first line of code in the subroutine should always serve as the entry point to a subroutine. The last line should always serve as the exit point. A subroutine has three distinct parts: entrance linkage, body of subroutine, and exit linkage. The entrance linkage of a subroutine must perform the following tasks. First, the return address just below the call must be preserved, either in a register, stack, or memory. Secondly, the registers of the programming model, which the subroutine will modify during subroutine execution, should be preserved. These two initialization steps should be accomplished with every subroutine. However, the first step may not exist within the actual subroutine itself, but rather in the main program as part of the subroutine call. Specific entrance linkage steps must be determined by the particular architecture of the specific machine. A single and unique task is then found in the body of the subroutine. Here, the lines of code you need to perform the task required of the subroutine are embedded. Following the body of the subroutine is the exit linkage. The exit linkage performs the reverse process of the entrance linkage. First, any active registers that were preserved at the beginning of the subroutine are now restored to their former values. Finally, some mechanism must be invoked to jump back to the calling point in the main program.

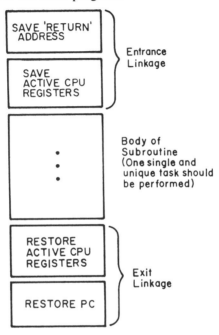

Figure 5.2   Subroutine Structure

   The individual steps required of any entrance and exit linkage are very machine-dependent. For example, in the PDP-11, the return address is saved by the subroutine call instruction: JSR. The first operand specifies the register in the programming model where the current contents of the program counter will be stored during the subroutine execution. Hence, this step of the entrance linkage exists as part of the subroutine call. Some machines, however, require code internal to the subroutine to save the current PC (e.g., HP 2100).

5.3.4   HP 2100 LINKAGE

In Example 5.5, the entrance linkage to the subroutine called ADDP depicts the HP 2100 assembly language instruction JSB ADDP at the line of code

labeled GO. In this language, the first line of the subroutine must contain a
NOP, because the return address will be stored in this line of code. The NOP
opcode in Example 5.5 will be replaced by the value of the address HERE.
Upon completion of the subroutine task, a jump instruction in the indirect
address mode will cause HERE to be loaded into the program counter. HERE
is the very next program line following the subroutine call.

Example 5.5 Subroutine Linkage in the HP 2100 Machines

```
/MAIN PROGRAM
                      •
                      •
                      •
GO              JSB ADDP    /CALL SUBROUTINE, NOW NEXT
HERE                        /MAIN PROGRAM INSTRUCTION.
                      •
                      •
                      •
/SUBROUTINE
ADDP            NOP         /SAVE SPACE FOR RETURN PC VALUE;
                      •     /SELF-MODIFYING INSTRUCTION
                            /NEEDED
                      •     /SUBROUTINE BODY NOW FOLLOWS
                      •
RETURN          JMP ADDP,I  /INDIRECT ADDRESS OBTAINS
                            /PC=HERE
```

Machines which execute subroutine calls and returns, as illustrated in
Example 5.5, have one major disadvantage. Any code which uses JSB (the
jump to subroutine) is necessarily self-modifying. The modified code is always
the first line of each subroutine. The NOP is replaced with the return address
for the subroutine. This replacement occurs in the program area. Programs
which modify themselves (in this case, using JSB) are potentially hazardous.
Furthermore, such code cannot reside in a ROM.

5.3.5 IBM 360/370 LINKAGE

The subroutine linkage for the IBM 360/370 illustrated in Example 5.6
accomplishes the same subroutine call as in the previous example. However,
self-modifying code is no longer required. The IBM 360 main program
requires us to define a register named RETURN. The EQU is an assembler
directive which is equivalent to the direct assignment statement in the PDP-
11. In Example 5.6, RETURN is defined as register 14. A subroutine call is
made with the assembly language instruction, BAL. The first operand must
contain the source of the return address. The second operand in the BAL

instruction contains the address of the first line of code in the subroutine. In contrast to the self-modifying code previously seen, the IBM 360/370 subroutine does not require a NOP in the first line. In the example shown, the first line, labeled ADDP, performs a loading operation (L is the mnemonic for LOAD). The number SIX is loaded into COUNT.

Example 5.6   Subroutine Linkage in the IBM 360/370

```
/MAIN PROGRAM
                    •
                    •
                    •
RETURN      EQU 14              ;SET UP RETURN ADDRESS REGISTER
            BAL  RETURN,ADDP    ;SUBROUTINE CALL VIA BRANCH AND
                                ;LINK INSTR.
            L    2,Y            ;SUBSEQUENT INSTRUCTION IN BODY
            A    INDEX,TWO      ;OF CALLING PROGRAM
                    •
                    •
                    •
/SUBROUTINE
ADDP        L    COUNT,SIX      ;FIRST LINE OF SUBROUTINE
                    •
                    •            ;BODY OF SUBROUTINE; SINGLE AND
                    •            ;UNIQUE TASK BEING PERFORMED
EXIT        BR   RETURN         ;RETURN TO MAIN PROGRAM; RETURN
                                ;ADDRESS FOUND IN REGISTER 7
```

The exit linkage of 360/370 subroutines uses the branch instruction (BR). The operand of this branch instruction contains the source of the return address. When the subroutine is completed and control returns to the main program, the return value of the PC (which is pointing just below the BAL instruction in the main program) is found in RETURN. The difference between the exit linkage in Examples 5.5 and 5.6 is obvious. The return address is found in a register in the IBM 360/370, while the return address in the HP2100 machine is found in the first line of code in the subroutine. Neither of these examples has illustrated the complete entrance and exit linkage steps illustrated in Example 5.1. Neither preserves or restores active registers which are integral elements in entry and exit linkage.

5.4   SUBROUTINE PROPERTIES

As with any body of code, subroutines possess properties which can increase system software performance. For example, a subroutine may be required to be relocatable anywhere in memory. Relocatable subroutines are very important in machines with limited memory or a multi-user or tasking environment where concurrent program execution is expected. In both cases, the subroutine will probably be moved around by the system software to relocate it into "new" available memory space. To relocate programs including subroutines, a relocating loader is used. This loader will place the subroutines after other programs and subroutines, and add the necessary starting address or relocation constants to the subroutine addresses referred to by the main program. A subroutine can be made relocatable by initially writing position-independent code. In that case, a relocatable loader may not be required because all addresses in the subroutine are expressed relative to a program counter's value.

A subroutine is a vivid illustration of many modules which can be affected by a change in program control flow. When a subroutine is called, the program counter is modified to cause a jump to the subroutine. When the subroutine is terminated, the program control flow returns to the calling point in the main program. If the only control flow occurs to/from a calling program, a user clearly understands when and under what circumstances a subroutine may be entered. However, predictable control flow is not always possible. A subroutine may be terminated prematurely by an interrupt request. In that case, the behavior of control flow is not predictably known. When the interrupt process is completed, the program execution should resume within the subroutine at the exit point to the interrupt process, and not at the end of the subroutine.

Subroutines which are non-self-modifying and which allow reentry without any execution errors are called *reentrant* subroutines. Non-self-modifying code never contains a store instruction whose destination operand is an instruction in the subroutine. A reentrant subroutine can be interrupted and called by an interrupting program, and still execute correctly upon returning to the subroutine. Many program applications are built around interrupt-based systems. In this environment, subroutine reentrancy is vital because a reentrant subroutine may only be partially executed at interruption time. When subroutine execution reconvenes at the interrupt point, it will execute properly (as intended by the programmer). Reentrant subroutines are generated by the programmer in a convenient manner using the stack since stack use enhances automatic reentrancy. Reentrant subroutines should use the stacks not only for parameter passage, but also for register preservation, as well as temporary storage (if not enough registers exist).

Self-modifying code in subroutines eliminates reentry. The HP 2100 assembly code example described previously is self-modifying. Hence, this is not a reentrant subroutine. The IBM 360/370 example is reentrant because this routine leaves the return address in a machine register instead of leaving it in program memory, as in the HP assembly code.

Sometimes a subroutine must be coded with the capability to call itself. This type of subroutine is a *recursive* subroutine if, in fact, it does call itself within the body of the subroutine. A recursive subroutine must be reentrant and thus must be pure code. Recursive and reentrant subroutines are very important, and we will return to these topics later. But in order to fully understand these features, we will first study stacks in greater detail.

5.5 STACKS

A stack is a contiguous set of addressable locations which holds data items and obeys certain entry/exit conventions. Stacks may be physically implemented in hardware as a set of general-purpose registers or in memory. Some machines allow a considerable amount of special hardware to carry out stack operations, while other computers provide the stacking means with fast single-line instructions using memory for the storage media. Regardless of how any stack is implemented, a stack must have the capacity to:

1. Maintain a linear array whose length can expand or contract without any constraints.
2. Command that words be added at only one end of the linear array. That end is called the top of the stack.
3. Command that words be removed from that same end of the array, the top of the stack.

The stacking commands are typically called **PUSH** for entering data onto the top of the stack, and **POP** for deleting data one at a time from the top of the stack. Some processors (6800, 6809, 68000) call the POP operation PULL. The PUSH and POP commands may store or retrieve any data type including bytes, words, or multiple words. Stacks can be organized to store any data size. Bytes in a two-byte word size memory are stored in one-half of a word size with the other half of the word possibly remaining vacant. Multiple word storage is accomplished by ensuring that the pointer skips the appropriate number of cells. In any event, the pointing and storage operations are sensitive to the specific machine, and a variety of stack manipulation instructions can be found in computers.

A pointer which keeps track of the top of the stack is called a stack pointer. A stack pointer does not contain data to be entered onto or retrieved from the stack, but rather contains an address of either the currently available stack location or the last used location in the stack.

Figure 5.3 illustrates a stack with data being stored in increasing memory locations. At first, the stack is pointing to location 4002. In the next stack operation, the datum 36 is added to the stack, and the stack pointer points to location 4004. In the final stacking operation, the datum 43 has been added to the stack at location 4006. Notice that the stack pointer only points to the last used location which is also the top of the stack. This particular stack adds datum toward increasing memory locations. Stacks in the PDP-11 are seldom organized with the top of the stack moving toward location 177777.

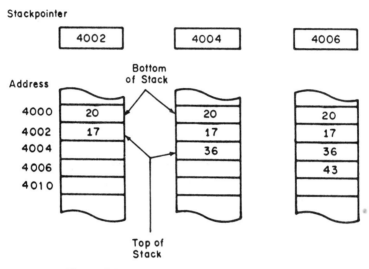

Figure 5.3   Push-Down Stack (Toward 177777)

The push-down stack, illustrated in Figure 5.4, performs a similar set of operations. However, in this push-down stack the datum is entered in decreasing memory locations as shown. This push-down stack direction is commonly encountered in the PDP-11. The stack area recommended by the manufacturer and used in the RT-11 operating system assumes that the bottom of the stack exists at 1000. The stack area then moves toward decreasing memory locations. The upper limit or top of the stack, using RT-11 in the PDP-11, is approximately location 400. A push-down stack is a last-in-first-out stack. In any machine, more than one stack may be used.

Stacks are used to accomplish a variety of tasks in a computer. The operating system software may use a stack to perform a dynamic storage allocation. Stacks can be used to activate as well as deactivate arrays for one or more user's program. Stacks can even be used by the operating system to activate or deactivate a user's program altogether. Finally, stacks are highly desirable for parameter passage from programs to subprograms, from high-level modules to low-level modules, from calling programs to subroutines, and from one

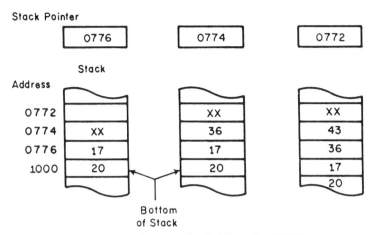

Figure 5.4   Push-Down Stack (Toward 000000)

subroutine to another subroutine. In any given computer, the stack manipulation operations should be consistently applied keeping in mind the system software stacking conventions as well as the hardware stacking conventions. A stacking convention must identify:

1. The direction of stacking (toward increasing memory locations or toward decreasing memory locations).

2. Whether the stack pointer points to the next available location or the previously accessed location.

3. The stack area to be used by individual subroutines and/or modules, as well as the stacking area of the system software.

Some convention should be adhered to throughout the system software and user software, because many computer stack pointers are manipulated not only by instructions in a user program, but also by hardware (for example, when the RESET line is asserted). The RESET line of many small machines causes an automatic stacking of the programming model registers onto a stack area. Some machines provide a hardware stack pointer and a software stack pointer. For instance, the 6809 microprocessor has two stack pointers: the S pointer for hardware stacking operations caused by interrupts and other external conditions, and the U pointer available as a user stack pointer. Other machines (such as the 68000) operate in either one of two modes, a system (or supervisor) mode or a user mode. In the user mode, a user stack pointer is available. In the supervisor or system mode, a supervisory stack pointer as well as a user stack pointer are available. (The 68000 invokes operating system software in the supervisor mode.)

A clear understanding of a machine's stack pointer capabilities is essential to error-free programming. Many side-effect problems of low level modules and/or subroutines are a direct result of the incorrect application of stack pointers. For example, it is certainly possible to implement the stack configuration of Figure 5.3 in the PDP-11. However, Example 5.7 illustrates how the PUSH operation can be inconsistent with the PUSH operation utilized in RT-11. In the unlikely event that your PDP-11 uses no system software similar to RT-11, any stacking configuration is permitted as long as you follow the same configuration throughout the program. Notice, however, that the PDP-11 stacking convention's direction grows toward decreasing memory locations, and the stack pointer points to the last used location. Hence, even though you may have a very simple computer system which requires no operating system software, you must still contend with the stacking direction of the JSR instruction. The JSR instruction automatically stores the program counter onto the stack (toward 000000). The system stack pointer in the PDP-11 designates register R6 for this purpose. Hence, R6 is not truly a general-purpose register.

Example 5.7   PDP-11 Stacking Consistency with RT-11

PUSH

Consistent	Inconsistent
MOV R0,-(SP)	MOV R0,(SP)+

POP

Consistent	Inconsistent
MOV (SP)+,R0	MOV -(SP),R0

The need for a consistent set of stack operations is made clearer by examining the facilities of the 68000. The 68000 has the capacity for system stacks as well as user-defined stacks. Both stacks normally grow toward decreasing memory locations, similar to the PDP-11. Hence, the register indirect with the predecrement mode is employed to push data onto the stack as in the following instruction.

```
MOVE D0,-(SP)    ;68000 CODE FOR A "PUSH"; MICRO-OPERATIONS
                 ;SAME AS PDP-11; D0 IS DATA REGISTER ZERO
```

This instruction pushes a word from D0 onto the active stack. The "active" stack depends on whether the machine is in the system or in the user mode.

To pull data from the stack, the appropriate move instruction for the 68000 must implement the address register indirect with post increment mode as follows:

```
MOVE (SP)+,D0    ;68000 CODE FOR A "POP" OR "PULL";
                 ;MICRO-OPERATIONS SAME AS PDP-11
```

This instruction retrieves the next word from the stack and transfers it to D0. These 68000 stacking directions are consistent with the stacking direction used by the microprocessor hardware RESET signal, exception processing sequences, and other 68000 facilities. When RESET is activated, it causes the 16-bit status register and the 32-bit program counter to be pushed onto the supervisor stack to preserve the state of the program. The same is true for most exception processing. (An exception processing sequence occurs when, for instance, an instruction fetch was attempted at an address which is illegal in the 68000.)

The instruction set of the 68000 contains two additionally useful instructions called LINK and UNLINK which manipulate the stack pointer and do more. As expected, the stacking conventions are consistent with the stack manipulations caused by hardware processes. The LINK instruction is a link and allocate space instruction. It causes the machine operations:

1. -(SP) ← An   ;An IS A FRAME POINTER USING REGISTER n
2. An ← SP   ;PERFORM LINK
3. SP ← SP+d   ;ALLOCATE PARAMETER SPACE ON STACK

First the stack pointer is decremented to point to the next available decreasing memory location on the stack. Then, a specified address register (containing the old frame pointer) is pushed onto the stack. In the next operation of the LINK instruction, the stack pointer is loaded into the specified address register, and finally, a 16-bit sign extended displacement is added to the stack pointer. This last operation allows for parameter passage opportunities.

The unlink (UNLK) instruction causes the following operations:

1. SP ← An   ;UPDATE STACK POINTER; DELETE D SPACES
2. An ← (SP)+   ;RESTORE OLD FRAME POINTER

The unlink instruction causes the stack pointer to be loaded from the specified address register. Next, the address register is loaded with a word pulled from the top of the stack. As expected, to be consistent, the 68000 link and unlink instructions push data onto the stack, first, by *decrementing* the stack pointer and, secondly, by *performing the storage operation*. The pull operation first takes the datum off the stack, and then updates the stack pointer. These predecrement and postincrement stacking operations are consistent throughout the entire instruction set of the 68000, matching hardware and system software stacking operations.

The entry and exit linkage supported by the instruction set of the 68000 is simple and straightforward. To emulate LINK and UNLINK, the PDP-11 would require an extra instruction to add and delete stack space. As already observed, the two instructions, LINK and UNLK (unlink), do much of the required pushing and popping. Example 5.8 illustrates a usage of both instructions for procedure calls. A frame pointer is in address register A3, and the stack pointer is in A7. A stack frame is a stack picture generated by a single procedure. Hence, the stack pointer should *always* remain at the top of the stack frame during procedure execution. Note that Figure 5.5 contains two stack frames, one for procedure A and one for procedure B.

Example 5.8 Using Link and Unlink in the 68000

High-Level Source Code	Compiler Generated Code	Comments
A: PROCEDURE (A)	A:	;CALL IS MADE IN
•		;PROCEDURE A, STEP 1
•	•	
•	•	
CALL B (C)	PEA <EA> OF C	;SAVE PARAMETER SPACE
•	JSR B	;CALL PROCEDURE B
•		;WITH ARG C
•	LEA 4(SP),SP	;CLEAN UP PARAMETER
END |A|	•	;SPACE, ADD 4 TO SP,
	•	;STEP 6
	•	
B: PROCEDURE (B)	B: LINK FP,PROCBALLOC	;CALLED PROCEDURE,
•	•	;STEP 3 g
•	•	;SAVE FRAME POINTER
•	•	;ON STACK, STEP 4
END |B|	UNLK FP	;CLEAN UP FRAME
		;POINTER, STEP 5
	RTS	;GO BACK TO
		;PROCEDURE A

Equivalent 68000 Assembly Code	
LEA $2000,A3	;A3 ← 2000 (INITIALIZE FRAME POINTER)
LEA $1FF0,SP	;SP ← 1FF0 (INITIALIZE STACK POINTER)
;PROCEDURE A STARTS HERE	
•	
•	
•	
PEA -6(A3)	;-(SP) ← A3-6, SET UP LOCAL SCRATCH
	;FOR PROCEDURE A
JSR PROCB	;CALL PROCEDURE B USING JUMP-TO-
•	;SUBROUTINE INSTRUCTION
•	
•	
UNLK A3	;RESTORE STACK POINTER (ADD 6 TO
	;A3)
RTS	;RETURN TO CALLING ROUTINE
	;(WHOEVER CALLED
	;PROCEDURE B)
;END OF PROCEDURE A	

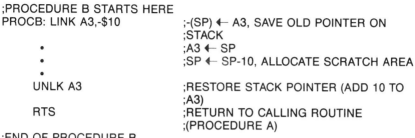

```
;PROCEDURE B STARTS HERE
PROCB: LINK A3,-$10        ;-(SP) ← A3, SAVE OLD POINTER ON
                           ;STACK
        •                  ;A3 ← SP
        •                  ;SP ← SP-10, ALLOCATE SCRATCH AREA
        •
      UNLK A3              ;RESTORE STACK POINTER (ADD 10 TO
                           ;A3)
      RTS                  ;RETURN TO CALLING ROUTINE
                           ;(PROCEDURE A)
;END OF PROCEDURE B
```

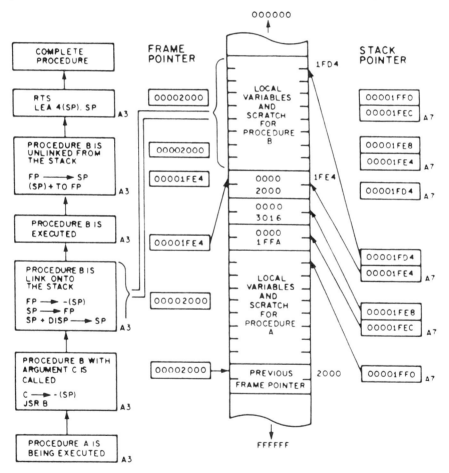

Figure 5.5   68000 Stack Picture

5.5.1 PDP-11 STACKING

In the PDP-11, stacking operations portrayed in Examples 5.9 and 5.10 illustrate a consistent stacking convention. In Example 5.9, the stacking operation causes registers R0, R1, and R2 to be pushed onto the stack, starting at location 0476. Notice that prior to this code execution, the stack pointer points to location 0500. At the end of this code execution, the stack pointer points to location 0472. That is, the stack pointer always points to the last used location. In an unstacking operation of the PDP-11, illustrated in Example 5.10, the three registers are unstacked or pulled off of a stack. Since the stack pointer is pointing to the last used location, the first instruction should be a MOV (SP)+,R2, and so on. The stacking and unstacking operations illustrated are useful in saving the programming model registers onto a stack prior to a subroutine execution, which must use registers R0, R1, and R2 for its own purposes. The stacking operations should be found in the beginning of a subroutine, and the unstacking operations should be found at the end of a subroutine. These examples illustrate part of the entrance and exit linkage for a subroutine structure depicted in Figure 5.2.

Example 5.9   A "PUSHING" Operation

```
            CODE
              •
              •
              •
STACK:    MOV R0,-(SP)
          MOV R1,-(SP)
          MOV R2,-(SP)
              •
              •
              •
```

Example 5.10   A "POPPING" Operation

```
            CODE
              •
              •
              •
UNSTACK:  MOV (SP)+,R2
          MOV (SP)+,R1
          MOV (SP)+,R0
              •
              •
              •
```

5.5.2 PASSING PARAMETERS IN THE PDP-11

Because we never know who has used the stack pointer last, it is important to make sure that any time a process uses the stack, that process must restore the stack pointer to its former position prior to process invocation. For safe parameter passage to and from subroutines, a procedure is illustrated in Figure 5.6. Assume that parameters are to be transferred to the subroutine. The subroutine also needs local storage. Furthermore, the subroutine uses some of the programming model registers and must save the old register contents before writing over them.

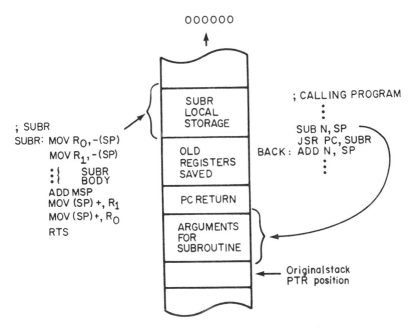

Figure 5.6 PDP-11 Stack Picture

   To invoke a consistent stacking configuration which reduces side effects, the calling program first makes room for the parameters to be transmitted to the subroutine. The SUB N,SP instruction in the calling program reserves space for the parameters. Next, the subroutine is called with JSR PC,SUBR. This instruction causes the program counter to be stored on the same stack using the stack pointer by which we previously reserved parameter space. Now the subroutine is entered. Its entry linkage causes any registers needed by the subroutine to be saved on the stack. Next, the subroutine reserves local storage on the stack for scratchpad area with the SUB M,SP instruction.

The stack picture (also called activation record or stack frame) created by the calling program and subroutine code helps minimize side effects which may cause the stack pointer to inadvertently write over important information should another process override this subroutine. For example, if during this subroutine execution, an interrupt occurs, the stack pointer will save the program counter above the top of the subroutine local storage area. Program control will exit the subroutine, handle the interrupt process, and return to the subroutine activity by popping the PC return address off the top of this stack (and not from the local storage area). Hence, subroutine program execution can resume without error because the stack pointer has been updated to point to the subroutine local storage again.

The subroutine body must also contain exit linkage instructions which essentially move the stack pointer to point to the PC return location. Any preserved registers must now be restored as we exit. In Figure 5.6, an ADD and two MOV instructions are required at the end of the subroutine body to deactivate the subroutine local storage area and to restore registers R1 and R0 to their original contents, respectively. When the subroutine exits to the main program (via RTS), the stack pointer is correctly updated to the PC return location. This "pointed-to" location will put the correct return address in the program counter (which is the label BACK in Figure 5.6). The calling routine should then update the stack pointer as needed.

Although our stack picture illustrates the parameter passage and subroutine local storage procedures using R6 or SP, it is also possible to use a register other than R6. The code in Example 5.11 illustrates such a method. In Example 5.11, the calling program passes three parameters to an "R3" stack using R3 as a stack pointer. Next a subroutine call is made with JSR R3,SUBR which causes the following:

```
STACK  ←  R3              ;SAVE R3 POINTER ON STACK
                          ;POINTED TO BY R6!
    R3  ←  PC             ;SAVE OLD PC IN REG R3
    PC  ←  ADDRESS (SUBR) ;JUMP TO SUBROUTINE
```

The entrance linkage in the subroutine, SUBR, saves active registers R0 and R1 on the stack, using R6 as the stack pointer. This subroutine needs two words for scratchpad, which are obtained with SUB #4,R6. In the body of the subroutine, these words will be used for temporary storage. The exit linkage of the subroutine restores the R6 stack pointer with ADD #4,R6. Also, the old contents of R1 and R0 are restored next. The last instruction of the subroutine, RTS R3, causes a return to the main program. The net effect of this instruction is:

```
PC ←  R3              ;RETURN TO CALLING SEQUENCE
R3 ←  STACK           ;CONTENTS OF TOP OF STACK
                      ;POINTED TO BY R6 LOADED INTO R3
```

Example 5.11   Using R3 as a PDP-11 "Stack" Pointer

```
;CALLING PROGRAM
            •
            •
            •
       MOV PARAM1,-(R3)  ;GET SUBROUTINE
       MOV PARAM2,-(R3)  ;PARAMETERS ONTO THE R3
       MOV PARAM3,-(R3)  ;PUSH-DOWN STACK
       JSR  R3,SUBR      ;CALL SUBROUTINE
BACK:  MOV (R3)+,PARAM3  ;GET SUBROUTINE
       MOV (R3)+,PARAM2  ;RESULTS OFF STACK
       MOV (R3)+,PARAM1
            •
            •
            •
;SUBROUTINE
SUBR:  MOV R0,-(SP)      ;SAVE ACTIVE REGISTERS
       MOV R1,-(SP)      ;FOR SUBROUTINE USAGE
       SUB #4,SP         ;SUBROUTINE LOCAL SCRATCHPAD
            •            ;TWO WORDS NEEDED
            •            ;BODY OF SUBROUTINE USING
            •            ;SCRATCHPAD AND R3 STACK
       ADD #4,SP         ;CLEAN UP R6 STACK POINTER
       MOV (SP)+,R1      ;RESTORE ACTIVE REGISTERS
       MOV (SP)+,R0      ;FOR MAIN PROGRAM
       RTS  R3           ;FIND RETURN ADDRESS IN R3
                         ;AND RESTORE OLD R3
```

Upon returning to the main program, the calling program executes three move instructions to acquire the results which were generated by the subroutine and passed back to the main program via the stack. The first move instruction, MOV (R3)+,PARAM3, pulls the first result off of the stack and transfers it to the PARAM3. (N and M of Figure 5.6 are equivalent to #6 and #4 in Example 5.11.) The JSR and RTS instructions can use any register in the programming model. However, always use the same register in JSR and RTS. It would be fatal to invoke RTS PC (instead of RTS R3) in the current example, because you would not necessarily return to the main program at the proper address.

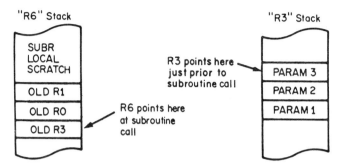

Figure 5.7   Stack Picture Using R3

5.5.3 THE VAX-11/780 STACKING IN PROCEDURE CALLS

A procedure call is a general-purpose routine that uses argument lists passed automatically by the processor. Data storage is then reserved only for local variables. A procedure call instruction in the VAX-11/780 provides several services. Among these is the ability to:

1. Save all of the registers in the CPU that the procedure will use, and only those registers, before entering the called procedure.

2. Pass an argument list to a procedure.

3. Maintain the stack, frame, and argument pointer registers.

The VAX-11/780 uses three instructions in its standard procedure calling interface. Two of the instructions implement the CALL to the procedure while the third implements the matching RETURN. The VAX manufacturers propose a convention with certain attributes for the interfaces between the modules. This convention does not necessarily apply to local routines, however. Within a single module, a programmer may use a variety of linkage and argument-passing techniques. However, the standard specifications include the following attributes between any module:

1. A calling sequence which constitutes the set of instructions at the call site and at the entry point.

2. The argument list, including the structure of the list, describing the actual arguments to the called procedure.

3. A function value return specifying the form and conventions on the use of the function value.

4. Which registers are preserved and who is responsible for preserving them.

5. A set of rules governing the use of the stack.

6. Any data types of arguments or argument descriptor formats.

7. How any exceptional processing conditions are to be signaled and handled in some modular fashion.

8. The stack unwinding process which specifies how the current execution sequences, including the stack popping operations, can be aborted cleanly.

The CALLG instruction in the VAX calls a procedure with the argument list in some arbitrary location pointed to by the AP register. The CALLS instruction calls a procedure with the argument list on the stack and also pointed to by the AP register. On return after a CALLS, this argument list is automatically removed from the stack. However, both call instructions specify the address of the entry point of the procedure being called. The entry point must consist of a word which is termed the "entry mask" followed by the procedure's instructions. Any procedure in the VAX terminates by executing an RET instruction. The entry mask specifies the subprocedures, register use, and any overflow enables. Integer overflow enable and other numeric overflow enables are permitted when bits 15 and 14 of the entry mask are set. The entry mask is a 16-bit word in which bits 12-15 specify the overflow enables. Bits 11-0 of the same word specify which registers in the VAX are to be preserved and later restored. The CALL instruction always preserves the program counter, stack pointer, frame pointer, and argument pointer registers.

It is not only interesting but instructive to observe how a CALL instruction in the VAX preserves the state of the machine on the stack. The actual structure of the stack is termed a call frame or stack frame. This stack frame contains the save registers, the save program status word, our register save mask, as well as several other control bits. Additionally, the stack frame provides the storage area for local variables. Since some condition handling may be required, a longword is also stacked at the top of the stack frame. The stack frame has the format shown in Figure 5.8.

Obviously, a procedure call in the VAX is a complex instruction which stores certain values into R0 and R1 (not shown), affects memory, and clears condition codes, as well as establishes a stack frame. Since a stack frame may be misaligned (not pointing to a longword), the CALLG and CALLS align the stack as well as create a stack frame. These very powerful CALL instructions also clear the condition codes, N, Z, V, and C. The RET or return from procedure instruction reverses the steps. It restores the stack pointer from the

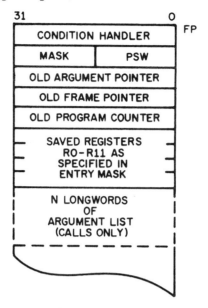

Figure 5.8   VAX-11/780 Stack Frame for Procedure Calls

frame pointer, restores the registers, drops the stack alignment (if required), and restores the program status word. The N, Z, V, and C flags are then restored to their prior bit settings. Once the program is executing the procedure, any local scratchpad area for the procedure can be acquired from the current frame pointer, if a CALLS (call procedure with stack argument list) instruction is invoked. The normal use of the stack frame is to push the argument list onto the stack in reverse order prior to the CALLS and to contain local variables. Then, on return the argument list and local variables are automatically removed from the stack—actually the entire frame is POPed. Registers R0 and R1 are always available for function return values, and, hence, are never saved.

5.5.4   STACK OPERATING GUIDELINES

The following guidelines are suggestions to minimize side effects and to maintain consistency. Although only suggestions, they can be successfully applied over and over again.

1. Know the upper/lower limits of your stack area. Never exceed either boundary. In some PDP-11 computers using RT-11, the programs are normally loaded at starting address 1000. A stack goes backward from this location toward 0000. Also, some PDP-11 hardware configurations

prevent a stack pointer from going lower than location 400. The stack boundaries vary widely from computer to computer.

2. Anticipate that a computer system stack pointer (e.g., R6 in the PDP-11) is manipulated by programs other than yours. You should maintain a stack configuration that causes no side effects and allows other programs to "stack above" your area on demand.

3. Comply with the stacking conventions implied by your computer system. Do not reverse PUSH and POP directions from program to program.

4. After a datum is removed from a stack, never assume that the vacated stack cell still contains meaningful data. System program interruptions may have just used the stack to overwrite this old data.

5. Do not write over someone else's stack area. Most computer systems permit multiple stacks (for your own program as well as for others). Debugging multiple stacking areas is extremely complicated.

6. Do not unstack so much data that you inadvertently pull from someone else's stack below you. Such data is obviously meaningless to your program and its destruction is not "nice."

7. Maintain a consistent stack picture. Before calling a subroutine, stack appropriate subroutine parameters and then save the return address. While in the subroutine, first preserve active registers, and then declare subroutine local storage. By using this structure, offsets to the subroutine parameter area are precise and definite.

8. Before you establish your own stack area in computers with multi-operating states (such as supervisor user modes in the 68000), save the system's software stack pointer. Restore it after subroutine execution so that, at all times, a proper return to the system software can be made at the end of your main program.

9. During execution of the subroutine body, try to leave the stack pointer at the top of your stack. (This is not always possible.) Use the index mode of addressing with the stack pointer. A system interruption process, then, will not enter your stack frame. Also, an external process will return the stack pointer to the top of your stack.

5.6   COROUTINES

For the most part, we have been examining control flow operations between levels of modules. One program may call another program just as a main program might call a subprogram. A calling program might need the services of a subroutine, which when completed returns to the calling program. Procedure A may call procedure B, which in turn, when complete, would return to procedure A. All of these situations so far assume that the called program returns back to the calling point in the calling program. The return operation, in fact, uses a RETURN instruction such as RTS in the PDP-11 or BR RETURN (PC return address) as found in IBM 360/370 programs. Such calls, in any event, are asymmetric calls.

An *asymmetric* call is one in which control passes from one module (A) to another module (B), and module (B) begins executing at its beginning. When the subprogram returns to A, execution begins not at the beginning of the main program, but at the statement following the call. In fact, if the main program executes further statements and desires the services of the subroutine or subprogram again, the subprogram begins execution at its beginning and returns to the main program at the point of the call. It does matter whether a program calls a subprogram, a procedure calls another procedure, a calling program calls a subroutine, and so on. Asymmetry refers to the flow of control in which one program always begins execution at its beginning. It always returns to the calling point of the "other" program. That calling point may vary, but the "beginning" point of the called program never varies.

There is a need for a symmetric control flow between two or more programs. Assume two procedures, A and B, each needing the services of the other at specific instances. Let procedure A first call procedure B. Procedure B begins execution. Upon completion, procedure B calls procedure A by returning to procedure A at A's calling point. Now procedure A resumes program execution. A little later, procedure A desires activity from procedure B. A call is made to procedure B. However, now procedure B is not entered at the beginning of procedure B, but rather at the point where procedure B returned to procedure A. Procedure B executes code. After further execution, procedure B desires the services of procedure A. Procedure B returns to procedure A, not at the very beginning of procedure A, but rather at the point where procedure A last called procedure B. Figure 5.9 depicts such a current control flow between two procedures.

Procedures A and B are called coroutines. Let's examine the return points after each call in both coroutine A and coroutine B. Notice that the "beginning" point of execution of either coroutine varies (depending on the last call). A coroutine call instruction is a *resume* instruction (to imply that execution always "resumes" where it was left off). Some machines have an actual RESUME instruction. The PDP-11 instruction, JSR PC,@(SP)+, performs the necessary resume operation. Unfortunately, many computers do not have a single instruction for resume as found in the PDP-11. The IBM 360/370 and the CYBER 70 must use more than one instruction.

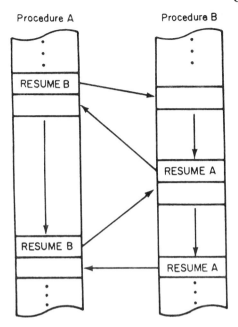

Figure 5.9   Flow of Control in Procedure Coroutine Calls

Assembly Language	Machine Operation	
JSR PC,@(SP)+	Temp ←	Top of Stack
	Top of Stack ←	Old PC
	PC ←	Temp

In order to execute resume calls in the PDP-11, the instruction uses a stack to remember the old PC return address. Notice, however, that the old PC return address varies in both coroutines. In a subroutine call, the subroutine is always entered at the same "beginning point" and the return from subroutine statement transfers control back to the main program at the calling point. Also, no matter where the call is made in the calling program, the call will always cause execution at the beginning of the subroutine. Neither the usual subroutine call nor the usual return instruction RTS will suffice for coroutines. If, however, a stack is used to remember each other's calling point, a resume operation simply needs to swap the old PC with the current top of the stack. The stack neither grows nor shrinks with resume instructions.

The call and return activity with coroutines is further explained with an example. Consider two programs, A and B, as in Example 5.12. Before coroutine activity begins, the top of the stack must be initialized properly.

Hence, in this example, the top of the stack contains program location 2200. The process begins with the execution of program A. The resume instruction encountered at program location 100 causes activity in program A to cease and control to transfer to program B. The JSR instruction at program location 100 causes the top of the stack contents to be placed in the program counter and places the old PC onto the top of the stack. Since the top of the stack contains location 2200, the program execution "resumes" at location 2200, which is program B. Now execution of program B continues until location 2706.

At location 2706, another resume instruction is encountered. This performs the identical swap on the stack with the current program counter and the old top of the stack. At this moment, the stack contains the quantity 102, so control is transferred to program A at location 102. Now in program A, the stack contains 2710, and program A continues execution until location 400, in which another resume instruction is encountered. At this point, the top of the stack is transferred into the program counter, and the program counter is saved in its place. This swapping action causes a transfer of control back to program B at one line below the previous calling point. Program B continues execution until location 3476. At this location, another resume instruction is encountered, which causes program flow to return to program A at location 402. The activity of the top of the stack in Example 5.12 is illustrated in Figure 5.10. Obviously, internal to the PDP-11 computer is a temporary register which must hold one of the operands during the swapping operation.

Example 5.12   A Pair of Coroutine Calls in the PDP-11

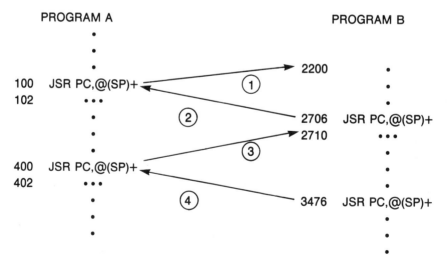

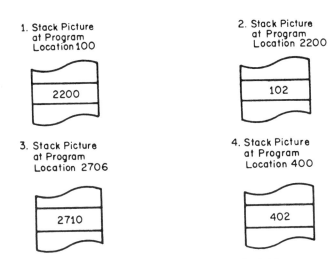

1. Stack Picture
   at Program
   Location 100

   2200

2. Stack Picture
   at Program
   Location 2200

   102

3. Stack Picture
   at Program
   Location 2706

   2710

4. Stack Picture
   at Program
   Location 400

   402

Figure 5.10 Top of Stack in Example 5.12

Knuth[2] suggests that we take the following viewpoint. Assume that a main program and a subroutine become a team of programs. Also assume that the relative importance of the activity of the main program is indistinguishable from that of any of the subroutines. The main program, at some point, desires activity of its team member, a subroutine. The subroutine begins execution and finds itself in need of services from the main program. Rather than stop at the usual point to end in the subroutine, this "novel" subroutine, which is now an equal team member, returns to the main program. This control flow moves back and forth at different points in all team members. In practice, then, the meaning of the names main program and subroutine begins to diminish. When this equal weighting of the relative importance of program segments exists, we should classify these segments' coroutines. The control flow of coroutines for procedures A and B has been illustrated by the resume instructions in Figure 5.9.

Coroutines are very likely to be found in modern operating systems which might require multi-pass algorithms. Even a two-pass assembler could also incorporate two coroutines instead of two passes. In fact, most n-pass algorithms could be programmed with n coroutines. The common property of such programs generally requires a very highly interactive interdependence among the procedures, modules, or subprograms. Recall that an assembler makes the first pass to build the symbol table, and another pass to assemble instructions.

---

[2]Donald E. Knuth, *The Art of Computer Programming, Volume 1/Fundamental Algorithms* (Reading, Mass.: Addison-Wesley, 1968).

It is conceivable that both passes can be combined into one pass using coroutines, in which one coroutine begins to assemble instructions until a symbol is encountered. At this point, the other coroutine builds a symbol table and returns back to the other coroutine to assemble further instructions. Although coroutines instead of two assembly passes are theoretically possible, difficulties arise when forward references are required for the symbols. Generally speaking, multi-pass algorithms can be combined into a single pass if the structure that results using coroutines does not create any forward referencing. Naturally, coroutines should be reentrant.

Consider the following problem. In order to interpret symbol strings, an assembler performs a lexicographic scan of each source statement at pass one. To provide clarity, the scanning steps could be separated from the main program flow. Scanning step subroutines would be cluttered with input/output parameters. A more concise approach must be to invoke coroutines. Let one coroutine perform the main assembly pass while another coroutine extracts one item at a time from the current input line as in Figure 5.11.

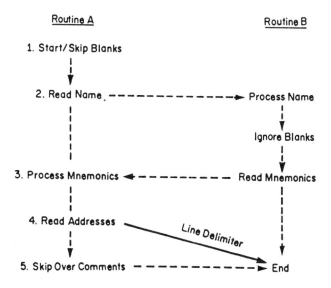

Figure 5.11   Coroutine Paths in an Assembly Process

In some instances, a one-pass process with coroutines can very likely be regenerated into an *n*-pass algorithm or process. However, we should understand the impact of each approach to assembly. Consider a very large program where a team effort requiring a number of people is involved. The first question that arises is, "How should each individual work effort be assigned so that parallel progress is achieved?" Secondly, "How should the problem be partitioned with the least amount of confusing interaction?" Here, a multi-pass algorithm could conceivably be easier to generate or understand than a one-pass algorithm. Obviously, a multi-pass algorithm can be partitioned into passes by assigning each pass to a different person. However, the same partitioning strategy holds true for assigning a coroutine activity to individuals. Each coroutine, then, can be assigned to one person, each person recognizing that the linkage is essentially a resume instruction.

Likewise, instead of assuming a program generation effort, we could consider a program execution effort. Suppose that the constraining factor is the ultimate size of memory space. A one-pass algorithm generally requires space to hold all the programs in memory simultaneously. This causes the memory requirements to increase rapidly, if not to exceed the physical limit of the computer itself. In contrast, a multi-pass algorithm could conceivably require much less memory. Suppose, further, that a computer memory system is partitioned both into a "fast" memory and a much larger but "slower" memory. Then, the program requirements for a single pass might reside in the fast memory, leaving most of the program resident in the slower memory. In effect then, the fast memory would beneficially execute a pass much faster if the entire multi-pass algorithm would require program execution in slower memory.

When translating a one-pass process with coroutines into a multi-pass process, some complications will arise when one coroutine receives inputs from another coroutine and then sends back crucial results to the other coroutine. Here, it may not be possible to convert the first coroutine into one pass and the other coroutine into another pass independently. Likewise, it is also true that not all multi-pass processes may not be translated into coroutines for the same reasons. A later pass through a process may require not only individual data of the previous pass, but it may also require accumulative data. In that event, partitioning a multi-pass process into coroutines is very unlikely.

5.7   REENTRANT CODE

A subroutine which can be reentered after it has been unexpectedly exited and can still behave correctly, generating correct results without any side effects, is called *serially reusable* code. A serially reusable subroutine must incorporate initialization of variables, otherwise each execution may yield a different result. A subroutine which produces different results with each execution is called *nonreusable*. Generating serially reusable code is not as difficult as generating reentrant code, although both must be non-self-modifying. A subroutine is serially reusable when, for example, it can be interrupted during instance A of its being entered. Then, it is entered totally anew at the beginning (at instance B) and executed, possibly to completion and return, but not necessarily. Subsequently control is returned to the point of interruption in instance A, and processing correctly continues from that point to completion of instance A. If it is also non-self-modifying (no internal subroutine code may contain store instructions whose operands are instructions, hence, cannot modify itself during execution), such code is denoted as *reentrant*. This does not necessarily imply that a reentrant subroutine can never create storage. Rather, storage cannot be created in the subroutine. A solution is to cause the calling routine to pass parameters by reference via, for example, an index register. Storage of variables, then, is made outside of the subroutine, leaving only *pure code* (non-self-modifying) internal to the subroutine.

A subroutine which is reentrant and/or serially reusable has a permanent part (an instruction sequence to be executed) and a temporary part (a pointer back to the calling program as well as data or results generated by a current activation). Each execution instance of a subroutine must have its own associated temporary information and permanent information. An execution instance is called an *activation*. The associated temporary information generated by the current activation is called the current activation record. The current activation record must obviously contain a pointer back to the calling program, as well as the data generated by the current activation. When instruction segments of a subroutine carefully separate the permanent and temporary parts throughout the subroutine, then the subroutine theoretically can support multiple and reentrant execution.

The following example illustrates why reentrancy is useful.

```
FIRST:                    ;BEGINNING OF SUBROUTINE
            •
            •
            •
        CMP B,A
        MOV R0,R1
GONE:   CLR R3
            •
            •
            •
        RTS PC        ;END OF SUBROUTINE
```

What would happen if just before the code labeled GONE is executed, this subroutine is interrupted, and program control exits to another area of your program? Nothing if you don't ever desire to return to GONE and resume executing code where the subroutine was exited. Never returning to a partially executed subroutine is hardly to be expected. Nearly always, program control will return to GONE and resume execution. Now, if R0 and R1 have been modified by some other code in the meantime, this reentered program execution is obviously meaningless. Someone must save R0 and R1 and restore them before execution resumes at GONE. Since this subroutine cannot anticipate such exits, the subroutine cannot also be expected to preserve R0 and R1. It must be by the calling code.

How does the "other routine" save R0 and R1? In most computers, preservation of R0 and R1 is made by pushing R0 and R1 on a stack, all performed by the interrupting routine. In other words, the entry linkage of a subroutine structure must also exist in any code which makes abrupt changes in the program control flow. Of course, a corresponding exit linkage must be provided to return us back to the previous executing code, such as GONE above. Exit/entry linkage is facilitated by stack operations, as we have seen earlier.

However, to do so, every subroutine above must have a consistent stack picture to support reentrancy and/or serial reusability. For example, consider the picture in Figure 5.12 which corresponds to the code above. During the execution of this subroutine, the stack pointer remains pointing to the top of the argument list as shown. Suppose this routine is now exited, and the new routine recognizes that it uses R0, R1, and R2. The new routine will first place GONE onto this stack, writing over the return address for the previous subroutine. Then R0, R1, and R2 will be preserved on the stack. Unfortunately, the new routine will return to the current subroutine and continue executing. However, this subroutine will not return to the main program properly because it has lost its return address (having been written over with GONE). In fact, the RTS PC line of code above will cause the program counter to be loaded with GONE instead of the correct return address.

The problem obviously lies with the stack pointer. During execution of our subroutine, the stack pointer should be left pointing to the top of the stack or location 0764. Then any exits will cause a return to this routine, which in turn will permit a final return to the main program. The subroutine, FIRST, could use the stack space in locations 1000 through 0764, inclusive, for its current activation record. The permanent part is to keep this activation record independent of any side effects. The stack pointer should be pointing at 0764, just in case the subroutine, FIRST, is exited and then reentered.

A more subtle requirement exists in reentrant coding. Reentrant code must not be self-modifying. We have already encountered some self-modifying code in a previous chapter including the subsequent remedies. As already observed, employment of the indirect addressing and index modes rather than the absolute mode of addressing is helpful. In fact, these two modes were invented primarily to facilitate the writing of reentrant programs.

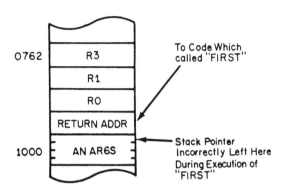

Figure 5.12   Bad Stack Picture

Suppose that we desire to pass parameters with a call-by-reference where an in-line parameter area is used. Recall that an in-line parameter area follows the calling program just below the subroutine call. If we were to consider that information in this parameter space as part of the temporary information of a subroutine, we destroy the rigid partitioning of temporary and permanent information suggested earlier for reentrant routines. Of course, if we use an index register to maintain the address, reentrancy is also facilitated. However, probably it is safer to store the parameter information associated with a subroutine call in the temporary information area of the called subroutine, instead of as part of the permanent information of the calling routine. A subroutine could then utilize a stack picture as in Figures 5.6 and 5.7. Entry and exit linkage is incorporated with the stack pointer. During subroutine execution, always point to the top of the current stack frame or activation record (to help reentrancy).

Another very common way to ensure that a routine is reentrant is to require that each and every independent user of the reentrant code provide his or her own data work space. The stack pointer obviously must be positioned at the top of the stack frame at every instance in order to preserve the appropriate return address. In so doing, no part of the reentrant program is thus modified. Any instruction part of the reentrant code must, of course, still be pure code or a pure procedure which is a synonym for non-self-modifying code. Reentrant code is very important in large computer systems with much memory as well as very small microcomputers, although for very different reasons.

5.7.1 REENTRANT CODE FOR MULTI-USER SYSTEMS

Any large computing installation or system must be a multi-programming or multi-user system by nature of its high cost. Programs which run in a multi-user system should be reentrant. Consider a main memory system snapshot shown in Figure 5.13. In this figure, the main memory contains, simultaneously, two editors, a compiler, some data space receiving input from a disk system, an operating system, output data buffer to a CRT, and user X and Y areas. This very dynamic configuration must be maintained without any program writing into or out of any other program in the memory. However, suppose this job mix requires more memory than that which is available. One solution would be to make some of these programs reentrant. For example, if we could invoke a reentrant editor, then only one copy would be required, and multi-users would not need more than one reentrant editor resident in main memory. This saves memory space. However, since memory cost is no longer significant, we are more concerned with the opportunity to support more users than the desire to keep memory costs down. Invoking reentrant code could then become a very desirable solution.

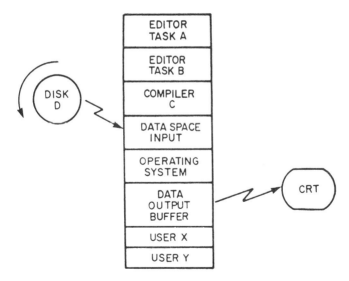

Figure 5.13 On-Line Memory Snapshot

5.7.2   CONSIDERATION IN MICROCOMPUTERS

Small computers are often assigned to a dedicated task, possibly with a single user. In this event, would reentrancy have any merit when there will never be any sharing of programs? In cases where the dedicated computer might be working in a hostile environment, the need for reentrant code still exists. Suppose a microcomputer was installed in a nuclear reactor site in which extreme temperature, vibration, and dirt could destroy any of the vital computation or I/O units. Or how about the automobile carburetion system which now uses a microcomputer. Carburetion, vacuum, exhaust gas, and ambient temperature are a few of the input parameters to this carburetion system. An output would be to throttle the gas mixture. If however, the program resides in some nonvolatile memory, what would happen if the volatile RAM (which we hope has a battery backup) lost power? You would not be very happy if you found yourself in Oshkosh without a new RAM. Most likely, the mechanic at the local gas station would not carry the necessary program to reload in your car's RAM space. To overcome this, the obvious, although not necessarily guaranteed, solution is to use a ROM instead of a RAM. However, this is a naive view. Code stored in a ROM does not imply that it must be reentrant.

Actually, in some computers reentrancy is enhanced indirectly by the hardware. Models 44 and 70 of the PDP-11 use a memory management unit (MMU) which distinguishes between lines of instructions and data. In fact, the MMU maintains two sets of memory address tables, one for the instruction space and the other for the data space. The management task rests upon the assumption that an item directed to the instruction register must be an instruction, whereas an item directed to the ALU is data. To maintain this strict partition, your program should not modify itself; otherwise, it would not belong in program space. The MMU won't even let you do it with its hardware. This leaves us with no alternative but to make our programs reentrant in the first place. However, the MMU separating instruction space from data space only discourages (not prohibits) self-modifying code.

5.7.3   EXECUTE INSTRUCTION

Unfortunately, some instructions are explicitly self-modifying. Certain input/output instructions which cause activity in the I/O unit of a computer system must change or modify an operand in the particular I/O instruction. The operand may be the name or the peripheral device number. Why this is so will be explained in the next chapter. In these situations, however, the instruction set may also contain a special EXECUTE instruction. Upon encountering the EXECUTE instruction, the program would jump to the I/O instruction code, directly execute this code, and return, as if an indirect call to a single instruction were made. The I/O instruction could then reside in data space, while the execute instruction could reside in program space. Then, even though the I/O address is actually a part of the instruction, and the instruction must make reference to more than one I/O (and thus be self-modifying), the EXECUTE instruction overcomes this self-modification by simply placing the I/O instruction in data space to begin with, and requesting the EXECUTE instruction to execute this "data." It is not true that only machines equipped with EXECUTE can support reentrant code. Other solutions are not only possible, but actually are more common. We defer the topic of I/O programming to the next chapter.

5.8 RECURSION

A subroutine which can call itself and execute properly is called a *recursive subroutine*. In computer programs, we find recursive procedures, recursive subprograms, as well as recursive functions, and even recursive modules. A *recurrence relation* is a rule which defines each element of a sequence in terms of its preceding elements. In this section, we will study recursion in greater detail, and we will refer primarily to subroutines. Regardless of which module is employed recursively, a recursive module must contain two distinct parts. That part of the module which does not participate in the recursion, but rather sets up the initial value of the expression or function, is called the *basis* part. The remaining code in the module belongs to the *recursive* part. Consider the factorial function $0! = 1$, $1! = 1$, $2! = 2$, $3! = 2*3 = 6$, and so on. We could express the function recursively as $F(n) = n*F(n-1)$ for non-negative n. Since $0!$ is valid, this recursive function makes no sense if we substitute 0 for n in the formula. The parentheses represent the basis part of this recursive function. In this case, we simply state that $F(0) = 1$. A recursive Pascal function for the factorial is illustrated in Example 5.13. Note that the statement "THEN FACT: = 1" represents the basis part of this recursive function.

Example 5.13   A Recursive Pascal Function

```
FUNCTION FACT(N:INTEGER):INTEGER;
BEGIN
    IF N = 0
        THEN FACT: = 1
        ELSE FACT: = N*FACT(N-1)
END;
```

Recursion is highly desirable because it often makes the evaluation of fairly complex algorithms comparatively straightforward and compact in program coding. As a result of such compact code, significant memory space is saved, although execution speed may decrease. However, the generation of a recursive routine is not always obvious. There are two important challenges we face for every recursive routine. First, we must identify the correct return address in each recursion. A recursive routine has the ability to nest its own calls. This nesting does not permit the return address to simply replace the return address of the previous call in the same physically designated space (whether in a register or a memory location). In other words, the return addresses in each nested call must be preserved on a stack. The second challenge we must deal with is the ability to store parameters of each nested call, separated from the previous parameter space. At least two copies of the results of a stack parameter storage are required. One copy must preserve the "old" results, and the other copy must preserve the "new" results. This is illustrated with the following PDP-11 assembly language program (Example 5.14).

Example 5.14   A Recursive Assembly Language Subroutine (PDP-11)

```
        MOV N,-(SP)      ;INPUT ARGUMENT
        JSR PC,FACTN     ;CALCULATE FACTORIAL OF N
DONE:   MOV (SP)+,FACTR  ;HERE'S THE ANSWER IN FACTR
        RTS PC           ;RETURN TO CALLING PROGRAM
FACTN:  MOV 2(SP),R2     ;R2 ← N, GET OLD PARAMETER BENEATH
                         ;RETURN ADDRESS ON STACK
        BEQ ZERFAC       ;N = 0?
        DEC R2           ;NO, R2 ← N-1
        MOV R2,-(SP)     ;PUSH R2 =N-1 ON TOP OF STACK
        JSR PC,FACTN     ;START RECURSIVE CALL
MORE:   MOV (SP)+,R2     ;POP (N-1)! INTO R2
        MUL 2(SP),R2     ;R2 ← (N-1)!∗N
        MOV R2,2(SP)     ;N! = (N-1)!∗N REPLACES N
LASTF:  RTS PC
ZERFAC: MOV #1,2(SP)     ;0! = 1
        RTS PC
```

This recursive subroutine takes advantage of the available stacking mechanisms of the PDP-11. Here, the basis part of the routine pushes the value of N onto a stack in the first line of code. Then the recursion process begins with the subroutine call to FACTN. Initially, a stack picture shown in Figure 5.14 is built. Assume that location 1000 representing, initially, the top of the stack has the value of N in it. In the first subroutine call, JSR PC, FACTN, a return address, DONE, is stored. The subroutine, FACTN, is now entered with the first line of code acquiring the value of N. Next, it is examined for zero (BEQ

ZERFAC). Then, N is decremented and pushed onto the stack. In this first pass, location 0774 now contains N-1.

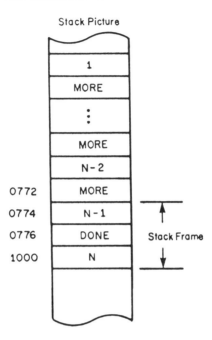

Figure 5.14   Stack Picture for Example 5.14 Before "MORE" Is Executed

This process continues first pushing the return address "MORE" on the stack, which is then followed by the next value, N-2, N-3, and so on. This process terminates when the value is zero. At this point, the stack picture in Figure 5.14 has now been completed. However, we have yet to compute the factorial function. All we have done is computed the operands necessary for the computation process, and stacked them so that the recursive function could implement the algorithm with this stack. Now the routine takes us to program location ZERFAC. This line pushes 0! onto the stack. Its position now is not at the top of the stack, but one location below the top of the stack. The next RTS instruction causes the program counter to be restored with MORE. Here, program execution begins to calculate the function 1!, 2!, etc. This is done recursively by executing the lines of code between MORE and LASTF. After N loops through this code, N! is found in location 1000. The final execution of LASTF causes the popping of DONE into the program counter, which returns us to the beginning code of this routine. Here, the N! found in location 1000 is moved to FACTR. The evaluated function is now complete. In this routine, the two parameters, N and N-1, as well as a return address, represent a stack frame. A stack frame is a segment of the stack picture which contains the parameters and new and old results of parameters necessary for the next recursive call.

Often, a software tool such as a compiler or an assembler must be called on to recognize mathematical expressions to determine their legality. For example, the MACRO-11 assembler does allow the expressions (A+B+C), A+A, (A−B+C), but does not consider −(A+B), B+−C, or A−(A+) legal. We can be more precise using the following rules to define the validity of expressions, and these rules, then, could furthermore cast into a recursive algorithm to recognize well-formed expressions. The rules are:

1. The chosen symbol is a legal expression.
2. (−symbol) is a legal expression.
3. If symbol is a legal expression, then (symbol) is also a legal expression.
4. If SYMBOLA and SYMBOLB are legal expressions, so are SYMBOLA + SYMBOLB as well as SYMBOLA − SYMBOLB.

Let's now restate the definitions of a valid expression, assuming that we desire a recursive examination. Obviously, we want to detect a valid string as in 1 or in 2. Also, when the first character in the string is "(" and the last is ")", then if the internal substring is legal, so is the expression within the parentheses. However, if none of the above is true, we should then scan the string to find strings such as A+B or A−B (assuming that A and B are both valid expressions). Finally, should none of the above apply, then the expression is not recognized as valid. The recursive statement can be translated into machine code by recognizing that the substrings or internal strings must first be validated, then parentheses are omitted or ignored if indeed they are paired.

Not all recursive algorithms can be elegantly coded. Some algorithms are extremely difficult. Others may not be supported by efficient hardware resources, such as a stack and stack manipulation instructions. For example, the PDP-11 stacking facilities are quite adequate for many recursive implementations. However, the IBM 360/370 must use alternate schemes because no hardware stack facilities exist. A software implementation of stacks must be made. In procedure calls which are recursive, we could put the return address in a register, and then leave it up to a procedure to store it in a safe place. Of course, if the procedure is recursive, it must put the return address somewhere else each time it is called, because the contents of the register will change with each nested call.

A hardware solution found in the CYBER 70 requires the call to store the return address in the first word of the procedure. The second word in the procedure then becomes the first executable statement. The procedure returns by jumping indirectly to this first word. Unfortunately, this technique will fail with the second call since the return address will be destroyed. The HP 2116 employs the same return address storage scheme, and, hence, cannot effectively implement recursive routines in this manner.

The point is that recursive programs must not be self-modifying, especially where the self-modification causes the loss of the subsequent return address. In this respect, recursive programs must obviously be reentrant. The safest way to implement recursive routines is through the use of stacks, saving the old and new arguments along with the return address on the stack with each call.

5.9 SUMMARY

In this chapter, we have studied the notion of program control via program structures as subroutines, coroutines, and modules in general. By now you should have learned how to:

1. Write resilient code which can be interrupted and reentered.

2. Minimize side effects on subroutine results by maintaining a stack picture.

3. Ensure that routines can be made reentrant.

4. Write recursive programs.

The most important concept of this chapter is the versatility of a stack for passing parameters. The stack operation guidelines provided for you should be seriously considered. Briefly, the best stack organization should be one which consistently does the following:

1. Saves the link on the stack.

2. Preserves any working registers on the stack.

3. Allocates space on the stack for any and all variables used temporarily by the routine.

4. Places any arguments transmitted to the called routine onto the stack in the same stack frame or activation record.

A paramount task is to make sure that code both returns from a subroutine properly and returns the generated results, all without side effects to other modules. The stack organization and the stacking operations proposed in this chapter are adequate.

Coroutines, reentrancy, and recursion, only introduced here, will become clearer in the next chapter. We will study the physical characteristics of I/O devices, handling input and output data, and control files in a multi-user environment.

5.10 KEY WORDS

actual parameter	linkage
call	module
call-by-reference	parameter areas
call-by-value	push-down stacks
cohesion	recursion
coroutine	resume
coupling	serially reusable
formal parameter	subroutine
invocation	subroutine structure

5.11 SUGGESTED READING

Andrews, Michael. *Programming Microprocessor Interfaces for Control and Instrumentation.* Englewood Cliffs, N.J.: Prentice-Hall, 1982.

Discussion of stacks specific to the 6809 8-bit microprocessor can be found on pages 138–159. Discussion concerning modern structured code and the modular facilities in the 6809 which support such code are found on pages 136–138. The designers of the 6809 intended that its instruction set handle stack manipulations, whether hardware or software generated, with extreme consistency. This instruction consistency regarding stacking operations is covered on pages 48–49. However, very little can be found in the text on reentrancy and recursion.

Calingaert, Peter. *Assemblers, Compilers, and Program Translation.* Rockville, Md.: Computer Science Press, 1979.

The general notion of program modules is carefully explained in Chapter 3. Here the degree of reusability important to software organization is characterized for nonreusable, serially reusable, reenterable, and recursive code. A lucid exposition of activation records amplifies the notion of reusability. The concepts of call-by-value and call-by-name complete the chapter.

Desautels, Edouard J. *Assembly Language Programming for PDP 11 and LSI 11 Computers: An Introduction to Computer Organization.* Dubuque, Ia.: Wm. C. Brown, 1982.

Some rather interesting recursive, reentrant, and coroutine examples can be found on pages 386–391 and 406–411, including a solution or two to homework problems. This textbook focuses solely on the PDP-11 computer.

Gear, C. William. *Computer Organization and Programming, 2nd Ed.* New York: McGraw-Hill, 1980.

Chapter 4 provides some vivid illustrations of subroutining, recursion, and parameter passage for the 360/370, 8080, as well as the PDP-11. Some useful comments about subprogram conventions and common statements are found on pages 193–197. The predominant focus is on the IBM 370, although some Cyber 170 passage techniques are illustrated. Pages 180–199 are especially helpful. Coverage of recursion and reentrancy on pages 201–203 is rather brief, but typical of most textbooks.

Knuth, Donald E. *The Art of Computer Programming, Volume 1/Fundamental Algorithms.* Reading, Mass.: Addison-Wesley, 1968.

This classic text is a very readable discourse covering the fundamental concepts of computer programming. It is highly recommended for its thorough coverage of many structured practices currently in vogue.

Leventhal, Lance. *6809 Assembly Language Programming.* Berkeley, Calif.: OSBORNE/McGraw-Hill, 1981.

Very clear examples illustrating the passing of parameters on stacks strictly for the 6809 microprocessor can be found on pages 11-8 through 11-14. There is very little discussion of reentrant and recursive subroutines. The author opted for directly illustrating reentrant programs via examples found on pages 10-7, 10-9, 10-11, 10-14, 11-6 through 11-7, and 11-11. These examples are very instructive.

Linz, Peter. *Programming Concepts and Problem Solving.* Menlo Park, Calif.: Benjamin/Cummings, 1983.

Chapter 6, on the structure of programs with subprograms, includes a discussion of parameter passage in Pascal. Some very instructive Pascal examples which describe a procedure to compute the mean and standard deviation can be found beginning on page 141. Pages 147–149 describe a procedure to print a bar graph for the frequency distribution, and pages 155–159 describe recursive calls. A complete Pascal routine to recognize well-formed expressions is illustrated on pages 156–160. A discussion on stacks and queues can be found on pages 222–237, again with informative Pascal examples.

Tannenbaum, Andrew S. *Structured Computer Organization.* Englewood Cliffs, N.J.: Prentice-Hall, 1976.

A conceptual coverage of the flow of control with procedures, subroutines, and coroutines is presented with clarity on pages 120–130. The towers of Hanoi problem including calling sequences for the IBM 370, Cyber 70, and PDP-11 can be found on pages 120–130.

Wegner, Peter. *Programming Languages, Information Structures, and Machine Organizations*. New York: McGraw-Hill, 1968.
    Some very abstract coverage of ALGOL procedure calls which are reentrant and recursive can be found on pages 35, 44, 56, 149, 228, and 258. The notion of static and dynamic relations between instances of activation of function modules is discussed in Chapter 4. This foundational work has carried over into much of today's assembly language programming. The resume call was first identified with ALGOL. Discussion of coroutines on pages 324–328 is rather descriptive. The text derives many of its examples with ALGOL and PL-1. However, it is very theoretical, with emphasis on general principles and concepts. Unfortunately, few figures can be found in this text, which makes reading sometimes difficult.

5.12   EXERCISES

5.1   What machine operations occur when a subroutine call and return are made?

5.2   Why should a macro definition or call be unlikely within a subroutine?

5.3   Midnight Software Engineering Corporation proposes that we eliminate JSR and RTS completely from computers. The following code is recommended in their place. Explain why you would not buy stock in this corporation.

```
;SUBROUTINE CALL
                    MOV #RETURN,R0
                    BR   SUBR
RETURN:             •
                    •
                    •
;SUBROUTINE
SUBR:               MOV R0,#SAVEPC
                    •               ;BODY OF SUBROUTINE
                    •
                    •
EXIT:               JMP $SAVEPC     ;RETURN TO CALLING
                                    ;PROGRAM
```

5.4   You are dissatisfied with MSE Corporation, but still desire to make an instruction set for a PDP-11 with fewer instructions (deleting JSR and RTS). Write two macros called "JSR" and "RTS" which mimic JSR and RTS, but now do not use a memory cell to save the PC.

5.5 Identify the formal and actual parameters in the subroutines of Example 5.1.

5.6 What method of parameter passage is being attempted below? Is the code correct?

```
;MAIN PROGRAM

            .ENABL AMA

            JSR PC,MIN
X:          .WORD 7
Y:          .WORD 2
Z:          .BYTE AC
;SUBROUTINE

            CMP X,Y

            BLE SMALL

            MOV Y,X
SMALL:      RTS PC
```

5.7 Describe the differences in the following:
  a. Subroutine call versus macro call.
  b. Subroutine definition versus macro definition.
  c. Macro dummy variable versus a subroutine formal parameter.
  d. Macro actual variable versus a subroutine actual parameter.

5.8 Identify each "storage" mechanism below as LIFO (last-in-first-out), FIFO (first-in-first-out), LILO (last-in-last-out), or otherwise. Explain carefully. Do multiple identities exist?
  a. Stack.
  b. A newspaper boy's coin changer device.
  c. RAM.
  d. ROM.
  e. A serial shift register.
  f. People going into and out of the San Diego museum or Cape Hatteras lighthouse.

5.9   The following stack manipulation code (and only that shown) is found in a subroutine. What's wrong with this subroutine?

```
;SUBROUTINE
            MOV    R0,-(SP)
            MOV    R1,-(SP)
              .
              .
              .
            MOV    (SP)+,DATA
              .
              .
              .
            MOV    (SP)+,R0
            MOV    (SP)+,R1
            RTS    PC
```

5.10   What characteristics should the displacement in the LINK instruction of the 68000 should have?

5.11   Generate the PDP-11 code which emulates the LINK and UNLINK of the 68000.

5.12   Write two subroutines: one to preserve R0-R5 onto a stack, and the other to restore R0-R5. Assume that the call to the first subroutine is JSR R5,PRESERV, and the call to the second subroutine is JSR R5,RESTORE.

5.13   Describe the stacking operations in the following. (Hint: See references at the end of the chapter.)
   a. VAX-11/70   f. NOVA ECLIPSE
   b. 8080   g. HP 3000
   c. 6800   h. HP 9000
   d. 6502   i. B5000
   e. Z80   j. CYBER 170

5.14   Generate PDP-11 code to push and pull data types which are 32 bits long. Use the fastest methods possible.

5.15   Explain why the figure below can inappropriately depict coroutine control flow. (Hint: Initialization?)

5.16 In Example 5.12, what instruction must be executed prior to initialization of any coroutine activity?

5.17 Some multi-pass algorithms are impossible to retranslate into a single pass using coroutines. One impossible case may occur when one pass requires cumulative information from another pass. If the above is true, explain why.

5.18 Generate two coroutines to repeat a character or a digit $n+1$ times, where the repetition factor immediately precedes the character or digit. For example, A3C541X becomes ACCCC444444XX.

5.19 Given the following procedure, determine if this procedure is recursive and reentrant.

```
real procedure SIGMA(I,J,K,G);
    value J,K;realG;integer I,J,K;
    begin I :=L;
        SIGMA :=if J>K then 0 else
        G + SIGMA(I,J+1,K,G)
    end
```

5.20 This "recursive" FORTRAN function to calculate N! will not work because its compiler makes storage allocation essentially static. (Note: Some FORTRAN compilers, namely Waterloo, can allow recursion.) Could you write a FORTRAN routine that does (and have it be recursive)?

```
    INTEGER FUNCTION FACT(N)
    IF (N.NE.0) GO TO 10
    FACT =1
    RETURN
10  FACT =N*FACT(N-1)
    RETURN              END
```

5.21 The following function-type procedure is supposed to be a recursive procedure. Is it? If not, what is not recursive about it? Is it reentrant? Is it serially reusable?

```
procedure SUM(A,K);
real array A;integer K;
begin integer I;real P;
     P :=0;
     for I :=1 step 1 until K do
     X :=X+A[I];
     sum :=X;
end
```

5.22 Some CRT's and pointers have automatic tab setting capabilities in hardware. Some don't. Generate a PDP-11 recursive program to insert spaces between the end of a character and the next tab. For example, suppose a tab is desired every 10 spaces. The following string of characters should be output so a new word begins at each tab.
Character string:

THETABISTENSPACES.

The output information is:

THE######TAB##########IS#########TEN######SPACES###

where # is inserted above to depict the nonprinting space character. Do not output #. Rather, output a space. Let R4 contain the current tab stop, and let R2 point to the output buffer string.

5.23 A Fibonacci number series can be expressed as:

$F(0) =0, F(1) =1, ..., F(N) =F(N-1) + F(N-2)$ $N>1$.

Generate a recursive routine to calculate the series. This series is often useful in ascertaining the performance of tree-searching algorithms.

5.24 The degree of *reusability* of a module is the extent to which it can be executed more than once with the same effect each time. Distinguish the degree of reusability of nonreusable, serially reusable, reenterable, and recursive modules. Carefully explain the impact of self-modification and variable initialization.

5.25 Find the permanent and temporary parts of the subroutine in Example 5.19.

5.26 Describe the salient differences between reentrant routines and recursive routines. Discuss activation records and static and dynamic relations.

5.27 How does indirect and/or indexed addressing support reentrant coding?

5.28 Side effects during evaluation of procedures in ALGOL can occur in the following:

  a. Assigning a value to an identifier declared in an enclosing block of the procedure.

  b. Jumping to a label in an enclosed block. Can this be done?

  c. Executing a procedure call in an enclosing block already possessing a side effect (a bad form of recursion).

  d. Assigning a value to an identifier already initialized by name.

Any procedure has a side effect if it modifies other (nonlocal) identifiers in memory during its own execution. List the ways side effects can occur in the following. (Hint: See Chapter 4 of Wegner, *Programming Languages, Information Structures, and Machine Organizations.*)

  a. FORTRAN programs

  b. Pascal procedures

  c. Ada procedures

  d. Assembly language subroutines or modules

5.29 In the following code, 2\$ is a local variable which is modified in the routine itself. Explain what happens at execution time as 2\$ takes on various values.

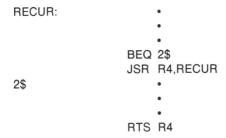

```
RECUR:                    •
                          •
                          •
             BEQ 2$
             JSR R4,RECUR
    2$                    •
                          •
                          •
             RTS R4
```

Chapter 6

INPUT/OUTPUT ORGANIZATION

> I shall be telling this with a sigh
> Somewhere ages and ages hence:
> Two roads diverged in a wood and I—
> I took the one less traveled by,
> And that has made all the difference.
>
> —Robert Frost

> The timing between the first and last detected bit of a character is nominally...less than 425 microinches.
>
> —ANSI-X3B1, 1969

> On a clear disk you can seek forever.
>
> —Jeff Mischkinsky

6.1 CHAPTER OBJECTIVES

In this chapter, we will learn about the general organization of input/output units, the fourth building block of a computer system. A computing system may be as trivial as a single microprocessor chip which turns on a light-emitting-diode. At the other extreme, complex applications include: room-filled computing centers for nuclear reactor sites, multi-floor centers for business in food processing (General Mills), and communications (AT&T). The input/output organization of a computing system depends not only on the complexity of the tasks, but also on the size of the system. In this chapter, we will focus upon the basic components of input/output organization, namely, direct control via data/status registers, indirect control via input/output processors/controllers, buffer storage, and their respective input/output programs. From these elements within an I/O unit, the reader will begin to understand interfaces from a programmer's standpoint.

309

The great disparity in the speed of data transmission among CPUs and I/O devices necessitates solutions in hardware, software, or both. To efficiently "interface" a device to a computer requires an understanding of temporary storage mechanisms, commonly called *buffers*. Much of this chapter focuses on the set-up and maintenance of buffers which expedite I/O transfers without degrading internal CPU performance. Such concurrency (multiple simultaneous activity) is often desirable to maximize the throughput of a computer system. To support concurrency, one dimensional arrays (stacks, queues, deques, circular buffers, etc.) support I/O transfer independent of CPU instruction execution. I/O overlap schemes are also important concurrency generating mechanisms.

Synchrony and control play major roles in input/output units. Seldom, if ever, will a peripheral device operate at precisely the same speed as the CPU clock. Hence, synchrony requires the slower device to either request service every *n*th CPU clock pulse or "store up" data in a buffer. One buffer may be a single register or several hundred registers or memory cells. In either case, transfer of control and synchrony to an I/O processor is necessary to match speeds and manage the buffer. Two closely related activities belonging to the I/O unit and peripheral devices are:

1. Transformation from external to internal representation and vice versa (often termed transduction as it changes the syntax while preserving the semantics).

2. Reception of bits into the computer as input and transmission of bits out of the computer as output.

6.2   BASIC PHYSICAL CHARACTERISTICS OF I/O AND AUXILIARY STORAGE

Nearly all computers provide the capability to handle one or more of the following I/O techniques.

Low Speed:
    a. program controlled transfer for sequential I/O operations.
    b. some excessive interrupt-driven I/O operations.

High Speed:
    a. specialized I/O units such as an auxiliary processor or selector channel.
    b. direct memory access.

Each application dictates whether a low-speed or high-speed I/O operation is required. It is unwise to connect high-speed devices through low-speed interfaces, and vice versa. Not only will a bad speed mismatch occur, but also the cost becomes prohibitive. For example, the speed of a paper tape reader is very slow relative to CPU speed. Connecting a paper tape reader to a high-speed interface of the computer makes little sense. High-speed interfaces are relatively expensive. A paper tape reader cannot effectively use a high-speed interface. Much of the high-speed I/O interface's time will be expended waiting for the slow-speed paper tape reader. Obviously, a paper tape reader should be connected to the low-speed interface.

6.2.1 TIMING

The timing property of an I/O device relates to its ability to perform synchronous or asynchronous data transfer. Synchronization with the computer's basic machine cycle is often assumed. I/O devices which transfer data synchronously with a computer do so in step with the computer's master clock. A data transfer may occur at every machine cycle or multiples of machine cycles. Devices which cannot do so must then perform asynchronous data transfer. Few I/O devices are synchronous. Hence, the I/O unit must often marry the asynchronous behavior of an I/O device to the synchronous behavior of the computer. To accomplish data transfer, resources in such an I/O unit must be able to temporarily store data if necessary and inform the receiver that the data buffer is full. The I/O unit must then execute the transfer (dump the buffer), and inform the transmitter that the buffer is empty. Such signaling is part of the "handshaking" among peripheral devices, I/O units, and the CPU.

6.2.2 CODING

It is highly unlikely that data entering an I/O device is directly available to the computer in a binary format (strings of 1's and 0's). The I/O unit must often encode or decode the data. Code translation basically takes noncompatible data (data in a state which cannot be directly processed) from one device into a state compatible for usage (processing in the case of a CPU) by the other device. For example, data found on a magnetic tape can be formatted, in which characters or numbers are 7, 8, or 9 bit strings. To process the same data, a CPU must use binary data in binary strings compatible in length with the word length of the computer (or a sub-multiple of the word length). A computer with a 16-bit word length can easily process an 8-bit and a 16-bit data item, but it takes more CPU effort to process a 3-bit data item (although it is still possible). The I/O unit performs some of the necessary translation, letting the CPU process better suited tasks.

The input/output unit of a computer system serves as the primary link between the central processing unit, memory unit, and the outside world. To the computer, the outside world consists of humans and peripheral devices. To a computer, a peripheral device is a *transducer of information representation.* For example, the cathode ray tube (CRT) displays characters and symbols which we hope are strings of intelligible English words. The CRT converts electrical signals (representing digital data) from the I/O unit into visible symbols. On the input side, a keyboard transforms our keystrokes into alphanumeric coded data, eventually to reside as binary strings somewhere in the computer system. Obviously then, the computer serves us best when the I/O, combined with a peripheral device, receives or transmits information recognizable by both system resources.

6.2.3 THE SPEED DISPARITY

In this chapter, we focus primarily on the organization of I/O to efficiently pass information into and out of a computer system. The relative speed of the device compared with that of the CPU is an important design criteria. Many peripheral devices process data extremely slowly, and thus waste computer time. When a slow device interfaces with a central processor which is extremely fast, the processor could be idle most of the time while waiting for the information.

Example 6.1 The Fast Salesman and the Slow Typewriter. The salesman from the Klickety Klack Typewriter Company has approached the Zippy Computer Company. "My typewriter can send and receive ten characters per second. At this phenomenal rate, we can quickly put an entire page of text into a computer." The engineer at Zippy Computer Company says, "But my computer can run at one million instructions per second. It just won't work with your slow typewriter." The salesman responds, "Why not use this technique? There's nothing else to do!"

1. TEST STATUS OF DEVICE (TYPEWRITER)
2. READY TO SEND? (ASCII available for transmission)
3. YES, SEND IT.
4. NO, GO BACK TO 1.
5. . . .

The engineer realized that the speed disparity solution would be achieved this way. However, he was unconvinced that the data was compatible between both machines. Furthermore, the salesman did not explain what would happen if the computer was not ready to receive a character.

An obvious solution is to allow some device to accumulate large amounts of data and then communicate such data to the processor at very high rates. High-speed storage such as a disk does just that, using a buffer. A *buffer* is an intermediate storage element that temporarily holds data for a busy receiving unit, CPU, or memory. A buffer may physically be a register, stack, special storage elements, or reserved memory locations.

6.2.4   INPUT/OUTPUT CONTROL

Not only do significant speed differences exist between the computer and peripheral devices, but also most devices require significant control over their operation. In the past and also in the microcomputers of today, the same control unit that commands CPU activity could also control input/output activity. But most large computing systems use separate control units called I/O processors or I/O controllers (IOC). I/O processors release the CPU to continue processing while I/O transfer takes place. Steps 1 and 2 in Example 6.1 crudely illustrate such control activity which an IOC might perform.

Direct Control. An I/O organization which operates under direct control has the capacity to make immediate transfers from the CPU to the peripheral device. Early computers and many microprocessors were designed to input or output data via a register in the CPU, typically the accumulator. Special I/O instructions effect the transfer to and from devices by name or number. That reserved name would become part of the I/O instruction. For example, the PDP-8 minicomputer I/O instruction has three fields: operation code (I/O), device name, and command.

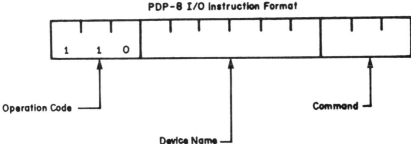

PDP-8 I/O Instruction Format

Typical I/O instructions for device 20 become SKIP20, CLEAR20, READ20, and WRITE20. The last two instructions transfer data into and out of the single accumulator. This same I/O instruction format (opcode, name, command) can be found in many first generation microprocessors. The 8080 uses the IN and OUT instructions, with the second byte specifying the device. 256 devices can be selected. A simple 8080 output program is illustrated in Example 6.2. The 68000, representative of third generation microprocessors, uses a MOVE instruction much like the PDP-11. Here, no special I/O instructions are provided.

Example 6.2 An 8080 Output Program.   The 8080 is interfaced to a CRT which has a data buffer register labeled CRTDB, and two flags to indicate the CRT status. CRTRB is a "ready" flag to indicate to the CPU that a character can be sent to the CRT (if the respective bit is set). CRTSB is another flag to inform the outputting element of the CRT status.

```
CRTSB    EQU 1           ;CRT SENSE FLAG
CRTRB    EQU 1           ;CRT READY FLAG
CRTDB    EQU 0           ;CRT DATA BUFFER REGISTER
         MVI B,CRTRB     ;TELL CRT, CPU READY TO SEND
RDY:     IN CRTSB        ;EXAMINE CRT STATUS; IS CRT
                         ;READY?
         ANA B           ;LOOK AT READY FLAG IN REG B
         JZ RDY          ;JUMP BACK TO RDY FLAG IF
                         ;STILL ZERO
WRITE:   OUT CRTDB       ;SEND CHARACTER NOW
```

6.2.5 INDIRECT CONTROL AND I/O PROCESSORS

This chapter is concerned not only with direct control where I/O transfers are made directly to a CPU register, but also with indirect control made possible with I/O processors. An I/O processor is, in many cases, a small CPU. The I/O processor is capable of storing or "buffering" large amounts of data, receiving commands from the CPU to control peripheral device behavior, as well as receiving status information from the peripheral device. Status information lets the CPU know that the peripheral is "busy," "free or available," "has completed its current task," or has a "full" or "empty" buffer. In the indirect control scheme, the CPU only needs to occasionally attend to the I/O process, leaving the intimate control of the peripheral behavior to the I/O processor.

Hardware internal to the I/O processor (rather than the CPU) could also initiate any mechanical operations required of the device. For example, if a magnetic tape unit were controlled by the I/O processor, the I/O processor could request that the tape move forward to fill the buffer with the next character whenever the buffer is empty. The controller could likewise reverse or rewind the tape, all with an occasional "command" from the CPU. One main objective of the I/O processor is to inhibit the CPU from wasting time while waiting upon some remote and slow mechanical motion.

6.2.6 SIMPLE PERIPHERAL CONTROLS

Peripheral devices need control signals which activate certain sequences within the peripheral itself. A typical I/O device is a combination of mechanical as well as electrical components. For instance, a paper tape reader uses eight light sensing devices to read eight holes, interpreted as bits. But the paper must also be moved. A capstan, much like that found in the magnetic tape or ordinary cassette, must be activated to cause forward or reverse movement of the paper tape. In fact, the sequence of steps taken by a paper tape reader are the following:

1. Activate the capstan motor to initiate tape motion and wait until tape comes up to speed.
2. Monitor a sprocket or "sense" hole to read data.
3. Deactivate capstan motor to stop tape.
4. Send character "read" from sensing devices to the computer.

Steps 1, 3, and 4 require a control signal which we might call "start motor," "stop motor," and "read data," respectively. These signals must enter the peripheral device to serve as control signal inputs to the paper tape reader. A sense signal emanating from the reader mechanism should identify the sprocket hole under the reader. A computer could control this sequence, but the internal mechanical parts cause the paper tape reader to move rather slowly. The tape motor must ramp up, often taking 50-100 milliseconds. In this "long" period of time between Steps 1 and 2, a CPU can execute several thousand instructions. Hence, it makes little sense to tie up a CPU in this activity.

On-Line Versus Off-Line. Although wasteful of CPU time, direct control could interface the CPU for the required sequence of tape motion control. However, indirect control via an IOC could do the same, without CPU direction. Of course, not all peripherals should be under direct control. Some peripherals may be considered *on-line*, which in fact is similar to direct control by the CPU, while others may be considered off-line. An *off-line* device can operate independently of the computer. Keypunching and line printer activities are essentially off-line tasks. Off-line tasks are executed when data can be first buffered or stored in sizable amounts somewhere temporarily before transmission takes place. Usually then, this buffering action reduces the inordinately frequent requests for CPU attention.

Off-Line Versus On-Line

There is very little distinction between on-line and off-line devices today. Even the terminology is considered archaic, because technological advances make such activity transparent. Multiple processor architectures/organizations already support high levels of concurrency so that slow-speed data transfers can occur in parallel with high-speed transfers. In the past, a printer or plotter that outputs from a magnetic tape that was prepared on *another* computer system would have been an example of off-line activity. Today, it is usual to overlap transfer activity among many CPU's, peripherals, and storage media, all on the *same* computer system. □

The software that transfers information for the CPU or I/O processor is called an *I/O program*. Example 6.2 for the 8080 is a very simple I/O program. An I/O program attempts to maximize the *I/O data throughput* or information passage per unit time while minimizing the CPU interruption. An I/O program is very machine-dependent. Hence, it is often written in assembly language. Not only must we know the details of the computer I/O unit, but we must also understand the operating behavior of the actual peripheral device. To a large extent, an I/O program is a function of the size of a computer system, and the particular control requirements and operating speeds of the peripheral devices. A large computer has a significant amount of hardware, including I/O processors, to make I/O transfers fast. Consequently, indirect control, which requires considerable intelligence outside of the CPU is possible with an I/O processor or controller which frequently populates such systems. Small computers, such as microcomputers, rely to a large extent on direct control, in which case much more intimate behavior of the I/O unit as well as device characteristics must be facilitated by the CPU. Whether direct or indirect control is implemented, the I/O program still performs the same tasks.

6.3 BASIC I/O PROGRAMMING

In this section, we briefly introduce some of the tasks required of I/O programs which perform input and output operations. The examples are deceptively simple. At this point, our sole purpose is to introduce elementary I/O programming steps, while simultaneously exposing their relative shortcomings. Generally, to communicate between the computer and an external device, four steps are required.

1. A computer or a peripheral device initiates a request for some service or task.

2. The requested system or device acknowledges the request.

3. The system or device is subsequently serviced.

4. The receiving element acknowledges the completion of the rendered service.

These I/O capabilities must be found, to some extent, in every computing system with an I/O unit. For example, if the peripheral device were a trivial light emitting diode (LED), the device would neither initiate a request nor acknowledge completion of the request. Also, the computer is not required to acknowledge any request. In this trivial I/O process (steps 1 and 4), a character would simply be transmitted to the light emitting diode. Of course, the computer must somehow leave the character "on" long enough for us to recognize it. A keyboard, on the other hand, could not acknowledge the completion of a rendered service (assuming the computer desires to read the input of a keystroke). A line printer, however, is an extremely fast device. During its I/O processing, it may inform the computer that it has just printed the last line, and is ready to receive an entirely new line of words. The computer would then acknowledge this request and service the line printer, transmitting an entire new line, possibly to a line buffer in the printer. The device would then acknowledge a "filled buffer," print out its contents, and repeat the process. All four steps above are executed. These are but a few examples where the four listed capabilities above are applicable.

Briefly, general information transfer techniques can be programmed I/O transfers or interrupt driven I/O transfers. Furthermore, a programmed I/O transfer may be an unconditional transfer or a conditional transfer. An unconditional programmed I/O transfer is simply a singly executed instruction to either input or output data as in Example 6.3. Here, a CRT display output achieved by a single instruction illustrates how fast and simple an unconditional transfer can be executed.

Example 6.3 PDP-11 CRT Display Output (Unconditional Transfer)

```
          •
          •
          •
DDBR =177566                          ;CRT DATA REGISTER
     MOVEB   @#CHAR,@#DDBR            ;SEND CHARACTER
          •
          •
          •
```

Not all devices can transfer and/or receive data "unconditionally." Consequently, an I/O process may need conditional transfers. A conditional transfer solicits a response from a device for a variety of reasons. In the previous example, we have ignored the possibility that the display may not be ready to receive another character. Sometimes, the device simply cannot service the request instantaneously. In that event, the program in Example 6.4 can be used.

Example 6.4   PDP-11 CRT Display Output (Conditional Transfer)

```
HI:        .ASCIZ  /HI/              ;ASCII STRING FOR GREETING
            .
            .
            .
  CDBR = 177566                      ;CRT DISPLAY DATA BUFFER
  CCSR = 177564                      ;CRT DISPLAY CONTROL REGISTER
            MOV     #HI,R2           ;STRING ADDRESS INTO REGISTER
                                     ;R2
OUTPUT: TSTB     @#CCSR              ;IS DEVICE BUSY?
        BPL      OUTPUT              ;BUSY/WAIT LOOP
        MOVB     (R2)+,@#CDBR        ;SEND A CHARACTER TO DEVICE
        BNE      OUTPUT              ;NEED ANOTHER CHARACTER?
            .                        ;NO, CONTINUE
            .
            .
```

In Example 6.4, a conditional I/O transfer is executed. The instruction TSTB is testing a bit in a status register of the CRT display. This single bit determines whether the device is busy or not. The routine remains in this tight loop until the device is free to receive a character. The MOVB instruction then outputs a character from R2 to the data buffer register, CDBR, of the CRT. In this conditional I/O transfer, the computer will obviously wait (and maybe for a long time) until the CRT can receive a new character. In this status register (CCSR), bit 7 serves as a "busy/done" or ready status flag. There may be more than one status flag for devices. A typical control and status register for a device is depicted in Figure 6.1. Bit 0 serves as a device enable signal. Bit 6 enables an interrupt for those devices which have interrupt capabilities. Bit 7 is a done/ready flag. Note that bit 7 conveniently resides in the sign bit position of a byte. A simple positive or negative conditional branch test could then serve to test this flag. In Example 6.4 the conditional branch instruction BPL OUTPUT is used to test bit 7.

For most simple devices, two registers can be found internal to the device: a data buffer register and a control/status register. The data buffer register temporarily latches the data to be communicated in either direction. The control/status register monitors the state of the device and latches necessary control signals which are required for an I/O activity. Status flags in bits 15-12 are typically interpreted as shown in Figure 6.1. The control signals reside in bits 7-0. This control/status register is common to PDP-11 organizations, and is not uncommon in many other computers.

Because microcomputers can be found in many diverse applications, direct interface between the microcomputer and a peripheral device is unlikely.

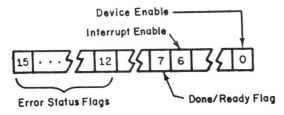

ERROR FLAG	INTERPRETATION
15	ERROR STATUS
14	DATA OVERRUN
13	FRAMING ERROR; STOP bit not found
12	PARITY ERROR ON RECEIVED CHARACTER

Figure 6.1   Typical Control/Status Register Flags

Communication between a microcomputer and a peripheral device is typically accomplished with special chips, designed to perform input/output transfer. However, a typical interface chip includes enough general features to allow interconnections to a variety of devices. The MC6822, Industrial Interface Adapter, is but one of a multitude of single-chip interfaces provided to the microprocessor community. This device, depicted in Figure 6.2, provides two parallel bidirectional ports between peripheral devices and the computer. Four control lines serve as the primary control signal communication paths between the control/status registers and the microprocessor. This particular device has two sets of data registers and control registers. Each register is eight bits wide. The control register contains both flags and control bits similar to that shown in Figure 6.1. This chip is programmable in that both port A and port B can be selected as either input or output ports. The control line signals can also be variously interpreted after preprogramming the chip.

The 6822 represents the low performance end of interface chips available to a microcomputer system designer. Even though an interface chip like the 6822 requires some setup or initialization, these minor steps do not constitute a significantly programmable I/O. An extensively programmable I/O device requires far more attention. For example, control words need to be sent to an I/O processor to indicate what operations to perform, and the device must return "status" information. Also, an intensive I/O process allows data to "fill" and "empty" a temporary holding zone or buffer. Such tasks of a programmable I/O process fall within the domain of an I/O processor. Commands sent to an I/O processor indicate how many characters to transfer, which memory locations to effect the transfer, as well as which direction to transfer (read or write). In addition, unique commands required of the specific physical device need to be generated to tell the printer, for example, when to move the printer head and where, or to tell a disk system when and where to move the disk arm, or even to select the next card of a card reader and advance the paper tape punch mechanism, etc. All such commands may actually be written and transmitted to the programmable I/O device via the I/O processor.

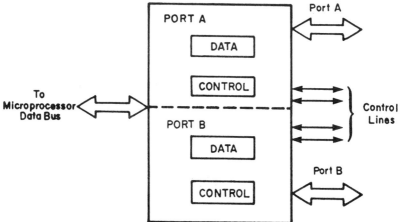

Figure 6.2 MC6822 Industrial Interface Adapter (IIA)

6.4 I/O SPECIFICATION STATEMENTS AND DEVICE HANDLERS

Previous examples have illustrated rudimentary I/O specification statements. An *I/O specification* consists of a set of rules or assignments of bits in an I/O word which serves as either a command word or a control word. The routine which initiates device activity, issues command words, and subsequently facilitates the input/output transfer is called a device *handler*. Each class of peripheral devices has a unique handler. A handler for a CRT would not function as a handler for a line printer, because handlers contain I/O specifications uniquely suited to the electrical and mechanical behavior of the particular peripheral device. To understand I/O specification statements, we must look at a few devices and their control/status words. Shortly we will be examining the general bit assignments for specific peripheral devices. Before we plunge into details, recognize that the I/O specification statements and device handlers can be very simple or very complex, depending on the kind of I/O unit a computer system has. Obviously, a direct control I/O simply requires:

1. An initialization of the control/status word.
2. The data transfer.

3. A monitor of the control/status register for another I/O transfer (if desired).

A peripheral device requires at least two registers: one for data transfer and the other for control/status. The descriptions of the general bit assignments for peripheral devices operating under the PDP-11 UNIBUS architecture can be found in Table 6.1. This 16-bit assignment is a general guide for the bit assignments to almost any control/status register in the UNIBUS interface. The specific assignment for the keyboard/reader status register fields is indicated in Table 6.2.

Table 6.1 General Bit Assignments for PDP-11 Peripheral Devices

Bits	Functions	Remarks
15-12	Error Flags or Status	Four bits are provided to indicate specific individual errors. If more error flags are required, an additional status word may be used.
11	Busy	When set, the device cannot accept another I/O transfer.
10-8	Unit Device Select	Where a controller is provided to allow more than one device per controller, these bits make a device selection. A multiple drive disk system is one example.
7	Ready	Hardware sets or clears this bit as well as bit 11. The CPU may interrogate both bits. Note, the ready bit is in the sign bit position. (Use BPL, BMI for tests.)
6	Interrupt Enable	Bit 6 set allows an interrupt as a result of a completed function or an error. The Interrupt is sent to the CPU only if bit 7 is set.
5-4	Memory Extension	The full 18 bits now specify the address for devices on UNIBUS.
3-1	Device Function	Specifies which operations a device is to perform (read, write, start motor, stop motor, ...).
0	Enable	When set, this bit allows device to perform a requested function. This is a master enable bit which affects most other bits.

6.4.1 DEVICE HANDLERS

A *device handler*, often referred to as a device driver, is a self-contained routine which performs the necessary assembly language instructions to initiate, execute, and terminate a peripheral device I/O transfer. Some input/output software of a computing system is integrated with the systems software at the factory. The manufacturer-supplied handlers are written for a wide variety of peripheral devices. Hence, such handlers can be quite versatile.

For example, Example 6.5 illustrates a test of a communication path between a teletype tape reader and a printer.

Table 6.2 Keyboard/Reader (Slow Speed) Status Register (TKS)

Bits	Functions	Remarks
15-12		Ignored here. Not used for slow speed-devices such as an ASR-33 teletype.
11	Busy	When set, terminal control is receiving a start bit or information bits. For read only operation.
10-8		No designation.
7	Ready	Character available in buffer when set. Cleared when data buffer is read by the CPU. Causes interrupt when bit 6 is set. Read only operation (no write).
6	Reader Interrupt Enable	When bit 7 is set, it enables interrupt.
5-1		No designation.
0	Paper Tape Reader Enable	Enables paper tape reader to read one character. Write only. Always reset (cleared) during the read operation.

Example 6.5 Tape Reader to Printer Test Routine (PDP-11)

```
        TKSTAT=777560           ;DEFINE STATUS AND
                                ;BUFFER REGISTERS
        TKBUF=777562            ;FOR READER/PRINTER;
                                ;SOME SYSTEMS
        TPSTAT=777564           ;MAY USE 1775XX INSTEAD
                                ;OF 777XXX
        TPBUF=777566
REPEAT: INC    @#TKSTAT         ;ENABLE PAPER TAPE
                                ;READER
IBUFFER: TSTB  @#TKSTAT         ;CHARACTER ARRIVE?
        BPL    IBUFFER          ;NO, CHECK 7TH BIT AGAIN
OBUFFER: TSTB  @#TPSTAT         ;PRINTER READY?
        BPL    OBUFFER          ;BRANCH IF NOT NO. CHECK
                                ;AGAIN
        MOVB   @#TKBUF,@#TPBUF  ;SEND READER BUFFER TO
                                ;PRINTER
        BR     REPEAT           ;DO IT ALL AGAIN
```

This device handler reads a single character from the paper tape reader and transmits it back out to a printer. Such a handler is useful in testing out the communications path between two devices. In this handler, as in most handlers, labels are used for the device names internal to the routine. Labels help make the routine understandable as well as make the routine generally applicable to other devices with simple program modification. For example, if we desire to apply this handler code to a high-speed reader and punch, we would simply need to change the device address assignments. The remaining code is also quite similar, but, the major contribution to the almost immediate reapplication of this handler lies in the status register bit assignments for many devices. Simply stated, these bit assignments are often identical from one device to another. In fact, Table 6.2 for the keyboard reader and status register looks very much like the bit assignments for a high-speed reader and punch. In particular, bits 7 and 11 are designated busy and ready bits in both status registers. Likewise, bit 0 is reserved for the device enable request.

Because the status register bit assignments follow a common assignment for many peripheral devices, nearly the same code can be used in all handlers. For instance, the REPEAT source statement above increments the status register. This places a 1 in bit 0 which enables a device. If TKSTAT (paper tape status register) were replaced with the high-speed reader status register address, this same code would apply. The sign bit or bit 7 in the status register of both devices designates the "ready" status of either device. Again, the same code can be used to test this particular status of many other devices. Of course, not all handlers can be so easily recoded. Some devices are extremely complicated. In those cases, more error bits (other than bits 15-12) may be required as well as a specific designation for bits 3-1 in the status register. In any event, a common bit assignment for the status/control applicable to many I/O devices is very important to manufacturers. In Example 6.6, this "echo" handler is a routine to accept 40 characters from a keyboard and transmit them to a teleprinter.

Coroutines are very desirable for I/O processing, especially when multiple peripheral devices are simultaneously active and interaction is high. To illustrate the mechanism of double-buffered I/O transfers, consider the following events which must be handled concurrently (reading devices 12 and 13). READ, WRITE, and PROCESS are commands to an operating system to perform the tasks of reading, writing, and processing the appropriately labeled devices. For example, WRITE 02 means "output data to device #02." At first, the following tasks occur:

COROUTINE A

```
WRITE 02
READ 12              {concurrently with device 13
PROCESS 13
```

Example 6.6   Echo Handler

```
;ACCEPT WITH AN IMMEDIATE ECHO AND PROCEED TO STORE 40
CHARACTERS FROM
;USER'S KEYBOARD. WHEN COMPLETE, OUTPUT CR AND LF. ECHO
ENTIRE STRING
;FROM STORAGE POINTED TO BY R0. R1 CONTAINS STRING LENGTH.
          R0=%0                      ;TEMPORARY SCRATCH AREA FOR
          R1=%1                      ;COUNTERS AND POINTERS
          CR=15                      ;DEFINE CARRIAGE RETURN SYMBOL (CR)
          LF=12                      ;DEFINE LINE FEED SYMBOL (LF)
          TKSTAT=177560              ;KEYBOARD STATUS REGISTER (BUFFER)
          TKBUF=TKS+2                ;KEYBOARD DATA REGISTER
          TPSTAT=TKB+2               ;READER STATUS REGISTER
          TPBUF=TPS+2                ;READER DATA REGISTER (BUFFER)
          .TITLE ECHO
START: MOV   #SAVE+2,R0              ;SET UP BUFFER AREA POINTER IN R0
                                     ;BEYOND CR & LF
       MOV   #40.,R1                 ;CHARACTER COUNT IN R1 FOR 40 CHARS
   IN: TSTB  @#TKS                   ;CHAR IN BUFFER?
       BPL   IN                      ;IF NOT BRANCH BACK AND WAIT UNTIL
                                     ;DATA READY (BUSY/WAIT LOOP)
 ECHO: TSTB  @#TPSTAT                ;CHECK TELEPRINTER READY STATUS
       BPL   ECHO                    ;NOT YET? GO BACK
       MOVB  @#TKBUF,@#TPBUF         ;ECHO CHARACTER BETWEEN DEVICES
       MOVB  @#TKBUF,(R0)+           ;STORE CHARACTER AWAY IN BUFFER
       DEC   R1                      ;UPDATE CHAR COUNT
       BNE   IN                      ;FINISHED INPUTTING?
       MOV   #SAVE,R0                ;SET UP BUFFER POINTER INCLUDING
                                     ;CR & LF NOW
       MOV   #42.,R1                 ;COUNTER OF BUFFER INCLUDING CR & LF
  OUT: TSTB  @#TPSTAT                ;CHECK TELEPRINTER READY STATUS
       BPL   OUT                     ;NOT READY, CHECK AGAIN TIL BIT 7 SET
       MOVB  (R0)+,@#TPBUF           ;OUTPUT CHARACTER
       DEC   R1                      ;UPDATE BUFFER COUNT IN R1
       BNE   OUT                     ;FINISHED OUTPUTTING?
       .WAIT                         ;YES. STOP
 SAVE: .BYTE CR,LF                   ;DATA AREA FOR "CARRIAGE RE TURN" AND
                                     ;"LINE FEED"
       .=.+40.                       ;DATA AREA FOR 40 CHARACTERS
       .END
```

Then, another set of tasks occurs as follows:

COROUTINE B

```
WRITE 01
READ 13            {concurrently with device 12
PROCESS 12
```

Coroutine A operates at first and executes at its exit point ("PROCESS 13"):

```
MOV #PCB,-(R6)   ;PCB IS PUSHED ONTO STACK TO PREPARE FOR
                 ;COROUTINE CALL PCB ← SP
JSR PC,@(R6)+    ;CONTROL FLOWS TO LOCATION PCB WHICH IS
                 ;ENTRY POINT TO COROUTINE B; THE RETURN
                 ;POINT OF COROUTINE A (PCA) IS PUSHED ONTO
                 ;STACK
```

Now coroutine B is operating. Upon completing its task, coroutine B transfers I/O control to coroutine A executing the following code at its exit point ("PROCESS 12"):

```
JSR PC,@(R6)+    ;PC IS EXCHANGED FOR PCA ON THE STACK;
                 ;CONTROL IS NOW RETURNED TO COROUTINE A;
                 ;THE RETURN POINT OF COROUTINE B IS
                 ;PUSHED ONTO STACK
```

6.5   DATA HANDLING VIA BUFFERING

Example 6.5 illustrates a rudimentary device handler routine. For many computer applications and certainly any medium or large-scale computer systems, the busy/wait loop required of the CPU for an I/O process is entirely unsatisfactory. A busy/wait loop is just too slow. In a computer system with sophisticated I/O traffic and devices, an I/O processor is used to circumvent speed disparity issues. An I/O program would then let the CPU continue program execution and relinquish control of a peripheral device to an I/O processor at a time convenient to both the CPU and the device. An I/O processor is like a data traffic cop directing data movement among CPU, memory, and I/O. Some I/O processors can even control the peripheral device while the computer is executing other code, thus supporting I/O overlap activity. However, an I/O program required of the I/O processor can become very involved. We immediately appreciate this when we consider that the program in Example 6.5 accomplishes only one character transfer at a time, tying up the CPU in the meantime. One simple solution would be to include some hardware in the I/O processor to retain several characters before transmission in either direction. Since a data buffer register can retain only one character at a time, this "single" character buffer is obviously quite inadequate. Obviously, extra hardware should include special storage, namely a buffer (with many registers).

6.5.1 BUFFERS

In an I/O process, a buffer scheme could be established by setting aside a few memory locations and demanding the I/O processor to keep these locations filled to capacity. A CPU can then retrieve or read characters from the device via this region at the most convenient time to the CPU. More importantly, the CPU can retrieve several characters at the speed of main memory references instead of at the speed of the transfer rates of the peripheral device (often called I/O references).

A buffer may physically be a register, special storage element, or simply reserved memory locations. The choice depends upon the speed of operation, available memory, and the cost of additional hardware. If a buffer is merely a register found in the I/O unit (and not in the CPU), data handling is straightforward although slow. If the buffer is a set of registers or a storage element with several locations, "buffering" is much more complicated. Here, we need to consider not only who can fill/empty a buffer, but in what direction and to what extent. Also, a buffer-full flag and buffer-empty flag are necessary. The *buffer-full* flag warns the sender (source of buffered data) that no more space exists. A *buffer-empty* flag tells the receiver (destination of buffered data) that no more data exists.

Buffers may be a stack (LIFO), a deque, or a queue (FIFO). We have already seen how the push-down stack of the PDP-11 can save and restore registers. Likewise, the stack can also buffer data, but its growth is only one dimensional. Nevertheless, stacks are useful because they maintain the list of data consistent with the stack user's need to know the last item entered. A *deque* or double-ended queue is a stack which can grow in both directions. Consider a deque as a stack with two stack pointers, one end growing upward and the other end growing downward as in Figure 6.3. A *queue*, also called a single-ended queue, has a first-in-first-out ordering. A queue adds on one end and removes from the opposite end. Note that the ordering in a queue is fixed and that queue information removal does not alter the ordering.

6.5.2 CIRCULAR BUFFERS

The circular buffer or ring employed as a queue is of prime importance to I/O processes, because adding or deleting data to such a buffer does not alter the ordering. More importantly, the circular buffer does not need to grow indefinitely. Rather, the circular buffer wraps around itself. Of course, data must not be destroyed in the filling process.

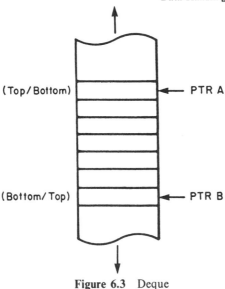

(Top/Bottom)   ←— PTR A

(Bottom/Top)   ←— PTR B

Figure 6.3 Deque

A circular buffer assumes a contiguous set of locations capable of adjoining the highest address location to the lowest. A track or a disk might have such an addressable structure. Random access memory can also be organized as a circular buffer. A circular buffer queue is logically depicted in Figure 6.4. As shown, the top of the buffer points to entry 0, which is the next data to remove. The "bottom" of the circular buffer points to the next location to insert data. When a peripheral device transfers data to the buffer for temporary storage, it will place data in the circular array location pointed to by BOTTOM. BOTTOM is then updated to point to the next location. In Figure 6.4, the circular buffer will rotate one position clockwise with each data access. A circular buffer could just as easily revolve in the opposite direction. Direction is unimportant as long as it stays the same. The circular buffer in Figure 6.4 is rather short.

Circular buffers do have some complications. An I/O routine should always check for the end of the buffer when updating pointers. In the event that a pointer is updated past the end of the list, the routine would cause the pointer to be reset to the first list entry, thus producing the circular effect. Another restriction to a circular buffer is that the peripheral device must not insert data faster than the CPU is able to remove data. Otherwise, the circular buffer overflows with a subsequent loss of data. One obvious solution is to increase the number of buffer locations and the size of the buffer. Two routines, listed in Example 6.7 for a VAX, first accept characters from a remote terminal, and subsequently pass those characters to some operating system call.

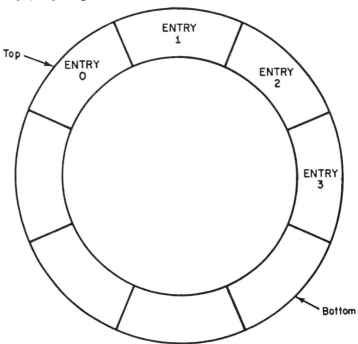

Figure 6.4   Circular Buffer

The first routine INBUF inserts a character into the circular buffer. Each character is a byte pointed to by an argument pointer. The buffer size is contained in BUFSIZE. R0 serves as the buffer-full flag to a subsequent calling sequence, and is zero if the buffer is full. If a character has been successfully transferred to the buffer, R0 equals one. The EDIV is an extended divide instruction which wraps the pointer around the buffer to ensure that the next "pointed-to" location at the bottom becomes the top of the circular buffer. The routine OUTBUF transfers a character from the buffer to the CPU or memory device.

6.5.3 BUFFER HARDWARE

Many computer systems are installed in a multi-user environment and, conceivably, each user may desire buffer storage for their own terminal. When multiple buffers are required, the operating system must coordinate storage activity for other purposes with these dynamic buffer storage requirements. In any event, buffer storage may become sizable. Hardware such as the buffer control unit (BCU) found in the IBM 370 becomes necessary. A BCU

Example 6.7 A VAX-11/780 Terminal Handler Using Circular Buffers

```
;FILL A CIRCULAR BUFFER POINTED TO BY R0 UP TO LENGTH #BUFSIZE
INBUF:      CLRQ      R0
            CMPL      #BUFSIZE,LENGTH
            BEQL      NOMORE
            MOVL      BOTTOM,R0
            MOVB      CHAR(AP),BUFFER[R0]
            INCL      LENGTH
            INCL      R0
            EDIV      #BUFSIZE,R0,R1,BOTTOM;PERFORM POINTER
                      ;WRAP-AROUND
            MOVZBL    #1,R0
NOMORE:     RET
;OUTPUT A CIRCULAR BUFFER AREA POINTED TO BY AP
OUTBUF:     CLRQ      R0
            TSTL      LENGTH
            BEQL      NOMORE
            MOVL      TOP,R0
            MOVB      BUFFER[R0],@CHARADR(AP)
            DECL      LENGTH
            INCL      R0
            EDIV      #BUFSIZE,R0,R1,TOP;PERFORM POINTER
                      WRAP-AROUND
            MOVZBL    #1,R0
NOMORE:     RET
```

includes logic circuitry to maintain an index array and control information for buffer storage. Buffer storage requirements must cooperate with main storage requirements. The BCU manages the buffer storage with the help of an index array that holds the entry for each block in the buffer. A main storage address in the 370 uses bits 11–31 as depicted in Figure 6.5a. Bits 11–27 are used by the buffer storage system to specify the row, address, and column number. The array index contains two rows and 128 columns to correspond with the buffer storage blocks. An index array entry is depicted in Figure 6.5b. Row address fields in Figure 6.5a contain the main storage address of the data block. Three bits in the index array entry designate the validity of high-order and low-order half-blocks. In addition, an OK bit specifies whether the corresponding positions in the buffer and index array are working properly.

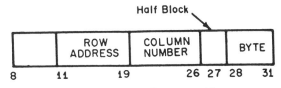

Figure 6.5a Main Storage Address

An indexed relationship is maintained between main storage and buffer storage as is depicted in Figure 6.6. Specific storage algorithms maintain the availability of upper and lower half-blocks for the CPU and buffer storage. The BCU also includes some storage protection and controls to perform data checking as data enters or leaves the buffer. Also, if any buffer component fails, a machine check interruption occurs upon reading an OK bit. It is important to note that the IBM 370 supports multi-length operands, including byte-oriented operands. Hence, operands for certain instructions (nonprivileged) will reside on byte boundaries. But CPU instructions must reside in or be aligned on half-word boundaries. Other instructions, such as the channel command words (CCW), must be aligned on double-word boundaries. These byte, half-word, and word boundary demands need attention. The BCU contains considerable error checking and correction circuitry which applies to all such stores and fetches. Hence, an elaborate relationship between main storage and buffer storage must be maintained. In general, the buffer storage system must be maintained on a column-wise basis, or each column of main storage will compete with the buffer storage for a position in that column of the buffer.

Buffers may be found as one-dimensional arrays (stacks, queues, deques, circular) or two-dimensional arrays (as in the IBM 370). Regardless of which buffer storage organization is used, the ultimate objective is to permit I/O transfer, independent of frequent CPU attention. This is called *I/O overlap* and always employs some type of buffer storage scheme, however trivial or complex it may be.

6.5.4 SEMAPHORES

Using a buffer by itself is not the final solution to many I/O operations (I/O overlapped or not). We have not answered such questions as, "Did we just fill the buffer?" or "Has the buffer just been emptied?" These questions are resolved by computer system software which keeps track of the buffer size. Some computers resort to special hardware which may reside in the I/O processor itself. In any case, remember that our problem stems from the fact

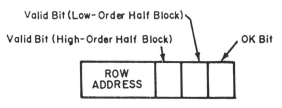

Figure 6.5b   Index Array Entry

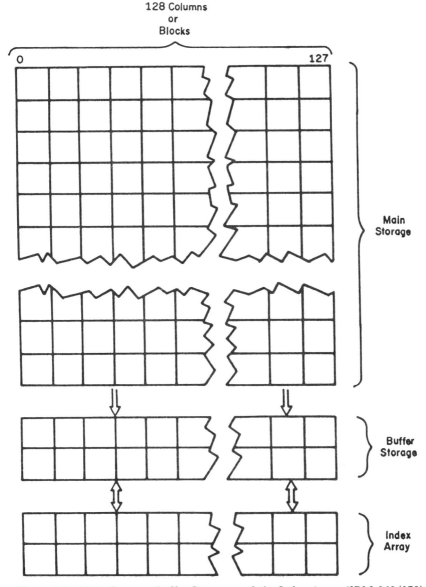

Figure 6.6   Main Storage, Buffer Storage, and the Index Array (IBM 360/370)

that two independent processes can change the contents of the same buffer. A peripheral may be filling the buffer while another storage element or CPU may be emptying it, and vice versa. In the previous VAX example, register R0 indicates when a buffer is full or when a character has been successfully inserted for the INBUF procedure. R0 is also used in the OUTBUF routine to indicate that the buffer is empty or a character has been successfully removed. The mechanism we are employing is actually called a semaphore by Dijkstra.[1]

A *semaphore* is a communications variable or a flag variable between two operations. Suppose our operations include filling and emptying a buffer, or P(3) and V(3), respectively. Let S be the semaphore variable to indicate a lock and unlock condition. One function of P(S) should cause one of the processes to wait. A Pascal procedure for P(S) is found in Example 6.8.

Example 6.8 A Pascal Semaphore

```
                        •
                        •
                        •
        IF S=0
                THEN wait and test S
                ELSE clear S
                        •
                        •
                        •
```

If the semaphore takes on one value (namely, "one" as in Example 6.8), the process is allowed to proceed, but, the semaphore is immediately set to its opposite value. If the semaphore has the opposite value, the process is not allowed, and must wait until somebody else changes the semaphore value.

6.5.5 TEST AND SET INSTRUCTIONS

The interval of time between S being tested and the time it is set to zero is, unfortunately, finite. For a semaphore to work properly, this operation of testing and setting must be *indivisible*. That is, no other process should be able to interfere with the current process's test and set operation. Why? Because S is a signaling variable to two or more processes using the same buffer area. Neither a process nor any other activity of the computer system should be able to affect S during the testing and setting operation. To be precise, no process can be allowed to test S between the time S is tested and found not to be zero and the time it takes to clear it to zero. Otherwise, the integrity of the value of S is damaged (or at least suspect).

---

[1] E. W. Dijkstra, "Cooperating Sequential Processes," in *Programming Languages*, ed. Elan Genuys (New York: Academic Press, 1968).

The 68000 microprocessor and the IBM 370 have a special instruction called test and set (TAS and TS, respectively) useful for semaphores. This instruction reads a byte from memory and sets the condition code on the basis of the information in the byte. Immediately thereafter, the byte is set to 11111111. In both machines, this test and set instruction is *noninterruptible* so that the indivisible property of the operation is retained.

A 68000 routine which facilitates a semaphore is indicated in Example 6.9. The routine remains in a tight loop while S is not zero, thus holding up one I/O process. When S is zero, the I/O process proceeds.

The VAX has two instructions, BBSSI and BBCCI, which "branch if bit set and set bit" and "branch if bit clear and clear bit," respectively. Both instructions can facilitate P(S) and V(S) semaphore activity, because the memory location currently being examined can be interlocked using a single bit as the semaphore. As such, more than one VAX processor or I/O device can cooperatively access shared buffers. However, only one at a time will be able to test and set or clear the semaphore. Example 6.10 illustrates the use of BBCCI in two processes to cooperate within a computer to share a buffer that only one process can access at a time. The routine assumes that a flag bit in memory is initially set, indicating the buffer is free to be used. Before either process accesses the buffer, each process tests the bit and branches to its code if the semaphore is set. If the semaphore is not set, the process continues waiting until set. Then the process clears the semaphore, accesses the buffer, finally setting only after its buffer activity is completed.

The VAX has two instructions, INSQUE and REMQUE, to insert and remove elements from a circular buffer, respectively. Like BBSSI and BBCCI, both are noninterruptable and can serve to fill/empty buffers using the Z and V flags in the condition code register to aid the process. INSQUE sets the Z flag if the entry inserted was the first in the queue, while REMQUE sets the Z flag if the entry removed was the last one. Also, REMQUE sets the V flag if there was no entry to remove. Even though the Z and V flags primarily serve as buffer empty/fill flags, the noninterruptable property of both instructions permits us to use buffers in the VAX with "semaphore" properties.

Example 6.9 A 68000 Semaphore

```
PHORE   TAS    S        ;WAIT HERE IF SEMAPHORE
                        ;IS NOT ZERO
        BNE    PHORE
         •               ;PERFORM DESIRED
         •               ;PROCESS NOW
         •
        CLR    S        ;CLEAR THE SEMAPHORE
```

Example 6.10   A VAX Semaphore

```
PHORE:  .LONG   1                 ;SET SEMAPHORE TO 1
          •                       ;BUFFER NOW OPEN TO
          •                       ;ANYONE
          •
;FIRST PROCESS (CPU) DESIRES BUFFER ACCESS
          •
          •
          •
WAIT1:  BBCCI   #0,PHORE,WAIT1 ;LOOP HERE UNTIL
          •                       ;SEMAPHORE IS SET
OK1:      •                       ;ACCESS SHARED BUFFER NOW
          •
        BISL    #1,PHORE          ;SET SEMAPHORE TO ONE
;SECOND PROCESS (I/O) DESIRES BUFFER ACCESS
          •
          •
          •
WAIT2:  BBCCI   #0,PHORE,WAIT2 ;LOOP HERE
          •
OK2:      •                       ;ACCESS SHARED BUFFER HERE
          •
        BISL    #1,PHORE          ;SET SEMAPHORE TO ONE
```

6.6   I/O TRANSFER VIA INTERRUPTS

Not all machines have a test and set instruction. Some machines rely solely upon the CPU to execute processes to fill and empty a buffer. In these machines, a *program* must switch the CPU between these processes and any other processes requiring attention. But many I/O processes cannot be initiated by a CPU-oriented program. They must be strictly initiated by an I/O peripheral. To invoke this change in program control flow, computer *hardware* supports an "interrupt" mechanism.

Furthermore, for most input/output operations, data transfer is an asynchronous task. That is, not only are individual data items transferable at a clock rate very much independent of the CPU clock, but each individual request for the data transfer may occur asynchronously. In such cases, we could not expect a device to transfer data every time just at the precise moment of the completion of a CPU instruction, because the request, as well as the synchronization, would not permit such fine interleaving of activity. However, such I/O operations can be partially interleaved between individual CPU instruction execution if interrupt-controlled I/O transfers are allowed (rather than program-controlled I/O transfers). An interrupt-controlled I/O transfer consists of the following steps.

1. A device initiates a service request by "interrupting" the computer.

2. When the computer can render service, the "interrupt" is acknowledged.

3. Program control jumps to an interrupt handler to service the device.

4. Upon completion of the rendered service, program control returns to the interrupted program, and the CPU resumes execution.

The interrupt process is illustrated in Figure 6.7 where we see how important it is to realize that the interruption is caused by hardware and not software (that is, a program). Note carefully that the interrupting point in the currently executing program is always unknown. Also, the CPU must acknowledge the interrupt before program control transfers to an interrupt handler. More importantly, the interrupt process (either with the handler or by other means) must save the current machine status and restore it when the interrupt servicing is completed. Some computers operate in a supervisor or user mode. For such machines, interrupt servicing is always executed in the supervisor mode (e.g., VAX, IBM 360/370, 68000). Whether interrupt handling is aided by hardware or not, a precise and consistent set of operations will occur every time. In the PDP-11, an interrupt causes the following equivalent operations using R6 as the stack pointer to save the processor status (PS) and the program counter (PC) (to preserve machine status).

```
MOV R7,-(SP)      ;SAVE PC
MOV PS,-(SP)      ;SAVE PROCESSOR STATUS
```

The actual "jump" to an interrupt handler is accomplished by retrieving an "interrupt vector" address from a preassigned memory location and placing it into the PC. The actual jumping mechanism is very machine-dependent and varies from one family to another. Also, the contents of the next consecutive location in memory are loaded into the processor status word. The actual locations, having been set aside by the manufacturer ahead of time, are designated by a system designer for each I/O device. The first location must contain the starting address of the interrupt handler routine. Within the interrupt handler itself, the last instructions must be a return-from-interrupt (RTI) which causes the following:

```
MOV (SP)+,PS      ;RESTORE OLD PROCESSOR STATUS
MOV (SP)+,R7      ;RESTORE OLD PC
```

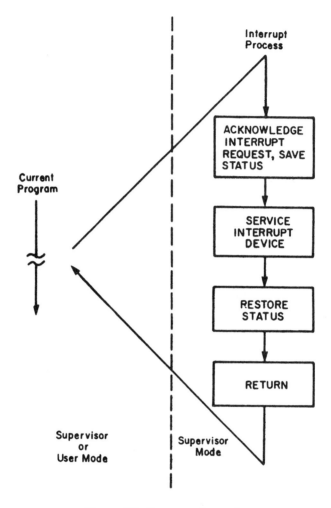

Figure 6.7   Interrupt Processing

Interrupt processing must be accomplished without interfering with the current CPU activity, other than to delay further current program execution. Neither active registers nor temporary CPU results should be lost. To ensure this, the computer either in hardware or the interrupting handler in software should preserve any previous results or contents of registers the handler uses internally within its routine. Software as well as hardware can execute preservation and restoration process operation.

Traps Versus Interrupts

Interruption, per se, is a general notion that applies to program control flow that makes abrupt changes in intended program tasks. Interruption may be invoked by software as well as hardware. A software interrupt could occur when instructions like SWI (in the 6800 and 6809) and TRAP (in the 68000, PDP-11, VAX, and IBM 360) are invoked. These instructions physically reside in a program and cause program control to divert to specific routines to handle, we hope, an uncommon condition. Such traps can be caused by floating-point overflow/underflow, integer overflow, an undefined opcode, stack overflow and fetching an instruction in an illegal address. Traps invoke "exception processing." Exception processing is a mechanism to handle program control flow in unexpected events. More importantly, software interrupts and traps are not normally used for I/O transfers. Another essential difference between traps and hardware interrupts is that traps are basically synchronous with the main program, while interrupts are totally asynchronous.

Hardware interrupts, of course, directly change program control flow caused not by a program, but rather by hardware, and usually as part of some I/O operation. Interruption is similar to an unanticipated procedure call or jump to subroutine, only now initiated by hardware. These hardware interrupts could occur by a disk which has been instructed to start transferring data. Here, when such data is available (the head is over the relevant track and sector), the disk could generate an interrupt to the CPU. At this point, the interrupt will stop main program execution and transfer control to a disk interrupt handler. Of course, when the service is completed, the handler must return control to the interrupted process exactly at the interrupted point.

Interrupts can both occur at any moment and by any I/O device capable of interrupting. Also, more than one I/O device may generate an interrupt, even while a previous device interrupt is being serviced. When this occurs, interrupts must be capable of nesting. This presents no problem if interrupt handlers are transparent. Furthermore, a transparent handler must be reentrant. A transparent handler must preserve the entire state of the interrupted process, including program counter, registers, condition codes, and stack pointers. Upon return, the interrupted process is returned to its previous uninterrupted state. As far as the interrupted process is concerned, if a handler is transparent, the interrupted process will have no recollection of the interrupt. Indeed, the interrupted process should take no special precautionary measures or even be concerned about the interrupt handling. If all I/O programs which handle interrupts are transparent, no side effects other than delay in execution time of the main program will occur. Interrupt handlers which are transparent ensure that no unexpected behavior and no side effects among the main program and other handlers will occur.

The nesting of interrupts is just as common as the nesting of subroutines. Likewise, just as stacks are useful to subroutine nesting, stacks with the same stacking principles can and do apply to nested interrupts. In fact, the concept of nesting is commonplace to computer science. A useful rule to consider is: *the inner nest should always be completed before its outer nest is completed.* Stack operating guidelines proposed in the previous chapter apply directly to nested interrupts. In the VAX, the stack picture, upon interrupt knowledge, contains both the status register and the program counter, as in Figure 6.8 where an interrupt has occurred just after another interrupt was acknowledged. The stack pointer is updated so that in the event another interrupt occurs while the current interrupt is being handled, the stack pointer again preserves the new program counter and status register. This nesting of the returned "state of the machine" can continue indefinitely (so long as memory space is available).

6.6.1   INTERRUPT ENABLE/DISABLE

A programming capability to prevent interruption must exist in a computer because some computer activity may never recover if interrupted. Such activity must remain indivisible (interrupted). The semaphore test and set process is one instance of such an indivisible noninterruptible activity. If, however, a TAS-like instruction does not exist in a computer, yet is still necessary, such an instruction can be emulated with several instructions. But even a TAS-like routine can still be interrupted, because interruption is commonly acknowledged at the end of every currently executing instruction in nearly all computers. So how are interrupts disabled over several instruction executions? The solution is to use another instruction which affects a special bit(s) in the processor status word, namely the interrupt-enable mask bit(s). Instructions such as enable-interrupt (CLI as in 6800) and disable-interrupts (SEI as in 6800) are used in some machines. These essentially control only a single bit (I) in the PSR as in Figure 6.9 for the 6800. Some computers provide more than one bit for interrupt enabling/disabling to allow "masking" or selectively discriminating one I/O device interrupt over another (as with the 68000, VAX, IBM 360/370).

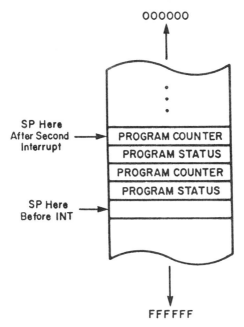

Figure 6.8   VAX Interrupt Stack Picture

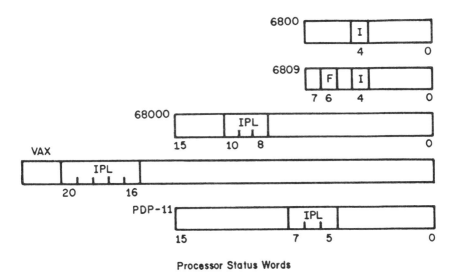

Figure 6.9   Interrupt Mask Bits in Status Words

6.6.2 INTERRUPT PRIORITY LEVELS

Not all I/O devices require immediate attention on an equal basis. Certainly, an interrupt to the computer to indicate that its power supplies are failing (thus asking the computer to save its status and vital registers somewhere) is more urgent than a TTY request. To enforce such a "priority," more than one bit in the PSW is designated for interrupt masking. In Figure 6.9, we see that the 68000 can provide eight priority levels, while the VAX can provide 32 priority levels, simply by setting a binary code in bits 8-10 and 16-20, respectively. A device at a higher interrupt level can block one with a lower interrupt level if they both appear simultaneously. Devices on the same level when generating simultaneous interrupts will cause the CPU to acknowledge the device closest to the CPU first. For example, if devices D4 and D5 in Figure 6.10 request interrupts, the CPU will acknowledge D4 first, effectively blocking D5 (if masking levels are appropriately declared).

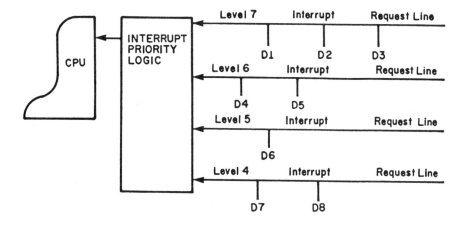

Figure 6.10   PDP-11 Interrupt Lines

The physical interrupt request signal from an I/O device can enter the CPU via more than one wire or line. To facilitate the eight levels of the 68000, three lines are required with an encoder between the eight devices and the 68000 chip, as in Figure 6.11. This multiple-line scheme is common among microprocessors. The three bits in the 68000 status word would mask out "lower" interrupt levels by ignoring 3-bit codes on IPL0, IPL1, and IPL2 whose binary values are less than the value of bits 8-10. The same interrupt priority organization can be found in the PDP-11 with bits 8-10 of its status word.

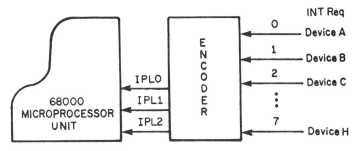

Figure 6.11   68000 Interrupt Priority Lines (IPL)

The designers of the PDP-11 chose to support a four-level hardware interrupt priority scheme and an eight-level "software" interrupt priority scheme. Bits 8-10 in the processor status word only correspond to software interrupt priorities. The hardware priority scheme is physically embedded in the I/O hardware interfaces, called the interrupt priority logic shown in Figure 6.10. An I/O device generating an interrupt causes its hardware priority level to be compared to the software level found in bits 8-10. Only if it equals or exceeds that level in the processor status (PS) word will the interrupt be serviced. The comparison is made by loading a new PS value from the device interrupt vector addresses.

The processor status word and interrupt control reside in the CPU of a computer. However, hardware does exist external to the CPU to control interrupts. In many I/O units and devices themselves, a control bit in the control/status register is specified as an interrupt enable bit. The I/O of a PDP-11 system designates the interrupt enable function (see Table 6.1). When set, an interrupt can be passed on to the CPU by the device (of course, only if the device itself has been enabled by bit 7 of the status registers). When cleared, an interrupt request is effectively blocked. Many computers utilize this "remote" interrupt enable/disable scheme. Microcomputers configured with interface adapter chips, as in Figure 6.2, designate a bit(s) in the interface chip control/status register for interrupt enable. The 6822 chip seen previously is one example.

Consider a clock interrupt handler for a PDP-11. We first initialize the clock's interrupt vector, which is at location 100, using MOV #CLOCK,@#100 and MOV #CLKSTAT,@#102. Then, we set bit 6 in the device register 177546 to enable the interrupt for the line clock, and continue computing. The interrupt handler in Example 6.11 is entered every 60th of a second, incrementing the double word length "seconds" location. Note that the clock PS (CLKSTAT) is programmed to have a priority 4 level.

Example 6.11   A PDP-11 Line Clock Interrupt Handler

```
CLKSTAT:   .WORD   200      ;SET CLOCK HARDWARE
                            ;PRIORITY TO 4
TICK:      INC     SEC+2    ;ANOTHER 60TH OF A
           BEQ     CARRY    ;SECOND
           RTI              ;RETURN FROM INTERRUPT
CARRY:     INC     SEC      ;ANOTHER SECOND
           RTI              ;RETURN FROM INTERRUPT
```

6.7   SOME INPUT/OUTPUT ORGANIZATIONS

The PDP-11 system block diagram in Figure 6.12 depicts a single bus organization centered around the UNIBUS, and to a large extent, the UNIBUS is a dedicated bus. That is, only one activity can occur on this bus. All memory, I/O devices, and even the CPU must be attached to the UNIBUS. One advantage of this bus structure is its simplicity. Incorporating a new I/O device into the system organization is just a matter of physically connecting cables from the device to the UNIBUS. To the CPU, one device "looks" just like any other device. There are some drawbacks to single bus structures like the UNIBUS. One significant shortcoming is the already mentioned restriction that only one bus transmission can be executed at a time. Yet, large computer installations exist primarily to support many users concurrently.

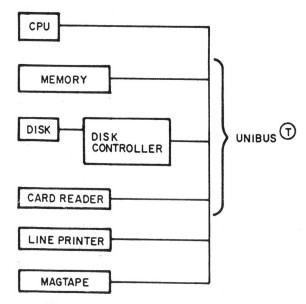

Figure 6.12   PDP-11 System Block Diagram

Hence, single bus organizations are more likely to be found in small computer installations. Realizing this, Digital Equipment Corporation designers (manufacturers of the PDP-11 and the larger VAX systems) made significant enhancements to their buses to speed up each bus and to support more concurrent activity in later systems.

In stark contrast to the PDP-11, the VAX computer systems were purposely designed to support significantly greater numbers of concurrent users. To do so, the VAX uses more than one bus. In the VAX-11/780 installation of Figure 6.13, the organization includes an SBI (synchronous backplane interconnect) which fans out to buses for memory devices via memory controllers to the existing UNIBUS and to a new MASSBUS. In addition, a console subsystem has a direct path to the CPU. The other devices are connected via the SBI through a CACHE memory to the CPU. (*CACHE memory* is a high speed storage element physically close to the CPU, and runs at speeds equivalent to CPU speeds.)

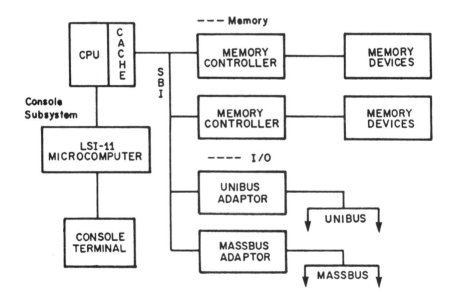

Figure 6.13   VAX-11/780 System Block Diagram

The IBM 370 system block diagram of Figure 6.14 has one bus for main memory, and channels (similar to buses) for I/O and memory devices. However, memory devices connected via channels do not serve the same purpose as main memory. Channel devices are slower secondary storage media. Each channel uses a *multiplexer* or switching device to select one device on a channel at a time, and to direct the flow of information between the I/O devices and the main storage. Channel selection is also possible with *selectors*, but facilities are more restrictive. Here, only one subchannel is allowed and the I/O device must transfer data in a burst mode (short but heavy streams of data). Disks are usually connected to a selector. Ordinarily, high speed devices operate with the channel in the burst mode while slower devices operate in a byte-multiplexed mode. Matching input/output devices to channel characteristics is important to a high performance 370 organization.

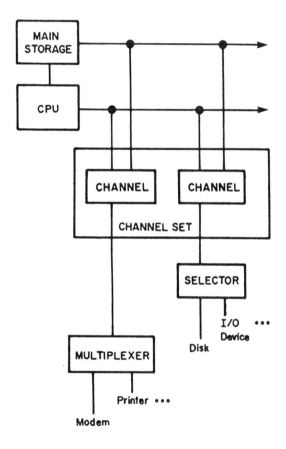

Figure 6.14   IBM 370 System Block Diagram

6.8   EXCEPTIONS AND INTERRUPTS IN THE VAX

It is a mistaken notion that a typical program will execute sequentially and completely once it is loaded in main memory. More often then not, a program will be interrupted by some other process. Upon responding to the other process, the CPU will return to the current program and resume execution. To do so requires more than a simple exit to the interrupting process. The CPU must save the state of the current program somewhere, remember where the state is stored, acquire the new executable code, process it, and finally restore the previous program and its state. All of these tasks must be executed before the previous program execution resumes. Exceptions and interruptions are only two of many mechanisms in a computer environment which cause program executions to suspend. Perhaps the best way to view such occurrences is as a change in the flow of control of events in a computer. Because events within the system may require the execution of particular modules of software outside of and external to the explicit flow of control, the processor forces a change in the flow of control from that which would be explicitly occurring otherwise in the currently executing process.

When events are relevant to the current process and normally invoke software in the context of the current process, the notification of these new events is called an *exception*. When events are not relevant to the current process, the notification is termed an *interrupt*. Although there are other differences between interrupts and exceptions, this is the major difference. From the system software standpoint, the processor is considered to be "executing on the interrupt stack"(IS). Interrupts have levels of priorities. A priority scheme is applied to interruption because certain events are more important than others. An event which must be processed and is of higher priority than the current event or process, should be allowed to interrupt the current event. However, less important interrupting events should not interrupt or bump the current event. As with almost all computers today, the VAX has a mechanism to assign interrupt priority levels (IPL).

6.8.1   EVENT HANDLING

When control flow exits to an event relevant to the current process, these exceptions are handled by the operating system (which is described in Chapter 8). An event change can cause the processor to change modes. A mode is a "state" of the computer system. For example, a computer may be in a supervisory mode in which case, the operating system is using privileged instructions. Or, a computer may be in the user mode in which case the process of executing some object code for a user is occurring. Other modes are possible. In any case, an exception in the VAX reflects a signal to the originating mode. This signal in some ways is described by a vector which is a list of longwords. The first entry in the list is the count of the other longwords. The second entry is the type of exception. The remaining entries are stack parameters, program counter value and the program status longword (PSL). All of these longwords identify the current state of the process for eventual preservation. In the VAX three kinds of exceptions are possible.

The *trap* exception condition occurs at the end of the instruction. Now since the exception may cause an exit from the current code, an eventual return to this same code requires the processor to save or store the current PC contents (more precisely, the address of the next instruction that normally would have been executed). Many trap conditions are possible. For example, an arithmetic overflow, a floating point underflow, and divide error may cause a trap. In some instruction sets a trap can be enabled or disabled by a single instruction. In the VAX, BISPSW and BICPSW, which selectively set and clear one or more program status word bits, respectively, are two such instructions.

A *fault* is an exception condition that occurs during an instruction rather than at the end of an instruction. This exception condition does not modify the registers and memory but rather leaves them in a consistent state. In so doing, the elimination of the fault condition and the eventual restarting of the instruction will produce the correct results. However, restoration may not be complete. In the VAX, restoration will be enough to restart the current instruction. A fault condition, which may also result in an interrupt during the time of the fault, requires special handling. The state of the process that faults may not be the same as that state of another process that was interrupted at the same point.

An exception condition which occurs during an instruction execution and which can potentially leave registers and memory locations in an indeterminate state is called an *abort*. In such an event, it is most likely impossible to restart, simulate, or even undo the offending situation. An abort exception is obviously more fatal than a fault exception. Traps, faults and aborts are found in the 68000, 68010, and 68020 microprocessors. The exception vectors for a VAX are depicted in Figure 6.15.

The IPL facilitates the arbitration of interrupt priorities. Recall from an earlier chapter that the PSL reserves bits $<20:16>$ for IPL. These bits designate the IPL of the current process. Only when the interrupting process has a higher IPL will the processor allow the interrupt request to be serviced. When the IPL is higher, the processor does not necessarily raise the IPL bits to the new level. Interrupt requests may come from a variety of sources.

Devices, input/output controllers, other processors, and even the same processor may request an interrupt. In a multiprocessor environment, special care must be taken when "other" processor interruptions occur. Often a multiprocessor system is designed so that one processor does not affect the priority level of another processor. A system user, then, should not assume that interrupt priority levels can be used to synchronize access to shared resources such as a common memory data base. The interrupt priority levels of the VAX are shown in Figure 6.16. Hardware interrupts are nearly always of a higher priority than software level interrupts. Some hardware interrupts are even nonmaskable. A nonmaskable interrupt cannot be disabled by any means.

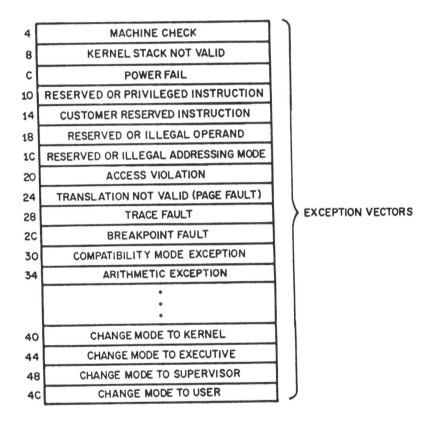

Figure 6.15   VAX Exception Vectors

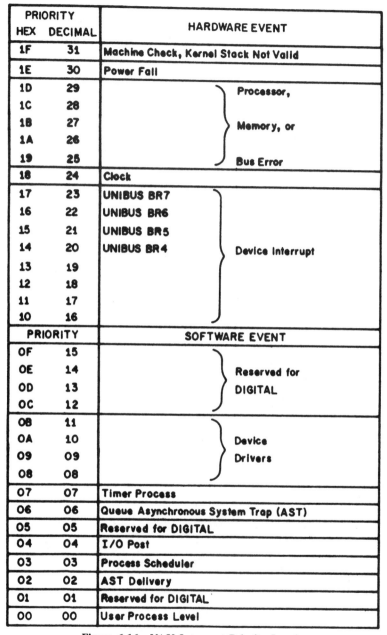

PRIORITY		HARDWARE EVENT
HEX	DECIMAL	
1F	31	Machine Check, Kernel Stack Not Valid
1E	30	Power Fall
1D	29	Processor,
1C	28	
1B	27	Memory, or
1A	26	
19	25	Bus Error
18	24	Clock
17	23	UNIBUS BR7
16	22	UNIBUS BR6
15	21	UNIBUS BR5
14	20	UNIBUS BR4 Device Interrupt
13	19	
12	18	
11	17	
10	16	
PRIORITY		SOFTWARE EVENT
OF	15	
OE	14	Reserved for
OD	13	DIGITAL
OC	12	
OB	11	
OA	10	Device
O9	09	Drivers
O8	08	
O7	07	Timer Process
O6	06	Queue Asynchronous System Trap (AST)
O5	05	Reserved for DIGITAL
O4	04	I/O Post
O3	03	Process Scheduler
O2	02	AST Delivery
O1	01	Reserved for DIGITAL
OO	OO	User Process Level

Figure 6.16   VAX Interrupt Priority Levels

6.9 SUMMARY

In this chapter, you have learned how to generate simple input/output programs. Recognize that each I/O device must often be programmed individually. Because I/O devices operate at much slower speeds and often asynchronously, different program control requirements are necessary. For example, the typical subroutine call no longer applies to an I/O device. Rather, a hardware interrupt request and an interrupt handler are used because the code, although very much like a subroutine, must save not only the program counter, but also the processor status. Requests for service may be random and response or acknowledgment may be delayed. The machine instruction set should include an RTI instruction which behaves much like the RTS instruction. (RTI not only restores the program counter, but also the processor status.)

Because of the asynchronous nature and relative speed disparity, I/O traffic via an interrupt controlled environment, instead of a program controlled environment, effectively increases the machine throughput. In other words, the CPU can execute the current program diverting to an I/O request only when needed by the I/O device. The interruption, then, effectively overlaps CPU processing with I/O activity. To facilitate this I/O overlap, a computer system employs buffers, which may be as simple as a single register or as complex as a large memory system. This "intermediate" storage allows the CPU to store or retrieve information at a rate comparable to CPU speeds. A device using the same buffer performs the same task, however, at speeds comparable to the I/O device transfer rates.

6.10 KEY WORDS

buffer	I/O specification
buffer register	interrupt priority
channels	interrupts
circular buffer	multiplexers
deque	programmed I/O transfer
device handler	queue
exception processing	semaphore
I/O process	software interrupts
I/O processor	status/control register
	traps

6.11 SUGGESTED READING

Digital Equipment Corporation. *VAX 11/780 Architecture Handbook Vol. 1.* Maynard, Mass.: Digital Equipment Corporation, 1977.

The detailed operations of the INSQUE and REMQUE for queues are found on pages 7–9 through 7–13. Interruption in a VAX system is only a small part of its exception processing capabilities. Chapter 12 discusses the general issue of exception processing. The return from exception or interrupt, REI, instruction is detailed on pages 12–13. Although the presentation is brief, as any manufacturer's handbook must be, the information is precise.

Eckhouse, Richard H., Jr., and Morris, L. Robert, *Minicomputer Systems: Organization, Programming and Applications (PDP-11),* 2nd Ed. Englewood Cliffs, N.J.: Prentice-Hall, 1979.

Stacks, deques, and queues are briefly analyzed on pages 160–166. Two FORTRAN queue manipulation routines and one PDP-11 queue/deque routine are provided to illustrate buffering possible in a PDP-11. I/O handler examples including a TTY keyboard, octal dump, software bootstrap, decktape search routines, and disk handler can be found in Chapter 7. Some interrupt-driven paper tape routines are also provided. All of the code is written at the assembly level. This chapter provides many real illustrations of I/O programming.

Kuck, David J. *The Structure of Computers and Computations, Vol. 1.* New York: John Wiley & Sons, 1978.

The earliest implementation of interrupts can be found in Babbage's Analytical Engine. Pages 347–351 describe Babbage's attempts as well as many types of interrupts, interrupt handling, and priorities found in modern machines.

Levy, Henry M., and Eckhouse, Richard H., Jr. *Computer Programming and Architecture: the VAX-11.* Bedford, Mass.: Digital Press, 1980.

A brief but useful discussion of circular lists or buffers including two circular buffer management routines written in VAX assembly code can be found on pages 171–174. Interrupts are clearly described on pages 277–283, although no examples are given. The VAX allows for 15 software interrupt levels via a software interrupt summary register. This software priority level scheme is described briefly on page 282, and is quite similar to the PDP-11 software/hardware priority level scheme which includes more levels.

Lorin, Harold. *Introduction to Computer Architecture and Organization.* New York: John Wiley & Sons, 1983.

This very readable text examines computer organization and assembly language from the viewpoint of a compiler. Many organizational design issues are covered by considering the ease/difficulty which the inherent instruction set supports. Chapters 7, 8, and 9 especially illuminate program segmentation and linkage.

Struble, George W. *Assembler Language Programming: The IBM System/360 and 370.* Reading, Mass.: Addison-Wesley, 1975.
The IBM 360/370 input/output structure is clearly described on pages 408–415. The 360/370 I/O organization builds on a channel concept which is not completely explained in this text. However, channel programming can be found on pages 411–415. These concepts exemplify the I/O processing via indirect and off-line methods.

6.12 EXERCISES

6.1 Describe the general classes of I/O programming.

6.2 Which I/O devices are likely to perform I/O transfers on-line? Off-line?

magnetic tape	ASR 43 TTY
floppy disk	paper tape reader
hard disk	paper tape punch
line printer	analog to digital converter
LED	push button switch
plotter	CRT
game paddles	mouse

6.3 Describe the "busy/wait" approach to I/O processing.

6.4 Which I/O devices in Problem 6.2 are likely to execute unconditional data transfers?

6.5 What three essential tasks does an I/O processor perform?

6.6 Generate a PDP-11 assembly routine which maintains a circular buffer. Set up the storage structure properly.

6.7 What is a device handler?

6.8 A deque can be easily implemented if positive and negative autoindexing is available. Write assembly language routines to fill and empty a deque. Remember that information removed from the deque is erased at the source. (In the PDP-11, TST -(Rn) and (Rn)+ are very helpful.)

6.9 Why is the code for a circular buffer queue more involved than that of a deque?

6.10 Write FORTRAN subroutines to perform queue and deque operations.

6.11 Describe the differences between a stack, deque, and queue.

6.12 How can computers without a test and set instruction still generate semaphores? What may happen in multiple CPU organized systems?

6.13 Why must an interruptible handler be reentrant?

6.14 As with many computers, the PDP-11 has a TST instruction. How does TST differ from TAS?

6.15 Explain how the VAX's instructions INSQUE and REMQUE work with buffers. Note that both instructions are noninterruptible.

6.16 Often, as in multi-tasking, procedures should be made common to several jobs, but should not be allowed to be reentered. One example is a dynamic storage allocation procedure. An indicator should be provided to indicate that such a procedure is not currently in use. Suppose that an indicator does exist which can be set upon entrance to a procedure, reset upon exit, and also tested before entrance. What kind of instruction(s) is necessary to prohibit "reentrancy" as desired above?

6.17 Why is a circular buffer sometimes referred to as a doubly linked list? Does such a reference misuse the terminology?

6.18 What tasks are absolutely essential in every interrupt process?

6.19 If a hypothetical computer stacks the PC, performs a predecrement on the stack pointer, and then stacks the status register, how should an RTI or return-from-interrupt instruction behave? How should the JSR instruction behave? Why?

6.20 The interrupt process is often said to be no different than a subroutine call, except that the call is "forced" rather than "controlled," because the program transfers execution because of some external and program-independent event. Why does this sound reasonable?

6.21 Why does the RTS instruction inadequately emulate the RTI instruction?

6.22 Describe two ways of selectively disabling interrupts.

6.23 Write a PDP-11 routine to send a character out to a display which was just received by the computer via a keyboard stroke. (This is an echo program used to check out a CRT, keyboard, cables, and an I/O path, in general.) Assume the following:

Keyboard control status register	177560
Keyboard data buffer register	177562
CRT status register	177564
CRT data buffer register	177566

6.24 What is the major differrence between an exception and an interrupt?

6.25 What three general exception types are possible in the VAX? Describe them in detail.

6.26 How are exceptions handled?

6.27 When an interrupt occurs, what should any computer do? What does the VAX do?

6.28 Which interrupts should have the highest priority? Explain your choice carefully? Do you agree with the text?

6.29 What is the function of interrupt priority levels? How does the VAX "remember" what the current IPL is? Can anyone change that level?

6.30 In a computer other than the VAX or PDP-11 families, describe how exceptions are handled.

Chapter 7

ASSEMBLY LANGUAGE

The less we understand something, the more variables we require to explain it. Variables, like people, are often illegitimately charged with guilt by association.

—R.L. Ackoff

The way variables act may not be nearly as important as how they interact.

—R.L. Ackoff

May all your PUSHes be POPped.

—Old Irish blessing

7.1 CHAPTER OBJECTIVES

In this chapter, we examine the assembly language level. Since assembly language programming promises to offer some benefits over that of other programming levels, how those benefits can be achieved will be demonstrated. A specific assembler, the MACRO-11 for the PDP-11, is examined. Good and bad programming practices presented herein apply not only with MACRO-11, but with any assembly language. Clear and concise labels, symbols, and mnemonics are important. Equally effective is complete documentation. Documentation includes a "header" which lists the programmer's name, latest revision data, and details about the program. Also, a program, whether low-level or high-level, should have a recognizable structure such as, first, a set of declarations; second, the actual instructions or the body of the code; and last, a data area (if needed). The general structure of any assembly language program should be no different than that of a Pascal or other high-level language program.

A thorough understanding of the assembly process is important. Here, the reader must grasp the essential tasks being performed in each pass through (or

355

scan of) the source code. Assembly is basically a multi-pass sequential scanning through source statements beginning with the first and ending with the last. Mnemonics, symbols, and labels are translated into binary object code. For our convenience, assemblers list the assembled code alongside the respective source statements in hexadecimal or octal (as in the PDP-11). The listing of object code is often helpful during the analysis and debugging phase of programming.

The differences between assembly time and execution time are crucial. Here, the notion of a location counter (analagous to a program counter) is important. Just as the program counter keeps track of the object program during execution time, the location counter keeps track of the assembly program during assembly time. Coupled with the object code listing, the location counter is useful in the program analysis phase.

A good assembly language program makes effective use of the assembler's facilities. However, with such flexibility comes the potential hazard of generating vague and obscure statements, thus making another programmer's life difficult if the original code is to be revised. Not all facilities in an assembly language program are useful everywhere. Rather, judicious employment of infrequently encountered facilities needs to be made.

In this chapter, the reader will learn what a macro is, how macros can be defined, how they are called, and what the assembler does with a macro during the assembly process. The PDP-11 syntax in the previous chapter apply here. Also, the concepts of expressions, symbolic addresses, and the values assigned to them are necessary to the assembly process. During the study of these concepts, many examples help to illustrate certain programming practices.

The study of any assembler features is very machine-dependent. Hence, assemblers must be considered in the context of a specific machine. The underlying architecture of this chapter is that of the PDP-11, since this family of machines is representative of a wide class of computers. It is also worthwhile to contrast the assembler features available on PDP-11 machinery with those of other machines. Just as machines have their own nuances, so do assemblers.

A study of this chapter should lead you into a clear understanding of how macros are defined, expanded, and used in a program. To grasp these issues, you need to be aware that assembly time is distinctively different from execution time. Entirely different mechanisms come to bear in each instance. *Assembly time* is the interval during which translation from source code to object code occurs. *Execution time* is the interval during which object code is executed. Source code is never translated at execution time, and object code is never executed at assembly time.

The notion of execution time is markedly different than the notion of assembly time. This is easily understood when, for example, you realize that the instruction, INC A, is not the same as A = A + 1. First, INC A is a source statement which is translatable to object code and executed at run time. A = A + 1 is an assembler expression to add "one" to "A" at assembly time. Such concepts as expressions, direct assignments, symbolic expressions, *and* the sequential scanning process of an assembler (discussed in a previous chapter) need to be grasped, especially when defining and calling macros.

A macro is basically a textual substitution device. The assembly language programmer's macro call (generally a single source statement) is substituted (at assembly time) for several other source statements. Using macros has both advantages (often primarily shorter source programs and possibly faster programming) and disadvantages (longer assembly time and greater program/data memory space). Therefore, macros must be used judiciously.

Macros extensively use variable symbols which are variables assigned values at assembly time (not at execution time). In order to effectively employ macros, arguments must be "passed into" macros at assembly time. Likewise, the number, type, and usage of the arguments must be denoted. Hence, a macro is *defined* with dummy arguments or parameters and is *called* with actual arguments or parameters. Both dummy and actual arguments may be variable symbols. Therefore, it is important to understand the functioning of symbolic parameters, and how they are defined (with attributes) and referenced (as a set, global, or local symbol).

7.2 THE ASSEMBLY PROCESS

To accomplish tasks such as generating addresses, assigning symbols, building tables, keeping track of instructions, an assembler implements a two-step process. Basically, an assembler scans an assembly language program twice. Each scanning operation sequentially examines each source statement line by line. Because the values of labels and symbolic addresses cannot always be determined at the currently scanned line of that symbol, the assembler must make a second pass. For example, suppose the backward branch (BNE LOOP) in Example 3.9 was actually a forward branch. When the line BNE LOOP is being scanned in the first pass, the assembler would have no idea what value to assign to the symbolic name LOOP. A symbolic address that makes reference to a location further on in a program is called a *forward reference*. Assignment of the value for a forward reference cannot be made in the first scan or pass for that statement. The assembler simply does not know how far away LOOP is until it is found in the label field.

A backward reference, shown in Example 3.9, presents no problem to an assembler. Several solutions to the forward referencing problem are available.

One of these could be to insist that the programmer make no forward references, but this is hardly realistic. A second solution would be to generate a second pass by the assembler. This is the most common solution employed.

The several tasks of an assembler can be summarized as follows:

1. The assembler must assign a unique memory location to each machine language instruction and to each datum of that instruction. Instructions with two operands would be assigned three unique memory locations.

2. An assembler must recognize and verify the legal fields and the composition of each field of a statement in order to process each source statement correctly. Legal mnemonics and assembly directives are verified by scanning appropriate tables provided by the manufacturer and made resident in the assembler program. The assembler recognizes labels by the specified termination symbol (:). Symbolic addresses are recognized in the operation code field.

3. Assemblers detect rules of syntax errors and undefined symbol errors. Assemblers generate error messages. Assemblers generate the binary machine language program. Optionally, the assembler produces a listing of the source program with comments as documentation.

7.2.1 PASS ONE

During the first pass, no machine code is generated, because the address assignments are missing. These addresses will be determined as the program is scanned. The assignments for symbols and addresses are placed in a symbol table which is generated in this pass, as shown in Figure 7.1. Also, the assembler stores those symbols found in the label field and the corresponding addresses the assembler has assigned to them are stored in a symbol table. From Figure 7.1, the reader can see that the assembler also scans the operation code of the instruction. Each statement in an assembly language program may consist of one or more fields (label, operation, operand, and comment). In the operation field, the assembler must determine whether the operation is a machine language instruction or a pseudo-operation (such as .BLKW, .RADIX, .END, etc.). In any given assembly language program, the majority of activity in the first pass is the assignment of labels. Whenever the assembler finds a label, it enters the label in the symbol table and assigns to it an address equal to the contents of the current location counter. The location counter is then incremented and ready for the next statement. Note that the location counter is not incremented for some pseudo-operations (for instance, .END).

It is, however, incremented for every word required of a machine language instruction.

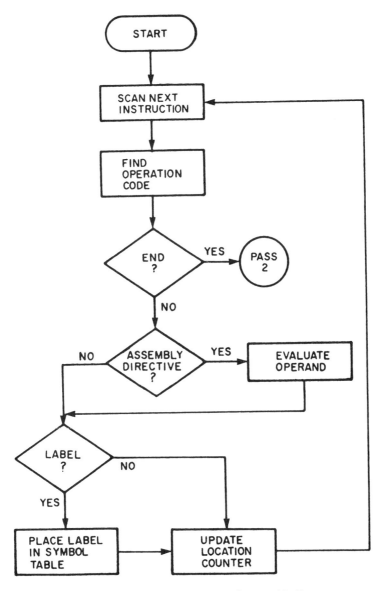

Figure 7.1   Flowchart of First Pass of Assembly Process

7.2.2 PASS TWO

The assembler terminates the first pass upon scanning the .END directive. It enters pass two as shown in Figure 7.2, again beginning with the first statement in the assembly language program. It sequentially scans each instruction now to find the operation code (both the machine language instruction as well as the pseudo-operation). Any operation code which requires an assigned value of the symbolic operand receives the value at this time. The entire

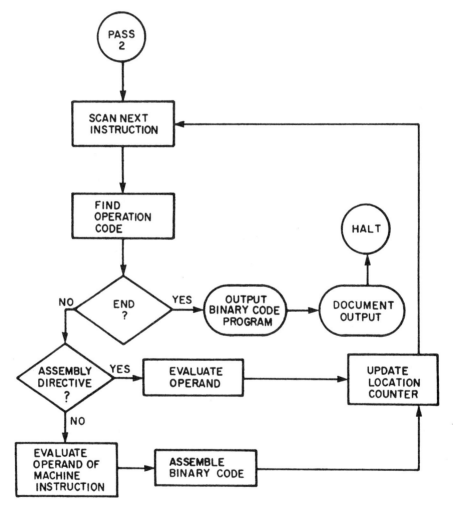

Figure 7.2   Flowchart of Second Pass of Assembly Process

instruction including its opcode and operands is now assembled. Essentially, this assembly requires the assembler to perform two table look-ups. One table look-up retrieves the operation code (in binary) from the manufacturer's operation code table. The second table look-up obtains the operand address by substituting the address found in the recently created symbol table for that symbolic operand. When both table look-ups are completed, the binary code for the instruction and the binary address for the operand are assembled in the proper position for that coded instruction. The assembled binary instruction is then placed in temporary storage in memory, and the location counter is incremented. This process continues in the second pass until the .END directive is again scanned. At this point, the assembly process halts.

The two-pass assembly process depicted in Figures 7.1 and 7.2 is a simplified view of the actual process. Not depicted are the steps taken by the assembler if an error in the assembly process occurs. What kind of errors could occur? The assembly process can only detect errors which violate the rules of syntax. The assembly process cannot detect logical errors or programming errors. The assembly process is simply a table look-up process. It cannot read a programmer's mind to determine what the intended task of the program is.

7.2.3   ERROR DETECTION

When an assembler translates an assembly language program into the object code, the assembler must be able to find the label field, the opcode field, and the operand field on each and every line of the assembly program (unless a line contains a label or consists entirely of a comment). An error of omission can be detected when the necessary component of each field is omitted. For example, in MACRO-11 a label is terminated by a colon. No space must exist between the colon and the label itself. If this rule of syntax is violated, an error message will be generated by the assembler. Also, in MACRO-11, fields must be delimited by a space. If no space exists between the operation and operand fields, an error message is also generated. *The syntax is a set of punctuation and grammar rules.* Hence, the assembler will detect such punctuation errors and generate a syntax error message. An assembler will also detect undefined symbols. An *undefined symbol* is encountered in an assembler when a name contained in the operation code is not found in the operation code table or symbol table. For example, if a programmer inadvertently misspelled the operation code MOV as MOVE, an undefined symbol error message would be generated. If the "." is omitted before a block assembly directive, an undefined symbol error message would be generated, or if the symbolic name is used in the label field more than once, an undefined symbol error message would be generated.

Since an assembler's only function can be to substitute numbers (binary opcodes and addresses) for symbols or names, an assembler has no means to check the validity of an assembly language program. At any programming level, it is the programmer's responsibility to write logically correct programs.

In the first pass, any symbol appearing in the label field of an instruction is assigned the current value of the location counter and is stored in the symbol table. The assembler's task would be simple if all instructions merely changed the location counter by one. In fact, there would be no reason to inspect other fields of the assembly language instructions in the first pass. This is not the case. Some assembly directives change the location counter by amounts that are determined by their operands (for example, .BLK). The second pass is similar to the first pass in the general flow of control as seen in Figure 7.2. In this second pass, the assembler no longer needs to examine the contents of the label field, and, hence, is omitted from the flowchart. Now the operation code field is examined to determine whether an instruction is a machine language instruction or a pseudo-instruction.

This determination is made via the search through the table associated with the manufacturer's mnemonic code with its binary code. Pseudo-instructions encountered in the second pass are similarly processed. In Example 3.9, the symbols START and LOOP are assigned the values 000000 and 000016 in pass one, respectively. If this program were located elsewhere in memory, the assigned values for the labels in the symbol table would be different.

7.3 PROGRAMMING PRACTICES

Programs at any language level, including the assembly level, eventually become public. Consequently, the program's author will not be the only one to use the program. More important, others may someday have to maintain or modify the code. A program that is poorly coded and documented often returns to plague its author endlessly. Furthermore, rarely does a user know much about the problem that another programmer is trying to solve. *A good assembly language program is well-structured, modular, and properly documented.* Of course, any program must be correct. Any other attributes assigned to a program reflect a "programming style." Careful annotation and commentary, lucid coding, and clear organization reflect a good programming style. The following practices are recommended.

1. Programs should not resemble spaghetti code. That is, program flow should not jump around erratically. Nested loops should be avoided and straight-line code encouraged.

2. Programs should be well-documented. Comments should be up-to-date, accurate, complete, concise, and understandable. Misleading or absent comments waste time and money. Do not use margin comments to simply make a literal translation of an instruction line. Rather, explain the effect of this line of code on a program. Use full-line comments where useful.

3. Programs should be modular. The length of a program should not exceed a written page. Program segments or modules should be well-defined and aimed at a specific task. Partition modular code by separating the code with blank lines for easy reading.

4. Entry and exit of modules should be clearly explained. Any parameters needed by one module and available from another module should be described by their full data and addressing specifications. For example, if bytes rather than words are needed by a module, the documentation for that module should clearly indicate a byte data size. Such affects on one module caused by another module should be nonexistent.

5. Many assembler languages allow a free format field specification. That is, one field could follow immediately after another field. Standardize source statement fields. MACRO-11 will list the program in a format that is easy to read (with clarity) if every programmer assigns:
   a. The label field at column 1
   b. The operation field at column 9
   c. The operand field at column 17
   d. The comment field at column 33
      unless a full line comment is desired.

6. Stay away from obscure assembly language instructions and capabilities. Avoid "tricky" instruction sequences (as in Example 5.3).

7. Do not write self-modifying programs. Such programs create havoc when re-entered after departing in the middle of a code segment. Partition data space from program space. Group all storage areas for constants, or the scratchpad, in one single segment of your code, and not interspersed within the executable code.

8. Always use symbols which have a mnemonic property. TEMP, CONST, and START are much better than X1, X2, and X3.

The following examples illustrate frequent programming errors and bad habits which should not exist.

In Example 7.1, a programmer desires to clear memory locations 2000 and 2004. Assume that the contents of location 2000 is 600. The sequence of

Example 7.1   Clearing Memory Locations

```
            •
            •
            •
     MOV    2000,R0    ;WRONG ADDRESS MODE
     CLR    (R0)+
     CLR    (R0)+
            •
            •
            •
```

instructions in our example actually clears locations 600 and 602, not 2000 and 2002. However, if one replaces the symbol 2000 with "#2000", the code will correctly clear locations 2000 and 2002. The simple omission of the # sign destroys the intent of the desired addressing mode. What was desired was the immediate addressing mode in the first instruction, but that is not what was coded. An assembler would not detect this error and object code would be generated.

Example 7.2   Immediate Address for a Destination?

```
           •
           •
           •
    ASL    R0
    MOV    R0,#20    ;DESTINATION ADDRESS
           •          ;MODE IS WRONG
           •
           •
```

In Example 7.2, a programmer wants to perform an arithmetic left shift of the contents of R0 and move the contents of R0 to location 20. This code does not work because the MOV instruction cannot employ the immediate addressing mode for a destination. The "#20" designates a constant. Assemblers would detect this error and generate an error message.

Example 7.3   An Illegal Instruction

```
            •
            •
            •
     ASLB   400(R2)+    ;QUESTIONABLE SYNTAX
            •           ;ILLEGAL ADDRESS MODE
            •
            •
```

Often, one desires to use the index mode of addressing and increment the register afterward. This is useful in handling arrays of data where it is necessary to obtain a second or a third table and proceed through that table, accessing the data and updating the pointer within the table simultaneously. The code in Example 7.3 does not work as intended. The programmer intended to perform an arithmetic shift left on a byte pointed to by the effective address, calculated by adding the number 400 to the contents of register R2. Next, the programmer wanted to increment the pointer in R2. This seemingly useful address mode just does not exist in MACRO-11. An assembler would detect this error. The solution to this requires two instructions:

```
ASLB    400(R2)    ;CORRECT POINTER
INC     R2         ;UPDATE
```

Example 7.4 Detecting the Phantom Error

```
                  •
                  •
                  •
START:    COM    ARG1
          MOV    ARG1,RESULT
          ADD    #300,RESULT
ARG1:                              ;NO ERROR MESSAGES
RESULT:                            ;GENERATED BY ASSEMBLER
                                   ;HERE
          .END   START
```

Errors can become very subtle and difficult to detect. In Example 7.4, a programmer intends to generate a result using a symbolic address, ARG1. He wants the result of the task to reside in the symbolic address location "RESULT", but he should have included two assembler directives for ARG1 and RESULT (namely, .BLKW 1) in the program. Since they were omitted in the code, the following occurs. The code will be assembled without detecting any errors. In fact, when ARG1 is encountered, it will be assigned the contents of the location counter. Since the .BLKW directive is missing, RESULT will be assigned the same contents as the location counter. If .BLKW were included in the source statement starting with ARG1, then the location counter would have been correctly incremented by 2, and RESULT would be assigned a different value. As it stands in the program of Example 7.4, both ARG1 and RESULT are assigned the same value. Hence, the program in Example 7.4 does not place the outcome of the activity in RESULT, but places the outcome in ARG1. The assembler, when encountering ARG1 and RESULT, just assumed that the programmer wanted to assign two symbolic names to the same value. This error is difficult to detect since the assembler will generate no error messages.

Example 7.5   An Incorrect Self-Modifying Program

```
;THIS INCORRECTLY WRITTEN PROGRAM ATTEMPTS TO ADD TEN
NUMBERS STORED IN
;MEMORY AT STARTING ADDRESS "A", LEAVING THE ACCUMULATED
RESULT IN "SUM".
;SELF-MODIFYING CODE IS USED TO COMPARE TWO OPERANDS, ONE
OPERAND BEING
;THE LINE OF CODE "ADD A,SUM"!
START:   MOV          ZERO,SUM     ;INIT SUM
ADDR:    ADD          A,SUM        ;ADD ANOTHER ARRAY ELEMENT
         CMP          ADDR,LIMIT   ;DONE YET?
         BEQ          DONE         ;YES, EXIT PROGRAM WITH
                                   ;RESULT IN "SUM"
         ADD          NUMR,ADDR    ;NO, MODIFY ADDRESS OF
                                   ;POINTER
         BR           ADDR         ;DO ADDITION AGAIN
DONE:    .EXIT
ZERO:    .WORD 0                   ;CONSTANT ZERO TO INIT "SUM"
SUM:     .BLKW 1                   ;RESULTANT "SUM" OUTPUT TO
                                   ;CALLER
NUMR:    .WORD 2                   ;A CONSTANT TO INCREMENT
                                   ;SOURCE OPERAND
LIMIT:   ADD A+,SUM                ;ADDRESS OF "ADD A,SUM" BY 1
                                   ;SYMBOLIC REPRESENTATION OF
                                   ;"ADD"
                                   ;INSTRUCTION AFTER FINAL
                                   ;LOOP
A:       (ARRAY OF 10 DATUM STARTS HERE)
         .END         START
```

Example 7.5 is an incorrectly written program which attempts to add ten numbers stored in consecutive locations in memory with the starting address "A". The result of this accumulated sum resides in "SUM". The flowchart of activity is indicated in Figure 7.3. The crucial instruction which is modified is the statement "ADD A,SUM". The statement "ADD NUMR,ADDR" modifies the above statement by attempting to increment the contents of the source operand A. The programmer checks for the last element in the array by

actually comparing two machine lines of code, assuming that each line represents an "operand." The programmer assumes that the pointer to the table of
ten numbers is also being updated by a simple addition process (ADD
NUMR,ADDR). But this attempt to update the table pointer is also wrong.
Adding the number 2 to the contents of ADDR each time indeed changes the
first word of the instruction, but the pointer exists, not in the first word, but in
the second word of this three-word instruction beginning with the label
ADDR. This self-modifying code is not only poorly written, but it is also
wrong. A different correctly written program to perform the same task is
shown in Example 7.6. However, neither program is recommended because
each still employs self-modifying code. In Example 7.6, the program location
and program contents with the symbol table are included to illustrate the
correct CMP procedure.

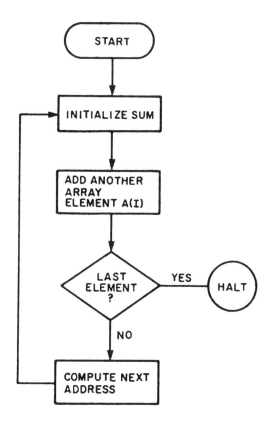

Figure 7.3 Summing Up the Elements of Array "A"

Example 7.6   A Correct Yet Self-Modifying Program

Program Location	Program Contents	Label	Opcode	Operand(s)	Comments
	000000		.ENABL	AMA	;ASSEMBLE ;ABSOLUTE ;CODE
	002000		.=1066+LC		;STARTING ;ADDRESS=2000
002000	016767 000032 000032	START:	MOV	ZERO,SUM	;INITIALIZE SUM
002006	066767	ADDR:	ADD	A,SUM	;ADD ANOTHER ;ARRAY ;ELEMENT
	000034 000024				
002014	026767 177770 000022		CMP	ADDR+2,LIMIT	;DONE YET?
002022	001404		BEQ	DONE	;YES, EXIT
002024	066767		ADD	NUMR,ADDR+2	;NO, MODIFY ;ADDRESS
	000012				;CODE MODIFIED ;HERE
˙	177756				
002032	000765		BR	ADDR	;LOOP
002034	000000	DONE:	.EXIT		;E.T. GO HOME
002036	000000	ZERO:	.WORD	0	;CONSTANT ZERO
002040	000000	SUM:	.WORD	0	;RESULTANT ;ZERO
002042	000002	NUMR:	.WORD	2	;CONSTANT TO ;GENERATE ;NEXT ADDRESS
002044	000176	LIMIT:	A-ADDR-4+18.		;LAST RELATIVE ;ADDRESS ;GENERATED
002046		A:	.BLKW	10.	;RESERVE 10 ;LOCATIONS ;FOR ARRAY A
	002000		.END	START	

SYMBOL TABLE

NUMR	002042	ADDR	002006	SUM	002040
A	002046	LIMIT	002044	START	002000
DONE	002034	ZERO	002036		

In Example 7.6, the instruction with the label ADDR is modified by adding 2 to the second word of this three-word instruction. The second word contains the source operand relative offset. As indicated by the instruction in program location 2024, the constant 2 is added to this second word, since this word contains the relative base address of the array A. The word labeled LIMIT contains the value which represents the address of the last element in array A which is assigned this value by the statement in program location 2044. Note that A-ADDR-4 represents the relative address generated for the initial instruction, and that the decimal 18 is "one less" than the number of elements.

In Example 7.7, the same task is executed with non-self-modifying code. To do so, general-purpose registers R0 and R1 are used for the "SUM" and "LIMIT" variables, respectively. Also, the instruction MOV A,R1 is used to initialize the register R1 with the address of A. Subsequent code determines whether the last element has been added in by comparing the last address of the element with R1. Since R1 is updated as each element is added, the compare instruction, "CMP A+20.,R1", will become negative and cause the program to stop. Otherwise, another element is added.

Example 7.7   Confusing Data with Addresses

Label	Opcode	Operand(s)	Comments
;THIS IS A PROGRAM TO SUM THE ELEMENTS OF THE ARRAY "A".			
;THE SUM IS LEFT IN R0.			
	R0=%0		;DEFINE REGISTER 0 AS SYMBOL ;R0
	R1=%1		;DEFINE REGISTER 1 AS SYMBOL ;R1
	.=1000+LC		;DEFINE STARTING ADDRESS
START:	CLR	R0	;INITIALIZE SUM
	MOV	A,R1	;ADDRESS OF "A" MOVED INTO ;R1
ADDR:	ADD	(R1)+,R0	;ADD IN VALUE
	CMP	A+20.,R1	;DONE?
	BPL	ADDR	;NO, CONTINUE
	.EXIT		
A:	.WORD	8.,9.,10.,1,2,3,4,5,6,7	
	.END	START	

SYMBOL TABLE
A   001020   ADDR   001006   R0   =%000000
R1   =%000001   START   001000

The program in Example 7.7 as listed is wrong because the symbol A, used in the MOV and CMP instructions, will incorrectly access the values of the numbers in the table instead of the address value for A. The programmer has

confused data with an address. The correct coding is a simple replacement of
"A" with "#A". Immediate addressing is desired each time A is invoked.

Does the program in Example 7.7, with "A" correctly addressed, now
execute properly? No. There still remain two subtle programming errors that
would not be detected by the assembler. First, no HALT instruction (or other
exiting/terminating statement at execution time) exists in the program. This
error of omission will not be detected by the assembler. During execution, the
PDP-11 computer will exit the loop, and the next code it will attempt to
execute is an instruction whose octal opcode is 000001, which is the value of
the first element in Table A and not a machine instruction. The computer will
stop executing the program and probably print an error message such as

TRAP TO 000010 FROM 001020

This indicates that the processor has found an illegal operation code. The
address 001020 indicates the approximate trouble spot in the program. The
"TRAP TO" is an error message from the computer to help diagnose the
probable cause of program failure.

Even if a HALT machine instruction was inserted at the end of the code, the
program still would not execute properly. There are ten elements in the table,
but the CMP instruction actually permits the addition of more than eleven
elements. The number "20." should be replaced with the number "18.", one
less than the number of elements in the table. This second programming error
is sometimes difficult to detect. A programmer should always carefully analyze loop exit parameters such as this counter. This error will not be detected
by an assembler. A correctly written non-self-modifying program is shown in
Example 7.8.

Example 7.8   A Correct Non-Self-Modifying Program

Label	Opcode	Operand(s)	Comments
;THIS IS A PROGRAM TO SUM THE ELEMENTS OF THE ARRAY "A".			
;THE SUM IS LEFT IN R0.			
	.ENABL	AMA	
	R0=%0		;DEFINE REGISTER 0 AS SYMBOL R0
	R1=%1		;DEFINE REGISTER 1 AS SYMBOL R1
	.=1000+LC		;DEFINE STARTING ADDRESS
START:	CLR	R0	;INITIALIZE SUM
	MOV	#A,R1	;ADDRESS OF "A" MOVED INTO R1
ADDR:	ADD	(R1)+,R0	;ADD IN VALUE
	CMP	#A+18.,R1	;DONE?
	BPL	ADDR	;NO, CONTINUE
A:	.WORD	8.,9.,10.,1,2,3,4,5,6,7	
	.END	START	
	.EXIT		

SYMBOL TABLE
| A | 001020 | ADDR | 001006 | R0 | =%000000 |
| R1 | =%000001 | START | 001000 | | |

7.4 SOME PROGRAMMING EXAMPLES

In the following examples, we are going to demonstrate some of the assembly language instructions in a few very simple tasks. The programs themselves are not complete. Consider each of them only as part of a larger program. A complete program would include code which initializes space in memory for temporary variables, the variables themselves, and instructions which terminate as well as initialize program execution. None of this necessary activity is shown in our examples. Furthermore, a complete assembly language program is fully documented with comments listed before (on-line comments), during (as field comments to the right of respective instructions), and after the body of executable instructions.

7.4.1 MULTIPLE-PRECISION ARITHMETIC

Example 7.9 Double-Precision Addition (Base 10)

$$
\begin{array}{r}
147 \quad 962 \\
+231 \quad 814 \\
\hline
379 \quad 776 \\
1 \swarrow \text{Carry}
\end{array}
$$

Before			After	
R0	962		R0	962
R1	814		R1	776
R3	147		R3	147
R4	231		R4	379

Assembly Language Code

```
            •
            •
            •
ADD    R0, R1    ;ADD LOWER HALF
ADC    R4        ;ADD CARRY TO UPPER DIGITS
ADD    R3, R4    ;ADD UPPER HALF
            •        ;NOTE! OVERFLOW IS NOT MONITORED HERE
            •
            •
```

In Example 7.9, we want to add numbers whose digits exceed the word length of a machine. We want to add decimal numbers which can be found in registers R0, R1, R3, and R4, as shown. The procedure for multiple-precision addition is to add the least significant words together, monitor a carry out of this addition operation, and add it to the upper digits. The numbers 962 and 814 are the least three significant digits of two 6-digit decimal numbers. The code to accomplish this is also shown in Example 7.9. (Note! We have not considered overflow.) It is then followed by three addition operations. The first ADD instruction adds the least significant digits together, and the next ADC instruction adds the carry to one of the most significant operands (in our case, we have chosen R4). The final operation adds the upper digits together.

Example 7.10   Double-Precision Complement

```
            •
            •
            •
NEG    R0    ;2'S COMPLEMENT HIGH-ORDER WORD
NEG    R1    ;2'S COMPLEMENT LOW-ORDER WORD
SBC    R0    ;PROPAGATE CARRY
            •
            •
            •
```

In Example 7.10, it is desired to form the 2's complement of a 32-bit number which resides with its high-order bits in R0 and its low-order bits in R1. To form the 2's complement of the 32 bits, it is necessary to consider the effect of the carry out of the most significant bits. A short program is found in Example 7.10 that performs the necessary operations on R0 and R1. First, the 2's complement of the high-order word is obtained with the NEG instruction. Recall that the NEG instruction sets the carry to a one if the 2's complemented result is nonzero. If the result is zero, the carry will be cleared. The next instruction forms a 2's complement of the low-order word. The third instruction in the code propagates the borrow from the low-order word into the high-order word, if necessary (with the SBC).

7.4.2 SIGNED AND UNSIGNED CONDITIONAL BRANCHES

Great care must be exercised when sorting data in either ascending or descending fashion. Data may be signed numbers, unsigned numbers, or alpha-numeric characters. It should be clear that in signed numbers, a negative number is always less than a positive number. For unsigned numbers, however, monitoring the flags when comparing the relative magnitudes of two numbers is markedly different. For example, consider the distinctive differences among the ordering of numbers in a 3-bit machine from Table 7.1.

Table 7.1 Ordering in a 3-Bit Machine

Ascending Order

Signed Numbers		Unsigned Numbers	
most positive	011	111	largest
	010	110	
	001	101	
	000	100	
	111	011	
	110	010	
	101	001	
most negative	100	000	smallest

Computers provide us with the option to test signed as well as unsigned numbers for such purposes as sorting or arranging. We have only seen one conditional branch (BLT). However, there are many more. Let's look at some simple cases which compare the relative "values" of two sets of numbers. Our problem is to determine the relative position of two numbers in an ascending array. If the first number is lower than the other number, we desire to branch (in the case of unsigned numbers). If the first number is of a lesser signed value than the second number, we also desire to branch.

Example 7.11 Conditional Branches

Suppose that

$$R3 = 177777$$
$$R4 = 077777$$

R3 contains the signed number, −1. R4 contains the largest positive 16-bit number. Let's pose the following questions:

Is R3 lower than R4?
Is R3 less than R4?

What conditional branch instructions should follow the CMP instruction in order to branch if the answer is yes? Those instructions are BLO for unsigned tests and BLT for signed tests. The instruction, CMP R3,R4, does the following (in octal). BLO should be used to answer the first question. BLT should be used for the second.

$$\text{CMP}\quad \text{R3,R4}\quad \rightarrow \quad \begin{array}{r} 177777 \\ +100001 \\ \hline 1 \longleftarrow 100000 \end{array}$$

Carry is "1", so the C flag
cleared to indicate that no
borrow is required.

All flags become

N	Z	V	C
1	0	0	0

In each program below, BLO and BLT are properly used for unsigned and signed conditional branches, respectively. Reversing their usage will cause an erroneous branch (such as assigning BLO to a signed conditional branch test). Notice that BLT tests the N and V flags. That is, if N XOR V is "1," the branch is taken. Otherwise, the next instruction is executed. BLO tests *only* the C flag. If C = 1, the branch is taken. Otherwise, the next instruction is executed. For signed number comparison tests, testing the C flag is not always sufficient. For unsigned number comparisons, testing the C flag alone is sufficient. Correct comparison of data types is so important that we will return to them in the next chapter.

Unsigned Conditional Branch Test	Signed Conditional Branch Test
(R3 "LOWER" THAN R4?)	(R3 "LESS" THAN R4?)
•	•
•	•
•	•
CMP R3,R4	CMP R3,R4
BLO ___	BLT ___
•	•
•	•
•	•

ACTION TAKEN	ACTION TAKEN
R3 is not lower than R4. *Branch is not taken* since BLO causes a branch if C flag is set.	R3 is less than R4. *Branch is taken* since BLT causes a branch if N XOR V is a "one".

7.5   MAKING THE ASSEMBLER WORK FOR YOU

By now, the reader should have begun to realize that the more the computer does and the less its user does, the better one can exploit the computer's advantages. Striving for this end is aided by powerful software support tools available to the programmer. Why program at the machine language level when the convenience and speed of assembly language programming are available? In fact, earlier chapters have only begun to scratch the surface of assembly language programming. It is now appropriate to view assemblers as a programming support tool. An assembler should help users to program faster. One reason should already be obvious. Meaningful symbols help programmers analyze and debug programs, thus generating the end result much more quickly and correctly. But are there other advantageous properties available to us? Absolutely!

More often than not, programmers find themselves writing similar code over and over again. This is typical of data processing. People even wonder why new programs must be invented. A natural question arises, "Is there a mechanism to write the code only once and ask the assembler in some fashion to insert it anywhere the code is to be desired?" Yes, using a macro is one method. It is incorrect to state that looping effectively does the same thing as a macro. Looping is an entirely different concept. With a loop, one segment of code is being repeatedly *executed* at execution time. Macros allow repeated copying of the code at *assembly* time.

Similar to loops, a macro is a form of shorthand notation. Unlike a loop, a macro is written once by the programmer, but could be assembled many times by the assembler. A macro allows for automatic iteration at assembly time rather than at execution time. With a macro, the programmer assigns a name to an instruction sequence or a segment of source statements. The macro name is then used in a source program instead of copying the same instruction sequences. A macro assembler replaces the macro name with the sequence of instructions found in the macro definition. For frequently used instruction sequences, the macro concept is very convenient because it relieves the drudgery of programming repetitive sequences. Using a macro, however, does not save memory space. Every time a macro is inserted in a program, it will generally consist of more than one source statement when expanded. The many advantages of macros include the following.

7.5.1   MACRO ADVANTAGES

1. Macros provide clearer program documentation.

2. Program changes are quicker every time the macro is called. The one-time change made in the macro definition causes the assembler to make that change every time that macro is used.

3. The programmer can amplify and even clarify an instruction set by building or including new commands or key words in the basic machine language instruction set. Emulating another computer using macros is common.

4. Macros help a programmer write shorter source programs. (However, seldom do shorter object code programs result.)

5. Once debugged, a macro ensures that an error-free sequence is used each and every time that macro is called.

Macros are not free. They do come at some expense. One of these is the need to learn something about implementing macros in an assembly language program. Other disadvantages of macros include the following.

7.5.2   MACRO DISADVANTAGES

1. A single macro could create many instructions (if called many times or even if it is called once when its definition is large).

2. Any time the macro is used, it must be expanded. Memory space could be wasted by the repeated use of instruction sequences.

3. Unless carefully considered, macros may affect program status register flags in surprising ways.

4. Macro processing is enormously costly in additional time to assemble.

7.5.3   THE SIMPLE MACRO

Many assemblers (but not all) have the ability to generate a segment of code upon a command from the programmer and to insert this code anywhere in a program. This facility is always found in a *macro assembler*. A macro is a pre-defined block of assembly language code that can be repeatedly inserted in a program. To do so, a macro must have a prescribed structure which follows the rules of syntax for the specific assembler. Macro assemblers assume that a macro definition contains:

1. A *header* or *name* of the macro as the beginning part of the macro.

2. The *body* of the macro definition consisting of the source code and character strings to be inserted into the program at the point of the macro call.

3. An assembler directive or pseudo-instruction to mark the *end* of the macro definition.

These three basic elements must exist in every macro definition. A *macro definition* is an assembler feature to allow a programmer to give a name to a contiguous piece of code to be assembled one or more times in the program. Consider a macro as an abbreviation for a piece of program code. Because macros are named blocks of code, anywhere the name is inserted in the operation field of an assembly language program, the assembler will duplicate the block of code. The macro assembler will insert neither the header nor the assembler directive terminating the macro definition. The macro definition should be found early in the program. (Otherwise, subsequent code may not recognize a call to insert the macro.) Good programming suggests that users place macro definitions at the very beginning of their code.

The general format of a macro definition in the MACRO-11 is:

```
.MACRO name a1,a2,...,an      { macro header (assembly directive)
   •
   •                          { macro body (source statements)
   •
.ENDM                         { terminator (assembly directive)
```

In this format, the first source statement is an assembly directive appropriately titled .MACRO. The actual name of the macro must follow .MACRO. Don't forget to leave a space after .MACRO. This name in the opcode field of the source program will be used as a "call" for the macro body.

The name inserted in the program tells the assembler to call this macro that has been previously defined. Following the name are the dummy arguments, a1,a2,...,an. Actual arguments are parameters to be passed into the macro when called. The general format of a *macro call* is:

LABEL: NAME a1,a2,...,an

A label in the source statement for the macro call is optional. However, the macro name and the same number of arguments should be used. The macro called "NAME" must be defined prior to its first call in the assembly program. Should more actual arguments be included (a1,...,an,an+1) in the macro call than are found in the macro definition (a1,...,an), the excess arguments may be ignored by most assemblers (but not all!). When fewer arguments are provided in the call than in the definition, assemblers may assign a null value to those missing arguments. Always consider the arguments in the macro definition as *dummy* parameters. The arguments in the macro call become *actual* arguments.

A simple macro definition is found in Example 7.12. The simple macro swaps the contents of A with the contents of B. Three lines of code are assumed in this macro. The header contains the assembler directive, .MACRO, with the macro name, SWAPIT, and with parameters, A, B, and C. The body of the macro contains source statements that perform the following steps. In this code, the computer transfers the contents of A into C temporarily. Then the contents of B are transferred to A. Finally, the contents of C are placed in B. When completed, this code has swapped the contents of A with B.

Example 7.12 SWAPIT

Macro Definition	Comments
.MACRO SWAPIT A,B,C	;NAME AND DUMMY PARAMETER LIST
MOV A,C	;TEMPORARILY STORE FIRST ARGUMENT
MOV B,A	;SWAP SECOND ARG WITH FIRST ARG
MOV C,B	;REPLACE FIRST ARG WITH SECOND ARG
.ENDM	;MACRO DEFINITION TERMINATOR

7.6 MACRO DEFINITION VERSUS MACRO CALL

In Example 7.12, the first time anything about this macro was to be encountered in the assembly program, it must have been encountered as a definition. The one exception is a call for a macro that has already been defined by the system macro library.[1] A macro definition not only names the desired segment of code, but also identifies the code itself with the terminating source statement. A macro definition is not the same as a macro call. It is impossible for any assembler to expand a macro before it is defined since assembly is essentially a sequential process. Assembler error messages may be generated, but this is not guaranteed from one assembler to another.

A *macro call* is a request to the assembler to insert the lines of code in the body of the macro at the actual calling position in a program. The assembler procedure which inserts the lines of code at the "calling point" in a program is termed a *macro expansion*. A macro expansion is accomplished at assembly

---

[1]MACRO-11 for the PDP-11 has some useful system macros such as .TTYIN and .TTYOUT. These two macros generate input and output sequences for a user's terminal. A good assembler has a library of many system macros available to a user.

time, not at program execution time. (The reader should realize that a macro name is a user-defined assembler directive.) In many assemblers, including MACRO-11, the macro expansion is done in the object code during pass two, rather than in the source code during pass one. The reader should realize, however, that the macro definitions will be consulted by the assembler during pass one, because the assembler needs to build the symbol table. In some assemblers, macros may be expanded at a time other than during pass two.

A macro call is accomplished by placing the macro name in the opcode field of an assembler source statement. The macro call must contain not only the name, but also the symbols of the arguments specified in the macro definition. Actual arguments are separated by a comma. (Spaces are also permissible as separators.) Realize that a macro definition does not cause the assembler to generate and insert code in a program. Only when the macro is called will that code be generated. Hence, an assembler may not recognize some programming errors (i.e., violation of assembler rules of syntax) until the macro with the embedded errors is called. The operands which follow the macro name represent the arguments of a macro call. Illustrations of macro calls and expansions of SWAPIT are found in Example 7.13. Every time the macro expansion occurs, the subsequent object code (without the comment fields) will contain that expansion. However, the object code contains neither the macro name nor the terminating assembler directive.

Example 7.13   Macro Calls and Expansion

Call	Expansion	Comments
a. SWAPIT X,T,Z	MOV X,Z	;RELATIVE ;ADDRESSES
	MOV T,X	;HERE; X, T, AND Z
	MOV Z,T	;ARE ACTUAL ;ARGUMENTS
b. SWAPIT HERE,THERE,PIVOT	MOV HERE,PIVOT	
	MOV THERE,HERE	
	MOV PIVOT,THERE	
c. SWAPIT H+4,T+3,PT	MOV H+4,PT	;SYMBOLIC ;EXPRESSIONS
	MOV T+3,H+4	;USED HERE NOW; ;SEE
	MOV PT,T+3	;SECTION 6.5

In Example 7.13, it is instructive to examine the actual arguments which follow each call. These arguments replace the dummy parameters of the macro definition. Each parameter in a macro is assigned a specific argument for each macro call. The same argument could be used in every macro call, but the relative position of an argument in the macro call is critical. In Example 7.12, the macro requires three parameters. However, each time the macro has been called in Example 7.13, the arguments have been changed. *An actual argument is a value assigned to the respective parameter in a macro call.* The arguments in Example 7.13 are no longer dummy arguments, but actual arguments. Notice from the expansions in Example 7.13 that the characters (length of the character string) substituted for a parameter need not be the same characters or even the same number of characters as in the dummy parameter. Furthermore, the substitution is made between character strings and not addresses. The macro processor of a macro assembler replaces all of the dummy parameter character strings with the respective actual argument character strings.

One should view arguments solely as character strings and not as addresses. Example 7.13c shows that the character strings can contain expressions such as H+4 or T+3. Upon substitution, those expressions will be found in the generated code. It is very convenient for macro assemblers to be able to generate nearly identical sequences by allowing macro definitions to provide formal characters and by allowing the programmer, at each macro call, to supply actual arguments. Of course, the generated code and expressions must be correct assembly language. Never expect a macro call to repair code which violates any rules of syntax of the specific assembly language.

7.6.1 USING MACRO PARAMETERS AS LABELS

In all of the previous examples, macro parameters appear only in the operand field of source statements. Substituting character strings in fields other than the operand field is also permissible. In fact, a substitution in the label field is allowed. In Example 7.14a, the first source statement in the macro definition now possesses a label, and the first parameter in the macro call is the character string designated for that label. In Example 7.14b, the macro call, SWAPIT, is embedded between the program segment just below an ASL instruction. (ASL R4 and COM R3 are not part of the macro.) Notice that the label will be assigned the character string "SWAP" when the expansion occurs. The macro expansion generated by the assembler at assembly time produces three source statements with the defined label in the first source statement.

Example 7.14   Macros with Label Parameters

a. Macro Definition   Comments

```
.MACRO       SWAPIT LABEL,X,Y,Z  ;PARAMETER LIST
                                 ;CONTAINS
LABEL: MOV   X,Z                 ;A LABEL
       MOV   Y,X
       MOV   Z,Y
       .ENDM
```

b. Macro Call   Comments

```
       •
       •
       •
ASL    R4            ;YOUR EXISTING PROGRAM
SWAPIT SWAP,X,Y,Z    ;MACRO CALL MADE HERE
COM    R3            ;YOUR EXISTING PROGRAM
       •
       •
       •
```

c. Macro Expansion   Comments

```
       •
       •
       •
       ASL   R4
SWAP:  MOV   X,Z     ;EXPANDED MACRO BODY
       MOV   Y,X     ;(CALL GENERATES THREE
       MOV   Z,Y     ;MORE LINES OF CODE)
       COM   R3
       •
       •
       •
```

Be careful when using labels in a macro definition, because these labels are almost always substitutable parameters. A problem occurs when the macro is called more than once (as macros are intended to be called). A label found in a macro definition which is *not* a substitutable parameter would then be redefined by the second call. A multiple-definition error could result in some assemblers.

An ill-defined macro is illustrated in Example 7.15. Here, the macro named ADBYTE and its subsequent expansions will request an assembler to define the label, ADDB, more than once (only, of course, if called more than once). Assemblers are designed to detect multiple-definitions of labels as errors and to flag this impending disaster. It is possible to get around this problem if nonsubstitutable labels must be used. Solutions can be found in Section 7.14, but the safest rule to follow is:

> Labels should be found in the parameter list.

Example 7.15   Multiple Labeling Within Macros

a. Macro Definition | Comments

```
        .MACRO ADBYTE    ADDEND,AUGEND,SUM
ADDB: MOVB  ADDEND,TEMP1              ;GET FIRST BYTE
      MOVB  AUGEND,TEMP2              ;GET SECOND BYTE
      ADD   TEMP1,TEMP2               ;ADD TWO BYTES
      MOVB  TEMP2,SUM                 ;SAVE SUM BYTE
      .ENDM
```

b. Macro Calls

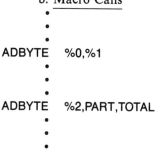

```
        ·
        ·
        ·
ADBYTE   %0,%1
        ·
        ·
        ·
ADBYTE   %2,PART,TOTAL
        ·
        ·
        ·
```

c. Macro Expansions in the Same Program

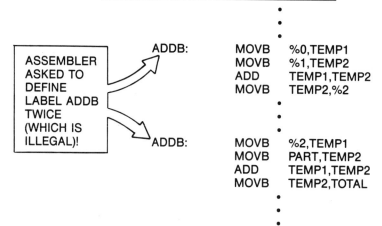

```
                                         ·
                                         ·
                                         ·
ADDB:    MOVB   %0,TEMP1
         MOVB   %1,TEMP2
         ADD    TEMP1,TEMP2
         MOVB   TEMP2,%2
                                         ·
                                         ·
                                         ·
ADDB:    MOVB   %2,TEMP1
         MOVB   PART,TEMP2
         ADD    TEMP1,TEMP2
         MOVB   TEMP2,TOTAL
                                         ·
                                         ·
                                         ·
```

ASSEMBLER ASKED TO DEFINE LABEL ADDB TWICE (WHICH IS ILLEGAL)!

7.6.2   MACRO PARAMETERS IN THE OPCODE FIELD

Since a macro expansion in simplest terms is a substitution of character strings, a programmer can substitute symbols with a machine language instruction in the opcode field of a source statement. This substitution is possible, even though a macro definition contains a symbol in the opcode field which is not a machine language instruction. If the macro expansion makes a substitution with a valid machine language instruction, the assembler will insert the machine language instruction found in the parameter list of the macro call. In Example 7.16, a simple macro replaces the operation code in the first source statement with the second parameter (OPCD) in the macro call. In Example 7.16c, the macro is expanded and the first source statement now contains the CLR opcode obtained from the argument list.

Any valid machine language instruction or assembly directive can be inserted in the opcode field. Remember that a macro assembler will only make the requested substitution. If the parameter list does not include valid opcodes or symbols, the expansion will still be made in pass two, but an assembler error will also be generated. Don't even try to execute the object code.

Example 7.16   A Macro with Opcode Parameters

a. Macro Definition   Comments

```
       .MACPO     ENDLOOP XLABEL,OPCD,CT
XLABEL: OPCD    CT
                   •                     ;BODY OF LOOP SOURCE
                   •                     ;STATEMENTS NOT SHOWN
                   •
       INC      CT
       .ENDM
```

b. Macro Call   Comments

```
          •                   ;YOUR EXISTING
          •                   ;SOURCE PROGRAM
          •
ENDLOOP   INITIAL,CLR,COUNT   ;CALL MACRO HERE; NOTE
                              ;"CLR"
CMP       COUNT,#100          ;EXISTING SOURCE PROGRAM
BEQ       OUT
          •
          •
          •
```

c. Macro Expansion		Comments
	•	;EXISTING SOURCE PROGRAM
	•	
	•	
INITIAL: CLR COUNT		;FIRST MACRO STATEMENT
	•	;BODY OF LOOP SOURCE
	•	;STATEMENTS NOT SHOWN
	•	
INC COUNT		;LAST MACRO STATEMENT
CMP COUNT,#100		;EXISTING SOURCE PROGRAM
BEQ OUT		
	•	
	•	
	•	

7.7 CONDITIONAL MACRO EXPANSION

At times, situations arise in which the expansion of a macro should depend on conditions within a program. Is it possible, then, to create a "switch" which enables or disables the expansion? Yes, macro assemblers provide this capability through the mechanism of a *conditional assembly* directive to inform the assembler whether to expand a macro or ignore it at any given point in the program, without having to remove the macro call. The macro call can always remain at the inserted positions in the source program, while the assembler tests a switch in the macro call to determine whether expansion is desired or not. The block of code between the condition delimiters in the macro definition is called a *conditional block*. Just as with a macro definition, a conditional block must always be delimited by two assembly directives. The first is a conditional assembly directive, and the last is a terminator directive. Conditional assembly code generally possesses the following form:

```
.IF COND,t      { Heading With Switch, Condition, and Test
    •
    •           { Conditional Block of Code to be Assembled
    •
.ENDC           { Source Statement Terminator
```

The conditional directive tests the condition "COND" to determine whether or not it is satisfied by "t". If "t" does satisfy that condition, the code within the assembler directives is expanded and object code is generated. Otherwise, the code including the conditional directive and terminator is not expanded by the assembler.

7.7.1 CONDITION TESTS

The condition to be tested can invoke one of the following tests:

1. Test the value of the argument expression.

2. Test the assigned value of the character strings.

3. Test the assembly environment.

Conditional assembly is useful for the following reasons. An assembly language programmer is permitted to have access to variables which can be set, changed, and tested *during assembly*. More important, the same variables can direct the assembler to jump around and even loop through the same source statements in the assembly language program. The examples provided give some indication of their utility. The conditional assembly feature can be used to save memory. Are there other ways to save memory? Yes, we could change the original source program. However, programs which undergo frequent changes increase the possibility of a programming error with each modification. Deleting or editing areas of code greatly affects the structure of the code itself. Often a programmer inadvertently removes too little or too much code. The risks involved with deleting code in large programs increase the probability of a subsequent error, thus destroying the correctness of modified code. Worse yet, if the programmer is asked at a later date to generate the original code, a record of this earlier code may be lost. Obviously, memory space is saved when such object code is omitted, but the source code still records the conditional directive and conditional block. Conditional assembly offers such attractive alternatives, especially when:

1. Memory space is limited, yet preservation of the original code is desired.

2. Data with different bit lengths are necessary in the parameter list.

3. Complex programs which require excessive diagnostics are needed with many test runs.

4. A programmer must add or delete extra variables at assembly time.

5. Code needs to be tailored to a particular situation, only known at translation time.

Remember that some conditional blocks may reside outside of a macro definition, while others must reside within the definition. However, most conditional blocks will be found within a macro definition. The BLANK (B), NOT BLANK (NB), IDENTICAL (IDN), and DIFFERENT (DIF) conditional block tests must always be found within a macro definition. Some IF directives of MACRO-11 are listed in Table 7.2. Most assemblers have one or more of the arithmetic, attribute, environment, and string test directives.

Table 7.2   Macro-11 Conditional Directives

Non-Symbolic

Type	Directive	Assemble Block If
Arithmetic	.IF EQ,t	t equals 0
	.IF NE,t	t is not equal to 0
	.IF GT,t	t is greater than 0
	.IF GE,t	t is greater than or equal to 0
	.IF LT,t	t is less than 0
	.IF LE,t	t is less than or equal to 0

Symbolic

Type	Directive	Assemble Block If
Attribute	.IF DF,t	t is defined
	.IF NDF,t	t is not defined
Environment	.IF B,<t>	macro argument t is blank (absent)
	.IF NB,<t>	macro argument t is not blank (present)
String	.IF IDN,<t1>,<t2>	t1 identical to t2 string
	.IF DIF,<t1>,<t2>	t1 not identical to t2 string

The *symbolic* conditional test determines the extent of the condition of the character strings delimited by the <character string>. The *arithmetic* condition test compares the parameter's numerical value with zero. The utility of conditional block assemblies can be seen in Example 7.17 which is a modification of an earlier macro definition named SWAPIT. This macro swaps the contents of two locations in memory. Suppose that the contents of the two memory locations are identical. Should this macro be expanded? No. Then why not omit the actual code when this useless task is not required? Notice that in Example 7.17c, six lines of object code are saved every time the body of code is not needed.

Example 7.17   A Conditional Block to Save Needless Object Code

   a. <u>Macro Definition</u>

```
.MACRO SWAPIT A,B,C
.IF DIF,<A>,<B>
MOV A,C
MOV B,A
MOV C,B
.ENDC
.ENDM
```

b. Macro Call

SWAPIT X,Y,Z   SWAPIT X,Y,Z
    •   •
    •   •
    •   •

c. Macro Expansion

(if X and Y   (if X and Y
are different)   are the same)
        •   •
        •   •
        •   SAVE   •
MOV   X,Z   OBJECT   •
MOV   Y,X   CODE   •
MOV   Z,Y   SPACE!   •
        •   •
        •
        •

It is important to recognize that macros without conditional directives may waste memory space. In fact, unconditional macro calls could consume memory space, sometimes at astronomical rates. Macro statements with conditional directives save programming time and memory space, but may trade memory for execution speed.

7.7.2 ARITHMETIC CONDITIONS

Conditional blocks may test for any valid relational operator of an assembler. In MACRO-11, six arithmetic relations, not equal, less than or equal, equal, less than, greater than or equal, and greater than (NE, LE, EQ, LT, GE, and GT) are permissible in a conditional block. These relational operators all compare the argument expression in the conditional block name with zero. The syntax rule applies when the .IF relation works on an expression as well as a symbol.

In Example 7.18, the beginning of the conditional block is marked by the .IF assembly directive, and the end of the conditional block is marked by the .ENDC assembly directive. (Do not use .ENDM.) The .IF directive must include a description of the logical condition. In this example, we are testing the argument SAMPLE to determine whether the value of the expression is not equal to zero using NE. If SAMPLE is not equal to zero, the code is assembled. If SAMPLE is equal to zero, the code is not assembled.

Example 7.18 Conditional Blocks and Expansion

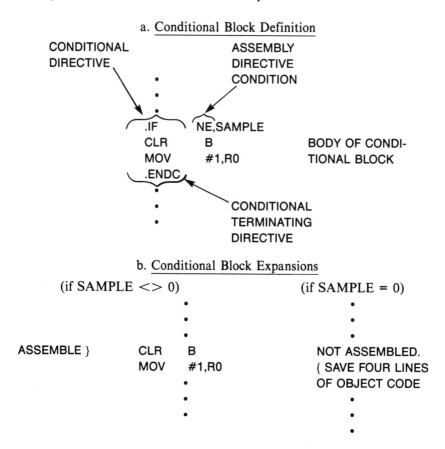

a. Conditional Block Definition

b. Conditional Block Expansions

(if SAMPLE <> 0)   (if SAMPLE = 0)

ASSEMBLE }   CLR   B   NOT ASSEMBLED.
             MOV   #1,R0   { SAVE FOUR LINES
                            OF OBJECT CODE

In Example 7.19, the expression Y+3 is tested to determine whether the expression is greater than or equal to zero. If Y+3 is greater than or equal to zero (which means that Y is −3, −2, −1 ...), then the code is assembled. Otherwise, the conditional block is skipped over during assembly time.

Example 7.19 A Conditional Block with an Expression

a. Conditional Block Definition

```
.IF      GE,Y+3
ADD      R0,R1
MOV      R1,#LARGE
.ENDC
```

b. Conditional Block Expansions

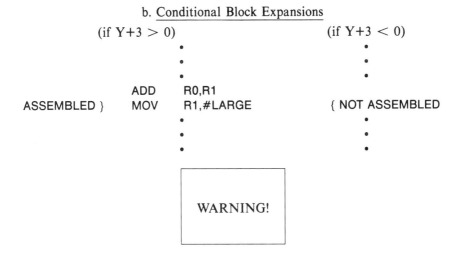

(if Y+3 > 0)

   •
   •
   •

ASSEMBLED }   ADD   R0,R1
              MOV   R1,#LARGE

   •
   •
   •

(if Y+3 < 0)

   •
   •
   •

{ NOT ASSEMBLED

   •
   •
   •

WARNING!

You should always assign the value of the parameter value early in your program, possibly at the very beginning. Of course, this is not always possible. Sometimes the condition is set only after source statements are assembled. Even so, always make the direct assignment *prior* to the conditional block. Otherwise, an assembly error will result.

7.7.3   SYMBOLIC CONDITIONS

Many data processing tasks in a computer handle non-numeric data. Consequently, a programmer cannot resort to an arithmetic condition test in a conditional block to invoke conditional assembly in such cases. Fortunately, besides tests for arithmetic conditions, tests for symbolic conditions can be made. A *symbolic* test determines whether a condition is true or the condition is not true. Of the six symbolic conditional directives listed in Table 7.2, the last four condition tests (B, NB, IDN, DIF) must be used within a macro definition.

7.7.4   CONDITION TESTS

7.7.4.1   BLANK (B)

A macro parameter substituted with blanks in the macro call will cause the generation of code. In Example 7.20, the macro named OMIT has three arguments (A, NOT, C). Internal to this macro is the conditional code block with a symbolic test of the argument NOT. If the later macro call OMIT X,Y,Z is made, the macro call will not generate any code, since Y is definitely not a blank symbol. If, however, the macro call OMIT A, ,4 is made, the macro assembler will generate one word of code (namely, MOV A,C).

Example 7.20 The BLANK Conditional Block Test

```
.MACRO    OMIT    A,NOT,C
.IF B,<NOT>
MOV       A,C
.ENDC
.ENDM
```

7.7.4.2 NOT BLANK (NB)

If a macro parameter is not substituted with blanks, the (NB) condition is true. Code will thus be generated. Consider Example 7.21. Now the macro call INSERT #100,INTO,PTR will generate one line of code (namely, MOV #100,PTR). The macro call INSERT #100, ,PTR will generate no code.

Example 7.21 The Not Blank Conditional Block Test

```
.MACRO    INSERT    A,YES,C
.IF NB,<YES>
MOV       A,C
.ENDC
.ENDM
```

7.7.4.3 IDENTICAL (IDN)

The identical (IDN) condition tests whether two macro type arguments are identical character strings after macro parameter substitution. If the strings are identical, the code is generated. In Example 7.22, the conditional test examines the arguments B and C. If after macro parameter substitution, the character strings for B and C are identical, the code will be assembled. The macro call, SAME R0,"/","/",R2, will cause two lines of code to be generated (namely, CLR R2 and MOV R2,R0). If the macro call SAME R0,"/","-",R2 were made, the condition test would fail and no code would be assembled.

Example 7.22 The Identical Conditional Block Test

```
.MACRO    SAME    A,B,C,D
.IF IDN,<B>,<C>
CLR       D
MOV       D,A
.ENDC
.ENDM
```

7.7.4.4   DIFFERENT (DIF)

In Example 7.23, the macro call DIF R0,"/","-",R2 will generate two lines of code. The macro call DIF R0,"/","/",R2 will not generate any code. This conditional test is the opposite of the IDN test.

Example 7.23   The Different Conditional Block Test

```
.MACRO    DIF    A,B,C,D
.IF DIF,<B>,<C>
MOV       A,D
CLR       A
.ENDC
.ENDM
```

7.7.4.5   DEFINED (DF)

The defined (DF) condition tests whether the argument in the macro call is a defined symbol. If the argument exists in the symbol table, it is defined and code will be generated. If the argument does not exist in the symbol table and consequently is not a defined symbol, the code will not be generated. In Example 7.24, if the symbol TOP is found in the symbol table prior to the macro call EXIST, the code will be assembled. In this example, storage for three words (X, Y, and Z) will be made. If at the time an EXIST macro call is made, TOP is not defined in the symbol table, no storage will be provided for X, Y, and Z.

Example 7.24   The Defined Conditional Block Test

```
.MACRO    EXIST    TOP,X,Y,Z
.IF DF,<TOP>
.WORD     X,Y,Z
.ENDC
.ENDM
```

7.7.4.6   NOT DEFINED (NDF)

If an argument is not defined (does not exist) in the symbol table, and the conditional test, not defined (NDF), is invoked, its conditional block of code is assembled. Otherwise, the block is ignored. In Example 7.25, if the symbol TOP is not found in the symbol table, the code .WORD X,Y,Z will be assembled and inserted instead of your program. If the symbol TOP is found in the symbol table at the time of this conditional block call in your program, the subsequent code will not be generated.

Example 7.25   The Undefined Conditional Block Test

```
.MACRO   EXIST
    •
    •
    •
.IF NDF,<TOP>
.WORD      X,Y,Z
.ENDC
    •
    •
    •
.ENDM
```

7.7.4.7   LOSING YOUR LABEL

Application of conditional blocks of code is straightforward. However, subtle expansion problems can arise in a program when conditional blocks contain labels. Consider Example 7.26. Here the conditional block definition contains the label SIZE in the second line of the body. When this conditional block is assembled (because the argument LIMIT is less than zero), the code will be expanded just as shown in Example 7.26b. However, if the condition test fails, the code will not be assembled in the program. As a consequence, the label SIZE no longer exists. Furthermore, any references to SIZE which may exist elsewhere in the program will result in an error message from the assembler. This error message will indicate that the programmer is attempting to use an undefined symbol. To prevent such an undefined symbol error, do the following in Example 7.26.

1. Do not use labels in conditional blocks. (Note, however, that such a rule only hampers the inherent flexibility of assembly language programming and is discouraged.)

2. Ensure that *all* references to the label SIZE in conditional blocks are prevented when LIMIT is less than zero.

3. Use the label SIZE elsewhere whenever LIMIT is not less than zero.

4. Use a direct assignment statement defining LIMIT prior to the conditional block call. This is not always possible since we frequently don't know what value to assign to the label.

5. Assign a local set symbol to the label (such as using the "?", to be described in Section 7.7).

Example 7.26   A Conditional Block with a Disappearing Label

a. Conditional Block Definition

```
        .IF     LT,LIMIT
        MOV     B,R3
SIZE:   INC     R3
        .ENDC
```

b. Conditional Block Expansions

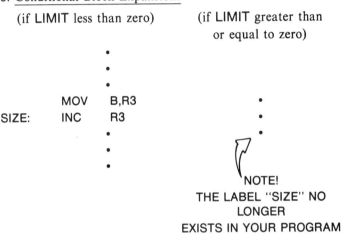

(if LIMIT less than zero)   (if LIMIT greater than
                                      or equal to zero)

```
·
·
·
        MOV     B,R3                      ·
SIZE:   INC     R3                        ·
        ·                                 ·
        ·
        ·
```

NOTE!
THE LABEL "SIZE" NO
LONGER
EXISTS IN YOUR PROGRAM

7.8 SYMBOLIC PARAMETERS, ATTRIBUTES, AND SEQUENCE SYMBOLS

The power of macro definitions and conditional assembly lies in the provision for manipulating variable symbols at assembly time. *Variable symbols* are variables which are given values during assembly of the program (and not during execution of the program). A very important kind of variable symbol is the *symbolic parameter*. The symbolic parameter is a dummy symbol used in the definition of a macro. The dummy arguments in a macro definition are, in fact, symbolic parameters. During expansion of the macro definition, the *actual arguments* will be placed properly in the assembly language program within the source statements precisely as specified. In Example 7.17, A,B,C are symbolic parameters (dummy arguments) and X,Y,Z are actual arguments.

7.8.1 SET SYMBOLS

Another very important class of variable symbols is the set symbol. A *set symbol* can assign arithmetic values, character values, or even logical values (0 or 1). Some assemblers call these binary values. *Local* set symbols inform the assembler that the symbols are specific to a macro expansion, and not to be used in other macro expansions. *Global* set symbols, in contrast to the previously defined local set symbols, inform the assembler that the values set in one macro can be used in another, or can be set and used outside of macros entirely. Set symbols can be set, changed, and tested. Thus such symbols are very convenient to control the assembly process itself.

In the PDP-11 assemblers, the question mark ("?") is a local set symbol. When preceding other symbols, the "?" informs the assembler that such annotated symbols belong to the macro using the symbols. In the following macro named SAVE, START and EXIT are *declared* local symbols by listing them in the macro's parameter list as shown. If a call makes no mention of START and EXIT (i.e., the parameter list contains only two arguments), the PDP-11 assembler replaces the symbols with values between 64$ and 127$.

	Macro Definition		
	.MACRO	SAVE	X,Y,?START,?EXIT
START:	MOV	X,Y	
	DEC	X	
	BNE	START	
EXIT:	.ENDM		

Macro Call	Comments
•	
•	
•	
SAVE X,Y	;TWO ARGUMENTS MISSING
•	
•	
•	
SAVE A,B	;TWO ARGUMENTS MISSING
•	
•	
•	

Macro Expansion			Comments
64$:	MOV	X,Y	;ASSEMBLER DEFINES THIS LABEL
	DEC	X	
	BNE	64$	;ASSEMBLER DEFINES THIS LABEL
65$:			
		•	
		•	
		•	
66$:	MOV	A,B	;ASSEMBLER DEFINES THIS LABEL
	DEC	A	
	BNE	66$	;ASSEMBLER DEFINES THIS LABEL
67$:			
		•	
		•	
		•	

7.8.2 ATTRIBUTES

Besides symbolic parameters and set symbols, the assembly language programmer has attributes at his disposal. An *attribute* is a property of a symbolic parameter, such as type and length (for example, integer and six digits). Attributes can be used by the macro call to adjust to the specific types and lengths of the actual parameters used in the macro expansion. An *attribute number* refers to a parameter list. This number enables the macro to determine how many parameters are actually supplied within a macro call. A macro, then, can adjust to variations in the number of parameters.

In PDP-11 assemblers, the .NARG directive defines an attribute number. In the macro below, up to seven items can be stored in the array, LIST. In the macro expansion, N becomes 5 to specify the given actual arguments (SCALE,23,47,19.,). Note that blank arguments result in the storage of 0's, and the label, "LIST", is an argument in this parameter list.

Macro Definition		
	.MACRO	TABLE LIST,D1,D2,D3,D4,D5,D6,D7
	.NARG N	
LIST:	.WORD	D1,D2,D3,D4,D5,D6,D7
	.BLKW	N-1
	.ENDM	

Macro Call	Comments
TABLE SCALE,23,47,19.,	;NOTE THE BLANK PARAMETER

Macro Expansion			Comments
SCALE:	.WORD	23,47,19.,0	;BLANK REPLACED WITH ZERO
	.BLKW	4	

7.8.3 SEQUENCE SYMBOLS

Conditional block codes are possible through the use of *sequence* symbols. The sequence symbol attached to the conditional directives, .IF ..., actually determines for the assembler whether or not to skip over the next source statements, thus omitting their expansion, or to actually physically expand the source code of the conditional block into the source program. In Table 7.2, the actual expression for "t" in each conditional directive is a sequence symbol.

7.9 SYMBOLIC EXPRESSIONS

So far, this chapter has been dealing with very simple symbolic expressions. The earlier exposures to expressions in the previous chapter illustrated simplistic single operator forms such as ADDR+2 and #A+20. These expressions designate addresses 2 or 20 locations below ADDR and A, respectively. From the current study of macros, repeat blocks, and conditional assembly, it is clear that much more sophisticated expressions are desired. Furthermore, you should realize that symbols can be and are used for much more than addressing. For instance, some earlier examples have demonstrated that symbolic names can be used for numbers.

7.9.1 ASSEMBLY PROCESS VERSUS PROGRAM EXECUTION

A programmer must be extremely careful to understand the difference between expressions used during the assembly process and expressions used during program execution. One writes the relationship, $A = A+1$, in a line of assembly code to cause the entry for A in the assembler's symbol table to be incremented by one. It does not cause a register or location to be incremented at program execution. In fact, $A = A+1$ is not recognized as any executable machine language code. Similarly, the line of assembly code, $A = A-1$, does not cause a location to be decremented at execution time. This table causes an entry, A, in the assembler's symbol table to be decremented. The reader is cautioned not to confuse $A = A+1$ with INC A. Likewise, do not regard $A = A-1$ as DEC A. The line of assembly code, $A = A+1$, is a source statement in assembly code to be used by the assembler to update a symbol. The line of assembly code, INC A, is an executable machine language code, and as a source statement will generate an object code, whereas $A = A+1$ generates no object code.

7.9.2 THE EFFECTS OF RELOCATION

There is a difference between symbols used for numbers in an assembler program and symbols used for addresses. This difference becomes obvious when object code is relocated to another area in memory (which frequently occurs when several programs are being executed simultaneously). The values of symbols used for numbers are not affected during relocation. Such values do not change. However, symbols used for addresses in a program have values that will change (as they must) when the object code is relocated elsewhere. The only symbols used for addresses which do not change when a program is relocated are symbols used for absolute addresses.

All symbols in the symbol table of the assembly process are distinguished as being either relocatable or absolute. In a machine language program, addresses which must be changed when a program is relocated are called relocatable addresses. All other addresses are called absolute. In MACRO-11, a word which contains an address within the source program is relocatable (e.g., INC COUNT), and must change when the program is moved. However, data, fixed addresses in memory, and numerical operation codes are absolute. The symbol table indicates relocatable entries by appending the letter R to each relocatable entry.

7.9.3 FORMING EXPRESSIONS

Any operand entry in an assembly language source statement may be an expression. Valid expressions include terms and arithmetic combinations of terms. The operations on terms and expressions which form new expressions are addition, subtraction, multiplication, and division. The assembly language symbols which represent addition, subtraction, multiplication, and division are

Expressions may be built from subexpressions in many assemblers by using parentheses. However, PDP-11 assemblers use "<" and ">" for left and right parentheses. Also in PDP-11 assemblers, no operator precedence exists. In other assemblers, multiplication and division typically take precedence over addition and subtraction (e.g., the IBM 360/370 assemblers). In the MACRO-11 assemblers, expressions are always evaluated from left to right, unless parenthesization is used. For example, 11.+4.*2. is 30 in decimal, because the expression is evaluated from left to right, so addition is performed before the multiplication. If the decimal value 19 is desired, the expression should be written as 11.+<4.*2.>. Certain rules apply to determine the types of expressions. Some of the more common guidelines are now listed.

1. An expression may not start with an arithmetic operator.

2. An expression may never contain two consecutive operators or two consecutive terms.

3. An expression composed entirely of numbers and absolutes or of absolute symbols will be considered absolute.

4. In general, combinations of relocatable (rel) terms or expressions and absolute (abs) terms or expressions allowed with the following operations are:

   a. rel+abs: relocatable expression
   b. rel-rel: absolute expression
   c. abs+abs: absolute expression
   d. abs∗abs: absolute expression
   e. abs/abs: absolute expression

5. The difference between two relocatable symbols is always absolute (as in 4b), since the difference between two addresses is, in effect, the number of locations between these two addresses. If both move, they will move the same amount. Hence, the number of locations between them will remain fixed.

6. If there is multiplication in an expression, the expression should contain at least one absolute term. In that case, just consider multiplication as repeated addition. Suppose that X, Y, and Z are relocatable. The expression $(2*X)-(3*Y)+Z$ is equivalent to $X-Y+X-Y+Z-Y$ since each subexpression is a difference between two relocatable operands, and each subexpression is absolute.

7.9.4   EXPRESSION EVALUATION IN A TWO-PASS ASSEMBLER

Two-pass assemblers pose some interesting hazards to the usage of expressions. The order in which symbols are *defined* and *used* must be strictly followed. Recall that two passes are needed in the assembly process, because a machine language instruction or source statement may refer to a symbolic address. Some symbolic addresses may be subsequently defined in the source program. However, not all symbolic addresses can be permitted to be defined later. Some values for the symbolic address must be known on the first pass. In these cases, the assembly process will fail if such values have not been previously defined.

Except for some assemblers which may generate a symbol table in a pre-pass, most two-pass assemblers will generate the symbol table in the first pass. That being so, symbols which modify entries in the same symbol table must be defined before being used. One frequent error is the wrong ordering of direct assignments as illustrated in Example 7.27.

Example 7.27a   An Incorrect Ordering

```
        •
        •
        •
    FIRST=SECOND        ;"FIRST" UNDEFINED IN
    SECOND=2            ;PASS ONE OF ASSEMBLER!
        •
        •
        •
```

Example 7.27b   The Correct Ordering

```
        •
        •
        •
        •
    SECOND=2            ;FIRST IS NOW PROPERLY
      FIRST=SECOND      ;DEFINED
        •
        •
        •
```

In the first assembly pass, FIRST remains undefined, even though a symbol table is being generated in the first pass. To eliminate this problem, simply exchange the order of the two lines.

Incorrect ordering of usage and definition of a symbol can lead to very subtle errors. Consider the following macro, RESERVE, which contains source statements to reserve words and bytes of storage. Note that the .BLKB directive uses a symbol (namely, FOUR) which is not defined until after the macro definition. In the first pass of an assembler, the symbol table will receive the four entries, TABLE, CONS1, CONS2, and FOUR, but the assembler has no idea of how many bytes to set aside for the array CONS2. Some assemblers will assign 0 to this undefined symbol. In pass two, FOUR is assigned the value "4." This assembly assignment now causes the address CONS1 to be two greater than the address CONS2. Since from pass one, address CONS1 was the same as CONS2, and from pass two these addresses are different, the assembler generates an error message called a *phase error*. One solution is found in Example 7.28b.

Example 7.28a A Macro with a Phase Error

```
        •
        •
        •
        .MACRO      RESERVE     TABLE,CONS1,CONS2,FOUR
TABLE:  .WORD       0,4,7       ;PHASE ERROR WILL OCCUR HERE
CONS2:  .BLKB       FOUR        ;"FOUR" IS NOT YET DEFINED!
CONS1:  .BLKW       16
        .ENDM
    FOUR=4
        •
        •
        •
```

Example 7.28b A Macro Without a Phase Error

```
        •
        •
        •
    FOUR=4
        .MACRO      RESERVE     TABLE,CONS1,CONS2,FOUR
TABLE:  .WORD       0,4,7
CONS2:  .BLKB       FOUR
CONS1:  .BLKW       16
        .ENDM
        •
        •
        •
```

7.10 NESTING MACROS

Since a macro is basically a procedure which performs a character string substitution, any valid character string or expression is allowed in the body of the macro, including *another* macro. This "recursive" feature of macros opens up entirely new programming vistas. A macro within a macro is called "*nesting*." Macros can be nested to any number of levels (hopefully, a finite number). Expansion of nested macros is then performed in a number of successive stages in the assembly process. However, remember that expansion occurs when a macro is called, not when it is defined. Also, expansion occurs only at program assembly time, not program execution time. Further, it is possible to define nested macros in any order. But calls to the outermost macros must occur *only* after all definitions of the respective inner macros.

Nested macro expansion is made clear in the following examples. Note! Recursive expansion is not allowed in most processes.

7.10.1 MACRO CALL WITHIN A MACRO CALL

A macro call within a macro call is then termed a *nested macro call*. Most macro assemblers allow users to nest macro calls. A macro may call itself or another macro. A macro call to itself is similar to a loop wherein the macro is actually expanded repeatedly. Macros which call themselves are *recursive macros*, which will be examined shortly.

For now, consider macro calls which only call other macros. In Example 7.29, the macro named POWER is intended to perform an arithmetic right shift on an operand N times. Within this macro is a call to another macro named COUNT. Both macro definitions are found in Example 7.29a. Suppose that just prior to the macro call of this program, a direct assignment of 4 to N is made. (A user does not want N to be undefined when the call is made.) Next, the macro, POWER, is called. This macro call, when expanded, will shift the contents of R1 to the right four places. In the intermediate expansion in Example 7.29b, the macro named POWER is expanded. COUNT is not yet expanded. This intermediate step lists the source statement, SHIFT: ASR R1, and the call to the macro named COUNT. The final generated code contains the fully expanded source statements for both macros. Notice that in Example 7.29b, the second and third source statements are expanded from the innermost macro (namely, COUNT).

Example 7.29 only illustrates a two-step macro expansion. Nested macro calls requiring three, four, or more expansion steps are also allowed. However, from this example, it is clear that very simple macros can be inserted into the body of more complicated macros, and this complexity can build upon itself from very simple macro source statements. The facility to create a macro expansion within a macro expansion is another translation mechanism for implementing multi-level computer machinery and virtual machines.

Example 7.29   A Nested Macro Call

	a. Macro Definitions		Comments
	.MACRO POWER X,N,?SSHIFT		;GET X∗2∗∗(-N)
SSHIFT:	ASR X		
	COUNT N,SSHIFT		
	.ENDM		
	.MACRO COUNT N,AGAIN		
	DEC N		;THIS IS A LOOP COUNTER
	BNE AGAIN		
	.ENDM		

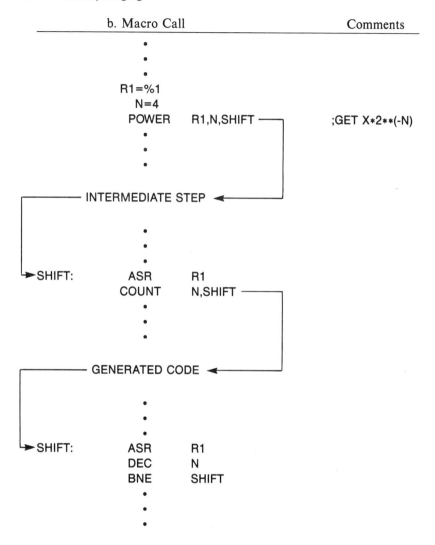

b. Macro Call		Comments

With nested calls, the relative positions of inner and outer macros are important. In Example 7.29, as with all nested macro calls, the body of a macro definition may contain calls for other macros which have not yet been defined. This structure is permissible. However, an embedded call must be defined before any call is issued to the outermost macro which contains the innermost or imbedded call. In Example 7.29, the macro definition for POWER and the macro definition for COUNT must appear in the assembly program before the call to POWER occurs.

7.10.2 MACRO DEFINITIONS WITHIN MACRO DEFINITIONS

In the previous section, a macro call was embedded within a macro call. Macro assemblers also permit users to embed a macro definition within another macro definition. Nested macros contain levels of assignment. The outermost macros are often called *first-level* macros. Macros directly inside of the outermost macros are then called *second-level* macros, and so on. Consider a macro with three levels. In Example 7.30, the task of this code is to compute the result, A + B + C / 2 − D / 2. The first-level macro, EXPR, performs a simple addition. The second-level macro, ASHIFT, performs a right shift and add. The third-level macro, SSHIFT, performs a right shift and subtract.

Example 7.30   Nested Macro Definition

(OBTAINS A + B + C / 2− D / 2)

a. Nested Definitions

```
.MACRO  EXPR TERM1,TERM2,TERM3,TERM4
ADD     TERM2,TERM1    AD,AUG ;COMBINE TWO TERMS
.MACRO  ASHIFT   TERM3
ASR     TERM3                 ;HALVE THIRD TERM
ADD     TERM3,TERM1           ;COMBINE THREE TERMS
.MACRO  SSHIFT   TERM4
ASR     TERM4                 ;HALVE FOURTH TERM
SUB     TERM4,TERM1           ;FORM FINAL EXPRESSION
.ENDM   SSHIFT                ;NOTE! NO OVERFLOW TEST
.ENDM   ASHIFT                ;NOTE! INPUTS ARE
                              ;MODIFIED
.ENDM   EXPR
```

	b. Call	"INTERMEDIATE" Expansion	Comments
EXPR	A,B,C,D	ADD B,A	
		ASHIFT C	;CAUSES ASHIFT TO BE DEFINED
ASHIFT	C	ASR C	
		ADD C,A	
		SSHIFT D	;CAUSES SSHIFT TO BE DEFINED
SSHIFT	D	ASR D	
		SUB D,A	;RESULT IN "B"!

c. Completed Expansion

- •
- •
- •

```
ADD   B,A
ASR   C
ADD   C,A
ASR   D
SUB   D,A    ;NOTE. THE INPUT PARAMETER
  •          ;IS REPLACED BY THE FORMED
  •          ;EXPRESSION
  •
```

To avoid confusion, the terminating directive for each macro includes the name of the macro (some macro assemblers may even require it). The innermost terminating directive applies to the innermost macro. Hence, .ENDM SSHIFT is the terminating statement for the macro named SSHIFT, and .ENDM ASHIFT is the terminating statement for ASHIFT. Every nested macro definition must contain a header and a terminating directive. These directives must always occur in pairs. When the nested macro is first encountered by the macro assembler, macro processing defines only the first-level macro. Thus, a macro call to a first-level macro is always permissible, but second-level and higher macros have not yet been defined. When EXPR is called in Example 7.30b, it will cause the second-level macro or ASHIFT to be defined. When ASHIFT is called, its expansion causes SSHIFT to be defined. When SSHIFT is called, it is expanded and the nested expansion is now completed. The general rule is:

> A macro definition which occurs inside another macro definition does not take effect (remains undefined) until the macro in which it has been defined has been *called* and *expanded*.

Why are calls to innermost macros illegal until outermost calls are made? When a macro assembler finds a macro definition, the macro definition body is stored without further examination. Hence, definitions occurring inside are not seen by the macro assembler until the surrounding macro is called. When the surrounding macro is called, its body is scanned by the assembler. This scanning action causes the embedded definitions to be found and expanded. In other words, when macro definitions are nested, the inner definitions cannot be called until the outer macro has been called and expanded.

7.11   RECURSIVE MACRO CALLS

The previous section illustrated how a macro call within a macro could invoke the calling of a different macro. This nesting concept can be carried even further. A macro call appearing within a macro definition which calls the same macro currently being defined is known as a *recursive macro*. A call to a recursive macro is handled in the following manner. The assembly process continues to expand the body of each call until some terminating statement tells the assembler to stop. Remember that when the definition of any macro is encountered by the assembler, the body in the macro definition is copied character by character into a special table of the assembler called the macro definition table. This copying is done without even being examined. The assembler, at this point, doesn't care whether the definition contains assembly language statements or another macro. A macro definition and expansion consist of character manipulations and nothing more. Extreme care must then be exercised to ensure that recursive macro calls will indeed terminate. It's the user's responsibility to ensure that recursive macro definitions contain directives to the assembler to stop expansion.

In Example 7.31, a programmer desires to build a table of three words. In his macro definition for BUILD, a call is found to the same macro, BUILD, in the first source statement of the definition. A macro call, as in Example 7.31b, generates the macro expansion in Example 7.31c. Note that in the first step of the macro expansion, a macro call for the same macro is found as well as the first word of the table. In the second step of the macro expansion, the BUILD macro is called again and two words of storage are now reserved. In the third step, a call to the same macro occurs with three reserved storage words. Do you see the problem? This process continues indefinitely, since no command to the assembler to cease this expansion process is found in the macro definition. The assembler is now running in a never-ending loop at assembly time! Most likely, the computer will stop only when all memory space is consumed by a very large table.

Example 7.31   Incorrectly Building Tables by Recursive Macros

        a. Macro Definition

```
.MACRO BUILD N
BUILD N
.WORD N
.ENDM
```

        b. Macro Call

```
     •
     •
     •
BUILD 3
     •
     •
```

c. Macro Expansion

First Step	Second Step	Third Step	
•	•	•	
•	•	•	
•	•	•	
BUILD 3	BUILD 3	BUILD 3	This goes on
.WORD 3	.WORD 3	.WORD 3	forever!
•	.WORD 3	.WORD 3	
•	•	.WORD 3	
•	•	.WORD 3	
•	•		
	•		

This careless macro programmer has built a very large table, indeed. Since some sort of a terminating statement is required, the programmer may be tempted to place a machine language instruction such as HALT in the macro definition. A machine language instruction, however, attempting to stop an assembly process does not stop the assembly process. The expansion above would only contain a very large number of HALT instructions. An assembler directive, not a machine language instruction, which tells the assembly process to terminate must be found in the macro definition. A "count" is needed in the assembly process and can be implemented by using conditional assembly. The conditional assembly pseudo-instruction, .IF, can be used to terminate the assembly expansion process.

In Example 7.32, the programmer has now included a conditional .IF statement, LT N, in its body. Now when the macro is called in Example 7.32b, the expansion proceeds only through four steps as shown in Example 7.32c. In the first step, the body of the macro is expanded once. Notice that in this first step of the macro expansion, the body has been expanded to include four source statements. The first word of the table (-3) is now specified. In the second step, the macro has been recursively called, and another word ($1-3$) is reserved in memory. In this same second step, a call to the macro remains, since the conditional assembly pseudo-instruction, .IF LT, is satisfied. The macro is recursively called again. In the third step, three words are now reserved and the pseudo-instruction test is still satisfied. Hence, a fourth macro expansion step occurs in which the table is now built up completely. Now the conditional assembly pseudo-instruction test fails and the macro is no longer called.

The reader should regard the actual parameter in the first call of BUILD to be an expression ("-3") and not the number, "-3." In the second call, the actual parameter is again regarded as an expression, this time "$1-3$." The assembly process continues until the .IF directive test fails. This occurs in the fourth expansion. When the fourth expansion is made (in the assembly process), the expression, $1+1+1-3$, is evaluated by the .IF statement. The test now fails because the expression, $1+1+1-3$, is numerically zero. When this test fails, the statements following the conditional assembly pseudo-instruction are *not* expanded. Notice that the table contains four machine words: 0, -1, -2, and -3.

Example 7.32   Building Tables by Recursive Macros Using Conditional Assembly

a. Macro Definition
```
.MACRO BUILD N
.IF LT,N
BUILD 1+N
.ENDC
.WORD N
.ENDM
```

b. Macro Call
```
.
.
.
BUILD -3
.
.
.
```

c. Macro Expansion

First Step	Comments
.IF LT,-3	;CONDITIONAL TEST PASSES
BUILD 1-3	
.ENDC	
.WORD -3	

Second Step	Comments
.IF LT,1-3	;CONDITIONAL TEST PASSES
BUILD 1+1-3	
.ENDC	
.WORD 1-3	
.WORD -3	

Third Step	Comments
.IF LT,1+1−3	;CONDITIONAL TEST PASSES
BUILD 1+1+1−3	
.ENDC	
.WORD 1+1−3	
.WORD 1−3	
.WORD −3	

Fourth Step	Comments
.IF LT,1+1+1−3	;CONDITIONAL TEST FAILS
BUILD 1+1+1+1−3	;AND CONDITIONAL BODY
.ENDC	;DISAPPEARS
.WORD 1+1+1−3	;THIS CODE IS SUBSTITUTED
.WORD 1+1−3	;IN THE TEXT FOR THE CALL
.WORD 1−3	
.WORD −3	

Example 7.33 illustrates another recursive macro definition to perform a multiplication of an operand, X, by $2**(-N)$. The recursion ends when the expression, N−COUNT, is equal to or less than zero. As long as N−COUNT is greater than zero, the macro will call itself. In Example 7.33b, the programmer wisely makes a direct assignment of 0 to COUNT prior to the call. Why? This direct assignment statement must be found prior to the macro call, otherwise, a phase error would result. In Example 7.33c, the macro is expanded three times. In the third macro expansion step, the expression N−COUNT, becomes numerically 0. Hence, recursion ceases and the assembly language program now contains three identical source statements (ASR NUMR). This macro is useful in computers which only have a single bit shift instruction rather than a multiple bit shift instruction.

Example 7.33   Multiple Shifts by Macro Recursion

a. Macro Definition	Comments
.MACRO POWER X,N	;GET X*2**(−N)
ASR X	
COUNT=COUNT+1	
.IF GT,N−COUNT	
POWER X,N	
.ENDC	
.ENDM POWER	

b. <u>Macro Call</u>

•
•
•

```
        COUNT = 0
                POWER        NUMR,3
                   •
                   •
                   •
```

c.   <u>Macro Expansion</u>

First Step	Comments
•	
•	
•	
ASR NUMR	
COUNT=COUNT+1	;COUNT BECOMES +1
.IF GT,N-COUNT	
POWER NUMR,N ┐	
.ENDC	

•
•
•

┌─────────────┐	
│ Second Step │◄────	Comments
└─────────────┘	

•
•

```
        ASR NUMR
        ASR NUMR
COUNT=COUNT+1              ;COUNT BECOMES +2
        .IF GT,N-COUNT
        POWER NUMR,N ┐
        .ENDC
```

•
•

┌─────────────┐	
│ Third Step │◄────	Comments
└─────────────┘	

•
•
•

```
ASR NUMR
ASR NUMR
ASR NUMR
   •                    ;EXPANSION IS NOW COMPLETE.
   •                    ;IF N IS LARGE, MEMORY
   •                    ;SPACE WILL BE CONSUMED
                        ;INEFFICIENTLY!
```

7.12   NESTING CONDITIONAL ASSEMBLY DIRECTIVES

7.12.1   ANDING CONDITIONS

Conditional assembly directives can be nested, just as has been seen with macro definitions and with macro calls. Care should be exercised, because for each .IF statement, there must also be a termination .ENDC statement. In other words, these source statements must occur in pairs. Also, if the outermost .IF is not satisfied, *all* conditional assembly blocks, including the inner blocks, are not assembled. If only one .IF statement is encountered and satisfied, the block of code for that block is assembled. However, should the assembler encounter an inner .IF, its condition is also tested by the assembler, and if and only if the outer and inner .IF tests are satisfied will the entire block of code be assembled. Consider nested .IF statements as logical AND circuits. When the first, second, and all remaining inner .IF statements are satisfied, the code for all nested .IF statements is assembled. If any inner .IF statement is not satisfied, no code within any of the .IF statements is assembled.

In Example 7.34, a programmer desires to set up a table with either one, three, or four words, depending on the value of K. In Example 7.34b, three macro calls are illustrated (for K=1, 2, and 5). In Example 7.34c, the macro expansions for each case depict the assembly process. Notice that this macro definition will reserve at least one word of storage, regardless of the outcome of the conditional assembly tests. For the case K=2, four words are assembled, namely .WORD 0, .WORD 1, .WORD 2, and .WORD 3. For K=5, one word is reserved.

Example 7.34   .IF WITHIN AN .IF

a. Macro Definition

	Comments
.MACRO SETAB K	;EXPAND MACRO ONLY IF
.WORD 0	;BOTH CONDITIONS ARE
.IF GE,K-2	;SATISFIED
.WORD 1	
.WORD 2	
.IF LE,K-4	;THIS CONDITIONAL TEST
.WORD 3	;IS NESTED INSIDE THE
.ENDC	;OUTER TEST
.ENDC	
.ENDM	

b. Three Different Macro Calls

```
    •                    •                    •
    •                    •                    •
    •                    •                    •
  K=1                  K=2                  K=5
  SETAB K              SETAB K              SETAB K
    •                    •                    •
    •                    •                    •
    •                    •                    •
```

c. Three Different Macro Expansions

```
    •                    •                    •
    •                    •                    •
    •                    •                    •
  .WORD 0              .WORD 0              .WORD 0
    •                  .WORD 1                •
    •                  .WORD 2                •
    •                  .WORD 3                •
                       .WORD 4
                         •
                         •
                         •
```

7.12.2 EXCLUSIVE-ORING CONDITIONS

Suppose that it is desired to conditionally assemble either one segment of code or another segment (but not both), all in the same macro definition. That is, if one assembly directive test passes, then its body of code is assembled. If the test fails, the block of code within the same definition is to be assembled. To do so, a simple solution is to combine the .IF with the .IFF sub-conditional assembly directive. The .IFF directive separates a conditional block into two sub-blocks. Only one of the two sub-blocks is actually expanded. In Example 7.35, the .IFF assembly directive is nested within the .IF assembly directive. Notice that only one .ENDC terminating statement is required when using .IF with .IFF.

Example 7.35 .IF AND .IFF

a. Macro Definition   Comments

```
.MACRO BRANCH RELADR
.IF GT,RELADR-128.          ;SUBBLOCK ONE, EXPAND
JMP RELADR                  ;ONLY IF THIS TEST IS TRUE
.IFF
BR RELADR                   ;SUBBLOCK TWO, EXPAND
.ENDC                       ;ONLY ABOVE IF TEST IS FALSE
.ENDM
```

b. Macro Calls

·   ·
·   ·
·   ·
RELADR=256.   RELADR=100.
BRANCH RELADR   BRANCH RELADR
·   ·
·   ·
·   ·

c. Macro Expansions

·   ·
·   ·
·   ·
JMP RELADR   BR RELADR
·   ·
·   ·
·   ·

In this example, the programmer desires to use a jump instruction if RELADR is greater than 128 (in decimal). If, however, RELADR is less or equal to 128, the programmer desires to use the relative branch instruction, BR RELADR. This macro can be called only after RELADR has been defined. The two cases for the macro call and macro expansion are depicted in Examples 7.35b and 7.35c. Notice that the programmer is only considering forward branches.

7.13 REPEAT BLOCKS

7.13.1 DEFINITE REPEAT BLOCKS (.REPT)

One main thrust of this chapter is to demonstrate how assemblers can effectively work for us. In most cases, the programmer wants the assembler to provide capabilities to speed up the programming process. Consider a programming task to build a table of 1000 parameters. Through the usage of the .REPT assembly directive, table construction can be rapid and simple. The *repeat block* is a block of code that is copied verbatim, source statement by source statement, over and over again. Such code is likely to be found in building tables with the .WORD, .BYTE, and other assembler data directives. The .REPT directive in the PDP-11 assembly language is used as follows:

```
.REPT Expression    { Header
  •
  •                 { Desired Block of Code
  •                 { to be Repeated
  •
.ENDR               { Terminating
                      Statement
```

The .REPT directive requires:

1. An expression

2. The block of code the programmer desires to repeat

3. The terminating directive, .ENDR

The terminating directive .ENDM is not allowed. All .REPT directives must be paired with the .ENDR terminating directive. The .REPT directive causes the assembler to assemble the code at assembly time, *not* at program execution time. The block of code is repeated over and over again, the number of times being equivalent to the *value* of the expression following the .REPT directive. In Example 7.36, a simple table of four words containing the number 2 will be assembled with the .REPT directive. The expanded code is shown in Example 7.36b. With .REPT, the table could be extended to any size, as long as memory exists to handle the table.

Example 7.36   The .REPT Directive

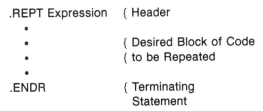

a. Repeat Block	b. Assembled Code
.REPT 4	.WORD 2
.WORD 2	.WORD 2
.ENDR	.WORD 2
	.WORD 2

In this example, using the .REPT as shown, no variation in the lines of text occurs, but expressions and definitions can be used within the .REPT directive to produce variable results, as shown next. Note that the .REPT directive can be found within a macro, although it is not necessary. In Example 7.36, the repeat block could have been found within the source program, instead of within the macro. As long as the .REPT is coded properly with an expression that has been defined prior to the use of .REPT, and the .ENDR directive terminates the block of code, the assembler will expand the code anywhere in the source program.

7.13.2 INDEFINITE REPEAT BLOCKS (.IRP)

Since computers are required to perform multiple processes simultaneously, it is often necessary to store the contents of programming model registers into some memory locations temporarily while a new task is being executed. Upon completion of the new process, the program should allow the registers to be restored from memory. The repeat directive .IRP (indefinite repeat), shown below, can be used to pass actual arguments into a repeat block with a convenient shorthand notation. An indefinite repeat block is similar to a macro definition with only one dummy argument. The form of the .IRP directive is as follows:

```
.IRP d,<a1,a2,...,an>        { Heading
    •
    •                        { Body of Code
    •                        { To Be Repeated
.ENDM                        { Terminating
                               Statement
```

The dummy argument is represented by d, and a1,a2,...,an are actual arguments to be passed into the repeat block. When the assembler encounters the .IRP directive during pass one, it will duplicate the repeat block n times. In the first copy, d will be replaced with a1. In the second copy, d will be replaced with a2, and so on. If no dummy argument is specified, the .IRP directive is flagged with an error code in the assembly listing. Example 7.37 restores the active registers R0, R1, R2, and R3 from the stack which is pointed to by R6 and represented by the symbol SP.

Example 7.37   Restoring Active Registers

    a. Macro Definition
```
.IRP GPR,<R0,R1,R2,R3>
MOV (SP)+,GPR
.ENDM
```

    b. Macro Expansion
```
    •
    •
    •
MOV (SP)+,R0
MOV (SP)+,R1
MOV (SP)+,R2
MOV (SP)+,R3
    •
    •
    •
```

7.13.3   USING THE LOCATION COUNTER IN REPEAT BLOCKS

Example 7.36 demonstrates the generation of a single table of data. Often, it is desired to create an array of addresses in several tables which are linked together by these addresses. An arrangement of data which contains pairs of addresses is called a *singly linked list*, and this address table is often used when a programmer recognizes the need to rearrange data. Rather than arrange data, per se, the programmer need only rearrange the pointers or addresses in the address table. In Example 7.38, the first word in each pair contains 4, while the second word contains the address of the next pair of words. The link is represented by "4." Notice that the data words, themselves, are not moved if this table is employed. Only the relative positions of each pointer are altered.

Example 7.38   Linked List Using .REPT

a. Repeat Block	b. Assembled Code	Comments
.REPT 12	•	
.WORD 4	•	
.WORD .+2	•	
.ENDR	.WORD 4	
	.WORD 2000	;POINTER TO FIRST TABLE
	.WORD 4	
	.WORD 2002	;POINTER TO NEXT TABLE
	.WORD 4	
	.WORD 2004	;POINTER TO NEXT TABLE
	.WORD 4	
	.WORD 2006	•
	.WORD 4	•
	•	•
	•	
	•	

7.13.4   ASSIGNMENT DIRECTIVES IN A .REPT BLOCK

The address table is generated with the use of an expression evaluator (namely, .+2) in the .WORD assembler directive of the repeat block. Recall that the PDP-11 assembler uses the special symbol "." to represent the location counter, and at assembly time "." changes with each source statement. Since this linked list contains pairs of words, the expression is incremented by 2. Example 7.38 assumes that when this code is assembled, the current value of the location counter is 2000. Here, the linked list consists of ten addresses. Hence, the expression with the .REPT directive is 12 (octal).

It is possible to redefine symbols using any legal assembler procedure besides the "." symbol. Because the "." symbol may confuse rather than clarify a programmer's intent, a programmer could use the "=" symbol, or the ":". The "=" symbol is available to make a *direct address*, much like the ":". However, recognize that using the ":" will cause a multiple-definition error. The assembler will generate such an error message. The "=" sign can be used to redefine a symbol with a subsequent "=" sign. The actual definitions are repeated in both pass one and pass two of the assembly process, with the symbol taking on the new value with its redefinition for any remaining lines of the program. In Example 7.39, the programmer computes an array of factorials, 1!,2!,3!,4!, and 5!. Recognize that the symbols FACT and N are neither locations nor names of locations, but rather symbolic addresses. These symbols receive assigned numeric values in the assembler's symbol table given by the "=" sign in the code.

Example 7.39   Generating a Factorial Table

a.
Repeat Block	Comments
•	
•	
•	
N=1	;INITIALIZE SYMBOL VALUES
FACT=1	
.REPT 5	
.WORD FACT	
N=N+1	;UPDATE SYMBOLS AT ASSEMBLY
FACT=FACT*N	;TIME, NOT PROGRAM EXECUTION
.ENDR	;TIME
•	
•	
•	

b. Assembled Code

```
      •
      •
      •
   .WORD 1
   .WORD 2
   .WORD 6
   .WORD 24
   .WORD 120
      •
      •
      •
```

Since the body of code in the repeat block can contain any valid source statement, even machine language instructions are possible. In Example 7.40, a block of data is being moved from one position in memory to another position in memory specified by PTR1 and PTR2 in the macro parameter list. Notice how the directive efficiently employs the MOV instruction in the autoincrement addressing mode. In this example, the user has traded program memory space for speed, because the MOV instruction will be repeatedly entered (50 times!) in the source program and eventually in the object code. A program containing a loop to execute this same task would have to execute additional instructions to increment the loop counter and test for the 50th iteration (which takes time).

Example 7.40   A Fast Block Move

```
.MACRO MOVBLK PTR1,PTR2
MOV # PTR1,R1
MOV # PTR2,R2
.REPT 50.
MOV (R1)+,(R2)+
.ENDR
.ENDM
```

7.14   CONCATENATION AND NUMERIC ARGUMENTS

As a special character, the single quote ("'") operates in the assembly process as a separating character. When the single quote precedes or follows a dummy argument, the single quote is deleted at expansion time. In its place, the real argument is substituted at the point where the single quote is deleted. When combining the single quote with a symbolic argument representing a numeric string, it is possible to generate informative labels. For example, consider the factorial example seen previously, and suppose it is now desired to label the factorial numbers as follows:

```
F1: .WORD 1
F2: .WORD 2
F3: .WORD 6
F4: .WORD 24
F5: .WORD 120
```

The macro definitions in Example 7.41 will generate this desired table with the respective labels. The table addresses are formed by appending the second argument of the macro label (L2) to the first argument of the label (L1) using L1'L2 in the label field of the macro. When TABLE is called and expanded, the desired result is found in Example 7.41c. To pass a numeric string as an argument, the unary operator backlash, "\", must precede the argument. When so used, the argument is treated as a numeric argument. In the macro TABLE, each numeral in the label F1,F2,... is then obtained. Remember that the number passed into the macro named LABEL is treated as a string argument. Hence, L2 (the number to be passed) cannot be updated in LABEL, because during macro expansion the characters representing the number, and not the number itself, are inserted. Therefore, two macros are necessary.

Example 7.41   Obtaining Variable Labels by Concatenation of Numeric Strings

a.

Macro Definition	Comments
.MACRO TABLE L1,L2	
LABEL L1,\L2	;PASS L2 AS A NUMERIC STRING
L2=L2+1	
.ENDM	
.MACRO LABEL L1,L2	
L1'L2: FACT=FACT*L2	;INSERT NUMERIC VALUE HERE
.WORD FACT	;USE NUMERIC VALUE HERE
.ENDM	

b.

Macro Call	Comments
•	
•	
•	
L2=1	;MAKE DIRECT ASSIGNMENTS
FACT=1	;BEFORE MACRO CALL
.REPT 5	
TABLE F,L2	
.ENDR	
•	
•	
•	

c. Macro Expansion

F1: .WORD 1
F2: .WORD 2
F3: .WORD 6
F4: .WORD 24
F5: .WORD 120

Example 7.42 illustrates how the apostrophe ("'") appends a character to the symbol R using the assembler directive .IRPC. This assembler directive appears next where d is a dummy argument, and "str" is the string of characters.

```
.IRPC d,str      { Heading
    •
    •            { Block of Code
    •            { To Be Repeated
    •
.ENDM            { Terminating
                   Statement
```

The .IRPC directive can be used in a repeat block. In the first copy, d is replaced by the first character of "str". In the second copy, d is replaced with the second character of "str", and so on. If no dummy argument is specified, the .IRPC directive is flagged with an error code in the assembly listing. In Example 7.42, the programmer is restoring registers R0, R1, R2, and R3 from the system stack. Note how the apostrophe separates the adjacent symbols in the argument list. During the macro expansion, the apostrophe is replaced with the appropriate string in each copy. What would happen if this macro statement was .IRPC X,0,1,2,3?

Example 7.42   Restoring Active Registers

a. Macro Definition
```
.IRPC X,0123
MOV (SP)+,R'X
.ENDM
```

b. Macro Expansion
```
    •
    •
    •
MOV (SP)+,R0
MOV (SP)+,R1
MOV (SP)+,R2
MOV (SP)+,R3
    •
    •
    •
```

7.15 SUMMARY

In this chapter, an in-depth view of programming at the conventional machine level is presented through assembly language programming. Here, the reader must master not only the syntax and semantics, but also grasp the essential distinction between assembly time and execution time. For example, at assembly time, variables may be expressions which are evaluated for assembly purposes (such as "ADDR+2" in Example 5.13). At execution time, however, ADDR+2 is not evaluated because the assembler has substituted ADDR+2 for binary object code.

An understanding of the process of assembly is important to good error-free programming. Assemblers first scan source statements to assign values to a symbol table. Later, another scan takes place to substitute mnemonics and symbols for opcodes and symbol table values. The ordering of these "binding" operations is essential. Binding cannot take place if the value is not yet known (defined) or is defined more than once. Knowing this, a programmer makes assignments early enough for error-free assembling. In this chapter, the following concepts should have been mastered:

1. Why assemblers are attractive to use.

2. The inherent power within an assembler to make programs clear and well-documented by the use of symbols, mnemonics, labels, and the rules of syntax which generate "standard" output.

3. How a two-pass assembler first generates a symbol table, and secondly performs a translation process between the symbol table and the mnemonic opcode table with the source program.

4. How to detect the subtle programming errors which frequently plague assembly language programmers.

A programmer now has the means to generate assembly language programs. The question of how well these programs are written, how clear they are, and whether they perform the desired task or not are matters to be addressed in the remaining chapters. Self-modifying code is programming in its worst form. Quality programming requires a thorough understanding of the concepts of structure and modularity. Exposure to such topics follows in the remaining chapters.

This chapter also focuses on macros. Most assembly language programmers would be happy just to master the defining and calling of macros. However, there is much more here than just macro definitions and expansions. Indeed, the reader will understand assembly language programming when:

1. The difference between symbolic addresses and their values is clear.

2. One writes error-free expressions.

3. Assembly language programs run the first time.

This chapter has devoted attention to the basic rules of syntax in assembly language programming. Making the assembler work rather than the programmer is often a matter of effective macro usage. Macros can save programming time, but only at the expense of memory and assembly time. Ill-defined macros (i.e., nested or recursive macros without terminators) can be very memory-expensive, if they assemble at all. Recognizing the difference between source statements for the assembly process and source statements for the execution process is vital. The following are important concepts for effective assembly language programming.

1. Macros are shorthand blocks of code that get substituted.

2. Macros are not separate code segments that get "called" like subroutines.

3. Macros are "substituted" for macro names at assembly time and not at execution time.

A crucial understanding of the differences between assembly time processes and run time processes must be gained. Several concepts examined in this chapter, such as the notion of an expression, sub-expressions, symbols, and symbolic parameters and their instances of assigned values, must be grasped within the framework of an assembly process. An assembly expression such as ADDR+1 is not the same as the machine instruction INC ADDR. The former is evaluated at assembly time, and the latter is executed at execution time.

7.16 KEY WORDS

absolute expression	dummy argument
assembly directive	execution time
assembly passes	expression
assembly process	forward reference
assembly time	literal
attribute	local set symbol
backward reference	location counter
conditional assembly	macro
delimiters	macro call

macro definition	rules of syntax
macro expansion	signed conditional branch
mnemonic	source program
nesting macros	source statements
object program	symbol table
parameter	symbolic address
phase error	symbolic expression
recursion	symbolic parameter
relative expression	undefined label
relocation	unsigned conditional branch
reserved character	variable symbols

7.17 SUGGESTED READING

Andrews, Michael. *Microprocessor Interfaces for Control and Instrumentation.* Englewood Cliffs, N.J.: Prentice-Hall, 1982.

> Pages 30–36 discuss some additional features about assemblers in general. The M6800 macro assembler which supports the 6809 is found on pages 117–128. Advanced programming concepts can be found in Chapter 5. This text focuses solely on the 6809 microprocessor and, hence, may be of limited value to assembly language programmers of other machines. However, the 6809 machine code is very similar to the mnemonics of the PDP-11 family including the addressing modes. It would be instructive to see how a microprocessor behaves with its CPU-limited computing resources.

Barron, D.W. *Assemblers and Loaders.* New York: American Elsevier, 1972.

> This short 61-page book quickly introduces the reader, through many easy-to-read examples about assemblers and how they work, to the notion of one-pass, two-pass, and meta-assemblers. The presentations, although brief, are self-contained explanations.

Campbell-Kelly, M. *Introduction to Macros.* New York: American Elsevier, 1973.

> Anyone who desires to use macros for implementing portable software ought to consult this short survey. Along with its illustrations of the uses of macros, the text also includes a brief coverage of the use of macros in high-level languages.

Caudill, P. "Using Assembly Coding to Optimize High-Level Language Programs." *Electronics*, February 1, 1979, pp. 121-124.

> This article describes why and how assembly coding can help speed up execution as well as reduce the number of instructions required in high-level language programs. Those who program general-purpose computers at the assembly language level will probably be writing system software which consists of compilers

and translators for high-level languages. This article identifies some of the techniques involved with generating better code.

Donovan, John J. *Systems Programming.* New York: McGraw-Hill, 1972.
If a programmer must generate an assembler from the start, this highly detailed discussion of how an assembler works should help. The focus is on algorithms and data bases; however, the text is illustrated with many examples, flowcharts, tables and programs. Pages 59–110 illustrate notions on searching and sorting in considerable depth. Pages 111–148 can help one to understand how to implement a macro processor. Detailed flowcharts illustrate the inner workings of a macro processor.

Eckhouse, Richard H., Jr., and Morris, L. Robert. *Minicomputer Systems: Organization, Programming, and Applications (PDP-11),* Englewood Cliffs, N.J.: Prentice-Hall, 1979.
Some interesting assembly language programming techniques are presented on pages 21–34. Here, self-modifying code is demonstrated. Similarly, the same program with and without self-modifying code with a good discussion can be found on pages 78–79 for the PDP-11. Minimal yet detailed coverage of macros and macro assemblers can be found on pages 112–119. The examples plunge into complicated detail without sufficient explanation. Read with caution.

Fisher, W.P. "Microprocessor Assembly Language Draft Standard." *Computer,* December, 1979, pp. 96–109.
A standard assembly language is proposed for small computers. The mnemonics of this language and its addressing modes are described in this article.

Gear, C. William. *Computer Organization and Programming.* New York: McGraw-Hill, 1980.
This text focuses on the IBM 360/370 series computers. However, Chapter 3 discusses the general principles of assembly language programming and contrasts them with system level programming. Detailed coverage of the pseudo-operations for such machines can be found in this chapter. Since the IBM 370 machines employ an assembler which differs considerably from others, it is instructive to review the assembler coverage for this machine and others on pages 138–150.

Gill, Arthur. *Machine and Assembly Language Programming of the PDP-11.* Englewood Cliffs, N.J.: Prentice-Hall, 1978.
Coverage on macros (pages 154–167) is brief, yet to the point. Numerous clear examples help, but explanations are short.

Kapps, Charles, and Stafford, Robert L. *Assembly Language for the PDP-11.* Boston, Mass.: Prindle, Weber & Schmidt, 1981.
This classroom textbook carefully builds complex concepts upon earlier material. It is well-organized and contains an extensive topical coverage with exercises for the beginning student as well as the professional. The main objective of this text is to help a student become proficient in assembly language programming. Examples in Chapters 1 through 4 support this claim. Chapter 9 provides an in-depth

coverage of macros and conditional assembly including repeat blocks. Many illustrative examples clearly explain much of the minute detail of MACRO-11. Motivation for using macros over loops and subroutines can be found on page 219.

Kent, William. "Assembler-Language Macroprogramming. A Tutorial Oriented Toward the IBM 360." *Computing Surveys*, Vol. 4, December, 1969, pp. 183–196.
This is a good introductory tutorial to the usage and implementation of macros in the IBM 360 assembler. The material includes attributes, global variables, and conditional assembly.

Leventhal, Lance. *6809 Assembly Language Programming*. Berkeley, CA: Osborne/McGraw-Hill, 1981.
More motivation for employing an assembler program instead of hand assembly can be found in the first chapter of this book including some disadvantages in Section 1.7. A myriad of details of assembly language programming of the 8-bit 6809 microprocessor consumes Chapters 2 through 10 of the remaining text. Later chapters cover very advanced material from tables and lists to stack programming and subroutines. Chapters 4 and 5 contain numerous assembly language programs.

Mano, M. Morris. *Computer System Architecture*, 2nd ed., Englewood Cliffs, N.J.: Prentice-Hall, 1982.
The extremely popular PDP-8 minicomputer, a classic von Neumann machine, opened the doors to a plethora of personal computers today. Chapter 6 examines the instruction mnemonics and the assembly language rules of this popular machine, and the material is covered with clarity.

PDP-11 MACRO-11 Language Reference Manual. Maynard, Mass.: Digital Equipment Corporation, 1980.
This is the authoritative reference for the MACRO-11 assembler. The reader should be familiar with the PDP-11 processor addressing modes and instruction set. The many features of MACRO-11 are described including source and command string control of assembly and listing functions, directives for conditional assembly and program sectioning, and user-defined and system macro libraries. The authors assert that the manual should only be used along with a system-specific user's guide as well as a linker or a task builder manual.

Struble, George W. *Assembler Language Programming: The IBM System/360 and 370*. Reading, Mass.: Addison-Wesley, 1975.
The notion of addressing of operands in assembler languages is critical to our understanding of this programming level. Pages 51-57 describe expressions, combinations of expressions, self-defining terms, and location counter reference. Although the text focuses on the rules of syntax for IBM 360/370 assemblers, many of the concepts carry directly over to many assemblers. An equally in-depth coverage of macro definitions and conditional assembly (again for the IBM OS assembler language) can be found on pages 375–387. The coverage of set symbols

and attributes describing local and global symbols can be found on pages 380–383.

Tannenbaum, Andrew S. *Structured Computer Organization.* Englewood Cliffs, N.J.: Prentice-Hall, 1976.

A brief coverage of macros including definitions, calls, expansions, and recursion can be found on pages 316–326. Some simple IBM 370 macros are compared with PDP-11 macros, but few examples can be found.

Wegner, Peter. *Programming Languages, Information Structures, and Machine Organization.* New York: McGraw-Hill, 1968.

General principles and concepts are emphasized in this reference, rather than any specific assembler. In fact, a strong theoretical treatment of assemblers can be found in this text. Readers desiring to expand their understanding to advanced topics can find the concepts of free and bound variables, table-driven programs, push-down definition, resource allocation, and assembly time operations scattered throughout the text. Pages 107–144 focus on assembler concepts. Theoretical coverage of macros is found in Sections 3.1 to 3.4. Some minor coverage of TRAC and GPM macro languages appears in other sections. A different perspective can be acquired from Wegner in comparison to most other references on macro assemblers.

Weller, Walter J. *Assembly Language Programming for Small Computers.* Lexington, Mass.: D.C. Heath, 1975.

This textbook covers the assembly language of Computer Automation's Alpha-Series minicomputers. The author has taken special care to ensure that the material covered maintains its generality of application to a wide range of mini-computers. Some examples of programs and subprograms in Chapter 8 attest to this. The instruction set of the Alpha Micro is markedly different from that of the PDP-11 family. Thus, the book serves as a contrast to that of the current textbook. Many of the examples are derived from the author's practical experiences with monitoring and data acquisition problems.

7.18 EXERCISES

7.1 Describe several functions of an assembler.

7.2 Does every assembly language source statement need a label? Which ones should?

7.3 A two-pass assembler accesses a table in both passes. What are those tables in each pass? Suppose that a symbol is not found in a table in either pass. What would the assembler do?

7.4 The ASR rounds down an odd number. How could we save the vacated bit?

7.5   Suppose that a 48-bit number is stored in registers R0, R2, and R5, with the most significant digits in R0 and the least significant digits in R5. Write a machine language program to execute the following.

a. An arithmetic left shift across all 48 bits.

b. An arithmetic right shift across all 48 bits.

c. A logical left shift across all 48 bits.

d. A logical right shift across all 48 bits.

7.6   Multiply two 8-bit positive integers using the ASL by repeated shifts and adds. Don't forget to initialize the carry flag if it is used.

7.7   32-bit signed numbers are stored in consecutive memory locations pointed to by R1. The first data word and every alternate word in memory pointed to by R1 contain the least significant sixteen bits of each 32-bit number. Write a program to add the first four 32-bit numbers together. The 32-bit sum should be found in memory just below the fourth operands. Do not be concerned with overflow. (Hint: Use R2 to point to the most significant bits of the 32-bit word. Add the least significant bits first.)

7.8   Which instruction pair will cause a branch in our computer for the following octal numbers?

a. CMP #77777, #177777
   BLT

b. CMP #77777, #177777
   BLO

7.9   Calculate the offsets needed for these branch instructions.

	Octal Location	Contents
a.	000102	COM R0
	000150	BR ?
b.	000102	BR ?
	000150	COM R0

7.10   Which languages are primarily descriptive? Which are primarily programming?

a. Machine languages

b. Microprogramming languages

c. Assembly languages

7.11 Describe at least five quality programming practices, even at the assembly level.

7.12 What address is in the PC after execution of each of these instructions? The location counter contains 000400 for the first word of the instruction.

a.   .−8   d.   BR .+10

                                      BR

b.   BNE .+2   e.   .−10.

c.   BR .0

7.13 Generate the octal code for the BNE instruction in the following instructions (assume LC=1000 at the BNE statement).

```
a.   LOOP:   CMP R0,R1
             MOV #10,SUM
             .BLKB 4
             BNE LOOP
b.   LOOP:   CLR R0
             ASL (R4)+
             .BLKW 2
             .BLKB 3
             BNE LOOP
```

7.14 The following code segments do *not* perform the same intended task in each case. Why?

```
a.   CLRB 2000(R0)+          CLRB 2000(R0)
                             INC R0
b.   MOV R2+4,R0             MOV R2,R0
                             ADD #4,R0
c.   MOV #100,R0             MOV 100,R0
d.   TEMP: .WORD 0           CLR TEMP
```

7.15 What is the difference between the following?

```
     SIX:   .WORD    6
            ADD      SIX,R
and
            SIX=6
            ADD      #SIX,R0
```

7.16 What is the appropriate quantity added to the location counter when each instruction below is scanned?

a. ADD   e. .BLKW 2

b. SUB#   f. .BLKB 6

c. MOV   g. .ENABL

d. MOV#   h. .END

7.17 A diehard desires to use the program in Example 7.6, despite its self-modifying code! He knows that the program, once self-modified because the code was executed, cannot be rerun until the second word of the instruction labeled ADDR is reset or initialized. Explain why the simple initializing statement

MOV   #A,ADDR+2

does not reestablish the instruction offset word (program location 002010) to its initial value of 000034.

7.18 In Example 7.7, the table of values for "A" begins immediately after the program. Answer the following questions.

a. What are the two octal words for CMP #A+18.,R1?

b. What is the octal code and its meaning in location 001004?

7.19 Division can be accomplished by repeated subtraction of the powers of the divisor, keeping a count of the number of subtractions at each level.

Example: To divide 221_{10} by 10, first try to subtract powers of 10 until a non-negative value is obtained, counting the number of subtractions at each power from then on. The result of the following step is negative,

$$221$$
$$-1000$$

negative result

so go to next lower power (count for $10^3=0$). The result of

$$221$$
$$-100$$

is positive so count for $10^2 = 2$. Now the result of the following step is negative,

$$21 \text{ count} = 2$$
$$-100$$

so reduce the power. The result of this next step is positive (increment count).

$$\begin{array}{r} 21 \\ -10 \\ \hline \end{array}$$

positive result

But the following step generates a negative result.

$$\begin{array}{r} 1 \text{ count} = 2 \\ -10 \\ \hline \end{array}$$

negative result

Now there is no lower power, so the remainder is 1 and the procedure stops. The quotient is 022_{10}, and the remainder is 1_{10}.

Using the method described above, write an assembly language program to perform unsigned division. Assume that R3, R2, R1, and R0 contain the divisor, quotient, dividend, and remainder, respectively.

7.20 Generate a short program to interpret the "∗" as the comment field delimiter instead of the ";" in MACRO-11.

7.21 List the several meanings of the "." in an assembler. Are any hazardous usages possible?

7.22 The symbols, "=", ".", and ":", appear to accomplish the same end results. That is, an "assignment" is made. Contrast the methods with regard to the assembly process. How can phase errors occur? How can they be prevented?

7.23 Assemblers may be one-pass or two-pass assemblers. What implications to programming at the assembly level arise? How can a one-pass assembler process forward references?

7.24 Explain why it is relatively easy for an assembler to detect syntax errors. Can an assembler ever be made to detect logical programming errors?

7.25 Why is self-modifying code discouraged? Let's say that our memory space is very precious (as it often is) and that a self-modifying program is faster and shorter than any other program performing the same task. Even in this situation, why is self-modifying code discouraged?

7.26 What is the chief distinction between .WORD and .BLKW, other than the name?

7.27 Which errors in Examples 4.17, 4.18, 4.19, 4.20, and 4.21 will be detected by the MACRO-11 assembler?

```
                    .WORD 2
                    .ENDM
```

7.28 Describe the difference between a macro call and a macro definition.

7.29 Suppose the macro, SWAPIT, in Example 7.12 is called as follows: "SWAPIT #10,#12,TEMP". Will the expansion be correctly assembled?

7.30 What is the difference between an argument and a parameter of a macro?

7.31 What precautions must be taken with LABEL in the macro below?

```
                .MACRO   LOAD   LABEL
        LABEL:  .WORD    0
                .WORD    1
                .WORD    2
                .ENDM
```

7.32 The TTY data and status register in the PDP-11 are addressable as 177566 and 177564, respectively. Generate a macro to write a single ASCII character to the TTY.

7.33 Generate a macro to perform double-precision addition by filling in the missing entries below (ignore overflow).

```
                .MACRO ADDDP X,Y
                ADD X,Y
                ADD        ,Y+2
```

7.34 Generate a macro to perform double-precision subtraction (ignore overflow).

7.35 What are the decimal and octal values for the following expressions? Assume the following direct assignment statements precede these expressions in the assembly program. What are the values if no direct assignments are made?

Direct assignment statements: A = 2, B = 3, and C = 7

a. A+B*C   d. <A/2>+<B-C>

b. A*B+C   e. <A-B/2>+<B-C/2>

c. <A*B>+<B*C>   f. C/A+2

7.36 How many bytes or words will the following macro calls reserve?

Macro Definition

```
            .MACRO    TABLE        STACK,S1,S2,S3,S4,S5,S6
            .NARG     N
STACK:      .WORD     S1,S2,S3,S4
            .BLKW     N-1
            .BYTE     S4,S5,S6
            .BLKB     1
            .ENDM
```

Macro Calls

a.   TABLE TOP,4,6,8,2,12.,16,19

b.   TABLE BOTTOM,1,6,2,3

c.   TABLE LIST

d.   TABLE ALL,1,2,3,4,18.,177650

7.37   Phase errors will occur in the source statements below. Identify them and reorder the statements to eliminate these phase errors.

```
            .BLKB K-D
            .WORD 4
D:          .BLKW I+J
            SUB R0,R1
            R0 =%0
            R1 =%1
             J =.+10
             K =I
             A =I+K
             I =4
            .BLKB A
            .END
```

7.38   Explain why a macro is, in fact, merely textual substitution code.

7.39   Find the errors in the following macros.

a.   ```
     MACRO   X,Y
     MOVE   X,Y
     .ENDM
     ```

b.   ```
     .MACRO    X,Y
     MOVE      X,X
     .ENDM
     ```

```
c.              .MACRO   MULT   A,B,C
                CLR C
        AGAIN:  DEC B
                BMI      OUT
                ADD      A,C
                BR       AGAIN
d.      .MACRO  ADDB
        CLR C
        ADD     A,B
        MOVE    B,C
        .ENDM
e.      .MACROSUM        A,B,C
        ADD     A,B
        MOV     B,C
        .END
```

7.40 Describe four conditional test types.

7.41 The conditional directive, ".IF NE,t", tests if t does not equal zero by comparing t with zero. What conditional directive can test whether t does not equal 3?

7.42 Which conditional assembly tests in MACRO-11 must be used inside a macro definition? Why?

7.43 What precautions should be taken with labels inside a conditional macro block?

7.44 Often we desire to know the number of times a macro is called. For example, a macro should print a message on a teletype when it is first called. Any subsequent call of that specific macro would not need this message. It would just waste paper. A conditional assembly statement which tests the number of calls could delete the message statements in subsequent calls. Generate a macro to print "HELLO" the first time called only.

7.45 Modify the code in Example 7.32 to start the table with −3 instead of 0.

7.46 What is a variable symbol? Describe one type found in MACRO-11. Why are they important?

7.47 What is a declared local symbol?

7.48 Describe the effects of the expression, "A=A−6", on an assembly program with respect to both the assembly process and the execution process.

7.49 What effect does relocation have on absolute addresses as well as on relative addresses?

7.50 Generate a recursive macro to multiply the contents of memory location, ALPHA, by 2^N. Assume that the datum size is a word and N is a positive integer less than 15. Do not worry about the case where ALPHA is zero and becomes zero after shifting.

7.51 Generate a recursive macro using the conditional, NE, to build a table of N words. Assume that the first word in the table is 000000.

7.52 Generate a recursive macro using the conditional, NE, to build a table of N bytes. Assume that the first byte is 000.

7.53 Modify your recursive macro definition in the two previous problems to "label" the top of each table, "TABLE".

7.54 Modify Problems 7.50 and 7.51 to label each datum in the table. Let the first datum be labeled 0, the second 1, and so on.

7.55 Generate a macro called BRANCH which assembles BR DIST if the relative distance to DIST is less than 255 bytes (decimal) and executes the instruction JMP DIST otherwise. Use a conditional block with .IFF. Do not consider forward branches.

7.56 What does the following macro do?

```
.MACRO CLEAN X
.REPT 2
ROR X
.ENDR
.IF LT,X
.EVEN
.IFF
.ODD
.ENDC
.ENDM
```

7.57 Generate macros to simulate the .EVEN and .ODD assembler directives without using .EVEN and .ODD.

7.58 What two assembler source statements must always occur in pairs?

7.59 The macro MULT computes the product of X and Y, placing the result in Z. Expand the macro and determine if any illegal assembly occurs. If so, modify the definition to be correctly assembled.

```
          .MACRO    MULT    X,Y,Z
          CLR   Z
LOOP:     DEC   Y
          BMI   DONE
          ADD   X,Z
          BR    LOOP
DONE:     .ENDM
```

7.60 Assume that a call is made and expand the following macro code.

a. Definition

```
          CHAR='A
LIST:
          .REPT 26.
          .BYTE CHAR
          CHAR=CHAR+1
          .ENDM
```

b. Definition

```
          .MACRO REPEAT X
          REPEAT X
          .WORD X
          .ENDM
```

7.61 Example 7.38 illustrates a "singly linked list." An array of addresses with each word containing the address of the next word is called a "circular list." Generate a repeat block for a circular list of 100 addresses.

7.62 Expand the following macro call. (Hint: \Y passes a number into the DEC macro. Also, DEC is a valid PDP-11 machine language instruction, but the symbol DEC in the macro name takes precedence.)

Macro Definition

```
          .MACRO CNT X,Y        .MACRO DEC X,Y
X'Y:      .WORD Y               CNT X,\Y
          .ENDM                 Y=Y+1
                                .ENDM
```

Macro Call

```
          N=0
          .REPT 4
          DEC A,N
          .ENDR
```

7.63 Expand the repeat blocks shown below.

```
a.              N=0
        A:      .REPT 4
                .WORD 0
                N=N+2
                .WORD A+N
                .ENDR

b.              NUM='0
        TABLE:  .REPT 12
                .BYTE NUM
                NUM=NUM+1
                .ENDR

c.              .IRP LOC,<A,B,C,D>
                MOV (R6)+,LOC
                .ENDR

d.              .IRPC LOC,ABCD
                MOV (R6)+,LOC'
                .ENDR
```

7.64 Generate a macro to do the following with a general-purpose register. (Note that, as it stands, this instruction is illegal.)

ASLB 400(Rn)+

7.65 The PDP-8 was a very popular scientific laboratory computer. However, its 12-bit word length often slowed the user down (because double-precision operations had to be employed). Impressed by its popularity, you have decided to reintroduce a 16-bit version of this machine called the PDP-8X with the following instructions.

a. LDA M   LOAD MEMORY INTO ACCUMULATOR A
b. STA M   STORE A INTO MEMORY
c. ADA M   ADD A TO MEMORY, RESULT IN A
d. SUBA M   SUBTRACT A FROM MEMORY, RESULT IN A
e. JMPZ M   JUMP TO M IF A IS 0
f. GOTO M   JUMP TO M UNCONDITIONALLY
g. ISZ M   INCREMENT AND SKIP IF M IS 0
h. CMA   1'S COMPLEMENT OF A
i. RAR   ROTATE "A" RIGHT ONE BIT

To "test" this machine, you decide to emulate it on a PDP-11. In emulation tests, you use several benchmark programs which have known performance on other computers. To emulate the PDP-8X, you generate macros for each instruction of the PDP-8X in the assembly language of the PDP-11. Generate a macro for each instruction above.

7.66   You want to make sure that the PDP-8X can execute every instruction of the PDP-11 (although more than one PDP-8X instruction may be needed to do so). Write a PDP-11 program to multiply two numbers. Use the macros you generated in the previous problem. Can it be done?

7.67   What mechanisms exist to make a variable length macro?

7.68   Generate a nested or recursive macro definition to evaluate the expression, "$\ldots((((a+bc)d+e)\,f+g)h+i)\ldots$" when called.

Chapter 8

THE OPERATING SYSTEM MACHINE LEVEL

Science is a good servant but a bad master, a good method for investigating and manipulating the material world, but no method at all for deciding what to do with the knowledge and power acquired thereby.

—M. D. Aeschliman

And here I stand with all my lore.
No wiser than I was before.

—Johann Wolfgang von Goethe

Maybe Computer Science should be in the College of Theology.

—R. S. Barton

Wisdom is knowing what to do with what you know.

—J. Winter Smith

8.1 CHAPTER OBJECTIVES

In this chapter, we examine the next level of machine organization for a computer system. All of the building blocks we have studied so far support this third-level abstraction: the *operating system machine level*. We suggest that a computer actually represents several abstract machine levels as in Figure 8.1. We are now most concerned with level 3. A level 3 machine uses an operating system running on a level 2 machine. The assembly language programs we generate at level 2 represent activity at the conventional machine level. But these level 2 programs, just like level 3 programs, are interpreted and, in fact, run at level 1 or the microprogramming machine level. Because levels of machines operate upon lower levels, a machine at any level (other than the lowest) can be looked upon as a virtual machine.

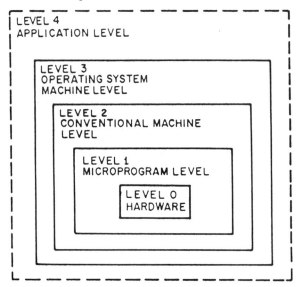

Figure 8.1 Machine Levels

Barron[1] contends that it is hard to tell what an operating system (OS) is, but we will recognize it when we see it. To a large extent, the ambiguity lies between what makes up an operating system and what services it provides. However, its primary goal, that of allowing users to accomplish data processing tasks, is well-known. The operating system primarily deals with *processes* (programs under execution), using machine resources called processors and memories. As such, the operating system takes a process through its various states using *commands* appropriate to this third level.

An operating system employs a command language by which users can address the system and indicate tasks to be performed. Its syntax specifies legal statements while its semantics specifies the meaning of the legal statements. The interface between the user and his or her computer system is a command system composed of statements, data structures, and complexes of modules. The interface contains, among other capabilities, control characters by which users at a terminal may perform editing tasks (create macros, delete characters, substitute parameters, etc.). In fact, a user may view the command language as a definition of the operating system's functional capabilities. The

---

[1]D. W. Barron, *Computer Operating Systems* (London: Chapman and Hall, 1971).

command system may be an integral component of the operating system or a separate processor. JCL/360 and the UNIX shell commands are representative of these cases, respectively.

In this chapter, the building blocks of level 3 will be identified. Many of these building blocks can be viewed as virtual subsystems (e.g., virtual memory, virtual I/O, etc.). For the most part, virtual I/O and virtual memory systems will be studied. Why do we classify such subsystems as virtual? A user at level 3 is no longer concerned with the intricacies of assembly language, machine language, or microprogramming language. The level 3 user employs "operating system" instructions which command activity of these virtual subsystems. (It is true, however, that these operating system instructions may be macros built from assembly language instructions or C-language statements.) In fact, operating system activity is often concerned with managing the systems (I/O devices, memory units, buffers, etc.), rather than strictly interpreting the operating system machine level instructions.

8.2 WHAT IS AN OPERATING SYSTEM?

A computer system at any given moment is typically processing several programs. In fact, these programs may be level 3, level 2, and even level 1 programs (if microprogramming is allowed on the machine). Such multiprogramming activity occurs with a memory composition of programs at one or more levels as shown in Figure 8.2. Notice that a user program at level 3 may require the operating system of a level 2 program, while that level 2 activity relies on an interpretation via the microprogram level 1. All of these processes must be handled simultaneously. In this chapter, we will study management topics of processes. The following questions are useful for consideration:

1. How is memory dynamically allocated among users?

2. How are several I/O devices such as line printers, disks, CRTs, and buffer areas allocated?

3. How are shared resources managed?

4. How are HLL users serviced?

5. How are I/O mechanical and electronic errors detected, and how is I/O traffic maintained?

6. How are computer system resources controlled?

7. How are shared data (leg multiple programs) managed?

8. How is operation caused to flow smoothly and without fatal interruption?

9. How are two or more concurrently executing programs kept out of each other's way?

10. How is an endless loop detected and terminated (possibly by interruption)?

The answer to all of these questions is "by the operating system." (In an introductory treatment of operating systems, it is impossible to answer all of these questions.) Operating systems may be simple or complex, depending on their environment. In the LSI-11, the RT-11 single-user operating system and DOS-11 (disk operating system) are modest versions of operating systems. With the IBM 370 series and the VAX, much more difficult tasks need to be handled. The Honeywell computer uses a MULTICS and GCOS operating system.

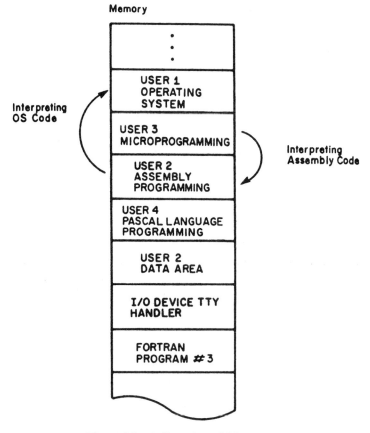

Figure 8.2   A Snapshot of Memory

The *operating system* in a VAX computer can be VAX/VMS or UNIX. In microcomputers, CP/M (a control program for microprocessors) MDOS are common. The list of operating systems is as long as the number of available computers. As yet, no universal or "meta" operating system has been discovered, dramatizing the fact that operating systems are still very machine-environment sensitive (and the ultimate computing machine still eludes us).

An operating system can be considered a collection of procedures and programs that performs system services and attempts to optimize the resources of the system. System services control resources available to processes to provide the communication among the processes and to perform the necessary coordination among input/output operations. Even though an operating system uses system services, primarily for users in the interests of managing I/O and memory, the same services are available for general use and can provide techniques to develop application programs. System services should become available on a restricted basis only to privileged users in order to protect the performance of the system and the integrity of other user processes. An operating system is like a traffic officer directing the efficient flow of programs through a computer system. Whereas the control unit of a computer represents a traffic officer of sorts in hardware by directing physical yet primitive resources (such as a register, ALU, counter, etc.), an operating system directs larger subsystems such as on-line memory, secondary storage, one or more CPU(s), and I/O interfaces. Consider the operating system as a police dispatcher managing activity at the level 3 or operating system machine level.

The snapshot of memory found in Figure 8.2 could just as easily represent the snapshot of user activity that could be found on a VAX-11/780 system depicted in Figure 8.3. Note the variety of devices representing machine resources at this third level. Who manages such resources? An operating system residing in a VAX would supervise its own operations, automatically calling in any programs, routines, or procedures, as well as data needed for the continuous throughput of all the jobs requested of the machine at any given time. An operating system even performs the start-up procedures for each job, instead of requiring a user to "restart" the computer each time a new job or process is encountered.

The VAX computer system depicted in Figure 8.3 consists of both software and hardware components. The hardware shown refers to physical components, CRT, memory, buses, and CPU. The software, however, refers to programs and files and is not easily portrayed in a figure. Nevertheless, as we already know, system software does exist. The purpose of any operating system (as part of the system software) is to execute legal user commands and allow the user full access to hardware and software resources provided by a computer system. For instance, the operating system allows a user to send text to the printer, read and process information from the TTY, or display information on the CRT. While doing this, the operating system performs internal chores such as managing the computer's memory space and disk space. Once a user enters into a dialogue with the operating system, the operating system activates any legal desired system services. A user-generated applications program that completes its activity causes the operating system to regain control and wait for a future command. An operating system could be viewed as an obedient servant ready to execute commands while managing the computer's resources.

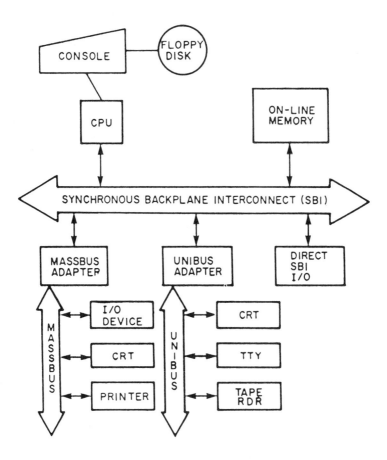

Figure 8.3   VAX-11/780 Organizational Structure

8.2.1 CLASSES OF OPERATING SYSTEM PROGRAMS

Any operating system uses three basic elements or programs: control programs, processing programs, and data management programs. These three classes of programs support the three principal tasks of any operating system: job control, program development, and data management. The *control programs* provide for the automatic control of the computer resources and serve as the supervisor or traffic officer. The control programs attempt to minimize necessary operator intervention while facilitating the orderly and efficient flow of jobs. In every operating system, some type of job control language (JCL) is used, although its style, format, and complexity will vary greatly. For our purposes, a job is synonymous with a process.

The *processing programs* may consist of language translators or interpreters which compile or interpret source programs. The PDP-11 MACRO-11 assembler is an example of such a processing program as is a FORTRAN compiler. Other examples of processing programs are service programs, utilities, and the I/O handlers seen earlier. These types of programs are necessary to accomplish the input/output that occurs.

The *data management programs* organize as well as control access to data. A data management program might specify the memory as well as the I/O resources necessary to supervise the allocation of data space, for instance. Data management programs relieve the programmer from having to code many detailed tasks, such as protecting one's data space from inadvertent use, organizing the data space, or transferring data. With regard to the later task, some functional overlap with processing programs is possible.

All of these programs and services invoked by the user via operating system commands depend on an organization of basic building blocks. Kernel instructions (e.g., in the UNIX shell) and certain macros are important, if not vital, here. At level 3, the basic building blocks include CPUs, data channels (or I/O processors), device controllers, I/O devices, and memory systems. In the next sections, these basic building blocks which comprise the computer organization at level 3 will be studied.

These blocks are the actual physical devices or resources of a computer system. An operating system supervises, manages, and/or otherwise controls or allocates physical space to a user without the user's knowledge. The programmer is concerned with the logically created data structures (files, records, data bases) and logically created devices (virtual I/O devices). Hence, such topics are not normally found in a text about computer organization. To the HLL programmer, significant entities are part of the logical world of variables and records arranged in various organizations as arrays, trees, sequential/indexed, etc., which are topics for a programming text. At the operating system level, significant entities are files, devices, programs, and processes (instances of execution of programs).

8.2.2   THE SIZE OF AN OPERATING SYSTEM

The operating system size is directly related to the number of I/O devices and their complexity (a TTY is much simpler than a line printer), the number of concurrent users, and the desired throughput of a system, the complexity of the file system, and the different types of jobs and choices the user is given. For example, is it limited or general use; uni- or multi-programmed, etc. RT-11 is a small operating system because it is single-user based. CP/M is a very small operating system. It runs on a microcomputer, has limited concurrent tasking (tasking is a system function, e.g., to specify an input or output operation), and recognizes that a microcomputer's main memory may be extremely small. CP/M is built *not* to consume valuable space. As a result, CP/M can only do so much. Far more instructions (operating system commands) can be found in 370/OS, VAX/VMS, or UNIX. However, much more main memory must be set aside for these.

If the memory space is available and high speed is ultimately desired, a memory-resident operating system is used. Here, all programs, subroutines, procedures, macros, and utility/handler programs are resident in main memory. Since all operating system programs have been preloaded, response to any request no longer depends on a reload of some operating system program from disk. If speed can be sacrificed or main memory is just too small, a disk-resident operating system may be used. Only those parts of the operating system are loaded as needed into main memory. Resident in main memory at all times is a small nucleus which loads other procedures from the disk as needed. For example, the CP/M operating system for small computers has routines that interpret OS commands and remain resident to main memory. These routines consist of built-in or permanent commands. Interpretive routines also reside in a user's disk for transient commands so that main memory is not totally consumed by operating system software. A user program would then contain instructions or commands to the operating system to call upon the resident routines.

8.2.3   PROCESS STATES

About 1964, the designers of the MULTICS system introduced the useful notion of a process to describe much of the operating system activity. Any process undergoes a series of discrete states caused by various events. Figure 8.4 depicts a state transition diagram for a single process. A *running* process currently is using a processor. A *ready* process could use a CPU if a CPU were available. A *blocked* process is waiting for some event before it can proceed. It is important to realize that several processes may be in various states in a computer. For example, a DMA processor may not be ready to transfer blocks of data until the starting address and count are established. When so established, the DMA processor is "ready." When the transfer takes place, the DMA process is "running."

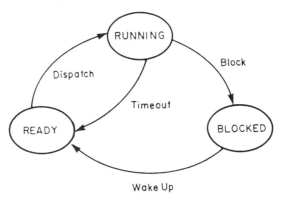

Figure 8.4 Process State Transition Diagram

An operating system maintains ready and blocked lists to ensure that the CPU is never idle. When first admitted, a process enters the bottom of the ready list. As earlier processes are completed, the next process on the ready list enters the run state (i.e., the process is given to a CPU), thus making a state transition from ready to running. Assigning the CPU to a ready process is called *dispatching*, and the operating system element performing this activity is called a dispatcher. A process that attempts to capture a CPU for a long period will be returned to the ready list. Hardware via an interrupting clock times every process allowing a specific time interval or quantum a slice.

A running process may also exit the running state by requesting some input/output activity. At this moment, the process voluntarily relinquishes the CPU and, in effect, blocks itself and enters the blocked state. (There are other ways to be blocked.) Upon completion of the I/O activity for the blocked process, the process enters the ready state. Of all the state transitions, the only state transition a user can initiate is a block.

An operating system uses a process control block (PCB) to capture process information such as (1) current state, (2) unique name/identifier, (3) scheduling priority, (4) pointers to process's memory, and (5) pointers to resources allocated to the process. The PCB is a data structure defining for the operating system key information about the process.

Among many activities possible with a process, some of the most likely operations include:

1. Creating a process
2. Dispatching a process
3. Destroying a process
4. Blocking a process
5. Waking up a process
6. Suspending a process
7. Resuming a process

It is possible for a process to spawn a new process. The created process is called the *child process*. Can you guess what the creating process is called?[2]

Processes, once destroyed, are removed from the computer, their PCBs are erased, allocated resources are returned to an "available state," and any knowledge of such processes (found in system lists or tables) is purged. Destroying a process is harsher than suspending a process. A suspended process normally returns to a resumed process very quickly. Suspension may occur because the priorities override the current process (CPU and/or primary memory need to make room for a higher priority process). Suspension and resumption are determined by many factors, including CPU scheduling algorithms.

8.2.4   PROCESSOR SCHEDULING

It is important in a multiprogramming environment to have a process running at all times to achieve maximum CPU utilization. The process ready list is one of many lists managed by the operating system. *Device* lists (lists of processes waiting for a specific device) may be maintained for each of the I/O devices in a computer system. Maintaining high system throughput requires a careful load balance among the CPU(s) and the several I/O devices. Algorithms designed to achieve maximum throughput realistically assume that process execution is a cyclic affair of CPU execution and I/O servicing. Bursts of CPU execution alternate with bursts of I/O servicing; however, measured durations of CPU bursts suggest a frequency curve much like that shown in Figure 8.5. Strategies depend on such histograms. Typically, CPU activity has a very large number of short bursts and a very small number of long bursts.

---

[2]A parent process.

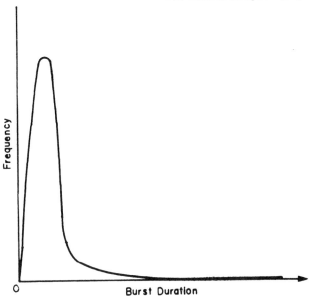

Figure 8.5 Histogram of CPU Burst Times

Two schedulers are often used, a long-term scheduler (most likely to handle the introductio⌐ of processes to the system) and a short-term scheduler (to select between ready processes in primary memory for execution). This is sometimes called macro and micro-scheduling, respectively. Long-term scheduling occurs minutes apart while short-term scheduling may occur as often as a few milliseconds apart. Some operating systems also have an intermediate scheduler, while others may have only one scheduler. All scheduling algorithms attempt to maximize CPU utilization and throughput while minimizing turnaround, waiting, and/or response time, even though these valid objectives are mutually impossible.

8.3 TWO VIEWS OF AN OPERATING SYSTEM

An operating system is a collection of system programs and system calls. A user views the operating system more as a collection of system programs. An operating system programmer primarily sees the system calls. The programmer sees only physical resources and devices that are to be made available to a user by converting them to logical entities. A user interfaces to the operating system mainly via the *command interpreter*, whose primary function is to acquire the next user command, interpret it, and initiate the action specified.

A user is more likely to work with one of many system programs (file modification/manipulation, status information, programming language support, program load/execute, and applications programs).

The command interpreter, also called a control card interpreter, command line interpreter, or shell (as in UNIX), runs at the initiation of a user job or when the user first logs into a time-sharing system. User commands at level 3 create, list, delete, execute, print, copy, and manipulate files, and so on. In a non-interactive environment, control cards often generate the commands, while in an interactive environment, commands may be generated via a terminal by the user.

Because operating systems are primarily event-driven, the operating system programmer structures an operating system to be interrupt-driven. Events are commonly signaled to the operating system by the onset of an interrupt. If, in fact, no users need responses, no jobs exist, and no I/O devices request service, the operating system will remain absolutely idle. Interrupts to the operating system may be derived from system calls, I/O device interrupts, or program errors (which may or may not cause abnormal termination of a process).

System calls are short code segments that implement some desired action. Such calls may initiate normal/abnormal termination of processes, request status (perhaps states of various responses such as available memory or time of day), and request additional resources (more memory or an I/O service).

Because of the asynchronous nature and speed disparity of I/O devices, I/O activity is often initiated and its completion noted by an I/O interrupt. Two kinds of service are likely. Upon initiation of I/O, the operating system may either do nothing else but wait for I/O completion before returning to the user process or, without waiting, the operating system may immediately return control to the user process. Each method has obvious advantages and disadvantages.

8.4   THE RT-11 OPERATING SYSTEM

The RT-11 operating system consists of a monitor/executive program for system control and supervision, several device handlers, a variety of utility programs for program/data creation and manipulation, and, finally, the interfaces necessary to support several programming language processes. Within the RT-11 operating system can be found a device handler for each of the PDP-11 supported hardware devices. Among the several programming language processors, RT-11 supports BASIC, FORTRAN, Pascal, APL, and others. The utility within RT-11 covers a range of resources. These programs allow a user to create and edit text, maintain other programs, as well as locate user-programming errors. Some utility programs available with the RT-11 operating system include:

1. An *editor*, which helps the user create and modify textual material. As with many editors, this editor can be used not only for creating an actual computer program, but also writing a letter for any other text the user wishes to create.

2. A *file maintenance program*, which assists a user in manipulating and maintaining programs and data. These programs help the user transfer files between devices, update them, and delete them.

3. A *debugging program* to uncover and correct errors in a user's program. Only syntactical errors can be uncovered, however.

4. A *librarian*, which assists the user in storing and retrieving frequently invoked programming routines.

5. A *linking program*, which converts a user's object module into the format suitable for loading and execution.

6. A *source comparison program*, which compares two ASCII files and outputs any differences to the user's specified output device.

7. A *dump program*, which outputs to a console or line printer all or any part of a file, an octal word, byte, or ASCII characters.

A language processor is a translating program (such as MACRO-11) which a user invokes to process a source program. In RT-11, a language processor exists for any programming language supported by the system. Both high-level and machine-level language processors may exist and even co-exist in main memory.

The PDP-11 computer main memory must contain at least part of the RT-11 operating system (namely, the monitor) at all times. The process of transferring an RT-11 monitor to main memory is called *bootstrapping the system*. In a PDP-11, this bootstrapping process is the only system operation required of a user at the operator's console. Otherwise, user activity no longer requires console interaction. User action with the PDP-11 now takes place mainly with keyboard and CRT interface. A file created by a user has a unique name that is composed of both a file name and file type. The file name and file type can be found in a volume directory which will identify the name, size, and creation date of each file residing in a specific volume and date of last update. Any operations performed that affect the contents of a volume will be directly reflected in a volume directory change. In order to provide the user with security against inadvertently destroying files, the RT-11 operating system provides a protection feature which requires the user to confirm certain system commands that might otherwise erase important information. These extra verification steps help to reduce inadvertent file purging.

As with the RT-11 monitor, any monitoring invokes a set of English command words to help a user quickly grasp its command language. Also, to expedite program creation, commands may exist either in a long format or a short format. In the long format the system should print prompting messages to the user. The long format obviously helps the user become familiar with the commands. Once familiarity is gained, a user may choose to resort to the briefer format. The general format of a command statement consists of a command, input, and output.

1. Command (Option): The first expression must be a command a user desires to initiate. Options are available to alter normal operation in case the default mechanism is not desired.

2. Input (Option): The next expression must be a device and file name serving as input information to be used as a result of the command operation. The current system volume serves as a default input device if not specified. A user must consistently indicate other volumes desired for input, as well as the file names and types of each input file.

3. Output (Option): A user must specify the device and file name as output information as a result of the command string. The current system volume also serves as a default output device. A user must explicitly indicate volumes for output as well as the file names and file types of the output types to be created.

Example 8.1 lists some of the RT-11 commands. These monitor commands are typical of monitor commands found in many computers. They assist the system user in managing the resources in any computer system.

Example 8.1   Some RT-11 Monitor Commands

ASSIGN	Changes a device physical name to a logical name.
DIRECTORY	Prints a list of user files in the current volume.
INITIALIZE	Clears a directory to ensure that enough room exists in current volume for new files.
SHOW	Prints a status of all current logical device name assignments.

8.5   FILE MANAGEMENT

A machine operating at level 3 manipulates "data structures" called files, which are, in fact, possibly homogeneous as well as logical collections of data elements. Arrays, lists, and queues are typical multi-element data structures. They are homogeneous, although not necessarily logical. They are commonly found in both high-level and assembly language programming. Collections of multi-element data which are not always homogeneous, but which are logical, are called *records*. Any record is in fact a logical data item in its own right. A record is characterized by its size, type, and initial value, and these character- istics are grouped to form a composite data structure. A record or file as a logical entity must be capable of being manipulated on the basis only of the knowledge of its structure.

Similar to the accessing requirements of queues described in Chapter 7, a record and file will also require sequences of instructions, offsets, and pointers to access the elements within them. We have seen that an array can be manipulated with the indexed addressing mode to step through elements of the array sequentially. The circular buffer, useful to pass information between two or more I/O routines, effectively uses the autoincrement and autodecre- ment forms of addressing. Records and files have similar useful addressing mechanisms. The mechanism, however, is not a mode, per se, as with address- ing modes in machine instructions. Rather, addressing, or more appropriately, manipulating records and files is accomplished with virtual instructions.

As we study file manipulation, we need to examine the structure of records and files. We identify a file as a basic data structure at level 3 because the user typically manipulates a collection of many data elements rather than a single character, queue, or stack. In fact, a user might be creating a new assembly program. The assembly program a programmer creates can be regarded as a file to an operating system. Of course, a file may also be strictly data. A data structure common to an inventory system might consist of the location of the warehouse, the supervisor's name, the time of day, and the collection of items stored in aisle 5, for example. This data structure might exist in several logical records, one record for each aisle in the warehouse. A sequence of these logical records could then be grouped into a file. If each record is exactly the same physical length, fixed length records are maintained, thus simplifying matters. Of course, not all records of a file need to be of the same length, in which case they are called *variable length records* as opposed to *fixed length records*.

8.5.1 FILE TYPES

Some files may be dedicated to a particular I/O device, mainly because the file structure lends itself to the unique property of that I/O device. We might have disk files, drum files, and keyboard files. Modern practice tends to separate a file from the storage device. Thus there is not a "disk file" but a file that first happens to be stored on a disk at this time, but could be stored on a tape, or on MBM, or in RAM pseudo-disk if that were "handy." This is the important abstraction point of device-independent I/O. For example, suppose a file called KYBD was designed. Since a CRT contains 80 columns, the file might consist solely of 80-character strings. Whenever the operating system *READ* instruction is executed on this file, the contents of the next keystroke are read into memory. Notice how the records would naturally contain 80-character strings and each record would, therefore, represent a screen line. (Note: The 80-character string length is an artificial instruction.) The main memory buffer, however, would store the contents of more than one line, since line reading is very slow. In fact, the entire screen may have been placed in the buffer before a user calls the KYBD file. Then the main memory resident KYBD file desired by the user could be copied into another buffer called the user's buffer in main memory, thus making more effective use of the KYBD reader, its file system, CPU, and the user's buffer in main memory.

The intimate operations involved with first reading a line and subsequently transferring it into a buffer is of no concern to an HLL programmer. His or her instruction is a simple READ of some file. However, the level 2 programmer implementing this READ operation would have to know much about the I/O device and main memory (e.g., a level 2 programmer works with assembly language instructions to set/clear control/status bits in an I/O register). These disparate considerations characterize activity at the different virtual machine levels.

A file type can be further characterized by its intent or function. Files may be programs, data, or both. Program files can be in source or object code. Source code can be FORTRAN, Pascal, Ada, BASIC, macros, etc. Object code can be compiled (from Pascal, FORTRAN, etc.) or interpreted (from BASIC). Furthermore, a file can be temporary (user code still in development), in which case it is called a working file, or a file can be a backup or a permanent file. Various operating systems denote file types in different ways. However, BAS, COM, FOR, and OBJ type files can be found in several operating systems today. Table 8.1 lists a few of them along with the operating system. Note that the names vary arbitrarily from computer system vendor to vendor.

8.5.2 FILE ACCESS INSTRUCTIONS

To ensure the integrity of the files in a multi-user environment, many operating systems require a user to first *open* a file before access can take place. In these operating systems, a virtual instruction is provided for just such a purpose. Likewise, once the file has been read or written, the user being finished with the file must *close* it. Again, an operating system instruction is provided. The need to open and close a file is important in a multi-user environment. Suppose user A had correctly opened and accessed a file and, while reading or writing, user B desires to access the same file. However, it would be disastrous for user B to manipulate data in the file which user A has just finished with (or is still using, for that matter), since user A upon returning to this modified data would have no knowledge of user B's access. The OPEN and CLOSE instructions serve as a type of semaphore to indicate to other users the current accessing status of a file. (In practice, OPEN accomplishes a "binding" and CLOSE accomplishes an "unbinding" of a file to/from a program.)

Table 8.1 Some File Types

File Types	Operating System		
	VAX/VMS	RT-11	CP/M
Basic Source Programs	BAS	BAS	BAS
Command Procedure Files	COM	COM	COM
Data Input/Output	DAT	DAT	
Directory Files	DIR	DIR	
FORTRAN Source Programs	FOR	FOR	
Macro Source Programs	MAR	MAC	
Assembled/Compiled Binary Object Programs	OBJ	OBJ	INT
Working File			*WRK
Backup File			*BAK
Text File			*TXT

Example 8.2 IBM 360/370 Operating System Instructions. The IBM 360/370 operating system invokes system software called QSAM (Queued Sequential Access Method), which is a collection of macro instructions for the operating system. There are many other access methods in 360 05. (In fact, QSAM is not the one most commonly used.) Four macro instructions (virtual I/O instructions) pertaining to input and output actions are shown below:

Level 3 Instruction	HLL Machine Operation
OPEN	Completes the action of the data control block and prepares for some file action (performs binding).
GET[3]	Retrieves a logical record.
PUT	Outputs a logical record.
CLOSE	Terminates file processing.

---

*User defined name

[3]GET and PUT access not from the file, but from the buffer in primary memory that has been pre-filled by the OS (input) or will be post-emptied by the OS (output); i.e., they unbind. In considering the OS, this is an important distinction. For one thing, it means each program I/O does not imply losing a time-slice.

The GET instruction physically loads a file from an I/O device or memory unit into a buffer area (if necessary) or main memory for on-line data processing. The PUT instruction performs a file movement or transfer in the opposite direction. OPEN, CLOSE, GET and PUT are typical level 3 virtual I/O instructions. Note that each is implemented with several assembly language instructions at level 2, each of which in turn is implemented by one or more microinstructions at level 1.

The GET, PUT, READ, and WRITE virtual instructions are actually mnemonics for *system calls*. Each is implemented using an instruction that posts a software interrupt, i.e., a supervisory call. In the IBM 370, it is the SVC instruction. In the PDP-11, it is a trap instruction. Such instructions allow a user to reach into the system library of routines, e.g., to perform an I/O activity.

8.5.3   SEQUENTIAL FILE ACCESS

File access may be organized as sequential, direct, or index-sequential. A *sequential* file always contains logical records which are ordered according to their physical placement in the storage medium. Assume that a magnetic tape is used for this storage. The logical records 8 through 13 depicted in Figure 8.6, indicate that a sequential file is comprised of logical records ordered in some ascending or descending sequence. That sequence is dependent solely on the order of storing the records. In Figure 8.6, obviously, the tenth record was stored just after the ninth, which was preceded by the eighth, and so on.

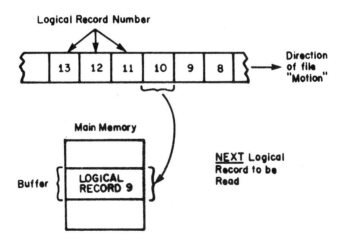

Figure 8.6   Reading a Sequential File

To read a sequential file, an I/O instruction must provide a specification of the file to be read and the main memory address where the record will be placed. Note that this reading operation transfers a record from the file to main memory without specifying the "file number." Obviously, consecutive sequential read instructions from the operating system will retrieve consecutive logical records from the same file. The record, then, will fill a buffer (hopefully, never completely) and remain there until the next read. This reading of a sequential file is entirely different from the reading of a direct access file, which we will examine next. (A direct access READ must specify which logical record in the read operation is to be acquired.) An operating system instruction to cause an output or a WRITE to a file accesses the buffer in main memory to transfer a record out to some file. Just like the sequential read, a consecutive sequential write instruction will produce consecutive logical records on the same file. Magnetic tapes are natural media for sequential file organization. A disk, however, can be organized with sequential files or direct access files. (Direct access in the past has been called random access.)

A major limitation of sequential access is that very rapid retrieval of records is impossible on most storage media. If a user desired to read logical record 16 on a magnetic tape just after the user read logical record 0, the storage medium must be read past the intermediate logical records. Obviously, the situation deteriorates quickly as the separation between logical records increases. On a magnetic tape, it is possible to have thousands of records in a file. Several seconds may elapse before the 950th record is to be retrieved when only the tenth record has just been read.

Sequentially accessed files are used primarily in batch processing systems. A computer operating system would not normally find a sequential file being used in a transaction-oriented processing system, because such systems need very fast access to data stored on auxiliary storage. Sequential files are still very useful in applications where the file organization naturally supports an ascending or descending sequence of stored data elements. For example, the personnel file at a large corporation organized by employee number or an inventory file structured with sequences of descending part numbers are typical applications for a sequential file.

8.5.4   RECORD BLOCKING

Records on a magnetic tape are always stored sequentially. This sequential organization implies that one record is stored after another. Likewise, when read sequentially, one record physically follows another. Magnetic tape records are separated by an interblock gap as shown in Figure 8.7. These interblock gaps or record gaps are typically .75 inches for 7-track tape and .56

inches for 9-track tape. The physical length of a single record depends very much on the tape speed as well as the size of main memory. The gaps are used for starting and stopping a tape during reading and writing operations. But because the density of the data stored on the tape may be high, the amount of tape used for interblock gaps may actually be much longer than the portion of the tape used to store a record. It is possible, then, to waste tape recording space.

To reduce wasted physical space and save a monstrous amount of time in physical I/O, *blocked* records may be used. Blocking assumes that more than one record exists between the interblock or record gaps. For example, in Figure 8.7 records 1 and 2 could conceivably be combined into one block, thus eliminating one interblock gap. The size of a block depends on the amount of main memory storage that can be used to store the block of records. Knowing the maximum block size is important because the entire block of records will be brought into main computer memory each time the tape file is read. Hence,

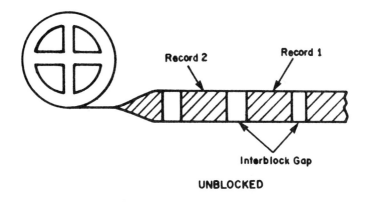

UNBLOCKED

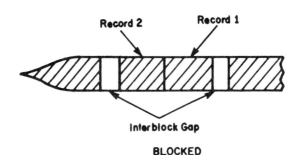

BLOCKED

Figure 8.7   Magnetic Tape Records

the main memory must be large enough to hold at least a single block. The purpose of blocking records is to:

1. Use the tape more efficiently by allowing more data to be stored on a reel of tape.

2. Read files faster because two or more logical records are read each time data is transferred from tape to main memory, and vice versa.

At this point it is significant to emphasize the significant differences between logical and physical I/O. Logical I/O is done by a program to/from buffer via MOV. Physical I/O is done by the operating system to/from devices such as buffer empty/fill requires as indicated by pointers. Concurrent processing by CPU and DMA are very important here because high system throughput can be achieved if semaphores are used properly.

8.6   ALLOCATION OF DISK STORAGE

So far, we have only studied how file access and organization relate to each other. Let's see how they relate to specific storage media. We want to understand how storage is allocated on a particular medium, the disk. The method of allocating storage on any specific medium is very sensitive to the speed and available physical space of the basic medium unit (the total usable length of tape on a magnetic tape reel, the number of sectors and tracks on a disk platter, the number of platters of an entire cylinder,...). To do so, we will examine the physical size of an allocation unit (for example, a linked list allocation or indexed allocation scheme). To a large extent, the I/O system services programs in an operating system are determined largely by the basic storage allocation unit. To relate this to a disk, we first study disk storage organization itself.

The disk is primarily a series of disk head positions or cylinders. Each cylinder may have one or more tracks equal to the number of surfaces. A cylinder with ten disk platters has ten tracks in each cylinder. Each track is further divided into sectors, and each sector may hold a certain number of words or data items. Sector size may be adjustable or fixed. In microcomputer systems, early marketed sectored floppy disks contained only thirteen sectors. Later marketed sectored floppy disks possess sixteen or more sectors. A programmer may choose to format a disk as thirteen or sixteen sectors, but this, of course, depends upon the installed operating system to begin with. The size of the unit of space is fundamental to any file system implementation.

Any disk has three choices for an allocation unit: the cylinder, the sector, or the track. The size of a sector usually (not always) determines the buffer size — at least the upper limit of it. Note that more than one record may fit into a sector. Although it might be reasonable to assign one cylinder as the basic allocation unit, 4.57 sectors would, of course, be an absurd allocation unit. How, then, can we reasonably allocate a unit of physical space on the disk to a file? The answer, of course, is to first estimate the average "size" of a typical file, and then attempt to make the storage allocation unit sufficiently large enough to store a complete file. At one extreme, if a file consisted of only a single character, using an entire cylinder or track would be totally wasteful. (But, most disks require a minimal number of characters for an I/O, often 8.) However, a single track in one sector might suffice, although several hundred bytes can be stored in each track. One major consideration of an operating system designer, then, is to determine whether a track or an entire cylinder is the appropriate allocation unit. In the former case, other tracks in the same cylinder could be available for other files.

Even after an allocation unit decision is made on the basis of the format of the sector, track, or cylinder, the file system generator must also consider whether a file is to be stored in consecutive allocation units or not. Figure 8.8 identifies file storage by consecutive sectors and non-consecutive sectors. In this single platter cylinder, each surface contains 13 sectors. A consecutive sector allocation scheme is employed in Figure 8.8a while a non-consecutive scheme is employed in Figure 8.8b. Notice that the non-consecutive scheme still assumes that a sector is the basic allocation, but a file may occupy non-consecutive sectors. Since many disks cannot access consecutive sectors because of timing this scheme may be more common than the consecutive. This is not to say that allocation for a file is not consecutive—only that access is often non-consecutive for good reasons.

If a file is allocated in terms of the number of units of tracks rather than sectors, consecutively allocated files will occupy consecutive tracks. But disk file systems generally allocate all the tracks in a cylinder before the next cylinder is allocated. Consecutively allocated files will occupy consecutive tracks. Files not consecutively allocated will then occupy tracks that may be found anywhere on the disk with no relation between their relative proximity.

It may be just as beneficial to match the logical record size to the allocation unit size. But this is just as difficult as matching the file size to the allocation unit size. A file may consist of screen reader data which could be sequences of 80 byte strings. If screen reader data is to be stored on a disk, tracks may be assigned to the first logical record (the first screen line) and subsequent lines assigned to remaining logical records. These tracks can be regarded as logically contiguous, even though they do not have to be physically contiguous. Contiguity depends on whether a consecutive or non-consecutive allocation scheme is assigned. In any event, we should recognize that the operating system looks upon a file much differently than a level 3 programmer does

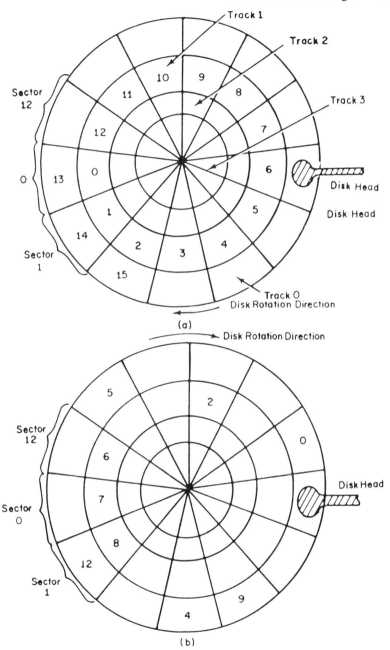

Figure 8.8   Disk Allocation Storage

(working in Pascal, for instance). The operating system assumes and views the file as an *ordered* collection of allocation units. This ordering may not be actually contiguous on the disk. In the I/O service software, of course, the operating system makes sure that the size of the physical allocation unit remains transparent to the level 3 program. A level 3 programmer views the file only as some linear sequence of CRT lines, print lines, and screen lines, etc. It makes no difference on which track, sector, or cylinder a logical record resides. The operating system, however, must contend with such physical details.

If a file has been allocated consecutively on a disk, an operating system need only determine the location of the starting address of the file, the sizes of the logical records, and the sizes of the physical blocks. Example 8.3 illustrates the procedure that a level 2 software must go through to calculate the exact disk address in order to issue the proper track and sector disk command to access logical record 162.

Example 8.3 Obtaining the Sector and Track of a Consecutively Allocated Disk File System.   Suppose a disk file system employs 16 sectors, 5 1/4" floppies, and each sector has 64 bytes apiece. Assume that each disk has 12 tracks. In what sector and track will logical record 162 be found if a record is 8 bytes?

1. Obtain the total number of bytes per track.

$$\frac{16 \text{ sectors}}{\text{track}} \quad * \quad \frac{64 \text{ bytes}}{\text{sector}} \quad = \quad \frac{1024 \text{ bytes}}{\text{track}}$$

2. Obtain the track location of logical record 162.

$$162 \quad * \quad \frac{8 \text{ bytes}}{\text{record}} \quad - \quad \frac{1024 \text{ bytes}}{\text{track}} \quad = \quad \begin{array}{l} 1 \text{ track with} \\ 272 \text{ bytes} \\ \text{remaining} \end{array}$$

3. Obtain the sector location.

$$272 \text{ bytes} \quad - \quad \frac{64 \text{ bytes}}{\text{sector}} \quad = \quad \begin{array}{l} 4 \text{ sectors with} \\ 16 \text{ bytes} \\ \text{remaining} \end{array}$$

Assume that the first track and first sector are called track 0 and sector 0, respectively. Logical record 162 is found on track 1 and sector 4.

8.7 FILE DIRECTORIES

In the early days of computers, files were primitively maintained by a user with a card deck. (The UNIVAC 1 had steel tapes.) Each user would then store away his or her private collection of card decks (or tapes) representing programs, data, or current activity in his or her desk. Any time a user desired data processing, the user merely submitted his or her card deck to operations personnel who then assembled a number of card decks from several users into one batch process. The sometimes huge collection of card decks was then loaded into a card reader for subsequent transfer to the central computer processing source. As computer installations and user requirements expanded, this "manual" sort of file management became totally ineffective.

Today, a computer keeps track of files using a file directory. The file directories of a computer system represent a table of file sources. The file directory, then, lets the computer's secondary memory, such as the disk, retain the several users' programs and data. The actual information in a file directory represents entries of user names, account numbers, and storage allocation decisions. In the file directory of Figure 8.9, an entry can consist of the file name, physical location, current length, type, access rights (permission to various users), history (file change event times), etc. Not all file directories are as comprehensive as that shown in Figure 8.9. However, the essential file entries in any directory must include at least a name, physical location, and version, as follows.

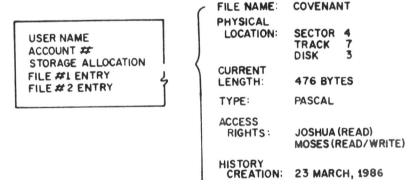

Figure 8.9   File Directory

1. A file *name*, which should be a descriptive title for a file, is generally limited to a few characters.

2. A *type* describes the type of information contained, such as found in Table 8.1.

3. A *version* indicates some historical landmark of the file, such as the number of the current version or last date entered.

In very small computers, a file directory may be very simple. Examples 8.4 and 8.5 list typical CP/M directories and RT-11 directories. Notice how little entry information is provided when compared with the file directory of Figure 8.9. These examples are representative of a subdirectory found in a hierarchical directory system, as in Figure 8.10. Hierarchical directory systems are used in large computer installations. The VAX/VMS, MULTICS, and UNIX operating systems employ a hierarchical directory system. At the highest level in the directory system is a system master directory. Beneath the system master directory can be found user directories, possibly similar to the directory listing of Figure 8.9. Below each user directory can be found user subdirectories that list information similar to that in Examples 8.4 and 8.5.

Example 8.4   A CP/M Directory on a Small Computer

Directory Entry.Format	Name.Type
LOAD.COM	GAME2.INT
TONE.TXT	PIP.COM
PROG1.BAS	DUMP.COM
GAME1.BAS	SYSGEN.COM
PROG.HEX	

Example 8.5   An RT-11 Directory

Name	Type	# of Blocks	Date
SWAP	.SYS	25	22-OCT-86
RT11SJ[a]	.SYS	67P	31-NOV-86
DL	.SYS	4	10-DEC-86
GAME	.BAC	32	11-DEC-86
ADDP	.MAC	1	12-DEC-86
TTYOUT	.OBJ	1	12-DEC-86

[a]RT11SJ is a protected file (67P).

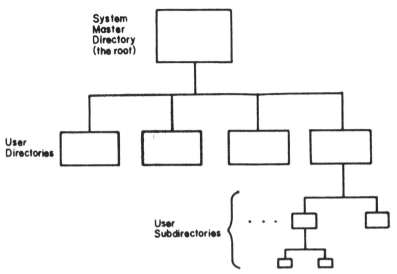

Figure 8.10   Hierarchical Directory System

A hierarchical system is beneficial when more than one "level" of user is maintaining a directory because partitioning file access is natural. An operating system could maintain a directory for itself. A user can also maintain a directory for his or her particular needs. The operating system could keep track of the availability of devices and possibly the current working status (for example, disk drive 7 disconnected, disk drive 2 in use, etc.). The user directory need only help a single user keep track of the physical location of his or her files. A user subdirectory merely maintains his or her listing of file names, type, and latest version.

Hierarchical directory systems are multilevel directories. A multilevel directory system is desirable not only when different privileged users each want to maintain a directory, but also when two or more people may share the same device for storing files and accidentally duplicate file names. Since both have access to the same set of files, one user could inadvertently modify or destroy another user's file without the other user's knowledge. User subdirectories, then, establish separate file directories for each system user, and eliminate such problems. Locating user files basically becomes a matter of searching through a two-level file directory. Passing from a user directory to a subdirectory could be accomplished only by providing a special LOGIN command with a subsequent password entered by the user (and known only by that user).

A system master directory should always reside in the computer system. No one should be capable of removing or directly changing the system master directory while a computer system is running. Otherwise, the system master may not represent the current status of system files. However, users may maintain directories of their own on a private floppy disk. In that event, many disk operating systems (DOS) maintain a disk directory file on each disk. When a user executes an operating system command similar to CATALOG, he or she is requesting a listing of all files on the current disk in use.

An operating system must keep track of the available space on any disk. To do so, two schemes are employed: a bit map and a hole table (as in Figure 8.11). The *bit map* indicates the specific track and sector where no records have been allocated. A "1" in the bit map indicates that the track and sector have already been reserved or occupied. A "0" in the bit map indicates that

Bit Map

Sector

Track	0	1	2	3	4	5	6	7	8	9	10	11	12
0	0	0	0	0	0	0	0	0	0	0	0	0	0
1	0	0	0	0	0	0	0	0	0	0	0	0	0
2	1	1	0	0	0	0	0	0	0	1	0	0	1
3	0	1	0	1	1	0	0	1	0	0	0	1	0

Hole Table

Sector	Track	Number of Sectors in Hole
0	0	13
0	1	13
2	2	7
10	2	2
0	3	1
2	3	1
5	3	2
8	3	3
12	3	1

Figure 8.11   Identifying Available Disk Sectors

the allocation unit is still available. The *hole table* lists the number of contiguous sectors on a track still unreserved and available starting with the first available sector. In the allocated storage of Figure 8.11, track 0 has no allocated sectors, hence all 13 sectors are available. Track 1 also has the entire track available. Sector 2, track 2, has this sector including six more sectors available. Hence, the number of sectors in the hole is seven. Sector 10, track 1, has sector 10 and sector 11 available, hence two sectors are in the hole. A hole represents any number of *contiguous* allocation units.

A hole table is useful for finding a hole of a particular length. Unfortunately, the same hole table requires much manipulation to make the hole search quick. In fact, the table must be sorted on hole length to permit a rapid lookup of a particular hole size. Also, the hole table itself varies in size, because the length of the hole table list fluctuates as files are created and destroyed. This is not desirable for a program that must search and sort a table whose length is unknown. A bit map, on the other hand, is an array of fixed-length rows and columns. This constant size makes sorting and searching easier. Furthermore, changing the status of one allocation unit from "occupied" to "available" changes only one entry in the bit map. A single allocation unit status may affect more than one entry in the hole table. Whether a hole table or a bit map is used, the operating system must still update either a bit map or a hole table every time the allocation status changes.

In RT-11, a user executing DIRECTORY will cause an output of the system volume directory like that shown in Example 8.5. However, in RT-11, while the user is developing programs, the operating system will be appending many system files to his or her file to support the program generation process. The user will often be surprised to find several files in his directory that he did not create himself. In that case, such temporary files created by the systems utilities programs could be deleted by special operating system instructions. Notice that the RT-11 DIRECTORY command essentially generates a catalog of user file names in one's current drive directory, even though the command CATALOG does not exist in RT-11. In many computer operating systems, the operating system considers a catalog as a directory. However, for each user, an operating system should always catalog permanent files being saved in some secondary memory. To do so requires file manipulation commands.

8.8 FILE MANIPULATION COMMANDS

With an operating system, a programmer should be able to create, rename, erase, copy, and print files. These tasks are all necessary for applications programming. All of these tasks, as well as often file handling tasks described in this section, are implemented by using operating system commands. An operating system *command* is an instruction in machine level 3 to invoke one or more processes, procedures, and/or programs to complete a level 3 task. A command differs from a machine instruction in that a command may invoke several assembly language instructions to complete a task. A typical command is a mnemonic more directly characteristic of the intended task request than the actual machine operation. For instance, if we want to rename a file, a command such as "newname = oldname" is used. Then in this command, RENAME causes the old file name to be replaced by the new file name. Commands may be resident or built-in, or they may be transient (available on files). A brief selection of file-handling commands for operating systems can be found in Example 8.6.

Example 8.6   File-Handling Commands

VAX/VMS	RT-11	CP/M	Comments
TYPE	TYPE	TYPE	Print out a file to specified device as is.
DIRECTORY	DIRECTORY	DIR	List all file names.
RENAME	RENAME	REN	Change a file name.
DELETE	DELETE	ERA	Erase a file.
		SAVE	Store a file from main memory.
COPY	COPY	PIP	Copy the specified file from one volume to another.
PRINT	PRINT		Print out a file's contents.
PURGE			Delete older versions of a file.
APPEND			Append a file(s) to the end of the first file.
CREATE/DIR			Create a new directory.

The resident or built-in commands reside in the operating system software in main memory. Hence, a user can always execute resident commands since this part of an operating system always resides in a computer. However, a transient command may not be available since it exists in a command file on some user's disk. The transient commands are often assembly language programs that can be copied, deleted, and even moved or actually executed as a command. In fact, a user can often create his or her own transient command. Each command should take one or more file names as parameters. Transient commands are sometimes called *private* commands. Systems that support the generation of private commands are useful when one wants to:

1. Generate a new command procedure to perform some useful set of commands.

2. Identify and set a decision-making task depending on some default.

3. Create user-recognizable names or synonyms to replace obscure command names or strings.

In the VAX-11 macro program, such private commands can be easily generated. The same facility exists in many operating systems that have a command interpreter. As an example, consider an applications program that frequently requires the computation of the hyperbolic tangent function. In the VAX/VMS command interpreter, a user could create a file named, appropriately, MATH, which is the file name for the set of procedures found in Example 8.7, to assemble, link, and run this VAX-11 macro program. A user makes this file a command file which can then be interpreted by the instruction

$ @MATH

This command causes the operating system to locate the file, MATH, and execute all commands contained within it.

Example 8.7   A Frequently Commanded Sequence (VAX/VMS) Developed as a Private OS Command

$macro/list tanh	;TANH IS THE FILENAME OF A
$link tanh	;SUB-PROGRAM WHICH COMPUTES THE
$run tanh	;HYPERBOLIC TANGENT

The process is actually similar to a macro expansion process found at the assembly language level, because the command interpreter at the operating system level executes each line just as it is encountered. As expected, such command files can also be parameterized by including dummy arguments, just as macros possess. And, as with macros, the actual argument will be automatically equated with the symbolic dummy arguments in the actual file command call. All of the file-handling commands for CP/M in Example 8.5 are built-in or resident operating system commands.

Whether the commands are transient or resident, to maintain a catalog or directory of a user's permanent files, an operating system should include, at the very least, the following level 3 instructions:

1. Create a permanent file.

2. Delete a permanent file.

3. Rename a permanent file.

Large computer systems that are expected to be employed by several users with varying privileged access should also include a level 3 command to change the protection status of any permanent file. It is quite common to allow each user to specify some secret password. Then a program attempting to access some permanent file must supply that same password before access is permitted.

8.9 MEMORY MANAGEMENT

In the early days of computers, main memory was very expensive. The IBM 650 and subsequent models seldom had more than 2,000 words of memory. Yet, even at the birth of computer machinery, programs grew to sizes much larger than 2,000 words. To overcome the problem, a programmer spent much time shrinking programs to a size capable of fitting into the tiny memory. As a result, the subsequent algorithms executed much more slowly, even though a better algorithm could have been used (but could not fit in memory). If a program just could not fit into memory all at once, the last resort was to separate the program into semi-autonomous modules.

With such limited memory a programmer would attempt to employ an overlay scheme so that each module could fit entirely in memory. Each module was made to be independent of all other modules (except for a root module). Also, once a module was entered, the structure of the module was such that its exit could occur only once. Every attempt was made to ensure that the module should need no other modules to complete its task. For instance, if the module needed a subroutine, that subroutine would have to reside within the module itself. No other module could call that subroutine unless it had a copy. These constraints, among many others, caused much programming grief.

In Figure 8.12, the memory overlay scheme assumes that a program has been broken up into modules or parts A, B, and C, each of which can fit into the available user space at any given time. (The permanent root module is not shown here.) Before program execution, the computer would first load module A into the available user space. When the system is done with module A, it would be transferred back out to secondary storage, and module B would be loaded. Upon completion of activity with module B, it would be returned to secondary storage, and module C would be loaded. Each part or overlay would be brought in and returned to secondary storage only when needed. Unfortunately, this scheme required a programmer to modify his or her total program to reduce or partition software into loadable sizes. Also, the programmer had to decide where each overlay was kept in secondary storage. Finally, the programmer also had to manage the overlay traffic between the main memory and secondary storage. This effort was accomplished all without the help of hardware or an operating system.

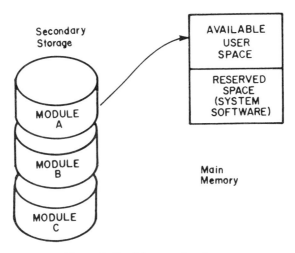

Figure 8.12   Memory Overlay

In 1961, an automatic overlay process was developed by researchers in England. They proposed to make the overlay process transparent to a programmer. Thus, the burden of generating overlays and managing them was now left to the computer. In subsequent years, several machines were designed with this feature and enhancements, which we now call *virtual memory*. Today several commercial machines are available with just such a capability, including the Burroughs 6700, IBM 370, 4341, PDP-11, and VAX. The actual process discovered was much different from the original manual memory overlay scheme. The concept developed by viewing address space as something distinct from memory locations (call it virtual memory). A program executing in a virtual memory would not necessarily need to be partitioned into short segments. Note that this also changed binding time to physical addresses.

Suppose we decide that a computer should have a 64K address space. That is, a user could access locations anywhere from 0 to 65,535. However, the same computer system may have an actual or physical main memory no larger than 4,096 words. Would it not be possible to employ some scheme that takes any 4,096 contiguous addresses in the 64K address space and "maps" them into the physical memory consisting of locations 0 through 4095? The simple mapping requires us to force any 4,096 contiguous locations onto locations 0 through 4095.

The address mapping process could take place either in software or hardware, but the preferred method is in hardware because it is faster. The actual mapping process must ensure that any address in a 4,096-word block of the address space would be found in its same relative position in locations 0 through 4095. The concept of virtual memory could be accomplished in any address space and main memory size. However, computers commonly maintain main memory size in powers of two. Hence, the contiguous block of locations in the address map entering the mapping process would then also need to be a power of two. Obviously, this mapping process cannot translate more address space locations into the main memory at any one time than the maximum number of physical locations available.

The crucial point is that the number of addressable words of the address space depends only on the number of bits in an address. If a 16-bit program counter is found in a computer, the address space conceivably could directly access 65,536 words of memory. The address space of this computer would then consist of numbers 0, 1, 2,..., 65,535. They may be regarded as virtual addresses. But the physical addresses in main memory, assuming only a 4K memory, would have the addresses 0, 1, 2,..., 4095. Here, the virtual memory assumes that the mapping process will take any 4,096 addressable words of the virtual address space into 4,096 words of physical memory. All of this occurs without a programmer's need to mentally segment the algorithm and then perform overlay bookkeeping.

8.9.1   PAGING

A virtual memory system managed by a mapping process that takes a virtual address space into physical address space is shown in Figure 8.13. In this virtual address system, a memory map exists which identifies the relationship between the virtual addresses and the physical addresses. This memory mapping is simply a one-to-one mapping of address spaces onto the actual memory addresses. The 4,096 contiguous addressable spaces are called a page. The page boundaries are 0-4095, 4096-8191, ... for the first and second pages, and so on. Managing a virtual memory scheme critically depends on whether a current instruction to be executed already resides in main memory or is somewhere else. In the case where the current instruction already exists in main memory, no extra management steps are necessary. However, when the instruction must be obtained from some other "page" in memory, the following sequence of steps would occur in this virtual memory scheme.

1. The current contents of main memory would be evicted from primary into secondary memory, probably another disk storage medium if any changes have been made to that page.

2. The page containing the necessary instruction would be determined by the mapping process.

3. The new page would now be loaded from virtual into main memory.

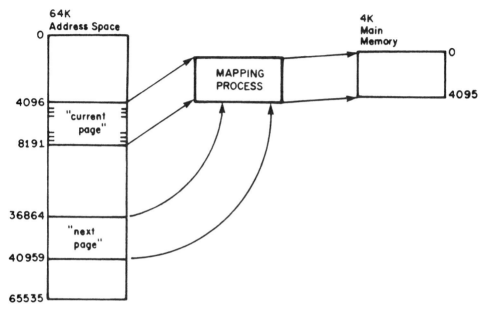

Figure 8.13 Page Mapping

The mapping process translates the virtual locations of the current page into physical locations 0 through 4095. More important, the virtual memory management process would appear transparent to the user with program execution continuing almost as if nothing had ever happened (except for some slight timing delay). This automatic overlaying of different address spaces into main memory is called a *paging process*. The actual contiguous locations or chunks of address spaces mapped onto main memory are called *pages*. In order for the automatic overlaying process to work effectively as a virtual memory, the secondary storage (for example, disk) must be large enough to store an entire program, including its data. Furthermore, a user could write a program just as though he or she actually had 65,536 locations in main memory. The computer hardware in the mapping process would cause the necessary address redefinitions without any user awareness. In fact, the user simply assumes that he or she has the full 64K space. This assumption is important because virtual memory can also be organized by a segmentation policy rather than a paging policy. (However, in a segmentation scheme, a programmer must *always* be sensitive to the existence of the segments and segment links.) In a virtual memory paging scheme, the entire paging mechanism remains transparent to the user programmer.

In Figure 8.13, the page mapping process depicted assumes that the 64K address space contains, in fact, sixteen virtual pages, each page 4K words long, and main memory contains only 4K words. However, main memory may be any size. Suppose that we expanded main memory to 16K words. Now it would be possible to load four pages into main memory at any given time. In Figure 8.14, the page mapping scheme assumes that the main memory has 16K physical locations which can hold four pages. The physical address space in main memory that contains a page is called a *page frame*. The 128K virtual address space contains 32 virtual pages of 4K words each. At any given moment, any four pages of the virtual address space can be found in main memory. In Figure 8.13, only one page frame can exist in main memory.

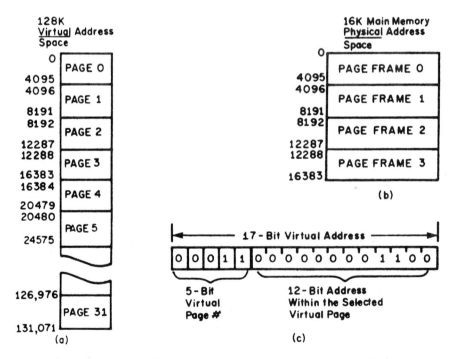

Figure 8.14a-c   128K Address Space with 32 Pages Each of 4K Words

In order to maintain the virtual memory system, a *page table* is used. A page table describes the current whereabouts of each virtual page in a virtual memory system. A page table must contain as many entries as there are virtual pages. Hence, the page table for Figure 8.14a must contain 32 entries. (How many entries would exist in a page table for Figure 8.13?) A page table is used to reference memory by generating the necessary physical address from its virtual address. A page table does not prohibit any addressing modes of specific instructions (direct, indirect, autoincrement, etc.). Addressing modes existing in the machine instruction set are views in level 2. In Figure 8.14c, the virtual address is seventeen bits long. The lower twelve bits determine an address within a selected virtual page. In our case, address 12 is being selected. The upper five bits specify the virtual page number. In Figure 8.14c, virtual page 3 is being selected.

The purpose of a page table is now described. Suppose that an operating system must determine the whereabouts of virtual page 3. Page 3 may be residing in main memory, in secondary memory, or both. To determine which possibility is true, the operating system scans the page table, which has one entry for each of the 32 virtual pages. The page table of Figure 8.15 contains 32 entries, each entry of which maintains four fields. The rightmost two bits comprise the page frame field, which designates the main memory page frame where virtual page 3 is currently mapped. The next field specifies the secondary memory address (if the page is currently in secondary memory). The operating system can determine whether a page is in secondary memory or in main memory by examining the residing field. Our example in Figure 8.15 indicates 888 at virtual page 3 is already in main memory and can be found in page frame 1. Can you tell what physical addresses this page now possesses? From Figure 8.14, we see that physical addresses 4096 through 8191 are specified for our current page number.

The last field (privileged/protection) in the leftmost bit of this page table entry specifies whether the page has restricted access. It is useful to prevent certain pages from being accessed by other users. This field is not necessary, but is very helpful. Notice that if the current page is in main memory, the secondary memory address field points to a location in main memory. However, if the current page being sought exists in secondary memory, this field points to a location in secondary memory.

Assuming that a current sought page is in main memory, how does its page table entry determine an actual physical address? Assume that the contents of address 12 in virtual page number 3 is desired (as in Figure 8.16). From the page table for the page 3 entry, we already know that this page exists in main memory. To access the actual location in main memory, we need to place a unique physical address into the MAR. Figure 8.16 illustrates the formation of the physical address. Our 17-bit virtual address contains the upper five bits which point to a location in the page table. It is virtual page 3. Now the

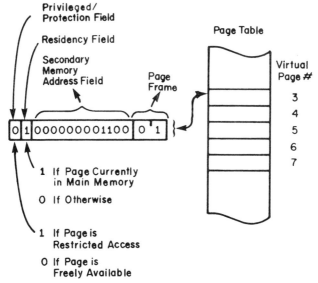

Figure 8.15   Page Table Entry for Fig. 8.14 with Four Fields

computer retrieves the page frame field and places these two bits into the upper two bits of the MAR. At the same time, the lower twelve bits of the virtual address are inserted into the lower twelve bits of the MAR. The 14-bit contents of our MAR now contains the physical address (which should be $4096 + 12 = 4108$). If virtual page 3 were not in main memory, the secondary address field would point to a location in secondary memory. In that event, the twelve bits would not necessarily point to location 12.

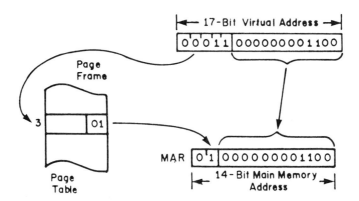

Figure 8.16   Virtual Address Translation to Physical Address

This address translation is temporarily suspended if the current page is not in main memory. In that event, the page must first be retrieved from secondary storage and placed somewhere in main memory. At that time, a page frame is assigned and the page table is updated. Now any access to main memory for this page will correctly load the MAR.

To access a main memory location, this virtual memory system must execute the following steps:

1. Obtain the next address from the user's program. It will always be a virtual address.

2. Determine whether the virtual page of this virtual address is in main memory or secondary memory from the page-resident field in the page table. Examine the residency field.

3. If the sought-after virtual page is already in main memory, load the lower twelve bits of the virtual address directly into the MAR. From the page table, load the page frame field into the upper bits of the MAR. The physical address is now formed.

4. If the page is in secondary memory, use the secondary memory address field to retrieve the page, load the page into primary memory, update the page table, and proceed to Step 3.

A page request for a page not found in main memory is called a *page fault*. Page faults cost time because the page must be retrieved from secondary storage and loaded into main memory. Also, the page table must be updated. A good operating system minimizes page faults. Several strategies can be employed. A page fault is also costly because it interrupts the operating system. When interrupted, the operating system must recognize this request for primary memory to be allocated, make a page replacement decision, and finally accomplish the transfer from secondary storage to main memory. All during this time, the currently executed program must be suspended until the transfer from secondary to main memory has been completed. Only when the transfer is complete can the suspended program resume.

8.9.2 PAGE SIZES

The best page length depends upon many factors of which the most commonly encountered program size is paramount. If this "ideal" length could be ascertained, the page size could be equal to this length or a multiple of it. However, no ultimately ideal length has been found in practice yet. Table 8.2 lists some of the more popular page lengths. Often, the critical page length is governed by the time needed to transfer a page from secondary storage to main memory. This transfer time must not be excessive. Recall that most of this time is consumed by the delay due to latency. Latency is the time it takes for the head of a disk arm to move over to the desired information. It includes the arm movement time, rotational delay, and head settling time. The average latency for a single head time is roughly approximate to the time required for the disk to move one-half of a revolution, which is of the order of 10 to 20 milliseconds. Because of the time involved, including transfer time, larger pages seem desirable. However, a larger page requires even greater main memory storage. Furthermore, if a large page is used, the average program may not fill that page, and considerable main memory space may be wasted. Incompletely filled pages lead to *internal fragmentation*. A last page unfilled is an external fragment.

Table 8.2   Common Page Sizes

Manufacturer	Model	Page Size	Word Size
DEC	PDP-10	512	36-bit Word
DEC	PDP-20	512	36-bit Word
DEC	VAX-11/780	128	16-bit Word
IBM	360/67	1024	32-bit Word
IBM	370/168	1024 or 512	32-bit Word
Honeywell	MULTICS	1024	36-bit Word

Main memory is said to be fragmented when its contents portray several unallocated locations or zones most likely at page ends. For example, a very fragmented main memory would exist in our virtual memory system of Figure 8.14b if each physical page were on the average only half filled. In this case, a 16K main memory would be used only 8K at a time, which is certainly a highly undesirable state of affairs! An obvious solution would be to divide the pages in half, using 2K word pages instead of 4K word pages. Now the 16K main memory could hold eight pages instead of four. A short page could exacerbate latency time for many secondary memory accesses. There is a practical limit to the minimum page length.

8.9.3   DEMAND PAGING

How does a computer system select which pages are to be retrieved from secondary storage and loaded into primary or main memory? The answer depends on assumptions made about the general behavior of programs and programming practices. Suppose we know nothing about a program's behavior. In that event, it would not matter which pages are selected. We would need to load the page containing the first instruction and begin program execution. When a subsequent instruction must be found on another page, the computer could then load this new page into primary memory. When the subsequent instruction cannot be found on either of these two pages, the computer would have to load another page, and so on. This process of loading pages into primary memory as they are needed is called *demand paging*. Such paging requests could be expected when a user's program is first encountered or when the computer has been initially turned on. Once a computer's memory is loaded with several programs, however, different paging schemes might be more suitable. Why? One reason is that we can now make assumptions about program behavior.

One reasonable assumption is that a program generally executes in a sequential manner using a set of contiguous locations. An astute programmer would not cause his or her program to jump about memory like spaghetti code, but rather keep his or her code concise and compact. Assuming, then, that a program may reside in a single page or at least within adjacent pages, a computer system could load several contiguous pages into main memory at a time, hoping that a user's program can be found within the pages already loaded. These pages constitute a special set. A working set is a collection of pages in primary memory at any time, t, used by K most recent memory references. Computer scientists observed that the $K+1$ most recent references made access to all of the pages used with the K most recent references. Hence, $W(K,t)$ can be described as a monotonically increasing function of K, with the limit of W approaching the maximum number of allowable main memory pages. The actual function may look like that shown in Figure 8.17.

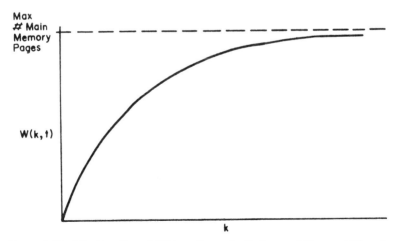

Figure 8.17   Working Set of K Most Recently Referenced Pages at Time t

Programs usually do not reference address space uniformly, but rather cluster about a small number of pages. Hence, the working set principle, assuming an ideal K can be found, can be effective. The function depicted in Figure 8.17 adequately describes the behavior of K with time. For small values of K, the slope of the curve is steep, indicating that the set changes slowly in time, reflecting the fact that most programs actually access a small number of pages and mostly in random fashion. As K increases, the slope of the curve likewise decreases. The decreasing slope for large K is justified by using a program that contains repetitive sequences such as a loop in one or two pages and that makes access to data in three or four other pages. The six total pages may be referenced very infrequently, especially if the loop contains several hundred instructions. Hence, the curve of Figure 8.17 tends to flatten out as K becomes large.

Since the content of any working set is not necessarily critical to any specific K, K may occupy a wide range of values without critically affecting the working set. Furthermore, a working set tends to vary slowly with time, instead of rapidly or even randomly. From this empirical observation, we could predict which pages will be most needed when a program is restarted (such as after an interrupt or at the beginning of a day's computer run). Those pages could be the last working set, and they could be loaded in advance of this program restart. But the I/O process for transferring secondary storage to primary memory can also occur while the CPU is running. Hence, if the CPU could anticipate this need, it could request a new working set and go about its own activity in the meantime. This concurrent behavior tends to increase the throughput of a machine.

Of course, loading pages in advance, depending on some prediction of their utility, fails to increase the machine throughput when a program is in the process of leaving one working set and entering another. In this transient state, the CPU may be bogged down with many page retrievals. There are arguments pro and con for bringing a working set into main memory in advance.

The page selection schemes observed so far address the issue of a single program. However, a computer that is time-shared has many different user programs in main memory, all in varying processing stages: some with a working set fully loaded and others with only a partial working set. Users may be swapped in and out of memory without knowing it. However, a CPU could easily be bogged down with swapping operations instead of processing operations. Hence, simplistic demand paging is not very attractive. However, demand paging does not aggravate the CPU throughput by burdening the CPU with unnecessary program transitions between one working set and another. In a demand paging scheme, only the actual pages needed are loaded at any given time. Statistically, this is only partly true because fewer pages are in a swapping state at any given time anyway.

8.10 PAGE REPLACEMENT STRATEGIES

In the last section, we examined how to select pages for transfer into main memory. In this section, we will examine what policies or strategies could be employed to remove or evict pages from main memory. Why? First of all, if we had completely filled main memory with pages and found ourselves lacking a required page, where could this new page be placed? Obviously, we have to write over an existing page in memory, which effectively removes that page. Just as before, we could apply the same arguments to selecting which pages to write over or withdraw. Assuming that we know nothing about program behavior, we could make a random choice of page replacement.

It makes more sense to evict a page that has been loaded long ago. The strategy that evicts the least recently loaded page and that is independent of the time this page was last referenced is called a *first-in-first-out* or FIFO algorithm. The computer can keep track of the loading history of each page by simply attaching a software or hardware "counter" to each virtual page. In software, this counter can be maintained in each entry of the page table. When we initialize the computer system, each counter is cleared to zero. When a page is brought in, the counter for every page in memory is incremented by one. The counter for this new page is cleared to zero. The FIFO algorithm would then select a page to evict on the basis of the highest counter reading. A page with the highest count value in the page table indicates that the page has been resident a very long time. Because of this, the algorithm tacitly assumes that this page is least likely to be used, and, hence, will be the first to be evicted.

This least recently loaded page algorithm is not entirely satisfactory. We can see this in the following example. Suppose a computer program consisted of a collection of procedures in some hierarchical level. Assume that the highest-level procedure is mainly a calling program to several lower-level procedures or modules. Let the calling program make frequent access to the lower-level modules. In order for this entire program to work, the highest-level procedure must be loaded first since it will make demands on other procedures only as needed. However, to make this program work, all of the procedures must be included in the current working set. Our dilemma is that the FIFO algorithm will evict the highest-level module first, since it will be in a page loaded at the start. Now the program will fail to execute. This leads to another page replacement strategy, which we will now examine.

Suppose that instead of evicting a page because it has been around a long time, we evict a page because it is seldom used. Taking this one step further, let's assume that the least recently used page will always be evicted first from the current working set. This *least recently used* or LRU algorithm assumes that the most infrequently accessed page will continue to have a high probability of idleness. On the basis of this assumption, the LRU algorithm evicts this dormant page every time. This algorithm behaves quite differently from the FIFO algorithm, and has its own drawbacks. Suppose that a program contains a rather large loop. In fact, let this looping program fill six virtual pages in a five-page main memory machine. Progressing through the loop the first time, the main memory will eventually encounter the last page, as in Figure 8.18. The next instruction not being found on this page will cause the operating system to replace the least recently used page with the new virtual page.

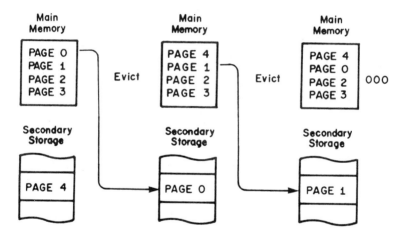

Figure 8.18   Worst Possible Program for an LRU Page Replacement Algorithm

In other words, page 0 will be evicted. Now, however, when the instructions of the new page are exhausted, the loop wants to return to the beginning of the program that has just been recently evicted. The operating system now evicts page 1, replacing it with page 0. The program executes instructions in page 0 until all instructions are exhausted. Now the operating system needs page 1 which was just evicted. This situation continues with every subsequent page, representing the worst possible situation for an LRU algorithm. Our problem with the LRU algorithm does not reflect a bad algorithm choice, but rather the available main memory is just too small. When main memory always exceeds the size of the working set, an LRU algorithm performs quite adequately, because it does tend to minimize page replacement traffic.

Page replacement strategies may combine attributes of both the LRU and FIFO algorithms or variations of them. The objective, however, of any page replacement strategy is to find room for a new page and adroitly identify a reasonable page to evict, assuming that no vacant page frame exists. Maximum usage and throughput demand that all page frames be filled with useful pages. If this does not occur, the computer system is probably maintaining a very fragmented main memory. Hence, operating system designers always invoke some algorithm that attempts to predict likely pages that are least useful. The criterion for the FIFO algorithm assumes that the least recently loaded page will also have the least adverse affect on the current working set and running program. The LRU algorithm assumes that the absence of its evicted page will likewise affect the running program only slightly.

Dynamic statistical studies of usage and residency time in main memory do produce more sophisticated page strategies. In any event, no matter which algorithm is used, so long as the average working set needed is larger than the number of available page frames in main memory, the algorithm will fail. Page faults will be quite frequent. Such a situation which generates such a frequent page faulting occurrence is called *thrashing*.

8.10.1 THE DIRTY BIT

Not all pages evicted from main memory need to be copied back into secondary storage. Can you determine which ones must be? Only those programs or pages that have been changed or written into should be returned to secondary storage. The others have a perfect copy in vertical memory on disk. Hence, pages that contain data are more likely to be modified than pages that contain program instructions. (Remember that self-modifying code is strongly discouraged and pure code is strongly encouraged.) Any page that has not been modified obviously already has an accurate copy of itself in secondary storage. Considerable savings in page transfer activity can be achieved if some method were possible to determine if a page has been modified. The simplest technique is to append an extra bit to the page entry in the page table. Then any page that has been modified in main memory will then be so indicated in this bit in the page table entry. A page that is clean has not been modified. A modified page is indicated by an appended bit called the *dirty bit*.

Suppose now that it is possible for the operating system to be hunting about for dirty pages to copy back into secondary storage. Then a simple scan of the dirty bit column in the page entries would immediately indicate to the operating system which pages could be copied. In that event, should the operating system forcibly stop execution of the current program and transfer dirty pages? No. Rather, the copying task could be performed concurrently when the CPU is executing instructions, because the CPU need only initiate the transfer, leaving the remaining task management to the I/O unit or memory management unit (DMA). A more elegant selection policy would be to take only those dirty pages that are most likely to be written out to secondary storage, instead of just any dirty page.

Even though a page became dirty again just after the transfer to secondary storage, the transfer costs to return the dirty page to main memory would still not be overly excessive. This is so mainly because the CPU merely initiates the transfer task, returning immediately back to its current process. However, if the operating system is poorly designed, it may frequently interrupt the CPU to maintain clean pages in secondary memory. The writing of dirty pages back to secondary storage merely to make dirty pages clean is called *sneaky writes*. Operating system designers carefully balance the sneaky write overhead against the page faults to determine what the best page replacement policy should be. Operating system designers often study simulations to determine tradeoffs as in Example 8.8. (The reader should consider the probability of memory interference during these "writeouts.")

Example 8.8 Sneaky Writes Versus Page Faults.   Assume that a CPU can resume program execution concurrently with a sneaky write. Also let an actual page reading time equal the actual page writing time. Also let the interval of CPU interruption to initiate a sneaky write cost X seconds, and a page fault cost Y seconds to fully recover (retrieve secondary storage page, update page table, and continue program execution). Note that Y is greater than X. On the average, we find that Z page faults occur per minute in our computer installation. The question is "How many sneaky writes could be allowed before performance degradation doubles?"

To answer this question, we should determine the differential cost between the time it takes to fully recover from a page fault and an initiation of a sneaky write. This differential cost is $Y-X$. We do not want to perform any more sneaky writes than necessary. So

$$N(Y-X)$$

represents the cost generated if N sneaky writes are allowed. If this cost is equated to ZY, we can determine the maximum number of sneaky writes at which level the degradation doubles. Hence,

$$ZY = N(Y-X) \qquad (8-1)$$

and solving for N we obtain the maximum number of sneaky writes at which degradation doubles.

$$N = (Y-X)/ZY \tag{8-2}$$

Example 8.8 assumes that the executing program does not get slowed down by memory needs that cannot be serviced during this "sneaky" activity. With only a few registers (as in the PDP-11), the probability of this idealism is very low. Perhaps this is the reason why very few commercially available systems really use this sneaky technique.

8.11 CACHE MEMORY

Virtual memory has been implemented to make the memory apparent to a user system seem very large. In order to effectively implement virtual memory, however, rapid load of immediately usable code and data into main memory is necessary. Paging, then, was introduced to allow the secondary storage to act as a temporary holding place for pages that will most likely become resident in main memory. The underlying concern was that if main memory was to have the physical capacity of an entire memory system, the memory system cost would rise astronomically. Since the cost per bit of typical secondary storage such as a disk or a drum is far less than that of main memory which is solid state, some of the memory space could be allotted to less costly disk storage. Hence, imbedded in the design of a memory system is a tradeoff between cost per bit versus the access speed of the storage medium.

Suppose that we introduce an additional but limited very fast memory reside between the CPU and main memory. Now let main memory serve as a sort of secondary storage as before, and let the small yet fast memory serve as "main memory." This memory, typically with far fewer storage addresses than main memory, is called *cache memory*. An effectively deployed cache memory is likely to have three characteristics:

1. A small memory storage between the CPU and main memory

2. Memory access speeds approximately equal to the CPU clock speed

3. Relatively fast address mapping and block replacement

Cache memory is useful only if programs behave a certain way. That is, program instruction executions must cluster about a few physically close instead of widely dispersed locations in memory. A cache memory may provide a significant speedup at only a modest increase in cost because most of the code currently in cache is likely to be needed immediately. Code resident elsewhere is unlikely to be needed by the current process.

Many computers today, including the IBM 370, the ILLIAC IV, CDC STAR, CRAY-1, and TI ASC, use a cache. Cache memory has appeared in one form or another in many high-performance scientific computers as well as business systems. The CYBER 172 has a "program stack" which serves as an instruction buffer. Effective cache implementations assume that a typical sequence of CPU-generated addresses will cluster around the high-order bits in the addresses. (This address-clustering assumption often applies to main memory and secondary storage.) Because clustering holds true for many programs, a cache memory is often found in the hierarchy of memory organizations.

Instead of main memory, the cache memory now provides the main source of CPU-generated addresses. A CPU-generated address found in cache is called a *hit*. An address not found in cache is called a *miss*. Let H represent the cache hit ratio which is the fraction of main memory addresses issued by the computer's control unit that can be satisfied by a cache access. And let T_c be the cache memory cycle time and T_m be the main memory cycle time. We say that the effective memory cycle time T_e is

$$T_e = H*T_c+(1-H)T_m \tag{8-3}$$

T_e is the effective memory cycle time seen both by the central processing unit and the control unit. Theoretically, then, the speedup due to the introduction of a cache memory to the total memory system becomes

$$S_c = T_m/T_e \tag{8-4}$$

If we substitute for T_e in the speedup equation, we obtain the equation

$$S_c = \frac{1}{1+H(\dfrac{T_c}{T_m}-1)} \tag{8-5}$$

A plot of the maximum possible cache speedup versus this hit ratio is indicated in Figure 8.19. In practice, it is possible to obtain hit ratios well over .9. Hence, caches are very effective memory system design options. Even as early as the 1960s, computer manufacturers, after incorporating large numbers of registers called scratchpads, recognized that expansion of these registers into a small yet fast cache memory was very beneficial.

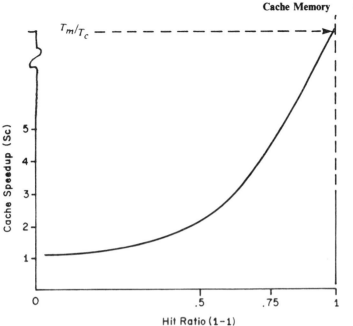

Figure 8.19   Maximum Possible Cache Speedup Versus Hit Ratio

Because a cache memory exists between the CPU and the main memory units, the cache should maintain images of many blocks of main memory. In so doing, any word access in the cache would be acquired much faster than the slower main memory. As long as the cache memory maintains a high hit ratio, subsequent memory accesses are expected to be made to the fast cache and not to the slower main memory. Of course, if an intelligent cache-filling algorithm is not used or a large cache access time to CPU clock time ratio exists, caching no longer becomes effective.

In principle, we could look at the cache relationship to main memory as similar to the main memory relationship to secondary storage. A cache memory would have its own cache tables. The cache should hold those parts of a user's program and data expected to be used most heavily, while the main memory would contain the less frequently accessed information. A cache generally assumes the main memory has been divided into blocks instead of pages, where blocks are typically either the same size or smaller than a page size. Most heavily used blocks are expected to be found in both cache and main memory. Now an operating system that makes a reference to some address space will transmit the virtual address to cache hardware. If that virtual address is a block referenced in cache memory, the addressed location is fetched from the cache. Otherwise, a cache block fault similar to a page fault will occur causing the needed block to be copied from main memory into the cache. There is no reason why we could not look upon a cache main memory as a two-level paging system. The two significant differences, however, between paging secondary memory into main memory and paging main memory into cache are the following:

1. Main memory, unlike secondary storage, has no latency such as found in a disk revolution. Hence, a main memory transfer is completed in microseconds instead of milliseconds. Because of this, a CPU when paging secondary storage will often perform a different task, returning to the main memory upon some interrupt, indicating that the page has been retrieved.

2. A cache memory, being very fast, is managed more often by a fast microprogram than software in an operating system.

The introduction of a cache memory raises many of the same selection problems generated by paging main memory and secondary storage. An algorithm is needed to determine which block to replace when cache is completely full. The solution again becomes a choice between a random replacement or a replacement based on prior knowledge of the history of resident cache blocks. Generally, the oldest or least recently used blocks will be replaced. Just as clean pages need not be written back into secondary storage, the cache memory system could be designed to cause the main memory to be written only when the CPU writes to the cache. In principle, these write-throughs attempt to maintain memory system performance by reducing the number of entire block writes back to main memory. Table 8.3 shows cache characteristics for two popular machines and indicates typical cache sizing parameters. Notice that cache access time is much shorter than main memory access time.

Table 8.3 Cache Characteristics

Computer	Main Memory Time T_m	Cache Time T_c	Cache Size (words)	Cache Block Size (words)
IBM 360/85	1.04 us	160 ns	$2K \rightarrow 4K$	8
IBM 370/165	2 us	160 ns	$1K \rightarrow 2K$	16

Since cache offers some very significant performance improvements with only a moderate cost, several investigators have studied both the hit ratios and the miss ratios (1-H) versus cache size. Typical measured plots as in Figure

8.20 demonstrate how much speedup is possible on an individual job. Observe that the cache size axis is a logarithmic instead of a linear scale. From Figure 8.20, we see that a doubling of the cache size from 512 bytes to 1024 bytes causes a 33% reduction in the cache miss ratio. Of course, as in main memory the same cache size doubling between 4096 to 8192 bytes causes only a relatively small change in the cache miss ratio.

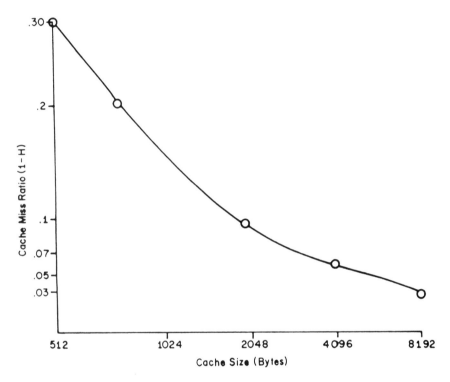

Figure 8.20   Typical Cache Miss Ratio Versus Cache Size

8.12   SEGMENTATION

Paging was introduced to provide a virtual memory that also facilitates memory sharing. At the same time, paging provides a uniform addressing scheme by partitioning virtual memory into pages that can then be mapped onto page frames in physical memory. Paging is only one of many reasonable schemes for implementing a virtual memory, but it has some shortcomings for memory sharing. Often, users want to share not only memory, but also programs and data occupying main memory at the same time. Remember that a typical memory snapshot might contain not only user segments of programs but also segments generated by compilers, constants and symbol tables generated by assemblers, and so on, as in Figure 8.21. When code segments are non-self-modifying or pure procedures, code sharing is safe. However, code that can be modified must be handled carefully (e.g., with semaphores).

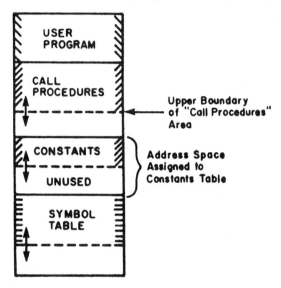

Figure 8.21   Linear-Address Space with Dynamic Space Requirements

There is no reason why the shared code must exist only in physical memory. It may also exist in virtual memory and, in that case, any one of several users desiring the same code segments could bring the code into physical memory. Now, one user's page table would have to identify the physical location of the shared code. Another user desiring access to the same code (segment) would have to set up in his or her own page table, or would have to access, the first user's page table entry for the shared code. Hence, two or more users can access the same physical space, even though shared data may reside in entirely different portions of virtual memory. Unfortunately, a scheme using only paging makes it difficult to support such sharing requirements. Segmentation does, primarily because the size of virtual memory space allocated to shared information is capable of dynamic change. A block of virtual memory is called a *segment* of memory.

Virtual memory space in a machine comprising segmented memory can have an addressing format as follows.

Segment Number	Page Number	Word Offset

The segment number indicates the segment location of a virtual memory address. The page number indicates which page the virtual memory location is in, and the word specifies the physical word address on the given page. A virtual word address can be formed as illustrated in Figure 8.22. Here, the segment number accesses a segment table. The output of the segment table identifies the upper bits of the address for a page table entry. The lower bits of the page table address are determined from the page number in the virtual word address. This page table address determines the upper bits of the physical address for the memory address register. The lower bits of the memory address register are obtained from the word in the lower bits of the virtual word address. The content of the memory address register contains the actual physical word address in main memory. The segment table entries consist of a segment number, an address in the segment, and the length of the segment.

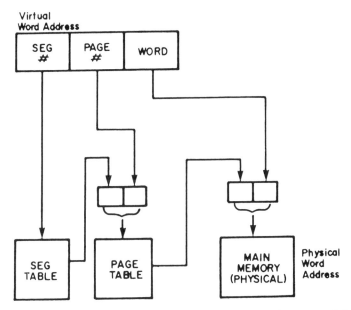

Figure 8.22 Obtaining the Physical Address in a Segmented Memory Scheme

Segments may be given symbolic names which are identified or evaluated when the segment is accessed. The evaluation of a segment name is called *binding*, a term historically referring to the mathematical process of assigning numerical values to symbolic addresses. Binding is still very important. A strict paging scheme slices virtual memory and physical memory into small blocks and binds the virtual memory to some physical memory (page frame) via the page table. Segmentation is also a slicing and binding scheme; however, virtual memory is now sliced into multipage blocks. Such blocks allow a segment to be of variable length (a key property of segmented memory). Hence, a paged virtual memory is only one-dimensional. However, segmentation generates a two-dimensional address space. One dimension is the segment number. The other dimension is the number of pages within each segment.

Of course, users could conceivably share memory with a paging scheme. However, the following difficulties arise. Suppose some pages were to be protected or at least characterized by privileged access. Once a page is "protected," the entire contents of that page become protected. But, as expected, programs do not always nicely fit into a page. Seldom is the page size ideally matched to the program size. Hence, protecting a page may restrict access not only to a program, but possibly to some other code that should not have been protected in the first place. What we actually need is a variable page size, but this is not possible in a paging scheme alone.

A segmented memory scheme handily supports variable page sizes. Because of this, the desired privileged access is easily accomplished (if, of course, a segment contains only a single program or constants table. Now only the code we want to be protected is actually protected. Likewise, only the code that should be shared will be shared. Segmentation is often called a variable-sized paging scheme. Recognize that, to be effective, a segment should always be identified with one unique function or activity, such as a constants table, a parsor tree, a compiler, etc. Unlike a page, which may contain many different symbol table generation programs or tables, a typical segment must have no functional duplicity.

Privileged access is a means to protect information. Protection can be denoted in the additional bit fields for both the page table and the segment table. These appended bits exist in a privilege/protection field or residency field for the page table entry of Figure 8.15. Such bits are actually called *descriptors*. Even though our earlier paging scheme provides us with protection bits, this is not always worthwhile. Why? Pages are often physical devices such as 128- , 256- , or 512-word ROMs or RAMs. Hence, any protection scheme or privileged access scheme would force its "description" on the entire device. A ROM would, of course, be a read only device. A RAM could be both read and write, however. The point is that the protection area must be strictly assigned by physical size and not by logical size. Segmentation helps us to partition logically separate code. Because a segment is, in fact, a single logical entity, a user must be conscious of this requirement and not add more than one function or task to a single segment. Otherwise, the advantage of the protection scheme could be lost.

As more space is needed, the user simply assigns himself or herself segments of virtual memory. The segment number field in the virtual memory address of course limits the total number of segments a user may have at any given time. But it is possible that a user may reach across the full virtual memory space, or even the total capacity of the memory system hierarchy including cache, main memory, and secondary storage. (However, most users require much less space.) When more than one program is loaded into a computer system at any given time, the operating system keeps track of which areas of physical memory are allocated to each program and lists the memory in a space table. A user request for more unallocated space causes the operating system to scan the space table and assign it to a user when so needed.

8.12.1 SEGMENT LIMITATIONS

Figure 8.22 represents the general technique of obtaining the physical word address from the virtual word address in a combined segmented and paged virtual memory. Within the virtual word address are descriptors identifying the page size and protection bits. Any virtual word address violation (trying to write into a protected zone) is checked at the segment table. Any page table not in main memory generates a page fault initiating a fetch from secondary memory. Finally, a page once available in main memory permits the physical word access.

Even with segmentation, is it possible to efficiently use memory all of the time? Not always. In fact, a segmented memory system produces the same problem that a page memory system does, that is, wasteful generation of unused main memory space. Suppose that at some point the memory system is completely filled up with several segments, each of a different length. Later on, the segments have been moved in and out of memory, all with different physical sizes. At some point, we could expect to find a short segment moved into the vacant space left by a very long segment. The remaining space is essentially unused. Suppose this occurs over many areas of the memory. The resultant memory will look somewhat like a checkerboard, where vacant or unused spaces can be found at the end of short segments that were placed in large segment holes.

An operating system could compact memory by collecting the useless small holes into one large hole. Then any new segments could be placed in this single large hole. Compaction does take time, however, especially if it is attempted after every hole is created.

Some hole management algorithms in an operating system attempt to minimize the number of small holes, while others indiscriminately try to reduce the number of holes. The *best-fit* algorithm always attempts to identify the smallest hole for an incoming segment. The purpose of the best-fit algorithm is to minimize useless space. The motivation behind the best-fit algorithm is the preservation of large holes as long as possible, just in case a large segment needs it. A *first-fit* algorithm simply scans the whole list and selects the first hole of sufficient size for the current inputted segment. This later algorithm takes much less time than the best fit algorithm. Both algorithms tend to decrease hole sizes equally well.

8.12.2   POPULARITY OF SEGMENTATION

Because segmentation easily supports protection by capturing the variable sizing of logical entities, it is commonly used in one form or another. In early Burroughs machines, a segment was simply a variable-sized page, which aimed toward business applications, and primarily executed ALGOL programs, which are naturally block structured. Segment blocks then conveniently matched the block structure of the main programming language. Digital Equipment Corporation (DEC) has employed both paging and segmentation schemes. As expected, DEC machines, as well as many others, can support different languages equally well. (However, early machine documentation described segmented memory, while later manufacturer's data described page schemes, even though the system remained unchanged.) The forerunner memory system of the Honeywell 645 and 6180 was a MULTICS segmented and paged virtual memory scheme built at MIT. IBM 370s also employ a virtual memory system with 2^{24}-bit bytes of virtual memory. The 370 provides various options of physical page sizes from 2K to 4K and between 16 and 256 segments of virtual memory.

8.13   VAX-VMS OPERATING SYSTEM

The VAX-VMS operating system has been designed to handle most multiprocessing tasks encountered. It is a general-purpose system intended to support concurrent execution of multiuser time-sharing, batch, and realtime applications. Typical activities of VAX-VMS include:

1. Virtual memory management

2. Event-driven priority scheduling

3. Shared-memory, file, and interprocess communication data

4. Programmed system services for process and subprocess control and interprocess communication

VMS invokes swapping, paging, and protection/sharing of both code and data. Memory is allocated dynamically so that throughput is maintained at a high rate. Application software can control physical memory allocated to executing processes, the protection pages, and swapping. This flexibility greatly adds to application software development. CPU time is normally allocated on a preemptive priority basis. Scheduling can rotate among processes, and demanding realtime processes do not have to compete with lower-priority processes for scheduling services. Because application software can allocate some services, realtime applications can control their virtual memory paging and execution. System security and privacy are also available in the VMS operating system. Memory access protection can be both between and within processes by allowing each process to have its own independent virtual address space that can be mapped to private pages or shared pages.

Several components and services make up VMS. The basic components include:

1. Processes that control initial resource allocation

2. Command interpreters

3. User-callable process control services

4. Memory management routines

5. Shared runtime library routines

6. File and record management services

Some VMS operating system jobs run as independent activities on the system, such as the job controller. It initiates and terminates user processes. Sometimes a user software must acquire the basic functions of VMS to perform program development, file management, and system information services. The command interpreter is used in this fashion. The memory management services perform much of the tasks described in Section 8.9. Routines to control mapping of virtual memory to system and user jobs are found in the image activator.

8.13.1 PROCESS VERSUS PROGRAMS

To understand VMS in a multiprogrammed application environment, four concepts must be described. They include the *image* (an executable program), *process* (image context and address space), *job* (detached process and its subprocesses, and *group* (set of jobs that can share resources.) Although a typical user has no need to understand these four concepts, they are important to the applications programmer.

The reader should understand the difference between an image and a process. An image is an executable program, created by translating source-language modules into object modules and linking the object modules together. Images are stored and can be retrieved from a file on disk. To run an image, the operating system must read the image file into main memory to execute it, and the environment in which an image executes is, in fact, its context. The complete context of an image is not just a user-generated set of object code. A complete image context includes definition of its resource allocation quotas (device ownership, file access, and maximum physical memory allocation). When an image is shared by two or more users concurrently, the image is said to be executing in two or more contexts.

The notion of a process contrasted with an image now becomes clear. An image context *and* the address space used by the image is called a *process*. It is then the function of the operating system to schedule processes and the process provides a context in which the image executes. A process can execute only one image at a time, even though the process can provide the context for serially executing any number of different images. One can easily see that a Pascal compiler is executable by two or more processes simultaneously, even though there may be only one copy of the compiler in main memory. In one context, the compilation process may have just begun. In another context, the compilation may be nearing completion. In a further context, the compiler may be performing some I/O tasks to another directory.

As stated earlier, a process can provide a context for serially executing a number of images. Consider the case where a user edits a file. Here, the system editor image executes in the context of the user's process. Upon compilation, the compiler image executes in the context of the user's process. From this viewpoint, one should be able to see how a process acts as a cover or "envelope" for a user's activities. To the operating system context switching becomes necessary and vital.

An image can also create *subprocesses* when executing in the context of a process. It is prudent to consider the subprocess as an auxiliary process in which a specific image executes. The image, of course, must also identify the image to be executed in the context of the subprocess and/or the source of commands to be interpreted in that process. A type of nesting occurs here, just as with nested subroutines. The *owner process* is the process executing the image that creates the subprocess. The owner process exercises complete control over execution of any subprocesses it creates even to the extent of declaring the privileges it will allow the subprocess to have. When the owner process terminates, all list subprocesses terminate.

When a user logs onto a system and requests services of the system using a command interpreter, the operating system creates a process called a *detached process*. In most cases, it is the operating system that creates detached processes but some privileged application program may also do so. Even so, a detached process is considered to have no owner. A detached process is not necessarily complete enough to be executable code by itself. When a detached process and all of its subprocesses it creates are considered together, this unit of code is called a *job*. It is jobs that an operating system considers as accounting entities to control resource allocation. The set of resources a job uses is its de facto authorized quotas. All processes of a job are scheduled independently.

8.13.2   RESOURCE ALLOCATION

The general classification of resources available to an operating system are the processor, memory, and peripherals. In a multiprogramming and multiprocessing environment it is easy to see that resources can be shared among several users. The system must manage them through the operating system functions. Furthermore each job can request different resources. The operating system enables the sharing of resources according to the individual needs of each job. But the operating system must do much more. It has to protect jobs and the data created by each job from inadvertent writing by another job. Job scheduling, memory management, device allocation, and I/O processing are part of the operating system resource allocation tasks. System managers do much of the scheduling, including setting quotas and limits to main memory space. Each user receives an authorization file entry from the system manager. The entry specifies total processor time usage, maximum number of subprocesses a job can create, the number of simultaneously open files, process virtual and physical memory usage, and number of simultaneous I/O transfers.

8.13.3   PRIVILEGES

Individual users in a multiprogramming environment need to have as much system access flexibility as possible. Computer system designers support this flexibility by assigning privileges. The basic privileges can then be found in a user authorization file. Sixty-four privileges can be granted or witheld in the VAX-VMS operating system. A job may have the right to alter priority of a process, execute a user-written program at a more-privileged access mode, execute operator functions (obviously not granted to everyone), create detached processes, and set up communicating facilities for cooperating processes. In most cases, when a user executes an image, the image acquires only those privileges granted directly to that user's job by the authorization file. However, there must be some exceptions to this rule and they are known images.

Known images are installed by the system manager and provide an additional set of dynamic privileges. One known image is the LOGIN image which has the privilege to access the user authorization file to obtain the user's privileges.

8.13.4   PROTECTION

A user's data file can be protected through the use of the user identification code (UIC), which has two numbers: a group number and a member number. A UIC is assigned by the system manager. When a user executes an image and is given or denied data access privileges, it is the UIC which determines the access. A protection code will apply to four types of accesses: read, write, execute, and delete. Access or denial is possible to an owner, group, world, and system. The world is essentially everyone on the system.

8.14   USER INTERFACES TO VAX I/O SERVICES

The VAX-VMS separates I/O services into two classes: I/O system services and record management services. Most users will invoke record management services. The I/O services provide for direct control over I/O processing resources of the operating system. Here, a programmer can perform device-dependent and device-independent processing. A programmer can also read and write blocks on mass storage media using physical (device-oriented), logical (volume-relative), or virtual (file-relative) addressing.

8.14.1   RECORD MANAGEMENT SYSTEM (RMS)

The VAX-11 RMS is the general-purpose file and record management programming tool for file and record processing. To facilitate typical user accesses in RMS, RMS provides device-independent access to file-structured I/O devices. Because processing logical records is most common, RMS automatically provides record blocking and unblocking. But users can also choose to select their own record blocking on file-structured volumes such as disk and magnetic tape. They must use a virtual block number for volume-independent processing.

8.15   SUMMARY

In this chapter, we have focused on the machine level above the assembly language. The level 3 virtual machine of this chapter executes "instructions" called commands mainly via an operating system. Just as we found machine language instructions to manipulate data among various microscopic resources (such as ALU and general-purpose registers), the dominant language at level 3 consists of commands. These commands, found in a typical operating system language, request activity of machine components at level 3. The basic component of a level 3 machine component is an I/O unit, CPU, and memory unit. Commands could be assembly language macros.

At this machine level, you should be able to answer the following questions regarding how tasks are accomplished.

1. How does an operating system manage resources?

2. What overall tasks does an operating system perform?

3. How does a level 3 virtual machine differ from a level 2 or level 1 virtual machine?

4. Why are files used at level 3? Are they physical or logical? Why?

5. How can memory appear very large to a user? What operating system features support virtual memory?

6. How does the computer orchestrate activity within its memory hierarchy?

In many ways, the control unit at level 1 relates to the physical elements of computer machinery, such as a gate, register, ALU, or memory location, just as an operating system at level 3 relates to the CPU, cache memory, main memory, secondary storage, and I/O units. Within the control unit resides one or more microprograms. These collections of very primitive instructions exert direct control of electronic circuits. An operating system program, unlike a microprogram, controls system behavior. Whereas a microprogram is built for machine convenience, the operating system is available for the user.

Is a level 3 machine the ultimate level? No. In fact, we could conceive of a machine that can be simulated by our host level 3 machine. Simulator software could even mimic the host machine (e.g., IBM's VM). However, most likely we would want to emulate an altogether different architecture on our current machine. Why? Perhaps we want to design a new machine and test it before we actually build the machine. Perhaps we want to explore new alternatives in computer system design. Whatever the reason, a perception of a virtual machine above level 3 is possible. Yet, no matter which level we are operating in, software connects each level to the next level. In this chapter, we have looked at the operating system level.

8.16   KEY WORDS

block	page fault
blocked process	process
checkerboard	process control block
command	race condition
direct access files	random access
dispatch	ready process
file	record
file access	relative organization
file organization	running process
fragmentation	segmentation
indexed allocation	sequential access
key	system calls
linked list allocation	virtual instruction
operating system	virtual machine

8.17   SUGGESTED READING

Coffman, E. G., Jr., and Denning, Peter J. *Operating Systems Theory*. Englewood Cliffs, N.J.: Prentice-Hall, 1973.

> This textbook focuses on operating systems mainly from a mathematical viewpoint emphasizing analytical models. Those who must design new operating systems would do well to understand the predictable performances of certain classes of operating systems found in this text.

Cohen, Leo J. *Operating System Analysis and Design*. Rochelle Park, N.J.: Hayden Book, 1970.

> This technical reference addresses the design of the operating system at a very abstract level, although it does provide a unifying and homogeneous point of view. Presentation tends to be brief and brisk. Sometimes the obscure nomenclature such as "worker" programs confuses the reader. Emphasis mainly upon the structure of a multiprogram executive runs throughout the textbook. Other than discussing files as the basic logical entity at this operating system level, a "transaction," which the author defines as an application program, is used.

Denning, Peter J. "The Working Set Model for Program Behavior," *CACM*, Vol. 11, pp. 323–333, May 1968.
> Machines invoking paging which do not use a working set model are contrasted with machines that do in this paper, which also provides more definition and analysis. Denning also covers scheduling, sharing, and resource allocation schemes.

Denning, Peter J. "Virtual Memory," *Computing Surveys*, Vol. 2, pp. 153–189, September 1970.
> This tutorial, with a bibliography of 84 entries, covers many topics concerned with virtual memory. As a tutorial, topics on segmentation, paging, storage utilization, demand paging, and working set models are clearly presented for the casual reader. This paper serves as a natural companion to "The Working Set Model for Program Behavior."

Deitel, Harvey M. *An Introduction to Operating Systems*. Reading, Mass.: Addison-Wesley, 1984.
> This is an excellent first-level text on operating systems which includes case studies on UNIX, VAX, CP/M, MVS, and VM. The notions of a process, processor, and processor states are clearly explained in Chapter Three.

Digital Equipment Corporation. *Introduction to RT-11*. Maynard, Mass., 1981.
> RT-11 is a single-user operating system. Precise details of its operation can be found in this manufacturer's documentation. Although examples abound in the many chapters, the presentation assumes much prior knowledge of operating systems in general. One great limitation of RT-11 is its single user feature.

Digital Equipment Corporation. *VAX-11 Software Handbook*. Maynard, Mass., 1978.
> Brief yet detailed discussion of the large mainframe operating system (VAX/VMS) for DEC's VAX machines is available directly from this manufacturer's documentation.

Gear, C. William. *Computer Organization and Programming*, 3rd Ed. New York: McGraw-Hill, 1980.
> Multiprogramming and multiprocessor topics can be found in Chapter Seven, where much discussion about paging and segmentation is also available. Only a small amount of discussion on segmentation and paging in the IBM 370 and PDP-11 can be found.

Kaisler, Stephen H. *The Design of Operating Systems for Small Computer Systems*. New York: Wiley Interscience, 1983.
> This advanced level text focuses upon the many aspects of operating systems giving not only the designer's view but also the user's view. The introductory material in Chapter One is especially helpful in this regard. Equally informative is the coverage of operating system command languages in Chapter Six.

Kuck, David J. *The Structure of Computers and Computations, Vol. One*. New York: John Wiley, 1978.

> This is an in-depth reference on the organization of computers with many interesting details that help us to compare different machines. Although written at a high level, the material on operating systems is lucid and informative.

Madnick, Stuart E., and Donovan, John J. *Operating Systems*. New York: McGraw-Hill, 1974.

> This is an introductory text on operating systems which stresses resource management functions more than virtual machine aspects. Like many operating system books, the major theme addressed is that of operating system-created environments for applications.

Peterson, James L., and Silberschatz, Abraham. *Operating System Concepts*. Reading, Mass.: Addison Wesley, 1983.

> This text presents the basic development of operating systems including their underlying concepts, all carefully organized into an in-depth presentation of accepted fundamentals with numerous figures and examples. A thorough coverage of concurrent processes is found in Chapter Eight.

Shaw, A. *The Logical Design of Operating Systems*. Englewood Cliffs, N.J.: Prentice-Hall, 1974.

> This introductory text emphasizes general principles rather than any specific machine. However, most of the algorithms presented are illustrated with ALGOL programs. There is an in-depth coverage of many interesting topics concerned with system organization, batch systems, sharing, resource control, deadlocks, and file systems, each of which is contained in a separate chapter.

Tanenbaum, Andrew S. *Structured Computer Organization*. Englewood Cliffs, N.J.: Prentice-Hall, 1976.

> Chapter Five focuses on the virtual machine at the operating system level, which the author also calls level 3. This chapter discusses virtual I/O instructions as well as virtual memory in a lucid manner. The text focuses on the significant differences of the virtual machine instructions for the PDP-11, CYBER 70, and IBM 370. The chapter also provides some insight into the use of virtual instructions for parallel processing tasks. As a whole, this chapter is highly recommended.

8.18   EXERCISES

8.1   What is the primary difference between user instructions or commands to the operating system and operating system routines?

8.2 Suppose files are to be organized as relative or direct files in a disk system, and assume that the maximum number of records is 50 in any file. What is the relative location of the following records?

Key	Record
147	1
121	2
375	4
962	6
37	3
29	5

8.3 Identify and explain four level 3 virtual machine instructions that would not be found at level 2.

8.4 Identify the available file types in the following:
   a. CP/M
   b. UNIX
   c. ZENIX
   d. MULTICS
   e. MP/M 86
   f. OASIS
   g. VAX/VMS
   h. 370/VM
   i. DOS-11

8.5 Describe the chief function of an operating system.

8.6 The following tasks are most likely to be handled by which principal class of operating system programs?
   a. Compile FORTRAN source code.
   b. Rewind a magnetic tape.
   c. Create a new assembler.
   d. Boot up a computer system.
   e. Keep a printer active.
   f. Delete a disk file.
   g. Process decks of cards.
   h. Remove a disk from a disk drive unit.
   i. Word processing.
   j. Execute a PAC-MAN game.

8.7 Does a typical user expect to find more or fewer "instructions" at level 4 compared with level 3?

8.8 Why do operating systems require a file access to be initiated by "opening" the file?

8.9 Obtain the sector and track for record 4000 on the following consecutively allocated disk file systems.

	# of Sectors	# of Tracks	Words/Sector	Words/Record
a.	100	14	64	8
b.	200	20	128	4
c.	64	8	256	12
d.	50	30	64	10

8.10 What is a system call?

8.11 What does the hole table look like for the following bit map?

	Sector						
Track	0	1	2	3	4	5	6
0	0	1	0	0	1	0	1
1	1	1	0	0	1	1	0
2	0	0	0	0	1	0	0
3	1	0	1	0	1	0	1
4	0	0	0	1	0	0	1

8.12 What are the advantages and disadvantages of storage allocation maintenance using a bit map? A hole table?

8.13 What are the chief reasons for using a multilevel directory? Would such a directory be found in an Apple or TRS-80 computer? Why not?

8.14 The following operations are most likely to be found at which machine level (1, 2, 3, 4)? Explain.

a. R2 ← R1+R3

b. Rewind tape

c. End-of-file detected

d. Square root routine

e. Macro call

f. OPEN file

g. .TTYIN macro definition

h. Overflow detect on V flag

i. 20 GOTO 1000

j. Coroutine resume

8.15 Why is it reasonable to classify an operating system command as a virtual assembly language instruction?

8.16 What is so attractive about considering the address space as distinct from the actual physical locations of memory?

8.17 A virtual memory using a paging scheme is organized around a 512-word page size, 8 virtual pages, and 2,048 words of main memory. The current page table is:

Secondary Memory

Virtual Page	Address	Page Frame
0	0	1
1	3741	3
2	1022	-
3	87	-
4	462	-
5	1320	-
6	4	2
7	2664	0
8	666	-

a. What is the main memory address of each of the following virtual addresses?

4, 1024, 630, 4020, 896

b. What is the meaning of the contents of the secondary address field in the page table entries for pages 2, 3, 4, and 5?

8.18 Describe three ways virtual storage can be implemented.

8.19 XYZ Computer Corporation decided to introduce a computer without a program counter. It took a survey of some "typical" programs and determined that a PC is not needed. After a year of widespread usage of the system, users began to complain that their operating system failed to achieve even respectable throughput. Many users gave up at their terminals when turnaround time approached agonizing minutes of waiting. Why?

8.20 Some clever operating system designers decided to combine the LRU algorithm with the FIFO page replacement algorithm. What "kinds" of programs were they trying to benefit with better page replacement performance? What "kinds" of programs would fail miserably?

8.21 Novel Operating Systems Corporation wants to take measurements on an existing computer installation (maybe yours) to determine how best to build a new page replacement algorithm. What meaningful statistical measures could they use? Why?

8.22 Assume that the cache memory cycle time is much smaller than main memory cycle time. Show that the speedup due to cache is approximately $1/(1-H)$.

8.23 Suppose our studies on cache memory design require a system speedup comparison test. We found the measured hit ratios for several programs on the average to be .91 for 4K bytes of cache and .96 for 12K bytes.

   a. What is the system speedup in each case if $T_c=100$ nanoseconds and $T_m=1.2$ microseconds?

   b. What percentage improvement in system speedup is obtained by using a 12K byte cache?

8.24 Show that the maximum cache speedup, S_c, is less than $K+1$ (where K is some positive number) if it is assumed that $H=K/(K+1)$.

8.25 Explain why a privileged access option is made available in files, records, pages, and segments in a computer system.

8.26 How is fragmentation different than checkerboarding?

8.27 Explain what type of software exists at each virtual machine level. Don't forget the fourth level. Can more than four virtual levels exist? Why?

Appendices

Appendix A
RT-11 FILE NAMES

File names must conform to the following format:

The actual file name consists of up to six letters and numbers and must begin with a letter. This name is followed by a dot (period) and the file type which consists of three letters. There are certain recognized file types which are standard with the system. Stay with the expected type of file when using standard file types.

Following are the standard file types:

.BAC   — BASIC compiled file

.BAK   — Editor backup file

.BAS   — BASIC source file

.BAT   — BATCH source file

.COM   — Indirect command file

.CTL   — BATCH control file

.DAT   — BASIC or FORTRAN Data file

.DBL   — DIBOL source file

.DIF   — SRCCOM output file

.DIR   — Directory listing file

.FOR   — FORTRAN source file

.LOG   — Batch log file

.LST   — Listing file

.MAC   — MACRO source file — The filetype you will use
             for your assembly language programs

.MAP   — Linker map file

.OBJ   — Object output file — What the assembler produces
             from your code

.REL   — Executable foreground program file — What runs
             on the system

.SAV   — Executable background program file
.SML   — System MACRO library

.SYS   — System files and handlers

.TXT   — Text files used for documentation

Cassette drives are named DD0: (note that this is a zero) and DD1: for drives zero and one, and the two RX02 disk drives (if we had them) are referred to by DY0: and DY1:. Note that the colon is an integral part of the name and must be included in the reference.

Appendix B
RT-11 KEYBOARD MONITOR COMMANDS

There are many keyboard monitor commands available in the RT-11 operating system, and there are many options associated with them. Following is a brief introduction to the commands most often used and a guide to the useful options associated with them.

Useful information for these commands:

(1) The system is set to look for data files on drive 1 (default) so a user need not specify the drivename on files unless you need to refer to a file on drive 0.

(2) The generic file reference is the asterisk *. To refer to all files with the same filename, enter your command with filename.* . To refer to all files with the same filetype, enter your command with *.filetype. To refer to all files on a volume, enter commands with *.* . Note that a command to DELETE *.* will result in the deletion of all files on the device. The commands that support the generic file reference are COPY, DELETE, DIRECTORY, HELP, PRINT, RENAME, and TYPE.

(3) The term volume refers to a storage device such as a cassette or disk, as a general term.

(4) If you make a typing mistake while entering a command, use the DELETE key to move back character by character to correct your mistake. The ^H does not work for correction on this sytem. ^U will take out the whole line.

You may enter multiple commands, separated by carriage returns, and the system will execute them one after another. There is a 134-character buffer to hold these commands, and if the buffer size is exceeded, you will hear a beep and no more characters will be accepted until one of the commands finishes execution. To stop execution of this buffer after the current job terminates, type ^C. To stop execution immediately (in the middle of the current job) type ^C^C.

COPY This command transfers files from one device to another, or concatenates files. The basic syntax is: COPY (source) devicename:filename.filetype (dest) devicename:filename. filetype example: COPY DD0:EXAM.TXT DD1:EXAM.TXT will copy the file EXAM.TXT from the file EXAM.TXT from drive 0 to the cassette on drive 1. Option: COPY/WAIT can be used to copy files between volumes that do not have the system on them. Type COPY/WAIT drivename: oldfile.filetype drivename:newfile.filetype and the monitor will instruct you as to which cassettes to insert in which drives to effect the copy.

DELETE This command deletes the files you specify. Syntax is: DELETE filename.filetype you may delete more than one file at one time, separating the files by commas, or using the generic file reference.

DIRECTORY This command will give you a directory of the volume you specify. The default will give you a directory of the cassette on drive 1. Note that if you wish a directory of the system cassette on drive 0, you must specify DD0: in the command. Syntax is: DIRECTORY devicename Example DIRECTORY DD0: Options available include: DIRECTORY/BRIEF will list just the files, whereas the standard directory lists lengths and dates created, if known. DIRECTORY/FULL will also list empty blocks on the volume. DIRECTORY/BADBLOCKS will return the address of any bad blocks that develop on the volume, and return a message if no bad blocks are detected /VOLUMEID added to the end of the directory command will add the name and owner of the volume to the directory. There are a great many more options available for those that are interested. Check the System User's Guide.

EDIT/KED filename.filetype You must add the /KED after EDIT. The Keypad editor is powerful and easy to use and is recommended for student use. Options: EDIT/KED/CREATE filename.filetype allows you to create a new file with the name you specify. EDIT/KED/OUTPUT:filenew.filetype fileold.filetype will rename the edited file (in this case to filenew) and leave the original file under the name (fileold) unchanged.

EXECUTE This command will assemble, link, load and run a file of filetype also. For example: EXECUTE/LIST/DEBUG filename will cause an assembly list to be printed, link the module with ODT, and bring your program up under ODT for debugging.

INITIALIZE This command initializes a volume in the specified device. Example: INITIALIZE DD1: will initialize a cassette placed in drive 1. Options: INITIALIZE/BADBLOCKS DD1: will search the cassette for any bad blocks before initialization (a really good idea). Any time the INITIALIZE command is given, the monitor will ask you Are you Sure? [Y/N] to make sure you really want to initialize the volume. Initialization causes the loss of any files stored on the volume. INITIALIZE/VOLUMEID DD1: will allow you to name your cassette (up to 12 characters) and give the owner's name (up to 12 characters). The system will ask you for these names when it is ready for them.

LINK This command will convert object modules into a format suitable to load and execute. Syntax is: LINK filename (in this case the filetype need not be specified--the system will look for type .OBJ) Option: LINK/DEBUG will link the ODT debugger with your file and when you RUN the resulting .SAV file, it will be run under ODT control.

MACRO This command assembles one or more source files and produces an object file ready to be linked and loaded. Syntax is: MACRO filename (in this case the default filetype is .MAC and you should enter your MACRO-11 programs with this filetype) To specify multiple source files to be assembled, separate the files with plus signs in the command line. The .OBJ file is created with the same filename as the source file, and will be put back on the data device. Options: LIST produces an assembly listing.

/CROSSREFERENCE adds cross-reference tables to the listing generated during assembly. If the /LIST/CROSSREFERENCE is placed after MACRO, the assembly listing is printed immediately on the printer; if the /LIST/CROSSREFERENCE is placed after the filename, a file of type LST is produced which may be TYPEd or PRINTed as desired. You may of course specify /LIST without /CROSSREFERENCE.

PRINT This command lists the contents of one or more files on the line printer. Syntax is: PRINT filename.filetype, [filename.filetype,...] Up to six files may be printed with one command, separating filenames by commas. If you have several files to print, you will save time this way. The generic file reference may be used to print all files of a certain name or type. If you wish a file printed that is not on drive 1, you

must specify the device name before the filename (i.e.   PRINT
DD0:FILE.TXT will print FILE.TXT from drive 0). Options:
PRINT/COPIES:n will print n copies of the specified files.

    RUN   This command loads a file from the system device and
starts execution.   Syntax is: RUN filename.filetype (default
filetype is .SAV)

    RENAME   This command assigns a new name to an existing file.
Syntax is: RENAME fileold.filetype filenew.filetype Default
device is drive 1, and device need be specified only if you need a
file on a different device.   Note that if you rename a file to
the name of a currently existing file on that volume, the original
contents of the file will be lost.

    SQUEEZE   This command consolidates all unused blocks on a
volume into a single area at the end of the volume.   You should
use this command if your data volume starts to get full.   Syntax
is: SQUEEZE DD1:   Some time will pass as the monitor recopies
everything to one end of your data cassette.

    TYPE   This command lists the contents of the specified file
on   the   CRT.   Syntax   is: TYPE
filename.filetype[,filename.filetype,...]   Up to six files may be
specified at one time, separating them with commas.   The generic
file reference may be used.

    All of the above commands are legitimate on either the
Working system or the Help system.   In addition, on the Help
system, the commands HELP and SHOW are enabled.   To use these
commands, the Help system must be the booted system on drive 0.

    HELP   This command lists information related to RT-11
commands regarding syntax, options, etc.   Syntax for this command
is: HELPtopics HELP * will list all the topics for which help is
available.HELP/PRINTER topic will send the information to the
line printer rather than the terminal.   Default is the terminal.
HELP topic OPTIONS will list all the options available for that
command.

    SHOW   This command prints information about the RT-11
system.   SHOW ALL will list configuration, devices and special
features.

Appendix C
MACRO-11 PROGRAMMING STYLE

    Your source program is composed of assembly-language
statements, each of which must be entirely on one line.   There
are four fields which may be present in each assembly-language
statement.

    The first is the label field.   A label is a name you give to
a line of your code.   The name may consist of up to six letters
or numbers, must begin with a letter and must be followed by a
colon.   This field, when present, is always placed at the left
margin.   A label is assigned the address of a memory location
when the code is assembled.   A label must be used whenever a
section of code needs to be branched to from some other
statement.   They can also be used to identify the end of a loop
or section of code.   Each label must be unique, otherwise an
assembly error will occur.

The next field is the opcode field. This specifies the action to be performed. It may be an instruction mnemonic (op code), a macro call (see below), or an assembler directive (see below). This field should be in column 9 (tab 1 on our terminals). An operator is terminated by a space or a tab. Sample opcodes include ADD, MOV, BGE. Check the PDP-11 Processor Handbook for the instruction set. This field must be present in each statement.

The third field is the operand field. It will be in column 17 (tab 2 on our terminals). When the opcode is an instruction, the operand field contains the operands required for the instruction. When the operator is a macro, the operand field contains any parameters that need to be passed.

The fourth field is the comment field. It will be in column 33 (tab 4 on our terminals; press the tab twice after the operand field to get to the right spot). A comment must begin with a semicolon. Following that, any character is legal. The assembler will ignore comments when your code is assembled. See below for a brief discussion of the importance and general style of comments.

Strictly speaking, there are no reserved words in MACRO-11. However, you will cause yourself a lot of grief if you use a label or variable that is the same as one of the opcode mnemonics, or one of the register names (Rn), or define your own macro with the same name as one of the system macros or none of the assembly directives.

Blank lines are legal, and are useful for delineating sections of your code. A line may consist of only a comment. Such lines at the head of your program or at the head of major sections may use the entire line, as long as they begin with a semicolon. Inside sections, extra lines of comments should reside in th comment field at tab 4, for ease of readability.

Comments are vitally important in assembly language programming. Comments on the code are as important as the code itself. It is impossible to go into someone's assembly language and figure out what it is doing without good comments. Each section of code should have a comment preceding it consisting of several lines telling what that section does. In the body of the code, the comments should spell out what is happening. It is not necessary to comment EVERY line. Certain lines are self-explanatory: MOV R1,NUM should not be commented as ;MOVE R1 TO NUM. A comment in this case of ;STORE RESULT IN NUM or even ;STORE RESULT would be enough to tell what is going on. There should be a comment at least every few lines, telling what is being done, what is in the various registers referred to, where the results are being stored, and what the conditions are for the various branches and jumps. Since in assembly language there are thousands of ways of achieving the same goal, your comments are there to let the reader know HOW you are going about achieving the desired results. It is important to comment your code as you are writing it, before you enter it into the machine.

MACROS--A macro is a section of code that has a name. There are predefined macros in the system library that you can use. You can also write your own. They are a tool that saves you from typing the same code many times. Macros are defined prior to the executable portion of your code and each one is given a name. Then, in your code when you wish that portion to appear, just type the name. During the assembly process, the actual code of the macro will be substituted for the name. This is NOT a subroutine. A subroutine causes a change in the flow of control, so that the program jumps from one section to another. It is done

EACH TIME the program executes. A macro is just the substitution of a named section of code for the name itself, and is done ONCE during assembly.

ASSEMBLY DIRECTIVE--An instruction to the assembler which specifies an operation to be done at assembly time. Examples are giving the program a title, or allocating data space.

The first line of your program should be a comment giving your name. The next line should be an assembly directive giving a title to your program. The format of this line is

.TITLE whatever you wish to call it the period must precede each assembly directive to distinguish it from a label. Next will be a line or lines identifying macros not defined in your program. There are a number of system macros that are available for you to use. Any of them that are used in the program must be named in the

.MCALL line. Those that you will use initially are:

.PRINT   This will print an ASCII message line on the terminal

.EXIT   This will return you to the monitor after the program has finished execution

The syntax of the line to name these is:

.MCALL .mac1, .mac2, .macn Following the identifying of exterior macros will be your own macros (if you have any), which must appear before the executable code.

Next will be any assignment of constants that is done in your program. If you wish NUM to have the value of 60 decimal, enter a line as follows: NUM = 60. The period indicates that this is a decimal quantity. If it was left off, the number would be interpreted as octal (base 8), in this case 48.

Next will come the executable code. Be sure to label the first line in order to give the .END directive something to refer to. You will now enter the lines of your program which represent the executable statements, macro calls, etc. When you wish execution to cease, use the .EXIT macro call to accomplish this.

Following the executable code will be the data space declarations. These are something like variable declarations in higher level languages, except in this case you are specifying exactly what space you want, and where it will be. Any data values or message strings will be defined here also.

After all the data space declarations will come the assembler directive:

.END label   The label is that of the line where you wish your program to begin execution. For this reason, separately assembled subroutines do not have a label following the .END directive. There must be a space separating the label from the .END (or use the tab).

This is the last line of code that the assembler will process. When you finish entering the code, you are ready to assemble, debug, link, load and run your program.

Appendix D
RT-11 THE KEYPAD EDITOR

To enter the Keypad Editor, type EDIT/KED filename.filetype. The drive name need not be specified if your file is on the cassette in drive 1. The KED program will load from drive O, then your file will be loaded from drive 1. Your file will be displayed on the screen and the cursor will be set at the beginning of your file. You are now ready to enter the various KED functions and commands. Your original file is renamed as a backup file (type .BAK) and the new edited version will be stored with the original name and filetype you specified. Should you wish to regain the version before the latest editing, the .BAK file will have it.

To create a new file under KED, type EDIT/KED/CREATE filename.filetype with the name you wish your new file to have. When KED is loaded, the cursor will flash in the upper left corner and wait for you to enter your lines.

The default function of KED is entering of characters, and anything you type that is not a specific function of KED will be entered at the cursor. You may enter carriage returns with the return key at the ends of your lines (otherwise the line will wrap around into the next line of copy without a carriage return). The keypad has the function keys for the various editing functions. The cursor movement is accomplished with the arrow keys on the main keyboard.

If you make a mistake in a function or a command, the console will signal you with a beep. Press (PF2) and a space will be cleared for an error message telling you about the problem. A second (PF2) will display a diagram of the keypad with the names of the functions. A third (PF2) will display a diagram of the keypad with the names of the functions. A third (PF2) will display a summary of the commands. To reenter normal mode, press the ENTER key on the keypad or type ^W to repaint the screen.

Occasionally the editor will need to refer to the cassette and you will hear the tape drive whirring. Attempting to enter characters at this time may result in an error. Just wait briefly for it to finish its read and then continue. Also if you enter cursor movement commands very fast, an error will occasionally show up in the form of added characters and a beep. You will have to delete those added characters.

Techniques that make the editing process speed along very easily: Use the SECTION command to jump to the desired sections 16 lines at a time. Reverse direction with the 4 and 5 keys to move through your file whichever direction you wish. Use the WORD command to skip through a line quickly. The BLINE moves you quickly to the beginning of the next line and the EOL moves you quickly to the next end-of-line. If you wish to change something that occurs in various places throughout your file, use the FIND to set a search model, the FINDNEXT and REPLACE to make the changes. A quick way to move a work or a line is to use DELWORD or DELLINE, move the cursor to where you want it, and UNDELWORD or UNDELLINE to write it back out. If you wish to move larger blOcks of copy, up to 512 characters, use the select range, cut and paste.

NAME   KEYS

Functions to delete and return copy:

DELCHAR ,   comma key on keypad deletes the
                             character under the cursor.

UNDEL-

CHAR   (PF1),   will return that deleted character at
                             the current cursor position.

DELWORD-   hyphen key on keypad deletes the rest of
                             the word from the cursor on to the right

UNDEL-

WORD   (PF1)-   will return the deleted word at the
                             current cursor position

DELLINE (PF4)   will delete the rest of the line to the
                             right of the cursor including the
                             carriage return

UNDEL-

LINE   (PF1)(PF4)   will return the deleted line

DELEOL   (PF1)2   on keypad will delete rest of line but
                             not the carriage return

            (PF1)(PF4)   will return deleted portion

            linefeed   on keyboard will delete portion of word
                             to the left of the cursor

            ^U   will delete portion of line to left of
                             cursor

Functions to move the cursor:

The arrow keys move the cursor up, down, left and right
by one space.

TOP   (PF1)5   moves cursor to the beginning

BOTTOM   (PF1)4   moves cursor to end of file

BLINE   O   moves cursor to next line

WORD   1   moves cursor to next word

EOL   2   moves cursor to end of line

SECTION   8   moves cursor to next section

The above four functions ordinarily move the cursor in
a forward direction.

To change the direction of these commands, use the
following functions:

ADVANCE   4   causes forward movement

BACKUP   5   causes backward movement

          This direction stays until you change it again.

          Other functions:

          ^W   repaints the screen

HELP   (PF2)   gives you the error message after you
                               hear a beep, or displays the keypad
                               diagram or a summary of commands. Use
                               ENTER to return to normal operation.

FIND-

NEXT   (PF3)   will move the cursor to the next
                               occurrence of a model string (see below)

     Building a select range: You can specify a certain section
of your file (1-512 characters) as a select range. Uses of this
select range are outlined below.

SELECT   .   The period on the keypad denotes the start of
                               the range. Use the right arrow to move the
                               range to the desired size. The range is in
                               reverse type as you create it. When you are
                               done, enter any function which uses the
                               range. To terminate a select range use
                               (PF1). (period).

          Functions that use a select range:

CUT   6   on keypad moves the select range into the
                               "paste buffer."

PASTE   (PF1)6   This restores the characters in the paste
                               buffer to the current location of the cursor.
                               This pair of functions allows you to move
                               sections of code from one place to another.

APPEND   9   on keypad adds the select range to the
                               contents of the paste buffer (otherwise a new
                               "cut" erases the previous contents)

CHNG-CASE (PF1)1   changes the select range from upper to lower
                               case or vice versa

FILL   (PF1)8   on keypad changes the width of your line of
                               copy according to the new right margin you
                               set with the "set wrap" command (see below)

     Entering a search model: You may use the FIND function to
find any words or characters that you set as a model. To do this
enter: FIND   (PF1)(PF3)   and a space will be cleared for you
to enter your search model. The findnext function (PF3) will
then search your file for the next occurrence of that string.

REPLACE   (PF1)9   on keypad erases and discards select range,
                               if one exists; otherwise, erases and discards
                               a search target, replacing it with the
                               contents of the paste buffer. You can use
                               this to correct all occurrences of a specific
                               error string in your file. To terminate a
                               search model, use 4 on the keypad.

Besides the functions there are a number of commands that can also be given to the Keypad editor. To enter command mode, type: (PF1)7 on keypad. The top two lines will be cleared and the message "Command:" will be given with a space for you to enter your command. Following the entry of your command, use ENTER key on keypad. DO NOT use return. This will cause an error. Commands you may find useful include:

EXIT   this ends the editing session, storing your file after the changes are made

QUIT   end session without making the changes

SET QUIET   if you cannot stand the beep, the editor will signal you of errors with a reversing of the screen

SET NOQUIET   restores the beep operation

SET SEARCH EXACT -- specifies exactly upper or lower case for a search model

SET SEARCH GENERAL -- is the default setting, and will ignore upper or lower case for the search model

SET SEARCH BOUNDED -- limits the search for the model to the page on which you are working

SET SEARCH UNBOUNDED -- is the default setting and will search the entire file for the model

SET WRAP nn   sets a right margin for your copy. nn is a number between 10 and 79. When you are in this setting, line ending is automatic if you exceed the right margin. It may also be used with a select range to rejustify your copy to a new line measure.

Appendix E
THE MACRO-11 ASSEMBLER

The MACRO-11 assembler takes your source program code as you have written it and converts it into machine-language code. During this process the assembler does the following things: Accounts for all instructions used within the source program and determines their relative positions in memory. Keeps track of all user-defined symbols and their values in a symbol table. Converts mnemonics into machine language (binary code).

Although assembly language code is primitive compared with higher-level languages such as FORTRAN and Pascal, it is one level above the binary code that the computer understands. The mnemonics (words representing the opcode such as ADD or MOV) aid the programmer in remembering the operations; the use of symbols is a very convenient aid to programming (otherwise the programmer would have to deal with actual addresses in place of the names).

Your object code will start in a relative location of zero in memory. The operation to be performed ((opcode) occupies one word (16 bits) of memory. The operands may take another word or two in memory. The variables that you declare (to put it in higher-level terms) each have their own address in memory. You will put labels on certain lines in order to specify jumps and branches, and these labels will refer to relative memory addresses.

During assembly, all the labels you specify will be converted into their actual relative memory addresses, and the "variables" will be replaced by the relative address in memory where the data will be stored.

Most assemblers require two passes through the program. The first pass sets up the symbol table and puts all labels and variable names in it, and also makes a count of the memory locations needed by the program (i.e., the commands and the data space required). On the second pass, the values (addresses in memory) are assigned to the labels and variables and the actual object code is generated.

To use the assembler once you have a source program written (the source program should have the filetype .MAC), call the assembler with the following command:

MACRO filename

The filetype .MAC is assumed. If you wish a listing generated that contains the object code, the source lines and possible errors, add the following after the filename /LIST.If you wish the cross-reference tables generated in this listing, which are tables of symbols used, macros called and errors detected, add (after the /LIST) /CROSSREFERENCE.The finished command to assemble a program and generate listing and cross-reference tables is: MACRO filename/LIST/CROSSREFERENCE You will get a message about the number of errors detected.   After the assembly process completes, if you wish a hard copy of the listing, type the command: PRINT filename.LST

The assembler takes your program of type .MAC and generates the object code of type .OBJ with the same filename, and if you request, a listing of type .LST with the same filename.   These new files will be put on your cassette.

The object code is still not ready to be run, however, and must be linked to produce an actual program that runs (see LINK.TXT).

There will be a more complete listing of the error messages produced by MACRO in the language manual in the lab, but here is a brief rundown of the error messages you may see:

A   Illegal argument (assembly directive);

               umatched delimiter;

               addressing errors;

               illegal forward reference;

               permissible range of a branch instruction (+/- 128) has been exceeded.

B   Bounding error. Instructions or word data are being assembled at an odd address.

D   Doubly-defined symbol referenced.

E   End directive not found.

I   Illegal character detected.

L   Line greater than 132 characters.

M   Multiply-defined symbol. A symbol is defined in two or more places.

O   Opcode error. Directive out of context. Attempt was made to expand a macro that is undefined.

P   Phase error. A label's definition varies from one pass to another.

Q   Questionable syntax. Arguments are missing, too many arguments specified, etc.

R   Register error. Invalid use of or reference to a register.

T   Truncation error. A number specified is too big to fit in the specified area, i.e., trying to put 1000. in a byte.

U   Undefined symbol. A symbol is referenced that has not been defined.

The most common errors you will likely see are the A, Q, R, and U. Misspellings will often cause the U error. Misplaced punctuation may cause the Q or A. Sometimes a line will be marked with more than one error. As in many other languages, the correction of one problem will often result in the elimination of several error codes. After you have worked down through your code, eliminating as many as you can figure out, reassemble it and work on any that still remain.

Assembly Directives—A directive is an instruction to the assembler that is implemented during the assembly process. Some of the directives you will be likely to use include:

.ASCII   Stores delimited string in memory as a sequence of ASCII code. Slashes are normally used as the delimiters. Control characters (such as a carriage return) may be specified by putting their octal ASCII code in angle brackets (<,>). .ASCII /VALUE IS:/<12><15>/$/ would store the following octal values in succesive bytes : 126,101,114,125,105,040,111,123,072,012,015.

                    The codes for carriage return and line feed were imbedded in the string.

.ASCIZ   Similar to the string above, except that a zero byte is automatically inserted at the end of the string. The reason for this can be seen by investigating the way the .PRINT macro works.

.BLKB exp   Allocates the number of bytes defined by exp (expression).

.BLKW exp   Allocates the number of words defined by exp. Both of the above are used to set aside space for results, or intermediate memory locations. Usually these lines will have a label so that the reserved locations can be easily referred to. Space reserved is initialized to zero.

.BYTE exp   Stores the value of exp in a byte.

.WORD exp   Stores the value of exp in a word. The above two commands may be used to define a number of bytes or words, separating the values by commas. The expression may be decimal, octal, ASCII or an arithmetic expression that evaluates to a number that is within the range of 8 or 16 bits.

.END exp   Indicates the end of the code. exp is the label of the line of code where you wish you program to begin execution.

.EVEN   Ensures that the next line, instruction or data, begins at an even location. Often used after ASCII strings to be sure the location of the next line is correct.

.ODD   Ensures that the location counter is at an odd location.

.LIST   "Turns on" assembly listing.

.NLIST   "Turns off" assembly listing.

.PAGE   Starts a new listing page.

.REPT exp   Repeat. Often used in initializing a group of words or bytes to have a certain value. exp is how many times it is to be repeated. This is followed on the next line(s) by the operation that is to be repeated.

.ENDR   The repeated block is closed by the .ENDR.

.TITLE   Assigns a name to the program module and puts headings on the assembly listing.

Appendix F
LINKING YOUR PROGRAM

Once your program has been assembled, it must be linked before it is ready to execute on the system. Linking has the following results: The relative addresses generated during the assembly are fixed (made absolute) in memory.

Several different program modules may be linked together to run as one program. Each of them has been assembled separately, each starting at relative address 0. The linker fixes the first address of the first program at location 1000, and fixes the absolute addresses of the rest of that program and the remainder of the modules relative to this.

System-defined macros that you have called in your program are now put in their proper places (this is called macro expansion) as sections of code. This also happens with user-defined macros. These are called global references, and the linker attempts to define all unresolved global references by first checking the user macro library, then the system macro library. Anything still undefined is generally given a value of 0.

The result of the linker's work is a program that is ready to be executed, which starts at memory location 1000. The linker takes a file of type .OBJ and produces a file of type .SAV with your filename. Any file of type .SAV is ready to be executed.

The syntax of the line is: LINK filename. The filetype is assumed to be .OBJ.

More than one file of type .OBJ may be linked by separating the filenames with commas. The .SAV file will have the name of the first file in the list.

Among options available with the linker are: LINK/DEBUG filename.

This links the debugging program ODT.OBJ with your program. Your program begins at location 1000, with ODT above it. You may now debug your program using the commands of ODT.

/MAP added to a link command prints a load map, which gives the absolute addresses of the various load modules.

/FILL:n fills any unused locations in the load modules with the octal value n. If not specified, the locations are filled with O. This may be used to determine if your program is erroneously referring to memory locations other than those you have specified.

/SLOWLY allows the largest possible use of memory in linking, at the price of a slower execution of the linking process. This should be used if you get a message of symbol table overflow.

Appendix G
DEBUGGING ASSEMBLY LANGUAGE WITH ODT

Once you have resolved all of your assembly errors, and you find you still have execution errors, it is time to use ODT to track them down. ODT (On-line Debugging Tool) allows you to examine the contents of registers and memory locations, and step through your program by lines, allowing you to narrow down and eliminate errors.

To call ODT, you must link it with your program, and ODT must reside on your system cassette. Enter the command: LINK/DEBUG filename and when the linking process is complete, enter the command: RUN filename.

You will get a message from ODT, and the ODT prompt, *. You may now enter the ODT commands to control the execution of your program. If you make a mistake entering an ODT command, the DELETE key will cancel the command and give you the prompt, allowing you to reenter it.

To examine any memory location, type the address of the location, followed by a slash. ODT will respond with the value in octal of the contents of that location. If you type a linefeed key, ODT will close that location and open the next one. If you type a return, ODT will close the location and return you to the * prompt. When the location is open, you may alter its value by typing an octal number, then a linefeed or return.

Since your program starts in location 1000, any locations you need to refer to which are shown on your program listing will have to have 1000 added to them. You can do this easily with the use of the relocation registers. If you have several modules, each assembly listing will start at relative address 0, but when executed will actually reside in sections of memory above 1000, relative to where the program module is located. (You may find out the relocation constants with the use of the load map which can be generated in the linking process.)

To use a relocation register, enter the following command: 1000;OR Note the O is zero. This loads the 0th relocation register with the value 1000. You may load any other module's relocation address in another relocation register, if needed.

Now, to refer to a relative address (which you read from your assembly listing), enter the command: 0,address/ where address is the relative address, and 0 specifies the 0th relocation register.

Entering an address followed by;G will begin program execution at the address. This address may be absolute or it may be relocation register, comma, relative address (example: 0,000022;G).

To examine the PSW (which includes the flags N, Z, V, and C) enter the command $S/ and it will return the value in octal of the entire PSW. You will have to convert this octal to binary to get the value of the flags which are the four least significant bits. For example, a PSW of 000312 would convert to 1010 in the four least significant bits, indicating that the negative and overflow bits were set.

To examine the contents of the 8 general-purpose registers, the commmand is $n/ where n is a value between 0 and 7. Contents of this register may be altered by typing a new value before the return. The linefeed key may not be used to step through the registers. Once a register location is open, you may use the @ command to open and examine the contents of the memory address pointed to by the register. Example follows: you type $1/ it returns 001124 you type @ it returns 0,000124/000001 which is the value at the address. The @ command may also be used when a memory location points to another address in memory. With @ entered before the return, ODT will then display the contents of the location pointed to.

One of the most helpful procedures in ODT is the ability to run your program up to a specified spot called a breakpoint, and then examine registers or memory to find out what the current values are. You may specify up to eight breakpoints in your program as follows: relocation register, relative address;nB to set the nth breakpoint

Example:

0,22;0B

0,40;1B   Will set breakpoints 0 and 1 to the relative
               addresses 22 and 40, respectively

If you now type 0,0;G your program will start at the beginning and run to the command at location 22 and stop (the command at 22 will not be executed). You may now examine registers and memory.

To continue on to the next breakpoint, you must reset the breakpoint you are currently on by the command: ;nB to reset the nth breakpoint   ;P will then cause program execution to resume, and continue to the next defined breakpoint. To reset all breakpoints, enter the command :   ;B

If the breakpoint is in a loop which you want to execute a certain number of times before stopping, the command: n;P will cause execution to stop in the nth occurrence of the breakpoint.

When you are examining the contents of a register or memory location, the backslash entered after ODT displays the contents of the location will display the low byte of the location and convert it to an ASCII character if possible. If it is not possible, a ? will be displayed.

To execute your program by single lines, enter the command: ;1S Now the n;P command will specify how many commands are to be executed before stopping. Breakpoints will be ignored. To reset to normal mode of operation, enter   ;S

With the use of ODT, an assembly listing showing the commands and their locations, and good comments on your program, you can trace exactly what is happening to your data as your program executes its various commands on it. Unlike higherlevel languages, which require extra print statements to allow you to trace the path of your data, assembly language under ODT can allow you direct access to data at each step of execution without any additional lines added to your program.

Remember that any changes you make to commands or data while under ODT are temporary. You must edit the changes into your .MAC file and reassemble and link to make them permanent.

To exit ODT, type ^C. Note that any time your program executes to completion under ODT, you will automatically be returned to monitor, and if you wish to reenter ODT, you must RUN filename again, and reset your relocation registers.

Appendix H
THE LSI11 INSTRUCTION SET

There are three types of instructions in MACRO-11 assembly language. These are the one-operand instructions, the two-operand instructions, and the program control instructions. The format used for these is the opcode in tab position 1 and the operand(s) in tab position 2. Double operands are separated by a comma (no space). Examples are given below.

The one-and two-operand instructions in most cases will operate on either words (16 bits) or bytes (8 bits). To specify operation on bytes, a B is appended to the opcode. Not all opcodes are defined on bytes (ADD for instance). Word operation is the default. The following commands will not work on bytes:

ADD   SUB   ASH   ASHC   XOR   SWAB

Some of these operations set the condition codes, which may then be used to activate conditional branch instructions. The condition codes are:

Z   When the result of the instruction is zero, the zero
        bit is set (i.e., value 1). Note that if the result is
        not zero, the bit will be cleared (i.e., value 0).

N   The most significant bit of the result is tested. If
        this bit is 1, the contents are assumed to be negative,
        and the N bit is set. If the result does not have the
        most significant bit set to 1, the N flag is cleared.

C   This is the carry bit, which is set on arithmetic
        operations when a carry is generated. The carry bit is
        also used in the rotate instructions as a 1 bit buffer.
        See individual instructions for some of the unusual
        features associated with this flag.

V   This bit is set if an overflow occurs (i.e., the
        result of the calculation is too large to be placed in
        the destination). This may be set by INC, DEC, ADD,
        etc. Both the C and V bits may be set by the same
        operation, such as an ADD instruction whose result
        exceeded 16 bits.

     In the chart below, when a flag is followed by an asterisk,
it means that it is set if appropriate (i.e., zero as a result of
the instruction).

ONE-OPERAND INSTRUCTIONS

                              flags set   flags cleared

CLR(B)   clear destination   Z   N V C
         contents of destination replaced by 0.
            CLR R0   clears register 0

COM(B)   complement dest.   N* Z* C   V
         replaces destination by its logical complement,
         each bit equal to 1 is set to 0 and vice versa.

INC(B)   increment destination   N* Z* V*
         adds 1 to the value of the destination

DEC(B)   decrement destination   N* Z* V*
         subtracts 1 from the value of the destination
               DEC OPER   decrements memory location at label
               OPER

NEG(B)   negate destination   N* Z* V*   C is set if
                                                  result = 0
         destination replaced by its 2's complement value.
         100000 is replaced by itself and the V flag set if this
         occurs.

TST(B)   test destination   N* Z*   V C
         destination is tested and flags are set accordingly.
         The value in the destination is not changed.

ASR(B)   arithmetic shift right   N* Z*   see below
         shifts all bits of destination right one place. The
         high order bit remains the same (retaining the sign of
         the operant). The C bit is loaded from the LSB. ASR
         performs signed division by 2.
               ASR R1   shifts right register 1

ASL(B)   arithmetic shift left   N* Z*   see below
shifts all bits of destination left one place. The low
order bit coming in is a zero. C is loaded for the
high order bit that is shifted out. ASL performs
signed multiplication with V set on overflow.

ROR(B)   rotate right   N* Z*   see below
rotates all bits of destination right one place. The
low order bit is loaded into the carry flag and the
previous contents of the carry flag are brought into
the high order bit. This is 17 (9) bit rotation.

ROL(B)   rotate left   N* Z*   see below
rotates all bits of destination left one place. High
order bit goes into the carry flag and previous
contents of C goes into the low order bit of the
destination.

SWAB   swap bytes   see below   V C
low order byte exchanged with high order byte.
N set if bit 7 of dest is set.
Z set if low order byte of result = O.

ACD(B)   add in carry   N* Z* C* V*
adds C bit to destination. Used for double precision
arithmetic.
C is set if dest. = 177777 and C = 1.
V is set if dest. = 077777 and C is 1 (this pushes the
destination into a negative value).

SBC(B)   subtracts carry   N* Z* V*   C*
subtracts C bit from destination. This is a borrow in
subtraction.
V is set if dest. = 100000 and C = 1
(neg. quantity goes to pos.).
C is cleared if dest. = O and C = 1.

TWO-OPERAND INSTRUCTION
    Note that in two-operand instructions, the source is always
given first, then the destination.

MOV(B)   move source to dest.   N* Z*   V
moves source operand to destination location. Previous
contents of destination are lost. Source is not
affected. MOVB into a register extends the sign to the
upper byte of the register.
          MOV   R1,R4   moves contents
          of register 1 to register 4.

CMP(B)   source - destination   N* Z* V*   C
result of subtracting destination from source is
computed. Result is ignored, but flags are set.
Destination and source are unchanged.

ADD   add source to dest.   N* Z* V* C*
source is added to destination. Original contents of
destination is lost. Source is unchanged . 2's
complement addition is performed. ADD #7,R3   adds 7
to R3 with result in R3.

SUB   subtracts source from   N* Z* V*   C*
          destination
result is left in destination. Contents of source
unaffected. C bit is set if there is a borrow. SUB
#4,RO   subtract 4 from register RO.

MUL   multiply   N* Z* C*   V
destination and source are multiplied and result is
stored in destination register. Destination must be a
register. If the register is even, the result is
stored in the register and the succeeding register. If
the register is odd, only the low order product is
stored. MUL @#OP,R2 multiply the value in OP by the
value in R2, storing result in R2 and R3.

DIV   divide   N* Z* V* C*
the 32-bit 2's complement integer in registers n and n+1
is divided by the source. n must be even. The quotient
is left in Rn. The remainder is left in Rn+1. C is
set if divide by zero is attempted.

BIT(B)   logical AND of source   N* Z*   V
and destination source and destination are unchanged.

BIC(B)   bit clear   N* Z*   v
clears each bit in destination that corresponds to a
set bit in the source. Original contents of
destination are lost. Source is unchanged.

BIS(B)   bit set   N* Z*   V
inclusive OR of source and destination. Result is in
destination. Source is unchanged.

XOR   exclusive OR   N* Z*   V
exclusive OR of register and destination is stored in
destination. Note that the source operand in this
instruction must be a register. Contents of this
register are unaffected. XOR R2,@#NUM exclusive OR
of R2 and value in memory cell with label NUM, stored
in NUM.

PROGRAM CONTROL INSTRUCTIONS

BR   branch relative
an unconditional branch to a location within plus 127
or minus 128 words (this is 400 octal bytes, for
instance the difference between memory locations 001200
and 001600). BR SECOND program jumps to the place in
your program labeled by SECOND and starts execution.

Conditional branches:

BNE   branch if not equal to zero (Z bit not set)

BEQ   branch if equal to zero (Z bit is set)

BPL   branch if plus (N bit not set)

BMI   branch if minus (N bit set)

BVC   branch if overflow clear (V bit not set)

BVS   branch if overflow set (V bit set)

BCC   branch if carry is clear

BCS   branch if carry is set

Signed conditional branches

BGE   branch if greater than or equal to zero (N and V either both clear or both set)

BLT   branch if less than zero (N or V set but not both)

BGT   branch if greater than zero (N or V set but not both)

BLE   branch if less than or equal to zero (N or V set but not both)

SOB   subtract 1 and branch if not equal to zero. This instruction only branches in the backward direction SOB R2,LOOP decrements R2 and jumps backward to LOOP if R2 <> 0

Unsigned conditional branches

BHI   branch if higher (C and Z clear)

BLOS   branch if lower or same (C or Z set)

BHIS   branch if higher or same (C clear)

BLO   branch if lower (C set)

JMP   jump unconditional. This may jump anywhere in your program. It is slower to execute than a branch. JMP LOOP causes a jump to LOOP in your program. The operand in this case may NOT be a register. Register deferred mode is OK, however.

JSR   jump to subroutine. The link register is the first operand, the address jumped to is the second. The link register is used by the program to return from the subroutine (it holds the return address). R6 (the stack pointer) should never be used as the link register as this will interfere with the stacking of subroutine calls. Usually the link register will be PC (R7). JST R3,PRNT causes a jump to subroutine PRNT, saving the return address in R3

RTS   return for subroutine. The register specified should be the same one used in the JSR instruction that you called the subroutine with. The register is loaded into the PC and execution resumes. RTS R6 returns flow of control to the address saved in R6

Set and clear condition bits (flags)

	C	V	Z	N	ALL
Set	SEC	SEV	SEZ	SEN	SCC
Clear	CLC	CLV	CLZ	CLN	CCC

USEFUL MACRO INSTRUCTIONS

.PRINT   print characters starting at a specified address (the operand) until finding a byte with value either 000 or 200. The characters are usually defined by .ASCII or .ASCIZ pseudo-ops. If the ending byte is 000, then a carriage return will be printed after the string. If there is no byte of 000 or 200, the macro will keep printing the ASCII character for each memory location. This is not good.

Example: .PRINT   #NAME
                           .
                           .
                           .
        NAME: .ASCII   / JOSEPH SCHMOE /<200>

.TTYIN control is passed to RT-11 which waits until a message
        is typed at the terminal followed by a carriage return.
        The first character of the message is placed in RO.
        Subsequent uses of .TTYIN place the next character of
        the message into RO. After all the characters of the
        message have been read (including the CR, and a line
        feed that .TTYIN sticks on there) the next .TTYIN will
        again wait for a message to be typed.

.TTYOUT the ASCII character corresponding to the value in the
        low order byte of RO is output to the screen.

It is termed "orthogonal" since almost all instructions work
with all addressing modes. The creative use of addressing modes
will save you many instructions in your programs.

Appendix I
RADIX-50 CHARACTER SET

Character	ASCII Octal Equivalent	Radix-50 Equivalent
Space	40	0
A-Z	101-132	1-32
$	44	33
.	56	34
Unused		35
0-9	60-71	36-47

Appendix J
ASCII TO RADIX-50 CHARACTER CONVERSION TABLE

The maximum Radix-50 value is:

$$47 * 50^2 + 47 * 50^1 + 47 = 174777.$$

The preceding table provides a convenient means of
translating between the ASCII character set and
its Radix-50 equivalents. For example, given the
ASCII string A1C, the Radix-50 equivalent is
(arithmetic is performed in octal):

           A = 003100
           1 = 002330
           C = 000003
          ───────────
         A1C = 005433

Single Character or First Character		Second Character		Third Character	
ASCII	Radix-50	ASCII	Radix-50	ASCII	Radix-50
A	003100	A	000050	A	000001
B	006200	B	000120	B	000002
C	011300	C	000170	C	000003
D	014400	D	000240	D	000004
E	017500	E	000310	E	000005
F	022600	F	000360	F	000006
G	025700	G	000430	G	000007
H	031000	H	000500	H	000010
I	034100	I	000550	I	000011
J	037200	J	000620	J	000012
K	042300	K	000670	K	000013
L	045400	L	000740	L	000014
M	050500	M	001010	M	000015
N	053600	N	001060	N	000016
O	056700	O	001130	O	000017
P	062000	P	001200	P	000020
Q	065100	Q	001250	Q	000021
R	070200	R	001320	R	000022
S	073300	S	001370	S	000023
T	076400	T	001440	T	000024
U	101500	U	001510	U	000025
V	104600	V	001560	V	000026
W	107700	W	001630	W	000027
X	113000	X	001700	X	000030
Y	116100	Y	001750	Y	000031
Z	121200	Z	002020	Z	000032
$	124300	$	002070	$	000033
.	127400	.	002140	.	000034
unused	132500	unused	002210	unused	000035
0	135600	0	002260	0	000036
1	140700	1	002330	1	000037
2	144000	2	002400	2	000040
3	147100	3	002450	3	000041
4	152200	4	002520	4	000042
5	155300	5	002570	5	000043
6	160400	6	002640	6	000044
7	163500	7	002710	7	000045
8	166600	8	002760	8	000046
9	171700	9	003030	9	000047

Appendix K
HEXADECIMAL AND DECIMAL CONVERSION TABLE

COLUMN 4		COLUMN 3		COLUMN 2		COLUMN 1	
15 BYTE			8	7 BYTE			0
15 CHAR 12		11 CHAR 8		7 CHAR 4		3 CHAR 0	
HEX	DEC	HEX	DEC	HEX	DEC	HEX	DEC
0	0	0	0	0	0	0	0
1	4096	1 _1_ 256		1	16	1 _3_ 1	
2	8192	2	512	2	32	2	2
3	12238	3	768	3	48	3	3
4	16384	4	1024	4 _2_ 64		4	4
5	20480	5	1280	5	80	5	5
6	24576	6	1536	6	96	6	6
7	28672	7	1792	7	112	7	7
8	32768	8	2048	8	128	8	8
9	36864	9	2304	9	144	9	9
A	40960	A	2560	A	160	A	10
B	45056	B	2816	B	176	B	11
C	49152	C	3072	C	192	C	12
D	53248	D	3328	D	208	D	13
E	57344	E	3584	E	224	E	14
F	61440	F	3840	F	240	F	15

Convert a decimal number to hexadecimal: What is the hexadecimal
equivalent of 421?
        Find the highest decimal number in the table equivalent to or less
than 421. From the table, we see that it is 256 in column 3. Hence, the
first or most significant hexadecimal character is 1. Now subtract 256
from 421 (421-256=65). Return to the table and repeat the previous step.
We find the highest decimal number in the table equivalent to or less than
65. That number is 64 (64 is less than 65) represented by 4 as the
hexadecimal character in column 2. Repeat the first step again,
subtracting 64 from 65, we find 1. The least significant hexadecimal
character is 1 in column 1. Therefore, the entire hexadecimal number is
141.

```
        141
        |||
        ||----->      256 = 2 from column 1
        |------>       64 = 4 from column 2
        |------>        1 = 1 from column 3
```

Convert a hexadecimal number to decimal: What is the decimal equivalent
of 3FA2?

        Start with the least significant hexadecimal character (2). Find its
decimal equivalent (2). Then moving from right to left, find the decimal
equivalent of A in column 2. It is 160. Next, find the decimal
equivalent of F in column 3. It is 3840. Finally, search for the decimal
equivalent of 3 in column 4. It is 12288. Remember to convert the next
character to decimal and so on. Add all of the decimal numbers together
to find the decimal equivalent of the entire hexadecimal number. The
decimal equivalent is 16290.

```
        3FA2
        ||||
        |||----->       2 from column 1
        ||------>     160 from column 2
        |------->    3840 from column 3
        -------->   12288 from column 4

    ANSWER --->   16290
```

Appendix L
OCTAL TO DECIMAL INTEGER CONVERSION TABLE

X =	0	1	2	3	4	5	6	7
0X	0	1	2	3	4	5	6	7
1X	8	9	10	11	12	13	14	15
2X	16	17	18	19	20	21	22	23
3X	24	25	26	27	28	29	30	31
4X	32	33	34	35	36	37	38	39
5X	40	41	42	43	44	45	46	47
6X	48	49	50	51	52	53	54	55
7X	56	57	58	59	60	61	62	63
10X	64	65	66	67	68	69	70	71
11X	72	73	74	75	76	77	78	79
12X	80	81	82	83	84	85	86	87
13X	88	89	90	91	92	93	94	95
14X	96	97	98	99	100	101	102	103
15X	104	105	106	107	108	109	110	111
16X	112	113	114	115	116	117	118	119
17X	120	121	122	123	124	125	126	127
20X	128	129	130	131	132	133	134	135
21X	136	137	138	139	140	141	142	143
22X	144	145	146	147	148	149	150	151
23X	152	153	154	155	156	157	158	159
24X	160	161	162	163	164	165	166	167
25X	168	169	170	171	172	173	174	175
26X	176	177	178	179	180	181	182	183
27X	184	185	186	187	188	189	190	191
30X	192	193	194	195	196	197	198	199
31X	200	201	202	203	204	205	206	207
32X	208	209	210	211	212	213	214	215
33X	216	217	218	219	220	221	222	223
34X	224	225	226	227	228	229	230	231
35X	232	233	234	235	236	237	238	239
36X	240	241	242	243	244	245	246	247
37X	248	249	250	251	252	253	254	255
40X	256	257	258	259	260	261	262	263
41X	264	265	266	267	268	269	270	271
42X	272	273	274	275	276	277	278	279
43X	280	281	282	283	284	285	286	287
44X	288	289	290	291	292	293	294	295
45X	296	297	298	299	300	301	302	303
46X	304	305	306	307	308	309	310	311
47X	312	313	314	315	316	317	318	319
50X	320	321	322	323	324	325	326	327
51X	328	329	330	331	332	333	334	335
52X	336	337	338	339	340	341	342	343
53X	344	345	346	347	348	349	350	351
54X	352	353	354	355	356	357	358	359
55X	360	361	362	363	364	365	366	367
56X	368	369	370	371	372	373	374	375
57X	376	377	378	379	380	381	382	383
60X	384	385	386	387	388	389	390	391
61X	392	393	394	395	396	397	398	399
62X	400	401	402	403	404	405	406	407
63X	408	409	410	411	412	413	414	415
64X	416	417	418	419	420	421	422	423
65X	424	425	426	427	428	429	430	431
66X	432	433	434	435	436	437	438	439
67X	440	441	442	443	444	445	446	447

X =	0	1	2	3	4	5	6	7
70X	448	449	450	451	452	453	454	455
71X	456	457	458	459	460	461	462	463
72X	464	465	466	467	468	469	470	471
73X	472	473	474	475	476	477	478	479
74X	480	481	482	483	484	485	486	487
75X	488	489	490	491	492	493	494	495
76X	496	497	498	499	500	501	502	503
77X	504	505	506	507	508	509	510	511
100X	512	513	514	515	516	517	518	519
101X	520	521	522	523	524	525	526	527
102X	528	529	530	531	532	533	534	535
103X	536	537	538	539	540	541	542	543
104X	544	545	546	547	548	549	550	551
105X	552	553	554	555	556	557	558	559
106X	560	561	562	563	564	565	566	567
107X	568	569	570	571	572	573	574	575
110X	576	577	578	579	580	581	582	583
111X	584	585	586	587	588	589	590	591
112X	592	593	594	595	596	597	598	599
113X	600	601	602	603	604	605	606	607
114X	608	609	610	611	612	613	614	615
115X	616	617	618	619	620	621	622	623
116X	624	625	626	627	628	629	630	631
117X	632	633	634	635	636	637	638	639
120X	640	641	642	643	644	645	646	647
121X	648	649	650	651	652	653	654	655
122X	656	657	658	659	660	661	662	663
123X	664	665	666	667	668	669	670	671
124X	672	673	674	675	676	677	678	679
125X	680	681	682	683	684	685	686	687
126X	688	689	690	691	692	693	694	695
127X	696	697	698	699	700	701	702	703
130X	704	705	706	707	708	709	710	711
131X	712	713	714	715	716	717	718	719
132X	720	721	722	723	724	725	726	727
133X	728	729	730	731	732	733	734	735
134X	736	737	738	739	740	741	742	743
135X	744	745	746	747	748	749	750	751
136X	752	753	754	755	756	757	758	759
137X	760	761	762	763	764	765	766	767
140X	768	769	770	771	772	773	774	775
141X	776	777	778	779	780	781	782	783
142X	784	785	786	787	788	789	790	791
143X	792	793	794	795	796	797	798	799
144X	800	801	802	803	804	805	806	807
145X	808	809	810	811	812	813	814	815
146X	816	817	818	819	820	821	822	823
147X	824	825	826	827	828	829	830	831
150X	832	833	834	835	836	837	838	839
151X	840	841	842	843	844	845	846	847
152X	848	849	850	851	852	853	854	855
153X	856	857	858	859	860	861	862	863
154X	864	865	866	867	868	869	870	871
155X	872	873	874	875	876	877	878	879
156X	880	881	882	883	884	885	886	887
157X	888	889	890	891	892	893	894	895

X =	Ø	1	2	3	4	5	6	7
16ØX	896	897	898	899	9ØØ	9Ø1	9Ø2	9Ø3
161X	9Ø4	9Ø5	9Ø6	9Ø7	9Ø8	9Ø9	91Ø	911
162X	912	913	914	915	916	917	918	919
163X	92Ø	921	922	923	924	925	926	927
164X	928	929	93Ø	931	932	933	934	935
165X	936	937	938	939	94Ø	941	942	943
166X	944	945	946	947	948	949	95Ø	951
167X	952	953	954	955	956	957	958	959
17ØX	96Ø	961	962	963	964	965	966	967
171X	968	969	97Ø	971	972	973	974	975
172X	976	977	978	979	98Ø	981	982	983
173X	984	985	986	987	988	989	99Ø	991
174X	992	993	994	995	996	997	998	999
175X	1ØØØ	1ØØ1	1ØØ2	1ØØ3	1ØØ4	1ØØ5	1ØØ6	1ØØ7
176X	1ØØ8	1ØØ9	1Ø1Ø	1Ø11	1Ø12	1Ø13	1Ø14	1Ø15
177X	1Ø16	1Ø17	1Ø18	1Ø19	1Ø2Ø	1Ø21	1Ø22	1Ø23
2ØØX	1Ø24	1Ø25	1Ø26	1Ø27	1Ø28	1Ø29	1Ø3Ø	1Ø31
2Ø1X	1Ø32	1Ø33	1Ø34	1Ø35	1Ø36	1Ø37	1Ø38	1Ø39
2Ø2X	1Ø4Ø	1Ø41	1Ø42	1Ø43	1Ø44	1Ø45	1Ø46	1Ø47
2Ø3X	1Ø48	1Ø49	1Ø5Ø	1Ø51	1Ø52	1Ø53	1Ø54	1Ø55
2Ø4X	1Ø56	1Ø57	1Ø58	1Ø59	1Ø6Ø	1Ø61	1Ø62	1Ø63
2Ø5X	1Ø64	1Ø65	1Ø66	1Ø67	1Ø68	1Ø69	1Ø7Ø	1Ø71
2Ø6X	1Ø72	1Ø73	1Ø74	1Ø75	1Ø76	1Ø77	1Ø78	1Ø79
2Ø7X	1Ø8Ø	1Ø81	1Ø82	1Ø83	1Ø84	1Ø85	1Ø86	1Ø87
21ØX	1Ø88	1Ø89	1Ø9Ø	1Ø91	1Ø92	1Ø93	1Ø94	1Ø95
211X	1Ø96	1Ø97	1Ø98	1Ø99	11ØØ	11Ø1	11Ø2	11Ø3
212X	11Ø4	11Ø5	11Ø6	11Ø7	11Ø8	11Ø9	111Ø	1111
213X	1112	1113	1114	1115	1116	1117	1118	1119
214X	112Ø	1121	1122	1123	1124	1125	1126	1127
215X	1128	1129	113Ø	1131	1132	1133	1134	1135
216X	1136	1137	1138	1139	114Ø	1141	1142	1143
217X	1144	1145	1146	1147	1148	1149	115Ø	1151
22ØX	1152	1153	1154	1155	1156	1157	1158	1159
221X	116Ø	1161	1162	1163	1164	1165	1166	1167
222X	1168	1169	117Ø	1171	1172	1173	1174	1175
223X	1176	1177	1178	1179	118Ø	1181	118Z	1183
224X	1184	1185	1186	1187	1188	1189	119Ø	1191
225X	1192	1193	1194	1195	1196	1197	1198	1199
226X	12ØØ	12Ø1	12Ø2	12Ø3	12Ø4	12Ø5	12Ø6	12Ø7
227X	12Ø8	12Ø9	121Ø	1211	1212	1213	1214	1215
23ØX	1216	1217	1218	1219	122Ø	1221	1222	1223
231X	1224	1225	1226	1227	1228	1229	123Ø	1231
232X	1232	1233	1234	1235	1236	1237	1238	1239
233X	124Ø	1241	1242	1243	1244	1245	1246	1247
234X	1248	1249	125Ø	1251	1252	1253	1254	1255
235X	1256	1257	1258	1259	126Ø	1261	1262	1263
236X	1264	1265	1266	1267	1268	1269	127Ø	1271
237X	1272	1273	1274	1275	1276	1277	1278	1279
24ØX	128Ø	1281	1282	1283	1284	1285	1296	1287
241X	1288	1289	129Ø	1291	1292	1293	1294	1295
242X	1296	1297	1298	1299	13ØØ	13Ø1	13Ø2	13Ø3
243X	13Ø4	13Ø5	13Ø6	13Ø7	13Ø8	13Ø9	131Ø	1311
244X	1312	1313	1314	1315	1316	1317	1318	1319
245X	132Ø	1321	1322	1323	1324	1325	1326	1327
246X	1328	1329	133Ø	1331	1332	1333	1334	1335
247X	1336	1337	1338	1339	134Ø	1341	1342	1343

X =	0	1	2	3	4	5	6	7
250X	1344	1345	1346	1347	1348	1349	1350	1351
251X	1352	1353	1354	1355	1356	1357	1358	1359
252X	1360	1361	1362	1363	1364	1365	1366	1367
253X	1368	1369	1370	1371	1372	1373	1374	1375
254X	1376	1377	1378	1379	1380	1381	1382	1383
255X	1384	1385	1386	1387	1388	1389	1390	1391
256X	1392	1393	1394	1395	1396	1397	1398	1399
257X	1400	1401	1402	1403	1404	1405	1406	1407
260X	1408	1409	1410	1411	1412	1413	1414	1415
261X	1416	1417	1418	1419	1420	1421	1422	1423
262X	1424	1425	1426	1427	1428	1429	1430	1431
263X	1432	1433	1434	1435	1436	1437	1438	1439
264X	1440	1441	1442	1443	1444	1445	1446	1447
265X	1448	1449	1450	1451	1452	1453	1454	1455
266X	1456	1457	1458	1459	1460	1461	1462	1463
267X	1464	1465	1466	1467	1468	1469	1470	1471
270X	1472	1473	1474	1475	1476	1477	1478	1479
271X	1480	1481	1482	1483	1484	1485	1486	1487
272X	1488	1489	1490	1491	1492	1493	1494	1495
273X	1496	1497	1498	1499	1500	1501	1502	1503
274X	1504	1505	1506	1507	1508	1509	1510	1511
275X	1512	1513	1514	1515	1516	1517	1518	1519
276X	1520	1521	1522	1523	1524	1525	1526	1527
277X	1528	1529	1530	1531	1532	1533	1534	1535
300X	1536	1537	1538	1539	1540	1541	1542	1543
301X	1544	1545	1546	1547	1548	1549	1550	1551
302X	1552	1553	1554	1555	1556	1557	1558	1559
303X	1560	1561	1562	1563	1564	1565	1566	1567
304X	1568	1569	1570	1571	1572	1573	1574	1575
305X	1576	1577	1578	1579	1580	1581	1582	1583
306X	1584	1585	1586	1587	1588	1589	1590	1591
307X	1592	1593	1594	1595	1596	1597	1598	1599
310X	1600	1601	1602	1603	1604	1605	1606	1607
311X	1608	1609	1610	1611	1612	1613	1614	1615
312X	1616	1617	1618	1619	1620	1621	1622	1623
313X	1624	1625	1626	1627	1628	1629	1630	1631
314X	1632	1633	1634	1635	1636	1637	1638	1639
315X	1640	1641	1642	1643	1644	1645	1646	1647
316X	1648	1649	1650	1651	1652	1653	1654	1655
317X	1656	1657	1658	1659	1660	1661	1662	1663
320X	1664	1665	1666	1667	1668	1669	1670	1671
321X	1672	1673	1674	1675	1676	1677	1678	1679
322X	1680	1681	1682	1683	1684	1685	1686	1687
323X	1688	1689	1690	1691	1692	1693	1694	1695
324X	1696	1697	1698	1699	1700	1701	1702	1703
325X	1704	1705	1706	1707	1708	1709	1710	1711
326X	1712	1713	1714	1715	1716	1717	1718	1719
327X	1720	1721	1722	1723	1724	1725	1726	1727
330X	1728	1729	1730	1731	1732	1733	1734	1735
331X	1736	1737	1738	1739	1740	1741	1742	1743
332X	1744	1745	1746	1747	1748	1749	1750	1751
333X	1752	1753	1754	1755	1756	1757	1758	1759
334X	1760	1761	1762	1763	1764	1765	1766	1767
335X	1768	1769	1770	1771	1772	1773	1774	1775
336X	1776	1777	1778	1779	1780	1781	1782	1783
337X	1784	1785	1786	1787	1788	1789	1790	1791

X =	Ø	1	2	3	4	5	6	7
34ØX	1792	1793	1794	1795	1796	1797	1798	1799
341X	18ØØ	18Ø1	18Ø2	18Ø3	18Ø4	18Ø5	18Ø6	18Ø7
342X	18Ø8	18Ø9	181Ø	1811	1812	1813	1814	1815
343X	1816	1817	1818	1819	182Ø	1821	1822	1823
344X	1824	1825	1826	1827	1828	1829	183Ø	1831
345X	1832	1833	1834	1835	1836	1837	1838	1839
346X	184Ø	1841	1842	1843	1844	1845	1846	1847
347X	1848	1849	185Ø	1851	1852	1853	1854	1855
35ØX	1856	1857	1858	1859	186Ø	1861	1862	1863
351X	1864	1865	1866	1867	1868	1869	187Ø	1871
352X	1872	1873	1874	1875	1876	1877	1878	1879
353X	188Ø	1881	1882	1883	1884	1885	1886	1887
354X	1888	1889	189Ø	1891	1892	1893	1894	1895
355X	1896	1897	1898	1899	19ØØ	19Ø1	19Ø2	19Ø3
356X	19Ø4	19Ø5	19Ø6	19Ø7	19Ø8	19Ø9	191Ø	1911
357X	1912	1913	1914	1915	1916	1917	1918	1919
36ØX	192Ø	1921	1922	1923	1924	1925	1926	1927
361X	1928	1929	193Ø	1931	1932	1933	1934	1935
362X	1936	1937	1938	1939	194Ø	1941	1942	1943
363X	1944	1945	1946	1947	1948	1949	195Ø	1951
364X	1952	1953	1954	1955	1956	1957	1958	1959
365X	196Ø	1961	1962	1963	1964	1965	1966	1967
366X	1968	1969	197Ø	1971	1972	1973	1974	1975
367X	1976	1977	1978	1979	198Ø	1981	1982	1983
37ØX	1984	1985	1986	1987	1988	1989	199Ø	1991
371X	1992	1993	1994	1995	1996	1997	1998	1999
372X	2ØØØ	2ØØ1	2ØØ2	2ØØ3	2ØØ4	2ØØ5	2ØØ6	2ØØ7
373X	2ØØ8	2ØØ9	2Ø1Ø	2Ø11	2Ø12	2Ø13	2Ø14	2Ø15
374X	2Ø16	2Ø17	2Ø18	2Ø19	2Ø2Ø	2Ø21	2Ø22	2Ø23
375X	2Ø24	2Ø25	2Ø26	2Ø27	2Ø28	2Ø29	2Ø3Ø	2Ø31
376X	2Ø32	2Ø33	2Ø34	2Ø35	2Ø36	2Ø37	2Ø38	2Ø39
377X	2Ø4Ø	2Ø41	2Ø42	2Ø43	2Ø44	2Ø45	2Ø46	2Ø47
4ØØX	2Ø48	2Ø49	2Ø5Ø	2Ø51	2Ø52	2Ø53	2Ø54	2Ø55
4Ø1X	2Ø56	2Ø57	2Ø58	2Ø59	2Ø6Ø	2Ø61	2Ø62	2Ø63
4Ø2X	2Ø64	2Ø65	2Ø66	2Ø67	2Ø68	2Ø69	2Ø7Ø	2Ø71
4Ø3X	2Ø72	2Ø73	2Ø74	2Ø75	2Ø76	2Ø77	2Ø78	2Ø79
4Ø4X	2Ø8Ø	2Ø81	2Ø82	2Ø83	2Ø84	2Ø85	2Ø86	2Ø87
4Ø5X	2Ø88	2Ø89	2Ø9Ø	2Ø91	2Ø92	2Ø93	2Ø94	2Ø95
4Ø6X	2Ø96	2Ø97	2Ø98	2Ø99	21ØØ	21Ø1	21Ø2	21Ø3
4Ø7X	21Ø4	21Ø5	21Ø6	21Ø7	21Ø8	21Ø9	211Ø	2111
41ØX	2112	2113	2114	2115	2116	2117	2118	2119
411X	212Ø	2121	2122	2123	2124	2125	2126	2127
412X	2128	2129	213Ø	2131	2132	2133	2134	2135
413X	2136	2137	2138	2139	214Ø	2141	2142	2143
414X	2144	2145	2146	2147	2148	2149	215Ø	2151
415X	2152	2153	2154	2155	2156	2157	2158	2159
416X	216Ø	2161	2162	2163	2164	2165	2166	2167
417X	2168	2169	217Ø	2171	2172	2173	2174	2175
42ØX	2176	2177	2178	2179	218Ø	2181	2182	2183
421X	2184	2185	2186	2187	2188	2189	219Ø	2191
422X	2192	2193	2194	2195	2196	2197	2198	2199
423X	22ØØ	22Ø1	22Ø2	22Ø3	22Ø4	22Ø5	22Ø6	22Ø7
424X	22Ø8	22Ø9	221Ø	2211	2212	2213	2214	2215
425X	2216	2217	2218	2219	222Ø	2221	2222	2223
426X	2224	2225	2226	2227	2228	2229	223Ø	2231
427X	2232	2233	2234	2235	2236	2237	2238	2239

X =	Ø	1	2	3	4	5	6	7
430X	2240	2241	2242	2243	2244	2245	2246	2247
431X	2248	2249	2250	2251	2252	2253	2254	2255
432X	2256	2257	2258	2259	2260	2261	2262	2263
433X	2264	2265	2266	2267	2268	2269	2270	2271
434X	2272	2273	2274	2275	2276	2277	2278	2279
435X	2280	2281	2282	2283	2284	2285	2286	2287
436X	2288	2289	2290	2291	2292	2293	2294	2295
437X	2296	2297	2298	2299	2300	2301	2302	2303
440X	2304	2305	2306	2307	2308	2309	2310	2311
441X	2312	2313	2314	2315	2316	2317	2318	2319
442X	2320	2321	2322	2323	2324	2325	2326	2327
443X	2328	2329	2330	2331	2332	2333	2334	2335
444X	2336	2337	2338	2339	2340	2341	2342	2343
445X	2344	2345	2346	2347	2348	2349	2350	2351
446X	2352	2353	2354	2355	2356	2357	2358	2359
447X	2360	2361	2362	2363	2364	2365	2366	2367
450X	2368	2369	2370	2371	2372	2373	2374	2375
451X	2376	2377	2378	2379	2380	2381	2382	2383
452X	2384	2385	2386	2387	2388	2389	2390	2391
453X	2392	2393	2394	2395	2396	2397	2398	2399
454X	2400	2401	2402	2403	2404	2405	2406	2407
455X	2408	2409	2410	2411	2412	2413	2414	2415
456X	2416	2417	2418	2419	2420	2421	2422	2423
457X	2424	2425	2426	2427	2428	2429	2430	2431
460X	2432	2433	2434	2435	2436	2437	2438	2439
461X	2440	2441	2442	2443	2444	2445	2446	2447
462X	2448	2449	2450	2451	2452	2453	2454	2455
463X	2456	2457	2458	2459	2460	2461	2462	2463
464X	2464	2465	2466	2467	2468	2469	2470	2471
465X	2472	2473	2474	2475	2476	2477	2478	2479
466X	2480	2481	2482	2483	2484	2485	2486	2487
467X	2488	2489	2490	2491	2492	2493	2494	2495
470X	2496	2497	2498	2499	2500	2501	2502	2503
471X	2504	2505	2506	2507	2508	2509	2510	2511
472X	2512	2513	2514	2515	2516	2517	2518	2519
473X	2520	2521	2522	2523	2524	2525	2526	2527
474X	2528	2529	2530	2531	2532	2533	2534	2535
475X	2536	2537	2538	2539	2540	2541	2542	2543
476X	2544	2545	2546	2547	2548	2549	2550	2551
477X	2552	2553	2554	2555	2556	2557	2558	2559
500X	2560	2561	2562	2563	2564	2565	2566	2567
501X	2568	2569	2570	2571	2572	2573	2574	2575
502X	2576	2577	2578	2579	2580	2581	2582	2583
503X	2584	2585	2586	2587	2588	2589	2590	2591
504X	2592	2593	2594	2595	2596	2597	2598	2599
505X	2600	2601	2602	2603	2604	2605	2606	2607
506X	2608	2609	2610	2611	2612	2613	2614	2615
507X	2616	2617	2618	2619	2620	2621	2622	2623
510X	2624	2625	2626	2627	2628	2629	2630	2631
511X	2632	2633	2634	2635	2636	2637	2638	2639
512X	2640	2641	2642	2643	2644	2645	2646	2647
513X	2648	2649	2650	2651	2652	2653	2654	2655
514X	2656	2657	2658	2659	2660	2661	2662	2663
515X	2664	2665	2666	2667	2668	2669	2670	2671
516X	2672	2673	2674	2675	2676	2677	2678	2679
517X	2680	2681	2682	2683	2684	2685	2686	2687

X =	0	1	2	3	4	5	6	7
520X	2688	2689	2690	2691	2692	2693	2694	2695
521X	2696	2697	2698	2699	2700	2701	2702	2703
522X	2704	2705	2706	2707	2708	2709	2710	2711
523X	2712	2713	2714	2715	2716	2717	2718	2719
524X	2720	2721	2722	2723	2724	2725	2726	2727
525X	2728	2729	2730	2731	2732	2733	2734	2735
526X	2736	2737	2738	2739	2740	2741	2742	2743
527X	2744	2745	2746	2747	2748	2749	2750	2751
530X	2752	2753	2754	2755	2756	2757	2758	2759
531X	2760	2761	2762	2763	2764	2765	2766	2767
532X	2768	2769	2770	2771	2772	2773	2774	2775
533X	2776	2777	2778	2779	2780	2781	2782	2783
534X	2784	2785	2786	2787	2788	2789	2790	2791
535X	2792	2793	2794	2795	2796	2797	2798	2799
536X	2800	2801	2802	2803	2804	2805	2806	2807
537X	2808	2809	2810	2811	2812	2813	2814	2815
540X	2816	2817	2818	2819	2820	2821	2822	2823
541X	2824	2825	2826	2827	2828	2829	2830	2831
542X	2832	2833	2834	2835	2836	2837	2838	2839
543X	2840	2841	2842	2843	2844	2845	2846	2847
544X	2848	2849	2850	2851	2852	2853	2854	2855
545X	2856	2857	2858	2859	2860	2861	2862	2863
546X	2864	2865	2866	2867	2868	2869	2870	2871
547X	2872	2873	2874	2875	2876	2877	2878	2879
550X	2880	2881	2882	2883	2884	2885	2886	2887
551X	2888	2889	2890	2891	2892	2893	2894	2895
552X	2896	2897	2898	2899	2900	2901	2902	2903
553X	2904	2905	2906	2907	2908	2909	2910	2911
554X	2912	2913	2914	2915	2916	2917	2918	2919
555X	2920	2921	2922	2923	2924	2925	2926	2927
556X	2928	2929	2930	2931	2932	2933	2934	2935
557X	2936	2937	2938	2939	2940	2941	2942	2943
560X	2944	2945	2946	2947	2948	2949	2950	2951
561X	2952	2953	2954	2955	2956	2957	2958	2959
562X	2960	2961	2962	2963	2964	2965	2966	2967
563X	2968	2969	2970	2971	2972	2973	2974	2975
564X	2976	2977	2978	2979	2980	2981	2982	2983
565X	2984	2985	2986	2987	2988	2989	2990	2991
566X	2992	2993	2994	2995	2996	2997	2998	2999
567X	2900	3001	3002	3003	3004	3005	3006	3007
570X	3008	3009	3010	3011	3012	3013	3014	3015
571X	3016	3017	3018	3019	3020	3021	3022	3023
572X	3024	3025	3026	3027	3028	3029	3030	3031
573X	3032	3033	3034	3035	3036	3037	3038	3039
574X	3040	3041	3042	3043	3044	3045	3046	3047
575X	3048	3049	3050	3051	3052	3053	3054	3055
576X	3056	3057	3058	3059	3060	3061	3062	3063
577X	3064	3065	3066	3067	3068	3069	3070	3071
600X	3072	3073	3074	3075	3076	3077	3078	3079
601X	3080	3081	3082	3083	3084	3085	3086	3087
602X	3088	3089	3090	3091	3092	3093	3094	3095
603X	3096	3097	3098	3099	3100	3101	3102	3103
604X	3104	3105	3106	3107	3108	3109	3110	3111
605X	3112	3113	3114	3115	3116	3117	3118	3119
606X	3120	3121	3122	3123	3124	3125	3126	3127
607X	3128	3129	3130	3131	3132	3133	3134	3135

X =	Ø	1	2	3	4	5	6	7
610X	3136	3137	3138	3139	3140	3141	3142	3143
611X	3144	3145	3146	3147	3148	3149	3150	3151
612X	3152	3153	3154	3155	3156	3157	3158	3159
613X	3160	3161	3162	3163	3164	3165	3166	3167
614X	3168	3169	3170	3171	3172	3173	3174	3175
615X	3176	3177	3178	3179	3180	3181	3182	3183
616X	3184	3185	3186	3187	3188	3189	3190	3191
617X	3192	3193	3194	3195	3196	3197	3198	3199
620X	3200	3201	3202	3203	3204	3205	3206	3207
621X	3208	3209	3210	3211	3212	3213	3214	3215
622X	3216	3217	3218	3219	3220	3221	3222	3223
623X	3224	3225	3226	3227	3228	3229	3230	3231
624X	3232	3233	3234	3235	3236	3237	3238	3239
625X	3240	3241	3242	3243	3244	3245	3246	3247
626X	3248	3249	3250	3251	3252	3253	3254	3255
627X	3256	3257	3258	3259	3260	3261	3262	3263
630X	3264	3265	3266	3267	3268	3269	3270	3271
631X	3272	3273	3274	3275	3276	3277	3278	3279
632X	3280	3281	3282	3283	3284	3285	3286	3287
633X	3288	3289	3290	3291	3292	3293	3294	3295
634X	3296	3297	3298	3299	3300	3301	3302	3303
635X	3304	3305	3306	3307	3308	3309	3310	3311
636X	3312	3313	3314	3315	3316	3317	3318	3319
637X	3320	3321	3322	3323	3324	3325	3326	3327
640X	3328	3329	3330	3331	3332	3333	3334	3335
641X	3336	3337	3338	3339	3340	3341	3342	3343
642X	3344	3345	3346	3347	3348	3349	3350	3351
643X	3352	3353	3354	3355	3356	3357	3358	3359
644X	3360	3361	3362	3363	3364	3365	3366	3367
645X	3368	3369	3370	3371	3372	3373	3374	3375
646X	3376	3377	3378	3379	3380	3381	3382	3383
647X	3384	3385	3386	3387	3388	3389	3390	3391
650X	3392	3393	3394	3395	3396	3397	3398	3399
651X	3400	3401	3402	3403	3404	3405	3406	3407
652X	3408	3409	3410	3411	3412	3413	3414	3415
653X	3416	3417	3418	3419	3420	3421	3422	3423
654X	3424	3425	3426	3427	3428	3429	3430	3431
655X	3432	3433	3434	3435	3436	3437	3438	3439
656X	3440	3441	3442	3443	3444	3445	3446	3447
657X	3448	3449	3450	3451	3452	3453	3454	3455
660X	3456	3457	3458	3459	3460	3461	3462	3463
661X	3464	3465	3466	3467	3468	3469	3470	3471
662X	3472	3473	3474	3475	3476	3477	3478	3479
663X	3480	3481	3482	3483	3484	3485	3486	3487
664X	3488	3489	3490	3491	3492	3493	3494	3495
665X	3496	3497	3498	3499	3500	3501	3502	3503
666X	3504	3505	3506	3507	3508	3509	3510	3511
667X	3512	3513	3514	3515	3516	3517	3518	3519
670X	3520	3521	3522	3523	3524	3525	3526	3527
671X	3528	3529	3530	3531	3532	3533	3534	3535
672X	3536	3537	3538	3539	3540	3541	3542	3543
673X	3544	3545	3546	3547	3548	3549	3550	3551
674X	3552	3553	3554	3555	3556	3557	3558	3559
675X	3560	3561	3562	3563	3564	3565	3566	3567
676X	3568	3569	3570	3571	3572	3573	3574	3575
677X	3576	3577	3578	3579	3580	3581	3582	3583

X =	0	1	2	3	4	5	6	7
700X	3584	3585	3586	3587	3588	3589	3590	3591
701X	3592	3593	3594	3595	3596	3597	3598	3599
702X	3600	3601	3602	3603	3604	3605	3606	3607
703X	3608	3609	3610	3611	3612	3613	3614	3615
704X	3616	3617	3618	3619	3620	3621	3622	3623
705X	3624	3625	3626	3627	3628	3629	3630	3631
706X	3632	3633	3634	3635	3636	3637	3638	3639
707X	3640	3641	3642	3643	3644	3645	3646	3647
710X	3648	3649	3650	3651	3652	3653	3654	3655
711X	3656	3657	3658	3659	3660	3661	3662	3663
712X	3664	3665	3666	3667	3668	3669	3670	3671
713X	3672	3673	3674	3675	3676	3677	3678	3679
714X	3680	3681	3682	3683	3684	3685	3686	3687
715X	3688	3689	3690	3691	3692	3693	3694	3695
716X	3696	3697	3698	3699	3700	3701	3702	3703
717X	3704	3705	3706	3707	3708	3709	3710	3711
720X	3712	3713	3714	3715	3716	3717	3718	3719
721X	3720	3721	3722	3723	3724	3725	3726	3727
722X	3728	3729	3730	3731	3732	3733	3734	3735
723X	3736	3737	3738	3739	3740	3741	3742	3743
724X	3744	3745	3746	3747	3748	3749	3750	3751
725X	3752	3753	3754	3755	3756	3757	3758	3759
726X	3760	3761	3762	3763	3764	3765	3766	3767
727X	3768	3769	3770	3771	3772	3773	3774	3775
730X	3776	3777	3778	3779	3780	3781	3782	3783
731X	3784	3785	3786	3787	3788	3789	3790	3791
732X	3792	3793	3794	3795	3796	3797	3798	3799
733X	3800	3801	3802	3803	3804	3805	3806	3807
734X	3808	3809	3810	3811	3812	3813	3814	3815
735X	3816	3817	3818	3819	3820	3821	3822	3823
736X	3824	3825	3826	3827	3828	3829	3830	3831
737X	3832	3833	3834	3835	3836	3837	3838	3839
740X	3840	3841	3842	3843	3844	3845	3846	3847
741X	3848	3849	3850	3851	3852	3853	3854	3855
742X	3856	3857	3858	3859	3860	3861	3862	3863
743X	3864	3865	3866	3867	3868	3869	3870	3871
744X	3872	3873	3874	3875	3876	3877	3878	3879
745X	3880	3881	3882	3883	3884	3885	3886	3887
746X	3888	3889	3890	3891	3892	3893	3894	3895
747X	3896	3897	3898	3899	3900	3901	3902	3903
750X	3904	3905	3906	3907	3908	3909	3910	3911
751X	3912	3913	3914	3915	3916	3917	3918	3919
752X	3920	3921	3922	3923	3924	3925	3926	3927
753X	3928	3929	3930	3931	3932	3933	3934	3935
754X	3936	3937	3938	3939	3940	3941	3942	3943
755X	3944	3945	3946	3947	3948	3949	3950	3951
756X	3952	3953	3954	3955	3956	3957	3958	3959
757X	3960	3961	3962	3963	3964	3965	3966	3967
760X	3968	3969	3970	3971	3972	3973	3974	3975
761X	3976	3977	3978	3979	3980	3981	3982	3983
762X	3984	3985	3986	3987	3988	3989	3990	3991
763X	3992	3993	3994	3995	3996	3997	3998	3999
764X	4000	4001	4002	4003	4004	4005	4006	4007
765X	4008	4009	4010	4011	4012	4013	4014	4015
766X	4016	4017	4018	4019	4020	4021	4022	4023
767X	4024	4025	4026	4027	4028	4029	4030	4031

X =	Ø	1	2	3	4	5	6	7
77ØX	4Ø32	4Ø33	4Ø34	4Ø35	4Ø36	4Ø37	4Ø38	4Ø39
771X	4Ø4Ø	4Ø41	4Ø42	4Ø43	4Ø44	4Ø45	4Ø46	4Ø47
772X	4Ø48	4Ø49	4Ø5Ø	4Ø51	4Ø52	4Ø53	4Ø54	4Ø55
773X	4Ø56	4Ø57	4Ø58	4Ø59	4Ø6Ø	4Ø61	4Ø62	4Ø63
774X	4Ø64	4Ø65	4Ø66	4Ø67	4Ø68	4Ø69	4Ø7Ø	4Ø71
775X	4Ø72	4Ø73	4Ø74	4Ø75	4Ø76	4Ø77	4Ø78	4Ø79
776X	4Ø8Ø	4Ø81	4Ø82	4Ø83	4Ø84	4Ø85	4Ø86	4Ø87
777X	4Ø88	4Ø89	4Ø9Ø	4Ø91	4Ø92	4Ø93	4Ø94	4Ø95

Octal		Decimal
1ØØØØ	=	4Ø96
2ØØØØ	=	8192
3ØØØØ	=	12288
4ØØØØ	=	16384
5ØØØØ	=	2Ø48Ø
6ØØØØ	=	24576
7ØØØØ	=	28672
1ØØØØ	=	32768
2ØØØØ	=	65536
3ØØØØ	=	98304
4ØØØØ	=	131Ø72
5ØØØØ	=	16384Ø
6ØØØØ	=	1966Ø8
7ØØØØ	=	229376
1ØØØØ	=	262144
2ØØØØ	=	524288
3ØØØØ	=	786432
4ØØØØ	=	1Ø48576
5ØØØØ	=	131Ø72Ø
6ØØØØ	=	1572864
7ØØØØ	=	1835ØØ8
1ØØØØØØØ	=	2Ø97152
2ØØØØØØØ	=	4194304
3ØØØØØØØ	=	6291456
4ØØØØØØØ	=	8388608
5ØØØØØØØ	=	1Ø48576Ø
6ØØØØØØØ	=	12582912
7ØØØØØØØ	=	1468ØØ64
1ØØØØØØØØ	=	16777216
2ØØØØØØØØ	=	33554432
3ØØØØØØØØ	=	5Ø331648
4ØØØØØØØØ	=	671Ø8864
5ØØØØØØØØ	=	8388608Ø
6ØØØØØØØØ	=	1ØØ663296
7ØØØØØØØØ	=	11744Ø512

Appendix M
ADDITION AND MULTIPLICATION TABLES

Addition	Multiplication

Binary Scale

```
         Ø + Ø = Ø                              Ø x Ø = Ø
Ø + 1 = 1 + Ø = 1                      Ø x 1 = 1 x Ø = Ø
         1 + 1 = 1Ø                              1 x 1 = 1
```

Octal Scale

		Addend								Multiplier						
	Ø	Ø1	Ø2	Ø3	Ø4	Ø5	Ø6	Ø7		1	Ø2	Ø3	Ø4	Ø5	Ø6	Ø7
A	1	Ø2	Ø3	Ø4	Ø5	Ø6	Ø7	1Ø	M	2	Ø4	Ø6	1Ø	12	14	16
u									u							
g	2	Ø3	Ø4	Ø5	Ø6	Ø7	1Ø	11	l	3	Ø6	11	14	17	22	25
e									t							
n	3	Ø4	Ø5	Ø6	Ø7	1Ø	11	12	i	4	1Ø	14	2Ø	24	3Ø	34
d									p							
	4	Ø5	Ø6	Ø7	1Ø	11	12	13	l	5	12	17	24	31	36	43
									i							
	5	Ø6	Ø7	1Ø	11	12	13	14	c	6	14	22	3Ø	36	44	52
									a							
	6	Ø7	1Ø	11	12	13	14	15	n	7	16	25	34	43	52	61
									d							
	7	1Ø	11	12	13	14	15	16					Product			

Sum

Appendix N
TABLE TO DETERMINE FORWARD BRANCHES

Steps Forward (Decimal)	Branch Operand (HEX)	Steps Forward (Decimal)	Branch Operand (HEX)	Steps Forward (Decimal)	Branch Operand (HEX)
1	Ø1	49	31	97	61
2	Ø2	5Ø	32	98	62
3	Ø3	51	33	99	63
4	Ø4	52	34	1ØØ	64
5	Ø5	53	35	1Ø1	65
6	Ø6	54	36	1Ø2	66
7	Ø7	55	37	1Ø3	67
8	Ø8	56	38	1Ø4	68
9	Ø9	57	39	1Ø5	69
1Ø	ØA	58	3A	1Ø6	7A
11	ØB	59	3B	1Ø7	7B
12	ØC	6Ø	3C	1Ø8	7C
13	ØD	61	3D	1Ø9	7D
14	ØE	62	3E	11Ø	7E
15	ØF	63	3F	111	7F
16	ØG	64	3G	112	7G

Steps Forward (Decimal)	Branch Operand (HEX)	Steps Forward (Decimal)	Branch Operand (HEX)	Steps Forward (Decimal)	Branch Operand (HEX)
17	11	65	41	113	71
18	12	66	42	114	72
19	13	67	43	115	73
2Ø	14	68	44	116	74
21	15	69	45	117	75
22	16	7Ø	46	118	76
23	17	71	47	119	77
24	18	72	48	12Ø	78
25	19	73	49	121	79
26	1A	74	5A	122	7A
27	1B	75	5B	123	7B
28	1C	76	5C	124	7C
29	1D	77	5D	125	7D
3Ø	1E	78	5E	126	7E
31	1F	79	5F	127	7F
32	2Ø	8Ø	5Ø		
33	21	81	51		
34	22	82	52		
35	23	83	53		
36	24	84	54		
37	25	85	55		
38	26	86	56		
39	27	87	57		
5Ø	28	88	58		
51	29	89	59		
52	2A	9Ø	5A		
53	2B	91	5B		
54	2C	92	5C		
55	2D	93	5D		
56	2E	94	5E		
57	2F	95	5F		
58	2Ø	96	6Ø		

Appendix O
TABLE TO DETERMINE BACKWARD BRANCHES

Steps Backward (Decimal)	Branch Operand (HEX)	Steps Backward (Decimal)	Branch Operand (HEX)	Steps Backward (Decimal)	Branch Operand (HEX)
−1	FF	−49	CF	−97	9F
−2	FE	−5Ø	CE	−98	9E
−3	FD	−51	CD	−99	9D
−4	FC	−52	CC	−1ØØ	9C
−5	FB	−53	CB	−1Ø1	9B
−6	FA	−54	CA	−1Ø2	9A
−7	F9	−55	C9	−1Ø3	99
−8	F8	−56	C8	−1Ø4	98
−9	F7	−57	C7	−1Ø5	97
−1Ø	F6	−58	C6	−1Ø6	96
−11	F5	−59	C5	−1Ø7	95
−12	F4	−6Ø	C4	−1Ø8	94
−13	F3	−61	C3	−1Ø9	93
−14	F2	−62	C2	−11Ø	92
−15	F1	−63	C1	−111	91
−16	FØ	−64	CØ	−112	9Ø

Steps Backward (Decimal)	Branch Operand (HEX)	Steps Backward (Decimal)	Branch Operand (HEX)	Steps Backward (Decimal)	Branch Operand (HEX)
-17	EF	-65	BF	-113	8F
-18	EE	-66	BE	-114	8E
-19	ED	-67	BD	-115	8D
-20	EC	-68	BC	-116	8C
-21	EB	-69	BB	-117	8B
-22	EA	-70	BA	-118	8A
-23	E9	-71	B9	-119	89
-24	E8	-72	B8	-120	88
-25	E7	-73	B7	-121	87
-26	E6	-74	B6	-122	86
-27	E5	-75	B5	-123	85
-28	E4	-76	B4	-124	84
-29	E3	-77	B3	-125	83
-30	E2	-78	B2	-126	82
-31	E1	-79	B1	-127	81
-32	E0	-80	B0	-128	80
-33	DF	-81	AF		
-34	DE	-82	AE		
-35	DD	-83	AD		
-36	DC	-84	AC		
-37	DB	-85	AB		
-38	DA	-86	AA		
-39	D9	-87	A9		
-50	D8	-88	A8		
-51	D7	-89	A7		
-52	D6	-90	A6		
-53	D5	-91	A5		
-54	D4	-92	A4		
-55	D3	-93	A3		
-56	D2	-94	A2		
-57	D1	-95	A1		
-58	D0	-96	A0		

Appendix P
POWERS OF TWO

2^n			n
		1	0
		2	1
		4	2
		8	3
		16	4
		32	5
		64	6
		128	7
		256	8
		512	9
	1	024	10
	2	048	11
	4	096	12
	8	192	13
	16	384	14
	32	768	15
	65	536	16
	131	072	17
	262	144	18
	524	288	19

2^n								n
					1	048	576	20
					2	097	152	21
					4	194	304	22
					8	388	608	23
					16	777	216	24
					33	554	432	25
					67	108	864	26
					134	217	728	27
					268	435	456	28
					536	870	912	29
				1	073	741	824	30
				2	147	483	648	31
				4	294	967	296	32
				8	589	934	592	33
				17	179	869	184	34
				34	359	738	368	35
				68	719	476	736	36
				137	438	953	472	37
				274	877	906	944	38
				549	755	813	888	39
			1	099	511	627	776	40
			2	199	023	255	552	41
			4	398	046	511	104	42
			8	796	093	022	208	43
			17	592	186	044	416	44
			35	184	372	088	832	45
			70	368	744	177	664	46
			140	737	488	355	328	47
			281	474	976	710	656	48
			562	949	953	421	312	49
		1	125	899	906	842	624	50
		2	251	799	813	685	248	51
		4	503	599	627	370	496	52
		9	007	199	254	740	992	53
		18	014	398	509	481	984	54
		36	028	797	018	963	968	55
		72	057	594	037	927	936	56
		144	115	188	075	855	872	57
		288	230	376	151	711	744	58
		576	460	752	303	423	488	59
	1	152	921	504	606	846	976	60
	2	305	843	009	213	693	952	61
	4	611	686	018	427	387	904	62
	9	223	372	036	854	775	808	63
	18	446	744	073	709	551	616	64
	36	893	488	147	419	103	232	65
	73	786	976	294	838	206	464	66
	147	573	952	589	676	412	928	67
	295	147	905	179	352	825	856	68
	590	295	810	358	705	651	712	69
1	180	591	620	717	411	303	424	70
2	361	183	241	434	822	606	848	71
4	722	366	482	869	645	213	696	72
9	444	732	965	739	290	427	392	73
18	889	465	931	478	580	854	784	74
37	778	931	862	957	161	709	568	75
75	557	863	725	914	323	419	136	76
151	115	727	451	828	646	838	272	77
302	231	454	903	657	293	676	544	78
604	462	909	807	314	587	353	088	79

					2^n						n
		1	208	925	819	614	629	174	706	176	80
		2	417	851	639	229	258	349	412	352	81
		4	835	703	278	458	516	698	824	704	82
		9	671	406	556	917	033	397	649	408	83
		19	342	813	113	834	066	795	298	816	84
		38	685	626	227	668	133	590	597	632	85
		77	371	252	455	336	267	181	195	264	86
		154	742	504	910	672	534	362	390	528	87
		309	485	009	821	345	068	724	781	056	88
		618	970	019	642	690	137	449	562	112	89
	1	237	940	039	285	380	274	899	124	224	90
	2	475	880	078	570	760	549	798	248	448	91
	4	951	760	157	141	521	099	596	496	896	92
	9	903	520	314	283	042	199	192	993	792	93
	19	807	040	628	566	084	398	385	987	584	94
	39	614	081	257	132	168	796	771	975	168	95
	79	228	162	514	264	337	593	543	950	336	96
	158	456	325	028	528	675	187	087	900	672	97
	316	912	650	057	057	350	374	175	801	344	98
	633	825	300	114	114	700	748	351	602	688	99
1	267	650	600	228	229	401	496	703	205	376	100

Appendix Q
POWERS OF SIXTEEN

					16^n		n
						1	0
						16	1
						256	2
					4	096	3
					65	536	4
				1	048	576	5
				16	777	216	6
				268	435	456	7
			4	294	967	296	8
			68	719	476	736	9
		1	099	511	627	776	10
		17	592	186	044	416	11
		281	474	976	710	656	12
	4	503	599	627	370	496	13
	72	057	594	037	927	936	14
1	152	921	504	606	846	976	15

Decimal Values

Appendix R
2ˣ IN DECIMAL

x	2^x	x	2^x	x	2^x
0.001	1.00069 33874 62581	0.01	1.00695 55500 56719	0.1	1.07177 34625 36293
0.002	1.00138 72557 11335	0.02	1.01395 94797 90029	0.2	1.14869 83549 97035
0.003	1.00208 16050 79633	0.03	1.02101 21257 07193	0.3	1.23114 44133 44916
0.004	1.00277 64359 01078	0.04	1.02811 38266 56067	0.4	1.31950 79107 72894
0.005	1.00347 17485 09503	0.05	1.03526 49238 41377	0.5	1.41421 35623 73095
0.006	1.00416 75432 38973	0.06	1.04246 57608 41121	0.6	1.51571 65665 10398
0.007	1.00486 38204 23785	0.07	1.04971 66836 23067	0.7	1.62450 47927 12471
0.008	1.00556 05803 98468	0.08	1.05701 80405 61380	0.8	1.74110 11265 92248
0.009	1.00625 78234 97782	0.09	1.06437 01824 53360	0.9	1.86606 59830 73615

Appendix S
10⁺ⁿ IN OCTAL

10^n	n	10^{-n}
1	0	1.000 000 000 000 000 000 00
12	1	0.063 146 314 631 463 146 31
144	2	0.005 075 341 217 270 243 66
1 750	3	0.000 406 111 564 570 651 77
23 420	4	0.000 032 155 613 530 704 15
303 240	5	0.000 002 476 132 610 706 64
3 641 100	6	0.000 000 206 157 364 055 37
46 113 200	7	0.000 000 015 327 745 152 75
575 360 400	8	0.000 000 001 257 143 561 06
7 346 545 000	9	0.000 000 000 104 560 276 41
112 402 762 000	10	0.000 000 000 006 676 337 66
1 351 035 564 000	11	0.000 000 000 000 537 657 77
16 432 451 210 000	12	0.000 000 000 000 043 136 32
221 411 634 520 000	13	0.000 000 000 000 003 411 35
2 657 142 036 440 000	14	0.000 000 000 000 000 264 11
34 327 724 461 500 000	15	0.000 000 000 000 000 022 01
434 157 115 760 200 000	16	0.000 000 000 000 000 001 63
5 432 127 413 542 400 000	17	0.000 000 000 000 000 000 14
67 405 553 164 731 000 000	18	0.000 000 000 000 000 000 01

Index

INDEX